Implementing Cisco IOS Network Security (IINS)

Catherine Paquet

Cisco Press

800 East 96th Street

Indianapolis, IN 46240

Implementing Cisco IOS Network Security (IINS)

Catherine Paquet

Published by:
Cisco Press
800 East 96th Street
Indianapolis, IN 46240 USA

Printed in the United States of America

First Printing April 2009

Library of Congress Cataloging-in-Publication Data:

Paquet, Catherine.
  Implementing Cisco IOS network security (IINS) / Catherine Paquet.
    p. cm.
  ISBN-13: 978-1-58705-815-8 (hardcover)
  ISBN-10: 1-58705-815-4 (hardcover)
  1. Computer networks--Security measures. 2. Cisco IOS. I. Title.

  TK5105.59.P375 2009
  005.8--dc22

                                    2009008780

ISBN-13: 978-1-58705-815-8

ISBN-10: 1-58705-815-4

Warning and Disclaimer

This book is designed to provide information about implementing Cisco IOS network security. It provides the information necessary to prepare for Cisco exam 640-553, Implementing Cisco IOS Network Security (IINS). For those who already possess a CCNA certification, passing exam 640-553 provides the additional certification of CCNA Security. Every effort has been made to make this book as complete and as accurate as possible, but no warranty or fitness is implied.

The information is provided on an "as is" basis. The authors, Cisco Press, and Cisco Systems, Inc., shall have neither liability nor responsibility to any person or entity with respect to any loss or damages arising from the information contained in this book or from the use of the discs or programs that may accompany it.

The opinions expressed in this book belong to the author and are not necessarily those of Cisco Systems, Inc.

Trademark Acknowledgments

All terms mentioned in this book that are known to be trademarks or service marks have been appropriately capitalized. Cisco Press or Cisco Systems, Inc., cannot attest to the accuracy of this information. Use of a term in this book should not be regarded as affecting the validity of any trademark or service mark.

Corporate and Government Sales

The publisher offers excellent discounts on this book when ordered in quantity for bulk purchases or special sales, which may include electronic versions and/or custom covers and content particular to your business, training goals, marketing focus, and branding interests. For more information, please contact: **U.S. Corporate and Government Sales**   1-800-382-3419   corpsales@pearsontechgroup.com

For sales outside the United States please contact: **International Sales**   international@pearsoned.com

Feedback Information

At Cisco Press, our goal is to create in-depth technical books of the highest quality and value. Each book is crafted with care and precision, undergoing rigorous development that involves the unique expertise of members from the professional technical community.

Readers' feedback is a natural continuation of this process. If you have any comments regarding how we could improve the quality of this book, or otherwise alter it to better suit your needs, you can contact us through email at feedback@ciscopress.com. Please make sure to include the book title and ISBN in your message.

We greatly appreciate your assistance.

Publisher: Paul Boger

Associate Publisher: Dave Dusthimer

Executive Editor: Brett Bartow

Project Editor: Seth Kerney

Copy Editor: Keith Cline

Editorial Assistant: Vanessa Evans

Cover Designer: Louisa Adair

Indexer: Tim Wright

Business Operation Manager Cisco Press: Anand Sundaram

Manager Global Certification: Erik Ullanderson

Managing Editor: Patrick Kanouse

Senior Development Editor: Christopher Cleveland

Technical Editors: Dave Chapman and Andrew Whitaker

Book Designer: Louisa Adair

Composition: Mark Shirar

Proofreader: Leslie Joseph

Americas Headquarters	Asia Pacific Headquarters	Europe Headquarters
Cisco Systems, Inc.	Cisco Systems (USA) Pte. Ltd.	Cisco Systems International BV
San Jose, CA	Singapore	Amsterdam, The Netherlands

Cisco has more than 200 offices worldwide. Addresses, phone numbers, and fax numbers are listed on the Cisco Website at www.cisco.com/go/offices.

CCDE, CCENT, Cisco Eos, Cisco HealthPresence, the Cisco logo, Cisco Lumin, Cisco Nexus, Cisco StadiumVision, Cisco TelePresence, Cisco WebEx, DCE, and Welcome to the Human Network are trademarks; Changing the Way We Work, Live, Play, and Learn and Cisco Store are service marks; and Access Registrar, Aironet, AsyncOS, Bringing the Meeting To You, Catalyst, CCDA, CCDP, CCIE, CCIP, CCNA, CCNP, CCSP, CCVP, Cisco, the Cisco Certified Internetwork Expert logo, Cisco IOS, Cisco Press, Cisco Systems, Cisco Systems Capital, the Cisco Systems logo, Cisco Unity, Collaboration Without Limitation, EtherFast, EtherSwitch, Event Center, Fast Step, Follow Me Browsing, FormShare, GigaDrive, HomeLink, Internet Quotient, IOS, iPhone, iQuick Study, IronPort, the IronPort logo, LightStream, Linksys, MediaTone, MeetingPlace, MeetingPlace Chime Sound, MGX, Networkers, Networking Academy, Network Registrar, PCNow, PIX, PowerPanels, ProConnect, ScriptShare, SenderBase, SMARTnet, Spectrum Expert, StackWise, The Fastest Way to Increase Your Internet Quotient, TransPath, WebEx, and the WebEx logo are registered trademarks of Cisco Systems, Inc. and/or its affiliates in the United States and certain other countries.

All other trademarks mentioned in this document or website are the property of their respective owners. The use of the word partner does not imply a partnership relationship between Cisco and any other company. (0812R)

About the Author

Catherine Paquet is a practitioner in the field of internetworking, network security, and security financials. She has authored or contributed to eight books thus far with Cisco Press. Catherine has in-depth knowledge of security systems, remote access, and routing technology. She is a Cisco Certified Security Professional (CCSP) and a Cisco Certified Network Professional (CCNP). Catherine is also a certified Cisco instructor with Cisco's largest training partner, Global Knowledge, Inc. She also works on IT security projects for different organizations on a part-time basis. Following her university graduation from the Collège Militaire Royal de St-Jean (Canada), she worked as a system analyst, LAN manager, MAN manager, and eventually as a WAN manager. In 1994, she received a master's degree in business administration (MBA) with a specialty in management information systems (MIS) from York University.

Recently, she has been presenting a seminar on behalf of Cisco Systems (Emerging Markets) on the topic of the business case for network security in 22 countries. In 2002 and 2003, Catherine volunteered with the U.N. mission in Kabul, Afghanistan, to train Afghan public servants in the area of networking.

Catherine lives in Toronto with her husband. They have two children, who are both attending university.

About the Technical Reviewers

David Chapman, CISSP-ISSAP, CCSP, is an independent information security consultant specializing in vulnerability assessments, penetration testing, and the design and implementation of secure network infrastructures. His protocol expertise includes TCP/IP, IPsec, 802.11 wireless, BGP, IPX, SNA, AppleTalk, Frame Relay, PPP, HDLC, LLC, and NetBIOS/SMB. David is the coauthor of *Cisco Secure PIX Firewalls*, from Cisco Press.

Andrew Whitaker, CCSP, is the Director of Enterprise InfoSec and Networking for TechTrain, where he performs penetration tests and teaches ethical hacking and Cisco courses. He has been working in the IT industry for more than 10 years, specializing in Cisco and security technologies, and has performed penetration tests for numerous financial institutions and Fortune 500 companies. Andrew is the coauthor of *Penetration Testing and Network Defense*, from Cisco Press.

Dedication

This book is dedicated to my father, Maurice Paquet, who passed away during this project. Just days before his death, from his hospital bed, this 92-year-old enthusiastic and incessant learner would ask the nurse to pass him his laptop! That was my dad: an inquisitive, lucid, articulate, and sensitive man. Dad, I miss you more than words can say.

Acknowledgments

I'd like to give special recognition to Dave Chapman and Andrew Whitaker for providing their expert technical knowledge in editing this book. They were not afraid to point out inaccuracies and make recommendations to improve the manuscript.

A big "thank you" goes out to the production team for this book. Brett Bartow, Seth Kerney, and especially Christopher Cleveland have been incredibly professional and a pleasure to work with. I couldn't have asked for a finer team.

Contents at a Glance

Contents

Icons Used in This Book

Command Syntax Conventions

The conventions used to present command syntax in this book are the same conventions used in the IOS Command Reference. The Command Reference describes these conventions as follows:

- **Boldface** indicates commands and keywords that are entered literally as shown. In actual configuration examples and output (not general command syntax), boldface indicates commands that are manually input by the user (such as a **show** command).

- *Italic* indicates arguments for which you supply actual values.

- Vertical bars (|) separate alternative, mutually exclusive elements.

- Square brackets ([ ]) indicate an optional element.

- Braces ({ }) indicate a required choice.

- Braces within brackets ([{ }]) indicate a required choice within an optional element.

Foreword

Cisco certification Self-Study Guides are excellent self-study resources for networking professionals to maintain and increase internetworking skills, and to prepare for Cisco Career Certification exams. Cisco Career Certifications are recognized worldwide, and provide valuable, measurable rewards to networking professionals and their employers.

Cisco Press exam certification guides and preparation materials offer exceptional (and flexible) access to the knowledge and information required to stay current in one's field of expertise, or to gain new skills. Whether used to increase internetworking skills or as a supplement to a formal certification preparation course, these materials offer networking professionals the information and knowledge required to perform on-the-job tasks proficiently.

Developed in conjunction with the Cisco certifications and training team, Cisco Press books are the only self-study books authorized by Cisco, and offer students a series of exam practice tools and resource materials to help ensure that learners fully grasp the concepts and information presented.

Additional authorized Cisco instructor-led courses, e-learning, labs, and simulations are available exclusively from Cisco Learning Solutions Partners worldwide. To learn more, visit http://www.cisco.com/go/training.

I hope you find this guide to be an essential part of your exam preparation and professional development, and a valuable addition to your personal library.

Drew Rosen
Manager, Learning & Development
Learning@Cisco
January 2009

Introduction

Network security is a complex and growing area of IT. As the premier provider of network security devices, Cisco Systems is committed to supporting this growing segment of the industry.

This book teaches you how to design, configure, maintain, and audit network security. It focuses on using Cisco IOS routers for protecting the network by capitalizing on its advanced features as a perimeter router, as a firewall, as an intrusion prevention system, and as a VPN device. By the end of this book, you will be able to select and implement the appropriate Cisco IOS services required to build flexible and secure networks. This book also introduces you to the concept of endpoint security.

This book provides you with the knowledge necessary to pass your CCNA Security certification because it provides in-depth information to help you prepare for the IINS exam. It also starts you on the path toward attaining your Cisco Certified Security Professional (CCSP) certification.

The commands and configuration examples presented in this book are based on Cisco IOS Releases 12.3.

Goals and Methods

The most important and somewhat obvious goal of this book is to help you pass the IINS exam (640-553). In fact, if the primary objective of this book were different, the book's title would be misleading; however, the methods used in this book to help you pass the CCNA Security exam are designed to also make you much more knowledgeable about how to do your job.

Although this book has more than enough questions to help you prepare for the actual exam, the method in which they are used is not to simply make you memorize as many questions and answers as you possibly can. One key methodology used in this book is to help you discover the exam topics that you need to review in more depth, to help you fully understand and remember those details, and to help you prove to yourself that you have retained your knowledge of those topics. So, this book does not try to help you pass by memorization, but helps you truly learn and understand the topics. The CCNA Security exam (640-553) is just one of the foundation topics in the CCSP certification, and the knowledge contained within is vitally important to consider yourself a truly skilled security specialist. This book would do you a disservice if it didn't attempt to help you learn the material. To that end, the book will help you pass the CCNA Security exam by using the following methods:

- Helping you discover which test topics you have not mastered

- Providing explanations and information to fill in your knowledge gaps

- Providing practice questions on the topics

Who Should Read This Book?

This book is not designed to be a general security topics book, although it can be used for that purpose. This book is intended to tremendously increase your chances of passing the CCNA Security exam. Although other objectives can be achieved from using this book, the book is written with two goals in mind: to improve your knowledge of Cisco IOS security and to help you pass the CCNA Security exam.

So why should you want to pass the CCNA Security exam? Because it is one of the milestones toward getting the CCSP certification; no small feat in itself. What would getting the CCSP mean to you? A raise, a promotion, recognition? How about to enhance your resumé? To demonstrate that you are serious about continuing the learning process and that you are not content to rest on your laurels? To have a chance of working in one of the most thrilling and fastest growing sectors of IT, network security? To please your reseller-employer, who needs more certified employees for a higher discount from Cisco? Or one of many other reasons.

Strategies for Exam Preparation

The strategy you use for CCNA Security might be slightly different from strategies used by other readers, mainly based on the skills, knowledge, and experience you already have obtained. For instance, if you have attended the IINS course, you might take a different approach than someone who learned firewalling via on-the-job training.

How This Book Is Organized

Although this book could be read cover to cover, it is designed to be flexible and allow you to move between chapters. However, if you do intend to read every chapter, the order in the book is an excellent sequence to use. Chapters 1 to 7 cover the following topics:

- **Chapter 1, "Introduction to Network Security Principles":** This chapter discusses how to develop a comprehensive network security policy to counter threats against information security. It also teaches you about possible threats and how to describe and implement the process of developing a security policy.

- **Chapter 2, "Perimeter Security":** This chapter discusses the concept of perimeter security and covers more precisely the physical installation of and administrative access to Cisco routers, the use of Cisco Security Device Manager (SDM), the use of Cisco routers to perform authentication, authorization, and accounting (AAA), the secure implementation of the management and reporting features of syslog, Simple Network Management Protocol (SNMP), Secure Shell (SSH), Network Time Protocol (NTP), and it examines how to secure a Cisco router with the Security Audit and One-Step Lockdown features of Cisco SDM.

- **Chapter 3, "Network Security Using Cisco IOS Firewalls":** This chapter teaches you how to configure firewall features, including access control lists (ACL) and Cisco IOS zone-based policy firewalls to perform basic security operations on a network. It explains the operations of the different types of firewall technologies and especially the technology used by Cisco routers and Cisco security appliances. The chapter provides thorough explanations on how to create static packet filters using ACLs and how to configure a Cisco IOS zone-based policy firewall.

- **Chapter 4, "Fundamentals of Cryptography":** This chapter introduces the concepts of cryptography and covers encryption, hashing, and digital signatures and how these techniques provide confidentiality, integrity, authenticity, and nonrepudiation. You will learn about algorithms, symmetric and asymmetrical encryption, digital signatures, and Public Key Infrastructure (PKI).

- **Chapter 5, "Site-to-Site VPNs":** This chapter introduces the concepts of site-to-site virtual private networks (VPN) using Cisco IOS. It covers topics such as concepts, technologies, and terms that IP Security (IPsec) VPNs use, Site-to-site IPsec VPN configuration using the command-line interface (CLI), and using Cisco SDM.

- **Chapter 6, "Network Security Using Cisco IOS IPS":** This chapter describes the functions and operations of intrusion detection systems (IDS) and intrusion prevention systems (IPS). It explains the underlying IDS and IPS technology embedded in the Cisco host- and network-based IDS and IPS solutions. Through this chapter, you will learn to configure Cisco IOS IPS using Cisco SDM.

- **Chapter 7, "LAN, SAN, Voice, and Endpoint Security Overview"**: This chapter focuses on several additional aspects of network security: LANs, storage-area networks (SAN), voice, and endpoints. This chapter emphasizes Layer 2 and host security to provide much more comprehensive coverage of the important issues involved in securing an enterprise. In this chapter, you learn about current endpoint protection methods, risks, and countermeasures for SANs security and for IP telephony. You will also read about how to protect your network against Layer 2 attacks.

In this chapter, you will learn how to develop a comprehensive network security policy to counter threats against information security. You will also learn about possible threats and how to describe and implement the process of developing a security policy. In this chapter, you will learn about the following topics:

- Core principles that are part of a secure network

- Attack methods and how to plan a defense in depth

- Principles behind operations security, security testing, secure life cycle, and business continuity planning

- Cisco Self-Defending Network strategy

- Firewall technologies

- Static packet filters using ACLs

CHAPTER 1

Introduction to Network Security Principles

The open nature of the Internet makes it increasingly important for growing businesses to pay attention to the security of their networks. As companies move more of their business functions to the public network, they need to take precautions to ensure that the data is not compromised or that the data does not end up in front of the wrong people.

Unauthorized network access by an outside hacker or disgruntled employee can cause damage or destruction to proprietary data, negatively affect company productivity, and impede the capability to compete. Unauthorized network access can also harm relationships with customers and business partners who might question the capability of a company to protect its confidential information.

Examining Network Security Fundamentals

It is increasingly difficult to establish and maintain a secure network computing environment. The challenge is more difficult because of increased availability requirements and growing regulatory requirements. This section explains the breadth of the challenge to establish and maintain a secure network environment.

The Need for Network Security

The easiest way to protect a network from an outside attack is to close it off completely from the outside world. A closed network provides connectivity only to trusted known parties and sites; a closed network does not allow a connection to public networks.

Because there is no outside connectivity, you can consider networks designed in this way to be safe from outside attacks. However, internal threats still exist. The Computer Security Institute (CSI) in San Francisco, California, estimates that 60 percent to 80 percent of network misuse comes from inside the enterprise.

The overall security challenge is to find a balance between two important needs:

- The need to open networks to support evolving business requirements and freedom of information initiatives

- The growing need to protect private, personal, and strategic business information

The Internet has created expectations for a company to build stronger relationships with customers, suppliers, partners, and employees. E-business challenges companies to become more agile and competitive. The benefit of this challenge is that new applications for e-commerce, supply chain management, customer care, workforce optimization, and e-learning have been created; applications that streamline and improve processes decrease turnaround times, lower costs, and increase user satisfaction.

E-business requires mission-critical networks that accommodate ever-increasing constituencies and demands greater capacity and performance. These networks also need to handle voice, video, and data traffic as networks converge into multiservice environments.

Internal Threats

Internal threats constitute the most serious of threats. Insiders, whether they are employees or contractors, have inside knowledge and inside access. They usually do not have to resort to technical means to achieve their security breaches. It is, in fact, unusual for inside attackers to engage in port scans or ping sweeps, because they already know where the resources exist in the network. Also, because inside attackers already have access to the network, they do not usually need to try to crack passwords or other things of this nature.

Technical defenses are usually ineffective against insider attacks. They are especially ineffective when administrators, or developers, or both have poor practices and do not harden the systems and applications according to the best practices of the vendor.

External Threats

External threats tend to rely on technical means to achieve their goals of breaching your security. For this reason, this book focuses mainly on external threats, because your technical defenses are most effective against them. Firewalls, routers with access control lists (ACL), intrusion prevention systems (IPS), and other technical controls can effectively reduce the number of external threats to which an organization is vulnerable.

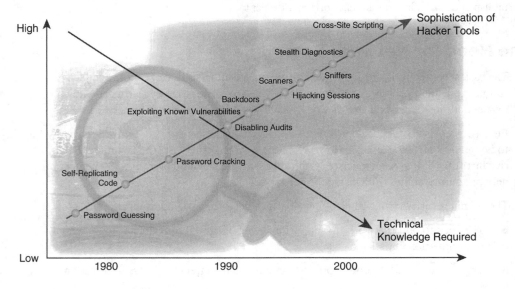

Figure 1-1   *Evolution of Hacker Tools*

Figure 1-1 illustrates how the increasing sophistication of hacking tools and the decreasing skill that is needed to use these tools have combined to pose increasing threats to open networks. With the development of large open networks, security threats in the past 20 years have increased significantly. Hackers have discovered more network vulnerabilities, and hacking tools have become easier to use. You can now download applications that require little or no hacking knowledge to implement. If troubleshooting applications that you use for maintaining and optimizing networks fall into the wrong hands, they can be used maliciously and pose severe threats.

Figure 1-2 shows the number of security events that occurred from 2004 to 2008 as reported in the *2008 CSI/FBI Computer Crime and Security Survey*. The numbers of security incidents cited in Figure 1-2 add up to a serious situation. Although it might appear as though the instances are decreasing, keep in mind that security measures continue to improve, and the damage done by the attackers can actually cost more nowadays with even fewer attacks.

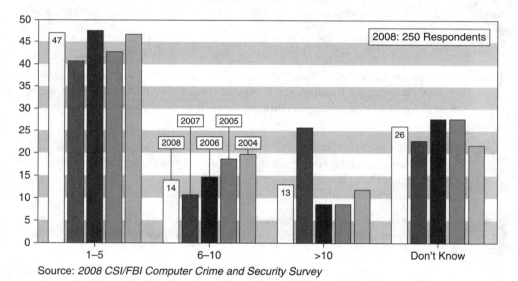

Source: *2008 CSI/FBI Computer Crime and Security Survey*

Figure 1-2   *Size of the IT Security Problem*

Note: The main sources of statistics in this sections are

- *2008 CSI/FBI Computer Crime and Security Survey* and *2008 Information Security Breaches Survey* (released by the U.K.'s Department for Business Enterprise & Regulatory Reform, BERR).

- The U.K. government website, http://www.berr.gov.uk/sectors/infosec/ infosecdownloads/page9935.html

- The actual report, http://www.berr.gov.uk/files/file45714.pdf

The CSI/FBI survey relates to U.S. statistics, and the BERR relates to statistics collected in the United Kingdom. Both documents are readily available for download from the Internet.

For 2008, the U.K.'s BERR reports that the total cost of security incidents is down overall by 35 percent. A large portion of this significant drop is attributable to the sharp decline in virus infections. The number of companies reporting to BERR a virus infection has gone to a level not seen since 2000.

■ Almost 18 percent of those respondents who suffered one or more kinds of security incident also said they had suffered a "targeted attack," defined as a malware attack that was aimed exclusively at their organization or at organizations within a small subset of the general population.

■ Financial fraud overtook virus attacks as the source of the greatest financial losses. Virus losses, which had been the leading cause of loss for seven straight years, fell to second place.

Note: For 2008, the BERR report lists virus infection in fourth place as the leading cause of loss.

■ If the separate categories that are concerned with the loss of customer and proprietary data are grouped together, that combined category would be the second-worst cause of financial loss. Another significant cause of loss was system penetration by outsiders.

■ Insider abuse of network access or email, such as trafficking in pornography or pirated software, edged out virus incidents as the most prevalent security problem, with 59 percent of the respondents reporting insider abuse, and 52 percent of respondents reporting virus incidents.

■ When the companies were asked generally whether they had suffered a security incident, 46 percent of respondents said yes, which is down from 53 percent in 2006 and 56 percent in 2005.

Note: According to the 2008 BERR report, 45 percent of small companies reported having been the victim of a security incident, compared to 72 percent for large companies and 96 percent for very large enterprises. The mean number of incidents reported by small business was 100 (with a median of 6); the large companies reported having been the victim of 200 incidents (with a median of 15), and the very large enterprises recorded more than 1300 incidents (with a median over 400).

■ The percentage of organizations reporting computer intrusions to law enforcement has continued to increase after reversing a multiyear decline over the past two years, standing now at 29 percent as compared to 25 percent in the 2006 report.

Research reveals that hackers are increasingly motivated by profit, as shown in Figure 1-3. In these instances, hackers are not looking for attention, so their exploits are harder to find. Few signatures exist or will ever be written to capture these "custom" threats. To be successful in defending your environments, you must employ a new model to catch threats across the infrastructure.

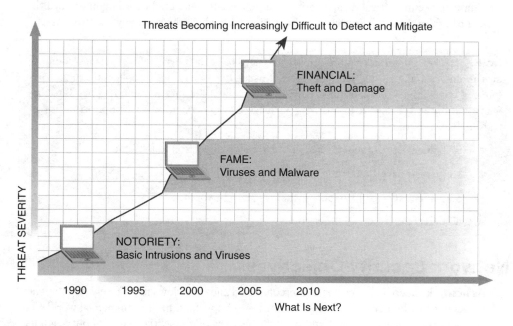

Figure 1-3 *The Evolution of Intent*

Application attacks, not lower-layer platform exploits, are the target of 75 percent of all attacks today. Most companies have many, perhaps hundreds, of different web applications, and their administrative interfaces are scattered throughout the IT environment. Current employees, ex-employees, contractors, integrators, or third-party outsourced developers, most of whom have never had any formal security training, might have written the code. In addition, web developers are constantly updating this code to respond to business needs, not security requirements.

There are no signatures or patches for your own customized application code. As a result, traditional firewalls, intrusion detection system (IDS) and IPS products, patch management tools, and remediation tools do nothing for custom applications. Even the best vulnerability scanners miss the majority of application security flaws in custom code because they use a database of static signatures to scan for known flaws.

This problem is compounded by the fact that the applications themselves are dynamic and complex, so new holes are almost certain to open up the moment you fix the old ones. The result is that unless you write and maintain perfect code, hackers can exploit vulnerabilities in your customized software to gain direct access to the critical data of your company.

Note: Cisco Flexible Packet Matching (FPM) provides an interface to catch attacks such as those previously mentioned. You can find more about FPM, which is beyond the scope of this CCNA Security book, at http://www.cisco.com/go/fpm.

In addition to protecting the data for company reasons, many companies must comply with regulatory mandates, with serious consequences if they cannot document their attempts to secure critical data, whether that data is customer credit card numbers, health records, or other sensitive, private information with which the company is entrusted.

> **Note:**   Hackers might have more opportunities to hack than ever before because companies are increasingly adding services for their users, customers, and suppliers through Internet connectivity. Look at these statistics from the 2008 Information Security Breaches Survey from the U.K.'s BERR on British businesses to understand the vast opportunities hackers have to strike:
>
> - 97 percent of respondents have a broadband connection to the Internet.
>
> - 93 percent have a corporate website.
>
> - 54 percent allow staff to access their systems remotely.
>
> - 42 percent use a wireless network.

Network Security Objectives

As networks become increasingly interconnected and data flows more freely, enabling networks to provide security services becomes very important. In the commercial world, connectivity is no longer optional, and the possible risks of connectivity do not outweigh its benefits. Therefore, security services must provide adequate protection to conduct business in a relatively open environment.

Basic Security Assumptions

Several new assumptions have to be made about computer networks because of their evolution over the years:

- Modern networks are very large, very interconnected, and run both ubiquitous protocols, such as IP, and proprietary protocols. Therefore, they are often open to access, and a potential attacker can often easily attach to, or remotely access, such networks. Widespread IP internetworking increases the probability that more attacks will be carried out over large, heavily interconnected networks, such as the Internet.

- Computer systems and applications that are attached to these networks are becoming increasingly complex. In terms of security, it becomes more difficult to analyze, secure, and properly test the security of the computer systems and applications, even more so when virtualization is involved. When these systems and their applications are attached to large networks, the risk to computing dramatically increases.

Basic Security Requirements

To provide adequate protection of network resources, the procedures and technologies that you deploy need to guarantee three things, sometimes referred to as the CIA triad:

- **Confidentiality:** Providing confidentiality of data guarantees that only authorized users can view sensitive information.

- **Integrity:** Providing integrity of data guarantees that only authorized subjects can change sensitive information; this might also guarantee the authenticity of data.

- **System and data availability:** System and data availability provides uninterrupted access by authorized users to important computing resources and data.

When designing network security, a designer must be aware of the following:

- The threats (possible attacks) that could compromise security

- The associated risks of the threats (that is, how relevant those threats are for a particular system)

- The cost to implement the proper security countermeasures for a threat

- A cost versus benefit analysis to determine whether it is worthwhile to implement the security countermeasures

Confidentiality

You usually manage the risk of confidentiality breaches by enforcing access control in various ways. The following are examples of this type of enforcement:

- Limiting access to network resources using network access control, such as physical separation of networks, restrictive firewalls, and VLANs

- Limiting access to files and objects using operating system-based access controls, such as UNIX host security and Windows domain security

- Limiting user access to data by application level controls, such as different user profiles for different roles

- Limiting the readability of information should there be a breach, through encryption

Confidentiality breaches can occur when an attacker attempts to obtain access to read-sensitive data. It can be extremely difficult to detect these attacks because the attacker can copy sensitive data without the knowledge of the owner and without leaving a trace.

A confidentiality breach can occur simply because of incorrect file protections. For instance, a sensitive file could mistakenly be given global read-access permissions. It is difficult to track an unauthorized copying or examination of the file without some type of audit mechanism running that logs every file operation. However, if users had no reason to suspect unwanted access, they would probably never examine the audit file.

Integrity

The basic meaning of *data integrity* is data that has not been subjected to unauthorized change. Other definitions of integrity add freshness of information, or authenticity of source, or both to integrity (protection against change).

The following are some examples of where data integrity would be helpful:

- Changing grades in a school database

- Modifying figures that are displayed online for the financials of a company

- Defacing a web server

Integrity violations can occur when the attacker attempts to change sensitive data without proper authorization. For example, the attacker obtains permission to write to sensitive data and changes it or deletes it. The owner may not detect such a change until it is too late, perhaps when the change has already resulted in tangible loss. Many businesses treat integrity violations as the most serious threat to their business, because of the difficulty in detecting changes and the possible cascading consequences of late detection.

Availability

In general, *availability* refers to providing uninterrupted access to computing resources and data even during accidental or deliberate network or computer disruptions. The availability service is increasingly recognized as one of the most important security services and possibly the most difficult to provide.

Businesses can experience loss of profit and productivity when customers, suppliers, and employees cannot access critical sites or software applications. Several factors can affect the availability of resources, such as bandwidth bottlenecks, improperly configured networks, and host or client overload, any of which can be due to legitimate use, illegitimate use, or both.

Denial-of-service (DoS) attacks attempt to compromise the availability of a network, host, or application. They are considered a major risk because they can easily interrupt a business process and cause significant loss in productivity and possible revenue. These attacks are relatively simple to conduct, even by an unskilled attacker.

For example, a Montreal teenager was sentenced in 2001 for his admitted guilt in paralyzing the websites of companies such as Yahoo!, Amazon.com, eBay, E*Trade Financial, and Dell. His DoS attacks flooded the networks of the companies with fake information requests that caused networks to shut down, which resulted in lost business. This attack also reportedly caused stock prices to drop.

DoS attacks are usually the consequence of two things:

- A host or application fails to handle an unexpected condition, such as maliciously formatted input data, an unexpected interaction of system components, or simple resource exhaustion.

- A network, host, or application is unable to handle an enormous quantity of data, causing the system to crash or brings it to a halt. It is difficult to defend against such an attack because it is difficult to distinguish legitimate data from attacker data.

The following are two examples of DoS attacks:

- An attacker sends a poisonous packet (an improperly formatted packet or a packet which the receiving device improperly processes) to a device, which causes it to crash or halt upon receipt. This attack can cause all communications to and from the device to be disrupted.

- An attacker sends a continuous stream of packets, which overwhelms the available bandwidth of some network links; in most cases, it is impossible to differentiate between an attacker and legitimate traffic, and it is impossible to trace an attack quickly back to its source. In general, success correlates to bandwidth resources, and whoever has more bandwidth, prevails. If attackers compromise many systems in the Internet core, they might be able to take advantage of virtually unlimited bandwidth to unleash packet storms at their targets. This type of attack has already happened on the Internet and is called a distributed DoS (DDoS) attack.

Data Classification

To optimally allocate resources and secure assets, it is essential that some form of data classification exists. By identifying which data has the most worth, administrators can make the greatest effort to secure that data. Without classification, data custodians find it almost impossible to adequately secure the data, and IT management finds it equally difficult to optimally allocate resources.

Sometimes information classification is a regulatory requirement, and there can be liability issues that relate to the proper care of data that are factors. By classifying data correctly, data custodians can apply the appropriate confidentiality, integrity, and availability controls to adequately secure the data, based on regulatory, liability, and ethical requirements. When an organization takes classification seriously, it illustrates to everyone that the company is taking information security seriously.

The methods and labels applied to data differ all around the world, but some patterns do emerge. The following is a common way to classify data that many government organizations, including the military, use:

- **Unclassified:** Data that has little or no confidentiality, integrity, or availability requirements and therefore little effort is made to secure it.

- **Sensitive But Unclassified (SBU):** Data that could prove embarrassing if revealed, but no great security breach will occur.

- **Confidential:** Data that must comply with confidentiality requirements. This is the lowest level of classified data in this scheme.

- **Secret:** Data for which you take significant effort to keep secure. The number of individuals who have access to this data is usually considerably fewer than the number of people who are authorized to access confidential data.

- **Top secret:** Data for which you make great effort and sometimes incur considerable cost to guarantee its secrecy. Usually a small number of individuals have access to top-secret data, on condition that there is a need to know.

It is important to point out that there is no actual standard for private-sector classification. Furthermore, different countries tend to have different approaches and labels. Nevertheless, it can be instructive to examine a common, private sector classification scheme:

- **Public:** Companies often display public data in marketing literature or on publicly accessible websites.

- **Sensitive:** Data in this classification is similar to the SBU classification in the government model. Some embarrassment might occur if this data is revealed, but no serious security breach is involved.

- **Private:** Private data is important to an organization. You make an effort to maintain the secrecy and accuracy of this data.

- **Confidential:** Companies make the greatest effort to secure confidential data. Trade secrets and employee personnel files are examples of what a company would commonly classify as confidential.

Regardless of the classification labeling used, what is certain is that as the security classification of a document increases, the amount of staff that should have access to this document should decrease, as illustrated in Figure 1-4.

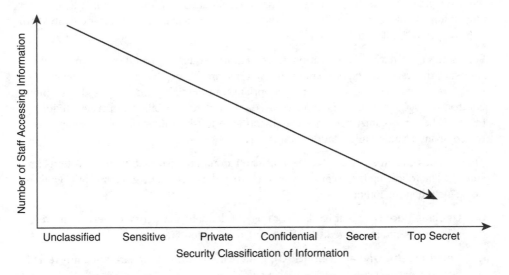

Figure 1-4   *Ratio: Staff Access to Information Security Classification*

Many factors go into the decision of how to classify certain data. These factors include the following:

- **Value:** Value is the number one criterion. Not all data has the same value. The home address and medical information of an employee is considerably more sensitive (valuable) than the name of the chief executive officer (CEO) and the main telephone number of the company.

- **Age:** For many types of data, its importance changes with time. For example, a general will go to great lengths to restrict access to military secrets. But after the war is over, the information is gradually less and less useful and eventually is declassified.

- **Useful life:** Often data is valuable for only a set window of time, and after that window has expired there is no need to keep it classified. An example of this type of data is confidential information about the products of a company. The useful life of the trade secrets of the products typically expires when the company no longer sells the product.

■ **Personal association:** Data of this type usually involves something of a personal nature. Much of the government data regarding employees is of this nature. Steps are usually taken to protect this data until the person is deceased.

Note: To understand further the *value* of information, think about the Federal Reserve Bank (commonly called *the* Fed) and the discount rate it sets. The discount rate is, in essence, the interest rate charged to commercial banks by the Fed.

Periodically, the Fed announces a new discount rate. Typically, if the rate is higher than the previous rate, the stock market reacts with sell-offs. If the discount rate is lower, the stock market rises.

Therefore, moments before the Fed announces the new discount rate, that information is worth gazillions of dollars. However, the value of this information drops to nothing when it hits the wire, because everyone then has free access to the information.

When an organization decides on a classification scheme, the next typical step is to decide how to classify the data, who is responsible for securing the data, and the level of security to be applied to the data. Generally, the information classification procedure is as follows:

Step 1.   Identify the administrator or custodian of the data.

Step 2.   Define how information is classified and labeled (the number of required classification levels).

Step 3.   Classify the data by its owner.

Step 4.   Specify exceptions to the classification policy.

Step 5.   Define controls to be applied to each classification policy.

Step 6.   Specify termination procedures for declassifying data or transferring the custody of the data.

Step 7.   Create an enterprise-awareness program.

Step 8.   (Optional) Audit compliance to classification policy.

Sometimes exigent circumstances, such as court orders, supersede a classification policy. In this situation, you make information available to officers of the court and attorneys and their staffs that would otherwise not be available for public view. To do otherwise would be to disobey a lawful order.

Certain government contracts require contractors to reveal confidential data before the contract is awarded. For example, if the defense department of a country awards a contract to an IT outsourcing company, they will likely insist on having a list of all individuals who will be working in their facility, and a lot of personal information about each of these individuals, to run background checks. In this instance, normal classification rules are set aside.

It is also the prerogative of senior management to declassify, reclassify, or even release classified data if it is required.

Note: While on the topic of court order, let's discuss e-discovery. In 2006, the U.S. Supreme Court amended the Federal Rules of Civil Procedure to create a category for electronic records that explicitly includes emails and instant message chats as records to be archived and produced in a timely manner when relevant in court.

For a classification system to work, there must be different roles that are fulfilled. The most common of these roles are as follows:

- **Owner:** The owner is the person who is ultimately responsible for the information, usually senior-level management who is in charge of a business unit. The owner classifies the data and usually selects custodians of the data and directs their actions. It is important that the owner periodically review the classified data because the owner is ultimately responsible for the data.

- **Custodian:** The custodian is usually a member of the IT staff who has the day-to-day responsibility for data maintenance. Because the owner of the data is not required to have technical knowledge, the owner decides the security controls but the custodian marks the data to enforce these security controls. To maintain the availability of the data, the custodian regularly backs up the data and ensures that the backup media is secure. Custodians also periodically review the security settings of the data as part of their maintenance responsibilities.

- **User:** Users bear no responsibility for the classification of data or even the maintenance of the classified data. However, users do bear responsibility for using the data in accordance with established operational procedures so that they maintain the security of the data while it is in their possession.

Security Controls

Once the owner classifies the data, the custodian is responsible for securing the data. If the custodian has only technical controls available to secure the data, the custodian is severely limited. Most inside attackers do not rely on technical means to accomplish their attacks. Therefore, if the only defense custodians have is a technical one, it is likely that they will fail at maintaining the security of the data.

In a comprehensive security program, organizations rely on a variety of controls to accomplish defense in depth. These controls fall into one of three categories:

- **Administrative:** Controls that are largely policies and procedures

- **Technical:** Controls that involve electronics, hardware, software, and so on

- **Physical:** Controls that are mostly mechanical

Note: If you are interested in the topic of IT management, look into the following framework:

Control Objectives for Information (COBIT) and related technology—COBIT offers a set of best practices for IT management and for IT governance.

ISO 27002—This list of information security best practices was known as the British Standard (BS) 7799. It eventually became an international standard, ISO 17799, and was recently revamped as ISO 27001. For more information, refer to http://www.iso.org.

ITIL—ITIL stands for IT Infrastructure Library. ITIL is also known as BS 15000 (British Standard 15000), and ISO 20000. This framework covers the Specification for Service Management and the Code of Practice for Service Management.

Administrative Controls

Administrative controls are largely policy and procedure driven. You will find many of the administrative controls that help with information security in the enterprise in the human resources department. Some of these controls are as follows:

- Security-awareness training

- Security policies and standards

- Change controls and configuration controls

- Security audits and tests

- Good hiring practices

- Background checks of contractors and employees

For example, if an organization has strict hiring practices that require drug testing and background checks for all employees, the organization will likely hire fewer individuals of questionable character. With fewer people of questionable character working for the company, it is likely that there will be fewer problems with internal security issues. These controls do not single-handedly secure an enterprise, but they are an important part of an information security program.

Technical Controls

Members of IT staffs tend to think of information security solely in terms of technical controls. Although technical controls are extremely important to a good information security program, they are not the only part. The following are examples of technical controls:

- Firewalls

- IPSs

- Virtual private network (VPN) concentrators and clients

- TACACS+ and RADIUS servers

- One-time password (OTP) solutions

- Smart cards

- Biometric authentication devices

- Network Admission Control (NAC) systems

- Routers with ACLs

Note: This book focuses on technical controls because of the Cisco family of products. However, it is important to remember that a comprehensive security program requires much more than technology.

Physical Controls

While trying to secure an environment with good technical and administrative controls, it is also necessary that you lock the doors in the data center. This is an example of a physical control. Other examples of physical controls include the following:

- Intruder detection systems

- Security guards

- Locks

- Safes

- Racks

- Uninterruptible power supplies (UPS)

- Fire-suppression systems

- Positive air-flow systems

When security professionals examine physical security requirements, protecting life safety (protecting human life) should be their number one concern. Good planning is needed to balance life safety concerns against security. For example, permanently barring a door to prevent unauthorized physical access might prevent individuals from escaping in the event of a fire.

Convergence of Physical and Logical Security

One of the best examples of the convergence of physical and logical security I have witnessed was during a technical visit with a Qatar bank in Doha in 2007. The bank was within weeks of the grand opening of their new head office. They had extensive physical security, using a mix of contactless smart cards and biometrics.

They had cleverly linked the login system for traders to the physical security system. For instance, a trader coming to work in the morning had to use his smart card to enter the building, to activate the turnstile, to call the exact floor where the elevator was to stop, and to be granted access through the glass doors of the trading floors. The movements of the traders were recorded by the physical security systems. Minutes later, upon logging in to perform the first trade of the day, the trading authentication, authorization, and accounting (AAA) system queried the physical security system about the location of the traders. The trader was granted access to the trading system only when the physical security systems confirmed to the trading AAA system that the trader was physically on the trading floor.

Controls are also categorized by the type of control they are:

- **Preventive:** The control prevents access.

- **Deterrent:** The control deters access.

- **Detective:** The control detects access.

All three categories of controls can be any one of the three types of controls; for example, a preventive control can be administrative, physical, or technical.

> **Note:**   A security control is any mechanism that you put in place to reduce the risk of compromise of any of the three objectives: confidentiality, integrity, and availability.

Preventive controls exist to prevent compromise. This statement is true whether the control is administrative, technical, or physical. The ultimate purpose for these controls is the prevention of security breaches.

However, a good security design also prepares for failure, recognizing that prevention will not always work. Therefore, detective controls are also part of a comprehensive security program because they enable you to detect a security breach and to determine how the network was breached. With this knowledge, you should be able to better secure the data the next time.

With effective detective controls in place, the incident response can use the detective controls to figure out what went wrong, allowing you to immediately make changes to policies to eliminate a repeat of that same breach. Without detective controls, it is extremely difficult to determine what you need to change.

Deterrent controls are designed to scare away a certain percentage of adversaries to reduce the number of incidents. Cameras in bank lobbies are a good example of a deterrent control. The cameras most likely deter at least some potential bank robbers. The cameras also act as a detective control.

> **Note:**   To be more concrete, examples of types of physical controls include the following:
>
> - **Preventive:** Locks on doors
> - **Deterrent:** Video surveillance
> - **Detective:** Motion sensor

Note: It is not always possible to classify a control into only one category or type. Sometimes there is overlap in the definitions, as in the case of the previously mentioned bank lobby cameras. They serve as both deterrent and detective controls.

Response to a Security Breach

To successfully prosecute an individual who breaches your security, it is necessary to establish three things in most countries:

■ **Motive:** Motive is concerned with why an individual performed the illegal act. As you investigate a computer crime, it is important to start with individuals who might have been motivated to commit the crime.

■ **Opportunity:** Having identified a list of suspects, the next thing to consider is whether they had the opportunity to commit the crime. For example, if you can establish that three of the suspects were all participating in a wedding at the time of the security breach, they may have been motivated, but they did not have the opportunity. They were probably busy doing something else.

■ **Means:** The means is an important thing to prove as well. Do not accuse someone who does not have the technical knowledge to accomplish the deed. Means is the ability to perform the crime. However, keep in mind that hacking tools have become easy for even a novice to use.

If you do not establish these three things, it is difficult to prove that the perpetrator is guilty of the offense. When you can establish motive, opportunity, and means, you have probably identified the guilty party.

Note: Different countries have different legal standards. Most countries and courts in the world accept this particular standard.

When working with computer data as part of a forensics case, you must maintain the integrity of the data if you will rely on the data in a court of law. It is difficult to maintain the integrity of the data in the virtual world of computers where it is trivial to change time stamps or any item of data. The flipping of a single bit can sometimes be all that is required to falsely establish an alibi. In Figure 1-5, by flipping a single bit, you can change the time stamp from October 2, 2008 to October 3, 2008 (where the bit pattern for 2 is *00000010* and the bit pattern for 3 is *00000011*). Therefore, strict procedures are required to guarantee the integrity of forensics data recovered as part of an investigation, such as keeping a proper chain of custody of the evidence.

Data collection is a volatile thing in the virtual world of computers. For this reason, a common procedure in response to security breaches is the immediate isolation of the infected system. Dumping the memory to disk is required because the system flushes the memory every time a device is powered off. Multiple copies of the hard drive are usually made after the device is powered down to establish master copies. These master copies are usually locked up in a safe, and investigators use working copies for both the prosecution and the

Figure 1-5   *Verifying Data Integrity*

defense. You can answer any charges of tampering with data by comparing working copies to the master copy that has been secured and untouched since the beginning of the investigation.

Laws and Ethics

This section describes key laws and codes of ethics that are binding on information systems security (infosec) professionals.

For many businesses today, one of the biggest considerations for setting security policies is compliance with the law. For that reason, it is important for INFOSEC professionals to be at least conversant in the basics of law.

In most countries, there are three types of laws:

- **Criminal:** Concerned with crimes, and its penalties usually involve the risk of fines or imprisonment, or both. If fines are paid, they are usually to the court and are used to defray court costs.

- **Civil (also called tort):** Focuses on correcting wrongs that are not crimes. An example of a civil law case is if one company sues another company for infringing on a patent. The penalty in civil law is usually monetary, although there can also be performance requirements such as ceasing to infringe on the patent. If money is awarded, it is given to the party who won the lawsuit. Imprisonment is not possible in civil law.

- **Administrative:** Involves government agencies enforcing regulations. For example, a company may owe its employees vacation pay. An administrative court could force the company to pay and would probably also levy a fine that is payable to the agency. Therefore, in administrative law cases, monetary awards are often split between the government agency and the victim whose wrongs have been righted.

Ethics involves a standard that is higher than the law. It is a set of moral principles that adherents follow to be considered ethical. These ethics are often formalized in codes appropriately entitled "codes of ethics" by the professions formalizing the code.

The information security profession has a number of codes that have been formalized:

- International Information Systems Security Certification Consortium, Inc (ISC)² code of ethics

- Computer Ethics Institute

- Internet Activities Board (IAB)

- Generally Accepted System Security Principles (GASSP)

ISC² Code of Ethics

The following is a brief overview of the ISC² code of ethics.

- **Code of ethics preamble**
  Safety of the commonwealth, duty to our principals, and to each other requires that we adhere, and be seen to adhere, to the highest ethical standards of behavior. Therefore, strict adherence to this Code is a condition of certification.

- **Code of ethics canons**
  Protect society, the commonwealth, and the infrastructure.
  Act honorably, honestly, justly, responsibly, and legally.
  Provide diligent and competent service to principals.
  Advance and protect the profession.

Computer Ethics Institute: 10 Commandments of Computer Ethics

The Computer Ethics Institute at the Brookings Institute has formalized its code of ethics as the 10 Commandments of Computer Ethics:

Step 1.   Thou shalt not use a computer to harm other people.

Step 2.   Thou shalt not interfere with other people's computer work.

Step 3.   Thou shalt not snoop around in other people's computer files.

Step 4.   Thou shalt not use a computer to steal.

Step 5.   Thou shalt not use a computer to bear false witness.

Step 6.   Thou shalt not copy or use proprietary software for which you have not paid.

Step 7.   Thou shalt not use other people's computer resources without authorization or proper compensation.

Step 8.   Thou shalt not appropriate other people's intellectual output.

Step 9.   Thou shalt think about the social consequences of the program you are writing or the system that you are designing.

Step 10.   Thou shalt always use a computer in ways that ensure consideration and respect for your fellow humans.

IAB Code of Ethics

The IAB has issued a statement that constitutes its code of ethics as follows:

The Internet is a national facility whose utility is largely a consequence of its wide availability and accessibility. Irresponsible use of this critical resource poses an enormous threat to its continued availability to the technical community. The U.S. government, sponsors of this system, suffers when highly disruptive abuses occur. Access to and use of the Internet is a privilege and should be treated as such by all users of this system. The IAB strongly endorses the view of the Division Advisory Panel of the National Science Foundation Division of Network, Communications Research and Infrastructure which, in paraphrase, characterized as unethical and unacceptable any activity which purposely:

- Seeks to gain unauthorized access to the resources of the Internet

- Disrupts the intended use of the Internet

- Wastes resources, such as people, capacity, and computer, through such actions

- Destroys the integrity of computer-based information

- Compromises the privacy of users

GASSP Code of Ethics

The GASSP code of ethics states that information systems and the security of information systems should be provided and used in accordance with the Code of Ethical Conduct of information security professionals.

The Code of Ethical Conduct prescribes the relationships of ethics, morality, and information. As social norms for using IT systems evolve, the Code of Ethical Conduct will change, and information security professionals will spread the new concepts throughout their organizations and products. Safeguards may require an ethical judgment for use or to determine limits or controls.

For example, entrapment is a process for luring someone into performing an illegal or abusive act. As a security safeguard, a security professional might set up an easy-to-compromise hole in the access control system, and then monitor attempts to exploit the hole. This form of entrapment is useful in providing warning that penetration has occurred. It can also provide enough information to identify the perpetrator.

Due to laws, regulations, or ethical standards, it may be unethical to use data that is collected via entrapment in prosecution, but it may be ethical to use entrapment as a detection and prevention strategy. You should seek both legal and ethical advice when designing your network security.

Locale-Specific Legal/Ethical Considerations

Companies must take into account the legal liability for the country in which they reside. Take, for example, an Internet service provider (ISP) that has hundreds of e-businesses that rely on them to run their websites with 100 percent uptime. If a hacker or a virus takes down this ISP, there is a chance for the ISP to be found liable, if it is discovered that the ISP did not take enough precautions or did not secure the network against internal or external threats.

In such cases, legal liability is likely to depend on what prevention technologies and practices are available and whether these technologies and practices are reasonably cost-effective to implement.

As a result, showing due diligence includes everything from implementing technologies such as firewalls, intrusion-detection tools, content filters, traffic analyzers, and VPNs, to having best practices for continuous risk-assessment and vulnerability testing.

Due care is concerned with the operations and maintenance of the secure mechanisms put in place by practicing due diligence.

Many U.S. government regulations have emerged to heighten the need for network and system security. The Gramm-Leach-Bliley Act (GLBA) of 1999 erased long-standing antitrust laws that prohibited banks, insurance companies, and securities firms from merging and sharing information with one another. The idea was that smaller firms would then be able to pursue acquisitions or alliances or both that would help drive competition against many of the larger financial institutions. Included in the GLBA were several consumer-privacy protections. Namely, companies must tell their customers what kinds of data they plan to share and with whom, and they must give their customers a chance to opt out of that data sharing.

On the healthcare side, the Health Insurance Portability and Accountability Act (HIPAA) of 2000 requires the U.S. Department of Health and Human Services to develop a set of national standards for healthcare transactions and provide assurance that the electronic transfer of confidential patient information will be as safe as, or safer, than paper-based patient records.

The Sarbanes-Oxley (SOX) Act of 2002 is a U.S. law in response to a number of major corporate and accounting scandals, including those affecting Enron, Tyco International, Peregrine Systems, and WorldCom. These scandals resulted in a decline of public trust in accounting and reporting practices.

The Security and Freedom through Encryption Act provides that people in the United States can use any kind of encryption. It also provides that any person in the United States can sell any encryption product within the United States. Furthermore, the U.S. government cannot mandate any kind of key escrow. The bulk of the 17-page bill deals with the export of encryption products.

Note: Most countries have similar laws. These particular laws are chosen as examples of laws worldwide.

The U.S. Congress originally passed the Computer Fraud and Abuse Act in 1986 with the intention of reducing hacking. It was amended in 1994, 1996, and lastly in 2001 by the Uniting and Strengthening America by Providing Appropriate Tools Required to Intercept and Obstruct Terrorism (USA PATRIOT) Act. The USA PATRIOT Act expired on December 31, 2005, but was amended and reauthorized in March 2006.

The USA PATRIOT Act increases the scope and penalties of this act by doing the following:

- Raises the maximum penalty for violations to 10 years for a first offense and 20 years for a second offense

- Ensures that violators need only to intend to cause damage and that damage was greater than $5000

- Enhances punishment for violations that involve any damage to a government computer that is involved in criminal justice or the military

- Includes damage to foreign computers that are involved in U.S. interstate commerce

- Includes state law offenses as priors for sentencing

- Expands the definition of loss to expressly include time spent investigating and responding to attacks, making damage assessment and restoration important

The U.S. Congress passed the Privacy Act of 1974 following revelations about the abuse of privacy during the administration of President Richard Nixon. It requires that the privacy of individuals be respected unless they consent to the release of their information in writing.

Note: If your organization conducts business in Europe, you should become familiar with the European Union Directive on Data Protection, EU 95/46/EC. It deals with the protection of individuals with regard to the processing of personal data and on the free movement of such data.

U.S. organizations wanting to share or transfer personal data with an E.U. counterpart should abide by the *U.S.-E.U. Safe Harbor principles,* which aim to harmonize data privacy between the United States and European countries.

The Federal Information Security Management Act (FISMA) of 2002 was intended to bolster computer and network security within the U.S. government and affiliated parties by requiring yearly audits. FISMA also brought attention within the U.S. government to cyber security, which the U.S. government had largely neglected previously.

The Economic Espionage Act of 1996 makes it a federal crime to misuse trade secrets. This law is intended to address corporate espionage, which is a huge security problem for companies with large R&D budgets.

Jurisdictional problems have plagued the prosecution of computer crimes for years. Attackers would simply launch their attacks from compromised computers in one country against computers in another country. It was most effective when the two countries in question had political difficulties. In response to these jurisdictional problems, cooperative efforts have started among the countries of the world. You can find examples of international cooperation in the sharing of law enforcement information in the G8, Interpol, and European Union, among others.

Ecotage

Imagine this nightmare scenario: A hacking group wants to create havoc for a U.S.-based organization it perceives to have a bad environmental record. The hacking group, located in a country friendly to the United States, wants to reduce the risk of prosecution by first hacking a system in a rogue country, and from that platform, unleash its attack against the U.S.-based organization.

Upon conducting an investigation, U.S. law enforcement agencies discover that the attack was launched from a country on unfriendly terms with the United States. They therefore realize that they will probably not receive full cooperation of the foreign country in tracking down the actual perpetrators.

Examining Network Attack Methodologies

Who are hackers? What motivates them? How do they do it? How do they manage to breach the measures we have in place to ensure confidentiality, integrity, and availability? Which best practices can we adopt to defeat hackers? These are some of the questions we try to answer next.

Adversaries, Motivations, and Classes of Attack

A *vulnerability* is a weakness in a system or its design that can be exploited by a threat. Vulnerabilities are sometimes found in the protocols themselves, as in the case of some security weaknesses in TCP/IP. Often, the vulnerabilities are in the operating systems and applications.

A *threat* is an external menace to that system. For example, a hacker actively scouting the Internet for a specific buffer-overflow vulnerability found in web servers would be considered a threat.

A *risk* is the likelihood that a particular threat using a specific attack will exploit a particular vulnerability of a system that results in an undesirable consequence. Although the roof of the data center might be vulnerable to being penetrated by a falling meteor, for example, the risk is minimal because the likelihood of that threat being realized is essentially almost none.

An *exploit* happens when computer code is developed to take advantage of a vulnerability. For example, suppose that a vulnerability exists in a piece of software, but nobody knows about this vulnerability. Although the vulnerability exists theoretically, there is no exploit yet developed for it. Because there is no exploit, there really is no problem yet.

Note: If you have a vulnerability, but there is no threat toward that vulnerability, you have no risk!

When you analyze system vulnerabilities, it helps to categorize them in classes to better understand the reasons for their emergence. You can categorize the main vulnerabilities of systems as one of the following:

- Design errors
- Protocol weaknesses
- Software vulnerabilities
- Misconfiguration
- Hostile code
- Human factor

These are just a few of the vulnerability categories. For each of these categories, many additional vulnerabilities could be listed.

People are social beings, and it is quite common for systems to be compromised through social engineering. Harm can be caused by people just trying to be "helpful." For example, in an attempt to be helpful, people have been known to give their passwords over the phone to attackers who have a convincing manner and say they are troubleshooting a problem and need to test access using a real user password. The end user must be trained, and reminded, that the ultimate security of a system depends on their behavior.

Of course, people often cause harm within organizations intentionally:

- Most security incidents are caused by insiders.
- Strong internal controls on security are required.
- Special organizational practices might need to be implemented.

An example of a special organizational practice that helps to provide security is the separation of duty, where critical tasks require two or more persons to complete them, thereby reducing the risk of insider threat. People are less likely to attack or misbehave if they are required to cooperate with others.

Unfortunately, users frequently consider security too difficult to understand. Software often does not make security options or decisions easy for end users. Also, users typically prefer "whatever" functionality to no functionality.

Adversaries

To defend against attacks on information and information systems, organizations must begin to define the threat by identifying potential adversaries. These adversaries can include the following:

- Nation or states

- Terrorists

- Criminals

- Hackers

- Corporate competitors

- Disgruntled employees

- Government agencies

Hackers comprise the most well-known outside threat to information systems. They are not necessarily geniuses, but they are persistent people who have taken a lot of time to learn their craft.

Many titles are assigned to hackers:

- **Hackers:** Hackers are individuals who break into computer networks and systems to learn more about them. Some hackers generally mean no harm and do not expect financial gain. Unfortunately, hackers may unintentionally pass valuable information on to people who do intend to harm the system.

- **Crackers (criminal hackers):** Crackers are hackers with a criminal intent to harm information systems. Crackers are generally working for financial gain and are sometimes called black hat hackers.

- **Phreakers (phone breakers):** Phreakers pride themselves on compromising telephone systems. Phreakers reroute and disconnect telephone lines, sell wiretaps, and steal long-distance services.

Note: When describing individuals whose intent is to exploit a network maliciously, these individuals are often incorrectly referred to as hackers. In this lesson, the term *hacker* is used, but might refer to someone more correctly referred to as a cracker, or black hat hacker.

- **Script kiddies:** Script kiddies think of themselves as hackers, but have very low skill levels. They do not write their own code; instead, they run scripts written by other, more skilled attackers.

- **Hacktivists:** Hacktivists are individuals who have a political agenda in doing their work. When government websites are defaced, this is usually the work of a hacktivist.

In computer security, a hacker is a person who specializes in work with the security mechanisms for computer and network systems.

The release of the movie *WarGames* in 1983 raised the public's awareness that computer security hackers (especially teenagers) could be a threat to national security. Unfortunately, this concern became real when a gang of teenage crackers known as the 414s broke into computer systems throughout the United States and Canada, including Los Alamos National Laboratory, Memorial Sloan-Kettering Cancer Center, and Security Pacific Bank. The case drew worldwide media attention, and a 17-year-old emerged as the spokesman for the gang. An American magazine, *Newsweek*, wrote an article in which the word *hacker* first appeared. Since that time, all forms of media refer to every class of attacker as a hacker.

Because of news coverage, the U.S. House of Representatives called for an investigation and new laws to cover computer hacking. Because of these laws, white hat, gray hat, and black hat hackers try to distinguish themselves from each other, depending on the legality of their activities.

When referring to the events of the 414 gang, Ken Thompson said the following:

I would like to criticize the press in its handling of the "hackers," the 414 gang, the Dalton gang, and so on. The acts that are performed by these kids are vandalism at best and probably trespass and theft at worst. ... I have watched kids testifying before Congress. It is clear that they are completely unaware of the seriousness of their acts.

In the academic hacker culture, a computer hacker is a person who enjoys designing software and building programs with a sense for aesthetics and playful cleverness. After 1980, this subculture coalesced with the culture of UNIX. Since the mid-1990s, it has been largely coincident with what is now referred to as the free software and open source movement.

Academic hackers usually work openly and use their real name, whereas computer security hackers prefer secretive groups and identity-concealing aliases. Also, their activities in practice are largely distinct. Academic hackers focus on creating new infrastructure and improving existing infrastructure (especially the software environment they work with), whereas computer security hackers primarily and strongly emphasize the general act of circumventing security measures.

The academic hacker community sees secondary circumvention of security mechanisms as legitimate if it is done to get practical barriers out of the way for doing actual work. However, the primary focus in these activities is not one of their interests. A further difference is that, historically, academic hackers were working at academic institutions and used the computing environment there. In contrast, the typical computer security hacker operates out of their home.

Within the academic hacker culture, the term *hacker* is also used for a programmer who reaches a goal by employing a series of modifications to extend existing code or resources. In a universal sense, a hacker also refers to someone who makes things work beyond perceived limits in a clever way.

The hobby hacking subculture relates to the home computing of the late 1970s. The hobbyist focuses mainly on computer and video games, software cracking, and the modification of computer hardware and other electronic devices, also known as modding.

Motivations

To defend against attacks on information and information systems, organizations must define the threat in terms of motivation. Motivations can include intelligence gathering, theft of intellectual property, denial of service (DoS), embarrassment of the company or clients, and pride in exploiting a notable target.

There are many different kinds of attackers. They mainly differ by how much funding they have and which targets they pick. You can roughly divide these attackers in to three groups:

■ Casual crackers (script kiddies)

■ Motivated or paid crackers (lone criminals, industrial spies, organized crime)

■ Military, government intelligence, information warfare, or cyberterrorism

Casual crackers pick almost any target and have low funding. Their motivation usually lies in learning, discovering, and generally exploiting things "because they were there." They are normally not capable of attacking highly secure systems because they lack the resources and knowledge. Still, they can produce substantial damage in money and lost time.

Motivated crackers are usually well paid and possess adequate resources. They are likely to attack carefully selected targets, based on the instructions of their employer. These actions are not always for profit. In recent history, attacks have been made to further a specific agenda. They can produce severe damage and can be extremely difficult to trace.

Military or government intelligence has almost unlimited funding. It is believed that, because of their state-of-the-art equipment, they can crack most low-end codes in nearly real time.

Classes of Attack and Methodology

The goal of any hacker is to compromise the intended target or application. Hackers begin with little or no information about the intended target, but by the end of their analysis, they have accessed the network and have begun to compromise their target. Their approach is usually careful and methodical, not rushed and reckless. The seven-step process that follows is a good representation of the methods that hackers use:

Step 1. Perform footprint analysis (reconnaissance).

Step 2. Enumerate applications and operating systems.

Step 3. Manipulate users to gain access.

Step 4. Escalate privileges.

Step 5. Gather additional passwords and secrets.

Step 6. Install back doors.

Step 7. Leverage the compromised system.

Caution: Hackers have become successful by thinking "outside the box." This methodology is meant to illustrate the steps that a structured attack might take. Not all hackers will follow these steps in this order.

To successfully hack into a system, as a first step hackers generally want to know as much as they can about the system. Hackers can build a complete profile or "footprint" of the company security posture. Using a range of tools and techniques, an attacker can discover the company domain names, network blocks, IP addresses of systems, ports and services that are used, and many other details that pertain to the company security posture as it relates to the Internet, an intranet, remote access, and an extranet. By following some simple advice, network administrators can make footprinting more difficult.

After the hacker has completed a profile, or footprint, of your organization, they use tools, such as those in the list that follows, to enumerate additional information about your systems and networks. All these tools are readily available to download, and the security staff should know how these tools work. Additional tools, introduced later in this chapter in the "Security Testing Techniques" section, can also be used to gather information and therefore hack:

- **Netcat:** Netcat is a featured networking utility that reads and writes data across network connections.

- **Microsoft EPDump and Microsoft Remote Procedure Call (RPC) Dump:** These tools provide information about Microsoft RPC services on a server.

- **GetMAC:** This application provides a quick way to find the MAC (Ethernet) layer address and binding order for a computer running Microsoft Windows locally or across a network.

- **DumpSec by SomarSoft:** This application is a security auditing program for Windows NT, Windows XP, and Windows 2000 or later systems.

- **Software development kits (SDK):** SDKs provide hackers with the basic tools that they need to learn more about systems.

Another common technique that hackers use is to manipulate users of an organization to gain access to that organization. There are countless cases of unsuspecting employees providing information to unauthorized people simply because the requesters appear innocent or to be in a position of authority. Hackers find names and telephone numbers on websites or domain registration records by footprinting. Hackers then directly contact these people by phone and convince them to reveal passwords. Hackers gather information without raising any concern or suspicion. This form of attack is called *social engineering*.

The next thing the hacker typically does is review all the information about the host that they have collected, searching for usernames, passwords, and Registry keys that contain application or user passwords. This information can help hackers escalate their privileges on the host or network. If reviewing the information from the host does not reveal useful information, hackers may launch a Trojan horse attack in an attempt to escalate their privileges on the host. This type of attack usually means copying malicious code to the user system and giving it the same name as a frequently used piece of software.

After the hacker has higher privileges, the next task is to gather additional passwords and other sensitive data. The targets now include such things as the local security accounts manager database or the active directory of a domain controller. Hackers use legitimate tools such as pwdump and lsadump applications to gather passwords from machines running Windows. By cross-referencing username and password combinations, the hacker is able to obtain administrative access to all the computers in the network.

If hackers are detected trying to enter through the "front door," or if they want to enter the system without being detected, they try to use "back doors" into the system. A back door is a method of bypassing normal authentication to secure remote access to a computer while attempting to remain undetected. The most common backdoor point is a listening port that provides remote access to the system for users (hackers) who do not have, or do not want to use, access or administrative privileges.

After hackers gain administrative access, they enjoy hacking other systems on the network. As each new system is hacked, the attacker performs the steps that were outlined previously to gather additional system and password information. Hackers try to scan and exploit a single system or a whole set of networks and usually automate the whole process.

In addition, hackers will cover their tracks either by deleting log entries or falsifying them.

Thinking Outside the Box

In 2005, David Sternberg hacked the Postal Bank in Israel by physically breaking into one of the bank's branches in Haifa, Israel, and connecting a wireless access point in the branch's IT infrastructure. Sternberg rented office space about 100 feet from the bank and proceeded to transfer funds to bank accounts in his name or in friends' names.

So instead of trying for months to break into the IT security of the bank, Sternberg thought outside of the box and broke through physical security to gain access to the IT system.

Sternberg was discovered when bank auditors noticed regular transfers from the main bank account to the same individual accounts.

I guess that Sternberg had not heard about the security axiom that says "predictability is the enemy of security."

The Principles of Defense in Depth

This section describes the concept of defense in depth.

It is often said that the security of a system is only as strong as its weakest link, which is universally understood by almost everyone, but is rarely addressed by security designers. The complexity of modern systems makes it difficult to identify all weak links, let alone identify the weakest one. Sometimes, it is desirable to eliminate a weak link or to augment its security.

Securing information and systems against all threats requires multiple, overlapping protection approaches that address the people, technology, and operational aspects of information technology. Using multiple, overlapping protection approaches ensures that the system is never unprotected from the failure or circumvention of any individual protection approach.

When a system is designed and implemented, its quality should always be questioned through design reviews and testing. Identification of various failure modes might help a designer evaluate the probability of element failure, and identify the links that are the most critical for the security of the whole system. Many systems have a security-based single point of failure, an element of functionality or protection, which, if compromised, would cause the compromise of the whole system. It is desirable to eliminate or at least harden such single points of failure in a high-assurance system.

Defense in depth is a philosophy that provides layered security to a system by using multiple security mechanisms:

- Security mechanisms should back each other up and provide diversity and redundancy of protection.

- Security mechanisms should not depend on each other, so that their security does not depend on other factors outside their control.

- Using defense in depth, you can eliminate single points of failure and augment weak links in the system to provide stronger protection with multiple layers.

The defense-in-depth strategy recommends several principles:

- **Defend in multiple places:** Given that insiders or outsiders can attack a target from multiple points, an organization must deploy protection mechanisms at multiple locations to resist all classes of attacks. At a minimum, you should include three defensive focus areas:
  - **Defend the networks and infrastructure:** Protect the local- and wide-area communications networks from attacks, such as DoS attacks. Provide confidentiality and integrity protection for data that is transmitted over the networks; for example, use encryption and traffic flow security measures to resist passive monitoring.
  - **Defend the enclave boundaries:** Deploy firewalls and intrusion detection systems (IDS) or intrusion prevention systems (IPS) or both to resist active network attacks.
  - **Defend the computing environment:** Provide access controls and host intrusion prevention systems (HIPS) on hosts and servers to resist insider, close-in, and distribution attacks.

- **Build layered defenses:** Even the best available information assurance products have inherent weaknesses. Therefore, it is only a matter of time before an adversary finds an exploitable vulnerability. An effective countermeasure is to deploy multiple defense mechanisms between the adversary and the target. Each of these mechanisms must present unique obstacles to the adversary. Further, each mechanism should include both protection and detection measures. These measures increase the risk of detection for adversaries while reducing their chances of success or makes successful penetrations unaffordable. One example of a layered defense is to have nested firewalls (each coupled with IDS or IPS) that are deployed at outer and inner network boundaries. The inner firewalls may support more granular access control and data filtering.

- **Use robust components:** Specify the security robustness (that is, strength and assurance) of each information assurance component as a function of the value of what it is protecting and the threat at the point of application. For example, it is often more effective and operationally suitable to deploy stronger mechanisms at the network boundaries than at the user desktop.

- **Employ robust key management:** Deploy robust encryption key management and public key infrastructures that support all the incorporated information assurance technologies and that are highly resistant to attack.

- **Deploy IDS or IPS:** Deploy infrastructures to detect and prevent intrusions and to analyze and correlate the results and react accordingly. These infrastructures should help the operations staff answer the following questions:
  Am I under attack?
  Who is the source?
  What is the target?
  Who else is under attack?
  What are my options?

To achieve high assurance in authentication, many trusted systems require "two-factor authentication"; they require a subject to include at least two types of proofs of identity, such as something they know and something they have. An example of two-factor authentication is an access control system that requires a smart card (something the user has) and a password (something the user knows). With two-factor authentication, a compromise of one factor does not lead to a compromise of the system. A password might become known, but it is useless without the smart card. Conversely, if the smart card is stolen, it cannot be used without the password.

Credit card processing centers use monitoring of usage patterns and spending limits to control possible damage. A stolen credit card is therefore subject to two layers of protection: Abnormal usage signatures are detected, and the thief cannot spend more than a predetermined amount of money with a stolen card.

You can configure the Cisco Adaptive Security Appliances (ASA) to require two layers of protection:

- The translation rules, without which no traffic can pass through the firewall

- The access rules, which specify the traffic that can pass over the firewall to the protected network if translation rules are in place

Note: Cisco ASA Software Version 7.0 and later no longer requires translation rules. To enforce this form of defense in depth, Network Address Translation (NAT) control must be enabled.

The defense-in-depth idea goes back to medieval castles, which offered multiple layers of defense to resist lengthy sieges. In addition to multiple layers of walls (perimeters), a medieval castle might use an array of the following protection mechanisms, often complementing each other:

- The barbican, which is a row of pointed wooden stakes that are placed across the front of the castle

- A moat, which is a ditch that is wide and full of water and which surrounds the castle walls

- A drawbridge, which is a bridge that crosses the moat and can be raised at the first sign of danger

- A portcullis, which is an iron grille that covers and protects the raised drawbridge

- A narrowed arched passageway to the inside that hinders and contains invaders

- The outer courtyard, called the bailey, which is another open area that is within the range of archers

- The inside court, which contains more walls and more archers

- The inside palace, which is another fortress within the castle and is where the nobles live

- The keep, which is the main commanding tower, is the oldest part of the castle and its final defense

Figure 1-6 shows another application of the defense-in-depth principle used in the context of an enterprise firewall, which must convey email from the Internet to the inside messaging system. In this network, email is relayed to an enterprise using two different email relays in series, the public email gateway and the inside email gateway, to avoid any implementation or configuration bugs that might be present in a single email relay. Both email relays are simple pieces of software that would both have to be compromised sequentially before the attacker can exploit the inside email gateway.

Figure 1-6 also illustrates an unfortunate side effect of defense in depth. By adding more layers of security, the complexity of the system increases, possibly reducing other aspects of its security (for example, ease of proper configuration) and reliability (a more complex system is more likely to fail). Careful balancing is needed to provide an optimal solution; each defense-in-depth decision must be analyzed for its side effects. Sometimes to maintain overall simplicity, only the most critical security mechanisms are backed up.

Figure 1-7 shows a series of Cisco ASAs that were deployed according to the defense-in-depth philosophy. If one Cisco ASA fails, the other Cisco ASA still protects the inside network. However, all Cisco ASAs are configured using the same management tool, such as Cisco Security Manager, which uploads a policy to both firewalls using an abstract definition of access rules.

If there is a defect in the management tool, it might generate faulty rules on all the devices under its control, nullifying the defense-in-depth potential of multiple devices in a series, because they would both pass unauthorized connections.

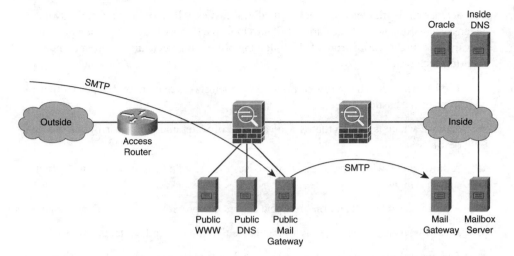

Figure 1-6   *Technical Example of Defense in Depth*

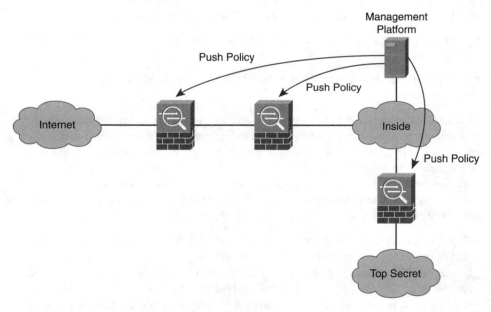

Figure 1-7   *Failed Attempt at Defense in Depth: Same Flaw Pushed to All Firewalls*

To counter this vulnerability, you can use two different Cisco Security Manager servers to configure different Cisco ASAs.

IP Spoofing Attacks

This section covers how hackers use IP spoofing to launch various types of attacks.

The prime goal of an IP spoofing attack is to establish a connection that allows the attacker to gain root access to the host and to create a backdoor entry path into the target system.

IP spoofing is a technique used to gain unauthorized access to computers whereby the intruder sends messages to a computer with an IP address that indicates the message is coming from a trusted host. The attacker learns the IP address of a trusted host and modifies the packet headers so that it appears that the packets are coming from that trusted host.

At a high level, the concept of IP spoofing is easy to comprehend. Routers determine the best route between distant computers by examining the destination address, and ignore the source address. In a spoofing attack, an attacker outside your network pretends to be a trusted computer by using a trusted internal or external IP address.

If an attacker manages to change the routing tables to divert network packets to the spoofed IP address, the attacker can receive all the network packets addressed to the spoofed address and reply just as any trusted user can.

IP spoofing can also provide access to user accounts and passwords. For example, an attacker can emulate one of your internal users in ways that prove embarrassing for your organization. The attacker could send email messages to business partners that appear to have originated from someone within your organization. Such attacks are easier to perpetrate when an attacker has a user account and password, but they are also possible when attackers combine simple spoofing attacks with their knowledge of messaging protocols.

Technical Discussion on IP Spoofing

Recall that TCP/IP works at Layer 3 and Layer 4 of the Open Systems Interconnection (OSI) model, IP at Layer 3 and TCP at Layer 4. IP is a connectionless model, which means that packet headers do not contain information about that transaction state that is used to route packets on a network. There is no method in place to ensure proper delivery of a packet to the destination.

The IP header contains the source and destination IP addresses. Using one of several tools, an attacker can easily modify the source address field. Note that in IP each datagram is independent of all others because of the stateless nature of IP. To engage in IP spoofing, hackers find the IP address of a trusted host and modify their own packet headers to appear as though packets are coming from that trusted host (source address).

TCP uses a connection-oriented design. This design means that the participants in a TCP session must first build a connection using the three-way handshake, as shown in Figure 1-8.

After the connection is established, TCP ensures data reliability by applying the same process to every packet as the two machines update one another on progress. The sequence and acknowledgments take place as follows:

1. The client selects and transmits an initial sequence number.
2. The server acknowledges the initial sequence number and sends its own sequence number.
3. The client acknowledges the server sequence number, and the connection is open to data transmission.

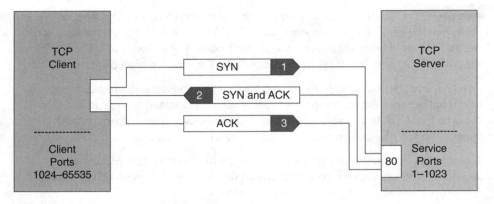

Figure 1-8 *TCP Three-Way Handshake*

Sequence Prediction

The basis of IP spoofing lies in an inherent security weakness in TCP known as *sequence prediction*. Hackers can guess or predict the TCP sequence numbers that are used to construct a TCP packet without receiving any responses from the server. Their prediction allows them to spoof a trusted host on a local network. To mount an IP spoofing attack, the hacker listens to communications between two systems. The hacker sends packets to the target system with the source IP address of the trusted system, as shown in Figure 1-9.

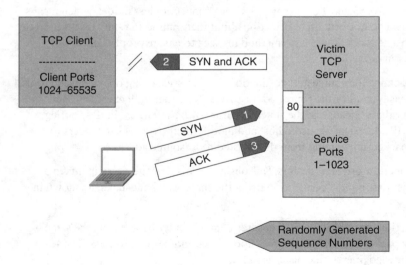

Figure 1-9 *Sequence Number Prediction*

If the packets from the hacker have the sequence numbers that the target system is expecting, and if these packets arrive before the packets from the real trusted system, the hacker becomes the trusted host.

To engage in IP spoofing, hackers must first use a variety of techniques to find an IP address of a trusted host and then modify their packet headers to appear as though packets are coming from that trusted host. Further, the attacker can engage other unsuspecting hosts to generate traffic that appears as though it too is coming from the trusted host, thus flooding the network.

IP spoofing attacks fall into one of two categories:

- **Nonblind spoofing:** This type of attack takes place when the attacker is on the same subnet as the victim. The attacker sniffs the sequence and acknowledgment numbers to eliminate the potential difficulty of calculating them accurately. The biggest threat of spoofing in this instance would be session hijacking. The attacker corrupts the data stream of an established connection, and then reestablishes the data stream with the attack machine using the correct sequence and acknowledgment numbers. Using this technique, an attacker could effectively bypass any authentication measures taken place to build the connection. A nonblind spoofing attack requires the use of a network packet sniffer.

- **Blind spoofing:** This type of attack is a more sophisticated attack because the sequence and acknowledgment numbers are unreachable. To circumvent this issue, the attacker sends several packets to the target machine to sample sequence numbers. This is a difficult task, but not impossible. Blind attacks rely on routing and transport protocols to compromise the target.

Both types of IP spoofing are forms of a common security violation known as a man-in-the-middle attack. In these attacks, a malicious party intercepts a legitimate communication between two friendly parties. The malicious host then controls the flow of communication and can eliminate or alter the information sent by one of the original participants without the knowledge of either the original sender or the recipient. In this way, an attacker can fool a victim into disclosing confidential information by "spoofing" the identity of the original sender, who is presumably trusted by the recipient.

IP spoofing is also part of most DoS and distributed DoS (DDoS) attacks because the attackers do not want to be easily identified.

Source Routing

Source routing is the ability of the source to specify within the IP header a full routing path between endpoints. However, the destination must reply along a reverse path back to the source, as shown in Figure 1-10.

With this mechanism, the attacker can locally create an interface with a bogus (spoofed) IP address, source connections from it using the source route options, and the target would return the packets along the reverse path to the spoofed address.

Two types of source routing, as defined in RFC 791, are possible:

- **Loose Source and Route Record (LSRR):** The sender specifies a list of IP addresses that the datagram must traverse, but the datagram can also traverse other routers between any two addresses in the list.

- **Strict Source and Route Record (SSRR):** The sender specifies the exact path that the IP datagram must follow.

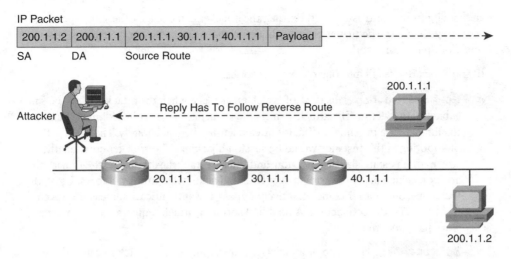

Figure 1-10   *IP Source Routing*

Note: Cisco IOS routers drop all source-routed packets if the **no ip source-route** global command is configured. Security devices, such as Cisco PIX 500 series security appliances and the Cisco ASA 5500 series appliances, drop such packets by default.

IP Source Route in Action

Looking at Figure 1-11, you see Harry the Hacker creating a packet, to be sent to Bob. Harry spoofs the source address of Alice and includes it in the source route option as its own IP address, thus appearing to be a router between Alice and Bob.

Harry generates spoofed packets that include this false source route and generously transmits them into the network. Routers between Harry and Bob read the IP packet header and forward the packets as instructed by the source route option. Bob eventually receives the packet, which he thinks originates from Alice. His reply will take the exact reverse route as it was specified in the original packet, instead of taking the more direct route to Alice. Through IP source routing, a hacker can circumvent filters and potentially gain access to internal hosts.

Such source route attacks cannot really take place over the Internet because most service providers and organizations block any packet that carries source route instructions in its header.

Man-in-the-Middle Attacks

A complex form of IP spoofing is called man-in-the-middle attack, where the hacker monitors the traffic and introduces himself as a stealth intermediary between the sender and the receiver.

Hackers use man-in-the-middle attacks to perform many security violations:

■   Theft of information

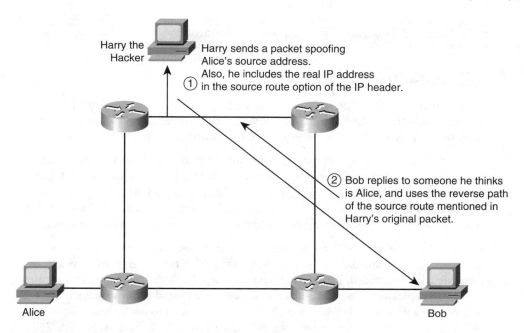

Harry the Hacker

Harry sends a packet spoofing Alice's source address. Also, he includes the real IP address ① in the source route option of the IP header.

② Bob replies to someone he thinks is Alice, and uses the reverse path of the source route mentioned in Harry's original packet.

Alice

Bob

Figure 1-11   *IP Source Routing Attack*

- Hijacking of an ongoing session to gain access to your internal network resources

- Analysis of traffic to derive information about your network and its users

- DoS

- Corruption of transmitted data

- Introduction of new information into network sessions

Note: A blind attack interferes with a connection that takes place from outside, where sequence and acknowledgment numbers are unreachable. A nonblind attack interferes with connections that cross wiring used by the hacker.

TCP session hijacking is a common variant of the man-in-the-middle attack. The attacker sniffs to identify the client and server IP addresses and relative port numbers. The attacker then modifies his or her packet headers to spoof TCP/IP packets from the client, and then waits to receive an ACK packet from the client communicating with the server. The ACK packet contains the sequence number of the next packet that the client is expecting. The attacker replies to the client using a modified packet with the source address of the server and the destination address of the client. This packet results in a reset that disconnects the legitimate client. The attacker takes over communications with the server by spoofing the expected sequence number from the ACK that was previously sent from the legitimate client to the server.

> **Note:**   This could also be an attack against confidentiality.

Confidentiality Attacks

Confidentiality breaches can occur when an attacker attempts to obtain access to read-sensitive data. These attacks can be extremely difficult to detect because the attacker can copy sensitive data without the knowledge of the owner and without leaving a trace.

A confidentiality breach can occur simply because of incorrect file protections. For instance, a sensitive file could mistakenly be given global read-access. Unauthorized copying or examination of the file would probably be difficult to track without having some type of audit mechanism running that logs every file operation. If a user had no reason to suspect unwanted access, however, the audit file would probably never be examined.

In Figure 1-12, the attacker is able to compromise an exposed web server. Using this server as a beachhead, the attacker then gains full access to the database server from which customer data is downloaded. The attacker then uses the information from the database, such as username, password, and email address, to intercept and read-sensitive email messages destined for a user in the branch office. This attack is difficult to detect because the attacker did not modify or delete any data. The data was only read and downloaded. Without some kind of auditing mechanism on the server, it is unlikely that this attack will be discovered.

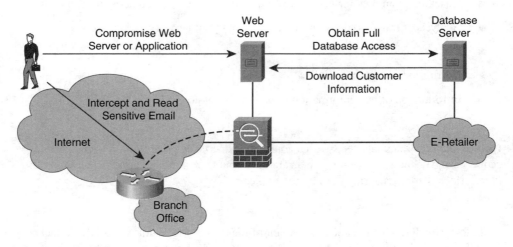

Figure 1-12   *Breach of Confidentiality*

Attackers can use many methods to compromise confidentiality, the most common of which are as follows:

■   **Packet sniffing:** Intercepting and logging traffic that passes over a digital network or part of a network.

■   **Port scanning:** Searching a network host for open ports.

■ **Dumpster diving:** Searching through company dumpsters or trash cans looking for information, such as phone books, organization charts, manuals, memos, charts, and other documentation that can provide a valuable source of information for hackers.

■ **Emanations capturing:** Capturing electrical transmissions from the equipment of an organization to deduce information regarding the organization.

■ **Wiretapping:** Monitoring the telephone or Internet conversations of a third party, often covertly.

■ **Social engineering:** Using social skills or relationships to manipulate people inside the network to provide the information needed to access the network.

■ **Overt channels:** Obvious and visible method of communications. Overt channels can be used for covert communication.

■ **Covert channels:** The ability to hide information within a transmission channel that is based on encoding data using another set of events.

Note: Many of these methods are used to compromise more than confidentiality. They are often elements of attacks on integrity and availability.

Port Scans and Ping Sweeps

As legitimate tools, port scan and ping sweep applications run a series of tests against hosts and devices to identify vulnerable services that need attention. IP addresses and port or banner data from both TCP and User Datagram Protocol (UDP) ports are examined to gather information.

In an illegitimate situation, a port scan can be a series of messages sent by someone attempting to break into a computer to learn which computer network services (each service is associated with a well-known port number) the computer provides. Port scanning can be automated to scan a range of TCP or UDP port numbers on a host to detect listening services. Port scanning, a favorite computer hacker approach, provides information to the assailant about where to probe for weaknesses. Essentially, a port scan consists of sending a message to each port, one at a time. The kind of response received indicates whether the port is being used and needs further probing.

The first step to protect against port scanning is to shut all unused ports on what can be a targeted computer, such as a server. Many server operating systems come with multiple ports open to provide a service, such as TCP port 80 for HTTP, or TCP ports 20 and 21 to provide FTP traffic. If the server is not providing FTP service, for example, make sure you disable TCP port 20 and 21.

Fingerprinting: Active Versus Passive
Scanning a network and its hosts to discover live hosts, open ports, and operating system version is called fingerprinting. Two types of fingerprinting exist:

- **Active fingerprinting:** Actively probing hosts and analyzing the nuances of the re-actions and replies of those hosts to pinpoint which operating systems and applica-tions are running on that host.

- **Passive fingerprinting:** Instead of sending packets to the targeted hosts, the hacker passively monitors the network traffic to determine the operating system in use.

A ping sweep, also known as an Internet Control Message Protocol (ICMP) sweep, is a ba-sic network scanning technique used to determine which IP addresses map to live hosts (computers). A ping sweep consists of ICMP echo requests (pings) sent to multiple hosts, whereas a single ping consists of ICMP echo requests sent to one specific host computer. If a given address is live, that host returns an ICMP echo reply. The goal of the ping sweep is to find hosts available on the network to probe for vulnerabilities. Ping sweeps are among the oldest and slowest methods used to scan a network. Moreover, firewalls limit the capability of an outside ping sweep to penetrate inside the corporate network.

Network Sniffer

In an Ethernet LAN, promiscuous mode is a mode of operation in which a network inter-face card (NIC) can receive and read every data packet that is transmitted. Promiscuous mode is the opposite of nonpromiscuous mode. When a NIC is operating in promiscuous mode, it passes all the traffic it receives to the CPU. When the NIC is not operating in promiscuous mode, it passes only the traffic whose destination MAC address matches the NIC MAC address to the CPU. Therefore, by operating in promiscuous mode, a NIC can then see more traffic than it would ordinarily be programmed to see.

A packet sniffer is a software application that uses a NIC in promiscuous mode to capture all network packets sent across a LAN. Packet sniffers work only in a single collision do-main unless a switch is compromised or an attacker launches a Layer 2 attack, such as Ad-dress Resolution Protocol (ARP) spoofing or a content-addressable memory (CAM) table overflow. These Layer 2 attacks are discussed in the "Mitigating Layer 2 Attacks" section in Chapter 7, "LAN, SAN, Voice, and Endpoint Security Overview."

Several network applications distribute packets in plaintext. Plaintext is information that is sent across the network without encryption. Sending plaintext in packets can be a prob-lem because if the packets are sniffed an attacker can easily read the contents.

A network protocol specifies the format and protocol operations. Because the specifica-tions for network protocols, such as TCP/IP, are widely published, a third party can easily interpret the packets and develop a packet sniffer. Numerous freeware and shareware packet sniffers are available that do not require the user to understand anything about the underlying protocols.

Emanations Capturing

TEMPEST is a U.S. government code word that identifies a classified set of standards for limiting electric or electromagnetic radiation emanations from electronic equipment. Mi-crochips, monitors, printers, and all electronic devices emit electromagnetic radiation

(EMI) through the air or through conductors (such as wiring or water pipes). For example, when you use a kitchen appliance while watching television, the static on your TV screen is caused by emanation.

During the 1950s, the U.S. government became concerned that emanations could be captured and then reconstructed. If the emanations were recorded, interpreted, and then played back on a similar device, it would be extremely easy to reveal the content of an encrypted message. Research showed it was possible to capture emanations from a distance, and as a response, the TEMPEST program was started.

The purpose of the program was to introduce standards that would reduce the chances of "leakage" from devices that are used to process, transmit, or store sensitive information. Government agencies and contractors use TEMPEST computers and peripherals (printers, scanners, tape drives, mice, and so on) to protect data from the monitoring of emanations. This protection is typically done by shielding the device, or sometimes a room or entire building, with copper or other conductive materials. There are also active measures for "jamming" electromagnetic signals.

Purchasing TEMPEST standard hardware is not cheap, and because of the cost, a lesser standard called ZONE has been developed. ZONE hardware does not offer the same level of protection as TEMPEST hardware, but it is less expensive.

Emanation standards are not just confined to the United States. The North Atlantic Treaty Organization (NATO) has a similar standard called the AMSG 720B Compromising Emanations Laboratory Test Standard. In Germany, the TEMPEST program is administered by the National Telecom Board. In the United Kingdom, Government Communications Headquarters (GCHQ) has a similar program.

Overt and Covert Channel

Overt and covert channels refer to the capability to hide information within or using other information:

- **Overt channel:** A transmission channel that is based on tunneling one protocol inside of another

- **Covert channel:** A transmission channel that is based on encoding data using another set of events

There are numerous ways that Internet protocols and the data that is transferred over them can provide overt and covert channels. The bad news is that firewalls generally cannot detect these channels; therefore, attackers can use them to receive confidential information in an unauthorized manner.

With an overt channel, one protocol is tunneled within another to bypass the security policy; for example Telnet over FTP, instant messaging over HTTP, and IP over Post Office Protocol version 3 (POP3). Another example of an overt channel is to use watermarks in JPEG images to leak confidential information.

One common use of overt channel is for instant messaging (IM). Most organization firewalls allow outbound HTTP but block IM. A user on the inside of the network can leak confidential information using IM over an HTTP session.

Note: You can use the advanced protocol inspection in the Cisco IPS products and Cisco ASA 5500 series appliances to counter attacks such as a hidden IM session being sent inside HTTP.

Steganography is another example of an overt channel. Steganography (the root is from the Greek word *steganos*, meaning "covered" or "secret") literally means *covered* or *secret* writing. The combination of CPU power and interest in privacy has led to the development of techniques for hiding messages in digital pictures and digitized audio.

For example, certain bits of a digital graphic can be used to hide messages. The key to knowing which bits are special is shared between two parties that want to communicate privately. The private message typically has so few bits relative to the total number of bits in the image that changing them is not visually noticeable. Without a direct comparison of the original and the processed image, it is practically impossible to tell that anything has been changed. Still, it might be detected by statistical analysis that detects non-randomness. This non-randomness in a file indicates that information is being passed inside of the file.

Note: Steganography is very difficult to detect or prevent.

With a covert channel, information is encoded as another set of events. For example, an attacker could install a Trojan horse on a target host. The Trojan horse could be written to send binary information back to the server of the attacker. The client, infected with the Trojan horse, could return to the hacker's server a ping status report in a binary format where a 0 would represent a successful ping over a one-minute period, and a 1 would represent two successful pings over a one-minute period. The hacker is keeping connectivity statistics for all the compromised clients he has around the world.

If ICMP is not permitted through a firewall, another idea is to have the client visit the web page of the attacker. The Trojan horse software, now installed on the client, has a "call home" feature that automatically opens a connection to TCP port 80 at a specific IP address, the address of the hacker's web server. All this so that the hacker can keep precise statistics of how many compromised workstations he possesses around the world. One visit per day would be represented by a 1, and no visits would be represented by a 0. As you might imagine, this technique is usually quite limited in bandwidth.

Note: Covert channels are very difficult to detect or prevent.

Phishing and Pharming

In computing, phishing is an attempt to criminally acquire sensitive information, such as usernames, passwords, and credit card details, by masquerading as a trustworthy entity. Phishing is typically carried out by email or IM, and often directs users to enter details at a website, although sometimes phone contact is attempted. Phishing is an example of social engineering.

Note: A new variation on phishing is *spear phishing*. In this case, a hacker sends an email that appears genuine to all the employees of an organization and hopes that a few get hooked. As an example, the email could say: "This is Christina, your HR director. The Automatic Payment organization which processes your pay is unable to do so this week. Please email me directly your banking information, and I will ensure that your pay is directly deposited in your bank account for Thursday morning."

Pharming is an attack aimed at redirecting the traffic of a website to another website. Pharming is conducted either by changing the hosts file on a victim computer or by exploiting a vulnerable Domain Name System (DNS) server. Pharming has become a major concern to businesses hosting e-commerce and online banking websites.

Note: Antivirus software and spyware-removal software cannot protect against pharming. Additional methods are needed such as server-side software, DNS protection, and web browser protection.

Integrity Attacks

Integrity violations can occur when the attacker attempts to change sensitive data without proper authorization. For example, the attacker obtains permission to write to sensitive data and changes or deletes it. The owner might not detect such a change until it is too late, perhaps when the change has already resulted in tangible loss. Many businesses treat integrity violations as the most serious threat to their business, because of the difficulty in detecting changes and the possible cascading consequences of late detection.

As an example, a consolidator of credit card transactions proceeds to make a batch transfer to a bank of all the transactions that took place during the previous 24 hours. A hacker could intercept the batch upload, change the amount of some transactions, and proceed with the upload toward the bank, pretending to be the consolidator. Neither the consolidator nor the bank would know that some of the transaction totals were changed.

Hackers can use many types of attacks to compromise integrity:

- **Salami attacks:** A salami attack is a series of minor data security attacks that together result in a larger attack. For example, a fraud activity in a bank where an employee steals a small amount of funds from several accounts can be considered a salami attack. A key feature to the salami attack is its resistance to detection.

- **Data diddling:** This type of attack involves changing data before or during input into a computer. A virus, the programmer of the database or application, or anyone else involved in the process of storing information in a computer could change the data.

- **Trust exploits:** A trust exploitation refers to an individual taking advantage of a trust relationship within a network.

- **Password attacks:** A password attack is any attack that attempts to identify a user account, password, or both. A password attack often uses a method called a *brute-*

force attack; however, password attacks can also employ methods such as Trojan horse programs, IP spoofing, keyloggers, and packet sniffers.

- **Session hijacking:** This attack is the exploitation of a valid computer session, sometimes also called a *session key*, to gain unauthorized access to information or services in a computer system. TCP session hijacking is a common variant of the man-in-the-middle attack.

Note: Many of these attacks can be used to compromise confidentiality, availability, or both.

The sections that follow describe some of the different types of strategies used by hackers to compromise the integrity of the data.

Trust Exploitation

Although it is not an attack in itself, trust exploitation refers to an individual taking advantage of a trust relationship within a network.

An example of a trust exploitation, consider the network in Figure 1-13, where a system in the demilitarized zone (DMZ) of a firewall, such as Server A, has a trust relationship with a system on the inside of a firewall, such as Server B. When a hacker on the outside network compromises Server A, the attacker can leverage the trust relationship Server B has with Server A to gain access to Server B.

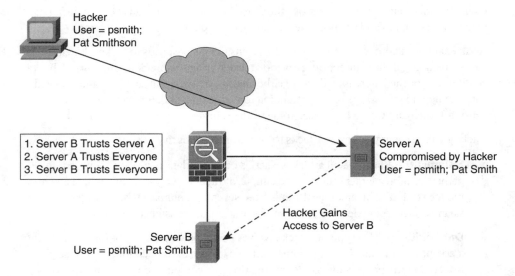

Figure 1-13   *Trust Exploitation*

Several trust models may exist in a network:

- Windows

- Domains
- Active Directory

- **Linux and UNIX**
  - Network File System (NFS)
  - Network Information Services Plus (NIS+)

The risk of trust exploitation can be reduced by introducing, among other techniques, tight constraints on trust levels within a network, such as forbidding traffic on the DMZ to access the inside network, or by insisting on strong authentication.

Port Redirection

A port redirection attack is a trust exploitation-based attack that uses a compromised host to pass traffic through a firewall that the firewall would otherwise drop. As an example, Figure 1-14 shows a firewall with three interfaces: Inside, Outside, and DMZ, with Host A on the DMZ interface. A host located on the outside interface can reach Host A, but cannot reach the host on the inside, Host B. Host A can reach both the host on the outside and Host B. If a hacker can compromise Host A, the hacker can install software on the DMZ host that redirects traffic from the outside host directly to the inside host (Host B). Although neither communication violates the rules implemented in the firewall, the outside host now has connectivity to the inside host through the port redirection process on the DMZ host. An example of an application that can provide this type of access is Netcat and fport.

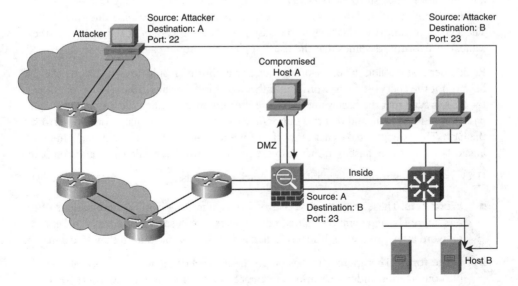

Figure 1-14 *Port Redirection Attack*

The primary way to mitigate port redirection is to use proper trust models that are network specific. If a system is under attack, a host-based intrusion prevention system (HIPS) can help detect a hacker and prevent the installation of such port redirect utilities on a host.

Password Attacks

Password attacks can be implemented using several methods, including brute-force attacks, Trojan horse programs, IP spoofing, keyloggers, and packet sniffers. Although packet sniffers and IP spoofing can yield user accounts and passwords, password attacks usually refer to repeated attempts to identify a user account, password, or both. These repeated attempts are called *brute-force attacks*.

To execute a brute-force attack, an attacker can use a program that runs across the network and attempts to log in to a shared resource, such as a server. When an attacker gains access to a resource, the attacker has the same access rights as the rightful user. If this account has sufficient privileges, the attacker can create a back door for future access, without concern for any status and password changes to the compromised user account.

Just as with packet sniffers and IP spoofing attacks, a brute-force password attack can provide access to accounts that attackers then use to modify critical network files and services. For example, an attacker compromises your network integrity by modifying your network routing tables. This trick reroutes all network packets to the attacker before transmitting them to their final destination. In such a case, an attacker can monitor all network traffic, effectively becoming a man in the middle.

Passwords present a security risk if they are stored as plaintext. You must encrypt passwords to overcome risks. On most systems, passwords are processed through an encryption algorithm that generates a one-way hash on passwords. You cannot reverse a one-way hash back to its original text. Most systems do not decrypt the stored password during authentication; they store the one-way hash. During the login process, you supply an account and password, and the password encryption algorithm generates a one-way hash. The algorithm compares this hash to the hash stored on the system. If the hashes are the same, the algorithm assumes that the user supplied the proper password.

Remember that passing the password through an algorithm results in a password hash. The hash is not the encrypted password, but rather a result of the algorithm. The strength of the hash is such that the hash value can be re-created only by using the original user and password information, and that it is impossible to retrieve the original information from the hash. This strength makes hashes perfect for encoding passwords for storage. In granting authorization, the hashes, rather than the plain password, are calculated and compared.

Hackers use many tools and techniques to crack passwords:

- **Word lists:** These programs use lists of words, phrases, or other combinations of letters, numbers, and symbols that computer users often use as passwords. Hackers enter word after word, at high speed, called a dictionary attack, until they find a match.

- **Brute force:** This approach relies on power and repetition. It compares every possible combination and permutation of characters until it finds a match. Brute force eventually cracks any password, but it might take a long, long time. Brute force is an extremely slow process because it uses every conceivable character combination.

- **Hybrid crackers:** Some password crackers mix the two techniques. This combines the best of both methods and is highly effective against poorly constructed passwords.

Password cracking attacks any application or service that accepts user authentication, including the following:

- NetBIOS over TCP (TCP 139)

- Direct host (TCP 445)

- FTP (TCP 21)

- Telnet (TCP 23)

- Simple Network Management Protocol (SNMP) (UDP 161)

- Point-to-Point Tunneling Protocol (PPTP) (TCP 1723)

- Terminal services (TCP 3389)

Note: RainbowCrack is a compilation of hashes that provide crackers with a list that they can use to attempt to match hashes that they capture with sniffers.

Availability Attacks

DoS attacks attempt to compromise the availability of a network, host, or application. They are considered a major risk because they can easily interrupt a business process and cause significant loss. These attacks are relatively simple to conduct, even by an unskilled attacker.

DoS attacks are usually the consequence of one of the following:

- The failure of a host or application to handle an unexpected condition, such as maliciously formatted input data or an unexpected interaction of system components.

- The inability of a network, host, or application to handle an enormous quantity of data, which crashes the system or brings it to a halt. Even if the firewall protects the corporate web server sitting on the DMZ from receiving a large amount of data and thus from crashing, the link connecting the corporation with its service provider will be totally clogged, and this bandwidth starvation will itself be a DoS.

Hackers can use many types of attacks to compromise availability:

- Botnets

- DoS

- DDoS

- SYN floods

- ICMP floods

- Electrical power

- Computer environment

Note: Many availability attacks can be used against confidentiality and integrity.

Botnets

Botnet is a term for a collection of software robots, or bots, which run autonomously and automatically. They run on groups of "zombie" computers controlled by crackers.

Although the term *botnet* can be used to refer to any group of bots, it is generally used to refer to a collection of compromised systems running worms, Trojan horses, or back doors, under a common command and control infrastructure. The originator of a botnet controls the group of computers remotely, usually through a means such as Internet Relay Chat (IRC).

Often, the command and control takes place via an IRC server or a specific channel on a public IRC network. A bot typically runs hidden. Generally, the attacker has compromised a large number of systems using various methods, such as exploits, buffer overflows, and so on. Newer bots automatically scan their environment and propagate using detected vulnerabilities and weak passwords. Sometimes a controller will hide an IRC server installation on an educational or corporate site, where high-speed connections can support a large number of other bots.

Several botnets have been found and removed from the Internet. The Dutch police found a 1.5-million node botnet and the Norwegian ISP Telenor disbanded a 10,000-node botnet. Large coordinated international efforts to shut down botnets have also been initiated. Some estimates indicate that up to 25 percent of all personal computers are part of a botnet.

DoS and DDoS Attacks

DoS attacks are the most publicized form of attack. They are also among the most difficult to eliminate. A DoS attack on a server sends an extremely large volume of requests over a network or the Internet. These large volumes of requests cause the attacked server to slow down dramatically. Consequently, the attacked server becomes unavailable for legitimate access and use.

DoS attacks differ from most other attacks because DoS attacks do not try to gain access to your network or the information on your network. These attacks focus on making a service unavailable for normal use. Attackers typically accomplish this by exhausting some resource limitation on the network or within an operating system or application. These attacks require little effort to execute because they typically take advantage of protocol weaknesses or because the attacks use traffic normally allowed into a network. DoS attacks are among the most difficult to completely eliminate because of the way they use protocol weaknesses and accepted traffic to attack a network. Some hackers regard DoS attacks as trivial and in bad form because they require so little effort to execute. Still, because of their ease of implementation and potentially significant damage, DoS attacks deserve special attention from security administrators.

System administrators can install software fixes to limit the damage caused by all known DoS attacks. However, as with viruses, hackers constantly develop new DoS attacks.

A DDoS attack generates much higher levels of flooding traffic by using the combined bandwidth of multiple machines to target a single machine or network. The DDoS attack enlists a network of compromised machines that contain a remotely controlled agent, or zombie, attack program. A master control mechanism provides direction and control. When the zombies receive instructions from the master agent, they each begin generating malicious traffic aimed at the victim.

DDoS attacks are the "next generation" of DoS attacks on the Internet. This type of attack is not new. UDP and TCP SYN flooding, ICMP echo request floods, and ICMP directed broadcasts (also known as Smurf attacks) are similar to DDoS attacks; however, the scope of the attack is new. Victims of DDoS attacks experience packet flooding from many different sources, possibly spoofed IP source addresses, which brings their network connectivity to a grinding halt. In the past, the typical DoS attack involved a single attempt to flood a target host with packets. With DDoS tools, an attacker can conduct the same attack using thousands of systems.

Figure 1-15 shows the process of a DDoS attack:

1. The hacker uses a terminal to scan for systems to hack.
2. After the hacker accesses handler systems, the hacker installs zombie software on them.
3. The zombies aim to scan, compromise, and infect agent systems.
4. When the hacker accesses agent systems, the hacker then loads remote-control attack software to carry out the DDoS attack.

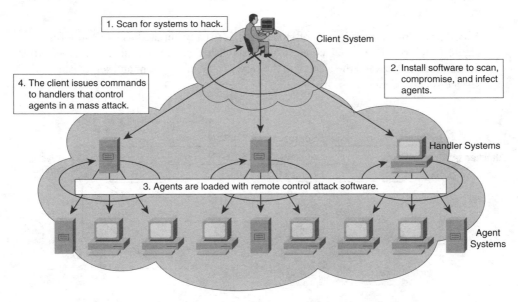

Figure 1-15   *DDoS Attack*

Note: *Stacheldracht*, which means "barbed-wire" in German, is a well-known tool used to conduct DDoS.

TCP SYN Flood Attack

Generally, in a TCP SYN flood, an attacker sends a flood of SYN segments to a target server but deliberately never completes the handshake. Servers have a limit to the number of half-open connections they will maintain before they eventually stop accepting new connections. In other words, the exhausting of the new connection resource acts as a DoS attack. The source address used on the SYN segment is usually forged, using a nonresponsive part of the address space and thus preventing resets (RST).

Cisco IOS Software has a TCP intercept capability designed to combat SYN flooding. When the Cisco IOS Software is configured to use intercept mode, which it is the default, it checks for incoming TCP connection requests and proxy-answers these requests on behalf of the destination server to ensure that the request is valid. After the TCP intercept has established a genuine connection with the client and the server, it then merges these two connections into a single source-destination session. It offers a zero window to the client to prevent it from sending data until the server sends a window offer back. In the case of bogus requests, TCP intercept uses aggressive timeouts on half-open connections and supports threshold levels for the number of outstanding and incoming TCP connection requests to protect servers while still allowing valid requests through. However, keep in mind that a severe attack might even have an impact on the router providing the TCP intercept protection. The Cisco ASAs implement a feature similar to TCP intercept, but using SYN cookies.

A TCP SYN flood attack, a form of DoS attack, is usually initiated using IP spoofing. Figure 1-16 shows how a TCP connection is established between a client and server. After the connection between the client and the server is open, the client and server can send service-specific data.

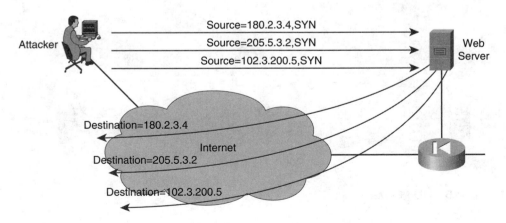

Figure 1-16   *TCP SYN Flood Attack*

An avenue of attack exists at the point where the server has sent the SYN-ACK to the client but has not yet received the ACK message. This condition is a half-open connection.

Now consider that the server has built in its system memory a data structure describing all pending connections. This data structure is a finite size and can overflow if too many half-open connections are created.

Hackers use IP spoofing to create half-open connections. The attacker sends SYN messages to the victim server. These messages appear to be legitimate but, in fact, refer to a client system that is unable to respond to the SYN-ACK messages. This means that the client never sends a final ACK message to the victim server and the connection remains half open.

The half-open connection data structure on the victim server eventually fills with messages, and the system is unable to accept any new incoming connections. Normally, a time-out period is associated with any pending connection. Half-open connections eventually expire, and the victim server recovers. However, the attacking system can simply continue sending IP-spoofed packets requesting new connections faster than the victim system can empty the table.

In most cases, the victim of such an attack has difficulty accepting any new incoming network connection. In these cases, the attack does not affect existing incoming connections or the ability to originate outgoing network connections. However, in some cases, the system might exhaust memory, crash, or be rendered otherwise inoperative.

The attacker obscures his or her location by making the source addresses in the SYN packets implausible. When the packet arrives at the victim server, there is no way to determine its true source. Because the network forwards packets based on destination address, the only way to validate the source of a packet is to use input source filtering, such as ACLs.

ICMP Flood/Smurf Attacks

Because ICMP can be a useful troubleshooting and diagnostic tool, it is often permitted by firewalls. Unfortunately, for the hosts behind such a firewall, bugs in the IP layers of the hosts can potentially be exploited.

Some DoS tricks that use ICMP are the ping of death, which uses packets that are too large, and another technique that causes ICMP fragments to fill the reassembly buffers of a device.

ICMP flooding attacks became popular because of amplification techniques such as the Smurf attacks, which use a spoofed broadcast ping to elicit a large number of responses that then bombard a target.

Smurf attacks use ICMP echo request packets directed at IP broadcast addresses from a remote site. The intent is to cause DoS. Three parties are involved in the attacks: the attacker, the intermediary, and the victim (the intermediary can also be a victim), as shown in Figure 1-17.

The intermediary receives an ICMP echo request packet that is directed to the IP broadcast address of its subnet. If the intermediary does not filter ICMP traffic directed to IP

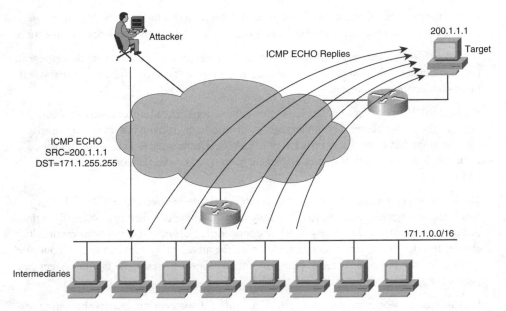

Figure 1-17   *Smurf Attack*

broadcast addresses, many of the machines on the network receive this ICMP echo request packet and send an ICMP echo reply packet back. If many of the machines on a network respond to this ICMP echo request, the result can be a severely loaded network.

Attackers create forged packets that contain the spoofed source address of the intended victim. When the machines at the site of the intermediary respond to the ICMP echo requests, they send replies to the victim machine. The victim is potentially subjected to severe network congestion.

Note: Smurf attacks were the reason that Cisco IOS Release 12.0 started shipping with a new default value in interface configuration. The **no ip directed-broadcast** command prevents sending a directed broadcast packet to the directly connected network of a router.

Electrical Power Attacks

There are three basic types of power attacks (or at least concerns), as shown in Table 1-1. Electrical power attacks would require that the hacker have physical access to your installation or to the grid. Regardless, organizations should be concerned about the constant and proper supply of electricity.

Table 1-1   *Basic Types of Power Attacks*

	Brief Period of Time	**Extended Period of Time**
Excessive Power	Spikes	Surges
Complete Loss of Power	Faults	Blackouts
Reduced Power	Sags	Brownouts

You can limit electrical supply problems by adhering to the following guidelines:

- Install UPSs for mission-critical Cisco network devices.

- Install backup generator systems for mission-critical supplies.

- Plan for and initiate regular UPS or generator testing and maintenance procedures based on the manufacturer suggested preventive maintenance schedule.

- Install redundant power supplies on critical devices.

- Monitor and alarm power-related parameters at the power supply and device levels.

Computer Environment Attacks

Environmental problems address everything that is of a physical nature that is not power. Such attacks require that the hacker have physical access to your building or to the supplier of that resource. The following are concerns that are of an environmental nature that an attacker can use to try to launch a DoS attack:

- **Temperature:** Computer systems require cool temperatures. Outages can happen because an air-conditioning system fails.

- **Air flow:** Computer-based systems do not like dust. The best data centers have a positive air-flow system in place wherein the air pressure within the data center is greater than the air pressure outside of the data center, causing the air to blow out instead of dust blowing in when a door is opened.

- **Humidity:** Electronic equipment does not tolerate water. Even the minor amounts of water found in humidity can damage equipment.

- **Water:** Water damages electronic equipment. Controls must be in place to protect the data center from floods.

- **Gas:** Gas is a flammable. It is important that electronic equipment does not create sparks in the presence of gas.

Mission-critical Cisco network equipment should be located in wiring closets or in computer or telecommunications rooms that meet the following minimum requirements:

- The room must be locked, with only authorized personnel allowed access.

- The room should not be accessible via a dropped ceiling, raised floor, window, ductwork, or point of entry other than the secured access point.

- If possible, use electronic access control, with all entry attempts logged by security systems and monitored by security personnel.

- If possible, security personnel should monitor activity using security cameras with automatic recording.

Take the following actions to limit environmental damage to Cisco network devices:

- Supply the room with dependable temperature- and humidity-control systems. Always verify the recommended environmental parameters of the Cisco network equipment with the supplied product documentation.

- Remove any sources of electrostatic and magnetic interferences in the room.

Best Practices to Defeat Network Attacks

Defending your network against attack requires constant vigilance and education. The following 10 practices represent the best insurance for your network:

- Keep patches current by installing them weekly or daily, if possible, to prevent buffer-overflow and privilege-escalation attacks.

- Shut down unnecessary services and ports.

- Use strong passwords and change them often.

- Control physical access to systems.

- Avoid unnecessary web page inputs. Some websites allow users to enter usernames and passwords. A hacker can enter more than just a username. For example, entering jdoe; rm -rf / might allow an attacker to remove the root file system from a UNIX server. Programmers should limit input characters and not accept invalid characters such as | ; < > as possible input.

- Perform backups and test the backed up files on a regular basis.

- Educate employees about the risks of social engineering and develop strategies to validate identities over the phone, via email, or in person.

- Encrypt and password-protect sensitive data.

- Implement security hardware and software such as firewalls, IPSs, VPN devices, antivirus software, and content filtering.

- Develop a written security policy for the company.

These methods are only a starting point for sound security management. Organizations must remain vigilant at all times to defend against continually evolving threats.

Examining Operations Security

Operations security is concerned with the day-to-day practices necessary to first deploy and later maintain a secure system. This section examines these principles.

Secure Network Life Cycle Management

The responsibilities of the operations team pertain to everything that takes place to keep a network, computer systems, applications, and the environment up and running in a secure and protected manner. After the network is set up, the operation tasks begin, including the continual day-to-day maintenance of the environment. These activities are regular in nature and enable the environment, systems, and applications to continue to run correctly and securely.

Operations within a computing environment can pertain to software, personnel, and hardware, but an operations department often focuses only on the hardware and software aspects. Management is responsible for the behavior and responsibilities of employees. The people within operations are responsible for ensuring that systems are protected and that they continue to run in a predictable manner.

The operations team usually has the following objectives:

- Preventing reoccurring problems

- Reducing hardware failures to an acceptable level

- Reducing the impact of hardware failure or disruption

This group should investigate any unusual or unexplained occurrences, unscheduled initial program loads, deviations from standards, or other odd or abnormal conditions that take place on the network.

Including security early in the information process, in the system design life cycle (SDLC), usually results in less-expensive and more-effective security when compared to adding it to an operational system.

A general SDLC includes five phases:

1. Initiation
2. Acquisition and development
3. Implementation
4. Operations and maintenance
5. Disposition

Each of these five phases includes a minimum set of security steps that you need to effectively incorporate security into a system during its development. An organization either uses the general SDLC or develops a tailored SDLC that meets their specific needs. In either case, the National Institute of Standards and Technology (NIST) recommends that organizations incorporate the associated IT security steps of this general SDLC into their development process.

Initiation Phase

The initiation phase of the SDLC includes the following:

■ **Security categorization:** This step defines three levels, such as low, moderate, and high, of potential impact on organizations or individuals should a breach of security occur (a loss of confidentiality, integrity, or availability). Security categorization standards help organizations make the appropriate selection of security controls for their information systems.

■ **Preliminary risk assessment:** This step results in an initial description of the basic security needs of the system. A preliminary risk assessment should define the threat environment in which the system will operate.

Acquisition and Development Phase

The acquisition and development phase of the SDLC includes the following:

■ **Risk assessment:** This step is an analysis that identifies the protection requirements for the system through a formal risk-assessment process. This analysis builds on the initial risk assessment that was performed during the initiation phase, but is more in depth and specific.

■ **Security functional requirements analysis:** This step is an analysis of requirements and can include the following components: system security environment, such as the enterprise information security policy and enterprise security architecture, and security functional requirements.

■ **Security assurance requirements analysis:** This step is an analysis of the requirements that address the developmental activities required and the assurance evidence needed to produce the desired level of confidence that the information security will work correctly and effectively. The analysis, based on legal and functional security requirements, is used as the basis for determining how much and what kinds of assurance are required.

■ **Cost considerations and reporting:** This step determines how much of the development cost you can attribute to information security over the life cycle of the system. These costs include hardware, software, personnel, and training.

■ **Security planning:** This step ensures that you fully document any agreed upon security controls, whether they are just planned or in place. The security plan also provides a complete characterization or description of the information system and attachments or references to key documents that support the information security program of the agency. Examples of documents that support the information security program include a configuration management plan, a contingency plan, an incident response plan, a security awareness and training plan, rules of behavior, a risk assessment, a security test and evaluation results, system interconnection agreements, security authorizations and accreditations, and a plan of action and milestones.

■ **Security control development:** This step ensures that the security controls that the respective security plans describe are designed, developed, and implemented. The security plans for information systems that are currently in operation may call for the development of additional security controls to supplement the controls that are already in place or the modification of selected controls that are deemed less than effective.

- **Developmental security test and evaluation:** This ensures that security controls that you develop for a new information system are working properly and are effective. Some types of security controls, primarily those controls of a nontechnical nature, cannot be tested and evaluated until the information system is deployed. These controls are typically management and operational controls.

- **Other planning components:** This step ensures that you consider all the necessary components of the development process when you incorporate security into the network life cycle. These components include the selection of the appropriate contract type, the participation by all the necessary functional groups within an organization, the participation by the certifier and accreditor, and the development and execution of the necessary contracting plans and processes.

Implementation Phase

The implementation phase of the SDLC includes the following:

- **Inspection and acceptance:** This step ensures that the organization validates and verifies that the functionality that the specification describes is included in the deliverables.

- **System integration:** This step ensures that the system is integrated at the operational site where you will deploy the information system for operation. You enable the security control settings and switches in accordance with the vendor instructions and the available security implementation guidance.

- **Security certification:** This step ensures that you effectively implement the controls through established verification techniques and procedures. This step gives organization officials confidence that the appropriate safeguards and countermeasures are in place to protect the information system of the organization. Security certification also uncovers and describes the known vulnerabilities in the information system.

- **Security accreditation:** This step provides the necessary security authorization of an information system to process, store, or transmit information that is required. This authorization is granted by a senior organization official and is based on the verified effectiveness of security controls to some agreed upon level of assurance and an identified residual risk to agency assets or operations.

Operations and Maintenance Phase

The operations and maintenance phase of the SDLC includes the following:

- **Configuration management and control:** This step ensures that there is adequate consideration of the potential security impacts due to specific changes to an information system or its surrounding environment. Configuration management and configuration control procedures are critical to establishing an initial baseline of hardware, software, and firmware components for the information system and subsequently controlling and maintaining an accurate inventory of any changes to the system.

- **Continuous monitoring:** This step ensures that controls continue to be effective in their application through periodic testing and evaluation. Security control monitoring, such as verifying the continued effectiveness of those controls over time, and reporting the security status of the information system to appropriate agency officials is an essential activity of a comprehensive information security program.

Disposition Phase

The disposition phase of the SDLC includes the following:

- **Information preservation:** This step ensures that you retain information, as necessary, to conform to current legal requirements and to accommodate future technology changes that can render the retrieval method of the information obsolete.

- **Media sanitization:** This step ensures that you delete, erase, and write over data as necessary.

- **Hardware and software disposal:** This step ensures that you dispose of hardware and software as directed by the information system security officer.

Principles of Operations Security

Certain core principles are part of the secure operations that are intended for information systems security (infosec). The following are among these principles:

- Separation of duties
  - Two-man control
  - Dual operator

- Rotation of duties

- Trusted recovery, which includes the following:
  - Failure preparation
  - System recovery

- Change and configuration controls

Separation of Duties

Separation of duties (SoD) is one of the key concepts of internal control and is the most difficult and sometimes the most costly control to achieve. SoD states that no single individual should have control over two or more phases of a transaction or operation, which makes deliberate fraud more difficult to perpetrate because it requires the collusion of two or more individuals or parties.

The term *SoD* is already well-known in financial systems. Companies understand not to combine roles such as receiving checks, approving discounts, depositing cash and reconciling bank statements, approving time cards, and so on.

In information systems, segregation of duties helps to reduce the potential impact from the actions/inactions of one person. You should organize IT in a way that achieves adequate SoD.

> **Note:**   SoD is also known as segregation of duties.

The two-man control principle uses two individuals to review and approve the work of the other. This principle provides accountability and reduces things such as fraud. Because of the obvious overhead involved, this practice is usually limited to sensitive duties considered potential security risks.

The dual-operator principle differs from the two-man control because the task involved actually requires two people. An example of the dual-operator principle is a check that requires two signatures for the bank to accept it, or the safety deposit bank where you have one key and the bank clerk has the second key.

> **Note:**   The dual-operator principle is a technical requirement, whereas two-man control is an administrative or policy decision.

Rotation of Duties

Rotation of duties is sometimes called job rotation. To successfully implement this principle, it is important that individuals have the training necessary to complete more than one job. Peer review is usually included in the practice of this principle.

For example, suppose that a job-rotation scheme has five people rotating through five different roles during the course of a week. Peer review of work occurs whether or not it was intended. When five people do one job in the course of the week, each person is effectively reviewing the work of the others.

The most obvious benefit of this practice is the great strength and flexibility that would exist within a department because everyone is capable of doing all the jobs. Although the purpose for the practice is rooted in security, you gain an additional business benefit from this breadth of experience of the personnel.

Trusted Recovery

One of the easiest ways to compromise a system is to make the system restart and compromise it before all of its defenses can be reloaded. For this reason, trusted recovery is a principle of operations security. The trust recovery principle states that you must expect that systems and individuals will experience a failure at some time and you must prepare for this failure. Because you anticipate the failure, you can have a recovery plan for both systems and personnel available and implemented. The most common way to prepare for failure is to back up data on a regular basis.

Backing up data is a normal occurrence in most IT departments and is commonly performed by junior-level staff. However, this is not a very secure operation because backup software uses an account that can bypass file security to back up the files. Therefore, junior-level staff members have access to files that they would ordinarily not be able to access. The same is true if these same junior staff members have the right to restore data.

Security professionals propose that a secure backup program contain some of the following practices:

■ A junior staff member is responsible for loading blank media.

■ Backup software uses an account that is unknown to individuals to bypass file security.

■ A different staff member removes the backup media and securely stores it on site while being assisted by another member of the staff.

■ A separate copy of the backup is stored off site and is handled by a third staff member who is accompanied by another staff member.

Note: One of the easiest ways for attackers to get their hands on a password file (or any other data) is to get a copy of the backup tape, because the backup tape is not always handled or stored securely.

Being prepared for system failure is an important part of operations security. The following are examples of things that help provide system recovery:

■ Operating systems and applications that have single-user or safe mode help with system recovery.

■ The ability to recover files that were open at the time of the problem helps ensure a smooth system recovery. The autosave process in many desktop applications is an example of this ability. A memory dump that many operating systems perform upon a system failure is also an example of this ability.

■ The ability to retain the security settings of a file after a system crash is critical so that the security is not bypassed by forcing a crash.

■ The ability to recover and retain security settings for critical key system files, such as the Registry, configuration files, password files, and so on, is critical for providing system recovery.

Change and Configuration Control

The goal of change and configuration controls is to ensure that you use standardized methods and procedures to efficiently handle all changes. To make changes efficient, you should minimize the impact of change-related incidents and improve the day-to-day operations.

A *change* is defined as an event that results in a new status of one or more configuration items. A change should be approved by management, be cost-effective, and be an enhancement to business processes with a minimum risk to the IT infrastructure and security.

The three major goals of change and configuration management are as follows:

■ Minimal system and network disruption

■ Preparation to reverse changes

■ More economic utilization of resources

To accomplish configuration changes in an effective and safe manor, adhere to the following suggestions:

■ Ensure that the change is implemented in an orderly manner with formalized testing.

■ Ensure that the end users are aware of the coming change (when necessary).

■ Analyze the effects of the change after it is implemented.

■ Reduce the potential negative impact on performance or security, or both.

Although the change control process differs from organization to organization, certain patterns emerge in change management. The following are steps in a typical change control process:

Step 1.   Apply to introduce the change.

Step 2.   Catalogue the proposed change.

Step 3.   Schedule the change.

Step 4.   Implement the change.

Step 5.   Report the change to relevant parties.

Network Security Testing

Security testing provides insight into the other SDLC activities such as risk analysis and contingency planning. You should document security testing and make them available for staff involved in other IT and security related areas. Typically, you conduct network security testing during the implementation and operational stages, after the system has been developed, installed, and integrated.

During the implementation stage, you should conduct security testing and evaluation on specific parts of the system and on the entire system as a whole. Security test and evaluation (ST&E) is an examination or analysis of the protective measures that are placed on an information system after it is fully integrated and operational. The following are the objectives of the ST&E:

■ Uncover design, implementation, and operational flaws that could allow the violation of the security policy

■ Determine the adequacy of security mechanisms, assurances, and other properties to enforce the security policy

■ Assess the degree of consistency between the system documentation and its implementation

Once a system is operational, it is important to ascertain its operational status. You can conduct many tests to assess the operational status of the system. The types of tests you use and the frequency in which you conduct them depend on the importance of the system and the resources available for testing. You should repeat these tests periodically and whenever you make a major change to the system. For systems that are exposed to constant threat, such as web servers, or systems that protect critical information, such as firewalls, you should conduct tests more frequently.

Security Testing Techniques

You can use security testing results in the following ways:

- As a reference point for corrective action

- To define mitigation activities to address identified vulnerabilities

- As a benchmark to trace the progress of an organization in meeting security requirements

- To assess the implementation status of system security requirements

- To conduct cost and benefit analysis for improvements to system security

- To enhance other life cycle activities, such as risk assessments, certification and authorization (C&A), and performance-improvement efforts

There are several different types of security testing. Some testing techniques are predominantly manual, and other tests are highly automated. Regardless of the type of testing, the staff that sets up and conducts the security testing should have significant security and networking knowledge, including significant expertise in the following areas: network security, firewalls, IPSs, operating systems, programming, and networking protocols, such as TCP/IP.

Many testing techniques are available, including the following:

- Network scanning

- Vulnerability scanning

- Password cracking

- Log review

- Integrity checkers

- Virus detection

- War dialing

- War driving (802.11 or wireless LAN testing)

- Penetration testing

Common Testing Tools

Many testing tools are available in the modern marketplace that you can use to test the security of your systems and networks. The following list is a collection of tools that are quite popular; some of the tools are freeware, some are not:

- Nmap

- GFI LANguard

- Tripwire

- Nessus

- Metasploit

- SuperScan by Foundstone, a division of McAfee

Note: Many other excellent tools exist. This list is only a representative sampling.

Some testing tools are actually hacking tools. Why not try on your network tools before a hacker does? Find the weaknesses on your network before the hacker does and before he exploits them. So, look at two tools that are commonly used.

Nmap is the best-known low-level scanner available to the public. It is simple to use and has an array of excellent features that you can use for network mapping and reconnaissance. The basic functionality of Nmap enables the user to do the following:

- Perform classic TCP and UDP port scanning (looking for different services on one host) and sweeping (looking for the same service on multiple systems)

- Perform stealth port scans and sweeps, which are hard to detect by the target host or IPSs

- Identify remote operating systems, known as OS fingerprinting, through its TCP idiosyncrasies

Advanced features of Nmap include protocol scanning, known as Layer 3 port scanning, which can identify Layer 3 protocol support on a host, such as generic routing encapsulation (GRE) support and Open Shortest Path First (OSPF) support, using decoy hosts on the same LAN to mask your identity.

Figure 1-18 shows a screen output of ZENMAP, the GUI for Nmap Security Scanner.

Tip: You can download the Nmap program from http://www.insecure.org/nmap.

SuperScan Version 4 is an update of the highly popular Microsoft Windows port scanning tool, SuperScan. It runs only on Windows XP and Windows 2000 and requires administrator privileges to run. Windows XP SP2 has removed support for raw sockets, which limits the capability of SuperScan and other scanning tools. Some functionality can be restored by entering the **net stop SharedAccess** command at the Windows command prompt.

The following are some of the features of SuperScan Version 4:

- Adjustable scanning speed

- Support for unlimited IP ranges

- Improved host detection using multiple ICMP methods

- TCP SYN scanning

- UDP scanning (two methods)

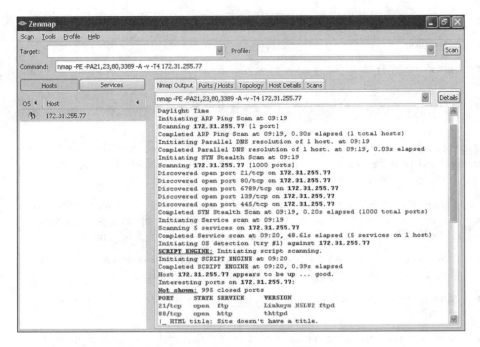

Figure 1-18 *ZENMAP (Nmap Security Scanner GUI)*

- Simple HTML report generation

- Source port scanning

- Fast hostname resolving

- Extensive banner grabbing

- Massive built-in port list description database

- IP and port scan order randomization

- A selection of useful tools (ping, traceroute, Whois, and so on)

- Extensive Windows host enumeration capability

Figure 1-19 shows a screen capture of SuperScan results.

Note: Visit http://www.remote-exploit.org/backtrack.html to download Backtrack 3, released in June 2008. Backtrack 3, a live CD, is packed with more than 300 security tools to test and secure your network.

Disaster Recovery and Business Continuity Planning

Business continuity planning and disaster recovery procedures address the continuing operations of an organization in the event of a disaster or prolonged service interruption that affects the mission of the organization. Such plans should address an emergency response phase, a recovery phase, and a return to normal operation phase. You should identify the

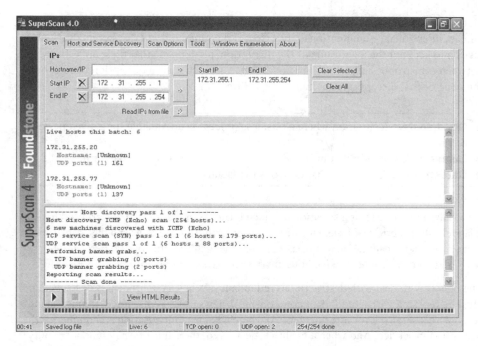

Figure 1-19   *SuperScan 4.0*

responsibilities of personnel and the available resources during an incident. In reality, contingency and disaster recovery plans do not address every possible scenario or assumption. Rather, they focus on the events most likely to occur and identify an acceptable method of recovery. Periodically, you should exercise the plans and procedures to ensure that they are effective and well understood.

Business continuity planning provides a short- to medium-term framework to continue the organizational operations. The following are objectives of business continuity planning:

- Moving or relocating critical business components and people to a remote location while the original location is being repaired

- Using different channels of communication to deal with customers, shareholders, and partners until operations return to normal

Disaster recovery is the process of regaining access to the data, hardware, and software necessary to resume critical business operations after a natural or human-induced disaster. A disaster recovery plan should also include plans for coping with the unexpected or sudden loss of key personnel. A disaster recovery plan is part of a larger process known as business continuity planning.

After the events of September 11, 2001, when many companies lost irreplaceable data, the effort put into protecting that data has changed. It is believed that some companies spend up to 25 percent of their IT budget on disaster recovery planning to avoid larger losses. Research indicates that of companies that had a major loss of computerized records, 43 percent never reopen, 51 percent close within two years, and only 6 percent survive long term.

Not all disruptions to business operations are equal. Whether the disruption is natural or human, intentional or unintentional, the effect is the same. A good disaster recovery plan takes into account the magnitude of the disruption, recognizing that there are differences between catastrophes, disasters, and nondisasters. In each case, a disruption occurs, but the scale of that disruption can dramatically differ.

Key Topic

- **Nondisaster:** A situation where a business process is unavailable for a given period of time
- **Disaster:** A situation that makes a facility unusable for an entire day or more
- **Catastrophe:** A situation that destroys the facility

Generally, a nondisaster is a situation in which business operations are interrupted for a relatively short period of time. Disasters cause interruptions of at least a day, sometimes longer. The significant detail in a disaster is that the facilities are not 100 percent destroyed. In a catastrophe, the facilities are destroyed, and all operations must be moved.

The only way to deal with destruction is redundancy. When a component is destroyed, it must be replaced with a redundant component. When service is disrupted, it must be insured with a service level agreement (SLA) wherein some compensation is acquired for the disruption in service. And when a facility is destroyed, there must be a redundant facility. Without redundancy, it is impossible to recover from destruction.

Redundant facilities are referred to as hot, warm, and cold sites. Each of these is available for a different price, with different resulting downtimes.

In the case of a hot site, a completely redundant facility is acquired with almost identical equipment. The copying of data to this redundant facility is part of normal operations, so that in the case of a catastrophe, only the latest changes of data must be applied so that full operations are restored. With enough money spent in preparation for a catastrophe, this recovery can take as little as a few minutes or even seconds.

Tip: Organizations that need to respond in seconds often employ global load balancing (GLB) and distributed storage-area networks (SAN) to respond quickly.

Warm sites are physically redundant facilities without the software and data standing by. Overnight replication would not occur in these instances, necessitating a disaster recovery team to physically go to the redundant facility and bring it up. Depending on how much software and how much data is involved, it can take days to resume operations.

A cold site is usually an empty data center with racks, power, WAN links, and heating, ventilation, and air conditioning (HVAC) already present, but no equipment. In this case, an organization would have to first acquire routers, switches, firewalls, servers, and so on to rebuild everything. Once you restore the backups to the new machines, operations can continue. This option is the least expensive in terms of money spent annually, but would usually take weeks to resume full operations.

Understanding and Developing a Comprehensive Network Security Policy

It is important to know that the security policy developed in your organization drives all the steps taken to secure network resources. The development of a comprehensive security policy prepares you for the rest of this course.

To create an effective security policy, it is necessary to also do a risk analysis to maximize the effectiveness of the policy. Also, it is essential that everyone be aware of the policy; otherwise, it is doomed to fail.

Security Policy Overview

Every organization has something that someone else wants. Someone might want that something for himself, or he might want the satisfaction of denying something to its rightful owner. Your assets are what need the protection of a security policy.

Determine what your assets are by asking (and answering) the following questions:

- What do you have that others want?

- What processes, data, or information systems are critical to you, your company, or your organization?

- What would stop your company or organization from doing business or fulfilling its mission?

The answers identify assets ranging from critical databases, vital applications, vital company customer and employee information, classified commercial information, shared drives, email servers, and web servers.

A security policy is a set of objectives for the company, rules of behavior for users and administrators, and requirements for system and management that collectively ensure the security of network and computer systems in an organization. A security policy is a "living document," meaning that the document is never finished and is continuously updated as technology and employee requirements change.

The security policy translates, clarifies, and communicates the management position on security as defined in high-level security principles. The security policies act as a bridge between these management objectives and specific security requirements. The security policy informs users, staff, and managers of their obligatory requirements for protecting technology and information assets. The security policy should specify the mechanisms that you need to meet these requirements. The security policy also provides a baseline from which to acquire, configure, and audit computer systems and networks for compliance with the security policy. Therefore, an attempt to use a set of security tools in the absence of at least an implied security policy is meaningless.

Key Topic

The three reasons for having a security policy are as follows:

- To inform users, staff, and managers
- To specify mechanisms for security
- To provide a baseline

One of the most common security policy components is an acceptable use policy (AUP). This component defines what users are allowed and not allowed to do on the various components of the system, including the type of traffic that is allowed on the networks. The AUP should be as explicit as possible to avoid ambiguity or misunderstanding. For example, an AUP might list the prohibited website categories.

Note: Some sites refer to an acceptable use policy as an *appropriate use policy*.

The audience for the security policy should be anyone who might have access to your network, including employees, contractors, suppliers, and customers. However, the security policy should treat each of these groups differently.

The audience determines the content of the policy. For example, you probably do not need to include a description of *why* something is necessary in a policy that is intended for the technical staff. You can assume that the technical staff already knows why a particular requirement is included. Managers are also not likely to be interested in the technical aspects of why a particular requirement is needed. However, they might want the high-level overview or the principles supporting the requirement. When end users know why a particular security control has been included, they are more likely to comply with the policy.

One document will not likely meet the needs of the entire audience of a large organization. The goal is to ensure that the information security policy documents are coherent with its audience needs.

Security Policy Components

Figure 1-20 shows the hierarchy of a corporate policy structure that is aimed at effectively meeting the needs of all audiences.

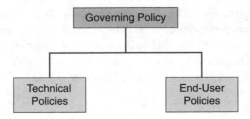

Figure 1-20   *Components of a Comprehensive Security Policy*

Most corporations should use a suite of policy documents to meet their wide and varied needs:

- **Governing policy:** This policy is a high-level treatment of security concepts that are important to the company. Managers and technical custodians are the intended audience. The governing policy controls all security-related interaction among business units and supporting departments in the company. In terms of detail, the governing policy answers the "what" security policy questions.

- **End-user policies:** This document covers all security topics important to end users. In terms of detail level, end-user policies answer the "what," "who," "when," and "where" security policy questions at an appropriate level of detail for an end user.

- **Technical policies:** Security staff members use technical policies as they carry out their security responsibilities for the system. These policies are more detailed than the governing policy and are system or issue specific (for example, access control or physical security issues). In terms of detail, technical policies answer the "what," the "who," the "when," and the "where" security policy questions. The "why" is left to the owner of the information.

Note: Cisco has created a tool to help you create customized security policies for your organization. Visit http://www.ciscowebtools.com/spb/ to find out more about Cisco Security Policy Builder.
Also, consider SANS security policies repository at http://www.sans.org/resources/policies.

Governing Policy

The governing policy outlines the security concepts that are important to the company for managers and technical custodians:

- The governing policy controls all security-related interactions among business units and supporting departments in the company.

- The governing policy aligns closely with existing company policies, especially human resource policies, but also any other policy that mentions security-related issues such as email, computer use, or related IT subjects.

- The governing policy is placed at the same level as all companywide policies.

- The governing policy supports the technical and end-user policies.

A governing policy includes the following key components:

- A statement of the issue that the policy addresses

- A statement about your position as IT manager on the policy

- How the policy applies in the environment

- The roles and responsibilities of those affected by the policy

- What level of compliance to the policy is necessary

- Which actions, activities, and processes are allowed and which are not
- What the consequences of noncompliance are

End-User Policies

The end-user policy is a single policy document that covers all the policy topics pertaining to information security that end users should know about, comply with, and implement. This policy may overlap with the technical policies and is at the same level as a technical policy. Grouping all the end-user policies together means that users have to go to only one place and read one document to learn everything that they need to do to ensure compliance with the company security policy.

Technical Policies

Security staff members use the technical policies in the conduct of their daily security responsibilities. These policies are more detailed than the governing policy and are system or issue specific (for example, router security or physical security issues). These policies are essentially security handbooks that describe what the security staff does, but not how the security staff performs its functions.

The following are typical policy categories for technical policies:

- General policies
  - **AUP:** Defines the acceptable use of equipment and computing services, and the appropriate security measures that employees should take to protect the corporate resources and proprietary information.
  - **Account access request policy:** Formalizes the account and access request process within the organization. Users and system administrators who bypass the standard processes for account and access requests can cause legal action against the organization.
  - **Acquisition assessment policy:** Defines the responsibilities regarding corporate acquisitions and defines the minimum requirements that the information security group must complete for an acquisition assessment.
  - **Audit policy:** Conducts audits and risk assessments to ensure integrity of information and resources, investigates incidents, ensures conformance to security policies, or monitors user and system activity where appropriate.
  - **Information sensitivity policy:** Defines the requirements for classifying and securing information in a manner appropriate to its sensitivity level.
  - **Password policy:** Defines the standards for creating, protecting, and changing strong passwords.
  - **Risk-assessment policy:** Defines the requirements and provides the authority for the information security team to identify, assess, and remediate risks to the information infrastructure that is associated with conducting business.
  - **Global web server policy:** Defines the standards that are required by all web hosts.

- Email policies
  - **Automatically forwarded email policy:** Documents the policy restricting automatic email forwarding to an external destination without prior approval from the appropriate manager or director.
  - **Email policy:** Defines the standards to prevent tarnishing the public image of the organization.
  - **Spam policy:** The AUP covers spam.

- Remote-access policies
  - **Dial-in access policy:** Defines the appropriate dial-in access and its use by authorized personnel.
  - **Remote-access policy:** Defines the standards for connecting to the organization network from any host or network external to the organization.
  - **VPN security policy:** Defines the requirements for remote-access IP Security (IPsec) or Layer 2 Tunneling Protocol (L2TP) VPN connections to the organization network.

- Telephony policies
  - **Analog and ISDN line policy:** Defines the standards to use analog and ISDN lines for sending and receiving faxes and for connection to computers.
  - **Personal communication device policy:** Defines the information security's requirements for personal communication devices, such as voicemail, IP phones, softphones, and so on.

- Application policies
  - **Acceptable encryption policy:** Defines the requirements for encryption algorithms that are used within the organization.
  - **Application service provider (ASP) policy:** Defines the minimum security criteria that an ASP must execute before the organization uses them on a project.
  - **Database credentials coding policy:** Defines the requirements for securely storing and retrieving database usernames and passwords.
  - **Interprocess communications policy:** Defines the security requirements that any two or more processes must meet when they communicate with each other using a network socket or operating system socket.
  - **Project security policy:** Defines requirements for project managers to review all projects for possible security requirements.
  - **Source code protection policy:** Establishes minimum information security requirements for managing product source code.

- Network policies
  - **Extranet policy:** Defines the requirement that third-party organizations that need access to the organization networks must sign a third-party connection agreement.
  - **Minimum requirements for network access policy:** Defines the standards and requirements for any device that requires connectivity to the internal network.
  - **Network access standards:** Defines the standards for secure physical port access for all wired and wireless network data ports.

- **Router and switch security policy:** Defines the minimal security configuration standards for routers and switches inside a company production network or used in a production capacity.
- **Server security policy:** Defines the minimal security configuration standards for servers inside a company production network or used in a production capacity.

- Wireless communication policy: Defines standards for wireless systems that are used to connect to the organization networks.

- Document Retention policy: Defines the minimal systematic review, retention, and destruction of documents received or created during the course of business. The categories of retention policy are, among others:
  - **Electronic communication retention policy:** Defines standards for the retention of email and instant messaging.
  - **Financial retention policy:** Defines standards for the retention of bank statements, annual reports, pay records, accounts payable and receivable, and so on.
  - **Employee records retention policy:** Defines standards for the retention of employee personal records.
  - **Operation records retention policy:** Defines standards for the retention of past inventories information, training manuals, suppliers lists, and so forth.

Standards, Guidelines, and Procedures

Security policies establish a framework within to work, but they are excessively general to be of much use to individuals responsible for implementing these policies. Because of this, other more detailed documents exist. Among the more important detailed documents are the standards, guidelines, and procedures documents.

Whereas policy documents are very much high-level overview documents, the standards, guidelines, and procedure documents are documents that the security staff will use regularly to implement the security policies.

Standards

Standards allow an IT staff to be consistent. They specify the use of specific technologies because no one can know everything. Standards also try to provide consistency in the network because it is unreasonable to support multiple versions of hardware and software unless it is necessary. The most successful IT organizations have standards to improve efficiency and to keep things as simple as possible.

Standardization also applies to security. One of the most important security principles is consistency. If you support 100 routers, it is important that you configure all 100 routers as similarly as possible. If you do not do this, it is difficult to maintain security. When you do not strive for the simplest of solutions, you usually fail in being secure.

Guidelines

Guidelines help provide a list of suggestions on how you can do things better. Guidelines are similar to standards, but are more flexible and are not usually mandatory. You will find some of the best guidelines available in repositories known as "best practices." The following is a list of widely available guidelines:

- National Institute of Standards and Technology (NIST) Computer Security Resource Center

- National Security Agency (NSA) Security Configuration Guides

- The Common Criteria Standard

- Rainbow Series

Procedures

Procedure documents are longer and more detailed than the standards and guidelines documents. Procedure documents include the details of implementation, usually with step-by-step instructions and graphics. Procedure documents are extremely important for large organizations to have the consistency of deployment that is necessary to have a secure environment. Inconsistency is the enemy of security.

Security Policy Roles and Responsibilities

In any organization, it is senior management, such as the CEO, which is always ultimately responsible for everything. Typically, senior management only oversees the development of a security policy. The creation and maintenance of a security policy is usually delegated to the people in charge of IT or security operations.

Sometimes the senior security or IT management personnel, such as the chief security officer (CSO), the chief information officer (CIO), or the chief information security officer (CISO), will have the expertise to create the policy, sometimes they will delegate it, and sometimes it will be a bit of both strategies. But the senior security person is always intimately involved in the development and maintenance of security policy. Guidelines can provide a framework for policy decision making.

Senior security staff is often consulted for input on a proposed policy project. They might even be responsible for the development and maintenance of portions of the policy. It is more likely that senior staff will be responsible for the development of standards and procedures.

Everyone else who is involved in the security policy has the duty to abide by it. Many of the policy statements will include language that refers to a potential loss of employment for violation of the policy. IT staff and end users alike are responsible to know the policy and follow it.

Risk Analysis and Management

Every process of security should first address the following questions:

■   Which are the threats the system is facing?

■   Which are the probable threats and what would be their consequence, if exploited?

The threat-identification process provides an organization with a list of threats, which a system is subject to in a particular environment.

Note: An interesting method of modeling security threats is the Attack Trees method by Bruce Schneier. You can find more information about this method at http://en.wikipedia. org/wiki/Attack_tree.

Risk analysis is a process that estimates the probability and severity of threats that a system needing protection faces. Risk analysis provides an organization with a prioritized list of risks, which the organization must mitigate, and allows an organization to focus on the most important threats first.

Risk Analysis

Risk analysis is the systematic study of uncertainties and risks. Risk analysts seek to identify the risks that a company faces, understand how and when they arise, and estimate the impact (financial or otherwise) of adverse outcomes. Risk managers start with risk analysis, and then seek to take actions that will mitigate these risks.

Two types of risk analysis are of interest in information security:

■   **Quantitative:** Quantitative risk analysis uses a mathematical model that puts numbers to the value of assets, the cost of threats being realized, and so on. Quantitative risk analysis provides an actual monetary figure of expected losses, which is typically based on an annual cost. You can then use this number to justify proposed countermeasures. For example, if you can establish that you will lose $1,000,000 by doing nothing, you can justify spending $300,000 to reduce that risk by 50 percent to 75 percent.

■   **Qualitative:** Qualitative risk analysis uses a scenario model. This approach is best for large cities, states, and countries to use because it is impractical to try to list all the assets, which is the starting point for any quantitative risk analysis. By the time a typical national government lists all of its assets, the list would have hundreds or thousands of changes and would no longer be accurate.

Quantitative Risk-Analysis Formula

Quantitative analysis relies on specific formulas to determine the value of the risk decision variables. These include formulas that calculate the asset value (AV), exposure factor (EF), single loss expectancy (SLE), annualized rate of occurrence (ARO), and annualized loss expectancy (ALE). The ALE formula is as follows:

The AV is the value of an asset. This would include the purchase price, the cost of deployment, and the cost of maintenance. In the case of a database or a web server, the AV should also include the cost of development. AV is *not* an easy number to calculate.

The EF is an estimate of the degree of destruction that will occur. For example, suppose that you consider flood a threat. Could it destroy our data center? Would the destruction be 60 percent, 80 percent, or 100 percent? The risk-assessment team would have to make a determination that evaluates everything possible, and then make a judgment call. For this example, assume that a flood will have a 60 percent destruction factor, because you store a backup copy of all media and data offsite. Your only losses would be the hardware and productivity.

As another example, consider data entry errors, which are much less damaging than a flood. A single data entry error would hardly be more than a fraction of a percent in exposure. The exposure factor of a data entry error might be as small as .001 percent.

Caution:
One of the ironies of risk analysis is how much estimating (guessing) is involved.

The SLE calculation is a number that represents the expected loss from a single occurrence of the threat. The SLE is defined as the AV * EF.

To use our previous examples, you would come up with the following results for the SLE calculations:

- **Flood threat**
  Exposure factor: 60 percent
  AV of the enterprise: US$10,000,000
  $10,000,000 * .60 = $6,000,000

- **Data entry error**
  Exposure factor: .001 percent
  AV of data and databases: $1,000,000
  $1,000,000 * .000001 = $10 SLE

The ARO is a value that estimates the frequency of an event and is used to calculate the ALE.

Continuing the preceding example, the type of flood that you expect could reach your data center would be a "flood of the century" type of event. Therefore, you give it a 1/100 chance of occurring this year, making the ARO for the flood 1/100.

Furthermore, you expect the data entry error to occur 500 times a day. Because the organization is open for business 250 days per year, you estimate the ARO for the data entry error to be 500 * 250, or 125,000 times.

Risk analysts calculate the ALE in annualized terms to address the cost to the organization if the organization does nothing to counter existing threats. The ALE is derived from multiplying the SLE by the ARO. The following ALE calculations continue with the two previous examples.

- **Flood threat**
  SLE: $6,000,000
  ARO: .01
  $6,000,000 * .01 = $60,000 ALE

- **Data input error**
  SLE: $10
  AROL: 125,000
  $10 * 125,000 = $1,250,000 ALE

A decision to spend $50,000 to enhance the security of our database applications to reduce data entry errors by 90 percent is now an easy decision. It is equally easy to reject a proposal to enhance our defenses against floods that costs $3,000,000.

When you perform a quantitative risk analysis, you will identify clear costs as long as the existing conditions remain the same. There is a list of expected issues, the relative cost of those events, and the total cost if all expected threats are realized. These numbers are put in to annual terms to coincide with the annual budgets of most organizations.

You then use these numbers in decision making. If an organization had a list of 10 expected threats, it could then prioritize the threats and address the most serious threats first. This prioritization enables management to focus their resources where it will do the most good.

For example, suppose an organization has the following list of threats and costs because of a quantitative risk analysis:

- **Insider network abuse:** $1,000,000 in lost productivity

- **Data input error:** $500,000

- **Worm outbreak:** $100,000

- **Viruses:** $10,000

- **Laptop theft:** $10,000

Decision makers could easily decide that it is of greatest benefit to address insider network abuse and leave the antivirus solution alone. They could also find it easy to support a $200,000 URL filtering solution to address insider network abuse and reject a $40,000 solution designed to enhance laptop safety. Without these numbers from a risk analysis, the decisions made would likely differ.

Tip: In cases that involve national security, it is not advisable to base decisions on cost.

Table 1-2 provides an example of threat identification for connecting an e-banking system to the Internet. It enumerates the following threats to the system, and the probability and severity of the impact on the bank should the threat materialize. The list of potential threats is by no means comprehensive, but includes the most obvious ones.

Table 1-2 *List of Potential Threats and Their Impact*

Threat	Description	Severity
Internal system compromise	The attacker could use the exposed e-banking servers to break into an internal bank system, causing substantial damage.	Extremely severe and likely, if untrusted software is used to pass data to the inside network.
Stolen customer data from an external server	The attacker could, by breaking into the exposed application server, steal all, or a substantial amount of, personal and financial data of the bank customers from the customer database.	Severe and likely, if the external server is vulnerable to intrusions, which could compromise the operating system or the application.
Phony transactions from an external server	The attacker could, by breaking into the external server, alter the code of the e-banking application, and run arbitrary transactions impersonating any legitimate user.	Severe and likely, if the external server is vulnerable to intrusions, which could compromise the operating system or the application.
Phony transactions if the customer PIN or smart card is stolen	The attacker could steal the identity of a customer and run malicious transactions from the compromised account.	Limited severity, because individual accounts are compromised; likely only if the stolen credentials are not detected quickly.
Insider attack on the system	A bank employee might find a flaw in the system to mount an attack.	Extremely severe and likely, because the bank has had its share of insider attacks on company data.
DoS attacks	DoS attacks could interrupt the service, because the attacker might compromise the availability of the application, cutting off legitimate users and potentially causing a public relations nightmare.	Severe and likely, because tools to perform such attacks are easy to find, and defense against such attacks is limited.

All the threats in Table 1-2 can lead to loss of reputation and customer trust.

After you identify threats and assess the risks, you must deploy a protection strategy to protect against the risks. There are two very different methods to handle risks:

■ **Risk management:** This method uses the deployment of protection mechanisms to reduce risks to *acceptable levels*. Risk management is perhaps the most basic and the most difficult aspect of building secure systems, because it requires good knowledge of risks, risk environments, and mitigation methods.

■ **Risk avoidance:** This method *eliminates* risk by avoiding the threats altogether, which is usually not an option in the commercial world, where controlled (managed) risk enables profits.

Dealing with Risk

There are actually four ways to deal with risk:

■ **Ignore:** This is not an option for an IT manager. The moment you become aware of a risk, you must acknowledge that risk and decide how to deal with it: accept this risk, transfer this risk, or reduce this risk.

■ **Accept:** This means that you document that there is a risk, but no action is taken to mitigate that risk because the risk is too far-fetched or the mitigation costs are too prohibitive.

■ **Reduce:** This is where we IT managers evolve. We are responsible for mitigating the risks. Four activities contribute to reducing risks:

■ **Limitation/avoidance:** Creating a secure environment by not allowing actions that would cause risks to occur such as, installing a firewall, using encryption systems and strong authentication, and so on
■ **Assurance:** Ensuring policies, standards, and practices are followed
■ **Detection:** Detecting intrusion attempts and taking appropriate action to terminate the intrusion
■ **Recovery:** Restoring the system to operational state

■ **Transfer:** This is buying insurance against a risk that cannot be eliminated or reduced further.

Risk Management

Continuing the example of a bank that wants to provide e-banking services and has identified threats and performed a risk analysis, risk management can be illustrated by high-level strategy decisions, which describe how to mitigate each risk to an acceptable level. Table 1-3 provides a list of the threats, the associated risk analysis, and the risk mitigation.

Table 1-3 *List of Threats, Risk Analysis, and Risk Mitigation*

Threat	Risk Analysis	Risk Mitigation
Internal system compromise	Extremely severe and likely, if untrusted software is used to pass data to the inside network	Provide the least amount of privilege access possible to the inside, and utilize a secure multitiered application which minimizes inside access
Stolen customer data from an external server	Severe and likely, if the external server is vulnerable to intrusions, which could compromise the operating system or the application	Keep all the customer data on inside servers, and only transfer data to the outside on demand

Table 1-3   *List of Threats, Risk Analysis, and Risk Mitigation*

Threat	Risk Analysis	Risk Mitigation
Phony transactions from an external server	Severe and likely, if the external server is vulnerable to intrusions, which could compromise the operating system or the application	Design the external server application so that it does not allow arbitrary transactions to be called for any customer account
Phony transactions if the customer PIN or smart card is stolen	Limited severity, because only individual accounts are compromised; likely only if the stolen credentials are not detected quickly	Use a quick refresh of revocation lists and have a contract with the user which forces the user to assume responsibility for stolen token cards
Insider attack on the system	Extremely severe and likely, because the bank has had its share of insider attacks on company data	Strictly limit inside access to the application and provide strict auditing of all accesses from the inside
DoS attacks	Severe and likely, because tools to perform such attacks are easy to find, and defense against such attacks is limited	Provide high-performance connectivity to the Internet, deploy of quality of service (QoS), implement high availability by using multiple Internet connections, and protect the server by hardening and implementing firewall DoS defense methods

Using the risk-avoidance approach, the company would decide not to offer the e-banking service at all because they deem it too risky. Such an attitude might be valid for most military organizations, but is usually not an option in the commercial world. Organizations that can manage the risks, and not avoid them, are traditionally the most profitable.

A different way of thinking about security might be this: "If we can figure out a way to provide a service securely, we will earn a lot of money." This attitude moves away from the paranoid thinking of many risk analysts, who might try to find a reason *not* to deploy a certain service. Sometimes it can help to take a fresh look at what risk management is all about.

Security Diminishing Returns and Residual Risk

Earlier I mentioned that a way to deal with risk is to reduce it by investing in security measures. The concept of diminishing returns applies to those security investments. Looking at Figure 1-21, you will notice that each additional security investment reduces risk (at least in theory). However, also notice that each additional security investment yields a lower additional risk reduction than the previous investment. In economics, this is what we call *diminishing returns*. Also, notice that regardless of how many resources you dedicate toward mitigating a risk, you can never reduce it to zero. There will always be *residual risk*. If that residual risk is unacceptable for your organization, you could consider buying insurance against it.

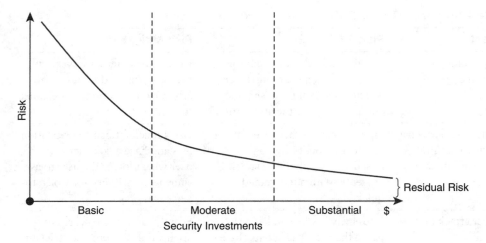

Figure 1-21 *Security Investment: Diminishing Returns and Residual Risk*

Principles of Secure Network Design

Business goals and risk analysis drive the need for network security. Regardless of the security implications, business needs must come first. If your business cannot function because of security concerns, you have a problem. The security system design must accommodate the goals of the business, not hinder them. Risk analysis includes two key elements:

- What does the cost-benefit analysis of your security system tell you?

- How will the latest attack techniques play out in your network environment?

Figure 1-22 illustrates the key factors you should consider when designing a secure network:

- **Business needs:** What does your organization want to do with the network?

- **Risk analysis:** What is the risk and cost balance?

- **Security policy:** What are the policies, standards, and guidelines that you need to address business needs and risks?

- **Industry best practices:** What are the reliable, well-understood, and recommended security best practices?

- **Security operations:** These operations include incident response, monitoring, maintenance, and auditing the system for compliance.

Realistic Assumptions

Historically, a huge percentage of security mechanisms are broken, misconfigured, or bypassed because the designer or implementer made unfounded assumptions about how and

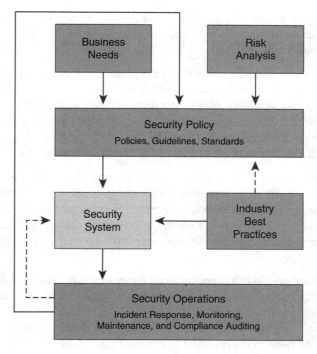

Figure 1-22 *Factors Affecting the Design of a Secure Network*

where the system will be used; for example, wrong assumptions were made about the users of the system, the attackers and threats, and the technology that is used to build the system.

A wrong assumption ends up being used as a bad axiom in all further design work; it might influence one design decision, and then propagate to other decisions that might depend on it. Wrong decisions are especially dangerous in early stages of secure system design, when threats are modeled and when risks are assessed. It is often easy to correct or enhance an implementation aspect of a system; however, design errors are either extremely hard or impossible to correct without substantial investments in time and technology.

The following is a summary of recommendations you should follow to avoid making wrong assumptions:

■ First, expect that any aspect of a system might fail, and evaluate how this failure affects the security of a system. It is possible for every single element of a system to fail; only the probability of failure might differ for different elements. When designing a system, perform "what-if" analysis for failures of every element, assess the probability of failure, and analyze all possible consequences of an element failure, taking into account consequent cascading failures of other elements.

■ As a part of the "anything can fail" mindset, identify any elements that "fail open." Fail open occurs when a failure results in a complete bypass of the security function of the element. Ideally, any security element should be fail-safe; if the element fails, it should default to a secure state, such as blocking all traffic across it.

- Try to identify all attack possibilities. The Attack Tree method is one successful method of top-down analysis of possible system failures, which involves evaluating the simplicity and probability of every attack.

- Realistically evaluate the probability of exploitation. An often-encountered philosophy is "if there is no exploit code available for a particular vulnerability, no one will be able to exploit it." This philosophy is true only for script kiddie attacks, and a sounder stance must be taken, such as "if a vulnerability exists, any skilled and focused attacker will easily write a tool to exploit it." The focus should be on the resources needed to create an attack tool, not on the obscurity of the vulnerability.

- Always account for technological advances if an attack is currently unlikely because the attacker needs many resources. As computer power increases, the probability of attacks might increase with an alarming rate. Many systems have been compromised because of unrealistic assumptions about how much computing power was necessary to mount successful attacks (the recommended lengths of cryptographic keys are a prime example).

- Assume that people will make mistakes. For example, end users might use a system improperly, compromising its security unintentionally. Likewise, attackers will not use common and well-established techniques to compromise a system; they might hammer the system with seemingly random attacks, looking for possible information on how the system behaves under unexpected conditions.

- Always check your assumptions with other people, who might have a fresh perspective on potential threats and their probability. The more people who question your assumptions, the more likely you can identify a bad assumption.

Incorrect Assumptions: Cautionary Tales

Three examples of wrong assumptions come from areas not directly related to network security.

The encryption of DVD movies, which uses a weak algorithm called Content Scrambling System (CSS), is an example of bad assumptions made about the scope of system use. The original assumption was that DVDs would be played only on hardware players, where the decryption keys could be stored in a tamper-resistant chip inside the player, making it extremely hard for even skilled attackers to compromise the DVDs. However, when software DVD players appeared, the DVDs were quickly reverse engineered, because making software tamper resistant is next to impossible against a determined attacker. The keys were recovered from one of the well-known players, and an algorithm was published on the Internet, together with the keys.

The response strategy of the DVD industry was to try to ban the publishing of the CSS algorithm and keys, but the decision of the court that the CSS algorithm source code was essentially free speech stopped much of their efforts.

Another example of a wrong or poor assumption was the lack of encryption of U.S. cellular traffic. When cellular phones were first introduced, the assumption was that scanners, which could intercept cellular traffic, were too expensive to mount any large-scale attacks against call confidentiality in cellular networks. In a couple of years, the price of these scanners dropped to the point that the scanners were available to almost anyone. Thus, bad assumptions compromised the protection policy of the cellular network.

The next-generation U.S. cellular service uses digital transmission, but the same assumption was made, that digital scanners are too expensive. As technology advances, the same story has unfolded for the digital transmissions.

Concept of Least Privilege

The least privilege concept is a philosophy in which each subject, user, program, host, and so on should have only the minimum necessary privileges to perform a certain task.

The rationale behind the concept is that having too many privileges for a task can result in doing more damage than would be otherwise possible, whether the damage is intentional or unintentional. Using the least privileges always narrows down the window of vulnerability, because it reduces the number of possible side effects of a task. Least privilege also simplifies a system when you analyze it for possible flaws, because if you allow only a very limited number of prescribed actions and system states, the potential for unwanted interactions within a system is limited.

In practice, the least privilege concept is often not followed, because a person or process must perform multiple tasks that require different privileges. Because the configuration of privileges in such an environment is often cumbersome, a person or process is given high (or even worse, the highest possible) privileges, which automatically enables them to perform a variety of tasks, including the tasks originally required. This configuration of privileges opens up a system to additional threats and interactions, which might not be expected.

Figure 1-23 shows an example of proper least privilege enforcement. A web server is located inside a firewall system and must be accessed by inside and outside users. No other access to the system is necessary, and the system does not need to open any connections itself (it is a simple static web server).

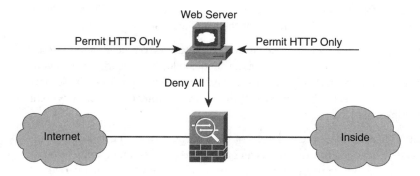

Figure 1-23   *Least Privilege Example*

In Figure 1-23, the firewall is configured to permit only HTTP connectivity to the server from the inside interface to the outside interface. The firewall denies all other connections to the server because they are not necessary. Also, the firewall prevents the web server from sourcing any connections because they are not required. An attacker who compromises the web server would be isolated on it because no connectivity is allowed from the web server.

In such a situation, many organizations would permit all access to the web server from the inside. This level of access opens up the server for insider attacks, or enables an attacker who manages to enter the protected network to also attack any service running on the web server.

You can see another example of least privilege enforcement by looking at the web server host itself. The host runs an exposed web server program, which is expected to be attacked by external crackers. Therefore, the web server program must be protected, and at the same time, other processes and data on the host must be protected from the attacker, who can potentially compromise the web server program. To protect the rest of the operating system, you can use several well-known techniques, all of which implement the least privilege concept:

- Run the web server program under a special username, which has minimal rights in the host operating system (it can listen on port 80 and it can access its data on disk).

- Set the file permissions in such a way that the web server program can access only its executable code (which is not owned by it, so it cannot be changed by it) and the documents it is serving (HTML, multimedia files).

- Configure the operating system to limit the web server program to be a part of the file system, disallowing it access to any other directories (for example, using the UNIX **chroot** system call).

Concept of Simplicity

Complexity is one of the biggest enemies of security. Complexity makes it hard for the designer or implementer to predict how parts of the system will interact, and makes the system extremely difficult to analyze from the security perspective. Simplicity of design and implementation should therefore be one of the main goals of the designer.

When you must implement a security mechanism, it is always recommended to use the simplest possible solution, which still provides an adequate level of security. When you need to put a very complex mechanism in place, consider replacing it with multiple simpler and easier-to-verify mechanisms, as long as the resulting protection strength is comparable to the original idea.

Also, simplicity is beneficial for the end users of the system. If the end user does not understand the system adequately, the system can be compromised through unintentional misuse. It is important to note that end users do not need to be aware of the internal workings of the system, but the usage instructions should be simple and concise, as far as security is concerned.

You can find an example of design and implementation simplicity in the formulation of a user security policy.

Two ways to formulate the same security policy that relates to the end-user responsibilities are as follows:

- **Complex rule:** All end users will participate in risk mitigation by enforcing discretionary access control on file system objects in such a way as to prevent external subjects from violating the integrity of the properties or contents of an object.

- **Simple rule:** When changing file permissions, ensure that only Cisco employees will have "write" access to that file.

An overly technical, confusing formulation alienates users, whereas a simple and concise formulation enables the user to easily comprehend the required procedures and understand why such protection must be put in place.

In short, simplicity in design often makes the implementation of security simpler.

You can also achieve simplicity by intentionally removing functionality from existing systems. This concept introduces the well-known practice of disabling all unnecessary services that a system offers. Disabling these services removes many potential attack possibilities. You could identify this as the enforcement of least privilege (running only the minimal necessary set of services), and it makes the system easier to analyze.

Another way to simplify security is to help simplify end-user functions. For example, if email needs to be encrypted when it goes to external business partners, a solution that would be the simplest for end users is to take the end users out of the equation and use technology to perform automated encryption of the email. A mail gateway can be configured to automatically encrypt all outgoing mail.

Security Awareness

Technical, administrative, and physical controls can all be defeated without the participation of the end-user community. To get accountants and secretaries to think about information security, you must regularly remind staff members about security. The technical staff also needs regular reminders because their jobs tend to emphasize performance rather than secure performance. Therefore, leadership must develop a nonintrusive program that keeps everyone aware of security and how to work together to maintain the security of their data. The three key components used to implement this type of program are awareness, training, and education.

An effective computer security-awareness and -training program requires proper planning, implementation, maintenance, and periodic evaluation. In general, a computer security-awareness and -training program should encompass the following seven steps:

Step 1. Identify program scope, goals, and objectives.

The scope of the program should provide training to all types of people who interact with IT systems. Because users need training that relates directly to their use of particular systems, you need to supplement a large organizationwide program with more system-specific programs.

Step 2. Identify training staff.

It is important that trainers have sufficient knowledge of computer security issues, principles, and techniques. It is also vital that they know how to communicate information and ideas effectively.

Step 3. Identify target audiences.

Not everyone needs the same degree or type of computer security information to do his or her job. A computer security-awareness and -training program that distinguishes between groups of people, presents only the information that is needed by the particular audience, and omits irrelevant information will have the best results.

Step 4. Motivate management and employees.

To successfully implement an awareness and training program, it is important to gain the support of management and employees. Consider using motivational techniques to show management and employees how their participation in a computer security and awareness program will benefit the organization.

Step 5. Administer the program.

Several important considerations for administering the program include visibility, selection of appropriate training methods, topics, materials, and presentation techniques.

Step 6. Maintain the program.

You should make an effort to keep abreast of changes in computer technology and security requirements. A training program that meets the needs of an organization today may become ineffective when the organization starts to use a new application or changes its environment, such as by connecting to the Internet.

Step 7. Evaluate the program.

An evaluation should attempt to ascertain how much information is retained, to what extent computer security procedures are being followed, and the general attitudes toward computer security.

A successful IT security program consists of the following:

1. Developing IT security policy that reflects business needs tempered by known risks
2. Informing users of their IT security responsibilities, as documented in agency security policy and procedures
3. Establishing processes for monitoring and reviewing the program

You should focus security awareness and training on the entire user population of the organization. Management should set the example for proper IT security behavior within an organization. An awareness program should begin with an effort that you can deploy and implement in various ways and be aimed at all levels of the organization, including senior and executive managers. The effectiveness of this effort usually determines the effectiveness of the awareness and training program and how successful the IT security program will be.

An awareness and training program is crucial because it is the vehicle for disseminating information that users, including managers, need to do their jobs. An IT security program is the vehicle that you use to communicate security requirements across the enterprise.

An effective IT security-awareness and -training program explains proper rules of behavior for the use of the IT systems and information of a company. The program communicates IT security policies and procedures that must be followed. This program must precede and lay the foundation for any sanctions that your company will impose for noncompliance. You should first inform the users of the expectations. You must derive accountability from a fully informed, well-trained, and aware workforce.

Security awareness efforts are designed to change behavior or reinforce good security practices. Awareness is defined in NIST Special Publication 800-16 as follows:

Awareness is not training. The purpose of awareness presentations is simply to focus attention on security. Awareness presentations are intended to allow individuals to recognize IT security concerns and respond accordingly. In awareness activities, the learner is the recipient of information, whereas the learner in a training environment has a more active role. Awareness relies on reaching broad audiences with attractive packaging techniques. Training is more formal, having a goal of building knowledge and skills to facilitate the job performance.

An example of a topic for an awareness session (or awareness material to be distributed) is virus protection. You can briefly address the subject by describing what a virus is, what can happen if a virus infects a user system, what the user should do to protect the system, and what users should do if they discover a virus.

Training strives to produce relevant and needed security skills and competencies by practitioners of functional specialties other than IT security (for example, management, systems design and development, acquisition, and auditing). The most significant difference between training and awareness is that training tries to teach skills that allow a person to perform a specific function, whereas awareness focuses the attention of an individual on an issue or set of issues. The skills that users acquire during training build on the awareness foundation (in particular, on the security basics and literacy material). A training curriculum does not necessarily lead to a formal degree from an institution of higher learning; however, a training course might contain much of the same material found in a course that a college or university includes in a certificate or degree program.

An example of training is an IT security course for system administrators, which should address in detail the management controls, operational controls, and technical controls that should be implemented. Management controls include policy, IT security program management, risk management, and life cycle security. Operational controls include personnel and user issues, contingency planning, incident handling, awareness and training, computer support and operations, and physical and environmental security issues. Technical controls include identification and authentication, logical access controls, audit trails, and cryptography.

Education integrates all the security skills and competencies of the various functional specialties into a common body of knowledge; adds a multidisciplinary study of concepts, issues, and principles (technological and social); and strives to produce IT security specialists and professionals capable of vision and proactive response.

An example of education is a degree program at a college or university. Some people take a course or several courses to develop or enhance their skills in a particular discipline. This is training as opposed to education. Many colleges and universities offer certificate programs, wherein a student may take two, six, or eight classes (for example, in a related discipline), and are then awarded a certificate upon completion. Often, these certificate programs are conducted as a joint effort between schools and software or hardware vendors. These programs are more characteristic of training than education. Those responsible for security training must assess both types of programs and decide which one better addresses their identified needs.

A successfully implemented training and awareness program, in conjunction with a good security operations practice, should result in many benefits to an organization. The technical staff should be better at implementing the technical controls. End users, executives, and everyone else should also do a better job of implementing the remaining administrative and physical controls. The resulting more thorough implementation of a well-designed set of controls is guaranteed to increase security.

Cisco Self-Defending Networks

In the past, threats from internal and external sources moved slowly and it was easy to defend against them. Now Internet worms spread across the world in a matter of minutes. Security systems, and the network itself, must react instantaneously. As the nature of threats to organizations continues to evolve, the defense posture taken by network administrators and managers must also evolve.

The Cisco Self-Defending Network strategy describes the Cisco vision for security systems and helps customers more effectively manage and mitigate the risks to their networked business systems and applications.

Changing Threats and Challenges

Figure 1-24 shows how the threats that organizations face have evolved over the past few decades, and how the growth rate of vulnerabilities reported in operating systems and applications is rising. The number and variety of viruses and worms that have appeared over the past three years is daunting, and their rate of propagation is frightening. There have been unacceptable levels of business outages and expensive remediation projects that consume staff, time, and funds that were not originally budgeted for such tasks.

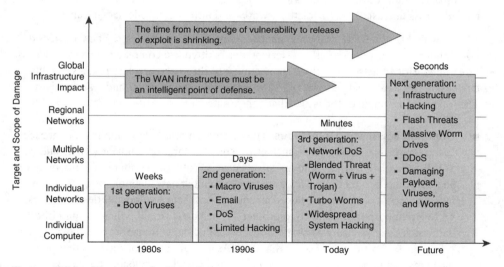

Figure 1-24 *Threat Evolution*

Figure 1-24 also shows that *blended threats* are evolving. A blended threat uses multiple means of propagation. These threats often have the characteristics of a virus; for example, they can attach themselves parasitically to email attachments. These threats self-replicate across a network with worm-like capability, and frequently search for and exploit a system or application vulnerability, or multiple vulnerabilities, to gain access to a host and deliver their payload. Some believe that blended threats might be evolving into "flash" threats that could exploit new, unknown vulnerabilities, and have the capability to propagate across the Internet in seconds, seriously affecting the Internet on a global scale.

Also, notice on Figure 1-24 that the trends are becoming regional and global in nature. Early attacks affected single systems or one organization's network. In contrast, more recent attacks are affecting entire regions. For example, attacks have expanded from individual DoS attacks from a single attacker against a single target to large-scale DDoS attacks emanating from networks of compromised systems known as botnets.

Threats are also becoming persistent. After an attack starts, attacks might appear in waves as infected systems join the network. Because infections are so complex and have so many end users (employees, vendors, and contractors), multiple types of endpoints (company desktop, home, and server), and multiple types of access (wired, wireless, VPN, and dialup), infections are difficult to eradicate.

Network-dependent enterprises constantly face security dilemmas in the typical business environment. You can no longer secure networks just by securing the network perimeter. Businesses have consolidated their data centers, converged internal networks, and embraced the Internet. Environments that were once self-contained and controlled are now open to partners through business-to-business extranets, retail outlet connections, and home-based employees. By extending the corporate network, the trust boundary has extended across untrusted intermediate networks and into uncontrolled environments.

The growing list of devices that access networks poses more problems. Many devices do not comply with corporate policies. Network users often use compliant devices to access other uncontrolled networks before connecting into the corporate network. As a result, devices on these external networks can become conduits for attacks and related misuse. The following are some of the issues that concern network security experts:

- **Common application interfaces:** The emergence of common application interfaces based on messaging protocols, such as Extensible Markup Language (XML) and SOAP, formally known as Simple Object Access Protocol, has increased e-commerce and corporate productivity. However, similar to most new technologies, these new message protocols have introduced an entirely new set of vulnerabilities and attack vectors that corporations need to protect. In the past, firewall policies would filter data carried across many network protocols. Now, single transport protocols, such as HTTP on TCP port 80, transport that data. As a result, much of the data that previously resided in packet headers now resides in the packet payload. This change creates significant processing challenges that make it easier for an attacker to evade classic network defenses.

- **Security hampering policy:** To meet the data confidentiality and integrity requirements of corporations, more applications are using Secure Sockets Layer (SSL), Transport Layer Security (TLS), and HTTPS protocols to encrypt application-level traffic. This trend makes it much harder for IT departments to enforce corporate access policies at the network perimeter, because they cannot inspect the packet payloads of those encrypted flows. Many organizations mistakenly assume that if they comply with regulations, their infrastructure is more secure, which is frequently not the case.

Following the law of unintended consequences, the very act of creating compliance can introduce new vulnerabilities. For example, worms and viruses can spread more effectively in a network supporting end-to-end VPNs because the intermediate nodes have no visibility into the traversing traffic. Such traffic can carry worms to sensitive corporate servers in a secure, encrypted packet. End-to-end VPNs can make it more difficult to remediate the problem and it can take longer to diagnose such an attack.

- **Blurred perimeters:** The wireless and mobile network within an enterprise now supports laptops, personal digital assistants (PDA), and mobile phones that have more than one network connection. These multihomed hosts are capable of establishing impromptu wireless networks to enable peer-to-peer communication. In addition, these devices effectively forward packets at the application level. As a result, network boundaries become much more ambiguous. To manage a secure system and maintain network availability, corporations must be able to extend a control point onto these mobile devices.

To illustrate the seriousness of network vulnerabilities, consider the effects of the SQL Slammer worm, first seen on January 25, 2003:

- Saturation point was reached within two hours of the start of infection.

- Infections doubled every 8.5 seconds.

- SQL Slammer spread 100 times faster than Code Red.

- At its peak, SQL Slammer scanned 55 million hosts per second.

- The number of hosts infected was between 250,000 and 300,000.

- Internet connectivity was affected worldwide.
Source: Cooperative Association for Internet Data Analysis (CAIDA) and the University of California at San Diego.

SQL Slammer compromised 90 percent of vulnerable systems within the first 10 minutes, and doubled in size every 8.5 seconds. Within the first 3 minutes, it achieved its maximum scanning rate of more than 55 million scans per second.

Building a Cisco Self-Defending Network

A Cisco Self-Defending Network uses the network to identify, prevent, and adapt to threats. Unlike point-solution strategies, in which you purchase products individually without consideration for which products work best together, a network-based approach is a strategic approach that meets the current challenges and evolves your security capability to keep ahead of the curve.

The following are key principles of a Cisco Self-Defending Network:

- Integrate security throughout the existing infrastructure. Security should be built in, not bolted on.

- There should be collaboration between security and the network so that they leverage off each other and work together.

■ The network should have the capability to intelligently evolve and adapt to emerging threats.

Cisco Self-Defending Network increases the value of your investment over time (contrary to point solutions, where the costs increase over time due to posture erosion, inconsistencies, and complexities).

A common infrastructure offers savings over time while supporting business transformations. A common infrastructure allows simplified management, which greatly reduces the evolution of gaps in controls that typically materialize over time. Management is more likely to be correctly and consistently performed when it is simplified, which allows the identification of gaps before they become disabling vulnerabilities in the posture.

The process of assessing the environment, identifying gaps, applying changes, and ultimately auditing those controls becomes much more efficient when you have more consistent controls and visibility.

An additional compelling argument for a Cisco Self-Defending Network design is the reality that introducing a common infrastructure falls within the scope of the other strategies for implementation. Specifically, each strategy is governed by product life cycle management. In spite of strategy differences, you can acquire the products that make up the infrastructure based on the traditional technology refresh cycles by which many IT organizations abide.

The Cisco Self-Defending Network approach is comprehensive and covers the following aspects of security using specific tools:

■ **Policy-based management** through Cisco Security Manager.

■ **Threat management** through Cisco Security Monitoring, Analysis, and Response System (MARS).

■ **Network security** through Cisco IOS Software, Cisco ASAs, and Cisco IPS Sensor Software.

■ **Endpoint security** through Cisco NAC appliances and Cisco Security Agent.

The following are additional benefits that result from this comprehensive, integrated approach:

■ **360 degree-visibility and protection:** Delivers comprehensive and proactive network defense
Infrastructurewide threat intelligence that is cost-effectively delivered across a variety of systems and devices.
Multivector threat identification captures policy violations, vulnerability exploits, and anomalous behavior.

■ **Simplified control:** Streamlines policy and management across the network
Networkwide policy management.
Infrastructurewide implementation across a variety of systems and devices.

■ **Proactive business protection:** Ensures the operations of the enterprise

Unparalleled collaboration and correlation across systems, endpoints, and management enables adaptive response to real-time threats.
Key element of the Cisco Self-Defending Network strategy.

This enhanced threat control and containment solution portfolio delivers comprehensive threat protection across the entire infrastructure, ensuring business continuity and strengthening the Self-Defending Network vision.

A Cisco Self-Defending Network starts with a secure network platform, as shown in Figure 1-25, which is a strong, secure, flexible base from which you build your own Cisco Self-Defending Network solution.

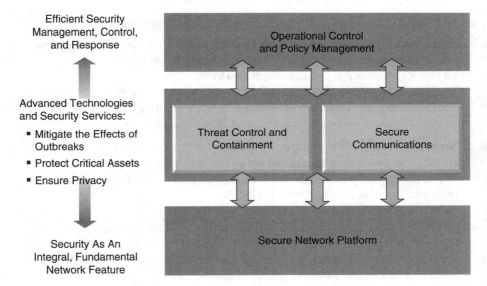

Figure 1-25 *Cisco Self-Defending Network Defined*

With security integrated into the very fabric of the network, security becomes an integral and fundamental network feature. The next step, as shown in Figure 1-25, is to layer advanced technologies and security services, where and when you need them, on to this platform. The following are solutions for advanced technologies and security services:

■ **Threat control and containment:** Keep your employees productive against a challenging and ever-changing threat landscape.

■ **Secure communications:** Ensure the confidentiality and privacy of all of your sensitive communications, whether it is data communication, voice communication, or wireless communication.

■ **Tools for operational control and policy management:** Add a suite of tools that comprise a framework for operational control and policy management that span your security end to end.

Whether you are a large enterprise or commercial customer, these solution components comprise a complete Cisco Self-Defending Network.

Threat Control and Containment

The Cisco Threat Control and Containment solution offers comprehensive protection for your network through networkwide visibility, simplified policy control, and proactive system protection.

The Cisco Threat Control and Containment solution is part of the Cisco Self-Defending Network, which protects the network, servers, endpoints, and information. The Cisco Threat Control and Containment solution regulates network access, isolates infected systems, prevents intrusions, and protects critical business assets. It counteracts malicious traffic such as worms, viruses, and malware before they affect your business, by using centralized policy, configuration, and threat event management.

The Cisco Threat Control and Containment Solution contains three elements:

- **Threat control for endpoints:** This element defends against threats most commonly introduced by Internet use, such as viruses, spyware, and other malicious content that may lead to data loss and degrade productivity.
  Cisco products that provide threat control for endpoints include the Cisco Security Agent for Desktops, Cisco ASA 5500 series (Content Security Edition), Cisco Integrated Services Routers, Cisco IPS, and Cisco NAC appliances.

- **Threat control for infrastructure:** This element safeguards your server and application infrastructure against attacks and intrusions. It also defends against internal and external attempts to penetrate or attack servers and information resources through application and operating system vulnerabilities.
  Products that provide threat control for the infrastructure include the Cisco Security Agent for Servers, Cisco IPS, Cisco firewall solutions including the Cisco ASA 5500 series and Cisco Catalyst 6500 series Firewall Services Module, Cisco ACE (Application Control Engine) Module, Cisco AVS Application Velocity System, XML security, Cisco Security MARS, and Cisco Security Manager.

- **Threat control for email:** This element protects your business productivity, resource availability, and confidential information by stopping email-initiated threats. Cisco provides solutions to protect from threats contained in email, such as the Content Security and Control Security Services Module used in the Cisco ASA firewall and the IronPort appliance.

Secure Communications

Ensuring the privacy and integrity of all information is vital to your business. You can achieve this through the use of IPsec and SSL VPNs. As your company uses the flexibility and cost-effectiveness of the Internet to extend its network to branch offices, telecommuters, customers, and partners, security is paramount. You must create a manageable, cost-effective communications infrastructure that will do the following:

- Improve productivity

- Enable new business applications

- Help you comply with information privacy regulations

- Enhance business efficiency

The Cisco Secure Communications solution is a set of products and security life cycle services that are an essential element of the Cisco Self-Defending Network. By incorporating capabilities that secure the network, the endpoints, and the applications and messages, this systems-based approach delivers comprehensive security of your communications. The solution has two major elements:

- **Secure communications for remote access:** This element provides highly secure, customizable access to corporate networks and applications by establishing an encrypted tunnel across the Internet.

- **Secure communications for site-to-site connections:** This element provides an Internet-based WAN infrastructure for connecting branch offices, home offices, or the sites of business partners to all or portions of your network.

Tip: The Cisco Secure Communications solution uses cryptography to ensure confidentiality.

Operational Control and Policy Management

Cisco network management systems help you automate, simplify, and integrate your network to reduce operational costs and improve productivity. Built to complement the popular CiscoWorks products, the tools within the network management systems provide innovative ways to centrally manage your network to achieve critical functions such as availability, responsiveness, resilience, and security in a consistent way.

These network management systems also help reduce the troubleshooting and planning time associated with the introduction of new services such as voice, wireless, and security management. Solutions-focused tools streamline network management systems, including the management of devices, configurations, users, and services.

The benefits of the different Cisco network management systems include the following:

- Increase speed and accuracy of policy deployment

- Gain visibility to monitor end-to-end security

- Respond to threats more rapidly

- Enforce corporate policy compliance

- Enable proper workflow management

Cisco Security Management Suite

The Cisco Security Management Suite is a framework of products and technologies designed for scalable policy administration and enforcement for the Cisco Self-Defending Network. This integrated solution can simplify and automate the tasks associated with security management operations, including configuration, monitoring, analysis, and response. There are two main components of the Cisco Security Management Suite: Cisco Security Manager and Cisco Security MARS.

Cisco Security Manager

Cisco Security Manager is a powerful but easy-to-use solution that enables you to centrally provision all aspects of device configurations and security policies for the Cisco family of security products. The solution is effective for managing even small networks consisting of fewer than 10 devices, but also scales to efficiently manage large-scale networks composed of thousands of devices. Scalability is achieved through intelligent policy-based management techniques that can simplify administration. Cisco Security Manager features include the following:

■ It enables administrators to effectively manage configuration for Cisco IPS 4200 series sensors, the Cisco ASA Advanced Inspection and Prevention Security Services Module (AIP-SSM), the Cisco Catalyst 6500 Series Intrusion Detection System Services Module 2 (IDSM-2), the Cisco IDS Network Module, the Cisco IPS AIM, and Cisco IOS IPS.

■ It responds faster to threats by enabling you to define and assign new security policies to thousands of devices in a few simple steps.

■ It has a rich graphical user interface that provides superior ease of use.

■ Multiple views provide flexible methods to manage devices and policies, including the ability to manage the security network visually on a topology map.

■ It contains extensive animated help for the new user, which reduces the learning time.

■ It enables you to centrally specify which policies are shared and automatically inherited by new devices to ensure corporate policies are implemented consistently, while providing optional flexibility.

■ It integrates with Cisco Secure Access Control Server (ACS) to provide granular roll-based access control to devices and management functions.

■ It integrates with Cisco Security MARS to correlate events with the associated firewall rules to help make quicker decisions and increase network uptime.

■ It enables you to assign specific tasks to each administrator during the deployment of a policy, with formal change control and tracking, and allows the security and network operations staff to work together as a single team with effective coordination.

Cisco Security MARS

Cisco Security MARS provides security monitoring for network security devices and host applications made by Cisco and other providers. Cisco Security MARS offers these benefits:

■ Greatly reduces false positives by providing an end-to-end view of the network

■ Defines the most effective mitigation responses by understanding the configuration and topology of your environment

■ Promotes awareness of environmental anomalies with network behavior analysis using NetFlow

■ Provides quick and easy access to audit compliance reports with more than 150 ready-to-use customizable reports

- Makes precise recommendations for threat removal, including the ability to visualize the attack path and identify the source of the threat with detailed topological graphs that simplify security response at Layer 2 and above

Tip: For training on Cisco Secure MARS, go to http://www.cisco.com/web/learning/le31/le29/learning_training_from_cisco_learning_partners.html.

Cisco Integrated Security Portfolio

A truly secure network requires multiple products and technologies that collaborate seamlessly across platforms and integrate tightly with the network infrastructure, as shown in Figure 1-26. No single product or technology can secure a network.

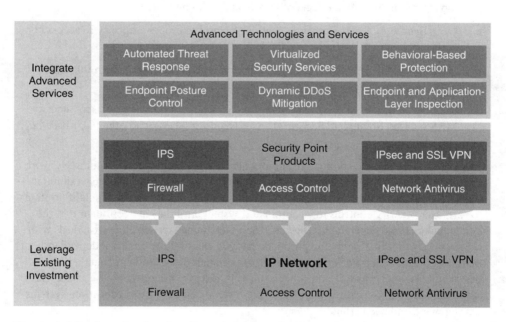

Figure 1-26 *Security Services Integrated into the Network*

Cisco offers the broadest portfolio of integrated security products in the industry. No other vendor has such a diversity of platforms. Benefits of a comprehensive Cisco architecture include the following:

- Increase speed and accuracy of policy deployment
- Gain visibility to monitor end-to-end security
- Respond to threats more rapidly
- Enforce corporate policy compliance
- Enable proper workflow management

The Cisco portfolio is designed to meet the requirements and diverse deployment models of any network and any environment. The following are some of these products:

- Cisco IOS platforms with integrated IPS, VPN, and stateful firewall to support secure IP connectivity

- Cisco ASA 5500 series appliances with integrated VPN to ensure perimeter security, access control, and IPS

- Cisco PIX 500 series security appliances with integrated VPN to ensure perimeter security and access control

- Appliance-based network IDS and IPS and integrated network IDS and IPS for Cisco IOS routers, Cisco PIX security appliances, and Cisco ASAs

- Cisco Security Agent endpoint protection software, which protects servers and desktops from the damaging effects of known and unknown threats

- Cisco Secure ACS, which ensures that users have the proper authority to access corporate resources

- Security modules for Cisco Catalyst 6500 series switches and Cisco 7600 series routers that provide security throughout the data center

- Security management products, including Cisco Security Manager, Cisco Security MARS, Cisco Router and Security Device Manager (SDM), and other GUI-based device managers

Most customers will not adopt all the components of the Cisco Self-Defending Network at one time, because it can be difficult to overhaul all the required subsystems simultaneously without disrupting the integrity of the IT services. Some customers might hesitate to turn over security controls to an automated system until they are confident that the system will operate dependably. The Cisco Self-Defending Network initiative deals with these concerns by first providing products that you can usefully deploy independently of one another and then by offering solutions that can link these products together as confidence builds in each product and subsystem. This initiative has proven to be a successful approach based on a combination of product development, product acquisition, systems development, and partnering.

Summary

To have a comprehensive security solution, it is important to cover all aspects of the operation of an organization. Comprehensive security requires suitable reliance on technical, physical, and administrative controls; implementing defense in depth; and developing an all-inclusive security policy. You will also be required to demonstrate forward thinking, taking into consideration the threats of tomorrow.

In this chapter you have learned that

■ To provide a comprehensive security solution, it is essential that there be a combination of technical, physical, and administrative controls in place.

■ Defense in depth is a philosophy used to provide layered security to a system by using multiple security mechanisms.

■ Operations security is concerned with the controls used to protect hardware, software, and media on a day-to-day basis.

■ A security policy is a set of objectives for the company, rules of behavior for users and administrators, and requirements for system and management that collectively ensure the security of network and computer systems in an organization.

■ Changing threats and challenges demand a new approach to network security, one that is quickly adaptable, such as the Cisco Self-Defending Network.

References

For additional information, refer to these resources:

Richardson, R. *2007 CSI Computer Crime and Security Survey*, http://i.cmpnet.com/v2.gocsi.com/pdf/CSISurvey2007.pdf

Harris, S. *CISSP All-in-One Exam Guide*, Third Edition (McGraw Hill Osborne, 2005)

The Jargon File, http://www.catb.org/~esr/jargon/html/index.html

McClure, S., Scambray, J., and Kurtz, G. *Hacking Exposed*, Fifth Edition (McGraw-Hill/Osborne, 2005)

SecurityFocus, http://www.securityfocus.com/

Verio, http://www.whois.net/

Uwhois, Universal WHOIS, http://www.uwhois.com/

Insecure.org, http://www.insecure.org/nmap/

Giacobbi, G. The GNU Netcat Project, http://netcat.sourceforge.net/

Security-Solutions.net, http://www.security-solutions.net/download/index.html

Microsoft Corporation. Windows 2000 Resource Kit Tools for Administrative Tasks. http://support.microsoft.com/kb/927229

SomarSoft Utilities, http://www.somarsoft.com/

Microsoft Corporation. Windows Server 2003 SP1 Platform SDK Web Install, http://tinyurl.com/cew8e

Kabay, M. E. *Salami Fraud*, http://www.networkworld.com/newsletters/sec/2002/01467137.html

NIST Publication 800-64 Rev. A. *Security Considerations in the Information System Development Life Cycle*

NIST Publication 800-42. *Guideline on Network Security Testing*

Tripwire, Inc., http://www.tripwire.com

GFI Security & Messaging Software, http://www.gfi.com

Tenable Network Security, http://www.nessus.org/download

Wood, C. *Information Security Policies Made Easy, Version 10* (Information Shield, 2005)

NIST Publication 800-29 Rev A. *NIST Engineering Principles for Information Technology Security*

Cisco Systems, Inc. *Security: Reduce IT Risk*, http://www.cisco.com/go/sdn

Wikipedia Foundation, Inc. *Attack Tree*, http://en.wikipedia.org/wiki/Attack_tree

Review Questions

Use the questions here to review what you learned in this chapter. The correct answers are found in the Appendix, "Answers to Chapter Review Questions."

1. Which are the three primary objectives of security?

   a. Integrity

   b. Confidentiality

   c. Antireplay functionality

   d. Authentication

   e. Availability

2. Which are the three categories of controls?

   a. Administrative

   b. Executive

   c. Managerial

   d. Technical

   e. Physical

3. Show that you understand the different types of controls by matching them with their related technology.

   Type of controls

   a. Preventive

   b. Deterrent

   c. Detective

   Technologies

   d. Motion sensor

   e. Video surveillance

   f. Lock

4. Match the different types of hackers and the like with their appropriate description.

   Hacker types

   a. White hat

   b. Black hat

   c. Gray hat

   d. Blue hat

   e. Cracker

f. Phreaker

g. Script kiddy

h. Hacktivist

Hacker descriptions

i. Bug testers

j. Hacker with little skill

k. Unethical hacker

l. Hacker of telecommunication systems

m. Ethically questionable hacker

n. Hacker with a political agenda

o. Synonymous with black hat hackers

p. Breaks security for nonmalicious reasons

5. Organize the following steps used to compromise targets and applications.

   a. Escalate privilege

   b. Leverage the compromise system

   c. Perform footprint analysis

   d. Install back doors

   e. Enumerate applications and operating systems

   f. Gather additional passwords and secrets

   g. Manipulate users to gain access

6. Which is an efficient way to protect against an integrity attack?

   a. Strong authentication

   b. Firewall

   c. Intrusion prevention system

   d. Cryptography

7. Which provides you with a site where only a communication link and electricity are provided?

   a. Warm site

   b. Cold site

   c. Hot site

   d. Backup site

8. Which of the following is (are) not part of the technical policies. Select all that apply?

   a. End-user policy

   b. Acceptable usage policy

   c. Email policy

   d. VPN access policy

   e. Network policy

   f. Wireless policy

9. Which are core goals and components of the Cisco Self-Defending Network approach?

   a. Threat management

   b. Appliance management

   c. Endpoint security

   d. Return on security investment

   e. Policy-based management

   f. Network security

10. Which layer of the OSI model is the current greatest target of security exploits?

   a. Application

   b. Session

   c. Transport

   d. Network

   e. Data link

   f. Physical

11. Which of the following statements is false regarding security issues of custom applications?

   a. Companies have many, perhaps hundreds, of different web applications or local databases.

   b. Employees and contractors may have written the code without security in mind.

   c. There are no signatures for those customized applications.

   d. There are no patches for those customized applications.

   e. These applications are often dynamic and complex.

   f. Hackers cannot exploit vulnerabilities in customized software because the application is resident on the inside network.

12. From the following items, which does a designer not need to care about when designing network security?

   a. The threats that could compromise security

   b. The impact on hackers of introducing a new security policy

   c. The associated risk of the threats

   d. How relevant those threats are for a particular system

   e. The cost to implement the proper security countermeasures for a threat

   f. A cost versus benefit analysis to determine whether it is worthwhile to implement a security countermeasure

13. What do you call an attack in which the attacker sends a continuous stream of packets from different sources toward the same destination?

   a. Denial-of-service attack

   b. Classification attack

   c. Distributed denial-of-service attack

   d. Ping of death

   e. Smurf attack

14. Reorder the classification levels of the private sector, from the least secure to the most secure document.

   a. Confidential

   b. Private

   c. Public

   d. Sensitive

15. Which of the following is not a criterion used to classify data?

   a. Value

   b. Age

   c. Useful life

   d. Copyright

   e. Personal association

16. Match each of the following information classification roles with its definition.

   a. Owner

   b. Custodian

   c. User

   Definitions

   d. Responsible for using the data

   e. Responsible on a day-to-day basis for the classified data

   f. Ultimately responsible for the data

17. Which of the following is a technical control?

   a. Network Admission Control system

   b. Security policies and standards

   c. Security audits

   d. Security awareness training

   e. Change and configuration management

18. Which of the following is not a characteristic of defense in depth?

   a. Security mechanisms back each other up.

   b. Security mechanisms do not depend on each other.

   c. Does not require IDS or IPS.

   d. The weakest links can be augmented so that single points of failure can be eliminated.

19. Match the specific man-in-the-middle attack with its specific characteristic.

   a. Nonblind attack

   b. Blind attack

   c. Network packet sniffer required

   d. Relies on routing and transport protocols to compromise target

20. Match the definition with the appropriate attack method.

   a. Searching a network host and open ports

   b. Capturing electrical transmission

   c. Hiding information within a transmission

   d. Intercepting traffic that passes over a digital network

   Attack Methods

   e. Packet sniffing

   f. Emanation capturing

g.   Cover channel

h.   Port scanning

21. Reorder the phases of a system development life cycle.

   a.   Operations

   b.   Initiation

   c.   Disposition

   d.   Acquisition

   e.   Implementation

22. Which of the following defines the steps that are taken when an outage occurs?

   a.   Business continuity planning

   b.   Disaster recovery planning

   c.   Service level agreement

   d.   Acceptable usage policy

23. Which of the following security concepts limits a user's rights to the lowest possible level needed to perform his tasks?

   a.   Need to know

   b.   Least privilege

   c.   Universal participation

   d.   Diversity of defense

24. Which of the following might not be a benefit of Cisco Self-Defending Networks?

   a.   Reduces initial acquisition costs

   b.   Reduces integration costs

   c.   Allows proactive and planned upgrades

   d.   Improves efficiency of security management

25. Which are the three elements of threat control and containment?

   a.   Threat control for endpoints

   b.   Threat control for infrastructure

   c.   Threat control for email

   d.   Threat control for applications

This chapter introduces the concept of perimeter security and covers the following topics:

- Physical installation of and administrative access to Cisco routers

- Features and uses of Cisco Router and Security Device Manager (SDM)

- Configuration of a Cisco router to perform authentication, authorization, accounting (AAA) authentication with a local database

- Operation of external AAA sources such as RADIUS and TACACS+ servers, and configuration of a Cisco router to perform AAA

- Secure implementation of the management and reporting features of syslog, Simple Network Management Protocol (SNMP), Secure Shell (SSH), and Network Time Protocol (NTP)

- Examination router configurations with the Security Audit feature of Cisco SDM and how to make the router and network more secure by using the One-Step Lockdown feature of Cisco SDM or the command **auto secure**

CHAPTER 2

Perimeter Security

A network perimeter is the border between a private, locally managed network and the public network, such as the Internet. Therefore, traffic originating from the outside destined for the inside of a closed network must transit through the network perimeter.

In this chapter, you will learn how to apply security policies to the perimeter routers, which includes securing administrative access to the router. You will also be introduced to the Cisco Router and Security Device Manager.

Securing Administrative Access to Cisco Routers

This section introduces how to secure Cisco routers using proven methods for physically securing the router and protecting the router administrative access.

General Router Security Guidelines

You should think about router security in terms of its physical security, the features and performance of the router operating system, the protection of the router configurations, and the elimination of potential abuse of unused ports and services through router hardening. The three main principles of router security are as follows:

- To provide physical security for a router, take the following actions:
  - Place the router in a locked room that is accessible only to authorized personnel, is free of electrostatic or magnetic interference, and has controls for temperature and humidity.
  - Install an uninterruptible power supply (UPS) and keep spare components available. This reduces the possibility of a denial-of-service (DoS) attack from power loss.
  - Configure the router with the maximum amount of memory possible. The availability of memory can help protect the network from some DoS attacks, while supporting the widest range of security services.
  - Store physical devices that connect to the router in a secure place.

- The security features in an operating system evolve over time; however, the latest version of an operating system might not be the most stable version available. To get the best security performance from your operating system, use the latest stable release that meets the feature requirements of your network. Also, keep a secure copy of the router operating system image and router configuration file as a backup.

■ Similar to many computers, a router has many services that are enabled by default. Many of these services are unnecessary and can be used by an attacker to gather information or for exploitation. You should disable unnecessary services to harden your router configuration.

Note: *Hardening a system* is an expression used in information system security to designate the steps taken to rid a system of known vulnerabilities by upgrading to a current operating system, applying current patches, and turning off unneeded applications on the system.

A router provides the capability to help secure the perimeter of a protected network. It is a device where you can implement security action that is based on the security policy of your organization.

To secure a network perimeter, you can deploy a router on its own. Scenario 1 of Figure 2-1 shows a typical topology where the router connects the private network to the Internet.

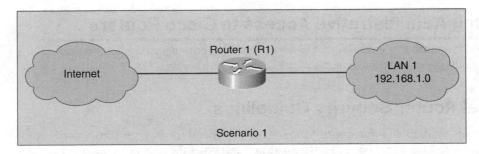

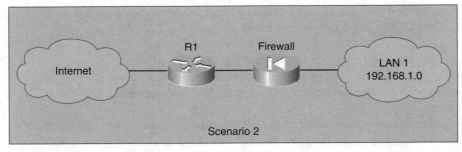

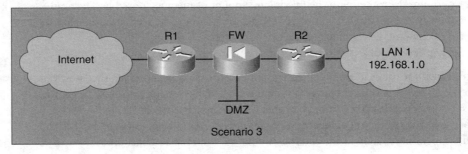

Figure 2-1   *Routers Enforcing Perimeter Security Policy*

You can also use a router as part of a defense-in-depth approach, as shown in Scenario 2 of Figure 2-1. This approach is preferred to that of using only a router because it is more secure. The router acts as the first line of defense and, in such a deployment, is known as a *screening router* or *perimeter router*. It passes all the connections that are intended for the internal LAN to the firewall. The firewall provides additional access control by tracking the state of the connections. By default, the firewall denies the initiation of connections from the outside (untrusted) networks to the inside (trusted) network but allows the internal users to establish connections to the untrusted networks and permits the responses to come back through the firewall. It can also perform user authentication (authentication proxy), where users have to be authenticated before they can gain access to network resources.

Another approach, shown in Scenario 3 of Figure 2-1, is to offer an intermediate area, often called the demilitarized zone (DMZ). The DMZ, attached to the firewall, can be used for servers that must be accessible from the Internet or some other external network. The firewall, located between the routers, is set up to permit the required connections (for example, HTTP) from the outside (untrusted) networks to the public servers in the DMZ. The firewall serves as the primary protection for all devices on the DMZ. In this situation, the router provides some protection by filtering some traffic, but leaves the bulk of the protection to the firewall.

Note: Note that the router R2 is not necessary in Scenario 3 for the topology to be secured or for the firewall to perform properly its duties regarding the DMZ.

Introduction to the Cisco Integrated Services Router Family

Cisco Integrated Services Routers (ISR) ship with the most comprehensive security services in the industry, intelligently embedding data, security, voice, and wireless in the platform portfolio for fast, scalable delivery of mission-critical business applications. The Cisco ISRs are an integral part of the Cisco Self-Defending Network. Engineered for delivering secure services, the Cisco ISRs offer a unique blend of both hardware-accelerated and software security features and offer solutions for the small office and teleworker and the branch office and small and medium-sized business (SMB).

Cisco Integrated Services Routers Models

Figure 2-2 shows Cisco ISRs and in which environment they are typically deployed.

The Cisco ISR family consists of the following:

■ **Cisco 800 series routers:** Extend to small offices and teleworkers, or to service providers to deploy as part of their managed network services, and deliver data, security, and wireless services concurrently and at broadband speeds, and offer built-in security. The Cisco 800 series also includes broadband routers that provide highly secure Internet access and corporate network connectivity to small remote offices and teleworkers.

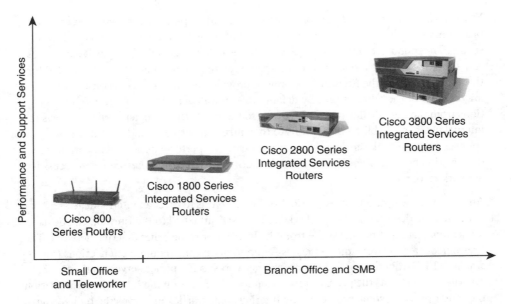

Figure 2-2 *Cisco Integrated Services Routers*

Note: Cisco had another 800 series router, but that became end-of-life in 2002. For more information, refer to http://www.cisco.com/en/US/products/hw/routers/ps380/prod_eol_notices_list.html.

■ **Cisco 1800 series routers:** These fixed-configuration routers are designed for secure broadband, Metro Ethernet, and wireless connectivity. This series of routers helps businesses reduce costs by enabling them to deploy a single device that provides multiple services, such as integrated router with redundant link, LAN switch, firewall, virtual private network (VPN), intrusion prevention systems (IPS), wireless technology, and quality of service (QoS), which are commonly performed by separate devices. The Cisco 1861 router includes a modular high-speed WAN interface card (HWIC) slot.

■ **Cisco 2800 series routers:** Designed to meet the expanding requirements of SMB offices and small to medium enterprise businesses in delivering secure, concurrent data, voice, and video services at wire-speed performance.

■ **Cisco 3800 series routers:** The architecture of these routers is designed to deliver the performance, availability, and reliability required for scaling mission-critical security, IP telephony, business video, network analysis, and web applications in the most demanding enterprise environments. Built for performance, the Cisco 3800 series ISRs deliver multiple secure, concurrent data, voice, and video services at wire-speed performance. The Cisco 3800 series ISR architecture builds on the powerful Cisco 3700 series Multiservice Access Routers.

Cisco Integrated Services Router Features

Cisco ISRs deliver additional options to enhance security in the network. Security-related features of the Cisco ISRs include the following:

- **Integrated security**

  The built-in, hardware-based encryption acceleration offloads the VPN processes to provide increased VPN throughput with minimal impact on the router CPU.
  The Cisco ISR series provides a built-in VPN encryption acceleration for IP Security (IPsec) Data Encryption Standard (DES), Triple Data Encryption Standard (3DES), and Advanced Encryption Standard (AES) 128-, 192-, and 256-bit key sizes. In addition, you can use an Advanced Integration Module (AIM) for VPN encryption.

  The Cisco NAC Network Module for ISRs brings Cisco NAC Appliance Server capabilities to Cisco 2800 and 3800 Series Integrated Services Routers. By extending the Cisco NAC Appliance portfolio to smaller locations, the Cisco NAC Network Module enables network administrators to manage a single device in the branch office for data, voice, and security.

  The Cisco IPS Network Module for Cisco routers includes innovative technologies that give users the confidence to take preventative actions on a broader range of threats. These technologies, including correlation and validation tools, greatly reduce the risk of dropping legitimate traffic.

  The Cisco Intrusion Prevention System Advanced Integration Module (AIM-IPS) integrates and brings inline Cisco IPS functionality to Cisco 1841, 2811, 2821, 2851, and 3800 series routers.

- **Unified network services**

  Packet voice digital signal processing (DSP) modules (PVDM) provide conferencing, transcoding, and secure voice features. With Secure Real-Time Transport Protocol (SRTP), the whole voice payload is encrypted while the header is still in plaintext to support features such as QoS.

  Media authentication and encryption in Cisco Survivable Remote Site Telephony (SRST) mode is supported beginning with the Cisco IOS Software Release 12.3(14)T and Cisco Unified CallManager Release 4.1.

- **Mobility**

  There are Cisco HWICs that provide access point functionality as an integrated secure 802.11 access point for modular Cisco ISRs.

  The third-generation (3G) wireless HWICs offer a compelling alternative to traditional wired backup solutions by using terrestrial cellular technology.

- **Application intelligence**

  The Cisco Wide Area Application Services (WAAS) network module is a powerful application-acceleration and WAN-optimization solution that accelerates the performance of any TCP-based application that is delivered across a WAN. Cisco WAAS allows customers to consolidate costly branch servers and storage into data centers and deploy new applications centrally while still offering near-LAN performance for remote users.

  Performance routing improves application performance by enabling a performance-aware infrastructure that selects the best path across the network.

- **Universal Serial Bus (USB) port**

  As of Cisco IOS Software Release 12.3(14)T, the USB eToken and USB flash support are available. The USB eToken feature provides secure configuration distribution and allows users to store VPN credentials for deployment. The USB flash feature allows users to store images and configurations using USB flash memory.

Note: The USB eToken uses smart card technology in a USB key to facilitate the authentication and configuration process of Cisco routers. The token itself and a PIN are necessary to access the configuration, keys, and credentials stored on the token. The token can also be used to securely provide the configuration to the router, because the configuration can be encrypted on the token. The eTokens are supplied by Aladdin Knowledge Systems and can be ordered by going to http://www.aladdin.com/etoken/cisco.

Configuring Secure Administration Access

Local access to a router, shown in Figure 2-3, usually involves a direct connection to a console port on the Cisco router using a PC or a laptop computer running terminal emulation software.

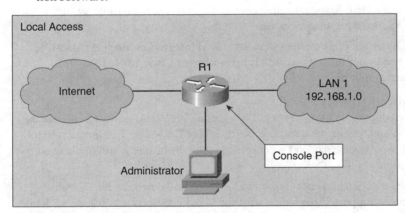

Figure 2-3 *Local Administrative Access*

Remote access typically involves allowing Telnet, Secure Shell (SSH), HTTP, HTTPS, or Simple Network Management Protocol (SNMP) connections to the router from a computer on the same subnet or different subnet. Figure 2-4 shows the topologies associated with both types of access.

It is preferable to allow only local access to the router because some remote-access protocols, such as Telnet, send the data, including usernames and passwords, to the router in plaintext. If an attacker can collect network traffic while an administrator is logged in remotely to a router, the attacker can capture passwords or router configuration information.

If remote access is required, it is recommended that you apply one of the following options:

- Establish a dedicated management network. The management network should include only identified administration hosts and connections to a dedicated interface on the router.

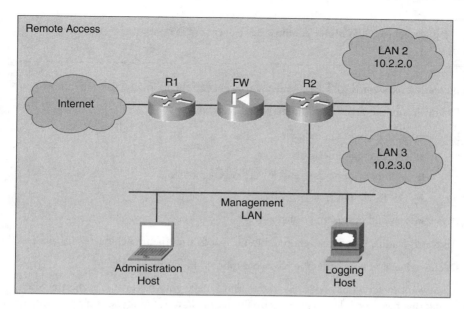

Figure 2-4   *Remote Administrative Access*

■   Encrypt all the traffic between the administrator computer and the router.

In either case, you can configure a packet filter to allow only the identified administration hosts and preferred protocols to access the router. For example, permit only SSH requests from the IP address of the administration host to initiate a connection to the routers in the network.

Note: For further information about the management LAN, read about "Secure Management and Reporting" in *Cisco SAFE: A Security Blueprint for Enterprise Networks* at http://www.cisco.com.

Configuring the Router Passwords

Configuring secure administrative access is an extremely important security task. If an unauthorized person were to gain administrative access to a router, the person could alter routing parameters, disable routing functions, discover and gain access to other systems in the network, or simply erase the startup configuration file and reload the router.

Strong passwords and similar secrets, such as SNMP community strings, are the primary defense against unauthorized access to your router. The first step to secure Cisco router administrative access is to configure secure system passwords. The best way to handle most passwords is to maintain them on a TACACS+ or RADIUS authentication server such as the Cisco Secure Access Control Server (ACS). However, routers can have locally configured passwords for privileged access and can have other password information in their configuration files. This section focuses only on configuring local passwords.

To gain access to the router and configure passwords, connect to the router using a console. A console is a terminal connected to a router console port. The terminal can be a dumb terminal or a PC with terminal emulation software, such as Microsoft HyperTerminal.

Key
Topic

> The first step to secure Cisco router administrative access is to configure secure system passwords.

When creating passwords for Cisco routers, always keep the following rules in mind:

- Establish a minimum of 10 characters for a password.

- Passwords can include the following:
    - Any alphanumeric character
    - A mix of uppercase and lowercase characters
    - Symbols and spaces

- Passwords should not use dictionary words.

- Password-leading spaces are ignored, but no spaces after the first character are ignored.

- Decide when and how often the passwords should be changed.

You might want to add your own rules to this list to make your passwords even safer, such as insisting that passwords be a sequence of alternating letters, numbers, and a symbol, for instance.

You can secure a router by using a password to restrict access. Using a password and assigning privilege levels is a simple way to provide terminal access control in a network. A password can be established on individual lines, such as the console, and to the privileged EXEC mode. Passwords are case sensitive.

By default, the console port does not require a password for console administrative access; however, you should always configure a console port line-level password. As shown in Example 2-1, you can use the **line console 0** command followed by the **login** and **password** subcommands to require login and establish a login password on the console line.

Example 2-1 *Configuring the Console Password*

```
R1(config)# line console 0
R1(config-line)# login
R1(config-line)# password M3rcury$09
```

By default, Cisco routers support up to five simultaneous vty (Telnet) sessions. On the router, the vty ports are numbered from 0 through 4. As shown in Example 2-2, you can use the **line vty 0 4** command followed by the **login** and **password** subcommands to require login and establish a login password on incoming Telnet sessions.

Example 2-2 *Configuring the Virtual Terminal Password*

```
R1(config)# line vty 0 4
R1(config-line)# login
R1(config-line)# password V3nus$2009
```

The **enable secret password** global command restricts access to the privileged EXEC mode. As shown in Example 2-3, you can use the **enable secret** global configuration command to configure the enable secret password. The enable secret password is always hashed inside the router configuration using a Message Digest 5 (MD5) hashing algorithm; it never appears in cleartext.

Example 2-3   *Configuring the Enable Secret Password*

```
R1(config)# enable secret M1lkyway$09
```

The enable password is also used to enter enable mode, but it is from earlier versions of Cisco IOS Software. By default, the enable password is not encrypted in the router configuration. The **enable password** global configuration command was kept for backward compatibility in case you downgrade the router to a version of Cisco IOS Software that does not support the **enable secret password** command. If both an enable password and an enable secret password are configured, the enable password is ignored. Example 2-4 demonstrates use of the **enable password** command.

Example 2-4   *Configuring the Enable Password*

```
R1(config)# enable password earth
```

If you forget the enable secret password, you have no alternative but to replace it using the Cisco router password recovery procedure specific to your Cisco equipment, which you can find in Cisco Document ID 6130 at http://www.cisco.com/en/US/products/sw/iosswrel/ps1831/products_tech_note09186a00801746e6.shtml.

With the exception of the **enable secret password**, all Cisco router passwords are stored in plaintext by default within the router configuration. You can view these passwords with the **show running-config** command. Sniffers can also see these passwords if your TFTP server configuration files traverse an unsecured intranet or Internet connection. If an intruder gains access to the TFTP server where the router configuration files are stored, the intruder is able to obtain these passwords.

As a safeguard against this possible exploit, the **service password-encryption** command encrypts all the passwords (except the previously hashed enable secret password) in the router configuration file, and will encrypt any passwords you set after entering this command until you turn the command off with the **no** form of the command. This method, which uses the Vigeneàre method explained in Chapter 4, "Fundamentals of Cryptography," is not as safe as MD5, which is used with the **enable secret** command, but prevents casual discovery of the router line-level passwords. Example 2-5 shows how to configure the **service password-encryption** command. To remove the **service password-encryption** command, use **no service password-encryption**.

Also by default, Cisco router auxiliary ports do not require a password for remote administrative access. Administrators sometimes use this port to remotely configure and monitor the router using a dialup modem connection. To combat this vulnerability, you can use the **line aux 0** command followed by the **login** and **password** subcommands to require login and establish a login password on an incoming auxiliary line.

Note: If you want to turn off the EXEC process for a specific line, such as on the auxiliary port, use the **no exec** command within the line configuration mode.

Example 2-5 *Configuring the* **service password-encryption** *Command*

```
R1(config)#service password-encryption
```

Setting Timeouts for Router Lines

By default, an administrative interface stays active (and logged in) for 10 minutes after the last session activity. After that, the interface times out and logs out of the session. It is recommended that you fine-tune these timers to limit the amount of time to within a two- or three-minute maximum.

You can adjust these timers using the **exec-timeout** command in line configuration mode for each of the line types that are used.

The syntax for this command is **exec-timeout** *minutes* [*seconds*]. Table 2-1 explains the variables.

Table 2-1 *exec-timeout Command Parameters*

Parameters	Description
minutes	This integer specifies the number of idle minutes before the session is timed out.
seconds	(Optional) This integer specifies the additional time interval in seconds.

Example 2-6 shows how to configure the console and auxiliary port timeouts for three and a half minutes.

Example 2-6 *Configuring Console and Auxiliary Timeouts*

```
R1(config)# line console 0
R1(config-line)# exec-timeout 3 30
R1(config-line)# exit
R1(config)# line aux 0
R1(config-line)# exec-timeout 3 30
R1(config)# line vty 0 4
R1(config-line)# exec-timeout 3 30
```

You can also use the Cisco Router and Security Device Manager (SDM), introduced later in this chapter, to configure the **exec-timeout** for the vty lines.

Configuring the Minimum Length for Router Passwords

Cisco IOS Software Release 12.3(1) and later allows you to set the minimum character length for all router passwords using the **security passwords** global configuration command. This command provides enhanced security access to the router by allowing you to specify a minimum password length (0 to 16 characters); this eliminates common passwords that are short and prevalent on most networks, such as lab and cisco. Example 2-7 demonstrates the **security passwords** command set for a minimum of 10 characters.

Example 2-7   *Example of the* **security passwords** *Command*

```
R1(config)# security passwords min-length 10
```

This command affects user passwords, enable passwords and enable secret passwords, and line passwords that are created after the command is executed. Existing router passwords remain unaffected.

It is highly recommended that you set your minimum password length to at least 10 characters. Never use a length of zero.

After the **security passwords** command has been enabled, any attempt to create a new password that is less than the specified length fails and results in an error message similar to this message:

Password too short - must be at least 10 characters. Password configuration failed.

Enhanced Username Password Security

Cisco routers can maintain a list of usernames and passwords for performing local login authentication.

Starting with Cisco IOS Software Release 12.0(18)S, system administrators can choose to use an MD5 hashing mechanism to encrypt a user password. MD5 hashing of passwords is a much better algorithm than the standard type 7 found in the **service password-encryption** command. The added layer of MD5 protection is useful in environments in which the password crosses the network or is stored on a TFTP server.

MD5 hashing of a Cisco IOS user password is accomplished with the **username secret** command in global configuration mode. Administrators can choose to enter a plaintext password for MD5 hashing by the router (option 0), or they can enter a previously encrypted MD5 secret (option 5). The syntax for the username secret command is as follows:

```
username name secret {[0] password ¦ 5 encrypted-secret}
```

Table 2-2 shows the parameters of the **username secret** command.

Table 2-2   *username secret Parameters*

Parameters	Description
name	This parameter specifies the username.
0	(Optional) This option indicates that the plaintext password is to be hashed by the router using MD5.
password	This parameter is the plaintext password to be hashed using MD5.
5	This parameter indicates that the encrypted-secret password was hashed using MD5.
encrypted-secret	This parameter is the MD5 encrypted-secret password that is stored as the encrypted user password.

Example 2-8 shows an example of the **username secret** command.

Example 2-8   *Example of the **username secret** Command*

```
R1(config)# username SecAdmin secret 0 Curium2008
R1(config)# username SecAdmin secret 5 $1$feb0$a104Qd9UZ./Ak00KTggPD0
```

Securing ROM Monitor

By default, Cisco IOS routers allow a break sequence during startup that forces the router into ROM monitor mode. Once the router is in ROM monitor mode, anyone can choose to enter a new secret password using the well-known Cisco password recovery procedure. This procedure, if performed correctly, leaves the router configuration intact. This scenario presents a potential security breach because anyone who gains physical access to the router console port can enter ROM monitor, reset the enable secret password, and discover the router configuration.

Note: As mentioned earlier, the specific steps for password recovery varies depending on which device is involved, and are beyond the mandate of this course. However, the generic steps are as follows:

Step 1.   Perform the password recovery procedure from the console port.

Step 2.   Use the power switch to turn off and then on the router to break its normal boot sequence

Step 3.   Send the break sequence to the router to force it to go in the ROM monitor mode.

Step 4.   Change the config-register for 0x2142; the normal config-register setting is 0x2102.

Step 5.   While still in the ROMMON mode, enter **reset** or **reload** to reboot the router.

Step 6. The router "not finding" a saved configuration in NVRAM will present you with the initial SETUP mode. Answer **no** (or **Ctrl-C**) to get out of this mode.

Step 7. At the router prompt, enter **enable**, followed by **copy startup-config running-config.**

Step 8. Enter **configure terminal.**

Step 9. At the configuration prompt, enter **enable secret** *password*, followed by **config-register 0x2102** to set it back to its default.

Step 10. Do **no shut** on each interface and exit the configuration mode.

Step 11. At the privilege mode, save the configuration file with the **copy running-config startup-config** command.

To find more about password recovery, check http://tinyurl.com/e3mjw.

You can mitigate this potential security breach by using the **no service password-recovery** global configuration command, as shown in Example 2-9. The **no service password-recovery** command is a hidden Cisco IOS command and has no arguments or keywords.

Example 2-9   no service password-recovery *Command*

```
R1(config)# no service password-recovery
WARNING:
Executing this command will disable password recovery mechanism. Do not execute
this command without another plan for password recovery.
Are you sure you want to continue? [yes/no]: yes
R1(config)#
```

Caution: If a router is configured with the **no service password-recovery** command, all access to ROM monitor mode is disabled. If the router flash memory does not contain a valid Cisco IOS image, you cannot use the **rommon xmodem** command to load a new flash image. To repair the router, you must obtain a new Cisco IOS image on a flash SIMM or on a Personal Computer Memory Card International Association (PCMCIA) card (Cisco 3600 series routers only). Refer to Cisco.com for more information about backup flash images.

When the **no service password-recovery** command is executed, the router boot sequence will look similar to the output shown in Example 2-10.

Example 2-10   *Router Boot Sequence After Configuring* **no service password-recovery**

```
System Bootstrap, Version 11.3(2)XA4, RELEASE SOFTWARE (fc1)
Copyright (c) 1999 by cisco Systems, Inc.
C2600 platform with 65536 Kbytes of main memory
```

Example 2-10   *Router Boot Sequence After Configuring* **no service password-recovery**

```
PASSWORD RECOVERY FUNCTIONALITY IS DISABLED
program load complete, entry point: 0x80008000, size: 0xed9ee4
```

Also, after the **no service password-recovery** command is executed, the **show running-config** command displays the **no service password-recovery** statement, as shown in Example 2-11.

Example 2-11   **show running-config** *Command Output After Configuring* **no service password-recovery**

```
Router# show running-config
!
version 12.0
service tcp-keepalives-in
service timestamps debug datetime localtime show-timezone
service timestamps log datetime localtime show-timezone
service password-encryption
no service password-recovery
!
hostname Boston
```

Note: To recover a device after the **no service password-recovery** command has been entered, press the **Break** key within five seconds after the image decompresses during the boot. You are prompted to confirm the Break key action. When you confirm the action, the startup configuration is erased, the password recovery procedure is enabled, and the router boots with the factory default configuration. If you do not confirm the Break key action, the router boots normally with the No Service Password-Recovery feature enabled.

Configuring Multiple Privilege Levels

Cisco routers enable you to configure various privilege levels for your administrators. You can configure different passwords to control which administrators have access to the various privilege levels. Configuring various privilege levels is especially useful in a help desk environment where you want certain administrators to be able to configure and monitor every part of the router (level 15), while you want other administrators to only monitor, and not configure, the router (customized levels 2 to 14). There are 16 privilege levels, 0 to 15; level 0 is reserved for the user-level access privileges, levels 1 to 14 are levels you can customize, and level 15 is reserved for enable mode privileges.

To assign privileges to levels 2 to 14, use the **privilege** command from global configuration mode:

privilege *mode* {**level** *level command* ¦ **reset** *command*}

Table 2-3 describes the parameters for this command and Example 2-12 demonstrates usage.

Table 2-3 **privilege** *Command Parameters*

Parameters	Description
mode	This command argument specifies the configuration mode. Use the Router(config)# **privilege ?** command to see a complete list of router configuration modes available on your router.
level	(Optional) This keyword enables setting a privilege level with a specified command.
level command	(Optional) This parameter is the privilege level that is associated with a command. You can specify up to 16 privilege levels, using numbers 0 to 15.
reset	(Optional) This keyword resets the privilege level of a command.
command	(Optional) Use this argument when you want to reset the privilege level.

Example 2-12 *Configuring Multiple Privilege Levels*

```
R1(config)# privilege exec level 2 ping
R1(config)# enable secret level 2 Cariboo2008
```

To assign a password to the custom privilege level, use the command **enable secret level** *level* password in global configuration mode.

To enter a custom privilege level, use the command **enable** *level* and enter the password that was assigned to the custom privilege level.

Example 2-12 sets the **ping** command to require privilege level 2 or above access and establishes Cariboo2008 as the secret password for privilege level 2. When you enter the **enable 2** command, as shown in Example 2-13, the router prompts you for the enable secret password for privilege level 2.

Use the **show privilege** command to display the current privilege level, as shown in Example 2-13.

Example 2-13 *Using the* **enable** *level and* **show privilege** *Commands*

```
R1> enable 2
Password: Cariboo2008
R1#show privilege
Current privilege level is 2
```

Configuring Role-Based Command-Line Interface Access

The role-based command-line interface (CLI) access feature allows you to create different "views" of router configurations for different users. Views define which commands are accepted from different users and what configuration information is visible to them. With role-based CLI access, you can exercise better control over Cisco networking devices.

> **Note:**   Before you create a view, you must enable authentication, authorization, and accounting (AAA) using the **aaa new-model** command or the Cisco SDM. AAA configurations are covered in the "Configuring AAA on a Cisco Router Using the Local Database" section of this chapter.

The steps used to configure and confirm a view are as follows:

Step 1.   Router> **enable view**

Step 2.   Router# **configure terminal**

Step 3.   Router(config)# **parser view** *view-name*

Step 4.   Router(config-view)# **secret 5** *encrypted-password*

Step 5.   Router(config-view)# **commands** *parser-mode* {**include** | **include-exclusive** | **exclude**} [**all**] [**interface** *interface-name* | *command*]

Step 6.   Router(config-view)# **exit**

Step 7.   Router(config)# **exit**

Step 8.   Router# **enable** [*view-name*]

Step 9.   Router# **show parser view** [**all**]

The last two steps allow you to preview the views that you have configured. The next few pages discuss these commands in detail.

The key commands specific to configuring views for role-based CLI are shown a little later in this section in Example 2-14. When a system is in "root view," it has all the access privileges as a user who has level 15 privileges. To configure any view for the system, you must be in the root view.

The difference between a user who has level 15 privileges and a root view user is that a root view user can configure a new view and add or remove commands from the view.

To access the root view, use first the **enable view** command and the **parser view** command:

```
R1> enable view
R1# configure terminal
R1(config)# parser view view-name
```

Table 2-4 shows the commands and parameters used to access and modify the root view.

Table 2-4   **enable view** *and* **parser view** *Command Parameters*

Parameters	Description
enable view	This command puts you in root view from where you create views and establish view attributes.
config term	This command puts you in global configuration mode.
parser view *view name*	This command creates a view and enters view configuration mode.
secret 0 | 5 *view-password*	This command configures a password for this view: secret 0 specifies that an unencrypted password follows. secret 5 specifies that an encrypted secret follows.

Next, you must assign the allowed commands to the selected view. Use the **commands** command in view configuration mode to assign the allowed commands. The syntax for this command is as follows:

```
R1(config-view)# commands parser-mode {include ¦ include-exclusive ¦ exclude}
[all] [interface interface-name ¦ command]
```

Table 2-5 shows the parameters used with the **commands** command.

Table 2-5   **commands** *Command Parameters*

Parameters	Description
commands	Adds commands or interfaces to a view
parser-mode	The mode in which the specified command exists (for example, EXEC mode)
Include	Adds a command or an interface to the view and allows the same command or interface to be added to an additional view
include-exclusive	Adds a command or an interface to the view and excludes the same command or interface from being added to all other views
Exclude	Excludes a command or an interface from the view
All	A "wildcard" that allows every command in a specified configuration mode that begins with the same keyword or every subinterface for a specified interface to be part of the view
interface *interface-name*	Interface that is added to the view
command	Command that is added to the view

Example 2-14 displays a complete configuration of a new view, called NetOps.

Example 2-14   *Commands to Enable Root View and to Create New Views*

```
R1> enable view
Password:
R1# configure terminal
Enter configuration commands, one per line.  End with CNTL/Z.
R1(config)# parser view NetOps
R1(config-view)# secret 0 hardtocrackpw
R1(config-view)# commands exec include ping
R1(config-view)# commands exec include all show
R1(config-view)# commands exec include telnet
R1(config-view)# commands exec include traceroute
R1(config-view)# commands exec include write
R1(config-view)# commands exec include configure
R1(config-view)# commands configure include access-list
R1(config-view)# commands configure include all interface
R1(config-view)# commands configure include all ip
```

To verify a view, use the **enable view** command. Enter the name of the view that you want to verify and provide the password to log in to the view. After you are in the view, use the question mark (**?**) command to verify that the commands available in the view are correct. Example 2-15 shows the commands only accessible from the NetOps view at the privilege mode and at the configuration mode.

Example 2-15   *Verifying Commands Available to the NetOps View*

```
R1# enable view NetOps
Password: hardtocrackpw
R1#
Jan  3 13:45:03.887: %PARSER-6-VIEW_SWITCH: successfully set to view 'NetOps'.
R1#?
Exec commands:
  configure    Enter configuration mode
  enable       Turn on privileged commands
  exit         Exit from the EXEC
  ping         Send echo messages
  show         Show running system information
  telnet       Open a telnet connection
  traceroute   Trace route to destination
  write        Write running configuration to memory, network, or terminal
R1# configure terminal
R1(config)#?
```

```
Configure commands:
  access-list  Add an access list entry
  do           To run exec commands in config mode
  exit         Exit from configure mode
  interface    Select an interface to configure
  ip           Global IP configuration subcommands
```

Securing the Cisco IOS Image and Configuration Files

The Cisco IOS resilient configuration feature enables a router to secure and maintain a working copy of the running image and configuration so that those files can withstand malicious attempts to erase the contents of persistent storage (NVRAM and flash storage).

A great challenge for network operators is the total downtime that is experienced after a router has been compromised and its operating software and configuration data are erased from its persistent storage. The operator must retrieve an archived copy (hopefully one is available) of the configuration and a working Cisco IOS image to restore the router. Recovery must then be performed for each affected router, adding to the total network downtime.

The Cisco IOS resilient configuration feature is intended to speed up the recovery process. This feature maintains a secure working copy of the router image and the startup configuration at all times. The user cannot remove these secure files. This set of Cisco IOS image and router running configuration files is referred to as the *bootset*.

The command sequence to save a primary bootset to a secure archive in persistent storage is as follows:

Step 1.   Router> enable

Step 2.   Router# configure terminal

Step 3.   Router(config)# secure boot-image

Step 4.   Router(config)# secure boot-config

Step 5.   Router(config)# end

Step 6.   Router# show secure bootset

Table 2-6 describes the key commands that are required to secure the Cisco IOS image and running configuration using the **secure boot-image** command:

```
R1(config)# secure boot-image
R1(config)# secure boot-config
```

Table 2-6 secure *Commands*

Command	Description
secure boot-image	This command enables Cisco IOS image resilience. When turned on for the first time, the running image (as displayed in the **show version** command output) is secured, and a syslog entry is generated. This command functions properly only when the system is configured to run an image from a disk with an Advanced Technology Attachment (ATA) interface. Images that are booted from a TFTP server cannot be secured. Because this command has the effect of "hiding" the running image, the image file is not included in any directory listing of the disk.
	If the router is configured to boot with Cisco IOS resilience and an image with a different version of Cisco IOS is detected, a message similar to this is displayed at boot:
	"ios resilience :Archived image and configuration version 12.2 differs from running version 12.3"
secure boot-config	This command takes a snapshot of the router running configuration and securely archives it in persistent storage.

Secured files do not appear in the output of a **dir** command that is issued from an executive shell because the Cisco IOS file system prevents the secure files in a directory from being listed. ROM monitor mode does not have any such restriction and can list and boot secured files. Because the running image and running configuration archives are not visible in the output from the Cisco IOS command **dir**, use the **show secure bootset** command to verify the archive existence.

Example 2-16 shows an example of the **show secure bootset** command output. This command is important to verify that the Cisco IOS image and configuration files have been properly backed up and secured.

Example 2-16   show secure bootset *Command Output*

```
R1# show secure bootset
IOS resilience router id FHK085031MD

IOS image resilience version 12.3 activated at 05:00:59 UTC Fri Feb 10 2006
Secure archive flash:c1841-advsecurityk9-mz.123-14.T1.bin type is image (elf) []
  file size is 17533860 bytes, run size is 17699528 bytes
  Runnable image, entry point 0x8000F000, run from ram

IOS configuration resilience version 12.3 activated at 05:01:02 UTC Fri Feb 10 2
006
Secure archive flash:.runcfg-20060210-050102.ar type is config
configuration archive size 4014 bytes
```

Configuring Enhanced Support for Virtual Logins

The Cisco IOS login enhancements feature allows you to better secure your Cisco IOS devices when creating a virtual connection, such as Telnet, SSH, or HTTP. In addition, you can slow down dictionary attacks and thereby protect your router from a possible DoS attack.

To better configure security when opening a virtual login connection, you should configure the login process with the following:

- Delays between successive login attempts

- Login shutdown if DoS attacks are suspected

- Generation of system logging messages for login detection

Delays Between Successive Login Attempts

A Cisco IOS device can accept virtual connections as fast as it can process these connections. Introducing a delay between login attempts helps to protect your router from a possible dictionary attack. You can enable delays in one of the following ways:

- The **login block-for** command: You must enter this command before issuing the **login delay** command. However, if you enter only the **login block-for** command, a login delay of 1 second is automatically enforced.

- The **login delay** command: This command enables you to specify the number of seconds to delay between login attempts.

- The **auto secure** command: If you enable the AutoSecure feature, a login delay of 1 second is automatically enforced.

Login Shutdown if DoS Attacks Are Suspected

If the configured number of connection attempts fails within a specified time period, the Cisco IOS device does not accept any additional connections for a period of time that is called the *quiet period*. Hosts that are permitted by a predefined access control list (ACL) are excluded from the quiet period.

You can specify the number of failed connection attempts that trigger the quiet period using the command **login block-for** in global configuration mode. You can specify the predefined ACL that is excluded from the quiet period using the command **login quiet-mode access-class** command in global configuration mode.

This functionality is disabled by default, and it is not enabled if the AutoSecure feature is enabled.

Generation of System Logging Messages for Login Detection

After the router switches to and from quiet mode, logging messages are generated. Also, if they are configured, logging messages are generated upon every successful or failed login request.

> **Note:**   When a session is running in quiet mode, messages sent to the sessions are not displayed on the terminal.

You can use the command **login on-success** in global configuration mode to generate log messages for successful login requests. The **login on-failure** command generates logs for failed login requests.

Logging messages for failed login attempts are automatically enabled when the **auto secure** command is issued, but are not automatically enabled for successful login attempts via the **auto secure** command.

All login enhancement features are disabled by default. You must issue the **login block-for** command, which enables default login functionality before using any other login commands. After you enable the **login block-for** command, the following defaults are enforced:

- The default login delay is one second.

- All login attempts made using Telnet, SSH, and HTTP are denied during the quiet period; that is, no ACLs are exempt from the login period until the **login quiet-mode access-class** command is issued.

Use the following command sequence to configure your Cisco IOS device for login parameters that help detect suspected DoS attacks and slow down dictionary attacks.

Step 1.   Router> **enable**

Step 2.   Router# **configure terminal**

Step 3.   Router(config)# **login block-for** *seconds* **attempts** *tries* **within** *seconds*

Step 4.   Router(config)# **login quiet-mode access-class** {*acl-name* | *acl-number*}

Step 5.   Router(config)# **login delay** *seconds*

Step 6.   Router(config)# **login on-failure log** [**every** *login*]

Step 7.   Router(config)# **login on-success log** [**every** *login*]

These commands are discussed in details in the next pages.

Table 2-7 describes the commands required to set the parameters for the quiet period.

Table 2-7 *Enabling Support for Virtual Logins*

Command	Description
login block-for *seconds* **attempts** *tries* **within** *seconds*	This command must be issued before any other login command can be used.
	This command configures your Cisco IOS device for login parameters that help provide DoS detection.
login quiet-mode access-class {*acl-name* | *acl-number*}	(Optional) This command specifies an ACL that is to be applied to the router when it switches to quiet mode. The devices that match a **permit** statement in the ACL are exempt from the quiet period.

Example 2-17 shows a configuration that will disable login for 150 seconds if more than 2 login failures occur within 100 seconds. This will help provides DoS detection. Example 2-17 also shows configuration that invokes an ACL that is named myacl. If this command is not enabled, all login requests would be denied during quiet mode.

Example 2-17 *Example of the* **login block-for** *and* **login quiet-mode** *Commands*

```
R1(config)# login block-for 150 attempts 2 within 100
R1(config)# login quiet-mode access-class myacl
```

To enable a login delay, use the **login delay** *seconds* command. To log the successful and failed attempts to login, use the following commands:

```
login on-failure log [every login]
login on-success log [every login]
```

Then, use the **show login** command to verify that the **login block-for** command is issued. Example 2-18 shows that the router is configured to block login hosts for 100 seconds if more than 15 (16 or more) login requests fail within 100 seconds. Five login requests have already failed.

Example 2-18 **show login** *Command Output*

```
Router# show login
A default login delay of 1 second is applied.
No Quiet-Mode access list has been configured.
All successful login is logged and generate SNMP traps.
All failed login is logged and generate SNMP traps.

Router enabled to watch for login Attacks.
If more than 15 login failures occur in 100 seconds or less, logins will be
disabled for 100 seconds.

Router presently in Watch-Mode, will remain in Watch-Mode for 95 seconds.
Present login failure count 5.
```

Example 2-19 is an output from the **show login** command to verify that the router is in quiet mode. This output shows that the **login block-for** command was configured to block login hosts for 100 seconds if more than 2 (3 or more) login requests fail within 100 seconds.

Example 2-19 **show login** *Command Output to Verify Quiet Mode*

```
Router# show login


A default login delay of 1 second is applied.
No Quiet-Mode access list has been configured.
All successful login is logged and generate SNMP traps.
All failed login is logged and generate SNMP traps.
Router enabled to watch for login Attacks.
If more than 2 login failures occur in 100 seconds or less, logins will be
disabled for 100 seconds.

Router presently in Quiet-Mode, will remain in Quiet-Mode for 93 seconds.
Denying logins from all sources.
```

Example 2-20 displays output from the **show login failures** command indicating all failed login attempts on the router.

Example 2-20 **show login failures** *Command Output*

```
Router# show login failures


Information about login failures with the device

Username       Source IPAddr   lPort Count   TimeStamp
try1           10.1.1.1         23    1       21:52:49 UTC Sun Mar 9 2003
try2           10.1.1.2         23    1      21:52:52 UTC Sun Mar 9 2003
```

Configuring Banner Messages

You should use banner messages to warn would-be intruders that they are not welcome on your network. Banners are very important, especially from a legal perspective.

Choosing what to place in your banner messages is important and should be reviewed by legal counsel before placing them on your routers. Intruders could have an argument in court cases if they were to argue that they have encountered a warning banner mentioning "Welcome to this site" or the like. All banners should rather warn that the access is strictly reserved to authorized personnel.

Banners are disabled by default, and you must explicitly enable them. Use the **banner** command from global configuration mode to specify appropriate messages.

Table 2-8   **banner** *Command Parameters*

Parameters	Description
exec	This parameter specifies and enables a message to be displayed when an EXEC process is created on the router (an EXEC banner).
incoming	This parameter specifies and enables a banner to be displayed when there is an incoming connection to a terminal line from a host on the network.
login	This parameter specifies and enables a customized banner to be displayed before the username and password login prompts.
motd	This parameter specifies and enables a message-of-the-day (MOTD) banner.
slip-ppp	This parameter specifies and enables a banner to be displayed when a Serial Line Internet Protocol (SLIP) or PPP connection is made.
d	This parameter represents the delimiting character of your choice (a pound sign, #, for example). You cannot use the delimiting character in the banner message.
message	This parameter represents message text. You can include tokens in the form $(*token*) in the message text. Tokens are replaced with the corresponding configuration variable.

Table 2-8 describes the parameters for the **banner** command, the syntax for which is as follows:

```
banner {exec ¦ incoming ¦ login ¦ motd ¦ slip-ppp} d message d
```

The following is a list of valid tokens for use within the message section of the **banner** command:

- **$(hostname):** Displays the hostname for the router
- **$(domain):** Displays the domain name for the router
- **$(line):** Displays the vty or tty (asynchronous) line number
- **$(line-desc):** Displays the description that is attached to the line

You can also use the Cisco SDM to configure banner messages.

Example 2-21 shows the configuration of a MOTD banner.

Example 2-21   *Configuring MOTD Banner*

```
R1(config)# banner motd %
WARNING: You are connected to $(hostname) on the Cisco Systems, Incorporated
network.
Unauthorized access and use of this network will be vigorously prosecuted. %
```

Introducing Cisco SDM

Cisco Router and Security Device Manager (SDM) is an intuitive, web-based tool that enables you to easily and reliably deploy and manage the services on Cisco IOS routers. Cisco SDM simplifies router and security configuration through smart wizards, which help users quickly and easily deploy, configure, and monitor Cisco routers without requiring knowledge of the Cisco IOS Software CLI.

Cisco SDM offers users the following benefits:

■   Smart wizards in Cisco SDM have built-in intelligence about recommended Cisco IOS configurations for different use scenarios.

■   Cisco SDM can recommend an optimum security configuration for a router that is based on the detection of such areas as LAN and WAN connections, ACLs, Network Address Translation (NAT), IP Security (IPsec) policies, and firewall rules.

■   Cisco SDM includes features such as WAN and virtual private network (VPN) troubleshooting, router security audit, and one-step lockdown that leverage the integration of routing, WAN access, and security technology.

■   For novices, Cisco SDM helps users that have limited CLI knowledge and security expertise to configure basic network security implementations. For experts, Cisco SDM has power tools that improve productivity.

■   As a device manager, Cisco SDM manages one device at a time.

■   Cisco SDM supports Cisco IOS Software Release 12.2(11)T6 or later.

■   Cisco SDM has no impact on router DRAM or CPU.

■   Cisco SDM works in conjunction with other management tools and the CLI over Telnet.

Refer to the *Cisco Router and Security Device Manager Version 2.4 User's Guide* for details on supported platforms and Cisco IOS Software requirements.

Note: To support Cisco SDM, make sure your security policy does not prohibit enabling a web server daemon on routers. Cisco SDM requires HTTP or HTTPS to be enabled.

Supporting Cisco SDM and Cisco SDM Express

Cisco SDM is a web-based tool that is supported on Microsoft Windows-based PC platforms. Refer to the Cisco Router and Security Device Manager Quick Start Guide at http://tinyurl.com/5n2rb7 for details on the operating systems and web browsers that Cisco SDM supports.

Cisco SDM is factory installed on some router models. If it is not installed on your router, it will either be available on a CD-ROM that is included with new routers or you can download it from Cisco.com. The install options allow you to install Cisco SDM Express, Cisco SDM, or both.

Note: As its name implies, Cisco SDM Express is a lightweight version of Cisco SDM that offers quick and easy router deployment for basic WAN access configurations. It is ideal as a router deployment tool for nonexpert users.

Note: As a rule of thumb, SDM Express is factory installed on router flash memory, and a Cisco SDM CD is bundled with the router, and can be sometimes preinstalled in flash. Currently, Cisco SDM ships with all new Cisco 850 series, Cisco 870 series, and Cisco 1800, 2800, and 3800 series ISRs.

Refer to the latest Cisco SDM datasheet, at Cisco.com, to confirm whether Cisco SDM is installed in flash.

Note: The Cisco SDM CD-ROM or the Cisco SDM image from the Cisco IOS Software Center (http://www.cisco.com/pcgi-bin/tablebuild.pl/sdm) supports the installation of Cisco SDM on a PC hard disk or router flash memory. When Cisco SDM is installed on a PC, no files are required in the router flash memory, and Cisco SDM can manage an installed base of Cisco routers that may not have enough flash memory space to load Cisco SDM files.

If the router is an existing router and is not configured with the Cisco SDM default configuration, you must configure the following services on the router for Cisco SDM to access the router properly:

- Set up a username and password that has privilege level 15:
  ```
  username name privilege 15 secret password
  ```

- Enable the HTTP server:
  ```
  ip http server
  ip http authentication local
  ip http secure-server (for enabling HTTPS access to Cisco SDM)
  ip http timeout-policy idle 600 life 86400 request 1000
  ```

- Define the protocol to use to connect to the Telnet and Secure Shell (SSH) vty lines:
  ```
  line con 0
   login local
  line vty 0 4
   privilege level 15
   login local
   transport input telnet ssh
  line vty 5 15
   privilege level 15
   login local
   transport input telnet ssh
  ```

> **Note:**   To enable HTTP over SSL, you do not need the **ip http server** command, but the **ip http secure-server** command is needed.

When you want to run Cisco SDM from your router, for Cisco SDM Version 2.2a and later, the following files must be loaded on the router flash memory:

- sdmconfig-*modelxxx*.cfg, where *modelxxx* is the model number of the router (this is, the manufacture default configuration file for the router)

- sdm.tar

- es.tar (for Cisco SDM Express and optional once Cisco SDM is installed)

- common.tar

- home.shtml

- home.tar

The file wlanui.tar is required if there are wireless interfaces to manage. Example 2-22 shows the content of the flash of a Cisco 2800 router.

Example 2-22   *Files Required to Run Cisco SDM from a Router*

```
router# show flash
-#- —length— — —-date/time— — — path
1      19312988 Dec 13 2005 01:23:50 +00:00 c2800nm-advsecurityk9-mz.124-5.bin
2          3317 Feb 8 2006 00:00:30 +00:00 startup.config
3          1646 Feb 8 2006 18:31:50 +00:00 sdmconfig-2811.cfg
4       4049920 Feb 8 2006 18:32:32 +00:00 sdm.tar
5        812544 Feb 8 2006 18:32:56 +00:00 es.tar
6       1007616 Feb 8 2006 18:33:14 +00:00 common.tar
7          1038 Feb 8 2006 18:33:24 +00:00 home.shtml
8        113152 Feb 8 2006 18:33:42 +00:00 home.tar
```

Launching Cisco SDM Express

On a new router, you can access Cisco SDM Express from your PC web browser by going to http://10.10.10.1. The factory default router configuration file that comes with Cisco SDM configures the router Ethernet IP address to 10.10.10.1.

If the proper files are loaded on the router flash memory, when you access the router for the first time, the Cisco SDM Express wizard appears. Just enter the required information, noting that some fields provide a default value.

When you launch Cisco SDM from the router, Cisco SDM checks the router configuration. If certain features are not configured, Cisco SDM Express launches instead. For example, when Cisco SDM sees the default configuration file on the router (sdmconfig-*modelxxx*.cfg, where *modelxxx* is the model number of the device), Cisco SDM Express is launched.

After you have completed the initial router configuration with Cisco SDM Express, the Cisco SDM Express Wizard is not presented again. If you need to make changes, you can edit the configurations using the full Cisco SDM tool.

You can find details about Cisco SDM Express in the *Cisco SDM Express 2.4 User's Guide* at http://tinyurl.com/47w5rk.

Launching Cisco SDM

SDM can run either as an application installed on your PC or from the router's flash through your PC's browser.

To launch Cisco SDM from an administrator PC, choose **Start > Programs (All Programs) > Cisco Systems > Cisco SDM > Cisco SDM**. Next, provide the IP address of the LAN interface on the router, as configured previously with the Cisco SDM Express Wizard, in the SDM Launcher window.

To launch Cisco SDM from the router flash memory, open an HTTP or HTTPS connection to the IP address of the Ethernet interface on the router. Follow the prompts, including entering your administrator credentials (username and password), to reach the Cisco SDM home page. Table 2-9 shows the browser requirements to run SDM.

Table 2-9   *Browser Requirements*

Software Type	Specifications
Browser	Microsoft Internet Explorer 5.5 or later.
	Netscape Navigator 7.1 or 7.2.
	Mozilla Firefox 1.0.5.
Java software	Java Virtual Machine (JVM) built-in browsers are required.
	Java plug-in Java 2 Standard Edition (J2SE) (Java Runtime Environment [JRE] Version 1.4.2_05 or later).

Navigating the Cisco SDM Interface

The home page, shown in Figure 2-5, appears each time you successfully log in to Cisco SDM.

Navigating the Cisco SDM user interface on the home page is done through the toolbar. Two of the modes on the toolbar, Configure mode and Monitor mode, are also used to navigate the interface. To select a mode, click the corresponding button in the toolbar. For each mode, a task panel is available that shows the wizard options available for that mode.

Configure mode provides wizards for the novice. Figure 2-6 shows the Configure mode task bar. More experienced users are able to perform tasks in any order and without the wizards. Monitor mode allows you to view the current status of the router.

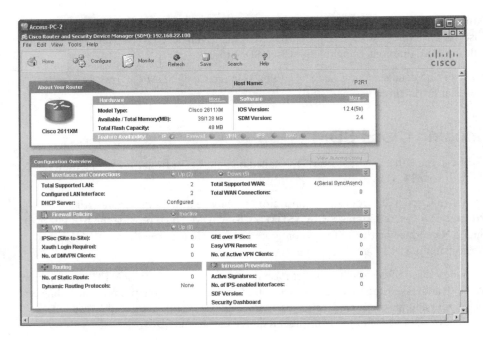

Figure 2-5   *SDM Home Page*

Figure 2-6   *Configure Mode: Task Bar*

Upon SDM startup, it synchronizes with the router running configuration. Subsequent commands applied using the CLI are not automatically reflected in SDM. In this case, you can use the Refresh button to resynchronize the router running configuration with Cisco SDM.

Click the **Save** button to save the running configuration to the startup configuration on the router.

Cisco SDM Wizards in Configure Mode

When you access a wizard, a dialog box appears if there is a new configuration that is not yet reflected in Cisco SDM. The dialog box states that you must perform a Refresh or Deliver before entering wizard mode. If you click Refresh, the running configuration of the router is reloaded into Cisco SDM. If you click Deliver, any work done in Cisco SDM is copied to the running configuration of the router. Click either the **Refresh** or **Deliver** button to perform the required function.

When the requested page appears, such as the Configure mode page, the wizards display on the left. In general, the following are functions that are available from the wizards in Configure mode:

- The Interfaces and Connections window displays the router interfaces and connections. The window also enables you to add, edit, and delete connections and to enable or disable the following types of connections:

  The LAN Wizard configures the LAN interfaces and DHCP.

  The WAN Wizard configures PPP, Frame Relay, and High-Level Data Link Control (HDLC) WAN interfaces.

- Firewall and ACL provide two wizards: a basic firewall wizard with inside and outside interfaces, and an advanced firewall wizard with inside, outside, and DMZ interfaces.

- For VPN, there are four wizards: IPsec VPN (site-to-site VPN), Cisco Easy VPN Remote, Cisco Easy VPN Server, and Dynamic Multipoint VPN (DMVPN).

- The Security Audit task contains two wizards: the Router Security Audit and a One-Step Lockdown Wizard.

- The Routing window displays the configured static routes and the configuration of the routing protocols. From this window, you can configure the Routing Information Protocol (RIP), Open Shortest Path First (OSPF), or Enhanced Interior Gateway Routing Protocol (EIGRP) routing protocol parameters, review the routes, add new static routes, edit existing static routes, and delete static routes.

- The NAT window enables you to view NAT rules, view address pools, and set translation timeouts. From this window, you can also designate interfaces as inside or outside interfaces.

- Starting with Cisco IOS Software Release 12.3(8)T, the Intrusion Prevention window allows you to enable or disable Cisco IOS Intrusion Prevention System (IPS) features on any interface in the router. If a Cisco Intrusion Detection System (IDS) Access Router Network Module (Cisco IDS Network Module) is installed in the router, this window displays basic status information for the module. If the Cisco IDS Network Module has been configured, you can also start the Cisco IDS Device Manager (IDM) software on the Cisco IDS Network Module and select the router interfaces that you want the Cisco IDS Network Module to monitor from this window.

Note: If Cisco SDM detects that the Cisco IDS Network Module has not been configured, it prompts you to open a session to the network module so that you can configure it. You can use Telnet or SSH for this session.

- The Quality of Service window allows you to configure QoS rules and policies for your router.

- The NAC window is used to protect data networks from computer viruses by assessing the health of client workstations, ensuring that they receive the latest available virus signature updates, and controlling their access to the network.

When you finish using a wizard, all the changes are automatically delivered to the router using generated CLI commands. You can choose whether to copy the running configuration to the startup configuration file.

For additional details on these tasks, refer to the *Cisco Router and Security Device Manager Version 2.4 User's Guide*.

Configure Mode: Advanced Configuration

At the bottom of the Cisco SDM configuration task bar is an Additional Tasks option, shown in Figure 2-7. This option allows you to configure many advanced options for the router, such as router properties, router access, DHCP settings, Domain Name System (DNS) and Dynamic DNS (DDNS) settings, ACLs, AAA configuration, router provisioning, and IEEE 802.1x. Click **Additional Tasks** to enter this mode and configure one of these options. You can perform tasks in any order, and you can always see existing configurations.

You can choose **Additional Tasks > Router Properties** to define the overall attributes of the router, such as the router name, domain name, password, SNMP status, DNS server address, user accounts, router log attributes, vty settings, SSH settings, and other router access security settings.

After you click Additional Tasks, you can use the Router Access window to create and manage security policies to access and manage the router. You can create, edit, and delete role-based user access accounts and set up management access policies to limit the Telnet, SNMP, or Cisco SDM access to the router from specific hosts or networks.

For additional details on the features and functions available from the Additional Tasks windows, refer to the *Cisco Router and Security Device Manager Version 2.4 User's Guide*.

Monitor Mode

From Monitor mode, you can view information about your router, including the router interfaces, firewalls, and any active VPN connections. You can also view any messages in the router event log. Figure 2-8 shows Monitor mode.

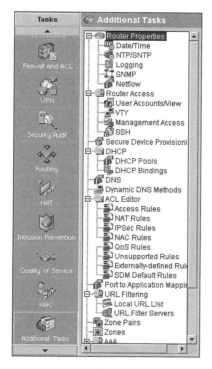

Figure 2-7   *Configure Mode: Additional Task Options*

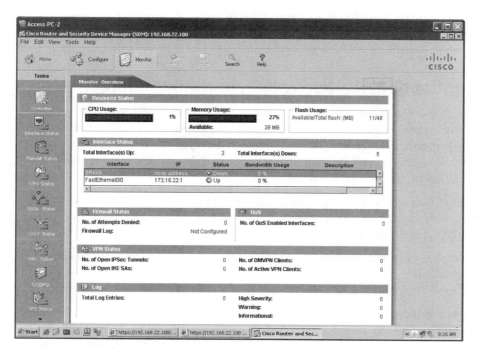

Figure 2-8   *Configure Mode: Task Bar*

The monitor function includes the following information:

■ The Monitor Overview window provides the router status, including a list of the error log entries.

■ Interface Status is used to select the interface and conditions to monitor (for example, packets and errors and whether you want to monitor them in or out).

■ Firewall Status displays a log with the number of entry attempts that the firewall denied.

■ VPN Status displays statistics about active VPN connections.

■ QoS displays QoS policy information on the interfaces.

■ NAC Status (not shown in Figure 2-8) displays information such as the number of active Network Admission Control (NAC) sessions on the routers.

■ Log contains the event log categorized by severity level, such as a UNIX syslog service.

Configuring AAA on a Cisco Router Using the Local Database

AAA is widely supported in Cisco IOS Software as an additional security service available for securing access to network devices and networks. One of the options you have when configuring your network to work with AAA is to use a local username and password database to provide security greater than a simple password. It is likely that smaller organizations will configure AAA to operate locally.

Authentication, Authorization, and Accounting

Access control is the way you control who is allowed access to the access server or router and which services they are allowed to use once they have access. AAA network security services provide the primary framework through which you set up access control on your router. AAA services provide a higher degree of scalability than the line-level and privileged EXEC authentication commands alone.

Unauthorized access in campus, dialup, and Internet environments creates the potential for network intruders to gain access to sensitive network equipment and services. The Cisco AAA architecture enables systematic and scalable access security.

Network and administrative access security in the Cisco environment, whether it involves campus, dialup, or IPsec VPN access, is based on a modular architecture that has three functional components:

■ **Authentication:** Authentication requires users and administrators to prove that they really are who they say they are. Authentication is established using a username and password, challenge and response, token cards, and other methods, such as "I am user *student* and my password *validateme* proves it."

- **Authorization:** After authenticating the user and administrator, authorization services decide which resources the user and administrator are allowed to access and which operations the user and administrator are allowed to perform, such as "User *student* can access host serverXYZ using Telnet."

- **Accounting and auditing:** Accounting records what the users and administrators actually did, what they accessed, and for how long they accessed it. Accounting keeps track of how network resources are used, such as "User *student* accessed host serverXYZ using Telnet for 15 minutes."

Introduction to AAA for Cisco Routers

Two examples of AAA implementation include authenticating remote users that are accessing the corporate LAN through dialup or Internet (IPsec VPN) connections as shown in Figure 2-9, and authenticating administrator access to the router console port, auxiliary port, and vty ports.

Cisco networking products support AAA access control using a local usernames and passwords database or remote security server databases. A local security database is configured in the router for a small group of network users with the **username** *xyz* **password** *strongpassword* command or, preferably, the **username** *xyz* **secret** *strongsecretpassword* command. A remote security database is a separate server that provides AAA services for multiple network devices and a large number of network users by running RADIUS or TACACS+ protocols.

Cisco provides four ways to implement AAA services for Cisco routers:

- **Self-contained AAA:** AAA services can be self-contained in the router or network access server (NAS) itself. This form of authentication is also known as local authentication.

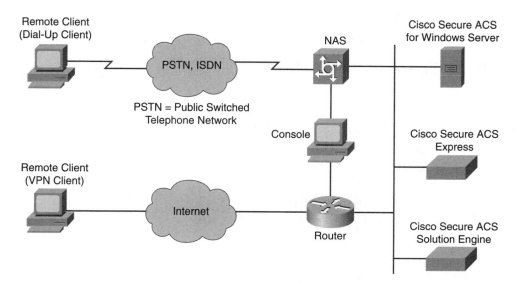

Figure 2-9 *Implementing Cisco AAA*

> **Note:**   The official Cisco definition of NAS is "network access server. Cisco platform (or collection of platforms, such as an AccessPath system) that interfaces between the packet world (for example, the Internet) and the circuit world (for example, the PSTN)."
> Source: Internetworking Terms and Acronyms, http://www.cisco.com/en/US/docs/internetworking/terms_acronyms/N12.html.

- Cisco Secure Access Control Server (ACS) for Microsoft Windows Server: AAA services on the router or NAS contact an external Cisco Secure ACS for Microsoft Windows system for user and administrator authentication.

- **Cisco Secure ACS Express:** This is an entry-level RADIUS and TACACS+ AAA server appliance. AAA services on the router or NAS contact an external Cisco Secure ACS Express device for user and administrator authentication. Cisco ACS Express is available as a one rack unit (RU), security-hardened appliance with a preinstalled Cisco Secure ACS Express license. Cisco ACS Express supports a maximum of 50 AAA clients and 350 unique user logons in a 24-hour period.

- **Cisco Secure ACS Solution Engine:** AAA services on the router or NAS contact an external Cisco Secure ACS Solution Engine for user and administrator authentication.

Using Local Services to Authenticate Router Access

If you have one or two NAS devices or routers that provide access to your network for a limited number of users, you can store username and password security information locally on the Cisco NAS devices or routers. This is referred to as local authentication on a local security database. The following are local authentication characteristics:

- Used for small networks

- Stores usernames and passwords in the Cisco router or Cisco NAS

- Users authenticate against the local security database in the Cisco router or Cisco NAS

- Does not require an external database

The system administrator must populate the local security database by specifying username and password profiles for each user that might log in.

Figure 2-10 shows how local authentication typically works.

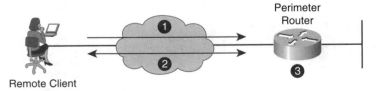

Figure 2-10   *Implementing Authentication Using Local Services*

1. The client establishes a connection with the router.

2. The router prompts the user for a username and password.

3. The router authenticates the username and password in the local database. The user is authorized to access the network based on information in the local database.

Authenticating Router Access

You can use AAA to secure two different types of router access mode. The mode refers to the format of the packets that are requesting AAA services:

■ **Character mode:** A user is sending a request to establish an EXEC mode process with the router, for administrative purposes.

■ **Packet mode:** A user is sending a request to establish a connection through the router with a device on the network.

With the exception of accounting commands, all the AAA commands apply to both character mode and packet mode.

For a truly secure network, you must configure the router to secure administrative access and remote LAN network access using AAA services.

Table 2-10 compares the router access modes, port types, and AAA command elements.

Table 2-10 *Router Access*

Access Type	Modes	NAS Ports	Specifications
Remote administrative access	Character (line or EXEC mode)	tty, vty, auxiliary, and console	**login, exec, enable**
Remote network access	Packet (interface mode)	async, group-async BRI and PRI	**ppp, network**

Configuring Local Database Authentication Using AAA

To configure AAA services to authenticate administrator access (character mode access) or network access (packet mode), follow these general steps:

■ Add usernames and passwords to the local router database for users who need administrative access to the router.

■ Enable AAA globally on the router, or confirm that it is already enabled.

■ Configure AAA/parameters on the router.

■ Confirm and troubleshoot the AAA configuration.

Configuring User Accounts Using Cisco SDM

The first step to configure AAA services for local authentication is to create users. Figure 2-11 shows the steps to use with Cisco SDM to create a user account in the local router database:

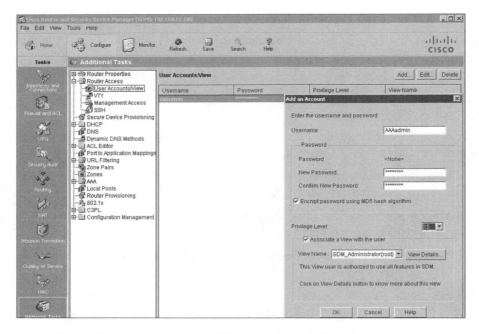

Figure 2-11   *Implementing Authentication Using Local services*

Step 1.   Choose **Configure > Additional Tasks > Router Access > User Accounts/View**.

Step 2.   Click **Add** to add a new user.

Step 3.   In the Add an Account window, enter the username and password in the appropriate fields to define the user account.

Step 4.   From the Privilege Level drop-down list, choose **15** unless you have defined lesser privilege levels.

Step 5.   If you have defined views, you can check the **Associate a View with the User** check box and choose a view from the View Name list that you want to associate with this user.

Step 6.   Click **OK**.

Cisco SDM will generate the following CLI command:

```
username AAAadmin privilege 15 secret 5 $1$f16u$uKOO6J/UnojZ0bCEzgnQi1 view root
```

Enabling and Disabling AAA Using Cisco SDM

The next step in configuring AAA is to make sure AAA is enabled. To verify the AAA configuration and to enable or disable AAA, choose **Configure > Additional Tasks > AAA**, as shown in Figure 2-12. AAA is enabled by default in Cisco SDM. If you click Disable, Cisco SDM displays a message telling you that it will make configuration changes to

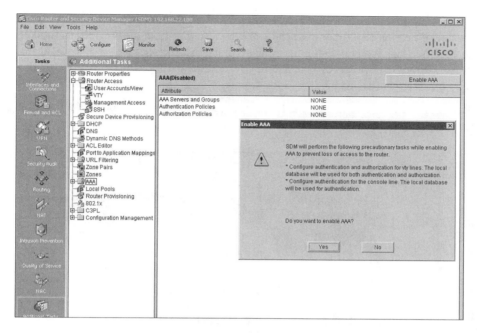

Figure 2-12   *Enabling and Disabling AAA Using Cisco SDM*

ensure that the router can be accessed after AAA is disabled. Disabling AAA will prevent you from configuring your router as an Easy VPN server, and will prevent you from associating user accounts with CLI views.

In the CLI, use the global configuration command **aaa new-model** to enable AAA. Use the **no** form of this command to disable AAA.

Configuring AAA Authentication Using Cisco SDM

A method list is a sequential list of authentication methods to query to authenticate a user. Method lists enable you to designate one or more security protocols to be used for authentication, thus ensuring a backup system for authentication in case the initial method fails.

When you first enable AAA, there is a default method list named default, which is automatically applied to all interfaces and lines, but which has no authentication methods defined. To configure AAA authentication, you must first either define a list of authentication methods for the default method, or configure your own named method lists and apply them to interfaces or lines. For flexibility, you can apply different method lists to different interfaces and lines. If an interface or line has a nondefault method list applied to it, that method overrides the default method list.

Cisco IOS Software uses the first method listed to authenticate users. If that method fails to respond, the Cisco IOS Software selects the next authentication method listed in the method list. This process continues until there is successful communication with a listed authentication method or until all methods defined in the method list have been exhausted.

It is important to note that the Cisco IOS Software attempts authentication with the next listed authentication method only when there is no response from the previous method. If authentication fails at any point in this cycle (meaning that the security server or local username database responds by denying the user access), the authentication process stops and no other authentication methods are attempted.

Follow these steps, shown in Figure 2-13, to configure the default method list for login authentication using the local database:

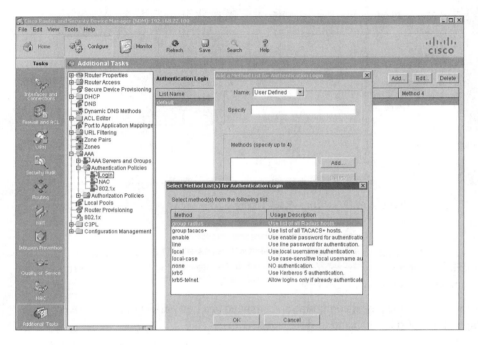

Figure 2-13   *Configuring AAA Authentication Using Cisco SDM*

Step 1.   Choose Configure > Additional Tasks > AAA > Authentication Policies > **Login** and click **Add**.

Step 2.   In the Add a Method List for Authentication Login window, verify that **Default** is selected in the Name drop-down list.

Step 3.   Click **Add**.

Step 4.   From the Select Method List(s) for Authentication Login window, choose **Local** from the method list.

Step 5.   Click **OK**.

Step 6.   Click **OK**.

The Cisco SDM will generate the following CLI command:

```
aaa authentication login default local
```

Note: Remember to save your work by clicking the **Save** button in the toolbar across the top.

Additional AAA CLI Commands

To further secure administrative access to the router, you can specify the maximum number of failed AAA login attempts that can occur before an account is locked out. Currently, you can configure this option only from the CLI.

To specify the maximum number of unsuccessful authentication attempts before a user is locked out, use the **aaa local authentication attempts max-fail** command in global configuration mode. To remove the number of unsuccessful attempts that was set, use the **no** form of this command. The complete syntax for this command is as follows:

```
aaa local authentication attempts max-fail number-of-unsuccessful-attempts
```

To display a list of all locked-out users, use the **show aaa local user lockout** command in privileged EXEC mode.

Example 2-23 shows that user1 is locked out.

Example 2-23   show aaa local user lockout *Command Output*

```
R1# show aaa local user lockout
               Local-user          Lock time
               user1               04:28:49 UTC Sat Dec 15 2007
```

Use the **clear aaa local user lockout** command in privileged EXEC mode to unlock a locked-out user. The complete syntax for this command is **clear aaa local user lockout** {username *username* | **all**}. To specify a single user to unlock, specify the username using the *username* parameter. To unlock all the users, use the **all** keyword. You might also consider using the **clear aaa local user fail-attempts username** *username* or the **clear aaa local user fail-attempts all** commands for cases in which you need to clear already logged unsuccessful attempts after the user configuration was changed.

Note: The **aaa local authentication attempts max-fail** command differs from the **login delay** command in how it handles failed attempts. The **aaa local authentication attempts max-fail** command locks the user account if the authentication fails. This account stays locked until it is cleared by an administrator. The **login delay** command introduces a delay between failed login attempts without locking the account.

When a user logs in to a Cisco router and uses AAA, a unique ID is assigned to the session. Throughout the life of the session, various attributes that are related to the session are collected and stored internally within the AAA database. These attributes can include the IP address of the user, the protocol that is used to access the router (such as PPP or SLIP), the speed of the connection, and the number of packets or bytes that are received or transmitted.

To display the attributes that are collected for a AAA session, use the **show aaa user** {all |
unique id} command in privileged EXEC mode.

Note: This command does not provide information for all of the users who are logged in
to a device, but only for those who have been authenticated or authorized using AAA, or
for those whose sessions are being accounted for by the AAA module.

As shown in Example 2-24, you can use the **show aaa sessions** command to show the
unique ID of a session.

Example 2-24   show aaa sessions *Command Output*

```
R1# show aaa sessions
Total sessions since last reload: 4
Session Id: 1
   Unique Id: 175
   User Name: tecteam
   IP Address: 10.30.30.2
   Idle Time: 0
   CT Call Handle: 0
```

Confirming and Troubleshooting the AAA Configuration

To configure AAA services to authenticate administrator access (character mode access) or network access (packet mode), follow these general steps:

■   Add usernames and passwords to the local router database for users that need admin-
     istrative access to the router.

■   Enable AAA globally on the router, or confirm that it is already enabled.

■   Configure AAA/parameters on the router.

■   Confirm and troubleshoot the AAA configuration.

Example 2-25 shows an example of what the running configuration would look like after
configuring AAA for local authentication using Cisco SDM and the CLI.

Example 2-25 *AAA Configuration*

```
aaa new-model
aaa local authentication attempts max-fail 10
!
!
aaa authentication login default local

enable secret 5 $1$x1EE$33AXd2VTVvhbWL0A37tQ3.
enable password 7 15141905172924
!
```

```
username admin1 password 7 14161606050A7B7974786B
username admin2 secret 5 $1$ErWl$b5rDNK7Y5RHkxX/Ks7Hr00
username AAAadmin privilege 15 view root secret 5 $1$0GGC$1Y.WBhh7UQso8cJSkvv2N0
!
```

To display information on AAA authentication, use the **debug aaa authentication** command in privileged EXEC command mode, as shown in Example 2-26. Use the **no debug aaa authentication** form of the command to disable this debug mode. Example 2-26 shows the debug output for a successful AAA authentication using a local database.

Example 2-26   *Displaying AAA Authentication Information*

```
R1# debug aaa authentication
113123: Feb 4 10:11:19.305 CST: AAA/MEMORY: create_user (0x619C4940) user=''
ruser='' port='tty1' rem_addr='async/81560' authen_type=ASCII service=LOGIN priv=1
113124: Feb 4 10:11:19.305 CST: AAA/AUTHEN/START (2784097690): port='tty1' list=''
action=LOGIN service=LOGIN
113125: Feb 4 10:11:19.305 CST: AAA/AUTHEN/START (2784097690): using "default" list
113126: Feb 4 10:11:19.305 CST: AAA/AUTHEN/START (2784097690): Method=LOCAL
113127: Feb 4 10:11:19.305 CST: AAA/AUTHEN (2784097690): status = GETUSER
113128: Feb 4 10:11:26.305 CST: AAA/AUTHEN/CONT (2784097690): continue_login
(user='(undef)')
113129: Feb 4 10:11:26.305 CST: AAA/AUTHEN (2784097690): status = GETUSER
113130: Feb 4 10:11:26.305 CST: AAA/AUTHEN/CONT (2784097690): Method=LOCAL
113131: Feb 4 10:11:26.305 CST: AAA/AUTHEN (2784097690): status = GETPASS
113132: Feb 4 10:11:28.145 CST: AAA/AUTHEN/CONT (2784097690): continue_login
(user='diallocal')
113133: Feb 4 10:11:28.145 CST: AAA/AUTHEN (2784097690): status = GETPASS
113134: Feb 4 10:11:28.145 CST: AAA/AUTHEN/CONT (2784097690): Method=LOCAL
113135: Feb 4 10:11:28.145 CST: AAA/AUTHEN (2784097690): status = PASS
```

Configuring AAA on a Cisco Router to Use Cisco Secure ACS

Cisco Secure Access Control Server (ACS) for Windows provides a centralized identity networking solution and simplified user management experience across all Cisco devices and security management applications. This section covers what Cisco Secure ACS is and what you can use it for, the requirements for installing Cisco Secure ACS for Windows, and the Cisco Secure ACS installation procedure.

Cisco Secure ACS Overview

Local implementations of AAA, explained in the previous section of this book, do not scale well. Most corporate environments have multiple Cisco routers and network access servers (NAS) with multiple router administrators and hundreds or thousands of users needing access to the corporate LAN. Maintaining local databases for each Cisco router and NAS for this size of network is not feasible.

To solve this challenge, you can use one or more Cisco Secure ACS systems (servers or engines) to manage the entire user and administrative access needs for an entire corporate network using one or more databases. External AAA systems, such as the Cisco Secure ACS for Windows or Cisco Secure ACS Solution Engine, communicate with Cisco routers and NASs using the TACACS+ or RADIUS protocols to implement AAA functions. This allows you to make changes to user accounts and passwords in a centralized place (the ACS server), and have all the Cisco routers and NASs in your network access this information.

Figure 2-14 shows the steps of the authentication and authorization process using an external Cisco Secure ACS system to provide AAA services to a network:

Step 1.   The client establishes a connection with the router.

Step 2.   The router prompts the user for a username and password.

Step 3.   The router passes the username and password to the Cisco Secure ACS (server or engine).

Step 4.   The Cisco Secure ACS authenticates the user. The user is authorized to access the router (administrative access) or the network based on information found in the Cisco Secure ACS database.

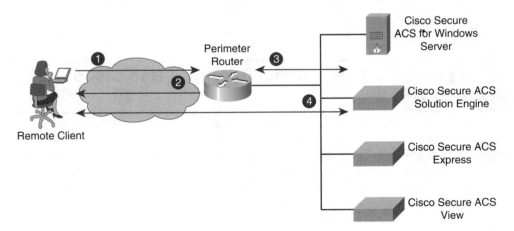

Figure 2-14   *Implementing Authentication Using External Servers*

Cisco Secure ACS is a highly scalable, high-performance ACS that operates as a centralized RADIUS and TACACS+ server that provides the following features:

- Extends access security by combining authentication, user access, and administrator access with policy control within a centralized identity networking solution

- Allows greater flexibility and mobility, increased security, and user-productivity gains

- Enforces a uniform security policy for all users regardless of how they access the network

- Reduces the administrative and management burden involved in scaling user and network administrator access to the network

Cisco Secure ACS uses a central database, which allows it to centralize the control of all user privileges and distribute them to hundreds or thousands of access points throughout the network. Cisco Secure ACS provides detailed reporting and monitoring capabilities of user behavior, access connections, and device configuration changes. This feature has become extremely important for organizations trying to comply with Sarbanes-Oxley Act regulations. Cisco Secure ACS supports a broad variety of access connections, including wired and wireless LAN, dialup, broadband, content, storage, VoIP, firewalls, switches, and VPNs.

You can leverage the Cisco Secure ACS framework to control administrator access and configuration for all the network devices in your network that support RADIUS and TACACS+. The following are some of the advanced features of Cisco Secure ACS:

- Automatic service monitoring

- Database synchronization and importing of tools for large-scale deployments

- Lightweight Directory Access Protocol (LDAP) user authentication support

- User and administrative access reporting

- Restrictions to network access based on criteria such as the time of day and the day of week

- User and device group profiles

- Token-based authentication

Cisco Secure ACS is an important component of the Cisco Identity Based Networking Services (IBNS) architecture. Cisco IBNS is based on port-security standards such as IEEE 802.1x and Extensible Authentication Protocol (EAP), and extends security from the perimeter of the network to every connection point inside the LAN. You can deploy new policy control, such as per-user quotas, VLAN assignments, and ACLs within this new architecture, because of the extended capabilities of Cisco switches and wireless access points to query Cisco Secure ACS over the RADIUS protocol.

Cisco Secure ACS is also an important component of Cisco Network Admission Control (NAC). Cisco NAC is an industry initiative sponsored by Cisco that uses the network infrastructure to enforce security-policy compliance on all devices seeking to access network computing resources, thereby limiting damage from viruses and worms. With NAC, customers can choose to allow network access only to compliant and trusted endpoint devices (for instance, PCs, servers, and personal digital assistants [PDAs]) and can restrict the access of noncompliant devices. Cisco NAC is part of the Cisco Self-Defending Network initiative and is the foundation for enabling NAC on Layer 2 and Layer 3 networks. Future phases extend endpoint and network security interoperation to include dynamic incident-containment capabilities. This innovation enables compliant system elements to report misuse emanating from rogue or infected systems during an attack. Thus, infected systems can be dynamically quarantined from the rest of the network to significantly reduce virus, worm, and blended-threat propagation.

Cisco Secure ACS is a powerful access control server with many high-performance and scalability features for any organization growing its WAN or LAN. The following lists the main benefits of Cisco Secure ACS:

- **Ease of use:** A web-based user interface simplifies and distributes the configuration for user profiles, group profiles, and Cisco Secure ACS configuration.

- **Scalability:** Cisco Secure ACS is built to support large networked environments with support for redundant servers, remote databases, and database replication and backup services.

- **Extensibility:** LDAP authentication forwarding supports the authentication of user profiles that are stored in directories from leading directory vendors, including Sun, Novell, and Microsoft.

- **Management:** Microsoft Windows Active Directory support consolidates Windows user name and password management and uses the Windows Performance Monitor for real-time statistics viewing.

- **Administration:** Different access levels for each Cisco Secure ACS administrator and the ability to group network devices together make it easier and more flexible to control the enforcement and changes of security policy administration over all of the devices in a network.

- **Product flexibility:** Because Cisco IOS Software has embedded support for AAA, Cisco Secure ACS can be used across virtually any network access server that Cisco sells (the Cisco IOS Software release must support RADIUS or TACACS+). Cisco Secure ACS is available in three options: Cisco Secure ACS Solution Engine, Cisco Secure ACS Express, and Cisco Secure ACS for Windows.

- **Integration:** Tight coupling with Cisco IOS routers and VPN solutions provides features such as Multichassis Multilink PPP and Cisco IOS Software command authorization.

- **Third-party support:** Cisco Secure ACS offers token server support for any one-time password (OTP) vendor that provides an RFC-compliant RADIUS interface, such as RSA, PassGo, Secure Computing, ActiveCard, Vasco, or CryptoCard.

■ **Control:** Cisco Secure ACS provides dynamic quotas to restrict access based on the time of day, network use, number of logged sessions, and the day of the week.

Cisco Secure ACS for Windows Requirements

The Cisco Secure ACS server must meet certain minimum hardware, operating system, and third-party software requirements. In addition, if you are upgrading from an earlier version of Cisco Secure ACS, you should refer to the Cisco Secure ACS upgrade requirements at http://tinyurl.com/8optuc.

Hardware Requirements

The server that will be running Cisco Secure ACS 4.2 must meet the following minimum hardware requirements:

■ Pentium IV processor that is 1.8 GHz or faster

■ 1 GB of RAM

■ At least 1 GB of free disk space; if you are running the database on the same computer, more disk space is required

■ Minimum graphics resolution of 256 colors at 800x600 pixels

Operating System Requirements

Cisco Secure ACS 4.2 for Windows supports the English-language versions of the following Microsoft Windows operating systems:

■ Windows 2000 Server, with Service Pack 4 installed

■ Windows 2000 Advanced Server, with the following conditions:
Service Pack 4 installed

Without Microsoft clustering service installed

Without other features specific to Windows 2000 Advanced Server enabled, such as Terminal Services.

■ Windows Server 2003 Service Pack 1, Enterprise Edition or Standard Edition

■ Windows Server 2003, R2, Standard Edition

■ Windows Server 2003, Service Pack 2

■ Windows Server 2003, R2, Service Pack 2

Note: ACS for Windows supports the multiprocessor feature on dual processor computers. Cisco Secure ACS 4.2 supports the Japanese Windows Server 2003.

You can apply the Windows service packs before or after installing Cisco Secure ACS. If you do not install a required service pack before installing Cisco Secure ACS, the Cisco Secure ACS installation program might warn you that the required service pack is not present. If you receive a service pack message, continue the installation, and then install the required service pack before starting user authentication with Cisco Secure ACS.

Virtualization Compatibility

Cisco has also tested ACS 4.2 on VMWare platform MWare ESX server 3.0.0.

Note: For the most recent information about supported operating systems and service packs, see the Cisco Secure ACS release notes at http://www.cisco.com/en/US/products/sw/secursw/ps2086/prod_release_notes_list.html.

Cisco Secure ACS Solution Engine

The Cisco Secure ACS Solution Engine, shown in Figure 2-15, is a one rack unit (RU), security-hardened appliance with a preinstalled Cisco Secure ACS license. The following lists the specifications of Cisco Secure ACS Solution Engine 4.2:

Figure 2-15   *Cisco Secure ACS Solution Engine*

- CPU 3.4-GHz Intel Pentium 4, 800-MHz FSB, 2-MB cache

- 1 GB of system memory

- 80-GB Serial Advanced Technology Attachment (SATA) hard drive

- Combination CD/DVD drive

- One RS-232 serial port and three USB 2.0 I/O ports (one front, two rear)

Compared to the Cisco Secure ACS for Windows product, the Cisco Secure ACS Solution Engine reduces the total cost of ownership by eliminating the need to install and maintain a Microsoft Windows server machine.

Cisco Secure ACS Express 5.0

Cisco Secure ACS Express 5.0 is intended for commercial (fewer than 350 users), retail, and enterprise branch office deployments. The product offers a comprehensive yet simplified feature set, a cutting-edge user-friendly GUI, and an attractive price point that allows you to deploy this product in situations where Cisco Secure ACS for Windows or Cisco Secure ACS Solution Engine might not be suitable.

Cisco Secure ACS Express 5.0 is available as a one RU, security-hardened appliance with a preinstalled Cisco Secure ACS Express license. Cisco Secure ACS Express 5.0 supports a maximum of 50 AAA clients and 350 unique user logins in a 24-hour period.

The following are some of the hardware specifications of Cisco Secure ACS Express 5.0:

- CPU Intel 352 Celeron D

- 1 GB of system memory

- 250-GB hard drive, CD/DVD drive

- 2-10/100/1000 onboard Ethernet network interface cards (NIC)

- One RS-232 serial port and three USB 2.0 I/O ports (one front, two rear)

- 1 PS/2 keyboard port and 1 PS/2 mouse port

Note: For information about Cisco Secure ACS Express 5.0, visit http://www.cisco.com/en/US/products/ps8543/index.html.

Cisco Secure ACS View 4.0

Cisco Secure ACS View 4.0 is an advanced reporting and alert tool for multiple Cisco Secure ACS servers. Much like Cisco Monitoring, Analysis, and Response System (MARS), which takes an enterprise approach to logging, Cisco Secure ACS View 4.0 takes a similar approach to monitoring Cisco Secure ACS servers. It has a web-based interface and a significant number of preprogrammed reports which make it a powerful addition to a distributed enterprise that has widely distributed resources and Cisco Secure ACS servers.

TACACS+ and RADIUS Protocols

The Cisco Secure ACS family of products supports both RADIUS and TACACS+ protocols, which are the two predominant AAA protocols that are used by Cisco security appliances, routers, and switches for implementing AAA.

Cisco Secure ACS supports both TACACS+ and RADIUS:

- TACACS+ remains more secure than RADIUS.

- RADIUS has a robust application programming interface and strong accounting.

TACACS+

TACACS+ is a Cisco enhancement to the original TACACS protocol. Despite its name, TACACS+ is a protocol that was designed from the ground up and it is therefore incompatible with any earlier version of TACACS. TACACS+ has been submitted to the Internet Engineering Task Force (IETF) as a draft proposal.

TACACS+ provides separate message types for AAA services. Because TACACS+ separates authentication and authorization, it is possible to use TACACS+ authorization and accounting, while using another method of authentication.

The extensions to the TACACS+ protocol provide more types of authentication requests and response codes than were in the original specification. TACACS+ offers multiprotocol support, such as IP and AppleTalk. Normal TACACS+ operation encrypts the entire body of the packet for more secure communications and uses TCP port 49.

RADIUS

RADIUS is an open IETF standard AAA protocol for applications such as network access or IP mobility that was developed by Livingston Enterprises. RADIUS works in both local and roaming situations and is commonly used for accounting purposes. RADIUS is currently defined by RFCs 2865, 2866, 2867, 2868, and many other related RFCs.

The RADIUS protocol hides the passwords during transmission between the NAS and RADIUS server, even with the PAP protocol, using a rather complex operation that involves Message Digest 5 (MD5) hashing and a shared secret. However, the rest of the packet is sent in plaintext.

RADIUS combines authentication and authorization as one process. Once users are authenticated, they are authorized, as well. RADIUS uses User Datagram Protocol (UDP) ports 1645 or 1812 for authentication and UDP ports 1646 or 1813 for accounting.

In addition, RADIUS is widely used by VoIP service providers. It is used to pass login credentials of a Session Initiation Protocol (SIP) endpoint (such as a broadband phone) to a SIP registrar using digest authentication, and then to a RADIUS server using RADIUS. RADIUS is also a common authentication protocol that is used by the 802.1x security standard.

The DIAMETER protocol is the planned replacement for RADIUS. DIAMETER is more secure than RADIUS because it uses Stream Control Transmission Protocol (SCTP) or TCP rather than UDP. It also provides for failover procedures, and offers a transition path for current RADIUS implementations.

Comparing TACACS+ and RADIUS

There are several differences between TACACS+ and RADIUS, as shown in the following list. Table 2-11 summarizes these differences.

Table 2-11 *TACACS+/RADIUS Comparison*

	TACACS+	RADIUS
Functionality	Separates AAA	Combines authentication and authorization
Standard	Mostly Cisco supported	Open/RFC
Transport protocol	TCP	UDP
CHAP	Bidirectional	Unidirectional
Protocol support	Multiprotocol support	No ARA, no NetBEUI
Confidentiality	Entire packet encrypted	Password encrypted

- **Functionality:** TACACS+ separates AAA functions according to the AAA architecture, allowing modularity of the security server implementation. RADIUS combines authentication and authorization, but separates accounting, thus allowing less flexibility in implementation than TACACS+.

- **Standard:** TACACS+ is a standard that is used mostly by Cisco customers. RADIUS is an open industry standard.

- **Transport protocol:** TACACS+ uses TCP. RADIUS uses UDP, which was chosen for the simplification of client and server implementations; however, it makes the RADIUS protocol less robust and requires the server to implement reliability measures such as packet retransmission and timeouts.

- **Challenge and response:** TACACS+ supports bidirectional challenge and response as used in Challenge Handshake Authentication Protocol (CHAP) between two routers. RADIUS supports unidirectional challenge and response from the RADIUS security server to the RADIUS client.

- **Protocol support:** TACACS+ provides more complete dialup and WAN protocol support. RADIUS does not support AppleTalk Remote Access (ARA) access, NetBIOS Extended User Interface (NetBEUI), NetWare Access Server Interface (NASI), and X.25 Packet Assembler/Disassembler (PAD) connections.

- **Confidentiality:** TACACS+ encrypts the entire packet body of every packet. RADIUS encrypts only the password attribute portion of the Access-Request packet, which makes TACACS+ more secure.

- **Customization:** The flexibility that is provided in the TACACS+ protocol allows many things to be customized on a per-user basis or per-group basis, including which commands a user can execute on a router. RADIUS lacks this flexibility, and therefore many features that are possible with TACACS+ are not possible with RADIUS.

- **Accounting:** TACACS+ accounting includes a limited number of information fields. RADIUS accounting can contain more information than TACAS+ accounting records, which is the key strength of RADIUS over TACACS+.

Installing Cisco Secure ACS for Windows

Before installing Cisco Secure ACS, it is important to prepare the server. You must consider third-party software requirements and the network and port requirements of the Cisco Secure ACS server and AAA devices.

Third-Party Software Requirements

Other than the software products that are described in the release notes, Cisco has not tested the interoperability of Cisco Secure ACS and other software products on the same computer. Cisco will only support interoperability issues with software products that are mentioned in the release notes. The most recent version of the Cisco Secure ACS release notes is posted on Cisco.com.

Network and Port Requirements

The network should meet the following requirements before you begin deploying Cisco Secure ACS:

■   For full TACACS+ and RADIUS support on Cisco IOS devices, AAA clients must run Cisco IOS Release 11.2 or later.

■   Cisco devices that are not Cisco IOS AAA clients must be configured with TACACS+, RADIUS, or both.

■   Dial-in, VPN, or wireless clients must be able to connect to the applicable AAA clients.

■   The computer running Cisco Secure ACS must be able to reach all AAA clients using ping.

■   Gateway devices between the Cisco Secure ACS and other network devices must permit communication over the ports that are needed to support the applicable feature or protocol.

■   A supported web browser must be installed on the computer running Cisco Secure ACS. For the most recent information about tested browsers, see the release notes for your Cisco Secure ACS product on Cisco.com.

■   All network cards in the computer running Cisco Secure ACS must be enabled. If there is a disabled network card on the computer running Cisco Secure ACS, installing Cisco Secure ACS may proceed slowly because of delays that are caused by the Microsoft CryptoAPI.

Configuring the Server

After successfully installing Cisco Secure ACS, you must perform some initial configuration. The only way to configure a Cisco Secure ACS server is through an HTML interface, as shown in Figure 2-16. To access the Cisco Secure ACS HTML interface from the computer that is running Cisco Secure ACS, you can use the Cisco Secure icon labeled ACS Admin that appears on the desktop or you can enter the following URL into a supported web browser: http://127.0.0.1:2002.

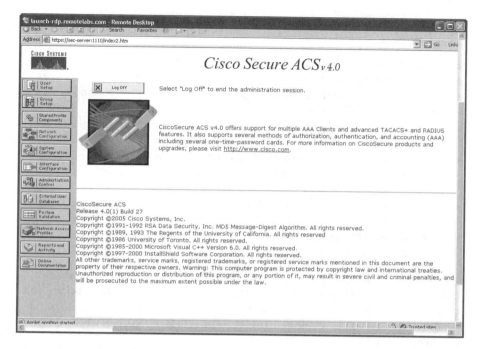

Figure 2-16 *Cisco Secure ACS 4.0 Home Page*

Note: You can also reach Cisco Secure ACS remotely *after* an administrator user account has been configured. To remotely access the Cisco Secure ACS, enter **http:**//*ip_address*[*hostname*]**:2002**. After the initial connection, a different port is dynamically negotiated.

The home page of Cisco Secure ACS is divided into frames. The buttons in the navigation bar represent a particular area or function that you can configure. When you click one of the buttons in the navigation bar, the window that opens enables you to access help on the right side of the window.

The following are the navigation buttons that are available in the navigation bar.

- **User Setup:** This option enables you to add a new user, search for an existing user, find users alphabetically or numerically, or simply list all users at once.

- **Group Setup:** This option enables you to configure any parameters that are common to a group of users. In this section, you can apply configuration from shared profile components and specific TACACS+ and RADIUS attributes.

- **Shared Profile Components:** This option allows you to specify shell command authorization sets and Cisco PIX Firewall shell command authorization sets. By creating these command authorization sets, you can control the commands a user can execute on a device by applying the command authorization set to the user profile in the TACACS+ settings or at the group level.

- **Network Configuration:** This option is where you add, delete, or modify settings for AAA clients.

- **System Configuration:** Under this option, you will find many subconfiguration links:
    - **Service Control:** Allows you to start and stop the Cisco Secure ACS services.
    - **Logging:** Allows you to configure logging, such as failed attempts, and TACACS+ and RADIUS accounting.
    - **Date Format Control:** Allows you to change the format of the date that is displayed on reports.
    - **Local Password Management:** Allows you to set password length and password options. You can also configure options for remote password change and logging of password changes.
    - **ACS Backup:** Allows you to schedule backups to be performed manually or automatically at specific times.
    - **ACS Service Management:** Enables you to determine how often to test the availability of ACS authentication services.

- **Interface Configuration:** This option allows you to configure user-defined fields that are recorded in accounting logs, configure TACACS+ and RADIUS options, and control the display of options in the user interface. What options are available depends on whether you have selected TACACS+ or a form of RADIUS when you entered your AAA client.

> **Note:** If you do not see RADIUS options here, you must add a AAA client that uses the RADIUS protocol. Interface Configuration is directly affected by the settings in Network Configuration.

- **Administration Control:** This option enables you to configure all aspects of Cisco Secure ACS for administrative access.

- **External User Databases:** This option enables you to configure the unknown user policy, configure authorization privileges for unknown users, and configure external database types.

- **Posture Validation:** Cisco Secure ACS supports the NAC initiative. NAC ensures that every endpoint conforms to the security policy before they are granted access to the network. The Posture Validation option enables you to configure NAC options.

- **Network Access Profiles:** This option enables you to classify access requests according to the IP address of a AAA client, membership in a network device group, protocol types, or other specific RADIUS attribute values sent by the network device through which the user connects. Cisco Secure ACS does not support network access profiles for TACACS+.

- **Reports and Activity:** Cisco Secure ACS keeps track of a lot of information. Use this option to view the following logs that Cisco Secure ACS keeps:
  TACACS+ accounting
  TACACS+ administration
  RADIUS accounting

VoIP accounting

Passed authentications

Failed attempts

Logged-in users

Disabled accounts

Cisco Secure ACS backup and restore

Remote Database Management Source (RDBMS) synchronization

Database replication

Administration audit

User password changes

Cisco Secure ACS service monitoring

- **Online Documentation:** This button provides access to documentation for Cisco Secure ACS online at Cisco.com.

Network Configuration

Before configuring a router, switch, or firewall as a TACACS+ or RADIUS client, you must add the AAA client to the Cisco Secure ACS server and specify the IP address and encryption key, as shown in Figure 2-17. The Network Configuration page is where you add, delete, or modify settings for AAA clients.

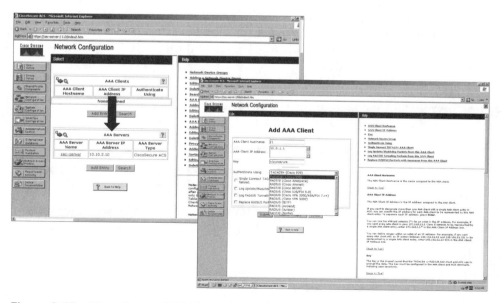

Figure 2-17   *Cisco Secure ACS Network Configuration*

Follow these steps to create a AAA client:

Step 1.   Click **Network Configuration** in the navigation bar. The Network Configuration page appears

Step 2.   In the AAA Clients section, click **Add Entry**.

Step 3.   Enter the client hostname in the AAA Client Hostname field. For example, enter the name of the router that will be a AAA client to the Cisco Secure ACS server.

> **Note:**   In the Cisco Secure ACS application, a client is a router, switch, firewall, or VPN concentrator that will be using the services of the Cisco Secure ACS server.

Step 4.   Enter the IP address in the AAA Client IP Address field.

Step 5.   Enter the key that the client will use for encryption in the Shared Secret field.

Step 6.   Choose the appropriate AAA protocol from the Authenticate Using drop-down list.

Step 7.   Complete other parameters as your needs require.

Step 8.   Click **Submit and Apply**.

Interface Configuration

The options available from the Interface Configuration navigation button, shown in Figure 2-18, enable you to control the display of options in the user interface. The following configuration links are available when you click the Interface Configuration button; the specific options you see depend on whether you have added TACACS+ or RADIUS clients to the Cisco Secure ACS server:

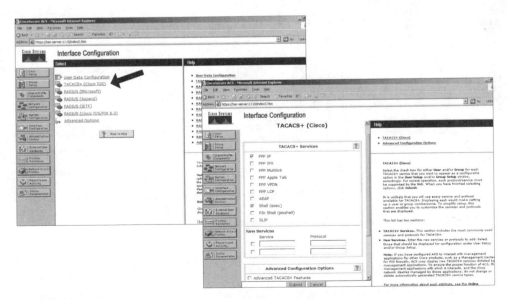

Figure 2-18   *Cisco Secure ACS Interface Configuration*

- User Data Configuration

- TACACS+ (Cisco IOS)

- RADIUS (Microsoft)

- RADIUS (Ascend)

- RADIUS (IETF)

- RADIUS (Cisco IOS/PIX 6.0)

- Advanced Options

Note: If you do not see RADIUS options in the list, you need to add a AAA client that uses the RADIUS protocol.

The User Data Configuration link enables you to customize the fields that appear in the user setup and configuration windows. Here you can add fields such as phone number, work location, supervisor name, or any other pertinent information.

The TACACS+ (Cisco IOS) link enables the administrator to configure TACACS+ settings and add new TACACS+ services. You can also configure advanced options that affect what you see in your user interface.

Configuring Cisco Secure ACS for External Databases

You can configure Cisco Secure ACS to forward authentication of users to one or more external user databases. Support for external user databases means that Cisco Secure ACS does not require you to create duplicate user entries in the Cisco Secure user database. In organizations in which a substantial user database already exists, Cisco Secure ACS can leverage the work already invested in building the database without any additional input. Figure 2-19 shows an example of Cisco Secure ACS External databases choices.

For most database configurations, except for Windows databases, Cisco Secure ACS supports only one instance of a username and password. If you configure Cisco Secure ACS to use multiple user databases with common usernames stored in each, you must be careful with the database configurations; the first database to match the authentication credentials of the user is the only one that Cisco Secure ACS uses for that user.

Note: It is recommended that there be only one instance of a username in all the external databases.

Follow these steps, shown in Figure 2-19, to configure Cisco Secure ACS to use external databases:

Step 1. Click the **External User Databases** button in the navigation bar. The External User Databases window appears with the following links:

- **Unknown User Policy:** This option enables you to configure the authentication procedure for users that are not located in the Cisco Secure ACS database.

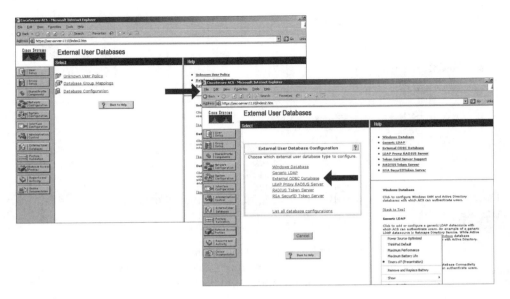

Figure 2-19   *Configuring Cisco Secure ACS for External Databases*

- **Database Group Mappings:** This option enables you to configure which group privileges external database users inherit when Cisco Secure ACS authenticates them. This means that in most cases when users are authenticated by an external user database, their actual privileges are drawn from Cisco Secure ACS and not the external database.

- **Database Configuration:** This option enables you to define all the external servers that you want Cisco Secure ACS to work with and authenticate users against.

Step 2.   Click **Database Configuration**. The External User Databases Configuration pane appears, displaying the following options:

- Windows Database

- Generic LDAP

- External ODBC Database

- LEAP Proxy RADIUS Server

- RADIUS Token Server

- RSA SecurID Token Server

Step 3.   To use the Windows database as an external database, click **Windows Database**. The External User Database Configuration pane appears.

Configuring a Windows Database as the External Database for Cisco Secure ACS

The Windows external database configuration has more options than other external database configurations. Because Cisco Secure ACS is native to the Windows operating system, you can configure additional functionality using the Windows external database option, functionality that you cannot configure with other external database options.

Step 4.   To configure the additional Windows database functionality, shown in Figure 2-20, click **Configure** from the External User Database Configuration pane. The Windows User Database Configuration window appears.

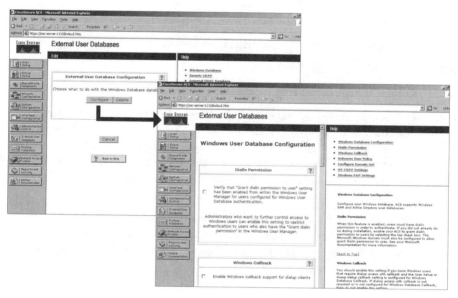

Figure 2-20   *Configuring the Windows Database*

Step 5.   If you want to have more control over who is able to authenticate to the network, you can configure the Dialin Permissions option. To configure this, in the Dialin Permission section, check the **Verify That "Grant dialin permissions to user" Setting Has Been Enabled from Within the Windows Users Manager for Users Configured for Windows User Database Authentication** check box. You must also make sure that the Grant Dial-in Permissions check box is checked in the Windows profile within Windows Users Manager.

Note: The Dialin Permissions option of Cisco Secure ACS applies to more than just the dialup connections. If a user has this option enabled, it applies to access permission in Windows 2000 and Windows 2003 R2.

Another option you can configure using the Windows external database is to map databases to domains. This option allows you to have the same username across different domains, all with different passwords.

Authenticating Users with the External Database

After you have configured Cisco Secure ACS to communicate with an external user database, you can configure Cisco Secure ACS to authenticate users with the external user database in one of two ways:

- **By specific user assignment:** You can configure Cisco Secure ACS to authenticate specific users with an external user database.

- **By unknown user policy:** You can configure Cisco Secure ACS to use an external database to authenticate users not found in the Cisco Secure user database. This method does not require you to define users in the Cisco Secure user database.

Follow these steps to configure the unknown user policy in Cisco Secure ACS:

Step 1. In the navigation bar, click **External User Databases**.

Step 2. Click Unknown User Policy.

Step 3. Choose the Check the Following External User Databases option.

Step 4. For each database that you want Cisco Secure ACS to use when attempting to authenticate unknown users, choose the database in the External Databases list and click the **Right Arrow** button to move it to the Selected Databases list. To remove a database from the Selected Databases list, choose the database, and then click the **Left Arrow** button to move it back to the External Databases list.

Step 5. To assign the order in which Cisco Secure ACS should use the selected external databases when attempting to authenticate an unknown user, click a database name in the Selected Databases list and click **Up** or **Down** to move it into the position you want.

Tip: Place the databases that are most likely to authenticate unknown users at the top of the list.

Step 6. Click **Submit**.

Figure 2-21 shows an example of an Unknown User Policy interface.

Group Setup

After a user has been authenticated to an external database, the authorization that takes place is up to Cisco Secure ACS. This can complicate things because users authenticated by a Windows server might require different authorizations than users authenticated by the LDAP server.

Because of this potential need for different authorizations, you should place users authenticated by the Windows server in one group and users authenticated by the LDAP server in another group. To do this, use database group mappings. Database group mappings enable you to map an authentication server, such as LDAP, Windows, ODBC, and so on, to a

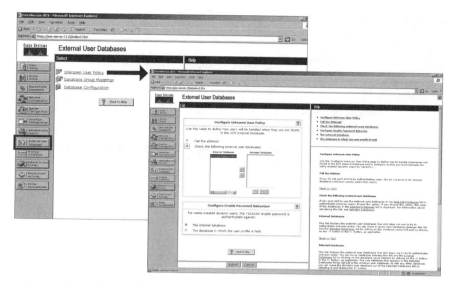

Figure 2-21 *Cisco Secure ACS Unknown User Policy Interface*

group that you have configured in Cisco Secure ACS. For some databases, a user can belong to only one group. For other databases, such as LDAP and Windows, support for group mapping by external database group membership is possible.

Key Topic

> Place users authenticated by the Windows server in one group and users authenticated by the LDAP server in another group.

One of the things you can configure in group setup is Per Group Command Authorization, which uses the Cisco Secure ACS to authorize which router commands the users that belong to a group can execute. In Figure 2-22, the group is permitted to execute any router commands except **show running-config**. This example is configured by doing the following:

Step 1.   Click **Permit** in the Unmatched Cisco IOS commands option.

Step 2.   Check the **Command** check box and enter **show** in the text box. In the Arguments text box, enter **deny running-config**.

Step 3.   For the Unlisted arguments option, click **Permit**.

Note: To access the Group Setup window, click **Group Setup** in the navigation bar.

User Setup

The configuration of user access is a critical task for configuring Cisco Secure ACS. Follow these steps to add a user account to the Cisco Secure ACS Server database:

Step 1.   Click **User Setup** in the navigation bar.

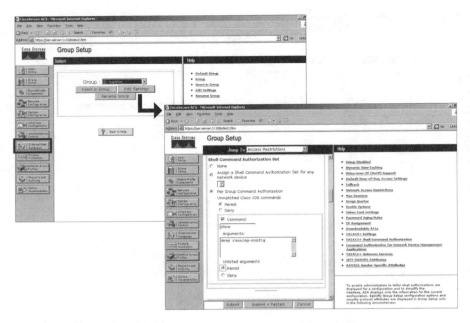

Figure 2-22 *Configuring Group Setup in Cisco Secure ACS*

Step 2. Enter a username in the User field and click **Add/Edit**.

Step 3. In the Edit pane, enter data in the fields to define the user account. Among the fields you will likely need are the user password fields, TACACS+ Enable Control, TACACS+ Enable Password, and TACACS+ Shell Command Authorization.

Step 4. Click **Submit**.

Note: If there are user properties that you do not see, you might need to modify the interface configuration. To modify the user interface, choose **Interface Configuration > User Data Configuration**.

Figure 2-23 shows how to accomplish user setup in Cisco Secure ACS.

Configuring TACACS+ Support on a Cisco Router

The next step in configuring the router for TACACS+ support is to specify a list of available Cisco Secure ACS servers that will provide TACACS+ services for the router. Follow these steps to use Cisco SDM to add a TACACS+ server to the router:

Step 1. From the Cisco SDM home page, choose **Configure > Additional Tasks > AAA > AAA Servers and Groups > AAA Servers**.

Step 2. In the AAA Servers pane, click **Add**. The Add AAA Server window appears. Choose **TACACS+** from the Server Type list box, as shown in Figure 2-24.

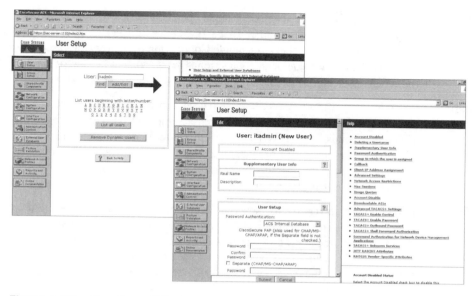

Figure 2-23 *User Setup Window in Cisco Secure ACS*

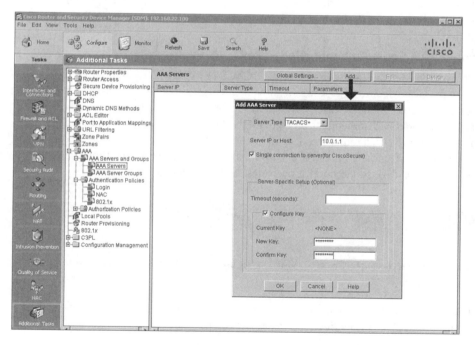

Figure 2-24 *Adding a AAA Server*

Step 3. Enter the IP address or hostname of the AAA server in the Server IP or Host field. If the router has not been configured to use a DNS server, enter an IP address.

Step 4.   If you want the router to maintain a single open connection to the TACACS+ server, rather than opening and closing a TCP connection each time it communicates with the server, check the **Single Connection to Server (for CiscoSecure)** check box. A single open connection is more efficient because it allows the TACACS+ server to handle a higher number of TACACS+ operations.

Step 5.   If you want to override AAA server global settings and specify a server-specific timeout value, in the Server-Specific Setup section enter a value in the Timeout (seconds) field. This field determines how long the router will wait for a response from this server before going on to the next server in the group list. If you do not enter a value, the router uses the value configured in the AAA Servers Global Settings window.

Step 6.   To configure a server-specific key, check the **Configure Key** check box and enter the key used to encrypt traffic between the router and this server in the New Key field. Reenter the key in the Confirm Key field for confirmation. If you do not check this option and enter a value, the router uses the value that was configured in the AAA Servers Global Settings window.

Step 7.   Click **OK**.

The resulting CLI command that Cisco SDM will generate following the preceding steps is **tacacs-server host 10.0.1.1 key** *secretkey*.

Creating a AAA Login Authentication Policy

After you enable AAA and configure the TACACS+ servers, you can configure the router to use the Cisco Secure ACS server to authenticate users logging in to the router. To configure the router to use the Cisco Secure ACS server for login authentication, you must create a user-defined authentication login method list or edit the default method list, and then apply this list to a router interface or line. The default method list is automatically applied to all interfaces and lines except those that have a user-defined method list explicitly applied. A user-defined method list overrides the default method list.

Note: The default login policy does not apply to Cisco SDM.

Follow these steps to use Cisco SDM to configure a user-defined authentication login method list:

Step 1.   From the Cisco SDM home page, choose **Configure > Additional Tasks > AAA > Authentication Policies > Login**.

Step 2.   In the Authentication Login pane, click **Add**.

Step 3.   To create a new authentication login method, choose **User Defined** from the Name drop-down list.

Step 4.   Enter the authentication login method list name in the Specify field. The example in Figure 2-25 enters TACACS_SERVER as the method list name.

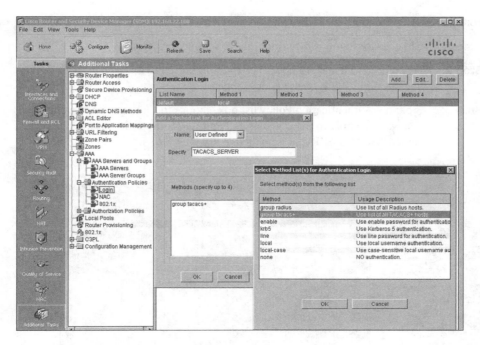

Figure 2-25   *Creating a AAA Login Authentication Policy*

Step 5.   Click **Add** to define the methods that this policy uses. The Select Method List(s) for Authentication Login window appears.

Step 6.   Choose **group tacacs+** from the method list, as shown previously in Figure 2-25.

Step 7.   Click **OK** to add group tacacs+ to the method list and return to the Add a Method List for Authentication Login window.

Step 8.   Click **Add** to add a backup method to this policy. The Select Method List(s) for Authentication Login window appears.

Step 9.   Choose **Enable** from the method list to use the enable password as the backup login authentication method.

Step 10.   Click **OK** to add enable to the method list and return to the Add a Method List for Authentication Login window.

Step 11.   Click **OK** to add the authentication login method list and return to the Authentication Login screen.

The resulting CLI command that Cisco SDM generates is **aaa authentication login TACACS_SERVER group tacacs+ enable.**

Applying an Authentication Policy

Once you create the authentication login method lists, you can apply the lists to lines and interfaces on the router.

Follow these steps to apply an authentication policy to a router line using Cisco SDM:

Step 1.   Choose **Configure > Additional Tasks > Router Access > VTY**.

Step 2.   From the VTY Lines window, click the **Edit** button to make changes to the vty lines. The Edit VTY Lines window appears.

Step 3.   From the Authentication Policy list box, choose the authentication policy that you want to apply to the vty lines. In Figure 2-26, the authentication policy named TACACS_SERVER is applied to vty lines 0 to 4.

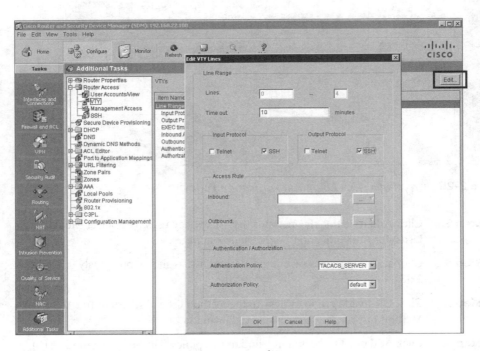

Figure 2-26   *Applying an Authentication Policy*

Example 2-27 shows the resulting CLI commands that Cisco SDM will generate in Figure 2-26.

Example 2-27   *AAA Authentication Policy on vty Lines*

```
Router(config)# line vty 0 4
Router(config-line)# login authentication TACACS_SERVER
```

You can also use the CLI to apply an authentication policy to lines or interfaces. Use the CLI command **login authentication** {**default** | *list-name*} in line configuration mode or interface configuration mode, where *list-name* is the name of the method list that was created and **default** is the default list.

Creating a AAA Exec Authorization Policy

Because the TACACS+ protocol allows you to separate authentication from authorization, you can configure a router to restrict the user to be able to perform only certain functions after successful authentication. You can configure authorization for both character mode (exec authorization) and packet mode (network authorization).

To configure the router to use the Cisco Secure ACS server for authorization, you must create a user-defined authorization method list or edit the default authorization method list. The default authorization method list is automatically applied to all interfaces except those that have a user-defined authorization method list explicitly applied. A user-defined authorization method list overrides the default authorization method list.

Tip: To avoid locking yourself out of the router, make sure you configure authorization on the Cisco Secure ACS *before* you configure the router for authorization.
Also as a precaution, you should consider logging on the router console in privilege mode before starting the authorization configuration.

Follow these steps to use Cisco SDM to configure the default authorization method list for character mode (exec) access:

Step 1.   From the Cisco SDM home page, choose **Configure > Additional Tasks > AAA > Authorization Policies > Exec**.

Step 2.   In the Exec Authorization pane, click **Edit**.

Step 3.   In the Edit a Method List for Exec Authorization window, click **Delete** to remove the local method.

Step 4.   In the Edit a Method List for Exec Authorization window, click **Add** to define the method that this policy uses, as shown in Figure 2-27.

Step 5.   From the Select Method List(s) for Exec Authorization window, choose **group tacacs+** from the method list.

Step 6.   Click **OK** to return to the Add a Method List for Exec Authorization window.

Step 7.   Click **OK** to return to the Exec Authorization pane.

The resulting CLI command that Cisco SDM will generate is **aaa authorization exec default group tacacs+**.

Creating a AAA Network Authorization Policy

Follow these steps to use Cisco SDM to configure the default authorization method list for packet mode (network) access:

Step 1.   From the Cisco SDM home page, choose **Configure > Additional Tasks > AAA > Authorization Policies > Network**.

Step 2.   In the Network Authorization pane, click **Add**.

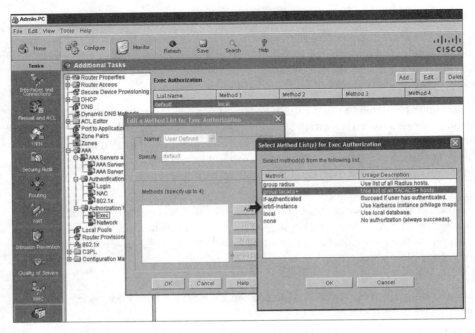

Figure 2-27   *Creating a AAA Exec Authorization Policy*

Step 3.   In the Add a Method List for Network Authorization window, choose **Default** from the Name drop-down list.

Step 4.   Click **Add** to define the methods that this policy uses.

Step 5.   From the Select Method List(s) for Network Authorization window, choose **group tacacs+** from the method list, as shown in Figure 2-28.

Step 6.   Click **OK** to return to the Add a Method List for Network Authorization window.

Step 7.   Click **OK** to return to the Network Authorization pane.

The resulting CLI command that Cisco SDM will generate is **aaa authorization network default group tacacs+**.

AAA Accounting Configuration

Cisco Secure ACS serves as a central repository for accounting information, essentially tracking events that occur on the network. Each session that is established through Cisco Secure ACS can be fully accounted for, and stored on, the server. This stored information can be very helpful for management, security audits, capacity planning, and network-usage billing.

Like authentication and authorization method lists, method lists for accounting define the way accounting will be performed and the sequence in which these methods are performed. The default accounting method list is automatically applied to all interfaces except those that have a named accounting method list explicitly defined. A defined accounting method list overrides the default accounting method list.

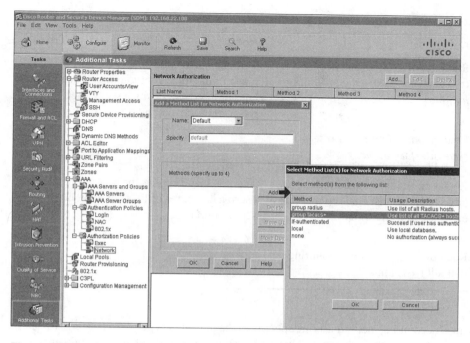

Figure 2-28 *Creating a AAA Network Authorization Policy*

AAA supports six different types of accounting: network, connection, exec, system, command, and resource.

Currently, AAA accounting can be configured only via the CLI.

To configure AAA accounting using named method lists, use the commands shown in Table 2-12 beginning in global configuration mode.

Table 2-12 *AAA Accounting Using Named Method Lists Procedure*

Step	Action	Notes
1.	Router(config)# **aaa accounting** {**system** | **network** | **exec** | **connection** | **commands** *level*} {**default** | *list-name*} {**start-stop** | **stop-only** | **none**} [*method1* [*method2...*]]	This command creates an accounting method list and enables accounting. The argument *list-name* is a character string used to name the list you are creating. To edit the default method list, use the **default** parameter. *level* refers to a specific privilege level, such as level 15. *list-name* refers to the name used to identify at least one of the accounting methods, explained below. *method* refer to **local**, **group tacacs+**, **group**, and so on.

Table 2-12   *AAA Accounting Using Named Method Lists Procedure*

Step	Action	Notes
2.	Router(config)# **line [aux	console	tty	vty]** *line-number* [*ending-line-number*] or Router(config)# **interface** *interface-type interface-number*	This command enters the line configuration mode or interface configuration mode for the lines or interface to which you want to apply the accounting method list.
3.	Router(config-line)# **accounting {arap	commands** *level* **| connection	exec} {default |** *list-name*} or Router(config-if)# **ppp accounting {default |** *list-name*}	This command applies the accounting method list to a line or set of lines, or to an interface or set of interfaces.

Named accounting method lists are specific to the indicated type of accounting. The **aaa accounting** parameters shown in Table 2-13 describes the types of accounting that can use named accounting method lists. The **aaa accounting** command enables you to specify how much information to record for accounting. Table 2-13 also describes the AAA accounting record types.

Table 2-13   aaa accounting *Command Parameters*

Parameter	Description
system	Performs accounting for all system-level events not associated with users, such as reloads. Note that when system accounting is used and the accounting server is unreachable at system startup time, the system will not be accessible for approximately 2 minutes.
default	Uses the listed accounting methods that follow this keyword as the default list of methods for accounting services.
network	This parameter creates a method list to enable accounting for all network-related service requests, including SLIP, PPP, PPP NCP, and ARAP protocols.
exec	This parameter creates a method list that provides accounting records about user EXEC terminal sessions on the network access server, including username, date, start and stop times.
connection	This parameter creates a method list that provides accounting information about all outbound connections made from the network access server.

Table 2-13   aaa accounting *Command Parameters*

Parameter	Description
commands	This parameter creates a method list that provides accounting information about specific, individual EXEC commands associated with a specific privilege level.
start-stop	This parameter instructs the TACACS+ server to send a start accounting notice at the beginning of the requested event and a stop accounting notice at the end of the event.
stop-only	This parameter instructs the TACACS+ server to send a stop record accounting notice at the end of the requested user process.
none	This parameter instructs the TACACS+ server to stop all accounting activities on this line or interface.

Note: System accounting provides information about all system-level events, such as when the system reboots or when accounting is turned on or off. System accounting does not use named method lists. For system accounting, you can define only the default method list.

AAA Configuration for TACACS+ Example

Example 2-28 shows the resulting running configuration of a router that has been configured for TACACS+ services using Cisco SDM and CLI commands.

Example 2-28   *Example of AAA Configuration for TACACS+*

```
aaa new-model
!
aaa authentication login TACACS_SERVER tacacs+ local
aaa authorization exec tacacs+
aaa authorization network tacacs+
aaa accounting exec start-stop tacacs+
aaa accounting network start-stop tacacs+
aaa accounting commands 15 default stop-only group tacacs+
!
!
tacacs-server host 10.0.1.11
tacacs-server key ciscosecure
!
line vty 0 4
 login authentication TACACS_SERVER
```

The following is an explanation of the commands displayed in Example 2-28:

- **aaa new-model:** Enables AAA

- **aaa authentication login TACACS_SERVER tacacs+ local:** Defines a AAA login policy entitled TACACS_SERVER that uses TACACS+ as the first authentication method and the local database as a second method if TACACS+ is unavailable

- **aaa authorization exec tacacs+:** Defines a AAA authorization policy that utilizes TACACS+ for access to an EXEC prompt

- **aaa authorization network tacacs+:** Defines a AAA authorization policy that utilizes TACACS+ for network access

- **aaa accounting exec start-stop tacacs+:** Defines a AAA accounting policy that utilizes TACACS+ for logging both start and stop records for user EXEC terminal sessions

- **aaa accounting network start-stop tacacs+:** Defines a AAA accounting policy that utilizes TACACS+ for logging both start and stop records for all network-related service requests

- **aaa accounting commands 15 default stop-only group tacacs+:** Defines a default **commands** accounting method list, where accounting services are provided by a TACACS+ security server, set for privilege level 15 commands with a stop-only restriction

- **tacacs-server host 10.0.1.11:** Configures the IP address of the TACACS+ server

- **tacacs-server key ciscosecure:** Configures an encryption key of ciscosecure to be used when communicating with the TACACS+ server

- **line vty 0 4:** Enters line configuration mode for vty 0 through vty 4

- **login authentication TACACS_SERVER:** Applies the AAA authentication policy named TACACS_SERVER to all five vty lines

Troubleshooting TACACS+

Use the **debug aaa authentication** command in privileged EXEC mode to get a high-level view of login activity. When the TACACS+ protocol is used on the router, you can also use the **debug tacacs** command for more detailed debugging information. To disable debugging output, use the **no** form of this command.

Example 2-29 provides sample output from the **debug aaa authentication** command for a TACACS+ login attempt that was successful. The information indicates that TACACS+ is the authentication method that was used.

Example 2-29 *Sample* **debug aaa authentication** *and* **debug tacacts+** *Output*

```
Router# debug aaa authentication


14:01:17: AAA/AUTHEN (567936829): Method=TACACS+
14:01:17: TAC+: send AUTHEN/CONT packet
14:01:17: TAC+ (567936829): received authen response status = PASS
14:01:17: AAA/AUTHEN (567936829): status = PASS
The following is sample output from the debug tacacs command for a TACACS+ login
attempt that was successful, as indicated by the status PASS:
Router# debug tacacs


14:00:09: TAC+: Opening TCP/IP connection to 192.168.60.15 using source
10.116.0.79
14:00:09: TAC+: Sending TCP/IP packet number 383258052-1 to 192.168.60.15
(AUTHEN/START)
14:00:09: TAC+: Receiving TCP/IP packet number 383258052-2 from 192.168.60.15
14:00:09: TAC+ (383258052): received authen response status = GETUSER
14:00:10: TAC+: send AUTHEN/CONT packet
14:00:10: TAC+: Sending TCP/IP packet number 383258052-3 to 192.168.60.15
(AUTHEN/CONT)
14:00:10: TAC+: Receiving TCP/IP packet number 383258052-4 from 192.168.60.15
14:00:10: TAC+ (383258052): received authen response status = GETPASS
14:00:14: TAC+: send AUTHEN/CONT packet
14:00:14: TAC+: Sending TCP/IP packet number 383258052-5 to 192.168.60.15
(AUTHEN/CONT)
14:00:14: TAC+: Receiving TCP/IP packet number 383258052-6 from 192.168.60.15
14:00:14: TAC+ (383258052): received authen response status = PASS
14:00:14: TAC+: Closing TCP/IP connection to 192.168.60.15
```

Example 2-30 shows sample output from the **debug tacacs** command for a TACACS+ login attempt that was unsuccessful, as indicated by the status FAIL.

Example 2-30 **debug tacacs** *Command for an Unsuccessful TACACS+ Login Attempt*

```
Router# debug tacacs


13:53:35: TAC+: Opening TCP/IP connection to 192.168.60.15 using source
192.48.0.79
13:53:35: TAC+: Sending TCP/IP packet number 416942312-1 to 192.168.60.15
(AUTHEN/START)
13:53:35: TAC+: Receiving TCP/IP packet number 416942312-2 from 192.168.60.15
```

```
13:53:35: TAC+ (416942312): received authen response status = GETUSER
13:53:37: TAC+: send AUTHEN/CONT packet
13:53:37: TAC+: Sending TCP/IP packet number 416942312-3 to 192.168.60.15
(AUTHEN/CONT)
13:53:37: TAC+: Receiving TCP/IP packet number 416942312-4 from 192.168.60.15
13:53:37: TAC+ (416942312): received authen response status = GETPASS
13:53:38: TAC+: send AUTHEN/CONT packet
13:53:38: TAC+: Sending TCP/IP packet number 416942312-5 to 192.168.60.15
(AUTHEN/CONT)
13:53:38: TAC+: Receiving TCP/IP packet number 416942312-6 from 192.168.60.15
13:53:38: TAC+ (416942312): received authen response status = FAIL
13:53:40: TAC+: Closing TCP/IP connection to 192.168.60.15
```

To display information from the TACACS+ helper process, use the **debug tacacs events** command in privileged EXEC mode. To disable debugging output, use the **no** form of this command.

Note: Use the **debug tacacs events** command with caution, because it can generate a substantial amount of output.
Also, because console ports communicate at 9600 bauds, it is recommended to send **debug** output to syslog server and enter **no logging console** on the router.

Example 2-31 shows sample output from the **debug tacacs events** command. The example shows the opening and closing of a TCP connection to a TACACS+ server, the bytes read and written over the connection, and the TCP status of the connection:

Example 2-31   debug tacacs event *Command Output*

```
Router# debug tacacs events



%LINK-3-UPDOWN: Interface Async2, changed state to up
00:03:16: TAC+: Opening TCP/IP to 192.168.58.104/1049 timeout=15
00:03:16: TAC+: Opened TCP/IP handle 0x48A87C to 192.168.58.104/1049
00:03:16: TAC+: periodic timer started
00:03:16: TAC+: 192.168.58.104 req=3BD868 id=-1242409656 ver=193 handle=0x48A87C
(ESTAB)
expire=14 AUTHEN/START/SENDAUTH/CHAP queued
00:03:17: TAC+: 192.168.58.104 ESTAB 3BD868 wrote 46 of 46 bytes
00:03:22: TAC+: 192.168.58.104 CLOSEWAIT read=12 wanted=12 alloc=12 got=12
00:03:22: TAC+: 192.168.58.104 CLOSEWAIT read=61 wanted=61 alloc=61 got=49
00:03:22: TAC+: 192.168.58.104 received 61 byte reply for 3BD868
00:03:22: TAC+: req=3BD868 id=-1242409656 ver=193 handle=0x48A87C (CLOSEWAIT)
expire=9
```

Example 2-31   debug tacacs event *Command Output*

```
AUTHEN/START/SENDAUTH/CHAP processed
00:03:22: TAC+: periodic timer stopped (queue empty)
00:03:22: TAC+: Closing TCP/IP 0x48A87C connection to 192.168.58.104/1049
00:03:22: TAC+: Opening TCP/IP to 192.168.58.104/1049 timeout=15
00:03:22: TAC+: Opened TCP/IP handle 0x489F08 to 192.168.58.104/1049
00:03:22: TAC+: periodic timer started
00:03:22: TAC+: 192.168.58.104 req=3BD868 id=299214410 ver=192 handle=0x489F08
(ESTAB)
expire=14 AUTHEN/START/SENDPASS/CHAP queued
00:03:23: TAC+: 192.168.58.104 ESTAB 3BD868 wrote 41 of 41 bytes
00:03:23: TAC+: 192.168.58.104 CLOSEWAIT read=12 wanted=12 alloc=12 got=12
00:03:23: TAC+: 192.168.58.104 CLOSEWAIT read=21 wanted=21 alloc=21 got=9
00:03:23: TAC+: 192.168.58.104 received 21 byte reply for 3BD868
00:03:23: TAC+: req=3BD868 id=299214410 ver=192 handle=0x489F08 (CLOSEWAIT)
expire=13
AUTHEN/START/SENDPASS/CHAP processed
00:03:23: TAC+: periodic timer stopped (queue empty)
```

Note: The TACACS messages are intended to be self-explanatory to IT service personnel only.

Implementing Secure Management and Reporting

In this section, you will learn the skills necessary to implement the management and re-porting features of Cisco IOS devices, including the following technologies:

- Syslog

- Network Time Protocol (NTP)

- Secure Shell (SSH)

- Simple Network Management Protocol Version 3 (SNMPv3)

In addition, you will examine some design aspects of a management infrastructure.

Planning Considerations for Secure Management and Reporting

Configuring logging for your Cisco routers is a straightforward operation when your net-work contains only a few Cisco routers. However, logging and reading information from hundreds of devices can prove to be a challenging proposition and can raise the following issues and considerations:

- What are the most important logs?

- How are important messages separated from routine notifications?

- How do you prevent tampering with logs?

- How do you ensure that time stamps match?

- What log data is needed in criminal investigations?

- How do you deal with the volume of log messages?

- How do you manage all the devices?

- How can you track changes when attacks or network failures occur?

Securing administrative access and device configurations is also a straightforward operation for smaller Cisco router networks. However, managing administrative access and device configurations for many devices can raise questions such as those listed.

Each of these issues is specific to your needs. To identify the priorities of reporting and monitoring, you must get input from management and from the network and security teams. The security policy that you implement should also play a large role in answering these questions.

From a reporting standpoint, most networking devices can send syslog data that can be invaluable when you are troubleshooting network problems or security threats. You can send this data to your syslog analysis host from any device whose logs you want to view. This data can be viewed in real time, on demand, and in scheduled reports. Depending on the device involved, you can choose various logging levels to ensure that the correct amount of data is sent to the logging device. You must also flag device log data within the analysis software to permit granular viewing and reporting. For example, during an attack, the log data that is provided by Layer 2 switches might not be as interesting as the data that is provided by the intrusion prevention system (IPS).

To ensure that log messages are synchronized with one another, clocks on hosts and network devices must be synchronized. For devices that support it, NTP provides a way to ensure that accurate time is kept on all devices. When you are dealing with an attack, seconds matter, because it is important to identify the order in which a specified attack occurred.

Configuration change management is another issue related to secure management. When a network is under attack, it is important to know the state of critical network devices and when the last known modifications occurred. Creating a plan for change management should be a part of your comprehensive security policy; however, at a minimum, you should record changes using authentication systems on the devices and archive configurations using FTP or TFTP.

Secure Management and Reporting Architecture

Figure 2-29 shows a management module with two network segments that are separated by a Cisco IOS router that acts as a firewall and a VPN termination device. The segment outside of the firewall connects to all of the devices that require management. The segment inside of the firewall contains the management hosts themselves and the Cisco IOS routers that act as terminal servers.

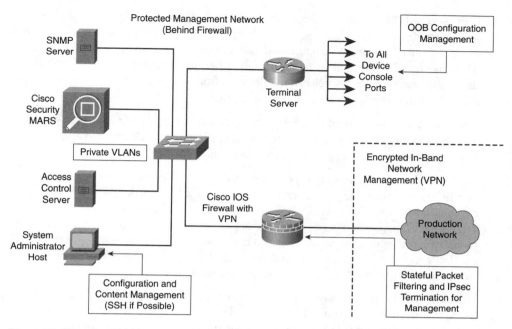

Figure 2-29 *Secure Management and Reporting Architecture*

The information flow between management hosts and the managed devices can take two paths:

- **Out-of-band (OOB):** Information flows within a network on which no production traffic resides.

- **In-band:** Information flows across the enterprise production network, the Internet, or both.

The connection to the production network is only provided for selective Internet access, limited in-band management traffic, and IPsec-protected management traffic from prede-termined hosts. In-band management occurs only when a management application does not function OOB, or when the Cisco device being managed does not physically have enough interfaces to support the normal management connection. This latter case employs IPsec tunnels. The Cisco IOS firewall is configured to allow syslog information into the management segment, and, in addition, Telnet, SSH, and SNMP, if these services are first initiated by the inside network.

Because the management network has administrative access to nearly every area of the network, it can be a very attractive target to hackers. The management module has been built with several technologies designed to mitigate such risks. The first primary threat is a hacker attempting to gain access to the management network itself. You can mitigate this threat only through the effective deployment of security features in the remaining mod-ules in the enterprise. All the remaining threats assume that the primary line of defense has been breached. To mitigate the threat of a compromised device, strong access control is implemented at the firewall, and at every other possible device, to prevent exploitation of the management channel. A compromised management device cannot even communicate with other hosts on the same management subnet because private VLANs (PVLAN) on the management segment switches force all traffic from the management devices directly to the Cisco IOS firewall, where filtering takes place.

Network administrators need to securely manage all devices and hosts in the network. Management includes logging and reporting information flow, including content, configurations, and new software, from the devices to the management hosts.

From an architectural perspective, providing OOB management of network systems is the best first step in any management and reporting strategy. Devices should have a direct local connection to such a network where possible, and where this is not possible (because of geographic or system-related issues), the device should connect via a private encrypted tunnel over the production network. Such a tunnel should be preconfigured to permit only the traffic required for management and reporting. The tunnel should also be locked down so that only appropriate hosts can initiate and terminate tunnels.

OOB management is not always desirable. Often, the decision depends on the type of management applications that you are running and the protocols required. For example, consider a management tool with the goal of determining the reachability of all the devices on the production network. If a critical link failed between two core switches, you would want this management console to alert an administrator. If this management application is configured to use an OOB network, it may never determine that the link has failed, because the OOB network makes all devices appear to be attached to a single OOB management network. With management applications such as these, it is preferable to run the management application in-band. In-band management needs to be configured in a secure manner.

SNMP management has its own set of security needs. Use SNMPv3 where possible, because SMNPv3 supports authentication and encryption. Keeping SNMP traffic on the management segment allows the traffic to traverse an isolated segment when it pulls management information from devices. To reduce security risks, SNMP management only pulls information from devices rather than being allowed to push changes to the devices. To ensure management information is pulled, each device is configured with a read-only SNMP community string. You can configure an SNMP read-write community string when using an OOB network; however, be aware of the increased security risk of a plaintext string that allows modification of device configurations if an earlier SNMP version is used.

Secure Management and Reporting Guidelines

The guidelines for OOB and in-band management of the architecture are as follow:

- **Management guidelines**
  Keep clocks on hosts and network devices synchronized.
  Record changes and archive configurations.
- **OOB management guidelines**
  Provide the highest level of security and mitigate the risk of passing unsecure management protocols over the production network.

- **In-band management guidelines**

  Apply only to devices that need to be managed or monitored.

  Use IPsec, SSH, or SSL when possible.

  Decide whether the management channel needs to be open at all times.

As a general rule, OOB management is appropriate for large enterprise networks. In smaller networks, in-band management is recommended as a means of achieving a more cost-effective security deployment. In such architectures, management traffic flows in-band in all cases and is made as secure as possible using tunneling protocols and secure variants to unsecure management protocols; for example, SSH is used whenever possible rather than Telnet.

To ensure that log messages are synchronized with one another, clocks on hosts and network devices must be synchronized. For devices that support it, NTP provides a way to ensure that accurate time is kept on all devices.

NTP is used to synchronize the clocks of various devices across a network. Synchronization of the clocks within a network is critical for digital certificates and for correct interpretation of events within the syslog data.

When in-band management of a device is required, consider these questions:

- **What management protocols does the device support?** Devices with IPsec should be managed by simply creating a tunnel from the management network to the device. This setup allows many insecure management protocols to flow over a single encrypted tunnel. When IPsec is not possible because it is not supported on a device, other, less-secure options must be chosen. For configuration of the device, SSH or Secure Sockets Layer (SSL) can often be used rather than Telnet to encrypt any configuration modifications made to a device. These protocols can sometimes also be used to push and pull data to a device instead of unsecure protocols such as TFTP and FTP. Often, however, TFTP is required on Cisco equipment to back up configurations or to update software versions. This fact leads to the second question.

- **Does this management channel need to be active at all times?** If not, you can place temporary holes in a firewall while the management functions are performed and then later remove them. This process does not scale with large numbers of devices, however, and should be used sparingly, if at all, in enterprise deployments. If the channel needs to be active at all times, such as with SNMP, the third question should be considered.

- **Do you really need this management tool?** Often, SNMP managers are used on the inside of a network to ease troubleshooting and configuration. However, SNMP should be treated with the utmost care because the underlying protocol has its own set of security vulnerabilities. If SNMP is required, consider providing read-only access to devices via SNMP, and treat the SNMP community string with the same care that you might use for a root password on a critical UNIX host. Know that by introducing SNMP into your production network, you are introducing a potential vulnerability into your environment. Finally, if you do need SNMP, use SNMPv3 authentication and encryption features.

■ **Is there a change management policy or plan in place?** If you are going to adopt new management methodologies, does everyone who needs access have access? Are old tools disabled? These issues should be dealt with in your change management policy.

Using Syslog Logging for Network Security

Syslog is the standard for logging system events. As shown in Figure 2-30, syslog implementations contain two types of systems:

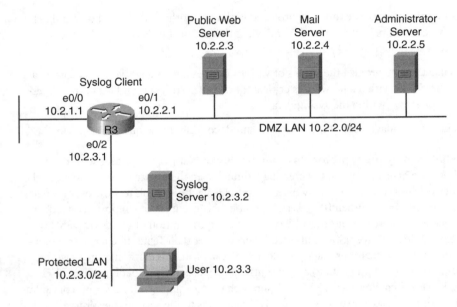

Figure 2-30 *Syslog Systems*

■ **Syslog servers:** These systems are also known as log hosts. These systems accept and process log messages from syslog clients.

■ **Syslog clients:** Syslog clients are routers or other types of Cisco equipment that generate and forward log messages to syslog servers.

Note: Performing forensics on router logs can become very difficult if your router clocks are not running the proper time. It is recommended that you use an NTP facility to ensure that all of your routers are operating at the correct time.

If not running your own NTP service, you should at least consider synchronizing on an authenticated public NTP service such as the one offered by the Canadian National Research Council at http://inms-ienm.nrc-cnrc.gc.ca/calserv/frequency_time_e.html#Authenticated.

Cisco Security Monitoring, Analysis, and Response System

The Cisco Security MARS is a Cisco security appliance that can receive and analyze syslog messages from various networking devices and hosts from Cisco and other vendors. Cisco Security MARS extends the portfolio of security management products for the Cisco Self-Defending Network initiative. Cisco Security MARS is the first purpose-built appliance for real-time security threat mitigation. Figure 2-31 shows the graphical user interface of Cisco Secure MARS.

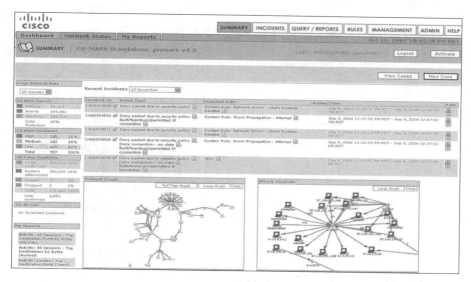

Figure 2-31 *Cisco Security MARS GUI*

Cisco Security MARS monitors many types of logging and reporting traffic that is available from the security and network products in the enterprise network, as shown in Figure 2-32. Cisco Security MARS combines all this log data into a series of sessions that it then compares to a database of rules. If the rules indicate that there might be a problem, an incident is triggered. By using this method, a network administrator can have the Cisco Security MARS appliance process most of the logging data from network devices and focus human efforts on the potential problems.

Note: For further information about the MARS product, consider the Cisco Press title *Security Threat Mitigation and Response: Understanding Cisco Security MARS* (ISBN-10: 1-58705-260-1).

Implementing Log Messaging for Security

Implementing a router logging facility is an important part of any network security policy. Cisco routers can log information regarding configuration changes, ACL violations, interface status, and many other types of events. Cisco routers can send log messages to

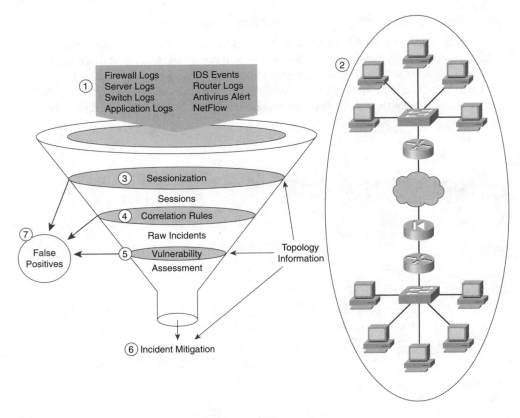

Figure 2-32   *Cisco Security MARS Process Flow*

several different facilities. You should configure the router to send log messages to one or more of the following items:

■ **Console:** Console logging is used when modifying or testing the router while it is connected to the console. Messages sent to the console are not stored by the router and, therefore, are not very valuable as security events.

■ **Terminal lines:** You can configure enabled EXEC sessions to receive log messages on any terminal lines. Similar to console logging, this type of logging is not stored by the router and, therefore, is valuable only to the user on that line.

■ **Buffered logging:** You can direct a router to store log messages in router memory. Buffered logging is a little more useful as a security tool but has the drawback of having events cleared whenever the router is rebooted.

■ **SNMP traps:** Certain router events can be processed by the router SNMP agent and forwarded as SNMP traps to an external SNMP server. SNMP traps are a viable security logging facility but require the configuration and maintenance of an SNMP system.

- **Syslog:** You can configure Cisco routers to forward log messages to an external syslog service. This service can reside on any number of servers, including Microsoft Windows and UNIX-based systems, or the Cisco Security MARS appliance. Syslog is the most popular message logging facility because this facility provides long-term log storage capabilities and a central location for all router messages.

Cisco router log messages fall into one of eight levels, as shown in Table 2-14. The lower the level number, the higher the severity level, as the log messages in the table denote.

Table 2-14   *Cisco Router Log Severity Messages*

Syslog Level	Definition	Example
0: LOG_EMERG	A panic condition normally broadcast to all users	Cisco IOS Software could not load.
1: LOG_ALERT	A condition that should be corrected immediately, such as a corrupted system database	Temperature too high.
2: LOG_CRIT	Critical conditions; for example, hard device errors	Unable to allocate memory.
3: LOG_ERR	Errors	Invalid memory size.
4: LOG_WARNING	Warning messages	Crypto operation failed.
5: LOG_NOTICE	Conditions that are not error conditions, but should possibly be handled specially	Interface changed state, up or down.
6: LOG_INFO	Informational messages	Packet denied by ACL
7: LOG_DEBUG	Messages that contain information normally of use only when debugging a program	Packet type invalid.

Note: When entering logging levels in commands, you must specify the level name or the level number.

Cisco router log messages contain three main parts:

- Time stamp

- Log message name and severity level

- Message text

Figure 2-33 shows a syslog entry example for a level 5 syslog message, indicating that someone has configured the router using the vty 0 port.

To enable syslog logging on your router using Cisco Router and Security Device Manager (SDM) follow these steps, shown in Figure 2-34:

Step 1.   Choose **Configure > Additional Tasks > Router Properties > Logging.**

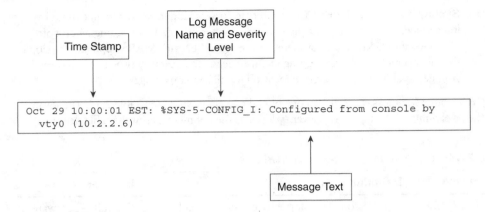

Figure 2-33   *Log Message Format*

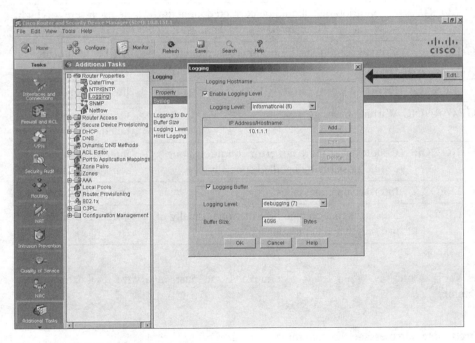

Figure 2-34   *Enabling Syslog Logging*

Step 2.   In the Logging pane, click **Edit** once syslog is highlighted.

Step 3.   In the Logging window, check the **Enable Logging Level** check box and choose the desired logging level from the Logging Level list box.

Step 4.   Click **Add**, and enter an IP address of a logging host in the IP Address/Hostname field.

Step 5.   Click **OK** to return to the Logging dialog box.

Step 6.   Click **OK** to accept the changes and return to the Logging pane.

Example 2-32 shows the resulting CLI commands that Cisco SDM will generate in Figure 2-35. In Example 2-32, the logging buffer is returned to its default value of 4096 bytes.

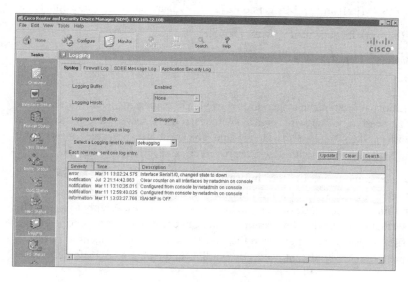

Figure 2-35 *Using Logs to Monitor Network Security*

Example 2-32 *Commands to Enable Syslog Logging on a Cisco Router*

```
logging host 10.0.1.1
logging trap informational
logging buffered 4096 debugging
logging on
```

Using Logs to Monitor Network Security

You can use Cisco SDM to monitor logging. Figure 2-35 shows the logging screen that appears when you choose **Monitor > Logging**.

From the Syslog tab, you can perform the following functions:

■ See the logging hosts to which the router logs messages

■ Choose the minimum severity level to view

■ Monitor the router syslog messages, update the screen to show the most current log entries, and erase all syslog messages from the router log buffer

Using SNMP to Manage Network Devices

SNMP was developed to manage nodes, such as servers, workstations, routers, switches, hubs, and security appliances, on an IP network. All versions of SNMP are application layer protocols that facilitate the exchange of management information between network devices. SNMP is part of the TCP/IP protocol suite. SNMP enables network administrators to manage network performance, find and solve network problems, and plan for network growth.

SNMP Version 1 (SNMPv1) and SNMP Version 2 (SNMPv2) are based on three concepts:

■ Managers (network management systems [NMS])

■ Agents (managed nodes)

■ MIBs

In any configuration, at least one manager node runs SNMP management software. Network devices that need to be managed, such as switches, routers, servers, and workstations, are equipped with an SMNP agent software module. The agent is responsible for providing access to a local MIB of objects that reflects the resources and activity at its node.

The SNMP manager can retrieve, or "get," information from the agent, and change, or "set," information in the agent, as shown in Figure 2-36. Sets can change variables (settings, configuration) in the agent device or initiate actions in devices. A reply to a set indicates the new setting in the device. For example, a set can cause a router to reboot, send a configuration file, or receive a configuration file. SNMP traps enable an agent to notify the management station of significant events by sending an unsolicited SNMP message.

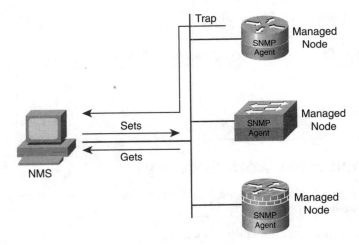

Figure 2-36 *SNMPv1/v2 Architecture*

The action of gets and sets are the vulnerabilities that open SNMP to attack.

SNMPv1 and SNMPv2 use a community string to access router SNMP agents. SNMP community strings act like passwords. An SNMP community string is a text string that can authenticate messages between a management station and an SNMP engine:

■ If the manager sends one of the correct read-only community strings, it can get information but not set information in an agent.

■ If the manager uses one of the correct read-write community strings, it can get or set information in the agent.

In effect, having set access to a router is equivalent to having the enable password of the router.

SNMP agents accept commands and requests only from SNMP systems using the correct community string. By default, most SNMP systems use public as a community string. If you configure your router SNMP agent to use this commonly known community string, anyone with an SNMP system is able to read the router MIB. Because router MIB variables can point to things such as routing tables and other security-critical parts of the router configuration, it is extremely important that you create your own custom SNMP community strings.

SNMPv3 Architecture

In its natural evolution, the current version of SNMPv3 addresses the vulnerabilities of earlier versions by including three important services: authentication, privacy, and access control.

SNMPv3 is an interoperable standards-based protocol for network management. SNMPv3 uses a combination of authenticating and encrypting packets over the network to provide secure access to devices. SNMPv3 provides the following security features:

- **Message integrity:** Ensures that a packet has not been tampered with in transit

- **Authentication:** Determines that the message is from a valid source

- **Encryption:** Scrambles the contents of a packet to prevent it from being seen by an unauthorized source

SNMP v3 provides for a combination of both, security model and security level, which determine the security mechanism that will be used when handling an SNMP packet.

A security model is an authentication strategy that is set up for a user and the group in which the user resides. Currently, Cisco IOS Software supports three security models: SN-MPv1, SNMPv2c, and SNMPv3. Meanwhile, a security level is the permitted level of security within a security model. The security level is a type of security algorithm that is performed on each SNMP packet. There are three security levels:

- **noAuth:** This security level authenticates a packet by a string match of the username or community string.

- **auth:** This level authenticates a packet by using either the Hashed Message Authentication Code (HMAC) with Message Digest 5 (MD5) method or Secure Hash Algorithms (SHA) method. This method is described in RFC 2104, *HMAC: Keyed-Hashing for Message Authentication.*

- **Priv:** This level authenticates a packet by using either the HMAC MD5 or HMAC SHA algorithms and encrypts the packet using the Data Encryption Standard (DES), Triple DES (3DES), or Advanced Encryption Standard (AES) algorithms.

Note: Only SNMPv3 supports the auth and priv security levels.

Table 2-15 identifies what the combinations of security models and levels mean.

Table 2-15 *AAA Accounting Using Named Method Lists Procedure*

	Level	Authentication	Encryption	What Happens
SNMPv1	noAuthNoPriv	Community string	No	Authenticates with a community string match
SNMPv2c	noAuthNoPriv	Community string	No	Authenticates with a community string match
SNMPv3	noAuthNoPriv	Username	No	Authenticates with a username
SNMPv3	authNoPriv	MD5 or SHA	No	Provides HMAC MD5 or HMAC SHA algorithms for authentication
SNMPv3	authPriv	MD5 or SHA	Yes	Provides HMAC MD5 or HMAC SHA algorithms for authentication; provides DES, 3DES, or AES encryption in addition to authentication

Enabling SNMP Options Using Cisco SDM

You can use Cisco SDM to enable SNMP, set SNMP community strings, and enter SNMP trap receiver information, as shown in Figure 2-37.

Note: SNMPv3 cannot be configured using Cisco SDM.

Follow these steps to enable SNMP options using Cisco SDM:

Step 1.   Choose **Configure > Additional Tasks > Router Properties > SNMP**.

Step 2.   Click the **Edit** button.

Step 3.   In the SNMP Properties window, check the **Enable SNMP** check box to enable SNMP support. Uncheck this box to disable SNMP support.

Viewing and Managing SNMP Community Strings Using Cisco SDM

SNMP community strings are like passwords that allow access to the information in MIBs. MIBs store data about router operation and are meant to be available to authenticated remote users. There are two types of community strings:

■ **Read-only community strings:** This type of community string provides read-only access to all objects in the MIB except the community strings.

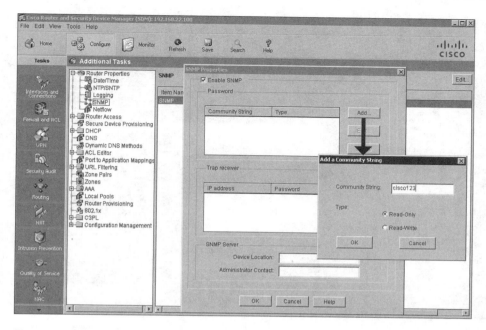

Figure 2-37 *Enabling SNMP with Cisco SDM*

■ **Read-write community strings:** This type of community string provides read-write access to all objects in the MIB except the community strings.

Follow these steps to use Cisco SDM to view and manage community strings:

Step 1.   Choose **Configure > Additional Tasks > Router Properties > SNMP**, and click **Edit** in the SNMP pane. The SNMP Properties window displays all the configured community strings and their types.

Step 2.   Click **Add** to create new community strings, click **Edit** to edit an existing community string, or click **Delete** to delete a community string.

Configuring Trap Receivers

You can also configure the devices to which a router sends traps. These devices are referred to as trap receivers. Follow these steps, shown in Figure 2-38, to use Cisco SDM to add, edit, or delete a trap receiver:

Step 1.   In the SNMP pane in Cisco SDM, click **Edit**. The SNMP Properties window displays.

Step 2.   To add a new trap receiver, click **Add** in the Trap Receiver section of the SNMP Properties window. The Add a Trap Receiver window displays.

Step 3.   Enter the IP address or hostname of the trap receiver and the password that is used to connect to the trap receiver. Typically, this is the IP address of the SNMP management station that monitors your domain. Check with your site administrator to determine the address if you are unsure of it.

Step 4.   Click **OK** to finish adding the trap receiver.

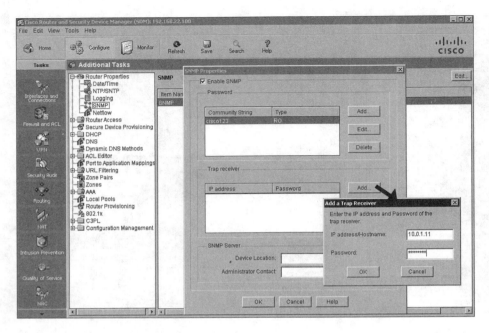

Figure 2-38   *SNMP Trap Receiver*

Step 5.   To edit an existing trap receiver, choose a trap receiver from the trap receiver list and click **Edit**. To delete an existing trap receiver, choose a trap receiver from the trap receiver list and click **Delete**.

Step 6.   When you are done managing the trap receiver list, click **OK** to return to the SNMP pane.

Still on Figure 2-38, in the SNMP Properties window you will also notice the SNMP Server Device Location field and the SNMP Server Administrator Contact field. Both of these fields are text fields that you can use to enter descriptive information about the SNMP server location and the contact information for a person managing the SNMP server. These fields are not required and do not affect the operation of the router.

The resulting CLI command that Cisco SDM will generate based on the example in Figure 2-37 and 2-38 is **snmp-server community cisco123 RO** and **snmp-server host 10.0.1.11 trap cisco123**.

Configuring an SSH Daemon for Secure Management and Reporting

The SSH daemon is a feature that enables an SSH client to make a secure, encrypted connection to a Cisco router. This connection provides functionality similar to that of an inbound Telnet connection, but it also provides strong encryption to be used with local authentication. The SSH daemon in Cisco IOS Software works with publicly and commercially available SSH clients. This feature is disabled if the router is not using an IPsec DES or 3DES Cisco IOS Software image.

Whenever possible, you should use SSH rather than Telnet to manage your Cisco routers. Cisco IOS Software Release 12.1(1)T and later support SSHv1, and Cisco IOS Release 12.3(4)T and later support both SSHv1 and SSHv2. Cisco routers configured for SSH act as SSH daemons. You must provide an SSH client, such as PuTTY, OpenSSH, or Tera Term, for the administrator workstation that you want to use to configure and manage routers using SSH.

Tip: Cisco routers with Cisco IOS Software Releases 12.1(3)T and later can act as both SSH clients and SSH daemons. This means that you could initiate an SSH client-to-server session from your router to a central SSH daemon system using the **ssh** command. SSH employs strong encryption to protect the SSH client-to-server session. Unlike Telnet, where anyone with a sniffer can see exactly what you are sending to and receiving from your routers, SSH encrypts the entire session.

Many vulnerabilities have been reported for SSH Version 1. It is therefore recommended to use SSH Version 2.

Complete the following tasks before you configure your routers for SSH daemon operations:

- Ensure that the target routers are running an IOS image which supports SSH, such as Release 12.1(1)T image or later with the IPsec feature set. For more information about which IOS supports SSH, refer to the Software Advisor at Cisco.com for a complete list.

- Ensure that the target routers are configured for local authentication, or for AAA services for username or password authentication, or both.

- Ensure that each of the target routers has a unique hostname.

- Ensure that each of the target routers is using the correct domain name of your network.

You can use Cisco SDM to configure an SSH daemon on a router, as shown in Figure 2-39.

To see the current SSH key settings, choose **Configure > Additional Tasks > Router Access > SSH**. The SSH key settings have two status options:

- **RSA key is not set on this router:** This notice appears if there is no cryptographic key configured for the device. If there is no key configured, you can enter a modulus size and generate a key.

- **RSA key is set on this router:** This option appears if a cryptographic key has been generated, in which case SSH is enabled on this router.

Note: The default configuration file that ships with a Cisco SDM-enabled router automatically enables Telnet and SSH access from the LAN interface and generates an RSA key.

To configure a cryptographic key if one is not set, click the **Generate RSA Key** button. The Key Modulus Size dialog box appears. Enter the modulus size that you want to give the key. If you want a modulus value between 512 and 1024, enter an integer value that is

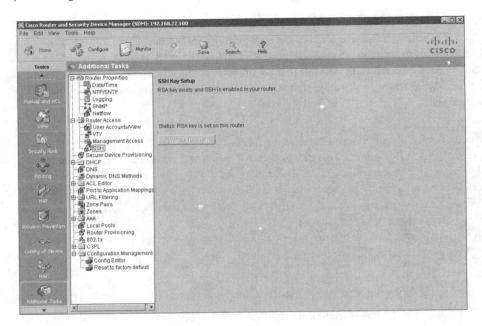

Figure 2-39 *Enabling SSH Using Cisco SDM*

a multiple of 64. If you want a value higher than 1024, you can enter 1536 or 2048. If you enter a value greater than 512, key generation can take a minute or longer.

After you enable SSH on the router, you must configure the vty lines to support SSH. To use Cisco SDM to configure SSH on the vty lines, choose **Configure > Additional Tasks > Router Access > VTY**, as shown in Figure 2-40. The VTY Lines window displays the vty settings on your router. The Property column contains the configured line ranges and the configurable properties for each range. The settings for these properties are contained in the Value column.

The window shows the following router vty settings:

■ **Line Range:** This setting displays the range of vty connections to which the rest of the settings in the row apply.

■ **Input Protocols Allowed:** This setting displays the protocols that are configured for input, which can be Telnet, SSH, or both Telnet and SSH.

■ **Output Protocols Allowed:** This setting displays the protocols that are configured for output, which can be Telnet, SSH, or both Telnet and SSH.

■ **EXEC Timeout:** This setting displays the number of seconds of inactivity after which a session is terminated.

■ **Inbound Access-Class:** This setting displays the name or number of the ACL that is applied to the inbound direction of the line range.

■ **Outbound Access-Class:** This setting displays the name or number of the ACL that is applied to the outbound direction of the line range.

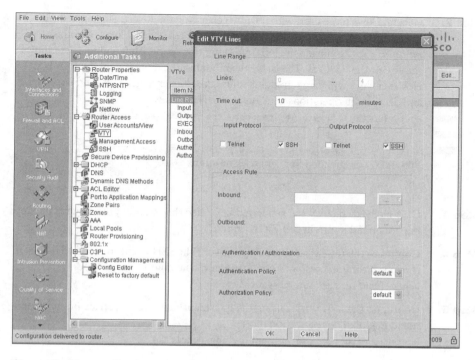

Figure 2-40 *vty Settings*

- **ACL:** If configured, this setting shows the ACL that is associated with the vty connections.

- **Authentication Policy:** This setting displays the AAA authentication policy associated with this vty line. This field is not visible if AAA is not configured on the router.

- **Authorization Policy:** This setting displays the AAA authorization policy associated with this vty line. This field is not visible if AAA is not configured on the router.

To change these settings, click the **Edit** button. The Edit VTY Lines window appears. From this window you can enable SSH on the vty lines by checking the **SSH** check box in the Input Protocol section or the Output Protocol section or both.

Follow these steps to configure your Cisco router to support an SSH daemon using the CLI:

Step 1.   Configure the IP domain name of your network using the **ip domain-name** *domain-name* command in global configuration mode:

```
Router(config)# ip domain-name cisco.com
```

Note: The domain name and the hostname are used for the generation of the RSA key pairs. If there are any existing key pairs, it is recommended that you overwrite them using the command **crypto key zeroize rsa**.

Step 2. Generate keys to be used with SSH by generating the Rivest, Shamir, and Adleman (RSA) keys using the **crypto key generate rsa general-keys modulus** *modulus-size* command in global configuration mode. The modulus determines the size of the RSA key. The larger the modulus, the more secure the RSA key. However, keys with large modulus values take longer to generate, and encryption and decryption operations take longer with larger keys:

```
Router(config)# crypto key generate rsa general-keys modulus 1024
```

Note: The minimum recommended key length is modulus 1024.

Step 3. Optionally, to display the generated keys, use the **show crypto key mypubkey rsa** command in privileged EXEC mode.

Step 4. Configure the time that the router waits for the SSH client to respond using the **ip ssh timeout** *seconds* command in global configuration mode:

```
Router(config)# ip ssh timeout 120
```

Step 5. Configure the SSH retries using the **ip ssh authentication-retries** *integer* command in global configuration mode:

```
Router(config)# ip ssh authentication-retries 4
```

Step 6. Enable vty inbound SSH sessions:

```
Router(config)# line vty 0 4
Router(config-line)# transport input ssh
```

The SSH protocol is automatically enabled when you generate the SSH (RSA) keys. Once the keys are created, you can access the router SSH daemon using your SSH client software.

Tip: If you are using a version of Cisco IOS Software that supports both SSHv1 and SSHv2, by default SSH runs in compatibility mode; that is, both SSHv1and SSHv2 connections are honored. If you are running Cisco IOS Release 12.3(4)T or later, you can use the **ip ssh version {1 | 2}** command to configure support for only one version of SSH.

The procedure for connecting to a Cisco router SSH daemon varies depending on the SSH client application that you use. Generally, the SSH client passes your username to the router SSH daemon. The router SSH daemon prompts you for the correct password. After the password has been verified, you can configure and manage the router as if you were a standard vty user.

Enabling Time Features

Because many things that are involved in the security of your network depend on an accurate date and time stamp, such as security certificates, it is important that the router maintains the correct time.

You can use Cisco SDM to configure the date and time settings of the router in three ways:

- Synchronize with the local PC clock

- Manually edit the date and time

- Configure NTP

Synchronizing Cisco SDM with the Local PC Clock

Follow these steps to synchronize the router time settings with the PC that is running Cisco SDM, as shown in Figure 2-41:

Step 1. From Cisco SDM, choose **Configure > Additional Tasks > Router Properties > Date/Time.**

Step 2. Click **Change Settings** to display the Date and Time Properties window.

Step 3. Click the **Synchronize with My Local PC Clock** radio button and click **Synchronize** to have Cisco SDM synchronize the time settings of the router with the local PC. Cisco SDM only synchronizes the time settings of the router when you click **Synchronize**. Cisco SDM does not automatically resynchronize the time settings with the PC during subsequent sessions. The Synchronize button is disabled if you did not choose the Synchronize with my local PC clock option.

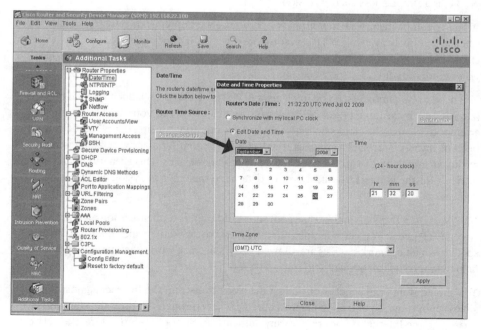

Figure 2-41 *Manually Configuring Date and Time Settings*

Note: You must configure the Time Zone and Daylight Savings settings on the PC before starting Cisco SDM so that Cisco SDM receives the correct settings when you click Synchronize.

Manually Editing the Date and Time

Follow these steps to use Cisco SDM to manually configure the time settings of the router (referring to Figure 2-41):

Step 1.   Choose **Configure > Additional Tasks > Router Properties > Date/Time**.

Step 2.   Click **Change Settings** to display the Date and Time Properties window.

Step 3.   From the Date and Time Properties window, click the **Edit Date and Time** radio button. You can choose the month and the year from the drop-down lists, and choose the day of the month in the calendar. The fields in the Time area require values in a 24-hour format. You can choose your time zone based on Greenwich mean time (GMT), or you can browse the list for major cities in your time zone. If you want the router to adjust time settings for daylight saving time and standard time, check the **Automatically Adjust Clock for Daylight Savings Changes** check box. This option appears only if you have selected a time zone that supports daylight savings time.

Network Time Protocol

NTP is a secure method to synchronize date and time settings for devices on the network. NTP uses UDP port 123 and is documented in RFC 1305. Simple Network Time Protocol (SNTP) is a simpler, less-secure version of NTP.

When you implement NTP in your network, you can set up your own master clock, or you can use a publicly available NTP server on the Internet. If you implement your own master clock, you should synchronize the private network to Coordinated universal time (UTC) via satellite or radio.

You need to be careful when you implement NTP. An attacker can launch a denial-of-service (DoS) attack by sending bogus NTP data across the Internet to your network in an attempt to change the clocks on network devices, possibly causing digital certificates to become invalid. Further, an attacker could attempt to confuse a network administrator during an attack by disrupting the clocks on network devices. This scenario would make it difficult for the network administrator to determine the order of syslog events on multiple devices.

NTP Version 3 (NTPv3) and later support a cryptographic authentication mechanism between NTP peers. You can use this authentication mechanism, in addition to ACLs that specify which network devices are allowed to synchronize with other network devices, to help mitigate such an attack.

You should weigh the benefits of pulling the clock time from the Internet against the possible risk of doing so and allowing unsecured packets through the firewall. Many NTP servers on the Internet do not require any authentication of peers. Therefore, the network administrator must trust that the clock itself is reliable, valid, and secure.

NTP allows routers on your network to synchronize their time settings with an NTP server. A group of NTP clients that obtain time and date information from a single source will have more consistent time settings. Cisco SDM allows you to view the NTP server information that has been configured, add new information, and edit or delete existing information, as shown in Figure 2-42.

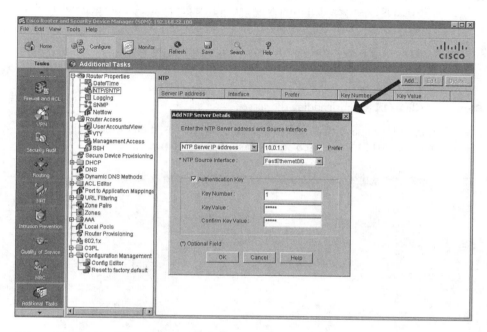

Figure 2-42   *Enabling NTP with Cisco SDM*

Follow these steps to add an NTP server using Cisco SDM:

Step 1.   Choose **Configure > Additional Tasks > Router Properties > NTP/SNTP**. The NTP pane appears, displaying the information for any configured NTP servers.

Note: If your router does not support NTP commands, the NTP/SNTP option will not appear in the Router Properties tree.

Step 2.   To add a new NTP server, click **Add**. The Add NTP Server Details window appears.

Step 3.   You can add an NTP server by name (if your router is configured to use a DNS server) or by IP address. To add an NTP server by IP address, enter the IP address of the NTP server in the field next to the NTP Server IP address option. If your organization does not have an NTP server, you might want to use a publicly available server, such as the server list that is described at http:/ /support.ntp.org/bin/view/Servers/WebHome.

Step 4.   From the NTP Source Interface drop-down list, choose the interface that the router will use to communicate with the NTP server. The NTP Source Interface is an optional field. If you leave this field blank, NTP messages will be sent out the closest interface per the routing table.

Step 5.   Check the **Prefer** check box if this NTP server has been designated as a preferred NTP server. Preferred NTP servers are contacted before nonpreferred NTP servers. There can be more than one preferred NTP server.

Step 6.   If the NTP server you are adding uses authentication, check the **Authentication Key** check box and enter the key number, the key value, and confirm the key value.

Step 7.   Click **OK** to finish adding the server.

The resulting CLI command that Cisco SDM will generate based on the example in Figure 2-43 is **ntp server 10.1.1.1 key cisco source fastethernet0/0 prefer**.

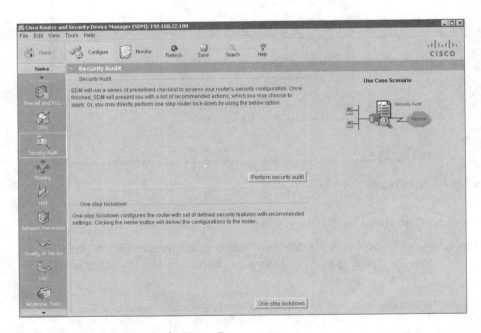

Figure 2-43   *Security Audit Home Page*

Note: It is possible to configure your Cisco IOS router as an NTP master, which other appliances will contact to synchronize on. The following commands are used to set the router as a NTP master.

```
router# conf t
router(config)# ntp authenticate
router(config)# ntp trusted-key 99
router(config)# ntp master
router(config)# key chain NTP
```

```
router(config-keychain)# key 99
router(config-keychain-key)# key-string TESTING
router(config-keychain-key)# end
```

Locking Down the Router

Cisco routers are initially deployed with services that are enabled by default. This section discusses the Cisco configuration settings that you should consider changing on your routers, especially on your perimeter routers, to improve security. The list of configuration settings discussed is not exhaustive, and it cannot be substituted for understanding on your part; it is meant to be a reminder of some of the things that are sometimes forgotten. Many of the services that you can enable on Cisco routers require careful security configuration. However, this section describes services that are enabled by default, or that are almost always enabled by users, and that might need to be disabled.

Consideration of these services is particularly important because some of the default settings in Cisco IOS Software are there for historical reasons; they made sense when they were chosen but would probably be different if new defaults were chosen today. Other defaults make sense for most systems but can create security exposures if they are used in devices that form part of a network perimeter defense. Still, other defaults are actually required by standards but are not always desirable from a security point of view.

Vulnerable Router Services and Interfaces

Cisco routers support many network services that may not be required in certain enterprise networks. The services that are listed here have been chosen for their vulnerability to malicious exploitation. These are the router services most likely to be used in network attacks. For ease of learning, the services are grouped as follows:

- Disable unnecessary services and interfaces
    - **Router interfaces:** You should limit unauthorized access to the router and the network by disabling unused open router interfaces.
    - **Bootstrap Protocol (BOOTP) server:** This service is enabled by default. This service allows a router to act as a BOOTP server for other routers. This service is rarely required and should be disabled.
    - **Cisco Discovery Protocol:** This service is enabled by default. Cisco Discovery Protocol is used primarily to obtain protocol addresses of neighboring Cisco devices and to discover the platforms of those devices. Cisco Discovery Protocol is media and protocol independent and runs on most equipment manufactured by Cisco, including routers, access servers, switches, and IP phones. This service should be disabled globally or on a per-interface basis if it is not required.
    - **Configuration autoloading:** This service is disabled by default. Autoloading of configuration files from a network server should remain disabled when not in use by the router.
    - **FTP server:** This service is disabled by default. The FTP server enables you to use your router as an FTP server for FTP client requests. Because it allows access

to certain files in the router flash memory, this service should be disabled when it is not required.

- **TFTP server:** This service is disabled by default. The TFTP server enables you to use your router as a TFTP server for TFTP clients. This service should be disabled when it is not in use, because it allows access to certain files in the router flash memory.

- **Network Time Protocol (NTP) service:** This service is disabled by default. When NTP is enabled, the router acts as a time server for other network devices. If NTP is configured unsecurely, an attacker can use it to corrupt the router clock and potentially the clock of other devices that learn time from the router. Correct time is essential for setting proper time stamps for IPsec encryption services, log data, and diagnostic and security alerts. If this service is used, restrict which devices have access to NTP. Disable this service when it is not required.

- **Packet Assembler/Disassembler (PAD) service:** This service is enabled by default. The PAD service allows access to X.25 PAD commands when forwarding X.25 packets. This service should be explicitly disabled when not in use.

- **TCP and UDPminor services:** These services are enabled in Cisco IOS Software before Release 11.3 and disabled in Cisco IOS Software Release 11.3 and later. The minor services are provided by small servers (daemons) running in the router. They are potentially useful for diagnostics but are rarely used. Disable this service explicitly.

- **Maintenance Operation Protocol (MOP) service:** This service is enabled on most Ethernet interfaces. MOP is a Digital Equipment Corp. (DEC) maintenance protocol that should be explicitly disabled when it is not in use.

- Disable and restrict commonly configured management services

  - **SNMP:** This service is enabled by default. The SNMP service allows the router to respond to remote SNMP queries and configuration requests. If required, restrict which SNMP systems have access to the router SNMP agent and use SNMPv3 whenever possible, because this version offers secure communication not available in earlier versions of SNMP. Disable this service when it is not required.

  - **HTTP or HTTPS configuration and monitoring:** The default setting for this service is Cisco device dependent. This service allows the router to be monitored or have its configuration modified from a web browser via an application such as the Cisco SDM. You should disable this service if it is not required. If this service is required, restrict access to the router HTTP or HTTPS service using ACLs.

  - **DNS:** This client service is enabled by default. By default, Cisco routers broadcast name requests to 255.255.255.255. Restrict this service by disabling it when it is not required. If the DNS lookup service is required, ensure that you set the DNS server address explicitly.

- Ensure path integrity

  - **Internet Control Message Protocol (ICMP) redirects:** This service is enabled by default. ICMP redirects cause the router to send ICMP redirect messages whenever the router is forced to resend a packet through the same interface on which it was received. Attackers can use this information to redirect packets to an untrusted device. This service should be disabled when it is not required.

- **IP source routing:** This service is enabled by default. The IP protocol supports source routing options that allow the sender of an IP datagram to control the route that a datagram will take toward its ultimate destination and, generally, the route that any reply will take. An attacker can exploit these options to bypass the intended routing path and security of the network. Also, some older IP implementations do not process source-routed packets properly, and it may be possible to crash machines running these implementations by sending datagrams with source routing options. Disable this service when it is not required.

- Disable probes and scans
  - **Finger service:** This service is enabled by default. The finger protocol (port 79) allows users throughout the network to obtain a list of the users currently using a particular device. The information that is displayed includes the processes running on the system, the line number, connection name, idle time, and terminal location. This information is provided through the Cisco IOS Software **show users** EXEC command. This command will also display the usernames of those that authenticate via AAA. Unauthorized persons can use this information for reconnaissance attacks. Disable this service when it is not required.
  - **ICMP unreachable notifications:** This service is enabled by default. This service notifies senders of invalid destination IP networks or specific IP addresses. This information can be used to map networks and should be explicitly disabled on interfaces to untrusted networks.
  - **ICMP mask reply:** This service is disabled by default. When this service is enabled, this service tells the router to respond to ICMP mask requests by sending ICMP mask reply messages containing the interface IP address mask. This information can be used to map the network, and this service should be explicitly disabled on interfaces to untrusted networks.

- Ensure terminal access security
  - **IP identification service:** This service is enabled by default. The identification protocol (specified in RFC 1413, *Identification Protocol*) reports the identity of a TCP connection initiator to the receiving host. An attacker can use this data to gather information about your network, and this service should be explicitly disabled.
  - **TCP keepalives:** This service is disabled by default. TCP keepalives help "clean up" TCP connections where a remote host has rebooted or otherwise stopped processing TCP traffic. Keepalives should be enabled globally to manage TCP connections and prevent certain DoS attacks.

- Disable gratuitous and proxy Address Resolution Protocol (ARP)
  - **Gratuitous ARP (GARP):** This service is enabled by default. GARP is the main mechanism that is used in ARP poisoning attacks. You should disable gratuitous ARPs on each router interface unless this service is needed.
  - **Proxy ARP:** This service is enabled by default. This feature configures the router to act as a proxy for Layer 2 address resolution. You should disable this service unless the router is being used as a LAN bridge.

- Disable IP-directed broadcast

This service is enabled in Cisco IOS Software before Release 12.0 and is disabled in Cisco IOS Software Release 12.0 and later. IP-directed broadcasts are used in the common and popular

Smurf DoS attacks and other related attacks. You should disable this service when it is not required.

Management Service Vulnerabilities

SNMP is a network protocol that provides a facility for managing the network devices through an NMS. SNMP is widely used for router monitoring and is frequently used for making changes to a router configuration. However, SNMPv1, which is the most commonly used version of SNMP, is often a security risk for the following reasons:

■ SNMPv1 and SNMPv2 use authentication strings called community strings, which are stored and sent across the network in plaintext. Most SNMP implementations send these strings repeatedly as part of periodic polling.

■ SNMPv1 is easily spoofed.

Because SNMP can retrieve a copy of the network routing table, and other sensitive network information, it is recommended that you disable SNMPv1 and SNMPv2 if your network does not require it, or use SNMPv3, which has much stronger security mechanisms.

Most Cisco IOS Software releases support remote configuration and monitoring using HTTP. The authentication protocol that HTTP uses sends a plaintext password across the network. With HTTPS, the session data is encrypted. Cisco SDM uses either HTTP or HTTPS. Access to the HTTP and HTTPS service should be limited by configuring an access class that allows access only to directly connected nodes.

By default, the Cisco router DNS lookup service sends name queries to the 255.255.255.255 broadcast address. Using this broadcast address should be avoided because it can allow an attacker to emulate one of your DNS servers and respond to router queries with erroneous data. The DNS lookup service is enabled by default. If your routers must use this service, ensure that you explicitly set the IP address of your DNS servers in the router configuration.

By default, Telnet sends authentication and commands in plaintext. SSH allows a management connection that is secure and encrypted. Whenever possible you should use SSH rather than Telnet to manage your Cisco routers.

Performing a Security Audit

Security Audit is a feature that examines your existing router configurations and then updates your router to make your router and network more secure. Security Audit is based on the Cisco IOS AutoSecure feature; Security Audit performs checks on, and assists in, the configuration of almost all of the Cisco AutoSecure functions.

Note: For a complete list of the functions that Security Audit checks for, and for a list of the Cisco AutoSecure features that Security Audit does not support, see the *Cisco Router and Security Device Manager 2.4 User's Guide.*

Security Audit operates in one of two modes, as shown in Figure 2-43:

■ **Security Audit:** A wizard that enables you to choose which potential security-related configuration changes to implement on your router

■ **One-Step Lockdown:** Automatically makes all recommended security-related configuration changes

Performing a Security Audit with the Security Audit Wizard

The Security Audit Wizard tests your router configuration to determine whether any potential security problems exist in the configuration, and then presents you with a screen that lets you determine which of those security problems you want to fix. Once you determine which security problems to fix, the Security Audit Wizard makes the necessary changes to the router configuration to fix those problems.

Follow these steps, shown in Figure 2-44, to perform a security audit:

Step 1.   From Cisco SDM choose **Configure > Security Audit**.

Step 2.   Click **Perform Security Audit**. The Welcome page of the Security Audit Wizard appears.

Step 3.   Click **Next**. The Security Audit Interface Configuration page appears.

Step 4.   The Security Audit Wizard needs to know which of your router interfaces connect to your inside network and which connect outside of your network. For each interface that is listed, check either the **Inside** or **Outside** check box to indicate where the interface connects.

Step 5.   Click **Next**.

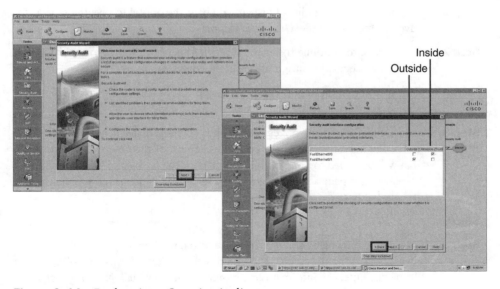

Figure 2-44   *Performing a Security Audit*

The Security Audit Wizard tests your router configuration to determine which possible security problems may exist. A window that shows the progress of this action appears, listing all of the configuration options that are being tested, and whether the current router configuration passes those tests, as shown in Figure 2-45.

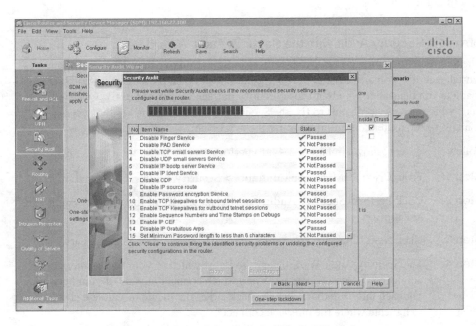

Figure 2-45   *Progress Window of the Security Audit Wizard*

Step 6.   When the security audit is finished, you have the option to save the report. To save this report to a file, click **Save Report**.

Step 7.   Click **Close** to continue fixing the identified security problems or to undo the configured security configurations in the router.

The Security Audit Report Card screen appears, as shown in Figure 2-46, showing a list of possible security problems.

Step 8.   Check the **Fix It** check boxes next to any problems that you want Cisco SDM to fix. For a description of the problem and a list of the Cisco IOS commands that will be added to your configuration, click the problem description link to display a help page about that problem. To fix all the presented problems, click the **Fix All** button.

Step 9.   Click **Next**.

Step 10.   Depending on which options you chose to fix, the Security Audit Wizard may display one or more screens that require you to enter information to fix certain problems. Enter the information as required, and then click **Next** for each of those screens.

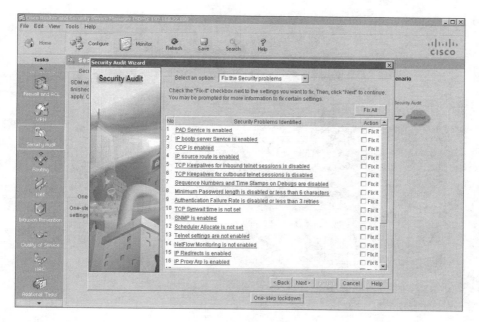

Figure 2-46 *Security Audit Report Card*

Step 11. The Summary page of the wizard shows a list of all the configuration changes that Security Audit will make. Click **Finish** to deliver those changes to your router.

Configuring One-Step Cisco Router Lockdown

The One-Step Lockdown feature tests your router configuration for any potential security problems and automatically makes the necessary configuration changes to correct any problems that were found.

Follow these steps to perform a one-step lockdown, shown in Figure 2-47:

Step 1. From Cisco SDM choose **Configure > Security Audit**.

Step 2. Click **One-Step Lockdown**.

Step 3. The SDM window appears asking whether you are sure you want to lock down the router. Click **Yes** to continue or click **No** to quit the process.

Step 4. The One-Step Lockdown window appears, showing the status of the lock-down process. When the One-Step Lockdown is finished, click **Deliver** to deliver the configuration to the router.

Step 5. The Commands Delivery Status window shows the status of delivering the commands to the router. After the configuration is delivered to the router, click **OK** to finish.

The One-Step Lockdown feature checks for and, if necessary, corrects the following items:

■ Disable finger service

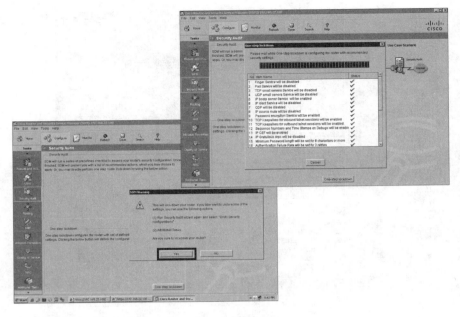

Figure 2-47 *Performing a One-Step Lockdown*

- Disable PAD service
- Disable TCP small servers service
- Disable UDP small servers service
- Disable IP BOOTP server service
- Disable IP identification service
- Disable Cisco Discovery Protocol
- Disable IP source route
- Enable password encryption service
- Enable TCP keepalives for inbound Telnet sessions
- Enable TCP keepalives for outbound Telnet sessions
- Enable sequence numbers and time stamps on debugs
- Enable IP Cisco Express Forwarding
- Disable IP GARPs
- Set minimum password length to less than six characters
- Set authentication failure rate to less than three retries
- Set TCP synwait time
- Set banner

- Enable logging
- Set enable secret password
- Disable SNMP
- Set scheduler interval
- Set scheduler allocate
- Set users
- Enable Telnet settings
- Enable NetFlow switching
- Disable IP redirects
- Disable IP proxy ARP
- Disable IP directed broadcast
- Disable MOP service
- Disable IP unreachables
- Disable IP mask reply
- Disable IP unreachables on null interface
- Enable Unicast Reverse Path Forwarding (RPF) on outside interfaces
- Enable firewall on all of the outside interfaces
- Set access class on HTTP server service
- Set access class on vty lines
- Enable SSH for access to the router
- Enable AAA

Note: One-Step Lockdown can cause a service disruption. Verify changes in a test environment before deploying in your production environment.

Cisco AutoSecure

Cisco AutoSecure is a Cisco IOS feature that lets you more easily configure security features on your router, so that your network is better protected. You can configure Cisco AutoSecure from the privileged EXEC mode using the **auto secure** command in one of two modes:

- **Interactive mode:** This mode prompts the user with options to enable and disable services and other security features. This is the default mode.

- **Noninteractive mode:** This mode automatically executes the Cisco **auto secure** command with the recommended Cisco default settings. This mode is enabled with the **no-interact** command option.

Example 2-33 shows an abstracted example of the first three steps of an interactive Cisco AutoSecure configuration.

Example 2-33   *Example of the Cisco AutoSecure Feature*

```
Router# auto secure
Is this router connected to internet? [no]:y
Enter the number of interfaces facing internet [1]:1
Enter the interface name that is facing internet:Serial0/0/0
Securing Management plane services..

Disabling service finger
Disabling service pad
Disabling udp & tcp small servers
Enabling service password encryption
Enabling service tcp-keepalives-in
Enabling service tcp-keepalives-out
Disabling the cdp protocol
```

Cisco SDM does not implement all the features of Cisco AutoSecure. As of Cisco SDM Version 2.4, the following Cisco AutoSecure features are not part of the Cisco SDM One-Step Lockdown feature:

- **Disabling NTP:** Based on input, Cisco AutoSecure will disable NTP if it is not necessary. Otherwise, NTP will be configured with MD5 authentication. Cisco SDM does not support disabling NTP.

- **Configuring AAA:** If the AAA service is not configured, Cisco AutoSecure configures local AAA and prompts for the configuration of a local username and password database on the router. Cisco SDM does not support AAA configuration.

- **Setting Selective Packet Discard (SPD) values:** Cisco SDM does not set SPD values.

- **Enabling TCP intercepts:** Cisco SDM does not enable TCP intercepts.

- **Configuring antispoofing ACLs on outside interfaces:** Cisco AutoSecure creates three named access lists to prevent antispoofing source addresses. Cisco SDM does not configure these ACLs.

The following Cisco AutoSecure features are implemented differently in Cisco SDM:

- **Disable SNMP:** Cisco SDM will disable SNMP; however, unlike Cisco AutoSecure, Cisco SDM does not provide an option for configuring SNMPv3.

Note: The SNMPv3 option is not available on all routers.

- Enable SSH for access to the router: Cisco SDM will enable and configure SSH on Cisco IOS images that have the IPsec feature set; however, unlike Cisco AutoSecure, Cisco SDM will not enable Secure Copy Protocol (SCP) or disable other access and file transfer services, such as FTP.

Chapter Summary

The following topics were discussed in this chapter:

- Routers can be used to secure the perimeters of your networks.

- Cisco SDM can be launched from router memory or from a Windows PC if it has been installed.

- AAA services provide a higher degree of scalability than line-level and privileged EXEC authentication.

- Cisco Secure ACS is a highly scalable, high-performance access control server that supports RADIUS and TACACS+.

- Because OOB management architectures provide higher levels of security and performance than in-band architectures, the decision to use an in-band solution must be carefully considered.

- Many services and interfaces are enabled by default on newly commissioned routers. These services and interfaces are vulnerable to attack and should be secured.

References

For additional information, refer to these resources:

Cisco Systems Inc. *Integrated Services Routers*, http://www.cisco.com/go/isr

Cisco Systems Inc. *Cisco Router and Security Device Manager Introduction*, http://www.cisco.com/go/sdm

Cisco Systems, Inc. *Cisco Router and Security Device Manager Quick Start Guide*, http://www.cisco.com/en/US/products/sw/secursw/ps5318/products_quick_start09186a0080511c89.html

Cisco Systems, Inc. *SDM Express 2.4 User's Guide*, http://www.cisco.com/en/US/docs/routers/access/cisco_router_and_security_device_manager/24/express/software/user/guide/esugd.html

Cisco Systems, Inc. *Tools & Resources: Software Download Cisco Security Device Manager*, http://www.cisco.com/pcgi-bin/tablebuild.pl/sdm

Cisco Systems, Inc. *Cisco Router and Security Device Manager 2.4 User's Guide 2.4*, http://www.cisco.com/en/US/products/sw/secursw/ps5318/products_user_guide_list.html

Cisco Systems, Inc. *Installing Cisco Secure ACS for Windows*, http://www.cisco.com/en/US/docs/net_mgmt/cisco_secure_access_control_server_for_windows/4.1/installation/guide/windows/install.html

Cisco Systems, Inc. *Cisco Secure Access Control Server for Windows: Release Notes*, http://www.cisco.com/en/US/products/sw/secursw/ps2086/prod_release_notes_list.html

Carroll, B., *Cisco Access Control Security: AAA Administration Services* (Cisco Press, 2004)

Cisco Systems, Inc. *Cisco Secure Access Control Server Express: Introduction*, http://www.cisco.com/en/US/products/ps8543/index.html

NTP RFC, http://www.faqs.org/rfcs/rfc1305.html

SNMP RFC, http://www.ietf.org/rfc/rfc2571.txt

Wikipedia. *Secure Shell*, http://en.wikipedia.org/wiki/Secure_Shell

Halleen, G. and Kellogg, G., *Security Monitoring with Cisco Security MARS* (Cisco Press, 2007)

Review Questions

Use the questions here to review what you learned in this chapter. The correct answers are found in the Appendix, "Answers to Chapter Review Questions."

1. What are the three areas of router security?

    a. Physical security

    b. Authentication server hardening

    c. Operating system

    d. Router hardening

2. Which of the following is the first step to secure Cisco router administrative access?

    a. Configure a AAA server

    b. Configure SDM access

    c. Configure secure system passwords

    d. Configure local database authentication

3. Which two statements are true about passwords?

    a. The console port does not require a password for console administrative access.

    b. Passwords can not include symbols and spaces.

    c. You can use either the enable password or the enable secret password to enter the enable mode when both are configured on a router.

    d. The enable secret password is always hashed inside the router configuration using a MD5 hashing algorithm.

4. How do you interpret the following console port command: **exec-timeout 3 30?**

    a. The connection closes after 3 minutes of inactivity and 30 minutes of absolute connectivity.

    b. The connection closes after 3 minutes and 30 seconds of inactivity.

    c. The connection closes after 3 hours of absolute connectivity and after 30 minutes of inactivity.

    d. The connection closes after 3 hours and 30 minutes of inactivity.

5. What is the purpose of the 5 in the following command: **username Admin secret 5 1feb0$a104Qd9UZ./Ak00KTggPD0?**

    a. The encrypted password will be converted to cleartext in the running-configuration using MD5.

    b. The user Admin has privilege level 5 in this router.

    c. The user Admin has 5 attempts to log in this router.

    d. The encrypted-secret password was hashed with MD5.

6. What is the purpose of the command **parser view**?

    a. It creates different views of router configuration for different users.

    b. It provides a root view of all commands.

    c. It configures a password for a view.

    d. It is used to enter commands accessible for that view.

7. Which command would you use to enable Cisco IOS resilience?

    a. secure boot-ios

    b. secure boot-config

    c. secure boot-image

    d. secure boot-flash

8. Which of the following is not a file required in flash if you want to run Cisco SDM from that router?

    a. sdm.tar

    b. common.tar

    c. home.html

    d. home.tar

9. True or False: Cisco SDM automatically synchronizes with the router configuration after a change?

    a. True

    b. False

10. Which SDM task would you use to configure One-Step Lockdown?

    a. Firewall and ACL

    b. Security Audit

    c. Intrusion prevention

    d. Additional tasks

11. What command is used to enable AAA on a router?

    a. aaa enable

    b. aaa authentication new-model

    c. aaa tacacs+

    d. aaa new-model

12. Which of the following is not supported by Cisco Secure ACS?

    a. StreetTalk Directory Services

    b. Novell Directory Services

    c. One-time passwords

    d. ODBC databases

13. Which portion of a RADIUS packet is sent in cleartext?

    a. All portions

    b. All portions except for the password

    c. All portions except for the CHAP password

    d. All portions except for the username

14. RADIUS is scheduled to be replaced by:

    a. PERIMETER

    b. CIRCUMFERENCE

    c. DIAMETER

    d. PI

15. What is meant by "out-of-band" management?

    a. The management traffic is sent through a control channel similar to the D channel in ISDN.

    b. The management traffic flows within a network on which no production traffic resides.

    c. The management traffic flows across the enterprise production network.

    d. The management traffic hogs most of the usable bandwidth.

16. What is the main advantage of Cisco Security MARS over a standard syslog server?

    a. Selective repository for syslog messages

    b. Limitless storage capacity

    c. Multipurpose response capabilities

    d. Central repository and analysis of syslog messages

17. Which is an advantage of using SSH rather than Telnet to establish a management connection to a router?

    a.   SSH is faster.

    b.   SSH uses less bandwidth.

    c.   SSH provides an encrypted connection.

    d.   SSH is readily available on all Cisco IOS routers.

18. Which of the following protocols is automatically enabled once RSA keys have been generated?

    a.   Telnet

    b.   SDM

    c.   SSH

    d.   HTTPS

19. What is the minimum recommended key length for RSA key pairs?

    a.   Modulus 1024

    b.   Modulus 512

    c.   56-bit encryption

    d.   128-bit encryption

20. What is the purpose of the **crypto key zeroize rsa** command?

    a.   To generate a new key pair

    b.   To establish the fully qualified domain name (FQDN)

    c.   To accept incoming connection on CON 0 and VTY 0

    d.   To override existing key pairs

This chapter teaches you how to configure firewall features, including access control lists (ACL) and Cisco IOS zone-based policy firewalls, to perform basic security operations on a network. At the end of this chapter, you will be able to do the following:

- Explain the operations of the different types of firewall technologies and describe the firewall technologies that are embedded in Cisco routers and Cisco security appliances

- Create static packet filters using access control lists

- Configure a Cisco IOS zone-based policy firewall on your network using the Cisco SDM Wizard

CHAPTER 3

Network Security Using Cisco IOS Firewalls

Implementing networkwide security can be a daunting task depending on the size and business of the company. Organizations must balance the cost in staff and equipment to implement a network security policy against the costs and possibility of network security breaches.

Cisco provides several router-based solutions for implementing firewall features: basic traffic filtering capabilities using access control lists (ACL), Cisco IOS Firewalls, and Cisco IOS zone-based policy firewalls. This chapter compares these three solutions.

Introducing Firewall Technologies

A firewall protects network devices from intentional hostile intrusion that could threaten information assurance (that is, availability, confidentiality, and integrity) or lead to a denial-of-service (DoS) attack. A firewall can protect a hardware device or a software program running on a secure host computer. This lesson introduces the firewall technologies that Cisco uses in routers and security appliances.

Firewall Fundamentals

The term *firewall* is a metaphor. By segmenting a network into different physical subnetworks, firewalls can limit the damage that can spread from one subnet to another, just as the fire doors and firewalls that are used in a building limit the spread of fire, heat, and structural collapse. In network security terms, a firewall is a software or hardware barrier between an internal (trusted) network and an external (untrusted) network. In this sense, a firewall is a set of related programs that enforce an access control policy between two or more networks.

In principle, as shown in Figure 3-1, a firewall is a pair of mechanisms that perform these two separate functions, which are set by policies:

■ One mechanism blocks bad traffic.

■ The second mechanism permits good traffic.

A firewall can be defined as follows:

A system or group of systems that enforces an access control policy between two networks. Because this definition is very generic, almost anything can be considered a firewall. Many network access technologies can be used to build a firewall:

■ Packet-filtering routers

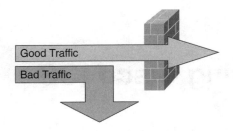

Figure 3-1 *Forward Acknowledgment*

- LAN switches

- Complex systems integrating many hosts into a firewall system

- Proxy servers

Firewalls mean different things to different organizations, and each organization has unique requirements. Nevertheless, all firewalls usually share some common properties:

- **Must be resistant to attacks:** The compromise of the firewall system should be very unlikely, because it would enable an attacker to disable the firewall or change its access rules.

- **Must be the only transit point between networks:** All traffic between networks must flow through the firewall. This requirement prevents a hacker from using a back-door connection to bypass the firewall and violate the network access policy.

- **Enforces the access control policy of an organization:** The access control policy should define what the firewall permits or denies.

Today, firewalls are such a mainstream technology that they are often considered a panacea for many security issues. While you should be aware of the benefits of the firewall model, you should also be aware of the many limitations that firewalls have and how to mitigate some of these limitations.

By performing network access control, you can use a firewall as a protective measure against the following:

- **Exposure of sensitive hosts and applications to untrusted users:** A firewall hides most of the functionality of a host and permits only the minimum required connectivity to a host. Complexity is thus reduced, and many possible vulnerabilities are not exposed.

- **Exploitation of protocol flaws:** You can program a firewall to inspect protocol messages and verify their compliance with the protocol, whether it is Layer 3, Layer 4, or a higher-layer protocol. The firewall limits what attackers can send to their target, preventing the delivery of malformed packets that are used in an attempt either to crash a system or to gain access to an application.

- **Malicious data:** A firewall can detect and block malicious data sent to clients or servers inside the application stream, thereby stopping it from infecting the server or the client. Because firewalls are located on critical interconnection points of the network, enforcing the network access policies is simple, scalable, and robust. Sometimes a small number of firewalls can handle most of the network access control needs of an organization.

Firewalls are often misunderstood, and false assumptions can be made about their capabilities. Although it is true that firewalls would not be necessary if host and application security could be made extremely robust, many organizations use firewalls as a replacement for host or application security. Such an attitude is extremely dangerous because it can completely ignore host and application security even in extreme cases, such as connecting a sensitive server inside an Internet firewall.

In general, firewalls have the following limitations:

- Because firewalls are used in critical points of the network, their misconfiguration can have disastrous consequences. Firewalls are often a single point of failure when it comes to security; a single mistake in a configuration rule or firewall code can compromise the network access policy.

- Many of the modern applications are firewall unfriendly because they are difficult to properly inspect. Compromises in rule design and inspection depth have to be made to support such applications, which might violate the policy of an organization. A typical example is a new application that opens dynamic sessions from the outside to the inside after the initial client request that was initiated from the inside to the outside. Multimedia applications such as those found with audio streaming and video-conferencing are examples of applications where the user opens one session from the inside to the outside requesting the feed. To support the streaming, however, additional sessions are opened from the outside to the inside, and by default the firewall will reject those new incoming requests. Once firewall vendors have a chance to study the new protocol, they can create a rule that will force the firewall to peek in the payload of the original outgoing packet to gain information about the additional sessions that will be created and to prepare for those new incoming sessions.

- End users, when faced with a restrictive firewall, might find their own methods of bypassing it. For example, inside users can dial out of the protected network to an Internet service provider (ISP) and create a backdoor connection to the protected network.

- Firewalls are placed at chokepoints, and can significantly affect performance if they inspect all the traffic.

- Tunneling unauthorized data over authorized connections (covert channels) is simple and generally impossible to detect. This activity usually requires the help of someone on the trusted side of the firewall.

Firewalls in a Layered Defense Strategy

In a layered defense scenario, firewalls provide perimeter security of the entire network and of internal network segments in the core. For example, system administrators can use a firewall to separate the human resources or financial networks of an organization from other networks or network segments within the organization.

A layered defense uses different types of firewalls that are combined in layers to add depth to the information defense of an organization, as shown in Figure 3-2. For example, traffic that comes in from the untrusted network first encounters a packet filter on the outer router. The traffic goes to the screened host firewall or bastion host system that applies more rules to the traffic and discards suspect packets. The traffic now goes to an interior screening router. The traffic moves to the internal destination host only after this routing. This type of demilitarized zone (DMZ) setup is called a *screened subnet configuration*.

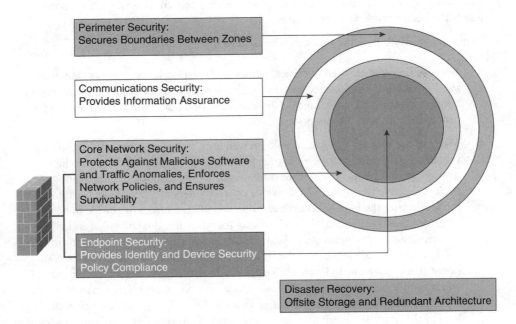

Figure 3-2   *Layered Defense Strategy*

Key Topic

Bastion host: A bastion host is a computer that is expected to be attacked and therefore is hardened. An example of a bastion host is firewall software installed on a workstation that is already running a commonly available operating system. The workstation would need to be hardened to protect against the potential vulnerability that the operating system has before the firewall being put in production.

Packet filter: An example of a packet filter is a router on which you have configured access lists to filter unwanted traffic.

The common misconception is that a layered firewall topology is all that you need to declare your internal network to be safe. This myth is probably encouraged by the booming firewall business; however, you need to consider the following factors when building a complete defense-in-depth environment:

■   A significant number of intrusions come from hosts within the network. For example, firewalls often do little to protect against viruses downloaded through email.

- Firewalls do not protect against rogue modem or rogue wireless access point installations. In addition, and most important, a firewall is not a substitute for informed administrators and users.

- Firewalls do not replace backup and disaster recovery mechanisms resulting from attack or hardware failure. An in-depth defense also includes offsite storage and redundant hardware topologies.

Defense in depth and diversity of defense are related topics. *Defense in depth* calls for multiple levels of defense, and *diversity of defense* calls for using different types of technologies in that defense.

An example of diversity of defense and defense in depth is using a perimeter router as a packet filter and using a stateful firewall to segment the unprotected segment from the protected segment.

Key Topic

Static Packet-Filtering Firewalls

Packet-filtering firewalls work primarily at the network layer of the Open Systems Interconnection (OSI) model, or the IP layer of TCP/IP, as shown in Figure 3-3. Packet-filtering firewalls are generally considered Layer 3 devices, but they typically have the capability to permit or deny traffic based on Layer 4 information, such as protocol, and source and destination port numbers, in addition to the Layer 3 source and destination IP address. Packet filtering uses rules and ACLs to determine whether to permit or deny traffic based on source and destination IP addresses, protocol, source and destination port numbers, and packet type. Packet-filtering firewalls are usually part of a router firewall.

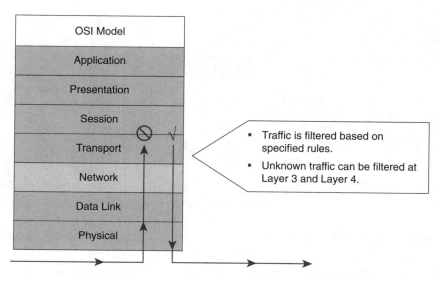

Figure 3-3 *How Static Packet Filters Mapped to the OSI Model*

Recall that services rely on specific ports to function, for example, Simple Mail Transfer Protocol (SMTP) servers listen to port 25 by default. Because packet-filtering firewalls filter traffic according to static packet header information, they are sometimes referred to as *static filters*. By restricting certain ports, you can restrict the services that rely on certain ports. For example, blocking port 25 on a specific workstation prevents an infected workstation from broadcasting email viruses across the Internet.

Packet-filtering firewalls are similar to packet-filtering routers but with some differences in implementation. Packet filters are very scalable, application independent, and have high performance standards; however, they do not offer the complete range of security solutions that are required in modern networks. For example, packet filter does not have the capability to understand dynamic protocols upon which a client request requires additional incoming connections to be initiated from the outside, toward the inside client.

Any device that uses ACLs can perform packet filtering. Cisco IOS router configurations commonly use ACLs, not only as packet-filtering firewalls but also to select specified types of traffic that is to be analyzed, forwarded, or influenced in some way. Later in this chapter, you will see examples of both ingress and egress filtering done with ACLs.

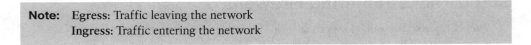

Note: **Egress:** Traffic leaving the network
Ingress: Traffic entering the network

Figure 3-4 shows a simple packet-filtering example using a Cisco router.

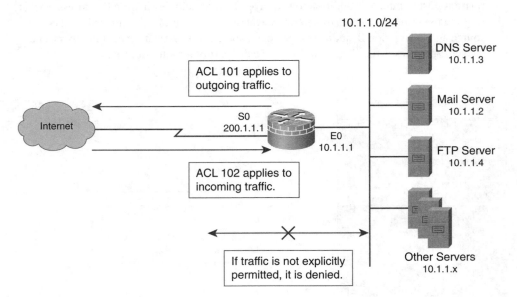

Figure 3-4   *A Static Packet Filter in Action*

In most network topologies, you need to protect the Ethernet interface connecting to the internal (inside) network, while the serial interface that connects to the Internet (outside) is unprotected. In Figure 3-4, the internal addresses that the firewall must protect are in the 10.1.1.0/24 subnet (on the Ethernet interface). The IP address of the Ethernet 0 interface is 10.1.1.1/24.

The particular network security policy shown in Figure 3-4 (ACL 101) allows all users from the inside to access Internet services on the outside. Therefore, all outgoing connections are accepted. The router checks only packets coming from the Internet (security policy ACL 102). In this case, the ACL allows Domain Name System (DNS), SMTP, FTP services, and the return of traffic initiated from the inside. ACL 102 denies access to all other services.

Packet-filter firewalls (or packet filters) use a simple policy table lookup that permits or denies traffic based on the following possible criteria:

- Source IP address

- Destination IP address

- Source port number

- Destination port numbers

- Synchronize/start (SYN) packet receipt

The firewalls are extremely fast because they do little computation. The rules are extremely easy to implement because they require little security expertise. Router manufacturers easily embed packet-filtering logic in silicon and, consequently, packet filtering is a feature of most routers. Packet-filtering firewalls are relatively inexpensive. Even if other firewalls are used, implementing packet filtering at the router level affords an initial degree of security at the network and transport layers.

Packet filters do not represent a complete firewall solution. However, they are a key element of a secure architecture.

The following are disadvantages of packet filters:

- Packet filtering is susceptible to IP spoofing. Hackers send arbitrary packets that fit ACL criteria and pass through the filter.

- Packet filters do not filter fragmented packets well. Because fragmented IP packets carry the TCP header in the first fragment and packet filters filter on TCP header information, all fragments after the first fragment are passed unconditionally. Decisions to use packet filters assume that the filter of the first fragment accurately enforces the policy.

- Complex ACLs are difficult to implement and maintain correctly.

- Packet filters cannot dynamically filter certain services. For example, sessions that use dynamic port negotiations are difficult to filter without opening access to a whole range of ports.

- Packet filters are stateless. They examine each packet individually rather than in the context of the state of a connection.

Application Layer Gateways

Application layer firewalls, also called proxy firewalls or application gateways, provide a higher level of security than packet-filtering firewalls because they allow the greatest level of control. Application-level proxy servers operate on Layers 3, 4, 5, and 7 of the OSI model, as shown in Figure 3-5.

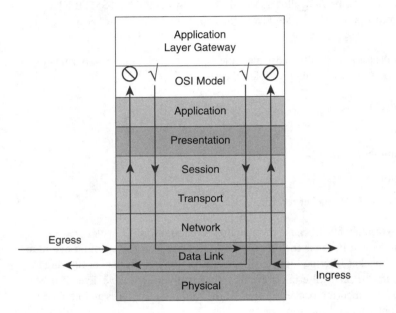

Figure 3-5   *Application Layer Gateway in Action*

Most application layer firewalls include specialized application software and proxy servers. A proxy is an application that does work on behalf of something else. Proxy services are special-purpose programs that manage traffic through a firewall for a specific service, such as HTTP or FTP. Proxy services are specific to the protocol that they are designed to forward, and they can provide increased access control, careful detailed checks for valid data, and generate audit records about the traffic that they transfer.

Proxy firewalls act as intermediaries between networks to determine whether to allow the communication to proceed. No direct connection exists between an outside user and internal network resources, because the original connection stops in the proxy and a new connection is set between the proxy and the outside destination. For this reason, the only IP address of the network that is visible from the Internet is the IP address of the outside interface of the proxy. The client connects to the proxy server and submits an application layer request. The application layer request includes the true destination and the data request itself. The proxy server analyzes the request and can filter or change the packet contents. The server makes a copy of each incoming packet, changes the source address, and sends the packet to the destination address. The destination server replies to the proxy server, and the proxy server passes the response back to the client.

Sometimes, application layer firewalls support only a limited number of applications, or even just one application. Some of the more common applications that an application layer firewall might support include email, web services, DNS, Telnet, FTP, Usenet news, Lightweight Directory Access Protocol (LDAP), and Finger.

Application layer firewalls provide several advantages:

- **Application layer firewalls authenticate individuals, not devices:** These firewalls typically allow you to authenticate connection requests before allowing traffic to an internal or external resource. This process enables you to authenticate the user requesting the connection instead of authenticating the device.

- **Application layer firewalls make it is harder for hackers to spoof and implement DoS attacks:** An application layer firewall enables you to prevent most spoofing attacks, and DoS attacks are limited to the application firewall itself. The application firewall can detect DoS attacks, and thus reduce the burden on your internal resources.

- **Application layer firewalls can monitor and filter application data:** You can monitor all data on a connection, so you can detect application attacks such as malformed URLs, buffer-overflow attempts, unauthorized access, and more. You can even control the commands or functions you allow an individual to perform based on the authentication and authorization information.

- **Application layer firewalls can provide detailed logging:** Using application layer firewalls, you can generate detailed logs and monitor the actual data that the individual is sending across a connection. This logging can prove extremely useful if a hacker finds a new type of attack, because you can monitor what the hacker does and how the machine does it, and then address the attack. Besides using logging for security purposes, you can use it for management purposes by keeping track of who is accessing what resources, how much bandwidth is used, and how often a user accesses the resources.

The topology in Figure 3-6 represents a typical proxy server deployment. The example in Figure 3-6 shows a client inside the network requesting access to a website. The client browser uses a proxy server for all HTTP requests. Network security policies force all client connections to go through the proxy server. As shown, the browser connects to the proxy server to make requests. Client-side DNS queries and client-side routing to the Internet are not needed when using a proxy server. The client has to reach only the proxy server to make the request.

When the proxy server receives the request from a client, it performs user authentication according to the rules applied to it and uses its Internet connection to access the requested website. It forwards only Layer 3 and Layer 4 packets that match the firewall rules. On the return route, the proxy server forwards only Layer 5 and Layer 7 messages and content that the server allows (that is, traffic that is not seen as malicious) according to the firewall rules.

In spite of how application layer firewalls work, this firewall provides only a limited number of services; however it provides the highest level of filtering for those specific protocols.

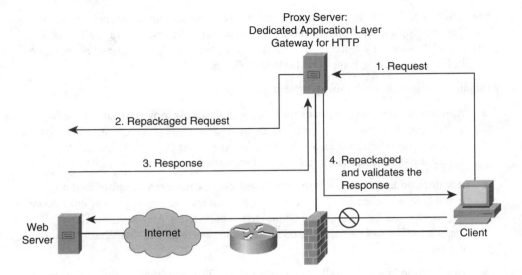

Figure 3-6 *Proxy Server Communication Process*

The main limitation of application layer firewalls is that they are process intensive because the server evaluates a significant amount of information embedded in many packets. This type of technology requires many CPU cycles and a lot of memory to process every packet that needs inspection, which sometimes creates throughput problems. In addition, the detailed logging can create disk space problems. To address these issues, you can use one of two solutions:

■   **A context transfer protocol:** Using a context transfer protocol, where identity-specific information tracks users, enables you to perform only authentication and authorization; you cannot monitor data on the connection, only whether the user is authorized to go on the Internet. With this solution however, we cannot talk per se of real firewalling because packets are not checked for their content, but rather based on the validity of the source and destination. It would be similar to a packet filter that has the capability of learning dynamically source and destination and match return traffic on that information it learned dynamically.

■   **Monitor only key applications:** With this solution, you limit the application layer firewall to process only certain application types (such as email, Telnet, FTP, or web services), and then, perhaps, process only connections to specific internal resources. The problem with this approach is that you are not monitoring all applications and connections, and this creates a security weakness.

Application layer firewalls typically do not support all applications, such as multimedia or peer-to-peer file sharing (to name a few). Instead, they are generally limited to one or a few connection types, typically common applications, such as email, Telnet, FTP, and web services. Therefore, you cannot monitor data on all applications: It monitors data only on applications it intrinsically understands.

Finally, application layer firewalls sometimes require you to install vendor-specific software on the client, which the firewall uses to handle the authentication process and any possible connection redirection. This limitation can create scalability and management problems if you must support thousands of clients.

Dynamic or Stateful Packet-Filtering Firewalls

Stateful packet filters, or stateful firewalls, are the most versatile and therefore the most common firewall technologies in use. Stateful filtering provides dynamic packet-filtering capabilities to firewalls. Stateful inspection is a firewall architecture that is classified at the network layer, although for some applications it can analyze traffic at Layers 4 and Layer 5, too, as shown in Figure 3-7. Some stateful firewalls can analyze traffic up to Layer 7 under special circumstances and additional configuration.

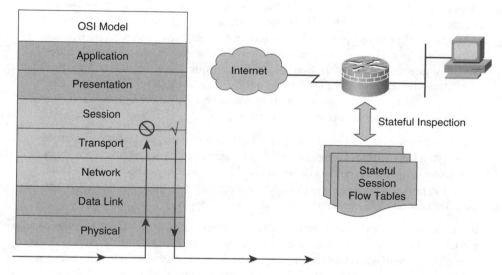

Figure 3-7   *Stateful Packet-Filtering Firewall*

Unlike static packet filtering, which examines a packet based on the information in its header, stateful inspection tracks each connection traversing all interfaces of the firewall and confirms that they are valid. Stateful packet filtering maintains a state table and allows modification of the security rules on-the-fly. The state table is part of the internal structure of the firewall and tracks all sessions and inspects all packets passing through the firewall. If packets have the expected properties that are predicted by the state table, the firewall allows them to pass. The state table changes dynamically according to traffic flow.

Stateful firewalls use a state table to keep track of the actual communication process. From a transport layer perspective, the firewall examines information in the headers of Layer 3 packets and Layer 4 segments. For example, the firewall looks at the TCP header for SYN, reset (RST), acknowledgment (ACK), FIN, and other control codes to determine the state of the connection. In this scenario, the session layer is responsible for establishing and tearing down the connection.

When an outside service is accessed, the stateful packet filter firewall "remembers" certain details of the request by saving the state of the request in the state table. Each time a TCP or User Datagram Protocol (UDP) connection is established for inbound or outbound connections, the firewall logs the information in a stateful session flow table. When the outside system responds to the request, the firewall server compares the received packets with the saved state to allow or deny network access.

The stateful session flow table contains the source and destination addresses, port numbers, UDP connection information and TCP sequencing information, and additional flags for each TCP connection associated with a particular session. This information creates a connection object against which the firewall compares all inbound and outbound packets. The firewall permits data only if an appropriate connection exists to validate the passage of that data.

More advanced stateful firewalls include the capability to parse FTP port commands and update the state table to allow FTP to work transparently through the firewall. Advanced stateful firewalls can also provide TCP sequence number randomization, and DNS query and response matching to ensure that the firewall allows packets to return only in response to queries that originate from inside the network. These features reduce the threat of TCP RST flood attacks and DNS cache poisoning. Some stateful firewalls can also check the validity of protocol commands to ensure that only more intrusive and dangerous commands are not admitted on our network.

There is a potential disadvantage of using stateful filtering that you must consider. Although stateful inspection provides speed and transparency, packets inside the network must make their way to the outside network. This can possibly expose internal IP addresses to potential hackers. Most firewalls incorporate stateful inspection, Network Address Translation (NAT), and proxy servers for added security.

To overcome this disadvantage, stateful firewalls keep track of the state of a connection and whether the connection is in an initiation, data transfer, or termination state. This information is useful when you want to deny the initiation of connections from external devices but allow your users to establish connections to these devices and permit the responses to come back through the stateful firewall.

Figure 3-8 shows a successfully established HTTP TCP session that leads to a dynamic ACL rule entry on the outside interface that permits response packets from the web server to the client.

Stateful packet-filtering firewalls are good to use for the following applications:

- **As a primary means of defense:** In most situations, a stateful firewall is used as a primary means of defense by filtering unwanted, unnecessary, or undesirable traffic.

- **As an intelligent first line of defense:** Networks use routing devices that support a stateful function as a first line of defense or as an additional security boost on perimeter routers.

- **As a means of strengthening packet filtering:** Stateful filtering provides more stringent control over security than packet filtering does, without adding too much cost.

- **To improve routing performance:** Stateful packet-filtering devices perform better than packet filters or proxy servers. Stateful firewalls do not require a large range of

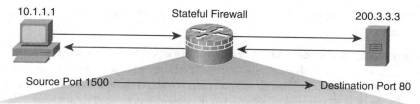

Inside ACL (Outgoing Traffic)	Outside ACL (Incoming Traffic)
permit ip 10.0.0.0 0.0.0.255 any	Dynamic: permit tcp host 200.3.3.3 eq 80 host 10.1.1.1 eq 1500 permit tcp any host 10.1.1.2 eq 25 permit udp any host 10.1.1.2 eq 53 deny ip any any

Figure 3-8 *Stateful Packet Filtering*

port numbers to allow returning traffic back into the network, providing that the firewall is familiar with the protocol and its behavior. The state table determines whether a packet is returning traffic. If it is not returning traffic, the filtering table filters the traffic.

- **As a defense against spoofing and DoS attacks:** Stateful packet filtering works on packets and connections. In particular, stateful firewalls track the state of the connection in the state table listing every connection or connectionless transaction. By determining whether packets belong to an existing connection or are from an unauthorized source, stateful firewalls allow only traffic from connections that are listed in the table. As an example, during the three-way handshake of a TCP session, the firewall tracks the flag and therefore can predict what the following exchange between the client and the server will be. When the firewall removes a connection from the state table (for instance, because of the connection termination following the TCP four-way handshake as a goodbye), the firewall does not allow any more traffic from that device. In addition, the stateful firewall can log more information than a packet-filtering firewall can, including when a connection was set up, how long it was up, and when it was torn down. This logging makes connections harder to spoof.

Stateful firewalls have the following limitations:

- **Stateful firewalls cannot prevent application layer attacks:** For example, your network might allow traffic to port 80 on a web server. Your stateful firewall examines the destination address in the Layer 3 packet and the destination port number in the segment. If there is a match, the stateful firewall allows the incoming and outgoing traffic. One problem with this approach is that the stateful firewall does not examine the actual contents of the HTTP connection.

- **Not all protocols are stateful:** UDP and Internet Control Message Protocol (ICMP) are not stateful, so stateful firewalls can provide only limited support for these protocols. For example, UDP has no defined process for how to set up, maintain, and tear down a connection. Routers define UDP connections on an application-by-application basis.

- **Some applications open multiple connections:** On earlier (more basic) stateful firewalls, if the client was inside the network and the server was outside the network, both stateful and packet-filtering firewalls had problems dealing with the data connection that the FTP server established to the client. You needed to open a whole range of ports to allow this second connection. Cisco IOS Firewall does not have this problem.

- **Stateful firewalls do not support user authentication:** Stateful firewall technology itself does not support user authentication. Add-on functionality is required to provide a feature such as proxy authentication.

Other Types of Firewalls

Over the years, variations of standards stateful firewalls have emerged. Some examples of those variations, which provide additional or restrictive features, are deep packet inspection (DPI) firewalls and Layer 2 firewalls.

Application inspection firewalls ensure the security of applications and services. Some applications require special handling by the firewall application inspection function. Applications that require special application inspection functions are those that embed IP addressing information in the user data packet or that open secondary channels on dynamically assigned ports.

The application inspection function works with NAT to help identify the location of the embedded addressing information. This arrangement allows NAT to translate embedded addresses and to update any checksum or other fields that are affected by the translation.

The application inspection function also monitors sessions to determine the port numbers for secondary channels. Many protocols open secondary TCP or UDP ports. The initial session on a well-known port negotiates dynamically assigned port numbers. The application inspection function monitors these sessions, identifies the dynamic port assignments, and permits data exchange on these ports for the duration of the specific session.

An application inspection firewall behaves in different ways according to each layer:

- **Transport layer mechanism:** From a transport layer perspective, the application inspection firewall acts like a stateful firewall by examining information in the headers of Layer 3 packets and Layer 4 segments. For example, the application inspection firewall looks at the TCP header for SYN, RST, ACK, FIN, and other control codes to determine the state of the connection.

- **Session layer mechanism:** From a session layer perspective, the application inspection firewall checks the conformity of commands within a known protocol. For example, when the application inspection firewall checks the SMTP message type, it allows only acceptable message types on Layer 5 (such as, DATA, HELO, MAIL, NOOP, QUIT, RCPT, RSET). In addition, the application inspection firewall checks whether the command attributes that are used (for example, length of a message type) conform to the internal rules. These rules often trust the RFC of a specific protocol.

- **Application layer mechanism:** From an application layer perspective, the application inspection firewall protocol is rarely supported. Sometimes application layer firewalls provide protocol support for HTTP, and the application inspection firewall can determine whether the content is really an HTML website or a tunneled application, such as Kazaa Media Desktop or eDonkey. In the case of a tunneled application, the application inspection firewall would block the content or terminate the connection. Future development will provide application inspection support for more protocols on an application inspection firewall.

There are several advantages of an application inspection firewall:

- Application inspection firewalls are aware of the state of Layer 4 and Layer 5 connections. For example, the application inspection firewall knows that a Layer 5 SMTP MAIL FROM command always follows a HELO command.

- Application inspection firewalls check the conformity of application commands at Layer 5.

- Application inspection firewalls have the capability to check and affect Layer 7.

- Application inspection firewalls can prevent more kinds of attacks than stateful firewalls can. For example, application inspection firewalls can stop an attacker from trying to set up a virtual private network (VPN) tunnel (triggered from inside the network) through an application firewall by way of tunneled HTTP requests.

Cisco PIX and Cisco ASA Adaptive Security Appliance Software Version 7.0 and Cisco Firewall Services Module Version 2.2 debut the capability to deploy a security appliance in a secure bridging mode as a Layer 2 device to provide rich Layer 2 through 7 security services for the protected network. This capability enables businesses to deploy security appliances into existing network environments without the need to readdress the network. Although the security appliance can be invisible to devices on both sides of a protected network, as shown in Figure 3-9, administrators can use an exposed IP address to manage the appliance.

Note: Layer 2 firewalls also known as transparent firewalls are sometimes referred to as *bumps in the wire* or as *stealth firewalls.*

Tip: Additional training is available on transparent firewalls in the Cisco Secure ASA Adaptive Security Appliance courses that are offered by Cisco Learning Partners.

Cisco Family of Firewalls

Cisco offers firewalls on different platforms:

- Cisco IOS Firewalls

- Cisco PIX 500 series Security Appliances

- Cisco ASA 5500 series Adaptive Security Appliances

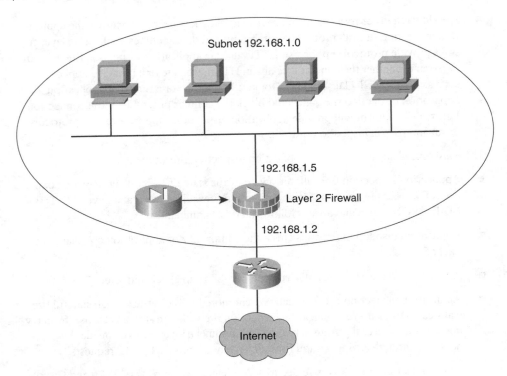

Figure 3-9   *Layer 2 Firewall*

- Cisco Firewall Services Module (FWSM)

The sections that follow describe these platforms in greater detail.

Cisco IOS Firewalls

A Cisco IOS Firewall is a specialized Cisco IOS feature that runs on Cisco routers. It is an enterprise-class firewall product that is rich with features for small and medium-sized businesses (SMB) and enterprise branch offices. The following are some of the main features of a Cisco IOS Firewall:

- Zone-based policy framework for intuitive policy management

- Application firewalling for web, email, and other traffic

- Instant messenger and peer-to-peer application filtering

- VoIP protocol firewalling

- Virtual routing and forwarding (VRF) firewalling

- Wireless integration

- Stateful failover

- Local URL whitelist and blacklist support

Another important feature of Cisco IOS Firewalls, deployed on specific models, is the assurance of its security standard known as FIPS 140.

The Federal Information Processing Standard (FIPS) 140 is a U.S. government and Canadian government standard that specifies security requirements for cryptographic modules. FIPS 140 has four levels of assurance. Level 1 is the lowest level, and Level 4 is the most stringent. Each level builds upon the one below it, so a Level 2 certification means that a product meets the requirements for both Level 1 and Level 2.

Note: To find out precisely the level of certification of different Cisco products, visit http://csrc.nist.gov/groups/STM/cmvp/documents/140-1/140val-all.htm.

Another benefit of Cisco security platforms is their conformance to Common Criteria.

The Common Criteria is an international standard for evaluating IT security. It was developed by a consortium of countries to replace a number of existing country-specific security assessment processes, and was intended to establish a single standard for international use. Currently, the Common Criteria is officially recognized by 14 countries, and evaluations can be conducted by any certified Common Criteria laboratory in a member country. To maintain the independent nature of the Common Criteria, evaluation results from a certified lab are submitted to the Common Criteria organization of the corresponding country for independent validation. This independent validation process, which distinguishes Common Criteria from some commercial certifications, ensures that the evaluation process is consistent across labs, and that it cannot be influenced by financial motives.

Table 3-1 illustrates for which security certifications the routers in the Cisco router family qualify.

Table 3-1   *Cisco Security Routers Certifications*

	FIPS	Common Criteria	
	140-2, Level 2	IPsec (EAL4)	Firewall (EAL4)
Cisco 870 ISR	✓	Pending	✓
Cisco 1800 ISR	✓	Pending	✓
Cisco 2800 ISR	✓	Pending	✓
Cisco 3800 ISR	✓	Pending	✓
Cisco 7200 VAM2+	✓	Pending	✓
Cisco 7200 VSA	✓	Pending	N/A
Cisco 7301 VAM2+	✓	Pending	✓
Cisco 7600 IPsec VPN SPA	✓	Pending	N/A
Catalyst 6500 IPsec VPN SPA	✓	Pending	N/A

Table 3-1 *Cisco Security Routers Certifications*

	FIPS	Common Criteria	
	140-2, Level 2	IPsec (EAL4)	Firewall (EAL4)
Cisco 7600	✓	Pending	✓

Check http://www.cisco.com for the latest certifications of Cisco hardware and software. You may also check the following:

For FIPS 140: http://csrc.nist.gov/groups/STM/cmvp/documents/140-1/140val-all.htm

For CVE: http://www.niap-ccevs.org/cc-scheme/

Note: Because it is not possible to "prove" that a product is secure, the greater the number of tests, the greater the confidence (or assurance) in its quality. To achieve the top certifications takes a considerable number of years and expense.

Cisco PIX 500 Series Security Appliances

The Cisco PIX 500 series Security Appliance delivers robust user and application policy enforcement, multivector attack protection, and secure connectivity services in cost-effective, easy-to-deploy solutions. These purpose-built appliances provide multiple integrated security and networking services:

- Advanced application-aware firewall services

- Market-leading VoIP and multimedia security

- Robust site-to-site and remote-access IPsec VPN connectivity

- Award-winning resiliency

- Intelligent networking services

- Flexible management solutions

The Cisco PIX 500 series Security Appliances scale to meet a range of requirements and network sizes. The Cisco PIX 500 series Security Appliances currently consists of five models: the PIX 501, 506E, 515E, 525, and 535. Figure 3-10 provides a visual reference of the PIX 500 family of products.

Note: In January 2008, Cisco announced the End-of-Life for the PIX products. Cisco will still be supporting this product until July 2013.

Note: Additional training is available for the Cisco PIX 500 series in the Cisco Secure ASA Adaptive Security Appliance courses that are offered by Cisco Learning Partners.

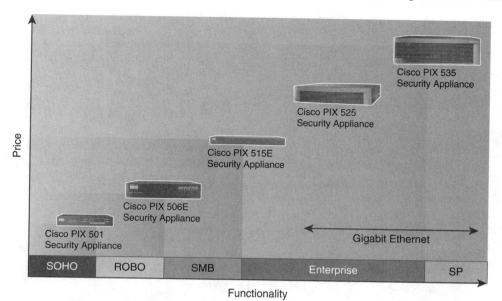

Figure 3-10   *Cisco PIX 500 Series Security Appliances*

Cisco ASA 5500 Series Adaptive Security Appliances

Cisco ASA 5500 series Adaptive Security Appliances are easy-to-deploy solutions that integrate world-class firewall, Cisco Unified Communications (voice and video) security, Secure Sockets Layer (SSL) and IPsec VPN, IPS, and content security services in a flexible, modular product family. Designed as a key component of the Cisco Self-Defending Network, the ASA 5500 series appliances provide intelligent threat defense and secure communications services that stop attacks before they affect business continuity. Designed to protect networks of all sizes, the ASA 5500 series appliances enable organizations to lower their overall deployment and operations costs while delivering comprehensive multilayer security.

The Cisco ASA scales to meet a range of requirements and network sizes, as shown in Figure 3-11. The Cisco ASA 5500 series appliances currently consist of five models: the Cisco ASA 5505, 5510, 5520, 5540, and 5550.

Note: Additional training is available for the ASA 5500 series Security Appliances in the Cisco Secure ASA Adaptive Security Appliance courses that are offered by Cisco Learning Partners.

Cisco Firewall Services Module

The Cisco Firewall Services Module (FWSM) is a high-speed, integrated firewall module (commonly called a "blade") for Cisco Catalyst 6500 switches and Cisco 7600 series routers and provides the fastest firewall data rates in the industry. Up to four FWSMs can be installed in a single switch chassis. Based on Cisco PIX Firewall technology, the Cisco FWSM offers large enterprises and service providers unmatched security, reliability, and performance.

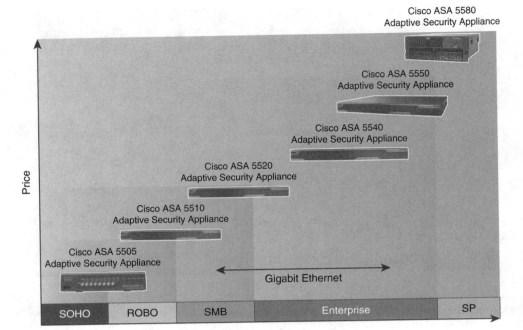

Figure 3-11   *Cisco ASA 5500 Series Adaptive Security Appliances*

Developing an Effective Firewall Policy

Best practice documents are a composite effort of security practitioners. This partial list is designed to be generic and serve only as a starting point for your own firewall security policy:

- Position firewalls at key security boundaries.

- Firewalls are the primary security device, but it is unwise to rely exclusively on a firewall for security.

- Deny all traffic by default and permit only services that are needed.

- Ensure that physical access to the firewall is controlled.

- Regularly monitor firewall logs. Cisco Security Monitoring, Analysis, and Response System (MARS) is especially useful in monitoring firewall logs.

- Practice change management for firewall configuration changes.

- Remember that firewalls primarily protect from technical attacks originating from the outside. Inside attacks tend to be nontechnical in nature, such as accidentally deleting a mission-critical data, or accidentally unplugging a device, thus creating a DoS attack, albeit an unintentional one.

Tip: For more information about firewall best practices, visit the following sites:
- http://www.principlelogic.com/docs/Firewall_Best_Practices.pdf
- http://www.nsa.gov/snac/index.cfm?MenuID=scg10.3.1
- http://iase.disa.mil/stigs/stig/index.html
- http://cisecurity.org/bench.html

Creating Static Packet Filters Using ACLs

Cisco provides basic traffic filtering capabilities with ACLs. You can configure ACLs for all routed network protocols to filter packets as the packets pass through a router or security appliance. There are many reasons to configure ACLs. For example, you can use ACLs to restrict the contents of routing updates or to provide traffic flow control. One of the most important reasons to configure ACLs is to provide security for your network.

This section outlines the types of ACLs available and provides guidelines that help create ACLs to provide network security.

ACL Fundamentals

ACLs provide packet filtering for routers and firewalls to protect internal networks from the outside world. ACLs filter network traffic in both directions by controlling whether to forward or block packets at the router interfaces based on the criteria that you specify within the ACLs. ACL criteria could be the source address of the traffic, the destination address of the traffic, the upper-layer protocol, or other information. Be aware, however, that sophisticated users (hackers) can sometimes successfully evade or fool basic ACLs because not only is authentication not required, but mainly because of the inability of an ACL to track the state of a connection.

ACLs provide a basic level of security for accessing your network. If you do not configure ACLs on your router, all packets passing through the router could get to all parts of your network. You can use ACLs on a router that is positioned between two parts of your network to control traffic entering or exiting a specific part of your internal network. An ACL on the router allows one host to access a part of your network and prevents another host from accessing the same area. The ACL shown in Figure 3-12 allows Host A to access the Human Resources network but prevents Host B from accessing the Human Resources network.

To provide the security benefits of ACLs, you should, at a minimum, configure ACLs at the perimeter of your networks. This configuration provides a basic buffer from the outside network, or from a less-controlled area of your own network, into a more sensitive area of your network. On these network edge routers, you should configure ACLs for each network protocol that is configured on the router interfaces.

You can use ACLs to mitigate many threats:

- IP address spoofing (inbound)
- IP address spoofing (outbound)
- DoS TCP SYN attacks (blocking external attacks)
- DoS TCP SYN attacks (using TCP intercept)
- DoS Smurf attacks
- Filtering ICMP messages (inbound)
- Filtering ICMP messages (outbound)

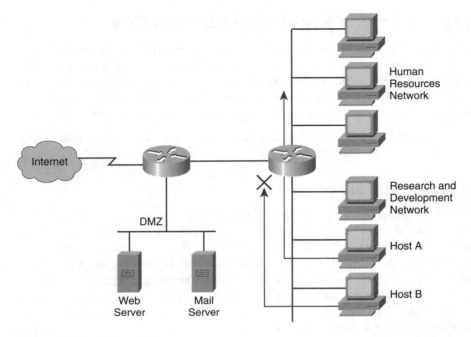

Figure 3-12 *Using ACLs*

■   Filtering traceroute

Cisco routers use ACLs as packet filters to decide which packets can access a router service or cross an interface. Packets that are allowed across an interface are permitted packets. Packets that are not allowed across an interface are denied packets.

An ACL enforces one or more corporate security policies. For example, a corporate security policy might only allow packets using source addresses from within the trusted network to access the Internet. Once this policy is written, you can develop an ACL that includes certain statements that, when applied to a router interface, can implement this policy.

Cisco router security depends strongly on well-written ACLs to restrict access to router network services and to filter packets as they traverse the router.

ACLs express the set of rules that give added control for packets that enter inbound interfaces, packets that relay through the router, and packets that exit outbound interfaces of the router. ACLs do not act on packets that originate from the router itself. Instead, ACLs are statements that specify conditions of how the router handles the traffic flow through specified interfaces.

ACLs operate in two ways:

■   **Inbound:** Incoming packets are processed before they are routed to an outbound interface. An inbound ACL is efficient because it saves the overhead of routing lookups if the packet will be discarded after it is denied by the filtering tests. If the packet is permitted by the tests, it is then processed for routing.

- **Outbound:** Packets arriving on the inside interface are routed to the outbound interface, and then they are processed through the outbound ACL.

Figure 3-13 shows an example of an outbound ACL. When a packet enters an interface, the router checks the routing table to see whether the packet is routable. If the packet is not routable, it is dropped.

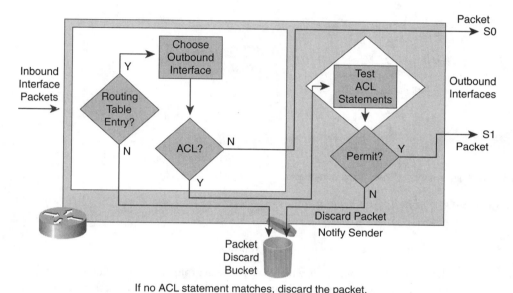

If no ACL statement matches, discard the packet.

Figure 3-13   *Outbound ACL Operation*

Next, the router checks to see whether the destination interface is grouped to an ACL. If the destination interface is not grouped to an ACL, the packet can be sent to the output buffer. Examples of outbound ACL operation are as follows:

- If the outbound interface is S0, which has not been grouped to an outbound ACL, the packet is sent to S0 directly.

- If the outbound interface is S1, which has been grouped to an outbound ACL, the packet is not sent out on S1 until it is tested by the combination of ACL statements that are associated with that interface. Based on the ACL tests, the packet is permitted or denied.

For outbound lists, *to permit* means to send the packet to the output buffer, and *to deny* means to discard the packet.

With an inbound ACL, when a packet enters an interface, the router checks to see whether the source interface is grouped to an ACL. If the source interface is not grouped to an ACL, the router checks the routing table to see whether the packet is routable. If the packet is not routable, the router drops the packet. Figure 3-14 shows an example of an inbound ACL.

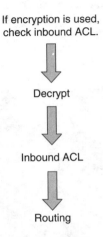

If encryption is used,
check inbound ACL.

Decrypt

Inbound ACL

Routing

If no ACL statement matches, discard the packet.

Figure 3-14   *Inbound ACL Operation*

Examples of inbound ACL operation are as follows:

■ If the inbound interface is E0, which has not been grouped to an inbound ACL, the packet is processed normally and the router checks to determine whether the packet is routable.

■ If the inbound interface is E1, which has been grouped to an inbound ACL, the packet is not processed and the routing table is not consulted until the packet is tested by the ACL that is associated with that interface. Based on the ACL tests, the packet is permitted or denied.

For inbound lists, *permit* means to continue to process the packet after receiving it on an inbound interface, and *deny* means to discard the packet.

Note: If encryption is used, the inbound ACL is checked first to see whether the encryption traffic is permitted. If permitted, the traffic is then decrypted and again compared to the ACL.

ACL statements operate in a sequential, logical order, as shown in Figure 3-15. They evaluate packets from the top down, one statement at a time. If a packet header and an ACL statement match, the rest of the statements in the list are skipped, and the packet is permitted or denied as determined by the matched statement. If a packet header does not match an ACL statement, the packet is tested against the next statement in the list. This matching process continues until the end of the list is reached.

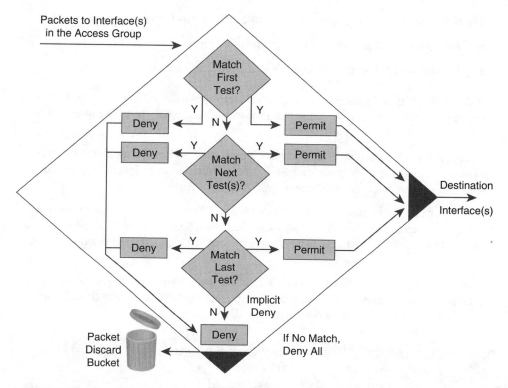

Figure 3-15 *Top-Down Process of Tests: Deny or Permit*

A final implied statement covers all packets for which conditions did not test true. This final test condition matches all other packets and results in a "deny" instruction. Instead of proceeding into or out of an interface, the router drops all of these remaining packets. This final statement is often referred to as the "implicit **deny any** statement." Because of this statement, an ACL should have at least one **permit** statement in it; otherwise, the ACL blocks all traffic.

Types of IP ACLs

Cisco routers support two types of IP ACLs:

- **Standard ACLs:** Standard IP ACLs check the source addresses of packets that can be routed. The result either permits or denies the output for an entire protocol suite, based on the source network, subnet, or host IP address.

- **Extended ACLs:** Extended IP ACLs check both the source and destination packet addresses. They can also check for specific protocols, port numbers, and other parameters, which allows administrators more flexibility and control.

The two general methods you can use to create ACLs are as follows:

- **Numbered ACLs:** Use a number for identification.

- **Named ACLs:** Use an alphanumeric string for identification.

Before Cisco IOS Software Release 11.2, you had to assign a number to each ACL as you created it. Since then, either a number or a name can identify Cisco ACLs and the protocols that they filter.

Using numbered ACLs is an effective method on smaller networks with more homogeneously defined traffic. Because each ACL type is limited to an assigned range of numbers, it is easy to determine the type of ACL that you are using.

Specifying an ACL number from 1 to 99 or 1300 to 1999 instructs the router to accept numbered standard IP Version 4 (IPv4) ACL statements. Specifying an ACL number from 100 to 199 or 2000 to 2699 instructs the router to accept numbered extended IPv4 ACL statements.

The named ACL feature allows you to identify IP standard and extended ACLs with an alphanumeric string (name) rather than the numeric representations. Named IP ACLs provide you more flexibility in working with the ACL entries.

Tip: The number of the ACL determines which protocol it is filtering.
1 to 99 and 1300 to 1999 define standard IP ACLs.

100 to 199 and 2000 to 2699 define extended IP ACLs.

Named ACLs have been available since Cisco IOS Software Releases 11.2. Names contain alphanumeric characters.

Names cannot contain spaces or punctuation and must begin with an alphabetic character.

Named ACLs enable you to add or delete entries within the ACL.

There are several benefits to IP access list entry sequence numbering:

- You can edit the order of ACL statements.

- You can remove individual statements from an ACL.

Where additions are placed in an ACL depends on whether you use sequence numbers. There is no support for sequence numbering in software versions earlier than Cisco IOS Software Release 12.3; therefore, all the ACL additions for earlier software versions are placed at the end of the ACL. This means that should you deny a protocol, for example, but then decide to add a **permit** statement for a specific host who needs to use that protocol, this new **permit** statement would be placed below the **deny** statement stipulating that all traffic for that application be denied. With older versions, it is a question of first match, not necessarily best match.

IP access list entry sequence numbering is a new edition to Cisco IOS Software that allows you to use sequence numbers to easily add, remove, or reorder statements in an IP

ACL. With Cisco IOS Release 12.3 and later, you can place additions anywhere in the ACL based on the sequence number, providing that you use an unused sequence number. You might need to resequence your access list if you need to create unused sequence numbers.

Earlier than Cisco IOS Release 12.3, only named ACLs allow the removal of individual statements from an ACL using the **no**{**deny** | **permit**} *protocol source source-wildcard destination destination-wildcard* command, where the *protocol source source-wildcard destination destination-wildcard* parameters match the line you are trying to remove. With numbered ACLs, you would have to remove the whole list and re-create it with the desired statements. With Cisco IOS Software Release 12.3 and later, you can also use the **no** *sequence-number* command to delete a specific access list entry.

Well-designed and well-implemented ACLs add an important security component to your network. Follow these general principles to ensure that the ACLs you create have the intended results:

- Based on the test conditions, choose a standard or extended, numbered or named ACL.

- Only one ACL per protocol, per direction, and per interface is allowed. Multiple ACLs are permitted per interface, but each must be for a different protocol or different direction.

- Your ACL should be organized with consideration for its top-down process. Organize your ACL so that the more specific references to a network or subnet appear before ones that are more general. Place conditions that occur more frequently before conditions that occur less frequently.

- Your ACL contains an implicit **deny any** statement at the end. Unless you end your ACL with an explicit **permit any** statement, by default, the ACL denies all traffic that fails to match any of the ACL lines. Every ACL should have at least one **permit** statement. Otherwise, all traffic is denied.

- You should create the ACL before applying it to an interface. With most versions of Cisco IOS Software, an interface that has an empty ACL applied to it permits all traffic.

- If you apply an ACL to an interface, the ACL filters traffic going through the router, but does not filter traffic that the router generates. You can apply ACLs on the router in other ways that will affect the traffic that the router generates, such as using the **access-class** command to control the traffic in and out of vty ports, which will be discussed later.

- You should typically place extended ACLs as close as possible to the source of the traffic that you want to deny. Because standard ACLs do not specify destination addresses, you must put the standard ACL as close as possible to the destination of the traffic you want to deny for the source to reach intermediary networks.

Note: ACLs that are applied to an interface do not filter traffic that is generated by the router.

ACL Wildcard Masking

Address filtering occurs when you use ACL address wildcard masking to identify how to check or ignore corresponding IP address bits. Wildcard masking for IP address bits uses the numbers 1 and 0 to identify how to treat the corresponding IP address bits, as follows:

- **Wildcard mask bit 0:** Match the corresponding bit value in the address

- **Wildcard mask bit 1:** Do not check (ignore) the corresponding bit value in the address

Note: A wildcard mask is sometimes referred to as an inverse mask.
Be aware, however, that you should use regular subnet masks if you are configuring ACLs on a PIX and ASA.

Figure 3-16 illustrates how wildcard bits are used to check the corresponding address bits.

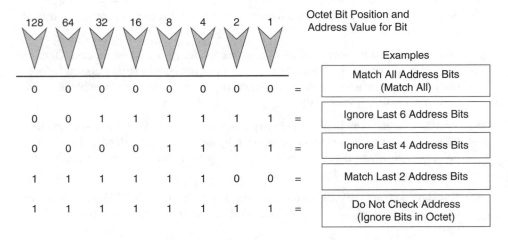

− 0 means to match the value of the corresponding address bit
− 1 means to ignore the value of the corresponding address bit

Figure 3-16   *Wildcard Bits: How to Check the Corresponding Address Bits*

By carefully setting wildcard masks, you can permit or deny tests with one ACL statement. You can select a single IP address or any IP address.

Example: Wildcard Masking Process for IP Subnets

In Figure 3-17, an administrator wants to test a range of IP subnets that is to be permitted or denied. Assume that the IP address is a Class B address (the first two octets are the network number), with 8 bits of subnetting (the third octet is for subnets). The administrator wants to use the IP wildcard masking bits to match subnets 172.30.16.0/24 to 172.30.31.0/24.

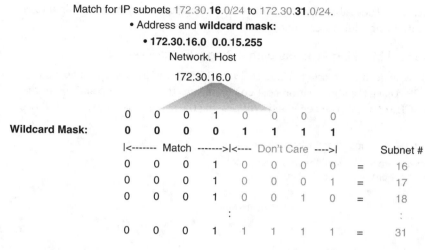

Match for IP subnets 172.30.**16**.0/24 to 172.30.**31**.0/24.
- Address and **wildcard mask:**
  - **172.30.16.0 0.0.15.255**
  Network. Host

Figure 3-17   *Wildcard Bits to Match IP Subnets 172.30.16.0 to 172.30.31.0*

To use one ACL statement to match this range of subnets, use the IP address 172.30.16.0 in the ACL, which is the first subnet to be matched, followed by the required wildcard mask.

First, the wildcard mask matches the first two octets (172.30) of the IP address using corresponding 0 bits in the first two octets of the wildcard mask.

Because there is no interest in an individual host, the wildcard mask ignores the final octet by using the corresponding 1 bit in the wildcard mask. For example, the final octet of the wildcard mask is 255 in decimal.

In the third octet, where the subnet address occurs, the wildcard mask of decimal 15, or binary 00001111, shown in bold, matches the high-order 4 bits of the IP address. In this case, the wildcard mask matches subnets starting with the 172.30.16.0/24 subnet. For the final (low-end) 4 bits in this octet, shown in gray, the wildcard mask indicates that the bits can be ignored. In these positions, the address value can be binary 0 or binary 1. Thus, the wildcard mask matches subnet 16, 17, 18, and so on up to subnet 31. The wildcard mask does not match any other subnets.

In Figure 3-17, the address 172.30.16.0 with the wildcard mask 0.0.15.255 matches subnets 172.30.16.0/24 to 172.30.31.0/24.

In some cases, you must use more than one ACL statement to match a range of subnets. For example, to match 10.1.4.0/24 to 10.1.8.0/24, use 10.1.4.0 0.0.3.255 and 10.1.8.0 0.0.0.255.

So, suppose that you want to block all IP traffic from the range of subnets of Figure 3-17, the access list could be this:

```
Router(config)# access-list 1 deny 172.30.16.0 0.0.15.255
```

The 0 and 1 bits in an ACL wildcard mask cause the ACL to either match or ignore the corresponding bit in the IP address. Working with decimal representations of binary wildcard mask bits can be tedious. For the most common uses of wildcard masking, you can use abbreviations. These abbreviations reduce how many numbers you are required to enter while configuring address test conditions.

Example: Wildcard Masking Process with a Single IP Address

In Figure 3-18, instead of entering 172.30.16.29 0.0.0.0, you can use the string **host 172.30.16.29**. Using the abbreviation **host** communicates the same test condition to the Cisco IOS ACL Software. The command syntax using the abbreviation **host** is as follows:

- 172.30.16.29 0.0.0.0 matches all of the address bits.
- Abbreviate this wildcard mask using the IP address preceded by the keyword **host** (host 172.30.16.29).

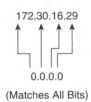

Wildcard Mask: 0.0.0.0

(Matches All Bits)

Figure 3-18 *ACL and the* **host** *Keyword*

```
Router(config)# access-list 2 permit host 172.30.16.29
```

And this is the same as entering the following:

```
Router(config)# access-list 2 permit 172.30.16.29 0.0.0.0
```

Should you enter the full host mask of 0.0.0.0, the router will convert the command for the host abbreviation automatically.

Example: Wildcard Masking Process with a Match Any IP Address

In Figure 3-19, instead of entering 0.0.0.0 255.255.255.255, you can use the word **any** by itself as the keyword. Using the abbreviation **any** communicates the same test condition to the Cisco IOS ACL Software. The command syntax using the keyword **any** is as follows:

```
Router(config)# access-list 3 permit 0.0.0.0 255.255.255.255
```

And this is the same as entering the following:

```
Router(config)# access-list 2 permit any
```

Tip: As a matter of fact, you can enter any valid host IP address, followed by the wildcard mask of 255.255.255.255 and the router will convert your entry to the keyword **any**, as demonstrated by the following test:

```
YYZ(config)# access-list 3 deny 192.168.16.214 255.255.255.255
YYZ(config)# do show access-list 3
Standard IP access list 3
    10 deny any
YYZ(config)#
```

- 0.0.0.0 255.255.255.255 ignores all address bits.
- Abbreviate expression with the keyword any.

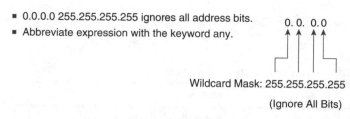

Wildcard Mask: 255.255.255.255

(Ignore All Bits)

Figure 3-19 *ACL and the* **any** *Keyword*

Using ACLs to Control Traffic

To configure numbered standard IPv4 ACLs on a Cisco router, you must create a standard IPv4 ACL and activate an ACL on an interface. The **access-list** command creates an entry in a standard IPv4 traffic filter list.

The following is the syntax for the **access-list** command:

```
Router(config)# access-list access-list-number {permit | deny | remark} source-
address [mask] [log]
```

To create an access list, use 1 to 99 for the *access-list-number* parameter. The first entry is assigned a sequence number of 10, and successive entries are incremented by 10. The default wildcard mask is 0.0.0.0 (only standard ACL). The **remark** argument lets you add a description to the ACL.

> **Caution:**   The **no access-list** *access-list-number* command removes the entire ACL.

The **log** option of the **access-list** command causes an informational logging message about the packet that matches the ACL entry to be sent to the console.

> **Tip:**   You control the level of messages that are logged to the console using the **logging console** command. You can also have the messages kept in buffer with the **logging buffered** command. The number of system error and debugging messages in the system logging buffer is determined by the configured size of the syslog buffer. This size of the syslog buffer is also set using the **logging buffered** command.

The logging message includes the ACL number, whether the packet was permitted or denied, the source address, and the number of packets. The message is generated for the first packet that matches, and then at five-minute intervals, including the number of packets permitted or denied in the previous five-minute interval.

The **ip access-group** command links an existing ACL to an interface. Only one ACL per protocol, per direction, and per interface is allowed. The syntax for this command is as follows:

```
Router(config-if)# ip access-group access-list-number  {in | out}
```

> **Note:**   To remove an IP ACL from an interface, first enter the **no ip access-group** command on the interface; then enter the global **no access-list** command to remove the entire ACL.

Table 3-2 provides an example of the steps required to configure and apply a numbered standard ACL on a router.

Table 3-2   *Numbered Standard ACL Configuration Procedure*

Step	Action	Notes

1.	Use the **access-list** global configuration command to create an entry in a standard IPv4 ACL:
	
	`RouterX(config)# access-list 1 permit`
	`172.16.0.0 0.0.255.255`
		Enter the global **no access-list** *access-list-number* command to remove the entire ACL.
		
		The example statement matches any address that starts with 172.16.x.x.
		
		Use the **remark** option to add a description to your ACL.

2.	Use the **interface** configuration command to select an interface to which to apply the ACL: `RouterX(config)# interface ethernet 1`	After you enter the **interface** command, the command-line interface (CLI) prompt changes from (config)# to (config-if)#.

3.	Use the **ip access-group** interface configuration command to activate the existing ACL on an interface:
	
	`RouterX(config-if)# ip access-group 1`
	`out`
		To remove an IP ACL from an interface, enter the **no ip access-group** *access-list-number* command on the interface.
		
		This example activates the standard IPv4 ACL 1 on the interface as an outbound filter.

Example: Numbered Standard IPv4 ACL: Deny a Specific Subnet

Table 3-3 describes the command syntax that is presented in Example 3-1 for the network topology shown in Figure 3-20.

Table 3-3   *Numbered Standard IPv4 ACL Example*

access-list Command Parameters	Description
1	ACL number that indicates this ACL is a standard list.
deny	Indicates that traffic that matches the selected parameters is not forwarded.
172.16.4.0	IP address of the source subnet.
0.0.0.255	Wildcard mask; 0s indicate positions that must match, 1s indicate "don't care" positions. The mask with 0s in the first three octets indicates those positions must match; the 255 in the last octet indicates a "don't care" condition.

Table 3-3 *Numbered Standard IPv4 ACL Example*

permit	Indicates that traffic that matches the selected parameters is forwarded.
any	Abbreviation for the IP address of the source. The abbreviation **any** indicates a source address of 0.0.0.0 and a wildcard mask of 255.255.255.255; all source addresses will match.

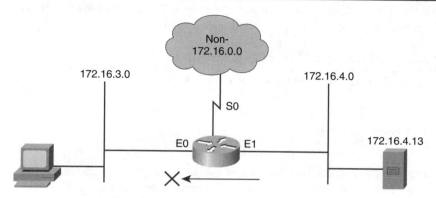

Figure 3-20 *Numbered Standard IPv4 ACL*

Example 3-1 *Numbered Standard IPv4 ACL*

```
r1(config)# access-list 1 deny 172.16.4.0  0.0.0.255
r1(config)# access-list 1 permit any
( implicit deny all = access-list 1 deny 0.0.0.0 255.255.255.255 )
r1(config)# interface ethernet 0
r1(config-if)# ip access-group 1 out
```

The ACL shown in Example 3-1 is designed to block traffic from a specific subnet, 172.16.4.0, and to allow all other traffic to be forwarded out E0. However, traffic from subnet 172.16.4.0 is not filtered when leaving by S0.

vty Access

To control traffic into and out of the router (not through the router), you protect the router virtual ports. A virtual port (or virtual terminal line) is commonly referred to as vty. By default, there are five such virtual terminal lines, numbered vty 0 through vty 4. You can configure Cisco IOS Software images to support more than five vty ports.

Restricting vty access is primarily a technique for increasing network security and defining which addresses are allowed Telnet access to the router EXEC process.

The command used to filter Telnet traffic is as follows:

```
Router(config-line)# access-class access-list-number {in ¦ out}
```

Filtering Telnet traffic is typically considered an extended IP ACL function because it filters a higher-level protocol. However, because you are using the **access-class** command to filter incoming or outgoing Telnet sessions by source address and apply filtering to vty lines, you can use standard IP ACL statements to control vty access.

In Example 3-2, you are permitting any device on network 192.168.1.0 0.0.0.255 to establish a virtual terminal session with the router. Of course, the user must know the appropriate passwords to enter user mode and privileged mode. In Example 3-2, we can only assume that the protocol used to exchange with the router is Telnet; however, other protocol can be filtered by the **access-class** command, such as Secure Shell (SSH).

Example 3-2   *Applying Standard ACLs to Control vty Access*

```
R1(config)# access-list 12 permit 192.168.1.0 0.0.0.255
!
R1(config)# line vty 0 4
R1(config-line)# access-class 12 in
```

Notice that identical restrictions have been set on every vty line (0 to 4) because you cannot control on which vty line a user will connect. The implicit **deny any** statement still applies to the ACL when it is used as an access class entry.

Numbered Extended IPv4 ACL

Use extended IPv4 ACLs, which are named or numbered 100 to 199 and 2000 to 2699, to provide more precise traffic-filtering control, because extended IPv4 ACLs check for the source and destination IPv4 address. In addition, with an extended ACL statement, you can specify the protocol and optional TCP or UDP application to filter traffic more precisely. To specify an application, you can configure either the port number or name of a well-known application.

Table 3-4 shows some well-known port numbers of IP protocols that you can use with extended access lists.

Table 3-4   *Well-Known Port Numbers and IP Protocols*

Well-Known Port Number (Decimal)	IP Protocol
20 (TCP)	FTP data
21 (TCP)	FTP control
23 (TCP)	Telnet
25 (TCP)	SMTP
53 (TCP/UDP)	DNS
69 (UDP)	TFTP
80 (TCP)	HTTP

To configure numbered extended IPv4 ACLs on a Cisco router, create an extended IPv4 ACL and activate that ACL on an interface. Use the **access-list** command to create an entry to express a condition statement in a complex filter. Table 3-5 explains the syntax of the command for configuring a numbered extended ACL shown here:

```
Router(config)# access-list access-list-number {permit | deny} protocol source
source-wildcard [operator port] destination destination-wildcard [operator port]
[established] [log]
```

Note: The syntax of the **access-list** command that is presented in Table 3-5 is representative of the TCP protocol form. Not all parameters and options are given. For the complete syntax of all forms of the command, refer to the appropriate Cisco IOS Software documentation available at Cisco.com.

To link an existing extended ACL to an interface, use the following command:

```
Router(config-if)# ip access-group access-list-number (in | out)
```

Only one ACL per protocol, per direction, and per interface is allowed.

Table 3-5 *Command Parameters for a Numbered Extended ACL*

access-list Command Parameters	Description
access-list-number	This parameter identifies the list using a number in the ranges of 100 to 199 or 2000 to 2699.
permit | deny	This parameter indicates whether this entry allows or blocks the specified address.
protocol	The *protocol* parameter can be IP, TCP, UDP, ICMP, GRE, or IGRP.
source and *destination*	These parameters identify the source and destination IP addresses.
source-wildcard and *destination-wildcard*	In the wildcard mask, 0s indicate positions that must match, 1s indicate "don't care" positions.
operator [*port* | *app_name*]	The operator can be **lt** (less than), **gt** (greater than), **eq** (equal), **neq** (not equal). The port number referenced can be either the source port or the destination port, depending on where in the ACL the port number is configured. As an alternative to the port number, well-known application names can be used (for example, **telnet, ftp, smtp**).
established	This option is for inbound TCP only. It allows TCP traffic to pass if the packet is a response to an outbound initiated session. This type of traffic has the acknowledgment (ACK) bits set. (See Example 3-4.)
log	This option sends a logging message to the console.

Table 3-6 describes the parameters of the **ip access-group** command.

Table 3-6   **ip access-group** *Command Parameters*

Parameter	Description
access-list-number	Indicates the number of the ACL that is to be linked to an interface
**in	out**	Selects whether the ACL is applied as an input or output filter; out is default

Example 3-3 shows the configuration for denying FTP access from subnet 172.16.4.0/24 to subnet 172.16.3.0/24, for the network depicted in Figure 3-21. All other traffic is allowed. By applying the ACL to the E0 interface in an outbound direction, traffic is dropped just before it would be transmitted out the E0 interface.

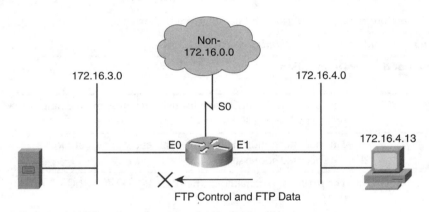

Figure 3-21   *Numbered Extended IPv4 ACL Example*

Example 3-3   *Numbered Extended IPv4 ACL Example*

```
r1(config)# access-list 101 deny tcp 172.16.4.0 0.0.0.255 172.16.3.0 0.0.0.255 eq 21
r1(config)# access-list 101 deny tcp 172.16.4.0 0.0.0.255 172.16.3.0 0.0.0.255 eq 20
r1(config)# access-list 101 permit ip any any
(implicit deny all)
(access-list 101 deny ip 0.0.0.0 255.255.255.255 0.0.0.0 255.255.255.255)
r1(config)# interface ethernet 0
r1(config-if)# ip access-group 101 out
```

In Example 3-4, the **established** parameter of the extended ACL allows responses to traffic that originate from the mail host, 200.1.1.2, to return inbound on the serial 0 interface. A match occurs if the TCP datagram has the ACK or reset (RST) bits set, which indicates that the packet belongs to an existing connection. Without the **established** parameter in the ACL statement, the mail host could only receive SMTP traffic but not send it.

Caution: ACLs using the keyword **established** are not a substitute of stateful firewall. The ACL only checks whether the established flag bit is turned on in the TCP header, without reference to other prior transmission. In other words, as long as the established bit is turned on and the other filtering criteria mentioned in the ACL entry are valid, the router will execute the action. It will not check to determine whether a proper TCP three-way handshake was done. It is therefore easy to fool the router using a packet-crafting tool.

Example 3-4   *Using the* **established** *Keyword*

```
Router(config)# access-list 102 permit tcp any host 200.1.1.2 established
Router(config)# access-list 102 permit tcp any host 200.1.1.2 eq smtp
Router(config)# interface serial 0
Router(config-if)# ip access-group 102 in
```

Displaying ACLs

When you finish the ACL configuration, use the **show** commands to verify the configuration. Use the **show access-lists** command to display the contents of all ACLs, as shown in Example 3-5. By entering the ACL name or number as an option for this command, you can display a specific ACL. To display the contents of only the IP ACLs, use the **show ip access-list** command.

Example 3-5   **show access-lists** *Command Output*

```
r1# show access-lists
Extended IP access list 102
  permit ip any host 128.88.1.6
Extended IP access list mailblock
  permit tcp any 128.88.0.0 0.0.255.255
    established
```

Note: Depending on your version of IOS, the **show access-lists** output might display sequence number like this:

```
YYZ# show access-list inside-servers
Extended IP access list inside-servers
    10 permit tcp any any eq 22
    20 permit tcp any any eq 443
    30 permit udp any any eq isakmp
    40 permit udp any any eq non500-isakmp
    50 permit esp any any
    60 permit udp any any eq ntp
```

The **show ip interfaces** command displays IP interface information and indicates whether any IP ACLs are set on the interface. In the **show ip interfaces e0** command output shown in Example 3-6, IP ACL 1 has been configured on the E0 interface as an inbound ACL. No outbound IP ACL has been configured on the E0 interface.

Example 3-6   show ip interfaces *Command Output*

```
r1# show ip interfaces e0
Ethernet0 is up, line protocol is up
  Internet address is 10.1.1.11/24
  Broadcast address is 255.255.255.255
  Address determined by setup command
  MTU is 1500 bytes
  Helper address is not set
  Directed broadcast forwarding is disabled
  Outgoing access list is mailblock
  Inbound  access list is 102
  Proxy ARP is enabled
<text omitted>
```

ACL Considerations

Before you start to develop any ACLs, consider the following basic rules:

- **Base your ACLs on your security policy:** Unless you anchor the ACL in a comprehensive security policy, you cannot be certain that it will effectively control access in the way that access needs to be controlled.

- **Write it out:** Never sit down at a router and start to develop an ACL without first spending some time in design. The best ACL developers suggest that you write out a list of things that you want the ACL to accomplish. Start with something as simple as "This ACL must block all Simple Network Management Protocol (SNMP) access to the router except for the SNMP host at 16.1.1.15."

- **Set up a development system:** Whether you use your laptop PC or a dedicated server, you need a place to develop and store your ACLs. Word processors or text editors of any kind are suitable, as long as you can save the files in ASCII text format. Build a library of your most commonly used ACLs and use them as sources for new files. ACLs can be pasted into the router running configuration (requiring console or Telnet access) or can be stored in a router configuration file. The system that you choose should support TFTP to make it easy to transfer any resulting configuration files to the router.

Note: Hackers love to gain access to router configuration development systems or TFTP servers that store ACLs. A hacker can discover a lot about your network from looking at these easily read text files. For this reason, it is imperative that the system where you choose to develop and store your router files be a secure system.

- Test: If possible, test your ACLs in a secure environment before placing them into production. Testing is a commonsense approach to any router configuration changes. Most enterprises maintain their own network test beds. Although testing might appear to be an unnecessary cost, over time it can save time and money.

You should consider several caveats when working with ACLs:

- **Implicit deny all:** All Cisco ACLs end with an implicit **deny all** statement. Although you might not actually see this statement in your ACLs, they do exist.

- **Standard ACL limitation:** Because standard ACLs are limited to packet filtering on only source addresses, you might need to create extended ACLs to implement your security policies.

- **Order of specific statements:** Certain ACL statements are more specific than others are; therefore, you need to place them higher in the ACL. For example, blocking all UDP traffic at the top of the list negates the blocking of SNMP packets lower in the list. Take care that statements at the top of the ACL do not negate any statements found lower in the list.

- **Directional filtering:** Cisco ACLs have a directional filter that determines whether they examine inbound packets (toward the interface) or outbound packets (away from the interface). Always double-check the direction of data that your ACL is filtering.

- **Modifying ACLs:** Cisco IOS Software Release 12.2 and earlier always appends new statements to an existing ACL to the bottom of the ACL. Because of the inherent top-down statement evaluation order of ACLs, these new entries can render the ACL unusable. When a new statement does render the ACL unusable, you must create a new ACL with the correct statement ordering, delete the old ACL, and assign the new ACL to the router interface. If you are using Cisco IOS Software Release 12.3 and later, you can use sequence numbers to ensure that you are adding a new statement into the ACL in the correct location. The ACL is processed top-down based on the sequence numbers of the statements (lowest to highest).

- **Special packets:** Router-generated packets, such as routing table updates, are not subject to outbound ACL statements applied to interfaces on the source router. If your security policy requires filtering these types of packets, inbound ACLs on adjacent routers or other router filter mechanisms using ACLs must do the filtering task.

- **Extended ACL placement:** If you use extended ACLs on routers too far from the source that you need to filter, packets flowing to other routers and interfaces might be adversely affected. Always consider placing extended ACLs on routers as close as possible to the source that you are filtering.

- **Standard ACL placement:** Because standard ACLs filter packets based on the source address, placing these ACLs too close to the source can adversely affect packets destined to other destinations. Always place standard ACLs as close to the destination as possible.

Configuring ACLs Using SDM

Rules define how the router will respond to a particular kind of traffic. Using Cisco Security Device Manager (SDM), you can create access rules that cause the router to block certain types of traffic while permitting other types, create NAT rules that define the traffic that is to receive address translation, and create IPsec rules that specify which traffic is to be encrypted.

Cisco SDM also provides default rules that are used in guided configurations, and that you can examine and use when you create your own access rules. It also allows you to view rules that were not created using Cisco SDM, called *external rules*, and rules with syntax that Cisco SDM does not support, called *unsupported rules*.

Use the SDM Rules (ACL) Summary window to view a summary of the rules in the router configuration and to navigate to other windows to create, edit, or delete rules. To access this window, choose **Configure > Additional Tasks > ACL Editor**, as shown in Figure 3-22.

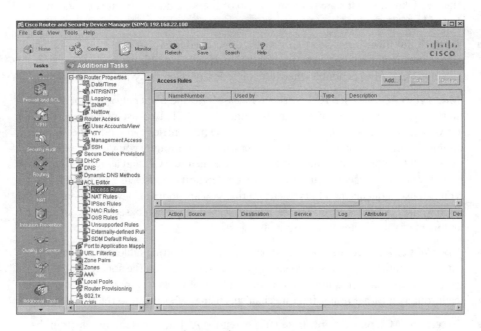

Figure 3-22 *SDM Access Rules Window*

Cisco SDM enables you to manage the following types of rules:

- **Access rules:** These rules govern the traffic that can enter and leave the network. You can apply access rules to router interfaces and to vty lines.

- **NAT rules:** These rules determine which private IP addresses are translated into valid Internet IP addresses.

- **IPsec rules:** These rules determine which traffic is encrypted on secure connections.

- **NAC rules:** These rules specify which IP addresses should be admitted to the network or blocked from the network. More precisely, it determines what access is granted to devices exempted from posture validation such as IP phones.

- **Firewall rules** (not shown in Figure 3-22): These rules can specify source and destination addresses and whether the traffic should be permitted or denied.

- **QoS rules:** These rules specify traffic that should belong to the quality of service (QoS) class to which the rule is associated.

- **Unsupported rules:** These are rules that were not created using Cisco SDM and that Cisco SDM does not support. These rules are read only, and cannot be modified using Cisco SDM.

- **Externally Defined rules:** These are rules that were not created using Cisco SDM, but that Cisco SDM supports. These rules cannot be associated with any interface using the SDM, however, they can be associated with an interface from the CLI.

- **Cisco SDM default rules:** These rules are predefined rules that are used by Cisco SDM wizards.

Creating Standard ACLs with Cisco SDM

Cisco SDM refers to ACLs as access rules. From Cisco SDM, you can create and apply standard rules (standard ACL) as shown in Figure 3-23.

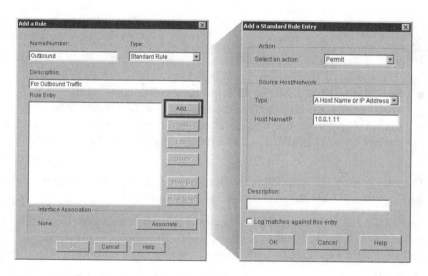

Figure 3-23 *Creating a Standard Rule*

Follow these steps to configure a standard rule using Cisco SDM:

Step 1.   Choose **Configure > Additional Tasks > ACL Editor > Access Rules.**

Step 2.   Click **Add.** The Add a Rule window appears.

Step 3.   In the Add a Rule window, enter a name or number in the Name/Number field.

Step 4.   From the Type drop-down list, choose **Standard Rule**. Optionally, enter a description in the Description field.

Step 5.   Click **Add**. The Add a Standard Rule Entry window appears.

Step 6.   From the Select an Action drop-down list, choose **Permit** or **Deny**.

Step 7.   From the Type drop-down list choose one of the following types of addresses:

■   **A Network:** Choose this option if you want the action to apply to all of the IP addresses in a network or subnet.

■   **A Host Name or IP Address:** Choose this option if you want the action to apply to a specific host or IP address.

■   **Any IP address:** Choose this option if you want the action to apply to any IP address.

Step 8.   Depending on what you chose from the Type drop-down list, complete the following fields:

■   **IP Address:** If you chose a network, enter the desired IP address in this field.

■   **Wildcard Mask:** If you chose a network, you must specify a wildcard mask to go with it. You can click the drop-down arrow to choose a wildcard mask from the Wildcard Mask drop-down list, or you can enter a custom wildcard mask in the field.

Caution: Remember, this is a wildcard mask, not a subnet mask.

■   **Host Name/IP:** If you selected a host name or IP address in the Type field, enter the name or the IP address of the host. If you enter a hostname, the router must be configured to use a DNS server, but once it has performed the DNS address resolution, the IP address will appear in the access list entry

Step 9.   Optionally, enter a description in the Description field. The description must be fewer than 100 characters.

Step 10.   Optionally, check the **Log Matches Against This Entry** check box. Depending on how the syslog settings are configured on the router, the matches are recorded in the local logging buffer, sent to a syslog server, or both.

Step 11.   Click **OK**.

Step 12.   Continue adding or editing rules until the standard rule is complete. If at anytime you need to rearrange the order of the rules listed in the Rule Entry list, use the **Move Up** and **Move Down** buttons.

After the Rule Entry list is complete, the next step is to apply the rule to an interface, as shown in Figure 3-24.

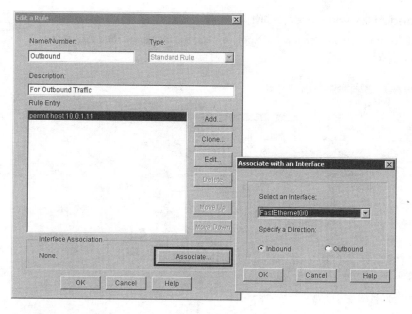

Figure 3-24   *Applying a Standard Rule to an Interface*

Follow these steps to apply the rule to an interface:

Step 1.   From the Add a Rule window, click **Associate**. The Associate with an Interface window appears.

Step 2.   From the Select an Interface drop-down list, choose the interface to which you want this rule to apply.

Step 3.   From the Specify a Direction section, click either **Inbound** or **Outbound**. If you want the router to check packets inbound to the interface, click **Inbound**. The router checks for a match with the rule before routing it; the router accepts or drops the packet based on whether the rule states permit or deny. If you want the router to forward the packet to the outbound interface before comparing it to the entries in the access rule, click **Outbound**.

Step 4.   If a rule is already associated with the interface and direction you selected, an information box appears. If this occurs, you have the following options:

- You can cancel the operation.

- You can continue with the operation by appending the new rule entries to the access rule that is already applied to the interface.

- You can disassociate the existing rule from the interface and associate the new rule.

Creating Extended ACLs with Cisco SDM

From Cisco SDM, you can also create and apply extended rules (extended ACLs) as shown in Figure 3-25.

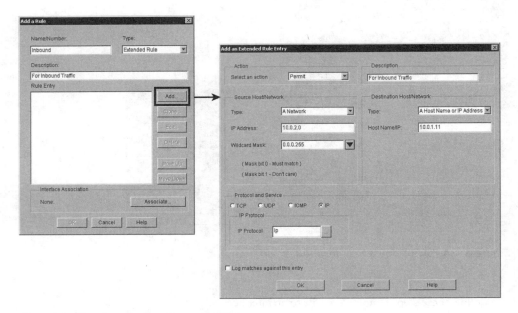

Figure 3-25   *Creating an Extended Rule*

Follow these steps to configure an extended rule:

Step 1.   Choose **Configure > Additional Tasks > ACL Editor > Access Rules**.

Step 2.   Click **Add**. The Add a Rule window appears.

Step 3.   In the Add a Rule window, enter a name or number in the Name/Number field.

Step 4.   From the Type drop-down list, choose **Extended Rule**. Optionally, enter a description in the Description field.

Step 5.   Click **Add**. The Add an Extended Rule Entry window appears.

Step 6.   From the Select an Action drop-down list, choose **Permit** or **Deny**. Optionally, enter a description in the Description field. The description must be fewer than 100 characters.

Step 7.   In both the Source Host/Network section and Destination Host/Network section, from the Type drop-down list, choose one of the following types of addresses:

   ■ **A Network:** Choose this option if you want the action to apply to all the IP addresses in a network or subnet.

   ■ **A Host Name or IP Address:** Choose this option if you want the action to apply to a specific host or IP address.

- **Any IP address:** Choose this option if you want the action to apply to any IP address.

Step 8.   Depending on what you selected from the Type drop-down list, complete the following fields:

- **IP Address:** If you selected a network, enter the desired IP address in this field.

- **Wildcard Mask:** If you selected a network, you must specify a wildcard mask to go with it. You can click the drop-down arrow to choose a wildcard mask from the Wildcard Mask drop-down list, or you can enter a custom wildcard mask in the field.

Caution: Remember, this is a wildcard mask, not a subnet mask.

- Hostname/IP: If you selected a hostname or IP address in the Type field, enter the name or the IP address of the host. If you enter a hostname, the router must be configured to use a DNS server.

Step 9.   In the Protocol and Service section, choose the protocol and service, if applicable, to which you want the entry to apply. The information that you provide differs from protocol to protocol. The following are the protocols you can choose, and the services or options that you must enter for each protocol:

- **TCP and UDP:** When you select either one of these protocols, you will be asked to provide source port information and destination port information. You can specify the source and destination port by name or number. If you do not remember the name or number, click the ... button and choose the value you want from the Service window. This field accepts protocol numbers from 0 to 65535. In addition, you must specify how you want the rule applied to the port:

    =:   The rule entry applies to the value that you enter in the field. In the CLI, this is stated as **eq.**

    !=:   The rule entry applies to any value except the one that you enter in the field. In the CLI, this is stated as **neq.**

    <:   The rule entry applies to all port numbers lower than the number you enter in the field. In the CLI, this is stated as **lt.**

    >:   The rule entry applies to all port numbers higher than the number you enter in the field. In the CLI, this is stated as **gt.**

    range: The entry applies to the range of port numbers that you specify in the fields. In the CLI, this is stated as **range.**

    It is not really necessary to set a source port value for a TCP connection. If you are not sure you need to use this field, you leave it set to **= any.** However, best practices recommend that you set the source port to greater than 1023 on inbound ACL to block crafted packets.

The content of the Service window will change depending on whether the ACE is filtering TCP, UDP, ICMP, or IP, as explained next.

- **ICMP:** When you select ICMP, you can choose **any** for the ICMP type or you can enter a type name or number. If you do not remember the name or number, click the ... button and choose the value from the Service window. This field accepts protocol numbers from 0 to 255.

- **IP:** If you select IP, the rule will apply to any protocol in the TCP/IP protocol suite. If you want to specify a specific protocol, you can enter it by name or number. If you do not remember the name or number of the protocol, click the ... button and choose the value you want from the Protocols window. This field accepts protocol numbers from 0 to 255.

Step 10.   Optionally, check the **Log Matches Against This Entry** check box. Depending on how the syslog settings are configured on the router, the matches will be recorded in the local logging buffer, sent to a syslog server, or both.

Step 11.   Click OK.

After the Rule Entry list is complete, the next step is to apply the rule to an interface, as shown previously in Figure 3-24.

Using ACLs to Permit and Deny Network Services

ACLs can be used to permit or deny different network services. ACLs can be used not only to filter user traffic, but also to filter routing updates, traffic originating from a vty session, ICMP messages, and many other uses. This section shows the different uses of ACLs.

Controlling Routing Updates

Cisco routers share routing table update information to provide directions on where to route traffic. ACLs can be used to limit which routes a router accepts (takes in) or advertises (sends out) to its counterparts.

Figure 3-26 shows examples of routing protocol entries using SDM. On the left, you can see an example of how to filter Open Shortest Path First (OSPF) or Enhanced Interior Gateway Routing Protocol (EIGRP). On the right, you can see how to filter Routing Information Protocol (RIP).

Example 3-7 shows an extended IP ACL that accepts only OSPF, EIGRP, and RIP traffic sourced from the IP address 192.168.1.1.

Example 3-7   *Extended IP ACL to Control Routing Updates*

```
r1(config)# access-list 120 permit émigré host 192.168.1.1 any
r1(config)# access-list 120 permit ospf host 192.168.1.1 any
r1(config)# access-list 120 permit udp host 192.168.1.1 any eq rip
r1(config)# interface fa0/2
r1(config-if)# ip access-group 120 in
```

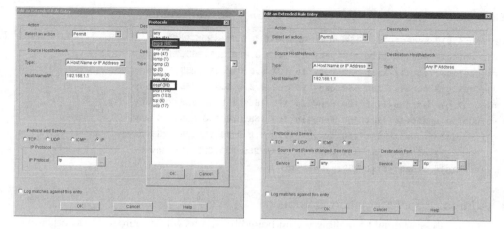

Figure 3-26   *ACL to Filter Routing Updates as Applied Using SDM*

IP Address Spoof Mitigation: Inbound

Generally, you should not allow any IP packets containing the source address of any internal hosts or networks inbound to a private network. Figure 3-27 shows how SDM can be used to configure an antispoofing rule detailed in Example 3-8.

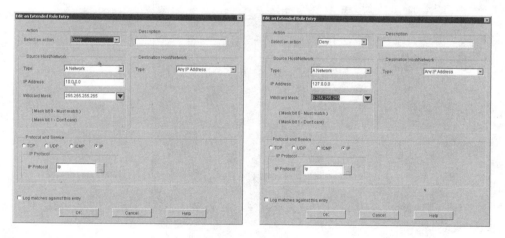

Figure 3-27   *SDM: Creating an Inbound Antispoofing Rule*

Example 3-8 shows ACL 150 for router r1. In this example, the ACL denies all packets containing the following IP addresses in their source field:

- Any local host addresses (127.0.0.0/8)

- Any reserved private addresses (RFC 1918, *Address Allocation for Private Internets*)

- Any addresses in the IP multicast address range (224.0.0.0/4)

Example 3-8   *ACL for Inbound IP Address Spoofing Mitigation*

```
r1(config)# access-list 150 deny ip 0.0.0.0 0.255.255.255 any
r1(config)# access-list 150 deny ip 10.0.0.0 0.255.255.255 any
r1(config)# access-list 150 deny ip 127.0.0.0 0.255.255.255 any
r1(config)# access-list 150 deny ip 169.0.0.0 0.255.255.255 any
r1(config)# access-list 150 deny ip 172.16.0.0 0.15.255.255 any
r1(config)# access-list 150 deny ip 192.168.0.0 0.0.255.255 any
r1(config)# access-list 150 deny ip 224.0.0.0 15.255.255.255 any
r1(config)# access-list 150 deny ip host 255.255.255.255 any
r1(config)# access-list 150 permit any any
```

IP Address Spoof Mitigation: Outbound

Generally, you should not allow any outbound IP packets with a source address other than a valid IP address of the internal network.

Figure 3-28 shows a partial configuration using SDM of an inbound spoofing protection.

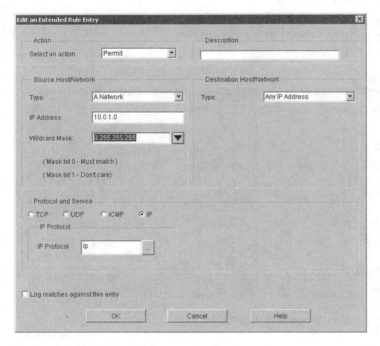

Figure 3-28   *Creating an Outbound Antispoofing Rule Using SDM*

Example 3-9 shows ACL 105 for router r1. This ACL permits only those packets that contain source addresses from the 10.0.1.0/24 network and denies all others.

Example 3-9   *ACL for Outbound IP Address Spoofing Mitigation*

```
r1(config)# access-list 105 permit ip 10.0.1.0 0.0.0.255 any
```

Note: Cisco routers running Cisco IOS Software Release 12.0 and later can use IP Unicast Reverse Path Forwarding (RPF) verification as an alternative IP address spoof-mitigation mechanism.

ICMP Filtering

Hackers use several ICMP message types to attack networks. Unfortunately, there are many legitimate ICMP messages as well. Various management applications use ICMP messages to gather information. Network management uses ICMP messages automatically generated by the router.

Filtering Inbound ICMP Packets

Hackers can use ICMP echo packets to discover subnets and hosts on the protected network and to generate DoS floods. Hackers can use ICMP redirect messages to alter host routing tables. Both ICMP echo and redirect messages should be blocked inbound by the router.

SDM can be used to filter ICMP messages, as shown in Figure 3-29.

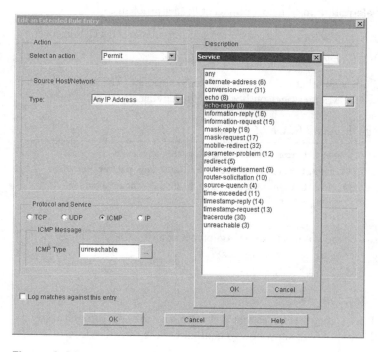

Figure 3-29   *SDM: Creating a Standard Rule*

The ACL statement shown in Example 3-10 permits necessary ICMP traffic and blocks all the others. The first line in access-list 112 ensures that inbound replies to our outbound echo requests (pings) will be allowed to come in. The second line in access-list 112 ensures that source-quench messages originating from a host located on the outside are allowed to come in to notify our inside host to reduce the pace at which it is sending packets to that outside host. The third line in access-list 112 ensures that ICMP messages originating from the outside and having for the destination an inside host, and bearing the news "unreachable," such as port unreachable, network unreachable, host reachable, and the like, are allowed to reach that inside host.

Example 3-10   *Filtering Inbound ICMP Messages*

```
r1(config)# access-list 112 permit icmp any any echo-reply
r1(config)# access-list 112 permit icmp any any source-quench
r1(config)# access-list 112 permit icmp any any unreachable
r1(config)# access-list 112 deny icmp any any
```

Filtering Outbound ICMP Packets

Several ICMP messages are required for proper network operation and should be allowed outbound:

- **Echo:** Allows users to ping external hosts

- **Parameter problem:** Informs the host of packet header problems.

- **Packet too big:** Required for packet maximum transmission unit (MTU) discovery

- **Source quench:** Throttles down traffic when necessary

As a rule, you should block all other ICMP message types outbound. The ACL in Example 3-11 permits all of these ICMP messages outbound while denying all others.

Example 3-11   *Filtering Outbound ICMP Messages*

```
r1(config)# access-list 114 permit icmp 16.2.1.0 0.0.0.255 any echo
r1(config)# access-list 114 permit icmp 16.2.1.0 0.0.0.255 any packet-too-big
r1(config)# access-list 114 permit icmp 16.2.1.0 0.0.0.255 any source-quench
```

Note: The examples shown are not meant to be comprehensive examples of router security best practices, but rather as used for pedagogical purpose.

Permitting Common Services

DNS, SMTP, and FTP are common services that you often have to allow through a firewall. Figure 3-30 and Example 3-12 show how to configure these three services.

Example 3-12   *Permitting DNS, SMTP, and FTP Using an ACL*

```
r1(config)# access-list 122 permit udp any host 172.16.2.2 eq domain
r1(config)# access-list 122 permit tcp any host 172.16.2.2 eq smtp
r1(config)# access-list 122 permit tcp any host 172.16.2.2 eq ftp
```

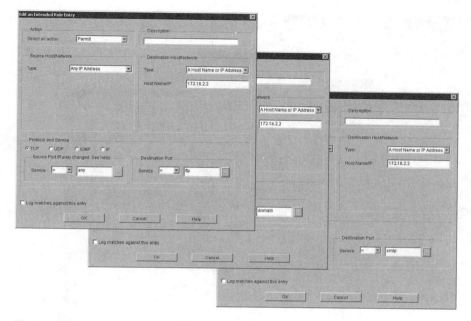

Figure 3-30 *Permitting DNS, SMTP, and FTP Using SDM*

Permitting Router Service Traffic

It is also quite common that you will need to configure a firewall to permit protocols that are necessary to administer a router. For example, it might be necessary to allow traffic through an internal router that permits router maintenance traffic from an outside device. Telnet, SSH, syslog, and SNMP are examples of services that a router may need to include. Figure 3-31 and Example 3-13 show how to allow these services.

Example 3-13 *Allowing Router Service Traffic Using an ACL*

```
r1(config)# access-list 180 permit tcp host 192.168.1.1 host 10.0.1.11 eq telnet
r1(config)# access-list 180 permit tcp host 192.168.1.1 host 10.0.1.11 eq 22
r1(config)# access-list 180 permit udp host 192.168.1.1 host 10.0.1.11 eq syslog
r1(config)# access-list 180 permit udp host 192.168.1.1 host 10.0.1.11 eq snmptrap
r1(config)# interface fa0/2
r1(config-if)# ip access-group 180 in
```

Note: SSH is preferred over Telnet whenever possible.

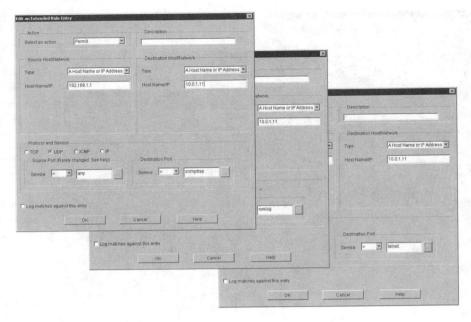

Figure 3-31 *Using SDM to Allow Router Service Traffic*

Configuring a Cisco IOS Zone-Based Policy Firewall

Zone-based policy firewalls change the original implementation of Cisco IOS Classic Firewall stateful inspection from the older interface-based model to a more flexible, more easily understood zone-based configuration model. This section focuses on the features of Cisco IOS zone-based policy firewalls and how to use the Cisco Router and Security Device Manager (SDM) to configure them.

Zone-Based Policy Firewall Overview

The original implementation of Cisco IOS Classic Firewall stateful inspection used an interface-based configuration model, in which a stateful inspection policy was applied to an interface. All traffic passing through that interface received the same inspection policy. This configuration model limited the granularity of the firewall policies and caused confusion of the proper application of firewall policies, particularly in scenarios when firewall policies must be applied between multiple interfaces.

Zone-based policy firewall (sometimes referred to as ZBF, or zone-policy firewall [ZPF]) changes the firewall from the older interface-based model to a more flexible, more easily understood zone-based configuration model. Interfaces are assigned to zones, and an inspection policy is applied to traffic moving between the zones, as shown in Figure 3-32. Figure 3-32 shows three zones:

- **Untrusted:** Represents the Internet

- **DMZ:** Contains the corporate servers access from the public

- **Trusted:** Represents the inside network

Interzone policies offer considerable flexibility and granularity, and thus enable you to apply different inspection policies to multiple host groups that are connected to the same router interface. The policies on Figure 3-32 are as follows:

- **Public:** DMZ policy that sets the rules for traffic originating from the untrusted zone with the DMZ as destination

- **DMZ:** Private policy that sets the rules for the traffic originating from the DMZ with the trusted zone as destination

- **Private:** DMZ policy that sets the rules for the traffic originating from the trusted zone with the DMZ as destination

- **Private:** Pubic policy that sets the rules for the traffic originating from the trusted zone with the untrusted zone as destination

Zone-based policy firewalls are configured with the Cisco Common Classification Policy Language (C3PL), which uses a hierarchical structure to define inspection for network protocols and the groups of hosts to which the inspection will be applied.

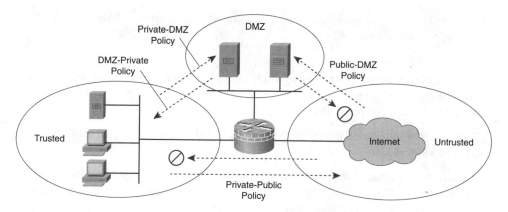

Figure 3-32   *Cisco IOS Zone-Based Policy Firewall*

Cisco IOS zone-based policy firewalls support the following features:

- Stateful inspection
- Application inspection
- URL filtering
- Per-policy parameter
- Transparent firewall
- Virtual routing and forwarding aware firewall

Key Topic

First-generation firewalls, packet filters, used only ACLs to control traffic. For this reason, it was relatively easy for attackers to breach a firewall, because no state data was examined. Second-generation firewalls, proxy firewalls, were concerned with the state of the connection, but they were application dependent. Third-generation firewalls, stateful packet filters, were developed to provide state tracking, application independence, and speed. Context-Based Access Control (CBAC), from the legacy Cisco IOS Firewall feature set, is an example of this type of third-generation firewall.

CBAC performs traffic filtering based on application-level protocol information. It does this filtering using stateful filters, whereby selected outbound traffic creates a temporary opening in the filter for replies to return through. This capability means that CBAC examines more than transport layer TCP or UDP ports. With FTP, it tracks the application as it opens ports for data connections, and allows the replies back through the firewall. With UDP, it tracks application ports and allows replies. With other application protocols, it tracks multiple connections that are created by negotiation on a control channel. Multimedia protocols, SQL*Net, and Remote Procedure Call (RPC) are examples of such traffic. CBAC can also perform Java blocking, based on server address. It does not perform Java or ActiveX content filtering.

The inspection by CBAC also allows it to prevent certain DoS attacks. For example, it detects and prevents SYN flooding, badly out of sequence TCP packets, large numbers of half-open connections, and high rates of new connections.

Note: CBAC can still be implemented on Cisco IOS Firewalls; however, interfaces that participate in a zone-based policy firewall cannot also participate in CBAC.

The legacy stateful inspection done by CBAC was very complicated because there was a combination of ACLs and inspection rules, all of which worked together to accomplish the stateful packet filtering done by the firewall.

The Cisco IOS zone-based policy firewall completely changes the way you configure a Cisco IOS Firewall.

The first major change to the firewall configuration is the introduction of a zone-based configuration. A Cisco IOS Firewall is the first Cisco IOS Software threat defense feature to implement a zone configuration model. Other features will adopt the zone model over time.

The classic Cisco IOS Firewall stateful inspection (CBAC) interface-based configuration model that you can configure using the **ip inspect** command will be maintained for a period of time, but few, if any, new features will be available.

A Cisco IOS zone-based policy firewall does not use the stateful inspection (CBAC) commands. You can use the two configuration models concurrently on routers but not on the same interfaces; you cannot configure an interface as a security zone member and for **ip inspect** simultaneously.

Zones establish the security borders of your network. A zone defines a boundary where traffic is subjected to policy restrictions as it crosses to another region of your network. The default policy of a zone-policy firewall between zones is to "deny all." If no policy is explicitly configured, all traffic moving between zones is blocked. This policy is a significant departure from the stateful inspection model, in which traffic is implicitly allowed unless it is explicitly blocked with an ACL entry.

The second major change is the introduction of a new configuration policy language known as C3PL. The C3PL structure is similar to the modular QoS CLI (MQC) structure in which class maps specify the traffic that is affected by the action that the policy map applies.

Note: Interface ACLs are still relevant and are applied before zone-based policy firewalls when they are applied inbound. Interface ACLs are applied after zone-based policy firewalls when they are applied outbound.

Zone-Based Policy Firewall Actions

The Cisco IOS zone-based policy firewall can take three possible actions when you configure it using Cisco SDM:

- **Inspect:** This action configures Cisco IOS stateful packet inspection.

- **Drop:** This action is analogous to deny in an ACL.

- **Pass:** This action is analogous to permit in an ACL. The pass action does not track the state of connections or sessions within the traffic; pass allows the traffic only in one direction. A corresponding policy must be applied to allow return traffic to pass in the opposite direction.

Note: The pass action does not perform stateful inspection.

Zone-Based Policy Firewall: Rule for Application Traffic

The membership of the router network interfaces in zones is subject to several rules governing interface behavior, as is the traffic moving between zone member interfaces:

- A zone must be configured before you can assign interfaces to the zone.

- You can assign an interface to only one security zone.

- Traffic is implicitly allowed to flow by default among interfaces that are members of the same zone.

- To permit traffic to and from a zone member interface, a policy allowing or inspecting traffic must be configured between that zone and any other zone.

- Traffic cannot flow between a zone member interface and any interface that is not a zone member. You can apply pass, inspect, and drop actions only between two zones.

- Interfaces that have not been assigned to a zone function as classical router ports and might still use classical stateful inspection (CBAC) configuration.

- If you do not want an interface on the router to be part of the zone-based firewall policy, it might still be necessary to put that interface in a zone and configure a "pass all" policy (sort of a dummy policy) between that zone and any other zone to which traffic flow is desired.

- From the preceding rules it follows that if traffic is to flow among all the interfaces in a router, all the interfaces must be part of the zoning model (each interface must be a member of a zone).

Table 3-7 shows a number of examples of different interface and configuration combinations.

Table 3-7 *Zone-Based Policy Firewall: Rules for Application Traffic*

Source Interface Member of Zone?	Destination Interface Member of Zone?	Zone Pair Exists?	Policy Exists?	Result
No	No	N/A	N/A	No impact of zoning/policy
Yes (zone 1)	Yes (zone 1)	N/A	N/A	No policy lookup (pass)
Yes	No	N/A	N/A	Drop
No	Yes	N/A	N/A	Drop

Table 3-7 *Zone-Based Policy Firewall: Rules for Application Traffic*

Yes (zone 1)	Yes (zone 2)	No	N/A	Drop
Yes (zone 1)	Yes (zone 2)	Yes	No	Drop
Yes (zone 1)	Yes (zone 2)	Yes	Yes	Policy actions

`Zone pair must have different zone as source and destination

Zone-Based Policy Firewall: Rule for Router Traffic

The rules for a zone-based policy firewall are different when the router is involved in the traffic flow, whether as the source of traffic or the destination. A zone-based policy firewall is used to control router administration where the router is the destination. Table 3-8 illustrates various scenarios that involve traffic in or out of the router.

Table 3-8 *Zone-Based Policy Firewall: Rules for Router Traffic*

Source Interface Member of Zone?	Destination Interface Member of Zone?	Zone Pair Exists?	Policy Exists?	Result
Router	Yes	No	N/A	Pass
Router	Yes	Yes	No	Pass
Router	Yes	Yes	Yes	Policy actions
Yes	Router	No	N/A	Pass
Yes	Router	Yes	No	Pass
Yes	Router	Yes	Yes	Policy actions

When an interface is configured to be a zone member, the hosts connected to the interface are included in the zone, but traffic flowing to and from the interfaces of the router is not controlled by the zone policies. Instead, all the IP interfaces on the router are automatically made part of the "self" zone when a zone-based policy firewall is configured. To limit IP traffic moving to the IP addresses of the router from the various zones on a router, policies must be applied to block, allow, or inspect traffic between the zone and the self zone of the router, and vice versa. If there are no policies between a zone and the self zone, all traffic is permitted to the interfaces of the router without being inspected.

If desired, you can define a policy using the self zone as either the source or destination zone. The self zone is a system-defined zone. It does not require any interfaces to be configured as members. A zone pair that includes the self zone, along with the associated policy, applies to traffic that is directed to the router or traffic that the router generates. It does not apply to traffic traversing the router.

The following are additional rules for zone-based policy firewalls that govern interface behavior when the router is involved in the traffic flow:

- All traffic to and from a given interface is implicitly blocked when the interface is assigned to a zone, except traffic to or from other interfaces in the same zone, and traffic *to* any interface on the router.

- All the IP interfaces on the router are automatically made part of the "self" zone when a zone-based policy firewall is configured. The self zone is the only exception to the default deny-all policy. All traffic to any router interface is allowed until traffic is explicitly denied.

- The only exception to the "deny by default" approach is the traffic to and from the router itself. This traffic is permitted by default. You can configure an explicit policy to restrict such traffic.

Configuring Zone-Based Policy Firewalls Using the Basic Firewall Wizard

The Basic Firewall Wizard of Cisco SDM helps you implement a firewall. The wizard walks you through creating the firewall by asking you for information about the interfaces on the router, whether you want to configure a demilitarized zone (DMZ) network, and what rules you want to use in the firewall, as shown in Figure 3-33.

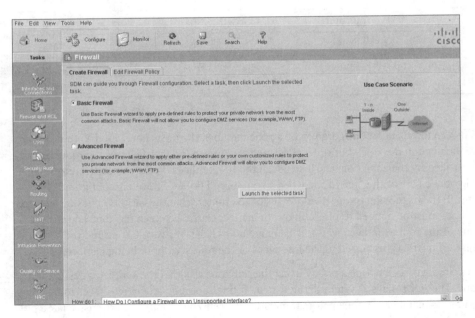

Figure 3-33 *Cisco IOS Firewall Wizard*

Follows these steps to configure a firewall using the Basic Firewall Wizard:

Step 1.   From Cisco SDM, choose **Configure > Firewall and ACL**.

Step 2.   From the Create Firewall tab, click the **Basic Firewall** option and click **Launch the Selected Task** button.

Step 3.   The Basic Firewall Configuration Wizard window appears (see Figure 3-34). Click **Next** to begin the configuration.

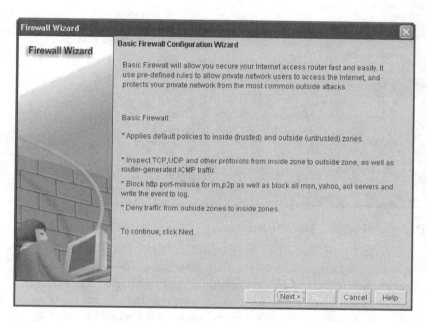

Figure 3-34   *Basic Firewall Configuration Wizard*

Note: If there is no Cisco IOS Classic Firewall configured, a zone-based policy firewall is created by the Basic or Advanced Firewall Wizards.

The first task you must perform to configure a basic firewall is to define inside (trusted) and outside (untrusted) interfaces. An outside (untrusted) interface is typically the router interface that is connected to the Internet or to your WAN. An inside (trusted) interface is typically a physical or logical interface that connects to the LAN. You can select multiple inside and outside interfaces.

The following steps are used for interface configuration:

Step 4.   From the Basic Firewall Interface Configuration window, check the **outside (untrusted)** check box and the **inside (trusted)** check box to identify each interface as an outside or an inside interface, as shown in Figure 3-35. Outside interfaces connect to your organization's WAN or to the Internet. Inside interfaces connect to your LAN. You can choose more than one of each.

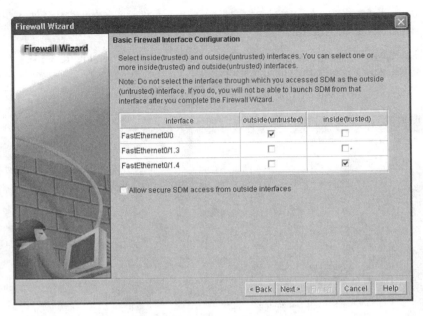

Figure 3-35   *Defining Inside and Outside Interfaces*

Step 5.   (Optional) Check the **Allow Secure Cisco SDM Access from Outside Interfaces** check box if you want users outside of the firewall to be able to access the router using Cisco SDM. Choosing this option permits secure HTTP access to the outside (untrusted) interface. Because it is a secure Cisco SDM connection to the firewall, you will not be able to browse the outside (untrusted) interface via HTTP after the firewall wizard completes the configuration. After you click **Next**, the wizard displays a screen that allows you to specify a host IP address or a network address. The firewall will be modified to allow access to the address you specify.

Step 6.   Click **Next**. If you checked the **Allow Secure SDM Access from the Outside Interfaces** check box, the Configuring Firewall for Remote Access window appears.

Step 7.   From the Configuring Firewall for Remote Access window, specify the source host or network from which Cisco SDM is allowed to remotely manage the router. To do this, choose **Network Address, Host IP Address,** or **Any** from the Type drop-down list, and then fill in the IP Address and Subnet Mask fields as appropriate.

The Basic Firewall Security Configuration window appears, as shown in Figure 3-36. Cisco SDM provides preconfigured application security policies that you can use to protect the network. Use the slider bar on the Basic Firewall Security Configuration window to choose the security level that you want and to view a description of the security that it provides.

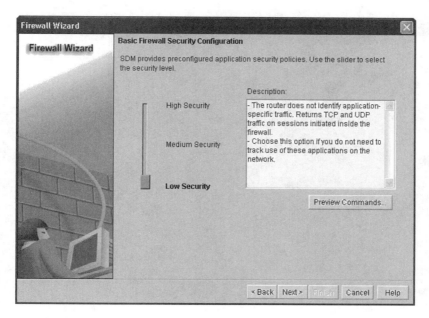

Figure 3-36 *Application Security Policy*

From the Basic Firewall Security Configuration window, you can click the **Preview Commands** button to view the Cisco IO commands that make up the chosen policy.

Note: The router must be configured with the IP address of at least one DNS server for application security to work.

The Firewall Configuration Summary window displays the policy name chosen, SDM_HIGH, SDM_MEDIUM, or SDM_LOW, and the configuration statements in the policy, as shown in Figure 3-37.

Example 3-14 shows the commands executed by the Basic Firewall Wizard.

Example 3-14 *Commands Executed by the Basic Firewall Configuration Wizard*

```
class-map type inspect match-any sdm-cls-insp-traffic
 match protocol cuseeme
 match protocol dns
 match protocol ftp
 match protocol h323
 match protocol https
 match protocol icmp
 match protocol imap
```

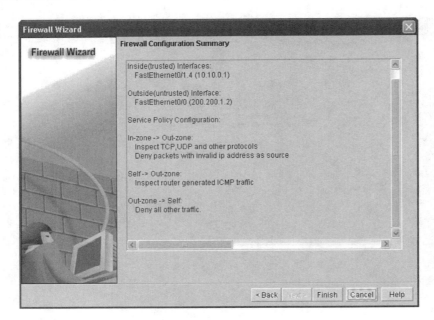

Figure 3-37   *Finishing the Basic Firewall Wizard*

```
 match protocol pop3
 match protocol netshow
 match protocol shell
 match protocol realmedia
 match protocol rtsp
 match protocol smtp extended
 match protocol sql-net
 match protocol streamworks
 match protocol tftp
 match protocol vdolive
 match protocol tcp
 match protocol udp
class-map type inspect match-all sdm-insp-traffic
 match class-map sdm-cls-insp-traffic
class-map type inspect match-any SDM_EIGRP
 match access-group name SDM_EIGRP
class-map type inspect match-any SDM_EIGRP_TRAFFIC
 match class-map SDM_EIGRP
class-map type inspect match-all SDM_EIGRP_PT
 match class-map SDM_EIGRP_TRAFFIC
class-map type inspect match-any sdm-cls-icmp-access
 match protocol icmp
class-map type inspect match-all sdm-icmp-access
 match class-map sdm-cls-icmp-access
```

Example 3-14 *Commands Executed by the Basic Firewall Configuration Wizard*

```
class-map type inspect match-all sdm-invalid-src
 match access-group 100
class-map type inspect match-all sdm-protocol-http
 match protocol http
!
!
policy-map type inspect sdm-permit-icmpreply
 class type inspect sdm-icmp-access
  inspect
 class class-default
  pass
policy-map type inspect sdm-inspect
 class type inspect sdm-invalid-src
  drop log
 class type inspect sdm-insp-traffic
  inspect
 class type inspect sdm-protocol-http
  inspect
 class class-default
policy-map type inspect sdm-permit
 class type inspect SDM_EIGRP_PT
  pass
 class class-default
!
zone security out-zone
zone security in-zone
zone-pair security sdm-zp-self-out source self destination out-zone
 service-policy type inspect sdm-permit-icmpreply
zone-pair security sdm-zp-out-self source out-zone destination self
 service-policy type inspect sdm-permit
zone-pair security sdm-zp-in-out source in-zone destination out-zone
 service-policy type inspect sdm-inspect
!
!
!
interface FastEthernet0/0
 description $FW_INSIDE$
zone-member security in-zone
!
!
interface Serial0/0/0
 description $FW_OUTSIDE$
zone-member security out-zone
!
!
```

Example 3-14 *Commands Executed by the Basic Firewall Configuration Wizard*

```
ip access-list extended SDM_EIGRP
 remark SDM_ACL Category=1
 permit eigrp any any
!
access-list 100 remark SDM_ACL Category=128
access-list 100 permit ip host 255.255.255.255 any
access-list 100 permit ip 127.0.0.0 0.255.255.255 any
access-list 100 permit ip 192.168.151.0 0.0.0.3 any
 !
```

Manually Configuring Zone-Based Policy Firewalls Using Cisco SDM

Cisco IOS zone-based policy firewalls are configured using C3PL, which uses a hierarchical structure to define inspection for network protocols and the groups of hosts to which the inspection applies.

There are four main steps to configure a Cisco IOS zone-based policy firewall:

Step 1.   Define zones.

Step 2.   Define class maps.

Step 3.   Define policy maps.

Step 4.   Define zone pairs and assign policy maps to zone pairs.

For a description of how you can implement a zone-based policy firewall, refer to the Zone-Based Policy Firewall Design Guide at Cisco.com.

Step 1: Define Zones

The first step in configuring a Cisco IOS zone-based policy firewall is to create zones. A zone, or security zone, is a group of interfaces to which you can apply a security policy. The interfaces in a zone should share common functions or features. For example, you might place two interfaces that connect to the LAN in one security zone, and the interfaces that connect to the Internet into another security zone.

For traffic to flow among all the interfaces in a router, all the interfaces must be a member of a security zone. It is not necessary for all router interfaces to be members of security zones.

Follow these steps to create a zone:

Step 1.   Choose **Configure > Additional Tasks > Zones**.

Step 2.   From the Zone panel, click **Add** to create a new zone, as shown in Figure 3-38.

Step 3.   The Add a Zone window appears. Enter a zone name in the Zone Name field.

Step 4.   Choose the interfaces that should participate in this zone by checking the check box in front of the interface name. Because physical interfaces can be

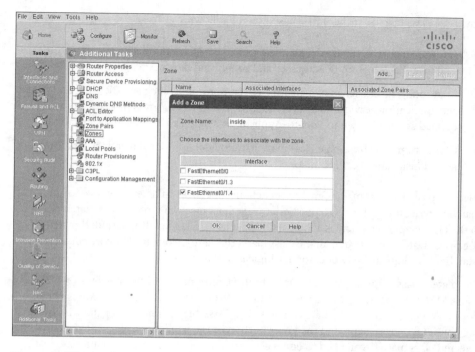

Figure 3-38 *Defining Zones with SDM*

placed in only one zone, they do not appear in the list if they have already been assigned to a zone. You can place virtual interfaces, such as Dialer interfaces or Virtual Template interfaces, in multiple zones, so these interfaces always appear in the list.

As you assign interfaces to zones, keep in mind the zone-based policy firewall rules that govern the interface behavior, such as described in Table 3-7.

Step 5.   Click **OK** to create the zone, and click **OK** at the Commands Delivery Status window.

After a zone has been created, you can change the interfaces that are associated with the zone, but you cannot change the name of the zone. Click **Edit** from the Zone panel to choose different interfaces for an existing zone. Click **Delete** from the Zone panel to remove a zone.

Note: A zone that is a member of a zone pair cannot be deleted.

Step 2: Define Class Maps

The next step in configuring a Cisco IOS zone-based policy firewall is to configure the class maps. Class maps identify traffic and traffic parameters that a Cisco IOS zone-based policy firewall selects for policy application. The policy maps define the actions to be taken on the traffic. Configuring a class map involves associating the class map with some traffic and setting attributes for the traffic.

Layer 3/4 class maps sort the traffic based on the following criteria:

■ **Access group:** A standard, extended, or named ACL can filter traffic based on source and destination IP addresses and source and destination ports.

■ **Protocol:** The class map can identify Layer 4 protocols such as TCP, UDP, and ICMP, and application services such as HTTP, SMTP, and DNS. Any well-known or user-defined service known to Port-to-Application Mapping (PAM) can be specified.

■ **Class map:** A subordinate class map that provides additional match criteria can be nested inside another class map.

Class maps can apply "match-any" or "match-all" operators to determine how to apply the match criteria. If match-any is specified, traffic must meet only one of the match criteria in the class map. Match-any is a logical OR operation, a logical disjunction. If match-all is specified, traffic must match all the class map criteria to belong to that particular class. Match-all is a logical AND operation, a logical conjunction.

To create a class map using Cisco SDM, choose **Configure > Additional Tasks > C3PL > Class Map > Inspection**, as shown in Figure 3-39. From the Inspect Class Maps panel, you can review, create, and edit class maps. The Class Map Name area of the window lists the configured class maps, and the lower portion of the window displays the details of the selected class map. If you need to edit a class map or see more detail about a class map, choose the class map from the list and click **Edit**.

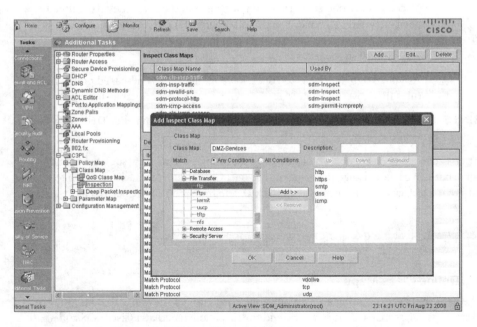

Figure 3-39　*Defining Class Maps Through SDM*

Note: A zone-based policy firewall also supports advanced Layer 7 application inspection. This topic is covered in the Cisco Securing Networks with Cisco Routers and Switches (SNRS) course.

Step 3: Define Policy Maps

Once you have created class maps, you create policy maps to which you apply class maps. Policy maps specify the actions to be taken when traffic matches the criteria. A policy map associates traffic classes with actions.

Inspection policy maps specify the action the router should take for traffic that matches the criteria in the associated class maps. The following are the actions a policy map supports:

- **Pass:** Traffic is allowed to pass from one zone to another, only in one direction. The router does not monitor the state of connections or session.

- **Drop:** The router drops unwanted traffic and can optionally log the event.

- **Inspect:** The router maintains state-based session and connection information so that the router permits traffic returning from a destination zone to a source zone.

Follow these steps to create a policy map using Cisco SDM:

Step 1.   Choose **Configure > Additional Tasks > C3PL > Policy Map > Protocol Inspection.**

Step 2.   From the Protocol Inspection Policy Maps panel, click **Add.**

Step 3.   Enter a policy name in the Policy Name field and optionally add a description in the Description field. The name and description that you enter will be visible in the Protocol Inspect Policy Maps window.

Step 4.   The Class Map and Action columns display the class maps that are associated with this policy map, and the action that the router should take for the traffic that the class map describes. Click **Add** to add a new class map to the list and configure the action.

Step 5.   The Associate Class Map window appears. In the Class Name field, enter the name of the class map you want to apply. If you do not know the name of the class map, or you want to create a new class map, click the down arrow to the right of the Class Name field. A pop-up menu appears that allows you to add a class map, select a class map, or choose the class-default, as shown in Figure 3-40.

Step 6.   After you have selected the class map, you must define the action that the policy map will take for traffic that matches this class map. From the Action section, click **Pass, Drop,** or **Inspect,** based on your needs for this class map.

Step 7.   Click **OK.**

Step 8.   If you want to add another class map to the policy, click **Add.** If you want to modify the actions of an existing class map, choose the class map from the Class Map list and click **Edit.** If you need to delete a class map, choose the

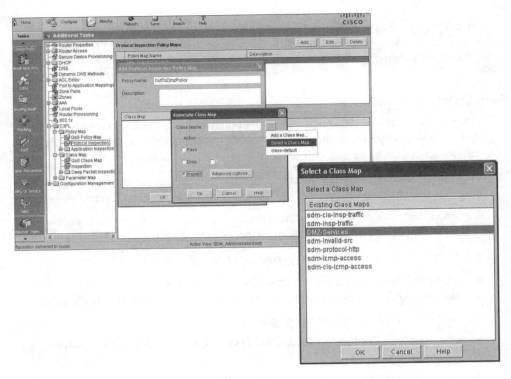

Figure 3-40   *Defining Policy Maps Through SDM*

class map from the Class Map list and click **Delete**. Use the **Move Up** and **Move Down** buttons to change the order in which the class maps are evaluated.

Step 9.   Click **OK**. At the Command Delivery Status window, click **OK**.

Step 4: Define Zone Pairs and Assign Policy Maps to Zone Pairs

A zone pair allows you to specify a unidirectional firewall policy between two security zones. The direction of the traffic is determined by specifying a source and destination security zone. The same zone cannot be defined as both the source and the destination.

If you want traffic to flow in both directions between two zones, you must create a zone pair for each direction. If you want traffic to flow freely among all interfaces, each interface must be configured in a zone.

Follow these steps to configure a new zone pair:

Step 1.   Choose **Configure > Additional Tasks > Zone Pairs**.

Step 2.   From the Zone Pairs panel, click **Add**. The Add a Zone Pair window appears, as shown in Figure 3-41.

Step 3.   In the Zone Pair field, enter a name for the zone pair. Choose a source zone from which traffic will originate, a destination zone to which traffic is to be sent, and the policy that determines which traffic can be sent across the zones.

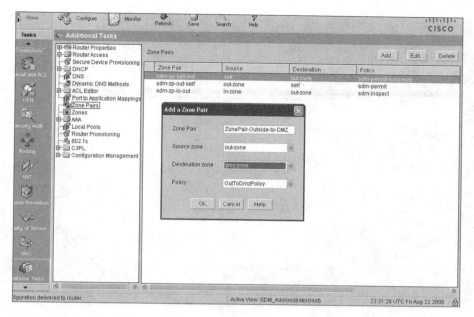

Figure 3-41 *Assigning Policy Maps to Zone Pairs*

The Source Zone and Destination Zone lists contain the zones configured on the router and the self zone. The self zone can be used when you are configuring zone pairs for traffic originating from the router itself, or destined for the router itself, such as a zone pair that is configured for SNMP traffic. The Policy list contains the name of each policy map that is configured on the router.

Step 4.   Click **OK** in the Add a Zone Pair window, and click **OK** in the Command Delivery Status window.

To edit a zone pair, from the Zone Pairs panel choose the zone pair you want to edit and click **Edit**. If you are editing a zone pair, you can change the policy map, but you cannot change the name or the source or destination zones.

After you have created the firewall, you can examine it by choosing **Configure > Firewall and ACL** and clicking the **Edit Firewall Policy** tab, as shown in Figure 3-42. A graphical view of the firewall displays in the context of the router interfaces. You can modify the firewall from this window if you need to.

Figure 3-43 shows, in a methodical manner, an example of what the resulting CLI commands might look like after configuring a Cisco IOS zone-based policy firewall that uses two interfaces and the default inspection parameters.

The class map named iinsprotocols is created and identifies three protocols that are to be inspected (HTTP, SMTP, and FTP). A policy map named iinspolicy is created that applies stateful inspection to the protocols that are listed in the iinsprotocols class map. Two zones, named private and internet, are created. Fastethernet0/0 is made a member of the private zone, and serial0/0/0 is made a member of the internet zone. Lastly, a zone pair

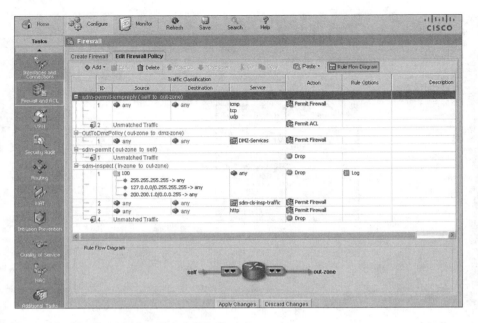

Figure 3-42 *Reviewing Firewall Policy*

```
class-map type inspect match-any iinsprotocols
 match protocol http
 match protocol smtp   ◄──────────────────── List of services defined in
 match protocol ftp                          the firewall policy
!
policy-map type inspect iinspolicy
 class type inspect iinsprotocols
  inspect   ◄──────────────────────────────── Apply action
!                                              (inspect = stateful inspection)
zone security private   ◄──────────────────── Zones created
zone security internet
!
interface fastethernet 0/0
 zone-member security private   ◄──────────── Interfaces assigned to zones
!
interface serial 0/0/0
 zone-member security internet
!
zone-pair security priv-to-internet source private destination internet
 service-policy type inspect iinspolicy   ◄── Inspection applied from
!                                             private to public zones
```

Figure 3-43 *Cisco IOS Zone-Based Firewall CLI Configuration*

named priv-to-internet is created with a source zone of private, a destination zone of "internet" zone, and the policy map named iinspolicy applied to it.

Monitoring a Zone-Based-Firewall

If the router runs a Cisco IOS image that supports the zone-based policy firewall feature, you can use the Cisco SDM to display the status of the firewall activity for each zone pair configured on the router. To display the firewall status information, choose **Monitor > Firewall Status**, as shown in Figure 3-44.

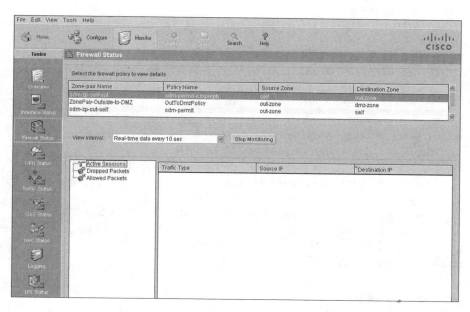

Figure 3-44   *Cisco IOS Zone-Based Firewall CLI Configuration*

The firewall policy list area displays the policy name, source zone, and destination zone for each zone pair. From the View Interval list box, choose one of the following options to specify how data should be collected:

■ **Real-time data every 10 sec:** Data is reported every 10 seconds. Each check mark on the horizontal axis of the Dropped Packets and Allowed Packets graph represents 10 seconds.

■ **60 minutes of data polled every 1 minute:** Data is collected every 1 minute, and the last 60 minutes result is displayed. Each check mark on the horizontal axis of the Dropped Packets and Allowed Packets graph represents 1 minute.

■ **12 hours of data polled every 12 minutes:** Data is reported every 12 minutes. Each check mark on the horizontal axis of the Dropped Packets and Allowed Packets graph represents 12 minutes.

Use the **show policy-map type inspect zone-pair session** command to examine the active connections in the zone-based policy firewall state table.

Example 3-15 output shows active connections from 10.0.2.12 to 172.26.26.51 port 80.

Example 3-15   show policy-map *Command Output*

```
R2# show policy-map type inspect zone-pair session
 Zone-pair: IINS-PAIR
  Service-policy inspect : HTTP-Policy
    Class-map: HTTP-Class (match-all)
      Match: access-group 110
      Match: protocol http
      Inspect
        Established Sessions
         Session 643BCF88 (10.0.2.12:3364)=>(172.26.26.51:80) http SIS_OPEN
          Created 00:00:10, Last heard 00:00:00
          Bytes sent (initiator:responder) [1268:64324]
         Session 643BB9C8 (10.0.2.12:3361)=>(172.26.26.51:80) http SIS_OPEN
          Created 00:00:16, Last heard 00:00:06
          Bytes sent (initiator:responder) [2734:38447]
         Session 643BD240 (10.0.2.12:3362)=>(172.26.26.51:80) http SIS_OPEN
          Created 00:00:14, Last heard 00:00:07
          Bytes sent (initiator:responder) [2219:39813]
         Session 643BBF38 (10.0.2.12:3363)=>(172.26.26.51:80) http SIS_OPEN
          Created 00:00:14, Last heard 00:00:06
          Bytes sent (initiator:responder) [2106:19895]
    Class-map: class-default (match-any)
      Match: any
      Drop (default action)
       58 packets, 2104 bytes
```

Summary

In this chapter, you have learned that a firewall is a set of rules designed to enforce an access control policy between two networks. You learned how to create firewall rules to implement your security policies. Cisco provides a range of firewall products that help you implement your security policies in a cost-effective way. ACLs provide packet-filtering capabilities for routers and firewalls to protect internal networks from the outside.

A zone-based policy firewall changes the firewall from the older interface-based model to a more flexible, more easily understood zone-based configuration model. Cisco IOS zone-based policy firewalls provide a more flexible way to implement your security policy and Cisco Router and Security Device Manager (SDM) makes it easier for you to configure and maintain the firewall capabilities of your routers.

References

For additional information, refer to these resources:

Deal, R. *Cisco Router Firewall Security* (Cisco Press, 2005)

Beaver, K. *Firewall Best Practices*, http://www.principlelogic.com/docs/ Firewall_Best_Practices.pdf

Morgan, B. and N. Lovering. *CCNP ISCW Official Exam Certification Guide* (Cisco Press, 2007)

Cisco Systems, Inc. *The Zone-Based Policy Firewall Design Guide*, http://www.cisco. com/en/US/products/sw/secursw/ps1018/products_tech_note09186a00808bc994.shtml

Review Questions

Use the questions here to review what you learned in this chapter. The correct answers are found in the Appendix, "Answers to Chapter Review Questions."

1. Which of the following is not a firewall?

   a. Static packet filters

   b. URL filters

   c. Application layer gateways

   d. Proxy servers

2. Which of the following is not a limitation or an issue for a stateful firewall?

   a. Stateful firewalls cannot prevent application layer attacks.

   b. Stateful firewalls can provide only limited support to protocols that are not stateful.

   c. Some applications open multiple connections and therefore are incompatible with some Stateful firewalls.

   d. Stateful firewall cannot provide a defense against spoofing attacks.

3. Match the following names and characteristics:

   a. Packet-filtering firewalls

   b. Application layer gateways

   c. Stateful packet filters

   d. Application inspection firewalls

   Characteristics

   1. Work primarily at the network level of the OSI model

   2. Are the most common firewalls

   3. Monitor sessions to determine the port numbers for secondary channels

   4. Were the first application layer firewalls

4. Which threats cannot be mitigated using ACLs?

   a. Malicious payloads

   b. DoS TCP SYN attacks

   c. ICMP message filtering

   d. IP address spoofing

5. Cisco routers are certified by which of the following? Select all that apply.

   a. FIPS 140

   b. NITS

   c. CMVP

   d. Common Criteria

6. Select the ACL numbers for a standard access list.

   a. 100–199

   b. 1–99

   c. 1300–1999

   d. 0–99

7. Which wildcard mask would match for IP subnets 172.30.16.0/24 to 172.30.31.0/24?

   a. 0.0.31.255

   b. 0.0.0.255

   c. 0.0.255.255

   d. 0.0.15.255

8. Which of the following is not an action of zone-based policy firewalls?

   a. Drop

   b. Reset

   c. Pass

   d. Inspect

9. Order the following steps for manually creating a zone-based policy firewall using Cisco SDM.

   a. Define class maps.

   b. Define zones.

   c. Define zone pairs and assign policy maps to the zone pairs.

   d. Define policy maps.

10. When using zone-based policy, for traffic to flow among all the interfaces in a router, all of the interfaces must be which of the following?

   a. Configured with the SDM Wizard

   b. A member of a security zone

   c. Placed in a virtual template

   d. A member of a dialer interface

11. What is the role of class maps?

    a. They group interfaces to which security policies will be applied.

    b. They allow to specify a unidirectional firewall policy between two security zones.

    c. They specify the actions to be taken when traffic matches the criteria.

    d. They identify traffic and traffic parameters that a Cisco IOS zone-based policy firewall selects for policy application.

12. Finish the sentence with the most accurate statement. CBAC...

    a. Performs traffic filtering based on application level protocol information

    b. Uses only ACLs to control traffic

    c. Is configured with the Cisco Common Classification Policy Language (C3PL)

    d. Uses a hierarchical structure to define inspection for network protocols

13. Which of the following is an accurate access list to allow outbound traffic of guests accessing to their incoming mail server?

    a. access-list 101 permit tcp any any eq 25

    b. access-list 101 permit tcp any eq 25 any

    c. access-list 101 permit tcp any eq 110 any

    d. access-list 101 permit tcp any any eq 110

14. Which of the following is not a caveat regarding ACLs?

    a. You need to use extended ACLs to implement security policies.

    b. Beware of the implicit **deny all** at the bottom of ACLs.

    c. Place more specific statements higher in ACLs.

    d. Ensure that statements at the top of ACLs do not negate statements found lower in the list.

This chapter introduces the concepts of cryptography and covers the following topics:

- Encryption, hashing, and digital signatures and how they provide confidentiality, integrity, and nonrepudiation

- Methods, algorithms, and purposes of symmetric encryption

- Use and purpose of hashes and digital signatures in providing integrity and nonrepudiation

- Use and purpose of asymmetric encryption and Public Key Infrastructure (PKI)

CHAPTER 4

Fundamentals of Cryptography

An IP Security (IPsec) virtual private network (VPN) is often used to connect branch of-fices, remote employees, and business partners to the resources of your company. It is a reliable way to maintain your company's privacy while streamlining operations, reducing costs, and allowing flexible network administration. This chapter provides a primer on the theory of cryptography; describes the fundamental concepts, technologies, and terms used with VPNs; and describes how to configure an IPsec site-to-site VPN tunnel using both the command-line interface (CLI) and the Cisco Router and Security Device Manager (SDM).

Examining Cryptographic Services

Cryptographic services are the foundation for many security implementations, and pro-vide confidentiality and integrity of data, when data might be exposed to untrusted par-ties. Understanding the basic functions of cryptography and how encryption and hashing provide confidentiality and integrity is important to creating a successful security policy. It is also important to understand the issues that are involved in key management.

Cryptology Overview

Cryptology is the science of the making and breaking of secret codes. Cryptology is bro-ken into two separate disciplines, as shown in Figure 4-1.

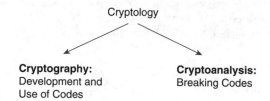

Figure 4-1 *Cryptology Disciplines: Cryptography and Cryptanalysis*

Cryptography is the development and use of codes, and cryptanalysis is the breaking of those codes. A symbiotic relationship exists between the two disciplines because each makes the other one better. National security organizations employ members of both dis-ciplines and put them to work against each other.

In the past, there have been times when each discipline has been ahead of the other. For example, during the Hundred Years' War between France and England, the cryptanalysts were ahead of the cryptographers. France believed that its cipher was unbreakable; however, the Englishmen were able to break it. Some historians believe that World War II largely turned on the fact that the winning side on both fronts was much more successful than the losing side at cracking the encryption of its adversary.

It is an ironic fact of cryptography that it is impossible to prove an algorithm secure. You can prove only that it is not vulnerable to known cryptanalytic attacks. If there are methods that have been developed but are unknown to the cryptanalysts, an algorithm might be able to be cracked. You can prove only invulnerability to known attacks, except for a brute-force attack.

All algorithms are vulnerable to brute force. If every possible key is tried, one of the keys has to work. Therefore, no algorithm is unbreakable. The best you can hope for are algorithms that are vulnerable only to brute-force attacks.

Note: Two separate techniques can be used to try to achieve secure communication. The first one is discussed in this chapter: cryptography, which is the science of encrypting a message.

The second technique is called *steganography*, which pertains to the method used to hide a message. The message is being hidden either within another message or by other means. Examples: The German Embassy in Washington, D.C., used steganography by hiding a message within a message. The first letter of each word of a telegram would make up a secret message. This method is referred to as using a null cipher. Another example of steganography was by Histiaeus, a Greek tyrant, who had the head of his most trusted slave shaved, tattooed a message on the scalp, waited for the hair to grow back, and then dispatched the slave to deliver the secret message. Obviously, the element of urgency wasn't there!

By comparison, when using cryptography, others are aware that a secret message is being transmitted, but hopefully they can't decipher the message. With steganography, third parties don't even know that a message is being transmitted.

If the topic of cryptography and steganography interests you, you must read this fascinating book *The Code Book: The Science of Secrecy from Ancient Egypt to Quantum Cryptography*, by Simon Singh (First Anchor Books Edition, 2000).

The History of Cryptography

The history of cryptography starts in diplomatic circles thousands of years ago. Messengers from a king's court would take encrypted messages to other courts. Occasionally, other courts not involved in the communication would attempt to steal any message sent to a kingdom they considered an adversary. Encryption was first used to prevent this information theft.

Not long after, military commanders started using encryption to secure messages. The messengers had challenges in many ways greater than that of the diplomatic messenger because killing the messenger to get the message was common. With the stakes so high, military commanders resorted to encryption to secure their military communications.

The cipher attributed to Julius Caesar was a simple substitution cipher that he used on the battlefield to quickly encrypt a message that could easily be decrypted by his commanders. Thomas Jefferson, the third president of the United States, was a man of many interests. Among his many inventions was an encryption system that he was believed to have used when serving as Secretary of State from 1790 to 1793.

Arthur Scherbius invented a machine in 1918 that served as a template for the machines that all the major participants in World War II used. He called the machine Enigma and sold it to Germany, estimating that if 1000 cryptanalysts tested 4 keys per minute, all day, every day, it would take 1.8 billion years to try them all.

During World War II, the Germans and Allies had machines modeled after the Scherbius machine. These were the most sophisticated encryption devices ever developed, and in response to it, the British arguably invented the world's first computer, the Colossus, to break the encryption that was used by the Enigma machine of Germany.

Ciphers

A cipher is an algorithm for performing encryption and decryption; they are a series of well-defined steps that you can follow as a procedure. Substitution ciphers simply substitute one letter for another. In their simplest form, substitution ciphers retain the letter frequency of the original message.

The cipher attributed to Julius Caesar is a simple substitution cipher. Every day has a different key, and that key is used to adjust the alphabet accordingly. For example, if today's key is five, an *A* is moved five spaces, resulting in an encoded message uses *F* instead. A *B* is a *G*, a *C* is an *H*, and so forth. The next day the key might be eight, and the process begins again, with an *A* now being *I*, *B* is *J*, and so on.

For example, if a message has 25 occurrences of the letter *S*, and *S* is replaced by the letter *Q*, there will 25 occurrences of the letter *Q*. If the message is long enough, it will be vulnerable to frequency analysis because it retains the frequency patterns found in the language. Because of this weakness, polyalphabetic ciphers were invented.

Vigenère Cipher

The Vigenère cipher, shown in Figure 4-2, is a polyalphabetic cipher that encrypts text by using a series of different Caesar ciphers based on the letters of a keyword. It is a simple form of polyalphabetic substitution and therefore invulnerable to frequency analysis.

The method was originally described in 1553 in a book by Giovan Batista Belaso. Mistakenly, Blaise de Vigenère, a French cryptographer, has been attributed with its invention, hence its name.

To illustrate how it works, suppose that a key of SECRETKEY is used to encode ATTACK AT DAWN. The *A* is encoded by looking at the row starting with *S* for the letter in the *A* column. In this case, the *A* is replaced with *S*. Then you look for the row that begins with *E* for the letter *T*. This results in *X* as our second character. If you continue this encoding method, the message ATTACK AT DAWN is encrypted as SXVRGDKXBSAP.

PLAIN TEXT LETTER (columns) / KEYWORD LETTER (rows)

	A	B	C	D	E	F	G	H	I	J	K	L	M	N	O	P	Q	R	S	T	U	V	W	X	Y	Z
A	A	B	C	D	E	F	G	H	I	J	K	L	M	N	O	P	Q	R	S	T	U	V	W	X	Y	Z
B	B	C	D	E	F	G	H	I	J	K	L	M	N	O	P	Q	R	S	T	U	V	W	X	Y	Z	A
C	C	D	E	F	G	H	I	J	K	L	M	N	O	P	Q	R	S	T	U	V	W	X	Y	Z	A	B
D	D	E	F	G	H	I	J	K	L	M	N	O	P	Q	R	S	T	U	V	W	X	Y	Z	A	B	C
E	E	F	G	H	I	J	K	L	M	N	O	P	Q	R	S	T	U	V	W	X	Y	Z	A	B	C	D
F	F	G	H	I	J	K	L	M	N	O	P	Q	R	S	T	U	V	W	X	Y	Z	A	B	C	D	E
G	G	H	I	J	K	L	M	N	O	P	Q	R	S	T	U	V	W	X	Y	Z	A	B	C	D	E	F
H	H	I	J	K	L	M	N	O	P	Q	R	S	T	U	V	W	X	Y	Z	A	B	C	D	E	F	G
I	I	J	K	L	M	N	O	P	Q	R	S	T	U	V	W	X	Y	Z	A	B	C	D	E	F	G	H
J	J	K	L	M	N	O	P	Q	R	S	T	U	V	W	X	Y	Z	A	B	C	D	E	F	G	H	I
K	K	L	M	N	O	P	Q	R	S	T	U	V	W	X	Y	Z	A	B	C	D	E	F	G	H	I	J
L	L	M	N	O	P	Q	R	S	T	U	V	W	X	Y	Z	A	B	C	D	E	F	G	H	I	J	K
M	M	N	O	P	Q	R	S	T	U	V	W	X	Y	Z	A	B	C	D	E	F	G	H	I	J	K	L
N	N	O	P	Q	R	S	T	U	V	W	X	Y	Z	A	B	C	D	E	F	G	H	I	J	K	L	M
O	O	P	Q	R	S	T	U	V	W	X	Y	Z	A	B	C	D	E	F	G	H	I	J	K	L	M	N
P	P	Q	R	S	T	U	V	W	X	Y	Z	A	B	C	D	E	F	G	H	I	J	K	L	M	N	O
Q	Q	R	S	T	U	V	W	X	Y	Z	A	B	C	D	E	F	G	H	I	J	K	L	M	N	O	P
R	R	S	T	U	V	W	X	Y	Z	A	B	C	D	E	F	G	H	I	J	K	L	M	N	O	P	Q
S	S	T	U	V	W	X	Y	Z	A	B	C	D	E	F	G	H	I	J	K	L	M	N	O	P	Q	R
T	T	U	V	W	X	Y	Z	A	B	C	D	E	F	G	H	I	J	K	L	M	N	O	P	Q	R	S
U	U	V	W	X	Y	Z	A	B	C	D	E	F	G	H	I	J	K	L	M	N	O	P	Q	R	S	T
V	V	W	X	Y	Z	A	B	C	D	E	F	G	H	I	J	K	L	M	N	O	P	Q	R	S	T	U
W	W	X	Y	Z	A	B	C	D	E	F	G	H	I	J	K	L	M	N	O	P	Q	R	S	T	U	V
X	X	Y	Z	A	B	C	D	E	F	G	H	I	J	K	L	M	N	O	P	Q	R	S	T	U	V	W
Y	Y	Z	A	B	C	D	E	F	G	H	I	J	K	L	M	N	O	P	Q	R	S	T	U	V	W	X
Z	Z	A	B	C	D	E	F	G	H	I	J	K	L	M	N	O	P	Q	R	S	T	U	V	W	X	Y

Figure 4-2 *The Vigenère Cipher*

Note: When using the Vigenère cipher and the message is longer than the key, just repeat the key.

In transposition ciphers, no letters are replaced, they are simply rearranged. An example of this type of cipher is taking the message THE PACKAGE IS DELIVERED and transposing it to read DEREVILEDSIEGAKCAPEHT. In this example, the key is to reverse the letters.

Another example of a transposition cipher is the rail fence cipher, shown in Figure 4-3. In this transposition, the words are spelled out as if they were a rail fence. The example in Figure 4-3 uses a key of three to illustrate how this could be done.

The message THE COVER IS BLOWN FLEE AT ONCE would be encoded as TOIOLTEHCVRSLWFEAOCEEBNEN using this method of transposition. Once again, no letters were changed; they were just rearranged.

The one-time pad was invented and patented by Gilbert Vernam in 1917 while working at AT&T. The primary design of the one-time pad was meant to overcome the weaknesses of using the Vigenère cipher. Vernam's idea was a stream cipher that would apply the exclusive OR (XOR) operation to plaintext with a key, but still using the Vigenère cipher. Joseph Mauborgne, a captain in the U.S. Army Signal Corps, contributed the idea of using random data as a key. This combined idea is so significant that the National Security Agency (NSA) has called this patent "perhaps the most important in the history of cryptography."

Cipher Text:

```
T...O...I...O...L...T...E.H.C.V.R.S.L.W.F.E.A.O.C...E...E...B...N...E...N..
```

Rail Fence Cipher with a Key of Three:

```
T...O...I...O...L...T...E
.H.C.V.R.S.L.W.F.E.A.O.C.
..E...E...B...N...E...N..
```

In order to read the message, simply look diagonally, following the rail fence.

Clear Text = THE COVER IS BLOWN FLEE AT ONCE

Figure 4-3   *Rail Fence Cipher*

Figure 4-4 shows three one-time pads used in conjunction with the Vigenère cipher.

Sheet 1				
E	M	Z	F	O
Y	P	G	A	Q
R	N	C	V	X
T	L	B	I	H
J	S	U	D	K

Sheet 2				
N	S	D	F	Z
V	T	A	M	P
G	L	Y	E	X
B	R	W	U	I
Q	H	O	K	C

Sheet 3				
T	E	K	C	W
N	X	P	R	Z
I	B	Y	U	L
V	O	S	H	Q
G	M	F	J	A

Figure 4-4   *One-Time Pads*

In Figure 4-5, the plaintext "at dawn attack the high plains" is encrypted with Sheet 2 of the one-time pads, using the Vigenère cipher.

In Figure 4-6, the ciphertext is unencrypted using Sheet 2 of the one-time pads.

There are several difficulties inherent in using one-time pads in the real world. The first of these is the challenge of creating random data. Computers, because they have a mathematical foundation, are incapable of creating random data. In addition, if the key is used more than once, it is trivial to break. Key distribution is also challenging (for example, how do you distribute the pads?).

Note: RC4 is an example of a Vernam cipher that is widely used on the Internet. It is not a one-time-pad because the key used is not random. If you have used Wired Equivalent Privacy (WEP) with a wireless network, you have used RC4.

The Process of Encryption

Encryption is the process of disguising a message in such a way as to hide its original contents, as shown in Figure 4-7. With encryption, the plaintext readable message is converted to ciphertext, which is the unreadable, "disguised" message. Decryption reverses

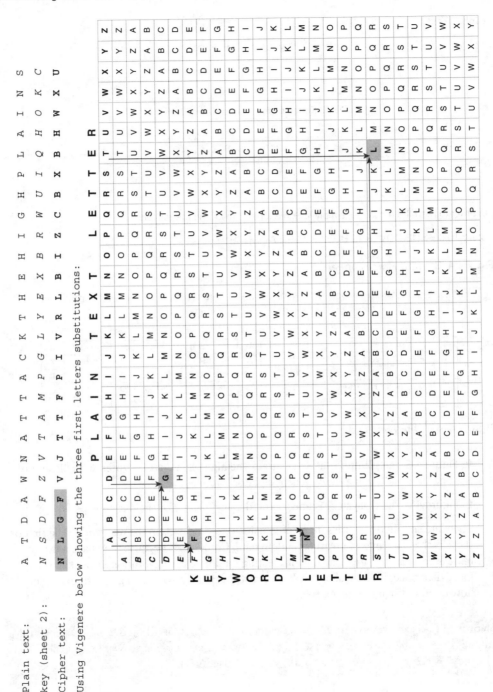

Plain text: A T D A W N A T T A C K T H E H I G H P L A I N S

key (sheet 2): N S D F Z V T A M P G L Y E X B R W U I Q H O K C

Cipher text: N L G F V J T T P I V R L B I Z X B X H W X U

Using Vigenere below showing the three first letters substitutions:

Figure 4-5 *Encryption Using One-Time Pad*

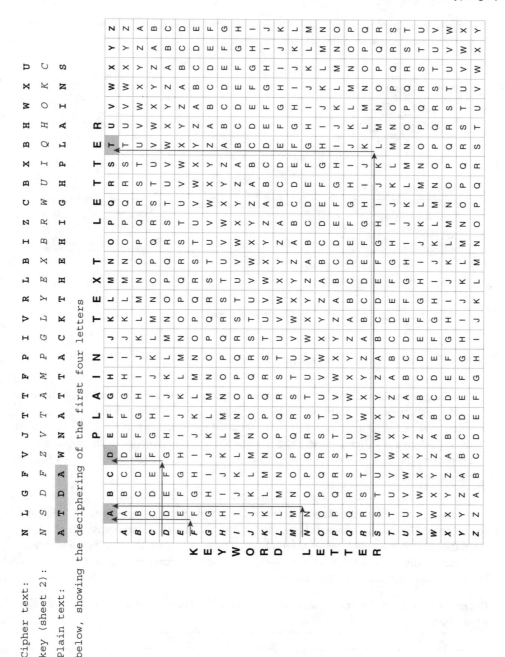

Figure 4-6   *Unencryption Using One-Time Pad*

the process. The purpose of encryption is to guarantee confidentiality so that only authorized entities can read the original message.

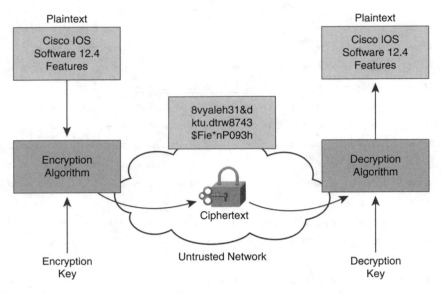

Figure 4-7   *Transforming Plaintext into Ciphertext*

Old encryption algorithms, such as the Caesar cipher or the Enigma machine, were based on the secrecy of the algorithm to achieve confidentiality. With modern technology, where reverse engineering is often simple, public-domain algorithms are often used. With most modern algorithms, successful decryption requires knowledge of the appropriate cryptographic keys; that is, the security of encryption lies in the secrecy of the keys, not the algorithm.

Nowadays, encryption algorithms such as the Triple Data Encryption Standard (3DES) and the Advanced Encryption Standard (AES) are readily distributed. So, because we all share the same algorithms, they have no need for protection (except for the fact that Western countries define cryptography as munitions, and therefore encryption algorithms are subject to the same export regulations as weapons.)

Because we all share algorithms, what we protect are the cryptographic keys used with the algorithms.

Classical ciphers are either transposition ciphers or substitution ciphers.

Recall that a transposition cipher exchanges the position of letters, whereas a substitution cipher replaces one letter with another letter based on a secret key.

Transposition rule:
1st Letter Goes in 3rd Position
2nd Letter Goes in 1st Position
3rd Letter Goes in 2nd Position

Clear Text: CHAMPLAIN

Grouping of 3 Letters: CHA MPL AIN

Applying Substitution: CHA MPL AIN

Cipher Text: **ACHLMPNAI**

Figure 4-8   *Example of a Transposition Cipher*

Figure 4-9 illustrates an example of a simple computer version of a substitution cipher, where the word WOLFE is translated in ASCII. The key MAJOR is also translated in ASCII. The key is applied to the cleartext using in this example the logical operation XOR. The result is ciphertext. The result of applying the key using again the XOR operation is the deciphering of the cipher text to its original cleartext.

Clear Text = WOLFE
Key = MAJOR
Substitution Algorithm: XOR

Exclusive or = Logical Operation of **Exclusive Disjunction**
(When the elements are the same, the result is 1, and when the elements are different, the result is 1.)

WOLFE in ASCII:	01010111	01001111	01001100	01000110	01000101
MAJOR in ASCII:	01001101	01000001	01001010	01001111	01010010
Cipher Text:	11100101	11110001	11111001	11110110	11101000

Re-applying the Key On the Cipher Text to Find the Clear Text:

Cipher Text:	11100101	11110001	11111001	11110110	11101000
MAJOR in ASCII:	01001101	01000001	01001010	01001111	01010010
Clear Text ASCII:	01010111	01001111	01001100	01000110	01000101

The clear text ASCII found in the last operation corresponds to WOLFE in ASCII.

Figure 4-9   *Computer Version of a Substitution Cipher*

XOR is a type of logical disjunction on two operands that results in a value of true if only one of the operands has a value of true. In other words, for the result to be true (result of 1), the two operands must be different (one operand has to be 0 and the other operand must be

1). In mathematics, operands are the input values used on the operation. With the formula 4 * 5, 4 and 5 are operands, and * (multiplication) is the operation.

Figure 4-9 is an example of both a substitution cipher and symmetrical encryption. Symmetrical encryption is discussed later in this chapter.

Encryption is usually used to provide confidentiality at an Open Systems Interconnection (OSI) layer, such as the following:

- Encrypt application layer data, such as secure email, secure database sessions (Oracle SQL*Net), and secure messaging (Lotus Notes sessions)

- Encrypt session layer data, using a protocol such as Secure Sockets Layer (SSL) or Transport Layer Security (TLS)

- Encrypt network layer data, using protocols such as those provided in the IPsec protocol suite

- Encrypt link layer data, using proprietary link-encrypting devices

Encryption Application Examples

The IP Security (IPsec) protocols can provide this encryption functionality for all the packets routed over an untrusted network. The encrypting IPsec peer takes a packet with the plaintext payload, encrypts the payload into ciphertext, and forwards the packet to the untrusted network. Its IPsec partner receives the ciphertext payload packet and decrypts the payload into the original plaintext. The two IPsec peers share the same encryption and decryption algorithm and proper keys.

The SSL protocol provides an encrypted channel on top of an existing TCP session. For example, HTTPS provides, among other services, confidentiality of the session between a web browser and a web server, using symmetric cryptography.

Both IPsec and SSL are used to set up a VPN. An IPsec VPN is application independent, and requires a specialized IP stack on the end system or in the packet path that includes IPsec. An SSL-based VPN supports only web-based applications, but the SSL software is included with all Internet browsers. Both SSL and IPsec are explained in more detail later in this book.

In contrast to IPsec and SSL, Layer 2 encryption, also known as data-link encryption, encrypts the whole frame, including the physical address fields located in the header of the frame, and therefore can be used only on point-to-point links where no network switching or routing equipment is required for path decision.

Note: IPsec implementation is a mandatory part of IPv6.

Cryptanalysis

Cryptanalysis is the practice of breaking codes to obtain the meaning of encrypted data. An attacker who tries to break an algorithm or encrypted ciphertext might use one of the following attacks:

- Brute-force attack

- Ciphertext-only attack

- Known-plaintext (the usual brute-force) attack

- Chosen-plaintext attack

- Chosen-ciphertext attack

- Birthday attack

- Meet-in-the-middle attack

The sections that follow describe these attacks in greater detail.

Brute-Force Attack

In a brute-force attack, an attacker tries every possible key with the decryption algorithm, knowing that eventually one of them will work. All encryption algorithms are vulnerable to this attack. On average, a brute-force attack will succeed about 50 percent of the way through the keyspace. The objective of modern cryptographers is to have a sufficiently large keyspace so that it takes too much money and too much time to accomplish a brute-force attack.

Note: As reported by Distributed.net in 1999, a Data Encryption Standard (DES) cracking machine was used to recover a 56-bit DES key in 22 hours using brute force. It is estimated that it would take 149 trillion years to crack Advanced Encryption Standard (AES) using the same method. You can find more information at http://www.distributed.net/des/.

Ciphertext-Only Attack

In a ciphertext-only attack, the attacker has the ciphertext of several messages, all of which have been encrypted using the same encryption algorithm, but the attacker has no knowledge of the underlying plaintext. The job of the attacker is to recover the ciphertext of as many messages as possible, or better yet, to deduce the key or keys used to encrypt the messages so as to decrypt other messages encrypted with the same keys. The attacker could use statistical analysis to achieve the result. Those attacks are no longer practical today because modern algorithms produce pseudorandom output that is resistant to statistical analysis.

Known-Plaintext Attack

In a known-plaintext attack, the attacker has access to the ciphertext of several messages, but also knows something about the plaintext underlying that ciphertext. With knowledge of the underlying protocol, file type, and some characteristic strings that might appear in the plaintext, the attacker uses a brute-force attack to try keys until decryption with the correct key produces a meaningful result. This attack may be the most practical attack, because attackers can usually assume the type and some features of the underlying plaintext, if they can only capture ciphertext. However, modern algorithms with enormous keyspaces make it unlikely for this attack to succeed, because on average an attacker would have to search through at least half of the keyspace to be successful.

Note: A known-plaintext attack was used in the cracking of the Enigma. During World War II, Alan Turing, a famous British crypto-mathematician, discovered that at around 6 a.m. each day the Germans were sending an encrypted weather report. Turing was sure that within the ciphertext captured around that time of day the word WETTER (weather in German) could be found. With the ciphertext equivalent to the plaintext WEATHER, Turing had a good start to continue reverse engineering the rest of the message.
In cryptanalysis, a sample of ciphertext suspected to be a resulting plaintext is called a *crib*.

Chosen-Plaintext Attack

In a chosen-plaintext attack, the attacker chooses what data the encryption device encrypts and observes the ciphertext output. A chosen-plaintext attack is more powerful than a known-plaintext attack because the attacker gets to choose the plaintext blocks to encrypt, allowing the attacker to choose plaintext that might yield more information about the key. This attack might not be very practical, because it is often difficult or impossible to capture both the ciphertext and plaintext, unless the trusted network has been broken into, and the attacker already has access to confidential information.

Chosen-Ciphertext Attack

In a chosen-ciphertext attack, the attacker can choose different ciphertexts to be decrypted and has access to the decrypted plaintext. With the pair, the attacker can search through the keyspace and determine which key decrypts the chosen ciphertext in the captured plaintext. For example, the attacker has access to a tamperproof encryption device with an embedded key. His job is to deduce the embedded key by sending data through the box. This attack is analogous to the chosen-plaintext attack. This attack might not be very practical, because it is often difficult or impossible to capture both the ciphertext and plaintext, unless the trusted network has been broken into, and the attacker already has access to confidential information.

Birthday Attack

The birthday attack gets its name from the amazing statistical probability involved in two individuals having the same birthday. According to statisticians, the probability that 2 people in a group of 23 people share the same birthday is greater than 50 percent.

This particular attack is a form of brute-force attack against hash functions. If some function, when supplied with a random input, returns one of k equally likely values, then by repeating the function with different inputs, the same output is expected after $1.2k^{1/2}$ number of times.

Tip: To test the birthday theory, input 365 in the place of k.

Meet-in-the-Middle

The meet-in-the-middle attack is a known-plaintext attack. Do not confuse this with the *man-in-the-middle attack*, which is discussed later. In a meet-in-the-middle attack, the attacker knows a portion of the plaintext and the corresponding ciphertext. The plaintext is encrypted with every possible key, and the results are stored. The ciphertext is then decrypted using every key until one of the results matches one of the stored values.

Encryption Algorithm Features

The following are features that a good encryption algorithm provides:

- Resists cryptographic attacks

- Supports variable and long key lengths and scalability

- Creates an avalanche effect

- Does not have export or import restrictions

A good cryptographic algorithm is designed in such a way that it resists common cryptographic attacks. The best way to break data protected by the algorithm is to try to decrypt the data using all the possible keys. The amount of time that such an attack needs depends on the number of possible keys, but is generally very, very long. With appropriately long keys, such attacks are usually considered unfeasible.

Variable-key lengths and scalability are also desirable attributes of a good encryption algorithm. The longer the encryption key, the longer it takes an attacker to break it. For example, a 16-bit key would mean that there are 65,536 possible keys, but a 56-bit key would mean there are 7.2×10^{16} possible keys. Scalability provides flexible key length and allows you to select the strength and speed of encryption that you need.

When changing only a few bits of the plaintext message causes its ciphertext to change completely, this is known as an *avalanche effect*. The avalanche effect is a desired feature of an encryption algorithm because it allows very similar messages to be sent over an untrusted medium, with the encrypted (ciphertext) messages being completely different.

You must carefully consider export and import restrictions when you use encryption internationally. Some countries do not allow the export of encryption algorithms, or allow only the export of these algorithms with shorter keys, and some countries impose import restrictions on cryptographic algorithms.

In January 2000, the restrictions that the U.S. Department of Commerce placed on export regulations were dramatically relaxed. Currently, any cryptographic product is exportable under a license exception unless the end users are governments outside of the United States or are embargoed. Visit http://www.bis.doc.gov/encryption/default.htm for more information about the current U.S. Department of Commerce export regulations.

Symmetric and Asymmetric Encryption Algorithms

An encryption algorithm, which is also called a cipher, is a mathematical function that is used to encrypt and decrypt data. Generally, there are two functions, one to encrypt and one to decrypt. If the security of an encryption system is based on the secrecy of the algorithm itself, the algorithm code must be heavily guarded. If the algorithm is revealed, every party that is involved must change the algorithm.

Modern cryptography takes a different approach: All algorithms are public, and cryptographic keys are used to ensure the secrecy of data. Cryptographic keys are sequences of bits that are input into an encryption algorithm together with the data to be encrypted. There are two classes of encryption algorithms, which differ in their use of keys:

■ **Symmetric encryption algorithms:** These use the same key to encrypt and decrypt data.

■ **Asymmetric encryption algorithms:** These use different keys to encrypt and decrypt data.

Key Topic

A key is a required parameter for encryption algorithms

There are two concepts regarding keys:

■ **Symmetric encryption:** The same key encrypts and decrypts.
■ **Asymmetric encryption:** One key encrypts, a different key decrypts.

Symmetric Encryption Algorithms

Symmetric encryption algorithms are algorithms in which the encryption and decryption keys are the same, as shown in Figure 4-10. Therefore, the sender and the receiver must share the same secret key before communicating securely. The security of a symmetric algorithm rests in the secrecy of the symmetric key; by obtaining the key, anyone can encrypt and decrypt messages. Symmetric encryption is often called secret-key encryption. Symmetric, or secret-key, encryption is the more traditional form of cryptography. The typical key length range of symmetric encryption algorithms is 40 to 256 bits.

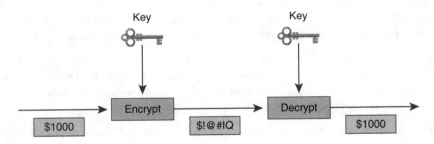

Figure 4-10 *Symmetric Encryption at Work*

The following are well-known encryption algorithms that use symmetric keys:

■ **DES:** 56-bit keys

■ **Triple Data Encryption Standard (3DES):** 112- and 168-bit keys

■ **AES:** 128-, 192-, and 256-bit keys

■ **International Data Encryption Algorithm (IDEA):** 128-bit keys

■ **The RC series (RC2, RC4, RC5, and RC6):**
  ■ **RC2:** 40- and 64-bit keys

- **RC4:** 1- to 256-bit keys
- **RC5:** 0- to 2040-bit keys
- **RC6:** 128-, 192-, and 256-bit keys

- **Blowfish:** 32- to 448-bit keys

The most commonly used techniques in symmetric encryption cryptography are block ciphers, stream ciphers, and message authentication codes (MAC).

Because symmetric algorithms are usually quite fast, they are often used for wire-speed encryption in data networks. Symmetric algorithms are based on simple mathematical operations and can easily be accelerated by hardware. Because of their speed, you can use symmetric algorithms for bulk encryption when data privacy is required (for example, to protect a VPN).

On the other hand, key management can be a challenge. The communicating parties must exchange the symmetric, secret key using a secure channel before any encryption can occur. Therefore, the security of any cryptographic system depends greatly on the security of the key exchange method.

Because of their speed, symmetric algorithms are frequently used for encryption services, with additional key management algorithms providing secure key exchange.

Asymmetric Encryption Algorithms

Asymmetric algorithms, also sometimes called *public-key algorithms*, are designed in such a way that the key used for encryption differs from the key used for decryption, as shown in Figure 4-11.

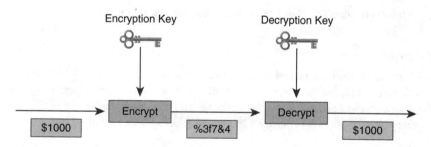

Figure 4-11 *Asymmetric Encryption at Work*

The decryption key cannot, in any reasonable amount of time, be calculated from the encryption key and vice versa. The typical key length range for asymmetric algorithms is 512 to 4096 bits. You cannot directly compare the key length of asymmetric and symmetric algorithms because the underlying design of the two algorithm families differs greatly.

Note: For further reference, consult the book *Applied Cryptography*, by Bruce Schneier. Mr. Schneier also maintains an informative and entertaining blog/newsletter, which you can subscribe to at http://www.crypto-gram.com.

The best-known asymmetric cryptographic algorithms are RSA, ElGamal, and elliptic curve algorithms.

Note: Rivest, Shamir, and Aldeman (RSA), who met while at the Massachusetts Institute of Technology (MIT), released the RSA algorithm in 1977.

Asymmetric algorithms can be up to 1000 times slower than symmetric algorithms. Their design is based on computational problems, such as factoring extremely large numbers or computing discrete logarithms of extremely large numbers. Because they lack speed, asymmetric algorithms are typically used in low-volume cryptographic mechanisms, such as digital signatures and key exchange. However, the key management of asymmetric algorithms tends to be simpler than that of symmetric algorithms, because usually one of the two encryption or decryption keys can be made public.

Because symmetric ciphers are faster than asymmetric algorithms, they are used for bulk data encryption.

Block and Stream Ciphers

Algorithms can operate in two modes:

- **Block mode:** The algorithm can work on only fixed chunks of data.
- **Stream mode:** The algorithm can process data bit by bit.

Block Ciphers

Block ciphers transform a fixed-length block of plaintext into a block of ciphertext of the same length. Applying the reverse transformation to the ciphertext block, using the same secret key, results in decryption. Currently, the fixed length, also known as the block size, for many block ciphers is typically 128 bits. DES has a block size of 64 bits.

Note: *Block size* refers to how much data is encrypted at any one time, whereas *key length* refers to the size of the encryption key. For example, DES encrypts blocks in 64-bit chunks, including an 8-bit parity check, thus yielding a 56-bit effective key strength.

Block ciphers usually result in output data that is larger than the input data because the ciphertext must be a multiple of the block size. To accomplish this, block algorithms take data one chunk at a time (for example, 8 bytes) and use padding to add artificial data (blanks) if there is less input data than one full block.

The following are common block ciphers:

- DES and 3DES, running in Electronic Code Book (ECB) and Cipher Block Chaining (CBC) mode

- AES

- IDEA

- Secure and Fast Encryption Routine (SAFER)

- Skipjack

- Blowfish

- RSA

Stream Ciphers

Unlike block ciphers, stream ciphers operate on smaller units of plaintext, typically bits. With a stream cipher, the transformation of these smaller plaintext units varies, depending on when they are encountered during the encryption process. Stream ciphers can be much faster than block ciphers, and generally do not increase the message size, because they can encrypt an arbitrary number of bits.

Common stream ciphers include the following:

- DES and 3DES, running in output feedback (OFB) or cipher feedback (CFB) mode

- RC4

- Software Encryption Algorithm (SEAL)

Algorithms can operate in two modes:

- **Block mode:** The algorithm can work on only fixed chunks of data (for example, 64 bit) requiring padding to align data to block size.
- **Stream mode:** The algorithm can process data bit by bit. Stream mode keeps data size constant; block mode has bigger ciphertext size.

Key Topic

Encryption Algorithm Selection

Choosing an encryption algorithm is one of the most important steps of building a cryptography-based solution. You should consider two main criteria when selecting an encryption algorithm for your organization:

- **Trust in the algorithm by the cryptographic community:** Most new algorithms are broken quickly, so algorithms that have been resisting attacks for a number of years are preferred. Inventors and promoters often oversell the benefits of new algorithms. The truth is that there are few or no revolutions in cryptography.

- **Protection against brute-force attacks:** If the algorithm is considered trusted, there is no shortcut to break it, and the attacker must search through the keyspace to guess the correct key. The algorithm must allow key lengths that satisfy the confidentiality requirements of an organization. For example, although DES is considered trustworthy, its key is shorter than 3DES or AES, and therefore could be easier to break than its more recent successors.

The following symmetric encryption algorithms are considered trustworthy:

- DES

- 3DES

- IDEA

- RC4

- AES

Because of its short key length, DES is considered a good protocol to protect data for a short time. 3DES is a better choice when you want to protect data with an algorithm that is very trusted and has higher security strength.

AES is a valid choice, being regarded as a good algorithm, although it is not proven to the degree that 3DES is. Because AES is more efficient, you can use AES in high-throughput, low-latency environments, especially when 3DES cannot handle the throughput or latency requirements. In time, AES is expected to gain more and more trust, when more time has passed and more attacks have been attempted against it.

RSA and Diffie-Hellman (DH) are considered trustworthy for confidentiality.

Other algorithms, such as elliptical curve cryptography (ECC), are generally considered immature in cryptographic terms.

For symmetric algorithms, each bit in a key doubles the difficulty of finding the key. But with asymmetric algorithms, such as RSA, each additional bit only nominally increases the difficulty of factoring the composite number that is used by the algorithm. Therefore, symmetrical and asymmetrical keys compare as follow:

- An 80-bit symmetric key is considered equal to a 1024-bit key using the RSA algorithm.

- A 112-bit symmetric key is considered equal to a 2048-bit key using the RSA algorithm.

- A 128-bit symmetric key is considered equal to a 3072-bit key using the RSA algorithm.

For more information about the comparison of the key strengths of symmetric algorithms to RSA, refer to http://www.rsasecurity.com/rsalabs/node.asp?id=2004.

Cryptographic Hashes

Hashing is a mechanism used for data integrity assurance. Hashing is based on a one-way mathematical function. Functions hash (digest) data into a fixed-length digest (fingerprint). Hashes are functions that are relatively easy to compute, but *significantly* harder to reverse. Grinding coffee is a good example of a one-way function: It is easy to grind coffee beans, but it is almost impossible to put all the tiny pieces back together to rebuild the original beans.

Figure 4-12 illustrates how hashing is performed. Data of arbitrary length is input into the hash function, and the result of the hash function is the fixed-length hash, known as either the digest or fingerprint. Hashing is similar to the calculation of cyclic redundancy check (CRC) checksums, but it is much stronger cryptographically. That is, given a CRC value, it is easy to generate data with the same CRC. However, with hash functions, it is computationally infeasible for an attacker to have two different sets of data that would come up with the same fingerprint.

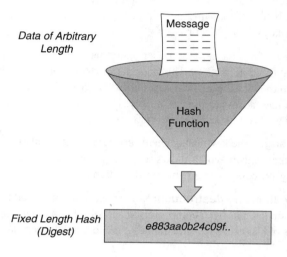

Figure 4-12 *Cryptographic Hashes*

The hashing process is not reversible—ONE WAY FUNCTION with a fixed-length output. If you hash the word "Hello" with MD5 (covered later), the output, called the *message digest*, will be 128 bits long. If you process the Oxford dictionary through MD5, the message digest will be 128 bits long. It is impossible to take a message digest of 128 bits long and try to reverse engineer it into a 1200-page dictionary; thus the expression that hashing is a one-way function.

Note: Hashing is covered in detail later in the "Examining Cryptographic Hashes and Digital Signatures" section.

Key Management

Key management is often considered the most difficult part of designing a cryptosystem. Many cryptosystems have failed because of mistakes in their key management, and all modern cryptographic algorithms require the services of key management procedures. In practice, most attacks on cryptographic systems will be aimed at the key management level, rather than at the cryptographic algorithm itself.

Key Management Components

Key management consists of the following components:

- **Key generation:** In a modern cryptographic system, key generation is usually automated and not left to the end user. The use of good random number generators is needed to ensure that all keys are likely to be equally generated so that the attacker cannot predict which keys are more likely to be used.

- **Key verification:** Almost all cryptographic algorithms have some weak keys that should not be used, and with the help of key verification procedures, you can regenerate these keys if they occur.

- **Key storage:** On a modern multiuser operating system that uses cryptography, a key can be stored in memory. This presents a possible problem when that memory is swapped to the disk, because a Trojan horse program, installed on the PC of a user, could then have access to the private keys of that user. A possible solution is to store the key on a USB stick and require a password to unlock that key.

- **Key exchange:** The key management procedures should also provide a secure key exchange mechanism, which allows secure agreement on the keying material with the other party, probably over an untrusted medium.

- **Key revocation and destruction:** Key revocation notifies all the interested parties that a certain key has been compromised and should no longer be used. Key destruction erases old keys in such a manner that malicious attackers cannot recover them.

Key management deals with the secure generation, verification, exchange, storage, revocation, and destruction of keys.

Keyspaces

The keyspace of an algorithm is the set of all possible key values. A key that has n bits produces a keyspace that has 2^n possible key values. By adding one bit to the key, you effectively double the keyspace. For example, DES with its 56-bit keys has a keyspace of more than 72,000,000,000,000,000 (2^{56}) possible keys, but by adding 1 bit to the key length, the keyspace doubles, and an attacker needs twice the amount of time to search the keyspace.

As previously mentioned, almost every algorithm has some weak keys in its keyspace that enable an attacker to break the encryption via a shortcut. Weak keys show regularities in encryption or poor encryption. For instance, DES has four keys for which encryption is the same as decryption. This means that if one of these weak keys is encrypted twice, the original plaintext is recovered.

The weak keys of DES are those that produce 16 identical subkeys. This occurs when the key bits are

- Alternating 1s + 0s (0101010101010101)

- Alternating F + E (FEFEFEFEFEFEFEFE)

- E0E0E0E0F1F1F1F1

- 1F1F1F1F0E0E0E0E

It is unlikely that such keys would be chosen, but implementations should still verify all keys and prevent weak keys from being used. With manual key generation, you must take special care to avoid defining weak keys.

Key Length Issues

If the cryptographic system is trustworthy, the only way to break it is with a brute-force attack. A brute-force attack is a search through the entire keyspace, trying all the possible keys, to find a key that decrypts the data. If the keyspace is large enough, the search should require an enormous amount of time, making such an exhaustive effort unfeasible. On average, an attacker has to search through half of the keyspace before the correct key is found. The time that is needed to accomplish this search depends on the computer power available to the attacker. However, current key lengths can easily make any attempt insignificant, because it would take many millions or billions of years to complete the search when a sufficiently long key is used.

With modern algorithms that are trusted, the strength of protection depends solely on the length of the key. Choose the key length so that it protects data confidentiality or integrity for an adequate period of time. Data that is more sensitive and needs to be kept secret longer must use longer keys.

The funding of the attacker should also affect your choice of key length. When you assess the risk of someone breaking the encryption algorithm, you must estimate the resources of the attacker and how long you must protect the data. For example, if the attacker has $1 million of funding, and the data must be protected for one year, classic DES is not a good choice because it can be broken by a $1 million machine in a couple of minutes. However, it would take an attacker some million years or more to crack 168-bit 3DES or 128-bit RC4, which makes either of these key length choices more than adequate.

Performance is another issue that can influence the choice of key length. You must find a good balance between the speed and protection strength of an algorithm, because some algorithms, such as RSA, run slower with larger key sizes. Strive for adequate protection, while enabling unhindered communication over untrusted networks.

Because of the rapid advances in technology and cryptanalytic methods, the key size needed for a particular application is constantly increasing. Go to the National Institute of Standards and Technology (NIST) website at http://www.keylength.com/en/4/ to see updated key length recommendations.

Example of the Impact of Key Length

Part of the strength of the RSA algorithm is the difficulty of factoring large numbers. If a 1024-bit number is hard to factor, then a 2048-bit number is going to be even harder to factor. Even with the fastest computers available today, it would take many lifetimes to factor a 1024-bit number that is a factor of two 512-bit prime numbers. Of course, this advantage is lost if an easy way to factor large numbers is found. However, cryptographers consider this possibility unlikely, and the rule "the longer the key, the better" is valid, except for possible performance reasons.

As of 2005, the best known attack on 3DES required around 2^{32} known plaintexts, 2^{113} steps, 2^{90} single DES encryptions, and 2^{88} memory operations. This is not currently practical. If the attacker seeks to discover any one of many cryptographic keys, there is a memory-efficient attack that will discover one of 2^{28} keys, given a handful of chosen plaintexts per key and around 2^{84} encryption operations. This attack is highly parallelizable and verges on the practical, given billion-dollar budgets and years to mount the attack, although the circumstances in which it would be useful are limited.

Introducing SSL VPNs

Transport Layer Security (TLS) and its predecessor, Secure Sockets Layer (SSL), are cryptographic protocols that provide secure communications on the Internet for such things as web browsing, email, Internet faxing, instant messaging, and other data transfers. SSL and TLS have some slight differences, but the protocol remains largely the same. Originally developed by Netscape, SSL has been universally accepted on the World Wide Web.

The SSL and TLS protocols support the use of a variety of different cryptographic algorithms, or ciphers, for use in operations such as authentication between the server and client, transmitting certificates, and establishing session keys. Symmetric algorithms are used for bulk encryption, asymmetric algorithms are used for authentication and the exchange of keys, and hashing is used as part of the authentication process.

Note: SSL was developed by Netscape. SSL 3.0 was the basis used by the IETF to develop TLS. Although closely related, SSL and TLS are not interchangeable. Two parties wishing to communicate must use the same protocol.

SSL-based VPNs provide remote-access connectivity from almost any Internet-enabled location using a standard web browser and its native SSL encryption. They do not require any special-purpose client software to be preinstalled on the system. Therefore, SSL-based VPNs are capable of "anywhere" connectivity from company-managed desktops and non-company-managed desktops, such as employee-owned PCs, contractor or business partner desktops, and Internet kiosks. All the software required for application access across the SSL VPN connection is dynamically downloaded as needed, minimizing the maintenance of desktop software.

SSL VPNs and IPsec VPNs are complementary technologies that you can deploy together to better address the unique access requirements of diverse user communities. Both offer access to virtually any network application or resource. SSL VPNs offer additional features such as easy connectivity from desktops outside your company's management, little or no desktop software maintenance, and user-customized web portals upon login.

Figure 4-13 gives a simplified explanation of the key steps in establishing an SSL session:

Step 1.   The user makes an outbound connection to TCP port 443.

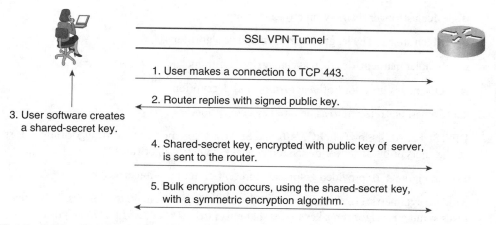

Figure 4-13 *SSL Tunnel Establishment*

Step 2. The router responds with a digital certificate, which contains a public key that is digitally signed by a trusted certificate authority (CA).

Step 3. The user computer generates a shared-secret, symmetric key that both parties will use.

Step 4. The shared secret is encrypted with the public key of the router and transmitted to the router. The router software is able to easily decrypt the packet using its private key. Now both participants in the session know the shared-secret key.

Step 5. The key is used to encrypt the SSL session.

Note: SSL uses encryption algorithms with key lengths from 40 to 256 bits.

Examining Symmetric Encryption

Modern encryption algorithms rely on encryption keys to provide confidentiality of encrypted data. With symmetric encryption algorithms, the same key is used to encrypt and decrypt data. The sections that follow describe the principles behind symmetric encryption, provide examples of major symmetric encryption algorithms, and examine their operations, strengths, and weaknesses.

Symmetric Encryption Overview

Symmetric encryption algorithms are the most commonly used form of cryptography. Because of the simplicity of their mathematics, they are extremely fast when compared to asymmetric algorithms. Also, because symmetric encryption algorithms are stronger, they can use shorter key lengths, which help increase their speed of execution in software.

Some of the characteristics of symmetric algorithms are as follows:

- Faster than asymmetric algorithms.

- Much stronger than asymmetric algorithms.

- Much shorter key lengths than asymmetric algorithms.

- Simpler mathematics than asymmetric algorithms.

- One key is used for both encryption and decryption.

- Sometimes referred to as private-key encryption.

DES, 3DES, AES, Blowfish, RC2/4/6, and SEAL are common symmetric algorithms. Most of the encryption done worldwide today uses symmetric algorithms.

Earlier, Figure 4-10 provided graphical representation of a symmetrical key.

Modern symmetric algorithms use key lengths that range from 40 to 256 bits. This range gives symmetric algorithms keyspaces that range from 2^{40} (1,099,511,627,776 possible keys) to 2^{256} ($1.5 * 10^{77}$) possible keys. This large range is the difference between whether or not the algorithm is vulnerable to a brute-force attack. If you use a key length of 40 bits, your encryption is likely to be broken easily using a brute-force attack. In contrast, if your key length is 256 bits, it is unlikely that a brute-force attack will be successful, because the key space is too large.

On average, a brute-force attack will succeed halfway through the keyspace. Key lengths that are too short can have the entire possible keyspace stored in RAM on a server cluster of a cracker, which makes it possible for the algorithm to be cracked in real time.

Assuming that the algorithms are mathematically and cryptographically sound, Table 4-1 illustrates ongoing expectations for valid key lengths. What is also assumed in such calculations is that computing power will continue to grow at its present rate and the ability to perform brute-force attacks will grow at the same rate.

Table 4-1   *Acceptable Key Lengths in Bits*

	Symmetrical Key	Asymmetrical Key	Digital Signature	Hash
Protection up to 3 years	80	1248	160	160
Protection up to 10 years	96	1776	192	192
Protection up to 20 years	112	2432	224	224
Protection up to 30 years	128	3248	256	256
Protection against quantum computers	256	15424	512	512

Caution: If a method other than brute-force is discovered against a particular algorithm, the key lengths in Table 4-1 become obsolete.

Note: Note the comparatively short symmetric key lengths, illustrating that symmetric algorithms are the strongest type of algorithm.

DES: Features and Functions

Data Encryption Standard (DES) is a symmetric encryption algorithm that usually operates in block mode, in which it encrypts data in 64-bit blocks. The DES algorithm is essentially a sequence of permutations and substitutions of data bits, combined with the encryption key. The same algorithm and key are used for both encryption and decryption. Cryptography researchers have scrutinized DES for nearly 35 years and have found no significant flaws.

Because DES is based on simple mathematical functions, it can easily be implemented and accelerated in hardware.

DES has a fixed key length. The key is actually 64 bits long but only 56 bits are used for encryption, the remaining 8 bits are used for parity; the least significant bit of each key byte is used to indicate odd parity.

A DES key is always 56 bits long. When you use DES with a weaker encryption of a 40-bit key, it actually means that the encryption key is 40 secret bits and 16 known bits, which make the key length 56 bits. In this case, DES actually has a key strength of 40 bits.

DES Modes of Operation

To encrypt or decrypt more than 64 bits of data, DES uses two different types of ciphers:

- **Block ciphers:** Operate on fixed-length groups of bits, termed blocks, with an unvarying transformation

- **Stream ciphers:** Operate on individual digits one at a time with the transformation varying during the encryption

DES uses two standardized block cipher modes:

- Electronic Code Book (ECB)

- Cipher Block Chaining (CBC)

Figure 4-14 illustrates the differences between ECB mode and CBC mode.

ECB mode serially encrypts each 64-bit plaintext block using the same 56-bit key. If two identical plaintext blocks are encrypted using the same key, their ciphertext blocks are the same. Therefore, an attacker could identify similar or identical traffic flowing through a communications channel, and use this information. The attacker could then build a catalogue of messages, which have a certain meaning, and replay them later, without knowing their real meaning. For example, an attacker might capture a login sequence of someone with administrative privilege whose traffic is protected by DES-ECB and then replay it. That risk is undesirable so CBC mode was invented to mitigate this risk.

In CBC mode, shown in Figure 4-15, each 64-bit plaintext block is exclusive ORed (XORed) bitwise with the previous ciphertext block and then is encrypted using the DES key. Because of this process, the encryption of each block depends on previous blocks.

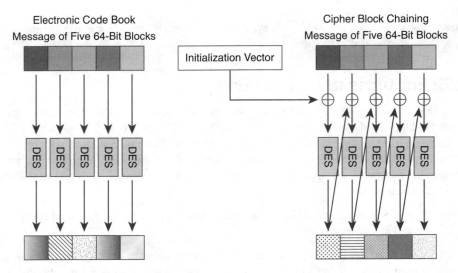

Figure 4-14   *DES ECB Versus CBC Mode*

Encryption of the same 64-bit plaintext block can result in different ciphertext blocks. CBC mode can help guard against certain attacks, but it cannot help against sophisticated cryptanalysis or an extended brute-force attack.

In CBC mode, each 64-bit plaintext block is XORed bitwise with the previous ciphertext block and then is encrypted with the DES key. Therefore, the encryption of each block depends on previous blocks, and because the key changes each time, the same 64-bit plaintext block can encrypt to different ciphertext blocks. The first block is XORed with an initialization vector, which is a public, random value prepended to each message to bootstrap the chaining process.

Note: Currently the Cisco IPsec implementation uses DES and 3DES in CBC mode.

In stream cipher mode, the cipher uses previous ciphertext and the secret key to generate a pseudorandom stream of bits, which only the secret key can generate. To encrypt data, the data is XORed with the pseudorandom stream bit by bit, or sometimes byte by byte, to obtain the ciphertext. The decryption procedure is the same: The receiver generates the same random stream using the secret key, and XORs the ciphertext with the pseudorandom stream to obtain the plaintext.

To encrypt or decrypt more than 64 bits of data, DES uses two common stream cipher modes:

- **Cipher Feedback (CFB):** CFB is similar to CBC and can encrypt any number of bits, including single bits or single characters.

- **Output Feedback (OFB):** OFB generates keystream blocks, which are then XORed with the plaintext blocks to get the ciphertext.

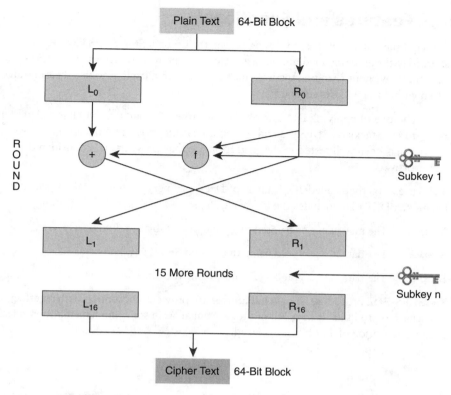

Figure 4-15   *Cipher Block Chaining (CBC) Mode*

DES Security Guidelines

You should consider doing several things to protect the security of DES-encrypted data:

- Change keys frequently to help prevent brute-force attacks.

- Use a secure channel to communicate the DES key from the sender to the receiver.

- Consider using DES in CBC mode. With CBC, the encryption of each 64-bit block depends on previous blocks. CBC is the most widely used mode of DES.

- Verify that a key is not part of the weak or semi-weak key list before using it. DES has 4 weak keys and 12 semi-weak keys. Because there are 2^{56} possible DES keys, the chance of picking one of these keys is small. However, because testing the key has no significant impact on the encryption time, it is recommended that you test the key. The keys that should be avoided are listed in Section 3.6 of Publication 74 of the Federal Information Processing Standards, http://www.itl.nist.gov/fipspubs/fip74.htm.

Note: If possible, use 3DES rather than DES. You should use DES only for very short-term confidentiality.

3DES: Features and Functions

With advances in computer processing power, the original 56-bit DES key became too short to withstand even medium-budget attackers. One way to increase the DES effective key length, without changing the well-analyzed algorithm itself, is to use the same algorithm with different keys several times in a row.

The technique of applying DES three times in a row to a plaintext block is called 3DES. Brute-force attacks on 3DES are considered unfeasible today, and because the basic algorithm has been well tested in the field for more than 35 years, it is considered very trustworthy.

3DES uses a method called 3DES-Encrypt-Decrypt-Encrypt (3DES-EDE) to encrypt plaintext. 3DES-EDE includes the following steps:

Step 1.   The message is encrypted using the first 56-bit key, known as K1.

Step 2.   The data is decrypted using the second 56-bit key, known as K2.

Step 3.   The data is encrypted again, now using the third 56-bit key, known as K3.

The 3DES-EDE procedure, shown in Figure 4-16, provides encryption with an effective key length of 168 bits. If keys K1 and K3 are equal, as in some implementations, a less-secure encryption of 112 bits is achieved.

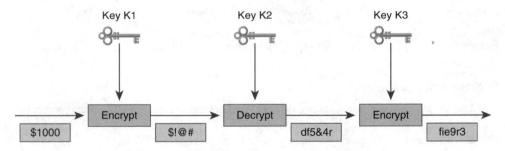

- EDE (Encrypt-Decrypt-Encrypt) Method – 3DES-EDE Method:
  - Data is encrypted using K1.
  - Data is decrypted using K2.
  - Data is encrypted using K3.
- If K1 = K3, Key Yields 112-Bit Key Length
- If K1 ≠ K3, Key Yields 168-Bit Key Length

Figure 4-16   *3DES Encryption Process*

The following procedure is used to decrypt a 3DES-EDE block:

Step 1.   Decrypt the ciphertext using key K3.

Step 2.   Encrypt the data using key K2.

Step 3.   Decrypt the data using key K1.

Note: Encrypting the data three times with three different keys does not significantly increase security. The 3DES-EDE method must be used. For example, it can be shown that encrypting data three times in a row using different 56-bit keys equals an effective 58-bit key strength and not the full 168-bit key strength, as you would expect.

AES: Features and Functions

For a number of years, it was recognized that DES would eventually reach the end of its usefulness. In 1997, the AES initiative was announced, and the public was invited to propose candidate encryption schemes, one of which could be chosen as the encryption standard to replace DES. There were rigorous reviews of 15 original candidates. Rijndael, Twofish, and RC6 were among the finalists. Rijndael was ultimately selected.

The Rijndael Cipher

On October 2, 2000, the U.S. National Institute of Standards and Technology (NIST) announced the selection of the Rijndael cipher as the AES algorithm. The Rijndael cipher, developed by Joan Daemen and Vincent Rijmen, has a variable block length and key length. The algorithm currently specifies how to use keys with a length of 128, 192, or 256 bits to encrypt blocks with a length of 128, 192, or 256 bits, which provides nine different combinations of key length and block length. Both block length and key length can be extended very easily in multiples of 32 bits.

The U.S. Secretary of Commerce approved the adoption of AES as an official U.S. government standard, effective May 26, 2002. AES is listed in Annex A of FIPS Publication 140-2 as an approved security function.

Note: Go to http://www.nist.gov/aes for more information about AES.

Rijndael is an iterated block cipher, which means that the initial input block and cipher key undergo multiple transformation cycles before producing output. The algorithm can operate over a variable-length block using variable-length keys; a 128-, 192-, or 256-bit key can be used to encrypt data blocks that are 128, 192, or 256 bits long, and all nine combinations of key and block length are possible. The accepted AES implementation of Rijndael contains only some of the capabilities of the Rijndael algorithm. The algorithm is written so that the block length or the key length or both can easily be extended in multiples of 32 bits, and the system is specifically designed for efficient implementation in hardware or software on a range of processors.

AES Versus 3DES

AES was chosen to replace DES and 3DES, because the key length of AES makes it stronger than DES and AES runs faster than 3DES on comparable hardware. AES is more efficient than DES and 3DES on comparable hardware, usually by a factor of five when it is compared with DES. Also, AES is more suitable for high-throughput, low-latency environments, especially if pure software encryption is used. However, AES is a relatively young algorithm, and, as the golden rule of cryptography states, a more mature algorithm is always more trusted. 3DES is therefore a more conservative and more trusted choice in terms of strength, because it has been analyzed for around 35 years.

AES Availability in the Cisco Product Line

AES is available in the following Cisco VPN devices as an encryption transform, applied to IPsec-protected traffic:

- Cisco IOS Release 12.2(13)T and later

- Cisco PIX Firewall Software Version 6.3 and later

- Cisco ASA Software Version 7.0 and later

- Cisco VPN 3000 Software Version 3.6 and later

Note: Note that Cisco announced late in 2007 the end-of-life of the VPN 3000 concentrators. However, Cisco will continue supporting them until 2012.

SEAL: Features and Functions

The Software Encryption Algorithm (SEAL) is an alternative algorithm to software-based DES, 3DES, and AES. SEAL encryption uses a 160-bit encryption key and has a lower impact on the CPU compared to other software-based algorithms. The SEAL encryption feature provides support for the SEAL algorithm in Cisco IOS IPsec implementations. SEAL support was added to Cisco IOS Software Release 12.3(7)T.

Note: Although the Cisco IOS Software Selector found at Cisco.com reports that the SEAL encryption feature became available in IOS Release 12.3(8)T10, it actually became supported in IOS Release 12.3(7)T.

Several restrictions apply to SEAL:

- Your Cisco router and the other peer must support IPsec.

- Your Cisco router and the other peer must support the k9 subsystem of the IOS (k9 subsystem refers to long keys). An example would be IOS c2600-ipbasek9-mz.124-17b.bin, which is the IP Base Security 12.4(17b) IOS for Cisco 2600.

- This feature is available only on Cisco equipment.

Caution: Your router and the other peer must not have hardware IPsec encryption.

Rivest Ciphers: Features and Functions

The RC family of algorithms is widely deployed in many networking applications because of their favorable speed and variable key length capabilities.

The RC algorithms were designed all or in part by Ronald Rivest. Some of the most widely used RC algorithms are as follows:

- **RC2:** This algorithm is a variable key-size block cipher that was designed as a "drop-in" replacement for DES.

- **RC4:** This algorithm is a variable key-size Vernam stream cipher often used in file encryption products and for secure communications, such as within SSL. It is not considered a one-time pad because its key is not random. The cipher can be expected to run very quickly in software and is considered secure, although it can be implemented insecurely, as in Wired Equivalent Privacy (WEP).

- **RC5:** This algorithm is a fast block cipher that has variable block size and variable key size. With a 64-bit block size, RC5 can be used as a drop-in replacement for DES.

- **RC6:** This algorithm is a block cipher that was designed by Rivest, Sidney, and Yin and is based on RC5. Its main design goal was to meet the requirement of AES.

Examining Cryptographic Hashes and Digital Signatures

Cryptographic hashes and digital signatures play an important part in modern cryptosystems. Hashes and digital signatures provide verification and authentication and play an important role in nonrepudiation. It is important to understand the basic mechanisms of these algorithms and some of the issues involved in choosing a particular hashing algorithm or digital signature method.

Overview of Hash Algorithms

Hashing is a mechanism that provides data-integrity assurance. Hashing is based on a one-way mathematical function: functions that are relatively easy to compute, but significantly harder to reverse, as explained earlier in this chapter using the coffee-grinding analogy.

The hashing process uses a hash function, which is a one-way function of input data that produces a fixed-length digest of output data, also known as a fingerprint. The digest is cryptographically very strong; it is impossible to recover input data from its digest. If the input data changes just a little bit, the digest changes substantially. This is known as the *avalanche effect*. Essentially, the fingerprint that results from hashing data uniquely identifies that data. If you are given only a fingerprint, it is computationally unfeasible to generate data that would result in that fingerprint.

Hashing is often applied in the following situations:

- To generate one-time and one-way responses to challenges in authentication protocols such as PPP Challenge Handshake Authentication Protocol (CHAP), Microsoft NT Domain, and Extensible Authentication Protocol-Message Digest 5 (EAP-MD5)

- To provide proof of the integrity of data, such as that provided with file integrity checkers, digitally signed contracts, and Public Key Infrastructure (PKI) certificates

- To provide proof of authenticity when it is used with a symmetric secret authentication key, such as IPsec or routing protocol authentication

Key Topic

Hashing algorithms are one-way processes.

A hash function, (H), is a transformation that takes an input (x), and returns a fixed-size string, which is called the hash value h. The formula for the calculation is $h = H(x)$.

A cryptographic hash function should have the following general properties:

- The input can be any length.

- The output has a fixed length.

- $H(x)$ is relatively easy to compute for any given x.

- $H(x)$ is one way and not reversible.

- $H(x)$ is collision free.

If a hash function is hard to invert, it is considered a one-way hash. Hard to invert means that given a hash value h, it is computationally infeasible to find some input, (x), such that $H(x) = h$. H is said to be a weakly collision-free hash function if given a message x, it is computationally infeasible to find a message y not equal to x such that $H(x) = H(y)$. A strongly collision-free hash function H is one for which it is computationally infeasible to find any two messages x and y such that $H(x) = H(y)$.

Figure 4-12, shown earlier in this chapter, illustrates the hashing process. Data of arbitrary length is input into the hash function, and the result of the hash function is the fixed-length digest or fingerprint. Hashing is similar to the calculation of CRC checksums, but is cryptographically stronger. That is, given a CRC value, it is easy to generate data with the same CRC. However, with hash functions, it is computationally infeasible for an attacker, given a hash value h, to find some input, (x), such that $H(x) = h$.

Figure 4-17 illustrates hashing in action. The sender wants to ensure that the message is not altered on its way to the receiver. The sending device inputs the message into a hashing algorithm and computes its fixed-length digest or fingerprint. This fingerprint is then attached to the message, the message and the hash are in plaintext, and sent to the receiver. The receiving device removes the fingerprint from the message and inputs the message into the same hashing algorithm. If the hash that is computed by the receiving device is equal to the one that is attached to the message, the message has not been altered during transit.

Hashing does not add security to the message. When the message traverses the network, a potential attacker could intercept the message, change it, recalculate the hash, and append it to the message. Hashing only prevents the message from being changed accidentally, such as by a communication error. There is nothing unique to the sender in the hashing

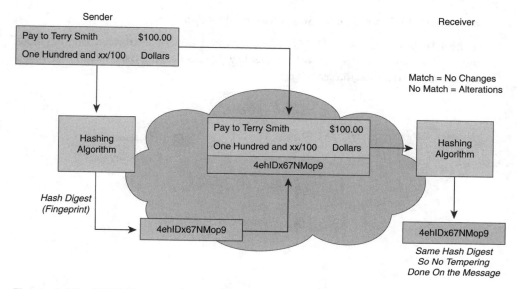

Sender

Receiver

Match = No Changes
No Match = Alterations

Figure 4-17   *3DES Encryption Process*

procedure; therefore, anyone can compute a hash for any data, as long as they have the correct hash function.

Thus, hash functions are helpful to ensure that data did not change accidentally, but it cannot ensure that data was not deliberately changed.

These are two well-known hash functions:

- Message Digest 5 (MD5) with 128-bit digests

- Secure Hash Algorithm 1 (SHA-1) with 160-bit digests

Overview of Hashed Message Authentication Codes

Hash functions are the basis of the protection mechanism of Hashed Message Authentication Codes (HMAC). HMACs use existing hash functions, but with a significant difference; HMACs add a secret key as input to the hash function. Only the sender and the receiver know the secret key, and the output of the hash function now depends on the input data and the secret key. Therefore, only parties who have access to that secret key can compute the digest of an HMAC function. This behavior defeats man-in-the-middle attacks and provides authentication of the data origin. If two parties share a secret key and use HMAC functions for authentication, a properly constructed HMAC digest of a message that a party has received indicates that the other party was the originator of the message, because it is the only other entity possessing the secret key.

Cisco technologies use two well-known HMAC functions:

- Keyed MD5, based on the MD5 hashing algorithm

■   Keyed SHA-1, based on the SHA-1 hashing algorithm

Figure 4-18 illustrates how an HMAC digest is created. Data of an arbitrary length is input into the hash function, together with a secret key. The result is the fixed-length hash that depends on the data and the secret key.

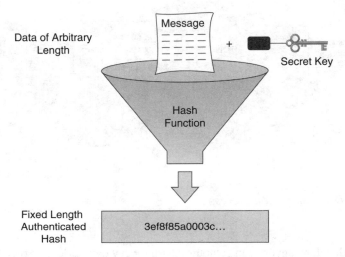

• Same procedure is used for generation and verification of secure fingerprints.

Figure 4-18   *HMAC Digest Creation*

Figure 4-19 illustrates HMAC in action. The sender wants to ensure that the message is not altered in transit, and wants to provide a way for the receiver to authenticate the origin of the message.

The sending device inputs data and the secret key into the hashing algorithm and calculates the fixed-length HMAC digest or fingerprint. This authenticated fingerprint is then attached to the message and sent to the receiver. The receiving device removes the fingerprint from the message and uses the plaintext message with the secret key as input to the same hashing function. If the fingerprint calculated by the receiving device is equal to the fingerprint that was sent, the message has not been altered. In addition, the origin of the message is authenticated, because only the sender possesses a copy of the shared secret key. The HMAC function has ensured the authenticity of the message.

Note: IPsec VPNs rely on HMAC functions to authenticate the origin and provide data integrity checking of every packet.

Cisco products use hashing for entity-authentication, data-integrity, and data-authenticity purposes:

■   IPsec gateways and clients use hashing algorithms, such as MD5 and SHA-1 in HMAC mode, to provide packet integrity and authenticity.

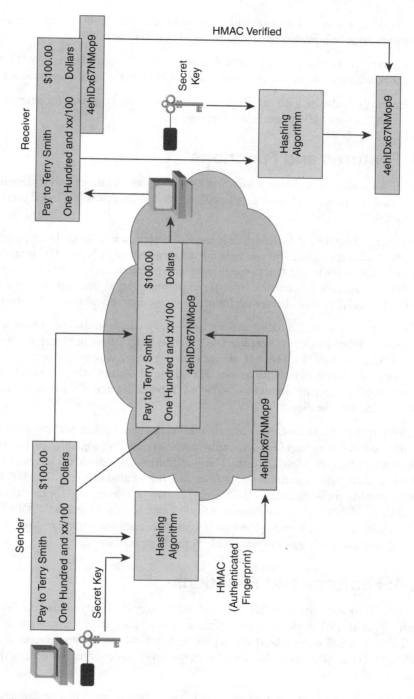

Figure 4-19 *HMAC in Action*

- Cisco IOS routers use hashing with secret keys in an HMAC-like manner, to add authentication information to routing protocol updates.

- Cisco software images that you can download from Cisco.com have an MD5-based checksum available so that customers can check the integrity of downloaded images.

- Hashing can also be used in a feedback-like mode to encrypt data; for example, TACACS+ uses MD5 to encrypt its session.

MD5: Features and Functions

The MD5 algorithm is a ubiquitous hashing algorithm that was developed by Ron Rivest and is used in a variety of Internet applications today. Hashing was illustrated previously in Figure 4-12.

MD5 is a one-way function that makes it easy to compute a hash from the given input data, but makes it unfeasible to compute input data given only a hash. MD5 is also collision resistant, which means that two messages with the same hash are very unlikely to occur. MD5 is essentially a complex sequence of simple binary operations, such as exclusive OR (XORs) and rotations, that are performed on input data and produce a 128-bit digest.

The main algorithm itself is based on a compression function, which operates on blocks. The input is a data block plus a feedback of previous blocks. 512-bit blocks are divided into 16, 32-bit sub-blocks. These blocks are then rearranged with simple operations in a main loop, which consists of four rounds. The output of the algorithm is a set of four, 32-bit blocks, which concatenate to form a single 128-bit hash value. The message length is also encoded into the digest.

MD5 is based on MD4, an earlier algorithm. MD4 has been broken, and currently MD5 is considered less secure than SHA-1 by many authorities on cryptography, such as the ICSA Labs (http://www.icsalabs.com). These authorities consider MD5 less secure than SHA-1 because some noncritical weaknesses have been found in one of the MD5 building blocks, causing uneasy feelings inside the cryptographic community. The availability of the SHA-1 and RACE Integrity Primitives Evaluation Message Digest (RIPEMD)-160 HMAC functions, which do not show such weaknesses and use a stronger (160-bit) digest, makes MD5 a second choice as far as hash methods are concerned.

SHA-1: Features and Functions

The U.S. National Institute of Standards and Technology (NIST) developed the Secure Hash Algorithm (SHA), the algorithm that is specified in the Secure Hash Standard (SHS). SHA-1 is a revision to the SHA that was published in 1994; the revision corrected an unpublished flaw in SHA. Its design is similar to the MD4 family of hash functions that Ron Rivest developed.

The SHA-1 algorithm takes a message of less than 2^{64} bits in length and produces a 160-bit message digest. The algorithm is slightly slower than MD5, but the larger message digest makes it more secure against brute-force collision and inversion attacks.

You can find the official standard text at http://www.itl.nist.gov/fipspubs/fip180-1.htm.

Note: SHA also has 224-, 256-, 384-, and 512-bit versions.

Because both MD5 and SHA-1 are based on MD4, MD5 and SHA-1 are very similar. SHA-1 should be more resistant to brute-force attacks because its digest is 32 bits longer than the MD5 digest.

SHA-1 involves 80 steps, and MD5 involves 64 steps. The SHA-1 algorithm must also process a 160-bit buffer rather than the 128-bit buffer of MD5. Therefore, it is expected that MD5 would execute more quickly, given the same device.

In general, when given a choice, SHA-1 is the preferred hashing algorithm. MD5 is arguably less trusted today, and for most commercial environments, such risks should be avoided.

When choosing a hashing algorithm, SHA-1 is generally preferred over MD5. MD5 has not been proven to contain any critical flaws, but its security is questionable today. You might consider MD5 if performance is an issue, because using MD5 might increase performance slightly, but not substantially. However, the risk exists that it might be discovered to be substantially weaker than SHA-1.

With HMACs, you must take care to distribute secret keys only to the parties that are involved, because compromise of the secret key enables any other party to forge and change packets, violating data integrity.

Overview of Digital Signatures

When data is exchanged over untrusted networks, several major security issues must be determined:

- **Has data changed in transit:** Hashing and HMAC functions rely on a cumbersome exchange of secret keys between parties to provide the guarantee of integrity.

- **Whether a document is authentic:** Hashing and HMAC can provide some guarantee of authenticity, but only by using secret keys between two parties. Hashing and HMAC cannot guarantee authenticity of a transaction or a document to a third party.

Digital signatures are often used in the following situations:

- To provide a unique proof of data source, which can be generated only by a single party, such as with contract signing in e-commerce environments

- To authenticate a user by using the private key of that user, and the signature it generates

- To prove the authenticity and integrity of PKI certificates

- To provide a secure time stamp, such as with a central trusted time source

Suppose a customer sends transaction instructions via an email to a stockbroker, and the transaction turns out badly for the customer. It is conceivable that the customer could claim never to have sent the transaction order, or that someone forged the email. The brokerage could protect itself by requiring the use of digital signatures before accepting instructions via email.

Handwritten signatures have long been used as a proof of authorship of, or at least agreement with, the contents of a document. Digital signatures can provide the same functionality as handwritten signatures, and much more.

Digital signatures provide three basic security services in secure communications:

- **Authenticity of digitally signed data:** Digital signatures authenticate a source, proving that a certain party has seen and has signed the data in question.

- **Integrity of digitally signed data:** Digital signatures guarantee that the data has not changed from the time it was signed.

- **Nonrepudiation of the transaction:** The recipient can take the data to a third party, which accepts the digital signature as a proof that this data exchange did take place. The signing party cannot repudiate that it has signed the data.

Note: To better understand nonrepudiation, consider using HMAC functions, which also provide authenticity and integrity guarantees. With HMAC functions, two or more parties share the same authentication key and can compute the HMAC fingerprint. Therefore, taking received data and its HMAC fingerprint to a third party does not prove that the other party sent this data; you could have generated the same HMAC fingerprint yourself, because you have a copy of the HMAC authentication key. With digital signatures, each party has a unique, secret signature key, which is not shared with any other party, making nonrepudiation possible.

To achieve the preceding goals, digital signatures have the following properties:

- **The signature is authentic:** The signature convinces the recipient of the document that the signer signed the document.

- **The signature is not forgeable:** The signature is proof that the signer, and no one else, signed the document.

- **The signature is not reusable:** The signature is a part of the document and cannot be moved to a different document.

- **The signature is unalterable:** After a document is signed, the document cannot be altered without detection.

- **The signature cannot be repudiated:** The signature and the document are physical things. The signer cannot claim later that they did not sign it.

Well-known asymmetric algorithms, such as Rivest, Shamir, and Adleman (RSA) or Digital Signature Algorithm (DSA), are typically used to perform digital signing.

In some countries, including the United States, digital signatures are considered equivalent to handwritten signatures, if they meet certain provisions. Some of these provisions include the proper protection of the certificate authority, the trusted signer of all other public keys, and the proper protection of the private keys of the users. In such a scenario, users are responsible for keeping their private keys private, because a stolen private key can be used to "steal" their identity.

Later in this chapter you will have the opportunity to delve deeper in the mechanic of digital signatures, but for now Figure 4-20 illustrates the basic functioning of digital signatures:

Step 1.   When someone wants to sign some data, they use a signature algorithm with their signature key. Only the signer knows this signature key. Therefore, you must keep the signature key secret.

Step 2.   Based on the input data and a signature key, the signature algorithm generates its output, which is called a digital signature.

Step 3.   The sending device then attaches the digital signature to the message and sends the message to the receiver.

Step 4.   The receiving device verifies the signature with the verification key, which is usually public.

Step 5.   The receiving device inputs the message, the digital signature, and the verification key into the verification algorithm, which checks the validity of the digital signature.

Step 6.   If the check is successful, the document has not been changed after signing and the document was originated by the signer of the document.

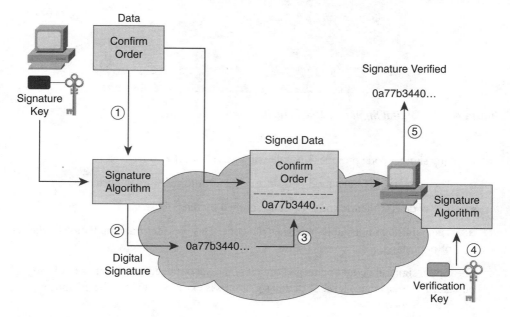

Figure 4-20   *Digital Signatures in Action*

Digital Signatures = Encrypted Message Digest

A digital signature is the result of encrypting, with the user's private key, the digest and appending that encrypted digest to the plaintext or encrypted message to verify the identity of the sender. The digest will be decrypted with the corresponding public key.

A digital signature provides authentication and integrity. If the recipient is successful at decrypting the digest using the public key of the sender, he has a proof of the origin of the message. Also, if both hashes have the same value—the hash calculated by the recipient upon receiving the message and the decrypted hash that was appended to the message in the first place—the recipient has proof that the message wasn't tampered with during transmission, and thus proof of its integrity.

Digital signatures are commonly used to provide assurance of the code authenticity and integrity of both mobile and classic software. In the case of Figure 4-21, the user is being warned that the digital certificate has expired or is no longer valid. The executable files, or possibly the whole installation package of a program, are wrapped with a digitally signed envelope, which allows the end user to verify the signature before installing the software.

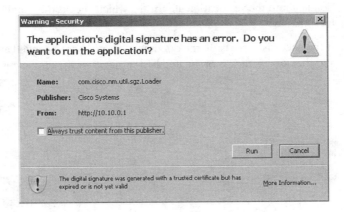

Figure 4-21   *Digital Signature Used During Software Installation*

Digitally signing code provides several assurances about the code:

- The code has not been modified since it has left the software publisher.
- The code is authentic and is actually sourced by the publisher.
- The publisher undeniably publishes the code. This provides nonrepudiation of the act of publishing.

The digital signature could be forged only if someone obtained the private key of the publisher. The assurance level of digital signatures is extremely high if the private key is protected properly.

The user of the software must also obtain the public key, which is used to verify the signature. The user can obtain the key in a secure fashion; for example, the key could be included with the installation of the operating system, or transferred securely over the network (for example, using the PKI and certificate authorities).

DSS: Features and Functions

In 1994, NIST selected the DSA as the Digital Signature Standard (DSS). DSA is based on the discrete logarithm problem and can only provide digital signatures.

DSA signature generation is faster than signature verification; however, with the RSA algorithm, signature verification is much faster than signature generation.

There have been several criticisms of DSA:

- DSA lacks the flexibility of RSA.

- The verification of signatures is too slow.

- The process by which NIST chose DSA was too secretive and arbitrary.

In response to these criticisms, the DSS now incorporates two additional algorithm choices:

- Digital Signature Using Reversible Public Key Cryptography, which uses RSA

- Elliptic Curve Digital Signature Algorithm (ECDSA)

Protection of the private key is of the highest importance when using digital signatures. If the signature key of an entity is compromised, the attacker can sign data in the name of that entity, and repudiation is not possible. To exchange verification keys in a scalable fashion, you must deploy a PKI in most scenarios.

You also need to decide whether RSA or DSA is more appropriate for the situation:

- DSA signature generation is faster than signature verification.

- RSA signature verification is much faster than signature generation.

Cisco products use digital signatures for entity-authentication, data-integrity, and data-authenticity purposes:

- IPsec gateways and clients use digital signatures to authenticate their Internet Key Exchange (IKE) sessions, if you choose digital certificates and the IKE RSA signature authentication method.

- Cisco SSL endpoints, such as Cisco IOS HTTP servers, and the Cisco Adaptive Security Device Manager (ASDM), use digital signatures to prove the identity of the SSL server.

- Some of the service-provider-oriented voice management protocols, for billing and settlement, use digital signatures to authenticate the involved parties.

Examining Asymmetric Encryption and PKI

Asymmetric encryption algorithms accomplish two primary objectives: confidentiality and authentication. Asymmetric algorithms are slower than symmetric algorithms because they use more complex mathematics. Because asymmetric algorithms are slower, they are usually used as key exchange protocols. The sections that follow cover the principles behind asymmetric encryption and provide examples of major asymmetric encryption algorithms, including Rivest, Shamir, and Adleman (RSA), Diffie-Hellman (DH), and Public Key Infrastructure (PKI).

Asymmetric Encryption Overview

To provide the two main objectives of confidentiality and authentication, asymmetric algorithms are based on considerably more complex mathematical formulas than symmetric algorithms. As a result, computation takes more time for asymmetric algorithms. Despite this slower computation trait, asymmetric algorithms are often used as key exchange protocols for symmetric algorithms, which have no inherent key exchange technology.

Also known as public key encryption, asymmetric algorithms have two keys: a public key and a private key. Both keys are capable of the encryption process. However, the complimentary matched key is required for decryption. For example, if a public key encrypts the data, the matching private key decrypts the data. The opposite is also true. If a private key encrypts the data, the corresponding public key decrypts the data.

Examples of public-key encryption algorithms are RSA, DSA, DH, ElGamal, and ECC. The mathematics differ with each algorithm, but they all share one trait: The mathematics can be complicated.

Figure 4-11, shown earlier, illustrates the mechanics of asymmetric encryption.

Asymmetric algorithms are designed in such a way that the key that is used for encryption is different from the key that is used for decryption. The decryption key cannot, in any reasonable amount of time, be calculated from the encryption key, and vice versa. The usual key length for asymmetric algorithms ranges from 512 to 4096 bits. Asymmetric algorithm key lengths cannot be directly compared to symmetric algorithm key lengths because the two algorithm families differ greatly in their underlying design.

To illustrate this point, it is generally thought that an encryption key of RSA that is 2048 bits is roughly equivalent to a 128-bit key of RC4 in terms of resistance against brute-force attacks.

The best-known asymmetric cryptographic algorithms are RSA, ElGamal, and elliptic curve algorithms.

The confidentiality objective of asymmetric algorithms is achieved when the encryption process is started with the public key. When the public key is used to encrypt the data, the private key must be used to decrypt the data. Only one host has the private key; therefore, confidentiality is achieved.

Caution: If the private key is compromised, another key pair must be generated to replace the compromised key.

In Figure 4-22, Alice and Bob exchange data with the goal of confidentiality. They follow these steps:

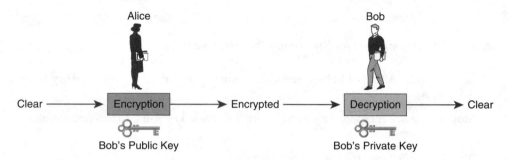

Figure 4-22   *Asymmetric Confidentiality Process*

Step 1.   Alice acquires Bob's public key.

Step 2.   Alice uses Bob's public key to encrypt a message, which is often a symmetric key, using an agreed upon algorithm.

Step 3.   Alice transmits the encrypted message.

Step 4.   Bob uses his private key to decrypt, and reveal, the message.

The authentication objective of asymmetric algorithms is achieved when the encryption process is started with the private key. When the private key is used to encrypt the data, the public key must be used to decrypt the data. Because only one host has the private key, only that host could have encrypted the message, therefore providing authentication of the sender.

Private key (encrypt) + Public key (decrypt) = Authentication.

Key Topic

In addition, no attempt is typically made to preserve the secrecy of the public key, so any number of hosts can decrypt the message. When a host successfully decrypts a message using a public key, it is trusted that the private key encrypted the message, which verifies who the sender is; this is a form of authentication.

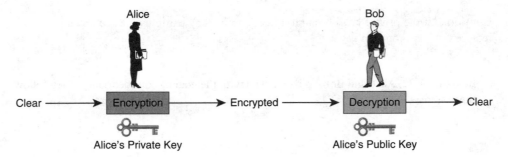

Figure 4-23 *Asymmetric Authentication Process: Signature*

In Figure 4-23, Alice and Bob exchange data with the goal of authentication. They follow these steps:

Step 1.   Alice encrypts the message, with her private key, using an agreed upon algorithm.

Step 2.   Alice transmits the encrypted message.

Step 3.   Bob acquires Alice's public key.

Step 4.   Bob uses Alice's public key to decrypt, and reveal, the message. With successful decryption, Bob has a proof of the authenticity of the origin of the message.

RSA: Features and Functions

RSA is one of the most common asymmetric algorithms. Ron Rivest, (discussed earlier in this chapter), Adi Shamir, and Len Adleman invented the patented public-key RSA algorithm in 1977. The patent expired in September 2000, and the algorithm is now in the public domain. Of all the public-key algorithms that were proposed over the years, RSA is by far the easiest to understand and implement.

The RSA algorithm is very flexible because it has a variable key length that allows speed to be traded for the security of the algorithm if necessary.

The RSA keys are usually 512 to 2048 bits long. RSA has withstood years of extensive cryptanalysis, and although the security of RSA has been neither proved nor disproved, it does suggest a confidence level in the algorithm. The security of RSA is based on the difficulty of factoring very large numbers, which is breaking large numbers into multiplicative factors. If an easy method of factoring these large numbers were discovered, the effectiveness of RSA would be destroyed.

The RSA algorithm is based on the fact that each entity has two keys: a public key and a private key. The public key can be published and given away, but the private key must be kept very secret. It is not possible to determine, using any computationally feasible algorithm, the private key from the public key and vice versa. What one of the keys encrypts, the other key decrypts, and vice versa.

RSA keys are long term and are usually changed or renewed after some months or even years.

Note: For those of you who enjoy crypto-mathematics, here is how RSA works. To generate an entity's RSA keys:

Step 1. Two very large prime numbers, p and q, are selected.

Step 2. A number n is computed via the formula: $n = p * q$

Step 3. The public key e is randomly chosen. It must be such that e and $(p - 1) * (q - 1)$ are relatively prime.

Step 4. The private-key d is chosen such that
$$ed = 1(\mathrm{mod}(p - 1)(q - 1))$$
In other words,
$$d = e - 1\mathrm{mod}\,((p-1)(q-1))$$

d and n are also relatively prime. The numbers e and n are the public key; the number d is the private key. The two primes, p and q, are no longer required. Therefore, they should be discarded and never revealed.

RSA works on numeric blocks smaller than n. To encrypt a message m, first the message must be divided into blocks smaller than n.

If P is the plaintext block, it is then encrypted with the use of the following formula:

$E = P^e\mathrm{mod}\,n$

To decrypt the message (where E is the ciphertext block), the following operation is performed:

$P = E^d\mathrm{mod}\,n$

The message could just as easily have been encrypted with d and decrypted with e; the choice is arbitrary and depends on the security service to be provided.

Factoring n reveals both keys to the attacker, but it is extremely difficult, and when long enough keys are used, practically unfeasible. So, feasible to break, but highly improbable.

The current signing procedures of digital signatures are not simply implemented by public-key operations. In fact, a modern digital signature is based on a hash function and a public-key algorithm. Figure 4-24 illustrates this procedure.

The signature process is as follows:

Step 1. The signer makes a hash or fingerprint of the document, which uniquely identifies the document and all of its contents.

Step 2. The signer encrypts the hash only with the private key of the signer.

Step 3. The encrypted hash, known as the signature, is appended to the document.

The verification process works as follows:

Step 1. The verifier obtains the public key of the signer.

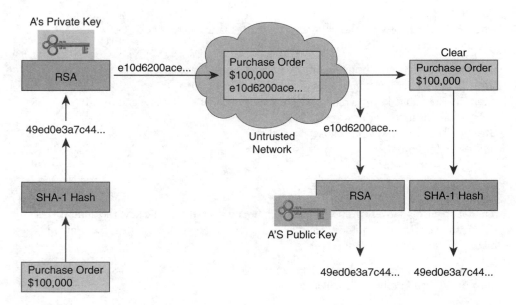

Figure 4-24 *RSA Digital Signatures*

Step 2. The verifier decrypts the signature using the public key of the signer. This step unveils the assumed hash value of the signer.

Step 3. The verifier makes a hash of the received document, without its signature, and compares this hash to the decrypted signature hash. If the hashes match, the document is authentic; that is, it has been signed by the assumed signer, and has not changed since it was signed.

This example shown using Figure 4-24 illustrates how the authenticity and integrity of the message is ensured, even though the actual text is public. Both encryption and digital signatures are required to ensure that the message is private and has not changed.

Note: The RSA algorithm is currently the most common method for signature generation and is used widely in e-commerce systems and Internet protocols in that role.

RSA is about 100 times slower than DES in hardware, and about 1000 times slower than DES in software. This performance problem is the main reason that RSA is typically used only to protect small amounts of data. RSA is mainly used for two services:

■ To ensure confidentiality of data by performing encryption

■ To perform authentication of data, nonrepudiation of data, or both by generating digital signatures

Note: RSA encryption is faster than decryption, and verification is faster than signing.

DH: Features and Functions

The Diffie-Hellman (DH) algorithm is the basis of most modern automatic key exchange methods. The Internet Key Exchange (IKE) protocol in IPsec VPNs uses DH algorithms extensively to provide a reliable and trusted method for key exchange over untrusted channels.

Whitfield Diffie and Martin Hellman invented the DH algorithm in 1976. Its security stems from the difficulty of calculating the discrete logarithms of very large numbers. The DH algorithm, shown in Figure 4-25, provides secure key exchange over unsecure channels and is frequently used in modern key management to provide keying material for other symmetric algorithms, such as DES, 3DES, and AES.

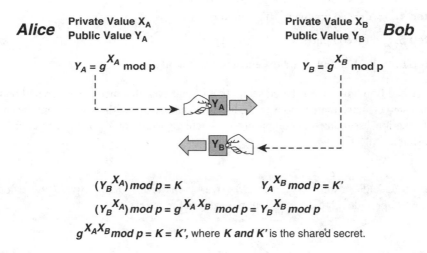

Figure 4-25 *Diffie-Hellman Key Exchange Algorithm*

To start a DH exchange, the two parties must agree on two nonsecret numbers. The first number is g, the generator, and the second number is p, the modulus. These numbers can be made public and are usually chosen from a table of known values. g is usually a very small number, such as 2, 3, and 4, and p is a very large prime number. Next, every party generates its own secret value. Then, based on g, p, and the secret value of each party, each party calculates its public value. The public value is computed according to the following formula:

$$Y = g^x \bmod p$$

In this formula x is the secret value of the entity, and Y is the public value of the entity.

After computing the public values, the two parties exchange their public values. Each party then exponentiates the received public value with its secret value to compute a common shared-secret value, represented by K and K' in Figure 4-25. When the algorithm completes, both parties have the same shared secret, which they have computed from their secret value and the public value of the other party.

No one listening on the channel can compute the secret value, because only g, p, Y_A, and Y_B are known; at least one secret value is needed to calculate the shared secret. Unless attackers can compute the discrete algorithm of the above equation to recover X_A or X_B, they cannot obtain the shared secret.

The following steps describe a DH exchange:

Step 1. Alice and Bob agree on generator g and modulus p.

Step 2. Alice chooses a random large integer X_A and sends Bob its public value, Y_A where $Y_A = g^{x(A)} \bmod p$.

Step 3. Bob chooses a random large integer X_B and sends Alice his public value, Y_B, where $Y_B = g^{x(B)} \bmod p$.

Step 4. Alice computes $K = Y_B{}^{x(A)} \bmod p$.

Step 5. Bob computes $K' = Y_A{}^{x(B)} \bmod p$.

Step 6. Both K and K' are the equal to $g^{x(A)x(B)} \bmod p$.

Alice and Bob now have a shared secret ($k = k'$) and even if someone has listened on the untrusted channel, there is no way the listener could compute the secret from the captured information, assuming that computing a discrete logarithm of Y_A or Y_B is practically unfeasible.

Note: RFC 2409 (http://www.ietf.org/rfc/rfc2409) and RFC 3526 (http://www.ietf.org/rfc/rfc3526) provide more details about the values of g and p.

PKI Definitions and Algorithms

With trusted third-party protocols, all individuals agree to accept the word of a neutral third party. In this way, the parties that need to validate each other rely on the in-depth authentication of an agreed upon third party, instead of performing their own authentication. Presumably, the third party does an in-depth investigation before the issuance of credentials, and, after this in-depth investigation, the third party issues credentials that are difficult to forge. From that point forward, all individuals who trust the third party simply accept the credentials that the third party issues.

In large organizations, it is impractical for all parties to continually exchange identification documents. For example, Cisco goes to reasonable measures to identify employees and contractors, and then issues an ID badge. This badge is relatively difficult to forge; measures are in place to protect the integrity of the badge and the badge issuance. Because of these measures, all Cisco personnel accept this badge as authoritative as to the identity of any individual.

If this method did not exist and 10 individuals needed to validate each other, 90 validations would need to be performed before everyone would have validated everyone else. The formula is n(n − 1), so 10(10 − 1) gives you the 90 validations. Adding a single individual to the group would require an additional 20 validations because each one of the original 10 individuals would need to authenticate the new individual, and the new individual would need to authenticate the original 10. This method does not scale well.

Note: Certificate servers are an example of a trusted third party.

In Figure 4-26, Alice applies for a driver's license. In this process, she will submit evidence of her identity and her qualifications to drive. Her application is approved and a license is issued.

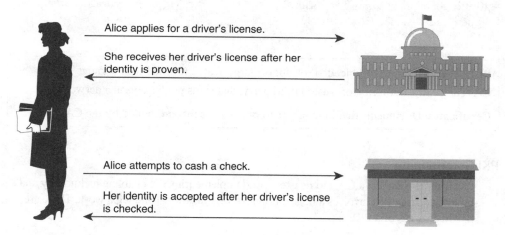

Figure 4-26   *Trusted Third-Party Example*

Later, Alice needs to cash a check at the bank. Upon presenting the check to the bank teller, the bank teller asks her for ID. The bank, because it trusts the government agency that issued the driver's license, verifies her identity, and cashes her check.

Note: Certificate servers function like the license bureau in this example. The driver's license is analogous to a certificate in a PKI or a technology that supports certificates.

A PKI provides a framework upon which you can base security services, such as encryption, authentication, and nonrepudiation. A PKI allows for very scalable solutions, and is becoming an extremely important authentication solution for VPNs. A PKI uses specific terminology to name its components.

PKI Terminology

When these concepts are applied in practice, it is important to understand the supporting framework. A PKI is the service framework that is needed to support large-scale, public-key-based technologies. PKI is a set of technical, organizational, and legal components that are needed to establish a system that enables large-scale use of public-key cryptography to provide authenticity, confidentiality, integrity, and nonrepudiation services.

Two very important terms must be defined when talking about a PKI:

- **Certificate authority (CA):** The trusted third party that signs the public keys of entities in a PKI-based system

- **Certificate:** A document that in essence binds together the name of the entity and its public key and that has been signed by the CA

Note: The certificate of a user is always signed by a CA. Moreover, every CA has a certificate, containing its public key, signed by itself. This is called a CA certificate, or more properly, a self-signed CA certificate.

Key Topic

PKI: A service framework needed to support large-scale PK-based technologies

CA: The central authority, or trusted third party, that signs public keys in a network

Certificates: Documents that bind names to public keys that are signed by the CA

PKI Components

PKI is more than just a CA and its users. And implementing the enabling technology and building a large PKI involves a huge amount of organizational and legal work. There are five main areas of a PKI:

- CAs for key management

- PKI users, such as people, devices, servers, and so on

- Storage and protocols

- Supporting organizational framework, known as practices and user authentication using local registration authorities (LRA)

- Supporting legal framework

Many vendors offer CA servers as a managed service or as an end-user product:

- VeriSign

- Entrust Technologies

- RSA

- Cybertrust

- Microsoft

- Novell

Certificate Classes

CAs, especially outsourced ones, can issue certificates of a number of classes, which determine how trusted a certificate is. A single outsourcing vendor (for example, VeriSign) might run a single CA, issuing certificates of different classes, and its customers will use the CA they need depending on the desired level of trust.

A certificate class is usually a number; the higher the number, the more trusted the certificate is considered. The trust in the certificate is usually determined by how rigorous the procedure was that verified the identity of the holder when the certificate was issued. For example, a class 0 certificate might be issued without any checks, such as for testing purposes. A class 1 certificate might require an email reply from the holder to confirm his wish to enroll. This confirmation is a weak authentication of the holder. For a class 3 or 4 certificate, the future holder must prove his identity and authenticate their public key by showing up in person, with at least two official ID documents.

PKIs also form different topologies of trust. In the simple model, a single CA, which is also known as the root CA, issues all the certificates to the end users, as shown in Figure 4-27. The benefit in such a setup is simplicity, but there are several pitfalls:

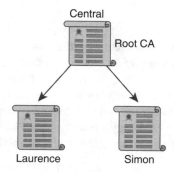

Figure 4-27 *PKI Topology Using a Single-Root CA*

- It is difficult to scale this topology to a large environment.

- This topology needs a strictly centralized administration.

- There is a critical vulnerability in using a single-signing private key; if this key is stolen, the whole PKI falls apart because the CA can no longer be trusted as a unique signer.

Because of its simplicity, VPNs that are managed by a single organization often use this topology.

Going beyond the single-root CA, topologies that are more complex can be devised that involve multiple CAs within the same organization. One such topology is the hierarchical

CA system, shown in Figure 4-28. With the hierarchical topology, CAs can issue certificates to end users and to subordinate CAs, which in turn issue their certificates to end users, other CAs, or both. Therefore, a tree of CAs and end users is built in which every CA can issue certificates to lower-level CAs and end users.

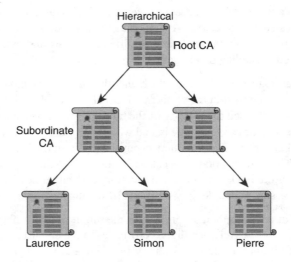

Figure 4-28   *PKI Topology Using Hierarchical CAs*

The main benefits of a hierarchical PKI topology are increased scalability and manageability; trust decisions can now be hierarchically distributed to smaller branches. This distribution works well in most large organizations. For example, a large company may have a root CA that issues certificates to level-2 CAs. These level-2 CAs issue the certificates to the end users. Because the root-signing key is seldom used after the subordinate CA certificates are issued, it is less exposed and therefore much more trusted. Also, if a subordinate CA has its private key stolen, only a branch of the PKI is rendered untrusted. All other users can consider this by no longer trusting that particular CA.

One issue with hierarchical PKI topologies lies in finding the certification path for a certificate (in other words, determining the chain of the signing process). The more CAs involved in establishing the trust between the root CA and the end user, the more difficult the task.

Another approach to hierarchical PKIs is called cross-certifying, as shown in Figure 4-29. In this scenario, multiple flat single-root CAs establish trust relationships horizontally, by cross-certifying their own CA certificates.

Some PKIs might offer the possibility or even require the use of two key pairs per entity:

■   One public and private key pair is intended only for encryption operations. The public key encrypts, and the private key decrypts.

■   The other public and private key pair is intended only for signing operations. The private key signs, and the public key verifies the signature.

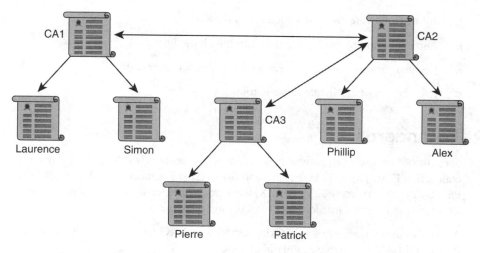

Figure 4-29   *PKI Topology Using Cross-Certifying CAs*

These keys are sometimes called "usage" or "special" keys. They may differ in key length and even in the choice of the public-key algorithm. If the PKI requires two key pairs per entity, a user has two certificates:

- An encryption certificate containing the public key of the user who encrypts the data

- A signature certificate containing the public key of the user who verifies the digital signature of the user

The following scenarios typically use usage keys:

- When encryption is used much more frequently than signing, a certain public and private key pair is more exposed due to its frequent usage. In this case, it might be a good idea to shorten its lifetime and change it more often, while having a separate signing private and public key pair with a longer lifetime.

- When different levels of encryption and digital signing are required, because of legal, export, or performance issues, usage keys allow you to assign different key lengths to the two pairs.

- When key recovery is desired (for example, a copy of a user's private key is kept in a central repository for various backup reasons), usage keys allow you to back up only the private key of the encrypting pair; the signing private key remains with the user, enabling true nonrepudiation.

The CA, with its private key, is the security-critical component in a PKI system. To make the operation of a CA simpler, and therefore more secure, many key management tasks are often offloaded to registration authorities (RA). RAs are PKI servers that perform management tasks on behalf of the CA, so that the CA can focus on the signing process.

Usually, the following tasks are offloaded to the RA:

■ Authentication of users when they enroll with the PKI

■ Key generation for users who cannot generate their own keys

■ Distribution of certificates after enrollment

PKI Standards

Standardization and interoperability of different PKI vendors is still an issue when inter-connecting PKIs. The X.509 standards and the Internet Engineering Task Force (IETF) Public-Key Infrastructure X.509 (PKIX) workgroup have made progress toward publishing a common set of standards for PKI protocols and data formats.

A PKI also uses a number of supporting services, such as Lightweight Directory Access Protocol (LDAP)-accessible X.500 directories.

Interoperability between a PKI and its supporting services is a concern because many ven-dors have proposed and implemented proprietary solutions, instead of waiting for stan-dards to develop. The state of interoperability can still be described as basic, even after 10 years of PKI software development.

Note: The IETF has formed a working group that is dedicated to promoting and standard-izing PKI in the Internet. The working group has published a draft set of standards detailing common data formats and PKI-related protocols in a network. The draft is accessible on the Internet at http://www.ietf.org/html.charters/pkix-charter.html, and you can consult this site for additional PKI information.

X.509 is a ubiquitous and well-known standard that defines basic PKI formats, such as cer-tificate and certificate revocation list (CRL) formats, to enable basic interoperability. The standard has been widely used for years with many Internet applications, such as SSL and IPsec.

The X.509 Version 3 (X.509v3) standard defines the format of a digital certificate. This format is already extensively used in the infrastructure of the Internet, in the following ways:

■ Secure web servers use X.509v3 for website authentication in the SSL and TLS protocols.

■ Web browsers use X.509v3 for services that implement client certificates in the SSL protocol.

■ User mail agents that support mail protection using the Secure/Multipurpose Internet Mail Extensions (S/MIME) protocol use X.509.

■ IPsec VPNs where certificates can be used as a public-key distribution mechanism for IKE RSA-based authentication use X.509.

Certificates are public information. Th
lic keys of entities and are usually pu!
users can easily access them.

In the CA authentication procedure
to securely obtain a copy of the p!
all the certificates issued by the C

The public key of the CA is also
itself. This certificate is also ca!
holder are the same entity. On'

Public-Key Cryptography St
which use public-key crypt
for the secure exchange of
of data, a signed piece of

The RSA Laboratories w_

The Public-Key Cryptography Standaru_
ries in cooperation with secure systems developer_
ating the deployment of public-key cryptography.

There are many defined PKCS standards:

- **PKCS #1:** RSA Cryptography Standard

- **PKCS #3:** DH Key Agreement Standard

- **PKCS #5:** Password-Based Cryptography Standard

- **PKCS #6:** Extended-Certificate Syntax Standard

- **PKCS #7:** Cryptographic Message Syntax Standard

- **PKCS #8:** Private-Key Information Syntax Standard

- **PKCS #10:** Certification Request Syntax Standard

- **PKCS #12:** Personal Information Exchange Syntax Standard

- **PKCS #13:** Elliptic Curve Cryptography Standard

- **PKCS #15:** Cryptographic Token Information Format Standard

Note: For more information about these standards, visit
http://www.rsa.com/rsalabs/node.asp?id=2124.

Public-key technology is becoming more widely deployed and is becoming the basis for
standards-based security, such as the IPsec and IKE protocols. With the use of public-key
certificates in network security protocols comes the need for a certificate management
protocol that PKI clients and CA servers can use to support certificate life cycle operations such as certificate enrollment and revocation, and certificate and CRL access. The

goal of the Simple Certificate
suance of certificates to net
wherever possible.

As shown in Figure 4-
tificate request usin
PKCS#7. After the
quest or sends t
can manually

nrollment Protocol (SCEP) is to support the secure is-
ork devices in a scalable manner, using existing technology

0, an end entity starts an enrollment transaction by creating a cer-
PKCS#10 and sends it to the CA or RA that is enveloped using the
CA or RA receives the request, it either automatically approves the re-
e certificate back, or it compels the end entity to wait until the operator
authenticate the identity of the requesting end entity.

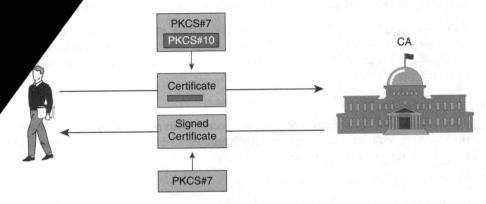

Figure 4-30 *Certificate Signing Request*

Certificate Authorities

The following features briefly describe CA-based solutions:

■   CAs are the trusted third party in PKI implementations.

■   The X.509 standard describes an identity and how to store an authentication key. Abstract Syntax Notation One (ASN.1) provides information about the format of the
X.509 certificate and the syntax of the fields in the certificate.

Distinguished names (DN) provide a way to identify an entity by using multiple fields to
provide hierarchical identification.

Note: An example of a distinguished name is
CN = Harry Wales, OU = Sales, DC = Fabrikarp, DC = COM

where,

■   CN = commonName

■   OU = organizationalUnitName

■   DC = domainComponent

The merging of the X.509 standard with public-key encryption allows the introduction of a trusted third party: the CA. The CA has a pair of asymmetric keys, a private key, and a public key. An X.509 certificate is created to identify the CA. The certificate of the CA contains the following information:

- The identity of the CA (for example, a subject containing the identity in the DN format)

- Other parameters (such as serial number, algorithms used, and validity period)

- The public key of the CA (for example, an RSA public key)

- The signature using the private key of the CA (for example, self-signing using the private key of the CA with RSA encryption and the SHA-1 hash algorithm)

Caution: The certificate is freely distributed. The receiver of the certificate should verify the authenticity of the certificate of the CA out-of-band.

In Figure 4-31, the following steps occur to retrieve the CA certificate:

Step 1. Alice and Bob request the CA certificate that contains the CA public key.

Step 2. Upon receipt of the CA certificate, Alice's and Bob's systems verify the validity of the certificate using public-key cryptography.

Step 3. Alice and Bob follow up the technical verification done by their systems by telephoning the CA administrator and verifying the public key and serial number of the certificate.

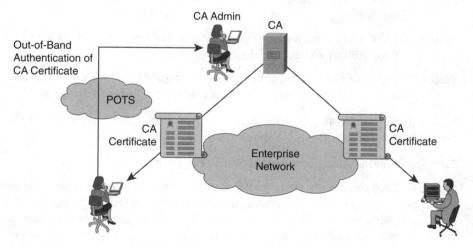

Figure 4-31 *Retrieving a CA Certificate*

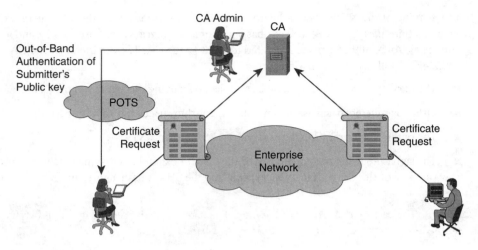

Figure 4-32   *Certificate Enrollment*

After retrieving the CA certificate, Alice and Bob perform the following steps to submit certificate requests to the CA, as shown in Figure 4-32:

Step 1.   Alice's and Bob's systems forward a certificate request that includes their public keys along with some identifying information. All of this information is encrypted using the public key of the CA.

Step 2.   Upon receipt of the certificate requests, the CA administrator telephones Alice and Bob to confirm their submittals and the public keys.

Step 3.   The CA administrator issues the certificate by adding some additional data to the certificate request, and digitally signing it all.

Step 4.   Either the end user manually retrieves the certificate or SCEP automatically retrieves the certificate, and the certificate is installed onto the system.

Having installed certificates signed by the same CA, Bob and Alice are now ready to authenticate each other, as shown in Figure 4-33:

Step 1.   Bob and Alice exchange certificates. The CA is no longer involved.

Step 2.   Each party verifies the digital signature on the certificate by hashing the plaintext portion of the certificate, decrypting the digital signature using the CA public key, and comparing the results. If the results match, the certificate is verified as being signed by a trusted third party, and the verification by the CA that Bob is Bob and Alice is Alice is accepted.

Compared to other authentication mechanisms, PKI has the following characteristics:

■   To authenticate each other, users have to obtain the certificate of the CA and their own certificate. These steps require the out-of-band verification of the processes. After this verification is complete, the presence of the CA is no longer required until one of the certificates that is involved expires.

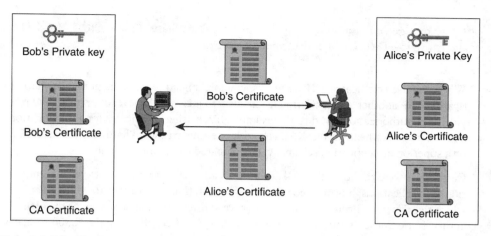

Figure 4-33 *Authentication Using Certificates*

- Public-key systems use asymmetric keys where one is public and the other one is private. One of the features of these algorithms is that whatever is encrypted using one key can only be decrypted using the other key. This provides nonrepudiation.

- Key management is simplified because two users can freely exchange the certificates. The validity of the received certificates is verified using the public key of the CA, which the users have in their possession.

- Because of the strength of the algorithms involved, you can set a very long lifetime for the certificates, typically a lifetime measured in years.

The disadvantages of using trusted third parties relate to key management:

- **A user certificate is compromised (stolen private key):** Other users should not accept compromised certificates. The only way to prevent the compromised certificates from being used is to keep a list of all revoked certificates. A server, not necessarily the CA server, must be accessible to users so that they can periodically download the latest CRL and use the list when authenticating other users. If the CRL lists the received certificate of the user, the authentication fails.

- **The certificate of the CA is compromised (stolen private key):** This invalidates all certificates signed by the CA. A single CA environment requires the creation of a new CA certificate and the creation of new user certificates. A hierarchical CA environment requires the use of an authority revocation list (ARL), where all child certificates of the compromised CA become invalid if the ARL lists the CA.

- **The CA administrator:** The human factor is an additional limitation of the CA-based solution. To lessen the impact, the CA administrator should follow strict rules when issuing certificates to users. A security policy should define the steps required to create certificates (for example, mandatory out-of-band verification of all initial enrollment procedures or verification steps for CA administrators before approving a certificate requests).

Note: Not covered in this book is the Online Certificate Status Protocol (OCSP) used as an alternative to a CRL. OCSP is described in RFC 2560.

When you use certificates in IP networks, you might need to combine public-key authentication with another authentication mechanism to increase the level of security and provide more authorization options. For example, IPsec using certificates for authentication and Extended Authentication (XAUTH) with one-time password hardware tokens would be a superior authentication scheme when compared to certificates alone.

Certificates were traditionally used at the application layer to provide strong authentication for applications; however, nowadays implementations can vary as to which layer on which they operate. Each application may have a different implementation of the actual authentication process, but they all use a similar type of certificate in the X.509 format.

SSL, which operates at the session layer of the OSI model, is probably the most widely used certificate-based authentication. SSL includes the negotiation of keys that are used to encrypt the SSL session. Many applications use SSL to provide authentication and encryption; the most widely used application is HTTPS. Other well-known applications that were using poor authentication and no encryption were modified to use SSL, such as Simple Mail Transfer Protocol (SMTP), LDAP, and Post Office Protocol Version 3 (POP3).

Email has experienced many extensions. One of the important extensions was the introduction of Multipurpose Internet Mail Extension (MIME), which allowed arbitrary data to be included in an email. Another extension was to provide security to entire mail messages or parts of mail messages. Secure/MIME (S/MIME) authenticates and encrypts email messages.

Pretty Good Privacy (PGP) is an application that was originally developed by Phil Zimmerman, a privacy advocate, so that end users could engage in confidential communications using encryption. The most frequent use of PGP has been to secure email.

Certificates are also used at the network layer, or at the application layer, by network devices. Cisco routers, Cisco VPN concentrators, and Cisco PIX firewalls can use certificates to authenticate IPsec peers.

Cisco switches can use certificates to authenticate end devices connecting to LAN ports. Authentication uses 802.1X between the adjacent devices. The authentication can be proxied to a central access control server (ACS) via the Extensible Authentication Protocol with TLS (EAP-TLS).

Cisco routers can also provide Telnet 3270 support that does not include encryption or strong authentication. Cisco routers can now use SSL to establish secure TN3270 sessions.

Figure 4-34 illustrates a network where certificates are used for various purposes. A single CA server can facilitate many applications that require digital certificates for authentication purposes.

Using CA servers is therefore a solution that simplifies the management of authentication and provides strong security due to the strength of cryptographic mechanisms used in combination with digital certificates.

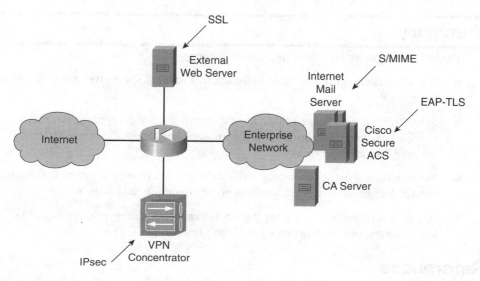

Figure 4-34   *Where Certificates Are Used*

Summary

The key points covered in this chapter are as follows:

- A cryptosystem is made up of a combination of hashing, symmetric, and asymmetric algorithms.

- Symmetric algorithms use a single key for encrypting and decrypting. Generally speaking, symmetric algorithms are the strongest and fastest algorithms and therefore are used for most encryption.

- Hashing algorithms use a one-way process designed to provide integrity. Usually, successful decryption of a digest provides proof of integrity and authenticity.

- Asymmetric algorithms use a key pair for the encrypting/decrypting process. One key encrypts, and the other member of the pair decrypts.

References

For additional information, refer to these resources:

Kahn, D. *The Codebreakers* (Scribner, 1996)

Singh, S. *The Code Book: The Science of Secrecy from Ancient Egypt to Quantum Cryptography* (Knopf Publishing Group, 1999)

U.S. Department of Commerce, http://www.commerce.gov

Kaliski, B. *TWIRL and RSA Key Size*, http://www.rsasecurity.com/rsalabs/node.asp?id=2004

Giry, D. *Cryptographic Key Length Recommendation*, http://www.keylength.com/en/3/

NIST. *AES*, http://www.nist.gov/aes

RSA Laboratories. *RSA Laboratories' Frequently Asked Questions About Today's Cryptography, Version 4.1* (RSA Security Inc., 2000)

Federal Information Processing Standards Publications. *FIPS PUB 180-1*, http://www.itl.nist.gov/fipspubs/fip180-1.htm

IETF. *Public-Key Infrastructure (X.509) (pkix)*, http://www.ietf.org/html.charters/pkix-charter.html

RSA Laboratories. *Crypto FAQ*, http://www.rsa.com/rsalabs/node.asp?id=2152

RSA Laboratories. *Public-Key Cryptography Standards (PKCS)*, http://www.rsa.com/rsalabs/node.asp?id=2124

Review Questions

Use the questions here to review what you learned in this chapter. The correct answers are found in the Appendix, "Answers to Chapter Review Questions."

1. Asymmetric encryption utilizes which of the following?

   a. A complex solution to leverage certificate

   b. Key pairs to accomplish encryption

   c. All types of authentication as long as they support PKI procedures

   d. A central authority that signs public keys in a network

2. Select all the desirable features of an encryption algorithm.

   a. Resistance to known cryptanalytic attack

   b. Short lengths and scalability of the key for easy storage

   c. No export or import restrictions

   d. Susceptible to the "avalanche effect"; a small change in plaintext causes substantial changes in ciphertext

3. Select all the asymmetrical algorithms.

   a. ElGamal

   b. DH

   c. Elliptic curve

   d. RC4

   e. IDEA

4. Which of the following does not apply to cryptographic hashes?

   a. They are based on one-way functions.

   b. They are used for integrity assurance.

   c. They hash arbitrary data into fixed-length digest known as a fingerprint.

   d. It is feasible for an attacker to have two different sets of data that would come up with the same fingerprint.

5. DES operates in which two block cipher modes?

   a. ECB

   b. CFB

   c. CBC

   d. OFB

6. Which algorithm is used in AES?

  a.   Twofish

  b.   RC6

  c.   RC4

  d.   Rijndael

7. Which of the following statements regarding public-key authentication is true?

  a.   When the private key is used to encrypt, the corresponding public key is used to decrypt.

  b.   Because the public key is present on only one system, authentication is assured when its private key decrypts the message.

  c.   Great effort is made to maintain the secrecy of the public keys.

  d.   Public-key scenario is used for producing fingerprint.

8. Which set of algorithms provides the most secure communication?

  a.   AES, SHA-1

  b.   3DES, SHA-1

  c.   3DES, MD5

  d.   AES, MD5

9. Which of the following statements best describe a digital signature?

  a.   A digital signature is a message digest encrypted with the sender's public key.

  b.   A digital signature is a message digest encrypted with the receiver's public key.

  c.   A digital signature is a message digest encrypted with the sender's private key.

  d.   A digital signature is a message digest encrypted with the receiver's public key.

10. Complete the sentence with the best statement: The Vigenère cipher is _____.

  a.   A polyalphabetic cipher

  b.   A polymorphic cipher

  c.   A polybius square cipher

  d.   An alphabetum cipher

11. Which protocol encrypts at the session layer of the OSI model?

  a.   IPsec

  b.   Enigma

  c.   SSL

  d.   MD5

12. Which statement is most accurate when describing aspects of a birthday attack?

  a. An attacker tries every possible key with the decryption algorithm.

  b. The attacker has the ciphertext of several messages, all of which have been encrypted using the same encryption algorithm.

  c. If some function, when supplied with a random input, returns one of k equally likely values, then by repeating the function with different inputs, the same output would be expected after $1.2k^{1/2}$ number of times.

  d. The attacker knows a portion of the plaintext and the corresponding ciphertext.

13. Which statement best describes MD5?

  a. MD5 is a one-way function that makes it difficult to compute a hash from the given input data, but makes it feasible to compute input data given only a hash.

  b. MD5 is a one-way function that makes it easy to compute a hash from the given output data, but makes it unfeasible to compute input data given only a hash.

  c. MD5 is a one-way function that makes it difficult to compute a hash from the given output data, but makes it feasible to compute input data given only a hash.

  d. MD5 is a one-way function that makes it easy to compute a hash from the given input data, but makes it unfeasible to compute input data given only a hash.

This chapter introduces the concepts of site-to-site virtual private networks using Cisco IOS features and covers the following topics:

- Concepts, technologies, and terms that IPsec VPNs use

- Site-to-site IPsec VPN configuration using the command-line interface

- Site-to-site IPsec VPN configuration using Cisco Security Device Manager

CHAPTER 5

Site-to-Site VPNs

The IP Security (IPsec) virtual private network (VPN) is an essential tool for providing a secure network for business communication. This chapter addresses the different protocols and algorithms that IPsec uses and the different security services that IPsec provides. This chapter also introduces the different VPN technologies and examines the various Cisco products available and the best practices that you should use with them.

VPN Overview

Historically, a VPN was an IP tunnel. Therefore, a generic routing encapsulation (GRE) tunnel is technically a VPN, even though GRE does not encrypt. Point-to-Point Tunnel Protocol (PPTP) is another good example of a VPN. With PPTP, a client makes a Point-to-Point Protocol (PPP) dial-up connection to an Internet service provider (ISP). Once connected to the ISP, the client sends IP packets, which carries PPP frames. This second connection is established from the client to the PPTP server at his corporate head office, as an example.

Encapsulating Versus Decapsulating Versus Tunneling

Encapsulation takes place when a data unit is passed to the next layer down on the OSI reference model. When a packet travels from a lower layer to an upper layer, we call this process *decapsulation*.

When a data unit travels sideways in the OSI model, we call that *tunneling*. PPTP is a tunneling protocol because it is the action of a PPP frame being carried inside of an IP packet, which is in turn encapsulated in a new frame.

Today, the use of a VPN implies the use of encryption. With a VPN, the information from a private network is transported over a public network, such as the Internet, to form a virtual network instead of using a dedicated Layer 2 connection, as shown in Figure 5-1. To remain private, the traffic is encrypted to keep the data confidential. For the purposes of this chapter, a VPN is defined as an encrypted connection between private networks over a public network, usually the Internet.

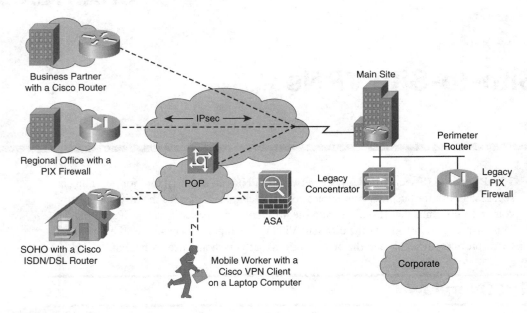

Figure 5-1 *Where VPNs Are Found*

Table 5-1 lists the primary Cisco products that can be used for VPN connectivity. Ensure that the router runs an IOS that supports VPN connectivity.

Table 5-1 *Cisco VPN Products*

VPN Application	Appropriate Cisco Product Choice
Dedicated VPN	Cisco VPN 3000 series concentrators (Note that the VPN 3000 is end-of-sale.)
	Cisco 7200 series routers
VPN-enabled routers series	Cisco SOHO 70 series routers and Cisco 800 series routers
	Cisco 1700 series modular access routers and Cisco 2600 series multiservice platforms
	Cisco 3700 series multiservice access routers and Cisco 3600 multiservice platforms
	Cisco 1800 series, Cisco 2800 series, and Cisco 3800 series integrated services routers
	Cisco 7200 series routers and Cisco 7300 series routers
	Cisco Catalyst 6500 series switches and Cisco 7600 series routers
	(Note that the SOHO 70, Cisco 800, 2600, and 3600 are end-of-sale.)
Firewall VPN	Cisco ASA 5500 series adaptive security appliances
	Cisco PIX 500 series security appliances

VPNs have many benefits:

- **Cost savings:** VPNs enable organizations to use cost-effective third-party Internet transport to connect remote offices and remote users to the main corporate site, thus eliminating expensive dedicated WAN links and modem banks. Furthermore, with the advent of cost-effective high-bandwidth technologies, such as digital subscriber line (DSL), organizations can use VPNs to reduce their connectivity costs while simultaneously increasing remote connection bandwidth.

- **Security:** VPNs provide the highest level of security by using advanced encryption and authentication protocols that protect data from unauthorized access.

- **Scalability:** VPNs enable corporations to use the Internet infrastructure within ISPs and devices, which makes it easy to add new users. Therefore, corporations are able to add large amounts of capacity without adding significant infrastructure.

- **Compatibility with broadband technology:** VPNs allow mobile workers, telecommuters, and people who want to extend their workday to take advantage of high-speed, broadband connectivity, such as DSL and cable, to gain access to their corporate networks, providing workers significant flexibility and efficiency. Furthermore, high-speed broadband connections provide a cost-effective solution for connecting remote offices.

VPN Types

Two basic types of VPN networks exist:

- Site to site
- Remote access

Site-to-Site VPNs

A site-to-site VPN, shown in Figure 5-2, is an extension of a classic WAN network. Site-to-site VPNs connect entire networks to each other; for example, they can connect a branch office network to a company headquarters network. In the past, a leased line or Frame Relay connection was required to connect sites, but because most corporations now have Internet access, these connections can be replaced with site-to-site VPNs.

In a site-to-site VPN, hosts do not have Cisco VPN Client software; they send and receive normal TCP/IP traffic through a VPN "gateway," which could be a router, firewall, Cisco VPN concentrator, or Cisco ASA 5500 series adaptive security appliance. The VPN gateway is responsible for encapsulating and encrypting outbound traffic for all the traffic from a particular site and sending it through a VPN tunnel over the Internet to a peer VPN gateway at the target site. Upon receipt, the peer VPN gateway strips the headers, decrypts the content, and relays the packet toward the target host inside its private network.

Remote-Access VPNs

Remote access is an evolution of circuit-switching networks, such as Plain Old Telephone Service (POTS) or Integrated Services Digital Network (ISDN). Remote-access VPNs,

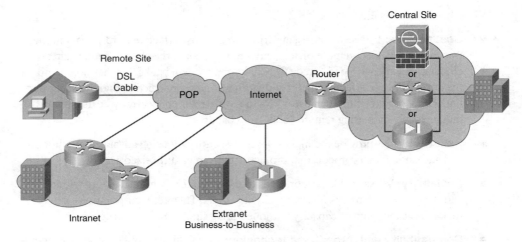

Figure 5-2 *Site-to-Site VPNs*

shown in Figure 5-3, can support the needs of telecommuters, mobile users, and extranet consumer-to-business traffic. Remote-access VPNs connect individual hosts who must access their company network securely over the Internet.

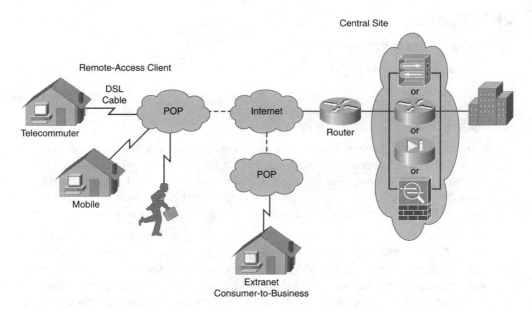

Figure 5-3 *Remote-Access VPN*

In the past, corporations supported remote users by using dial-in networks and ISDN. With the advent of VPNs, a mobile user simply needs access to the Internet to communicate with the central office. In the case of telecommuters, their Internet connectivity is typically a broadband connection such as DSL or cable.

In a remote-access VPN, each host typically has Cisco VPN Client software. Whenever the host tries to send any traffic, the Cisco VPN Client software encapsulates and encrypts that traffic before sending it over the Internet to the VPN gateway at the edge of the target network. Upon receipt, the VPN gateway behaves as it does for site-to-site VPNs.

Cisco IOS Secure Sockets Layer (SSL)-based VPN, shown in Figure 5-4, is a maturing technology that provides remote-access connectivity from almost any Internet-enabled location using a web browser and its native SSL encryption. SSL VPN provides the flexibility to support secure access for all users, regardless of the endpoint host from which they establish a connection. If application access requirements are modest, SSL VPN does not require a software client to be preinstalled on the endpoint host. This capability enables companies to extend their secure enterprise networks to any authorized user by providing remote-access connectivity to corporate resources from any Internet-enabled location.

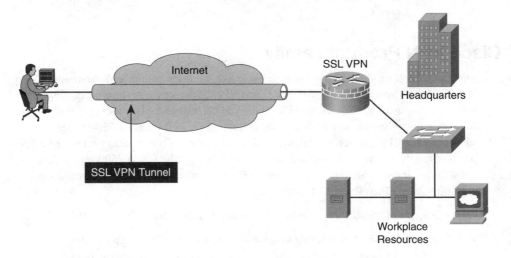

Figure 5-4   *SSL VPN*

SSL VPNs allow users to access web pages and services, including the ability to access files, send and receive email, and run TCP-based applications, without IPsec VPN Client software. SSL VPNs are appropriate for user populations that require per-application or per-server access control, or access from non-enterprise-owned desktops.

SSL VPN currently delivers two modes of SSL VPN access:

■ **Clientless:** In clientless mode, the remote user accesses the corporate network using the web browser on the client machine, so no applications needs to be installed locally on the user's laptop.

■ **Thin client:** In thin-client mode, the remote user downloads a Java applet by clicking the link provided on the corporate portal page or it could be configured for the Java applet to be downloaded. The Java applet acts as a TCP proxy on the client machine for the services made available to remote users.

In many cases, IPsec and SSL VPN are complementary because they solve different problems. This complementary approach allows a single device to address all remote-access user requirements.

The primary benefit of SSL VPN is that it is compatible with Dynamic Multipoint VPNs (DMVPN), Cisco IOS firewalls, IPsec, intrusion prevention systems (IPS), Cisco Easy VPN, and Network Address Translation (NAT).

The primary restriction of SSL VPN was that it was supported only in software, where the router CPU processed the SSL VPN connections. It used to be that the onboard VPN acceleration that was available in integrated services routers (ISR) accelerated only IPsec connections. However, the newer generation of VPN acceleration for ISR now also accelerates SSL connections.

Caution: SSL VPN does not support the same level of cryptographic security that IPsec supports.

Cisco VPN Product Family

The Cisco VPN product family, listed in Table 5-2, includes remote and site-to-site Cisco IOS VPN and firewall security routers, Cisco VPN 3000 series concentrators, Cisco PIX 500 series security appliances, and Cisco ASA 5500 series adaptive security appliances. Note that both the PIX and VPN 300 are end-of-sale. Cisco Catalyst 6500 series switches with VPN service modules (not shown in Table 5-2) were also part of the VPN product family. It is now end-of-sale and was replaced by the Cisco 7600 series/Catalyst 6500 Series Services Shared Port Adapter (SPA) Carrier-400, which can be configured with up to two Cisco IPsec VPN SPAs.

Characteristics of the different platforms include the following:

■   **Cisco VPN-enabled routers and switches:** Cisco VPN security routers and switches represent the best options for customers of all sizes looking to take

Table 5-2   *Cisco VPN Products*

Product Choice	Remote-Access VPN	Site-to-Site VPN
Cisco VPN 3000 series concentrators	Primary role	Secondary role
Cisco VPN-enabled routers	Secondary role	Primary role
Cisco PIX 500 series security appliances	Enhances existing Cisco PIX with VPN remote-access solution	Security organization owns the VPN solution
Cisco ASA 5500 series adaptive security appliances	Supports Cisco VPN 3000 concentrator features and more	Security organization owns the VPN solution

advantage of their existing network infrastructures to deploy VPNs and security while integrating all services into a single device with the widest selection of WAN and LAN interfaces.

- **Cisco VPN 3000 series concentrators:** Cisco VPN 3000 series concentrators offer both IPsec and SSL VPN connectivity on a single platform without the expense of individual feature licensing.

Note: Cisco VPN 3000 series concentrators and the PIX are end-of-sale. For details on the specifics for end-of-sale and end-of-life devices, refer to Cisco.com.

- Cisco ASA 5500 series adaptive security appliances: The Cisco ASA 5500 series adaptive security appliances are all-in-one security appliances that deliver enterprise-class security and IPsec VPNs to small and medium-sized businesses and large enterprise networks in a modular, purpose-built appliance. Cisco ASA 5500 series adaptive security appliances incorporate a wide range of integrated security services, including firewall, IPSs, and VPNs in an easy-to-deploy, high-performance solution, along with built-in hardware VPN acceleration. By integrating VPN and security services, the Cisco ASA 5500 series adaptive security appliances provide secure VPN connectivity and communications. Cisco ASA 5500 series adaptive security appliances are ideal for clients who are looking for the best-of-breed firewall combined with comprehensive VPN support. Cisco PIX 500 series security appliances are also an excellent option for organizations whose security policies recommend separate management of the security infrastructure to set a clear demarcation between security and network operation.

- **Cisco PIX 500 series security appliances:** Cisco PIX 500 series security appliances provide robust, enterprise-class, integrated network security services, including stateful inspection firewall, deep protocol and application inspection, IPsec VPNs, multivector attack protection, and rich multimedia and voice security.

Note: In most networks, you will find some devices already in place. In this case, it is important to verify whether interoperability between the different devices is possible. In a customer network, there may be a Cisco ASA 5500 series adaptive security appliance at one site and a Cisco router at another. A VPN tunnel can be established between these two devices as long as the software is at a minimum version. This site-to-site VPN interoperability is possible by choosing, at a minimum, the following software versions: Cisco IOS Release 12.2(8)T and Cisco ASA 5500 series adaptive security appliance Version 8.0. Note that the Cisco PIX does not support SSL VPN.

Cisco VPN-Enabled IOS Routers

With Cisco routers running Cisco IOS Software, organizations can easily deploy and scale site-to-site VPNs of any topology (from hub-and-spoke VPNs to the more complex, fully meshed VPNs). In addition, the Cisco IOS security features combine the VPN feature set with firewall, intrusion prevention, and extensive Cisco IOS capabilities, including quality of service (QoS), multiprotocol, multicast, and advanced routing support.

Cisco provides a suite of VPN-optimized routers. Cisco IOS Software for routers combines rich VPN services with industry-leading routing, delivering a comprehensive solution. The Cisco VPN software adds strong security using encryption and authentication. These Cisco VPN-enabled routers provide high performance for site-to-site, intranet, and extranet VPN solutions.

The Cisco IOS feature sets incorporate many VPN features:

- **Voice and Video Enabled VPN (V3PN):** Integrates IP telephony, QoS, and IPsec, providing an end-to-end VPN service that helps ensure the timely delivery of latency-sensitive applications such as voice and video.

- **IPsec stateful failover:** Provides fast and scalable network resiliency for VPN sessions between remote and central sites. With both stateless and stateful failover solutions available, options such as dead peer detection (DPD), Hot Standby Router Protocol (HSRP), Reverse Route Injection (RRI), and Stateful Switchover (SSO) help ensure maximum uptime of mission-critical applications.

- **DMVPN:** Enables the autoprovisioning of site-to-site IPsec VPNs, combining three Cisco IOS Software features: Next Hop Resolution Protocol (NHRP), multipoint GRE, and IPsec VPN. This combination eases the provisioning challenges for customers and provides secure connectivity between all locations.

- **IPsec and Multiprotocol Label Switching (MPLS) integration:** Enables ISPs to map IPsec sessions directly into an MPLS VPN. You can deploy this solution on colocated edge routers that are connected to a Cisco IOS Software MPLS provider edge (PE) network. This approach enables the ISP to securely extend its VPN service beyond the boundaries of the MPLS network by using the public IP infrastructure that securely connects enterprise customer remote offices, telecommuters, and mobile users from anywhere to the corporate network.

- **Cisco Easy VPN:** Simplifies VPN deployment for remote offices and teleworkers. The Cisco Easy VPN solution centralizes VPN management across all the Cisco VPN devices, thus reducing the management complexity of VPN deployments.

Cisco Adaptive Security Appliances

For VPN services, Cisco ASA 5500 series adaptive security appliances offer flexible technologies that deliver tailored solutions to suit remote-access and site-to-site connectivity requirements. Cisco ASA 5500 series adaptive security appliances provide easy-to-manage IPsec and SSL VPN-based remote-access and network-aware site-to-site VPN connectivity, enabling businesses to create secure connections across public networks to mobile users, remote sites, and business partners.

The Cisco ASA 5500 series adaptive security appliances form a high-performance, multi-function security appliance family delivering converged firewall, IPS, network antivirus, and VPN services. As a key component of the Cisco Self-Defending Network, Cisco

ASA 5500 series adaptive security appliances provide proactive threat mitigation that stops attacks before they spread through the network, control network activity and application traffic, and deliver flexible VPN connectivity while remaining cost-effective and easy to manage.

Compared to Cisco PIX 500 series security appliances, Cisco ASA 5500 series adaptive security appliances offer additional services, such Cisco SSL VPN, and in some models an expansion slot that can be populated with modules that provide intrusion prevention, or advanced inspection or increased port density. The following are some of the features of Cisco ASA 5500 series adaptive security appliances:

- **Flexible platform:** Offers both IPsec and SSL VPN on a single platform, eliminating the need to provide parallel solutions. In addition to VPN services, Cisco ASA 5500 series adaptive security appliances offer application inspection firewall and intrusion prevention services.

- **Resilient clustering:** Allows remote-access deployments to scale cost-effectively by evenly distributing VPN sessions across all the Cisco ASA 5500 series adaptive security appliances and Cisco VPN 3000 series concentrators without requiring any user intervention.

- **Cisco Easy VPN:** Delivers uniquely scalable, cost-effective, and easy-to-manage remote-access VPN architecture. Cisco ASA 5500 series adaptive security appliances dynamically push the latest VPN security policies to remote VPN devices and clients, making sure that those endpoint policies are current before a connection is established.

- **Automatic Cisco VPN Client updates:** Provides VPN client software the capability to automatically update, which enables Cisco VPN Client software operating on remote desktops to be automatically upgraded.

- **Cisco SSL VPN:** Offers Cisco SSL VPN with clientless and thin-client Cisco SSL VPN capabilities.

- **VPN infrastructure for contemporary applications:** Provides a VPN infrastructure capable of converged voice, video, and data across a secure IPsec network by combining robust site-to-site VPN support with rich inspection capabilities, QoS, routing, and stateful failover features, allowing businesses to take advantage of the many benefits that converged networks deliver.

- **Integrated web-based management:** Provides management of the Cisco ASA 5500 series adaptive security appliances using the integrated web-based Cisco Adaptive Security Device Manager (ASDM). Cisco ASDM manages all the security and VPN functions of the appliances.

Each Cisco ASA 5500 series adaptive security appliance supports a different number of VPN peers:

- **Cisco ASA 5505:** 10 IPsec VPN peers and 25 SSL VPN peers with the Base license. The Cisco ASA 5505 can be upgraded to the Security Plus license, which supports up to 25 concurrent remote-access clients (IPsec), and 25 VPN peers (IPsec or SSL).

- **Cisco ASA 5510:** 250 IPsec VPN peers and 10 SSL VPN peers. Up to 250 SSL VPN peers by installing an SSL VPN upgrade license.

- **Cisco ASA 5520:** 750 IPsec VPN peers and 10 SSL VPN peers. Up to 750 SSL VPN peers by installing an SSL VPN upgrade license.

- **Cisco ASA 5540:** 5000 IPsec VPN peers and 10 SSL VPN peers. Up to 2500 SSL VPN peers with the SSL VPN upgrade license.

- **Cisco ASA 5550:** 5000 IPsec VPN peers and 10 SSL VPN peers. Up to 5000 SSL VPN peers with the SSL VPN upgrade license.

- **Cisco ASA 5580:** 10,000 IPsec VPN peers and 10 SSL VPN peers. Up to 10,000 SSL VPN peers with the SSL VPN upgrade license.

VPN Clients

Cisco remote-access VPNs are able to use three IPsec clients: the Cisco VPN Software Client, the Cisco VPN 3002 Hardware Client, and the Certicom IPsec client, which is no longer sold but still works.

- **The Cisco VPN 3002 Hardware Client (legacy equipment):** A network appliance that connects small office, home office (SOHO) LANs to the VPN. The device comes in either a single-port or an eight-port switch version. The VPN 3002 Hardware Client replaces traditional Cisco VPN Client applications on individual SOHO computers.

- **The Cisco VPN Software Client:** Software that is loaded on the PC or laptop of an individual. The Cisco VPN Client, shown in Figure 5-5, allows organizations to establish end-to-end, encrypted VPN tunnels for secure connectivity for mobile employees or teleworkers. The Cisco Easy VPN feature allows the Cisco VPN Client to receive security policies from the central-site VPN device, the Cisco Easy VPN Server, when a VPN tunnel connection is made, minimizing configuration requirements at the remote location.

- **The Certicom client:** A wireless client that is loaded onto wireless personal digital assistants (PDA) running the Palm or Microsoft Windows Mobile operating systems. Certicom wireless client software enables companies to extend critical enterprise applications, such as email and customer relationship management (CRM) tools, to mobile professionals by enabling handheld devices to connect to corporate VPN gateways for secure wireless access.

Cisco has recently released a new generation of VPN client: the Cisco AnyConnect VPN Client. The Cisco AnyConnect VPN Client provides remote users with secure VPN connections to the Cisco 5500 Series adaptive security appliance running Cisco ASA Software Version 8.0 and later or Cisco ASDM Version 6.0 and later, using SSL VPN, and therefore it does not connect with a Cisco PIX device or with a Cisco VPN 3000 series concentrator. The Cisco AnyConnect VPN Client supports Windows Vista, Windows XP, Windows 2000, Mac OS X (Version 10.4 or later) on either Intel or PowerPC, and Red Hat Linux (Version 9 or later).

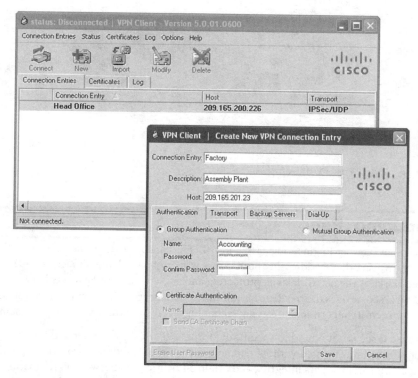

Figure 5-5 *Cisco VPN Software Client*

Cisco Hardware-Based Encryption

To enhance the performance and offload the encryption task to specialized hardware, the Cisco VPN family of devices offers the following hardware acceleration modules:

- **AIM:** A broad range of Cisco routers can be equipped with AIM. The AIM modules are installed inside the router chassis and offload encryption tasks from the router CPU.

- **Cisco IPsec VPN Shared Port Adapter (Cisco IPsec VPN SPA):** The Cisco IPsec VPN SPA, shown in Figure 5-6, delivers scalable and cost-effective VPN performance for Cisco Catalyst 6500 series switches and Cisco 7600 series routers. Using the Cisco 7600 series/Catalyst 6500 Series Services SPA Carrier-400, each slot of the Cisco Catalyst 6500 series switch or Cisco 7600 series router can support up to two Cisco IPsec VPN SPAs.

- **Enhanced Scalable Encryption Processing (SEP-E):** You can upgrade Cisco VPN 3000 series concentrators with SEP-E modules. The modules perform hardware encryption of Data Encryption Standard (DES) 0, Triple Data Encryption Standard (3DES), and Advanced Encryption Standard (AES) traffic.

- **Cisco PIX VPN Accelerator Card+ (VAC+):** The PIX Firewall VAC+ delivers hardware acceleration up to 425 Mb/s of DES, 3DES, or AES IPsec encryption throughput.

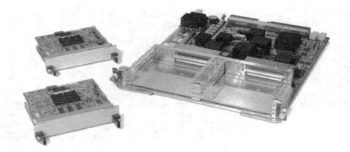

Figure 5-6   *Cisco IPsec VPN SPA*

Introducing IPsec

IPsec is an Internet Engineering Task Force (IETF) standard that defines how a VPN can be set up using the IP addressing protocol; it was originally defined in RFCs 2401 to 2412. IPsec works at the network layer, protecting and authenticating IP packets between participating IPsec devices (peers). IPsec is not bound to any specific encryption, authentication, or security algorithms or keying technology. IPsec is a framework of open standards.

Because IPsec is not bound to specific algorithms, IPsec allows newer and better algorithms to be implemented without patching the existing IPsec standards. IPsec provides data confidentiality, data integrity, and origin authentication between participating peers at the IP layer. IPsec secures a path between a pair of gateways, a pair of hosts, or a gateway and host, as shown in Figure 5-7.

IPsec provides the following essential security functions:

- **Confidentiality:** IPsec ensures confidentiality by using encryption. Data encryption prevents third parties from reading the data, especially data transmitted over public networks or over wireless networks.

- **Integrity:** IPsec ensures that data arrives unchanged at the destination; that is, that the data has not been manipulated at any point along the communication path. IPsec ensures data integrity by using checksums, which are a simple redundancy check. The IPsec protocol adds up the basic components of a message, typically the number of bytes, and stores the total value. IPsec performs a checksum operation on received data and compares the result to the authentic checksum. If the sums match, the assumption is that the data has not been manipulated.

- **Authentication:** Authentication ensures that the connection is made with the desired communication partner. IPsec uses Internet Key Exchange (IKE) to authenticate users and devices that can carry out communication independently.

Note: IKE is discussed in more detail in the section "IKE Protocol," later in the chapter.

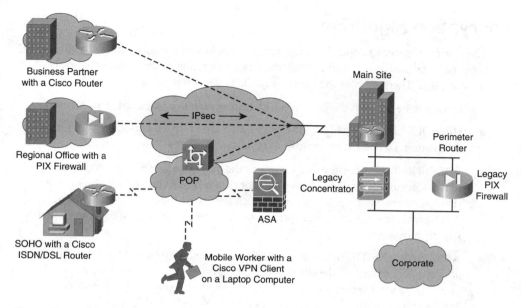

Figure 5-7 *How IPsec Can Be Used*

IKE uses several types of authentication:

- Username and password
- One-time password
- Biometric
- Pre-shared keys (PSK)
- Digital certificates

- **Antireplay protection:** Antireplay protection verifies that each packet is unique and is not duplicated. IPsec packets are protected by comparing the sequence number of the received packets with a sliding window on the destination host or security gateway. A packet that has a sequence number that comes before the sliding window is considered either late or a duplicate packet. Late and duplicate packets are dropped.

Essential services provided by IPsec are as follows:

- Confidentiality
- Integrity
- Authentication
- Antireplay

Key Topic

Encryption Algorithms

The degree of security depends on the length of the key of the encryption algorithm. The time that it takes to process all the possibilities is a function of the computing power of the computer. Therefore, the shorter the key, the easier it is to break the key.

The following are some of the encryption algorithms and key lengths that VPNs use:

- **DES:** DES was developed by IBM. DES uses a 56-bit key, ensuring high-performance encryption. DES is a symmetric key cryptosystem.

- **3DES:** The 3DES algorithm is a variant of the 56-bit DES. 3DES operates in a way that is similar to how DES operates, in that data is broken into 64-bit blocks. 3DES then processes each block three times, each time with an independent 56-bit key. 3DES provides significant encryption strength over 56-bit DES. 3DES is a symmetric key cryptosystem.

- **AES:** The National Institute of Standards and Technology (NIST) has recently adopted AES to replace the existing DES encryption in cryptographic devices. AES provides stronger security than DES and is computationally more efficient than 3DES. AES offers three different key lengths: 128-, 192-, and 256-bit keys.

- **Rivest, Shamir, and Adleman (RSA):** RSA is an asymmetrical key cryptosystem. It uses a key length of 512, 768, 1024, or larger. IPsec does not use RSA for data encryption. IKE uses RSA encryption only during the peer-authentication phase.

- **Software-Optimized Encryption Algorithm (SEAL) algorithm:** SEAL is a stream cipher, developed in 1993 by Phillip Rogaway and Don Coppersmith, and uses a 160-bit key for encryption.

Refer to the release notes of your specific security appliance version to confirm which algorithms are supported.

Encryption algorithms, such as DES and 3DES, explained in Chapter 4, "Fundamentals of Cryptography," require a symmetric shared-secret key to perform encryption and decryption. You can use email, courier, or overnight express to send the shared-secret keys to the administrators of the devices. But the easiest key-exchange method is a public-key exchange method between the encrypting and decrypting devices.

Diffie-Hellman Exchange

The Diffie-Hellman (DH) key agreement, explained in Chapter 4, is a cryptographic protocol that provides a way for two peers to establish a shared-secret key, which only they know, even though they are communicating over an unsecure channel.

That shared-secret key, created by Diffie-Hellamn, is then used as the encryption key to exchanged data.

Data Integrity

VPN data is typically transported over the public Internet. Potentially, this data could be intercepted and modified. To guard against this problem, you can use a data-integrity algorithm, explained in this previous chapter. A data-integrity algorithm adds a hash to the message, which guarantees the integrity of the original message. If the transmitted hash matches the received hash, the message has not been tampered with. However, if there is no match, the message was altered.

A Hashed Message Authentication Code (HMAC) is a data-integrity algorithm that guarantees the integrity of the message. At the local end, the message and a shared-secret key are sent through a hash algorithm, which produces a hash value. The message and hash are sent over the network.

As explained in this previous chapter, there are two common HMAC algorithms:

- **HMAC-Message Digest 5 (HMAC-MD5):** HMAC-MD5 uses a 128-bit shared-secret key of any size. The variable-length message and shared-secret key are combined and run through the HMAC-MD5 hash algorithm. The output is a 128-bit hash. The hash is appended to the original message and is forwarded to the remote end.

- **HMAC-Secure Hash Algorithm 1 (HMAC-SHA-1):** HMAC-SHA-1 uses a secret key of any size. The variable-length message and the shared-secret key are combined and run through the HMAC-SHA-1 hash algorithm. The output is a 160-bit hash. The hash is appended to the original message and is forwarded to the remote end.

Authentication

When you are conducting business long distance, it is necessary to know who is at the other end of the phone, email, or fax. The same is true of VPN networks. The device on the other end of the VPN tunnel must be authenticated before the communication path is considered secure. Three peer-authentication methods exist:

- **PSKs:** A secret key value is entered into each peer manually and is used to authenticate the peer. This is a shared secret that both parties must exchange ahead of time. See it as the secret password that they will be offering to each other to confirm the identity of the other party. At each end, the PSK is combined with other information to form the authentication key.

- **RSA signatures:** A hash value of the message, encrypted with the sender's private key. The encrypted hash is attached to the message and is forwarded to the remote end, and acts like a signature. At the remote end, the encrypted hash is decrypted using the public key of the sender. If the decrypted hash matches the recomputed hash, the signature is genuine.

- **RSA encrypted nonces:** A nonce is a random number generated by the peer. RSA encrypted nonces use RSA to encrypt the nonce value and other values. This method requires that the public key of the two peers be present on the other peer before the third and fourth messages of an IKE exchange can be accomplished. For this reason, public keys must be manually copied to each peer as part of the configuration process, and therefore this method is limited by the available memory of the receiver. This method is the least used of the three authentication methods.

IPsec Advantages

One of the greatest strengths of IPsec is that is implemented at Layer 3 of the Open Systems Interconnection (OSI) model. As a result, IPsec can protect nearly all application traffic because the protection is implemented irrespective of whether Layer 4, Layer 5, Layer 6, or Layer 7 is used.

Because in all the implementations of IPsec there is a plaintext Layer 3 header, there are no issues with routing. Therefore, IPsec runs over all Layer 2 protocols, too; ATM, Ethernet, Token Ring, Frame Relay, Synchronous Data Link Control (SDLC), High-Level Data Link Control (HDLC), and others all work with IPsec data. IPsec is truly a universal protocol that works in almost every circumstance.

IPsec is also extremely scalable, as proven by the innumerable large organizations that use it.

IPsec exceeds SSL in many significant ways:

- The number of applications supported

- Its encryption strength

- Its authentication strength

- Its overall security

Table 5-3   *IPsec Versus SSL*

	SSL	IPsec
Applications	Web-enabled applications, file sharing, email.	All IP-based applications.
Encryption	Moderate. (Key lengths range from 40 bits to 128 bits.)	Stronger. (Key lengths range from 56 bits to 256 bits.)
Authentication	Moderate. (One-way or two-way authentication.)	Strong. (Two-way authentication using shared secrets or digital certificates.)
Ease of use	Very high.	Moderate. (Can be challenging to nontechnical users.)
Overall security	Moderate. (Any device can connect.)	Strong. (Only specific devices with specific configurations can connect.)

The one area in which SSL excels is its ease of use and ease of deployment. When security is the issue, IPsec is the superior choice. If ease of deployment and support is the primary issue, you should consider SSL.

Cisco VPN products support both technologies to satisfy the largest number of customer requirements.

Table 5-3 summarizes the differences between SSL VPN and IPsec VPN.

IPsec Protocol Framework

IPsec is a framework of open standards. IPsec spells out the messaging to secure the communications but relies on existing algorithms. There are two main IPsec framework protocols, as depicted in Figure 5-8:

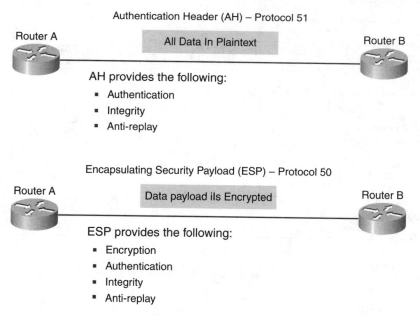

Figure 5-8   *IPsec Security Protocols*

- **Authentication Header (AH):** AH, which is IP protocol 51, is the appropriate protocol to use when confidentiality is not required or permitted. It provides data authentication and integrity for IP packets passed between two systems. It is a means of verifying that any message that is passed from Router A to Router B has not been modified during transit. It verifies that the origin of the data was either Router A or Router B. AH does not provide data confidentiality (encryption) of packets. All text is transported in the clear. If the AH protocol is used alone, it provides weak protection. Consequently, Encapsulating Security Payload uses the AH protocol to provide data encryption and tamper-aware security features.

■ **Encapsulating Security Payload (ESP):** ESP is a security protocol that can provide confidentiality and authentication. ESP, which is IP protocol 50, provides confidentiality by performing encryption on the IP packet. IP packet encryption conceals the data payload and the identities of the ultimate source and destination. ESP provides authentication for the inner IP packet and ESP header. Authentication provides data-origin authentication and data integrity. Although both encryption and authentication are optional in ESP, at a minimum, one of them must be selected.

Note: Figure 5-9 provides a visual representation of where IPsec fits in the layered model.

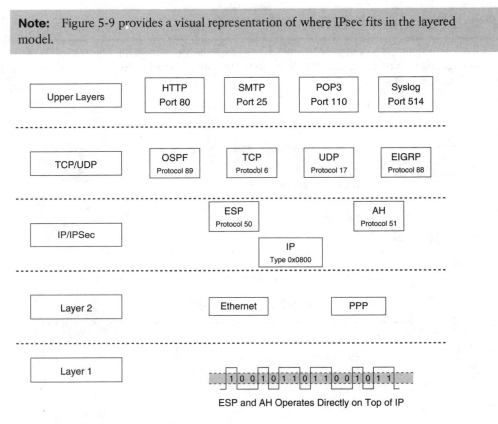

ESP and AH Operates Directly on Top of IP

Figure 5-9 *IPsec and the Layered Model*

Authentication Header

AH achieves authenticity by applying a keyed one-way hash function to the packet to create a hash, or message digest. The hash is combined with the text and is transmitted. The receiver detects changes in any part of the packet that occur during transit by performing the same one-way hash function on the received packet and comparing the result to the value of the message digest that the sender has supplied. The fact that the one-way hash also involves the use of a shared-secret key between the two systems means that authenticity is ensured.

The AH function is applied to the entire datagram except for any mutable IP header fields that change in transit; for example, Time to Live (TTL) fields that are modified by the routers along the transmission path. Figure 5-10 illustrates the AH process as follows:

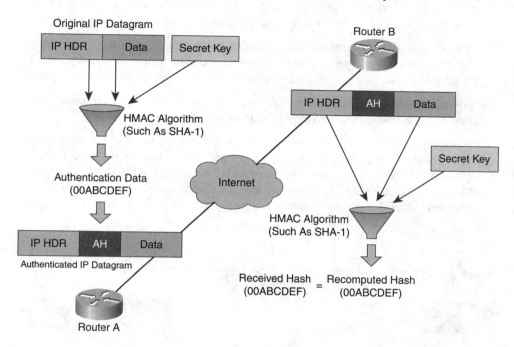

Figure 5-10   *AH Authentication and Integrity*

Step 1.   The IP header and data payload is hashed.

Step 2.   The hash builds a new AH header, which is prepended to the original packet.

Step 3.   The new packet is transmitted to the IPsec peer router.

Step 4.   The peer router hashes the IP header and data payload, extracts the transmitted hash from the AH header, and compares the two hashes. The hashes must match exactly. Even if 1 bit is changed in the transmitted packet, the hash output on the received packet changes and the AH header will not match.

AH supports the HMAC-MD5 and HMAC-SHA-1 algorithms.

Note: AH protects the entire IP packet, which includes the IP header, against tempering during transmission. Because NAT modifies the IP header, it is incompatible with AH. Fixes, such as tunnel mode, discussed later, remedies this problem.
Also, note that the PIX and ASA 7.x does not offer the AH option. Only ESP can be performed.

Encapsulating Security Payload

ESP provides confidentiality by encrypting the payload. It supports a variety of symmetric encryption algorithms. The lowest common algorithm for IPsec is 56-bit DES. Cisco products also support the use of 3DES and especially AES for stronger encryption.

ESP can also provide integrity and authentication of the datagrams. First, the payload is encrypted. Next, the encrypted payload is sent through a hash algorithm, HMAC-MD5 or HMAC-SHA-1. The hash provides authentication and data integrity for the data payload.

Optionally, ESP can also enforce antireplay protection by requiring that a receiving host set the replay bit in the header to indicate that the packet has been seen.

The original data is well protected by ESP because the entire original IP datagram is encrypted, as shown in Figure 5-11. An ESP header and trailer are added to the encrypted payload. With ESP authentication, the encrypted IP datagram and the ESP header and trailer are included in the hashing process. Lastly, a new IP header is prepended to the authenticated payload. The new IP address is used to route the packet through the Internet.

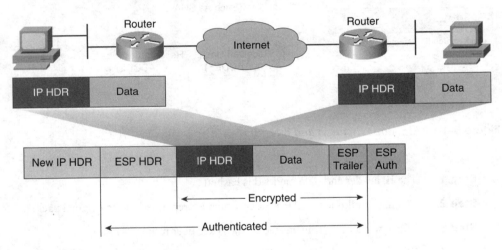

Figure 5-11   *ESP Protocol*

When both authentication (AH) and encryption (ESP) are selected, encryption occurs first. One reason for this order of processing is that it facilitates rapid detection and rejection of replayed or bogus packets by the receiving device. Before decrypting the packet, the receiver can authenticate inbound packets. By doing this, it can quickly detect problems and potentially reduce the impact of denial-of-service (DoS) attacks.

Tunnel Mode Versus Transport Mode

ESP and AH can be used in two different ways referred to as modes. The encapsulation can be done in tunnel mode or in transport mode. The encapsulation performed on an ESP packet with each mode is illustrated in Figure 5-12:

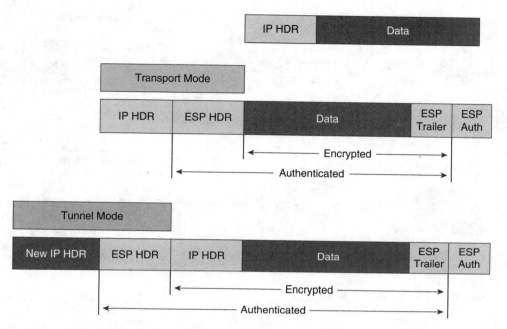

Figure 5-12 *Encapsulation with Tunnel and Transport Modes*

- **Transport mode:** In transport mode, security is provided only for the transport layer and above. Transport mode protects the payload of the packet but leaves the original IP address in the clear. The original IP address is used to route the packet through the Internet. ESP transport mode is used between hosts.

Note: Transport mode works well with GRE because GRE hides the addresses of the end stations by adding its own IP header.

- Tunnel mode: Tunnel mode provides security for the complete original IP packet. The original IP packet is encrypted, and then it is encapsulated in another IP packet. The outside IP address is used to route the packet through the Internet.

Tunnel Mode

ESP tunnel mode is used between a host and a security gateway or between two security gateways, as shown in Figure 5-13. For gateway-to-gateway applications, rather than load IPsec on all the computers at the remote and corporate offices, it is easier to have the security gateways perform the IP-in-IP encryption and encapsulation.

ESP tunnel mode is used in the IPsec remote-access application. At a home office, there might be no router to perform the IPsec encapsulation and encryption. In this case, an IPsec client running on the PC performs the IPsec IP-in-IP encapsulation and encryption. At the corporate office, the router de-encapsulates and decrypts the packet.

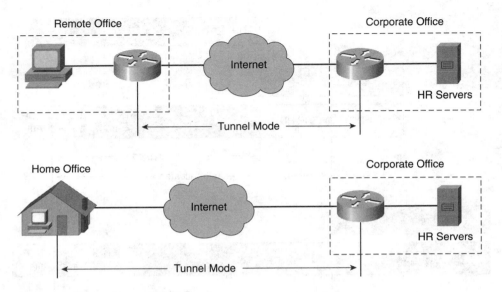

Figure 5-13   *IPsec Tunnel Mode*

IPsec Framework

IPsec is a framework of open standards that spells out the rules for secure communications. IPsec, in turn, relies on existing algorithms to implement the encryption, authentication, and key exchange. The following are some of the standard algorithms that IPsec uses:

- **DES:** Encrypts and decrypts packet data

- **3DES:** Provides significant encryption strength over 56-bit DES

- **AES:** Provides stronger encryption, depending on the key length that is used, and faster throughput

- **MD5:** Authenticates packet data, using a 128-bit message digest

- **SHA-1:** Authenticates packet data, using a 160-bit message digest

- **DH:** Allows two parties to establish a shared-secret key that is used by encryption and hash algorithms (for example, DES and MD5) over an unsecure communications channel

In Figure 5-14, there are four IPsec framework squares to be filled in. When you configure an IPsec gateway to provide security services, you must first choose an IPsec protocol. The choices are ESP or ESP with AH. AH can also be used alone. The second square is an encryption algorithm. Choose the encryption algorithm appropriate for the desired level of security: DES, 3DES, or AES. The third square is authentication. Choose an authentication algorithm to provide data integrity: MD5 or SHA. The last square is the DH algorithm group. Choose which group to use, DH Group 1 (DH1), DH Group 2 (DH2), or DH Group 5 (DH5). IPsec provides the framework, and the administrator chooses the algorithms that are used to implement the security services within that framework.

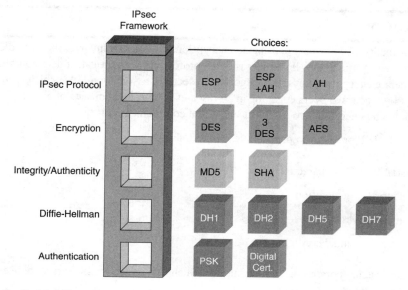

Figure 5-14   *IPsec Framework*

IKE Protocol

IPsec implements a VPN solution using an encryption process that involves the periodic changing of encryption keys. IPsec uses the IKE protocol to authenticate a peer computer and to generate encryption keys. IKE negotiates a security association (SA), which is an agreement between two peers engaging in an IPsec exchange, and consists of all the required parameters necessary to establish successful communication.

IPsec uses the IKE protocol to provide these functions:

■ Negotiation of SA characteristics

■ Automatic key generation

■ Automatic key refresh

■ Manageable manual configuration

To establish a secure communication channel between two peers, the IKE protocol uses the following three modes of operation:

■ **Main mode:** In main mode, an IKE session begins with one computer (the initiator) sending a proposal or proposals to another computer (the responder). The proposal sent by the initiator defines what encryption and authentication protocols are acceptable, how long keys should remain active, and whether Perfect Forward Secrecy (PFS) should be enforced. There are three exchanges typical of the main mode:
   ■ The first exchange between the initiator and the responder establishes the basic security policy. The responder chooses a proposal best suited to the security situation and then sends that proposal to the initiator.
   ■ The next exchange passes DH public keys between the two users. DH key exchange is a cryptographic protocol that allows two parties that have no prior knowledge of each other to establish a shared-secret key over an unsecure communications channel. All further negotiation is encrypted within the IKE SA.
   ■ The third exchange authenticates an Internet Security Association and Key Management Protocol (ISAKMP) session. Once the IKE SA is established, IPsec quick mode negotiation begins.

■ **Aggressive mode:** Aggressive mode compresses the IKE SA negotiation phases described thus far into three packets. In aggressive mode, the initiator passes all data that is required for the SA. The responder sends the proposal, key material, and ID and authenticates the session in the next packet. The initiator replies by authenticating the session. Negotiation is quicker, and the initiator and responder IDs pass in plaintext.

■ **Quick mode:** Quick mode IPsec negotiation takes place after successful IKE SA negotiation. Quick mode is similar to aggressive mode IKE negotiation, except that negotiation is protected within an IKE SA. Quick mode negotiates the SA for the data encryption and manages the key exchange for that IPsec SA.

To establish a secure communication channel between two peers, the IKE protocol executes the following phases:

- **IKE Phase 1:** In IKE Phase 1, two IPsec peers perform the initial negotiation of SAs. In this phase, the SA negotiations are bidirectional; data may be sent and received using the same encryption key. In IKE Phase 1, the transform sets, hash methods, and other parameters are determined. Optionally, IKE Phase 1 can include authentication, in which each peer in the SA negotiation is able to verify the identity of the other. Even if the SA negotiation data stream between the two IPsec peers is compromised, there is little chance that the encryption keys could be guessed and thus the traffic decrypted.

- **IKE Phase 2:** In IKE Phase 2, SAs are negotiated by the IKE process ISAKMP on behalf of other services, such as IPsec, that need encryption key material for operation. Quick mode negotiates the IKE Phase 2 SAs. In this phase, the SAs that IPsec uses are unidirectional; therefore, a separate key exchange is required for each data flow.

Note: Other, optional parameters are sometimes negotiated between IKE Phase 1 and IKE Phase 2, such as level of DH, encryption algorithms, and methods of authentication.

IKE Phase 1

The basic purpose of IKE Phase 1, shown in Figure 5-15, is to negotiate IKE policy sets, authenticate the peers, and set up a secure channel between the peers. IKE Phase 1 occurs in two modes: main mode and aggressive mode.

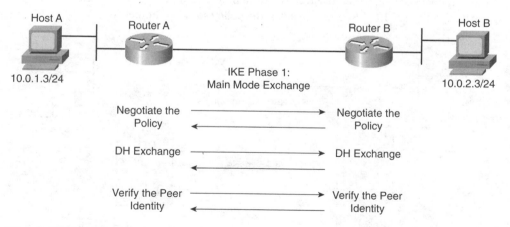

Figure 5-15 *IKE Phase 1*

Main mode has three two-way exchanges between the initiator and receiver:

- **First exchange:** Peers negotiate and agree on the algorithms and hashes that will be used to secure the IKE communications.

- **Second exchange:** DH generates public and private values. The peers exchange their public values, and the result is a shared secret. The shared-secret key is used to generate all the other encryption and authentication keys.

- **Third exchange:** The identity of the other side is verified. The main outcome of main mode is a secure communications path for subsequent exchanges between the peers.

Note: In aggressive mode, fewer exchanges are done, and the exchanges have fewer packets. As an example, with aggressive mode, the peers will exchange their identity and a hash of the PSK even though DH have not been negotiated yet, and therefore there is no shared secret to send data in an encrypted format.

IKE Phase 1: Example

When you are trying to make a secure connection between Host A and B through the Internet, a secure path (a tunnel) is established between Router A and Router B. Through the tunnel, the encryption, authentication, and other protocols are negotiated.

First Exchange: IKE Policy Is Negotiated

Rather than negotiate each protocol individually, the protocols are grouped into sets, called IKE policy sets. IKE policy sets are exchanged during the IKE main mode, first exchange phase. If a policy match is found between peers, main mode continues. If no match is found, the tunnel is torn down.

In Figure 5-16, Router A sends IKE policy sets 10 and 20 to Router B. Router B compares its set, policy set 15, with those received from Router A. In this instance, there is a policy match. Policy set 10 of Router A matches the policy set 15 of Router B.

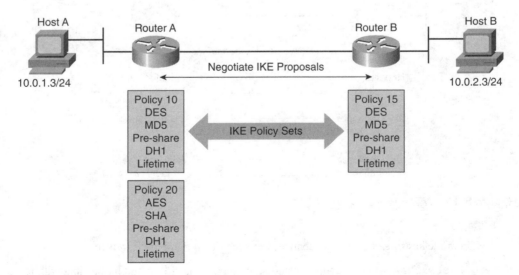

Figure 5-16   *First Exchange: IKE Policy Is Negotiated*

In a point-to-point application, each end may need only a single IKE policy set to be defined. However, in a hub-and-spoke environment, the central site may require multiple IKE policy sets to satisfy all the remote peers.

Second Exchange: DH Key Exchange

When the IKE policy is agreed on, including the size of the prime number to be used for DH, the two peers run the DH key exchange protocol, as shown in Figure 5-17. The result of DH will be the creation of a shared secret that is needed by the various encryption and hashing algorithms upon which IKE and IPsec will ultimately agree.

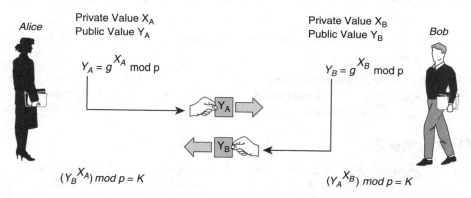

Alice
Private Value X_A
Public Value Y_A

$Y_A = g^{X_A} \bmod p$

Private Value X_B
Public Value Y_B

$Y_B = g^{X_B} \bmod p$

Bob

$(Y_B{}^{X_A}) \bmod p = K$

$(Y_A{}^{X_B}) \bmod p = K$

Figure 5-17 *Second Exchange: DH Key Exchange*

Several levels of DH key exchanges are available in Cisco IOS Software:

- **DH Group 1:** A key exchange that uses a 768-bit prime number. This group is the usual choice when the encryption algorithm is DES.

- **DH Group 2:** A key exchange that uses a 1024-bit prime number. This group is the usual choice when using 3DES for encryption.

- **DH Group 5:** A key exchange that uses a 1536-bit prime number. DH 5 should be used with AES.

- **DH Group 7 (elliptic curve cryptography [ECC]):** A key exchange that generates IPsec keys when the elliptic curve field is 163 bits. This group was designed to be used with low-powered hosts such as PDAs.

Third Exchange: Authenticate Peer Identity

When you are conducting business over the Internet, it is necessary to know who is at the other end of the tunnel. The device on the other end of the VPN tunnel must be authenticated before the communications path is considered secure. The last exchange of IKE Phase 1 authenticates the remote peer, as illustrated in Figure 5-18.

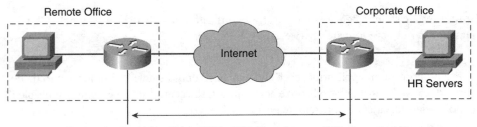

Peer Authentication Using Either PSKs, RSA Signatures or RSA-Encrypted Nonces

Figure 5-18 *Third Exchange: Authenticate Peer Identity*

There are three data origin authentication methods:

- **PSKs:** PSKs are a secret key value that is entered into each peer manually and is used to authenticate the peer.

- **RSA signatures:** RSA signatures are the exchange of digital certificates that is used to authenticate the peers.

- **RSA encrypted nonces:** Nonces are random numbers that are generated by each peer and are encrypted and then exchanged between peers. The two nonces are used during the peer-authentication process.

IKE Phase 2

The purpose of IKE Phase 2 is to negotiate the IPsec security parameters, as shown in Figure 5-19, that will be used to secure the IPsec tunnel. IKE Phase 2 performs the following functions:

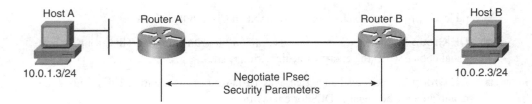

Figure 5-19 *IKE Phase 2*

- Negotiates IPsec security parameters, known as IPsec transform sets

- Establishes IPsec SAs

- Periodically renegotiates IPsec SAs to ensure security

- Optionally performs an additional DH exchange

IKE Phase 2 has one mode, called quick mode. Quick mode occurs after IKE has established the secure tunnel in Phase 1. It negotiates a shared IPsec transform, derives shared-secret keying material that the IPsec security algorithms will use, and establishes IPsec

SAs. Quick mode also exchanges nonces that are used to generate new shared-secret key material and prevent replay attacks from generating false SAs.

Quick mode also renegotiates a new IPsec SA when the IPsec SA lifetime expires. Basically, quick mode refreshes the keying material that creates the shared-secret key based on the keying material derived from the DH exchange in Phase 1.

Earlier, the text mentioned Perfect Forward Secrecy (PFS). The basic principle of PFS is that new keys (shared secrets) cannot be derived from older keys. The idea is that if keys are compromised, previous and subsequent keys are secured because they were generated from scratch and not derived. Therefore, PFS exists when a DH exchange is done at each rekeying interval, which is preferable, but might not be necessary, instead of deriving the new keys from the previous keys.

IKE negotiates matching IPsec policies.

Key Topic

Note: Because a picture is worth a thousand words, Figure 5-20 is the visual representation of IPsec I created to teach students the sequence of events when tunnels are being built. The process starts at the bottom of the figure with IKE Phase 1, followed by IKE Phase 2, and finally with the two unidirectional IPsec tunnels coming up to exchange the encrypted data.

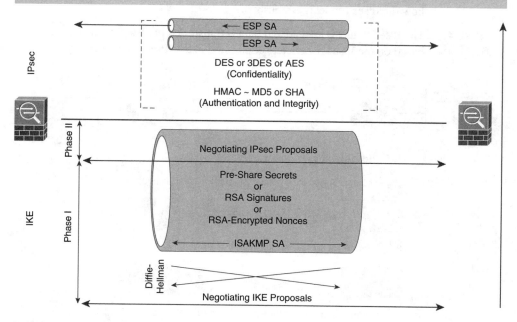

Figure 5-20   *Visual Representation of IPsec Tunnels Being Built*

Building a Site-to-Site IPsec VPN

Building a site-to-site IPsec VPN is an essential part of many plans to meet the security requirements of customers. In the next few pages, you will learn how to use the command-line interface (CLI) to configure a site-to-site IPsec VPN to securely connect two or more subnets over the Internet or an intranet. You will also learn how to test that configuration using the CLI.

Site-to-Site IPsec VPN Operations

IPsec VPN negotiation can be broken down into five steps, as shown in Figure 5-21, including Phase 1 and Phase 2 of Internet Key Exchange (IKE):

Step 1.   An IPsec tunnel is initiated when Host A sends "interesting" traffic to Host B. Traffic is considered interesting when it travels between the IPsec peers and meets the criteria that is defined in the crypto access control list (ACL).

Step 2.   In IKE Phase 1, the IPsec peers (routers A and B) negotiate the established IKE SA policy. Once the peers are authenticated, a secure tunnel is created using ISAKMP.

Step 3.   In IKE Phase 2, the IPsec peers use the authenticated and secure tunnel to negotiate IPsec SA transforms. The negotiation of the shared policy determines how the IPsec tunnel is established.

Step 4.   The IPsec tunnel is created and data is transferred between the IPsec peers based on the IPsec parameters configured in the IPsec transform sets.

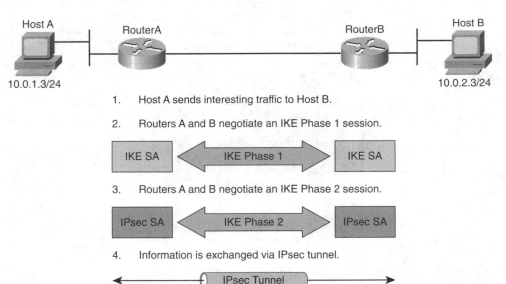

Figure 5-21   *Site-to-Site IPsec VPN*

Step 5.   The IPsec tunnel terminates when the IPsec SAs are deleted or when their life-time expires.

Configuring IPsec

Follow these steps to configure a site-to-site IPsec VPN:

Step 1.   Create a crypto ACL. The crypto ACL defines which traffic should be sent through the IPsec tunnel and be protected by the IPsec process.

Step 2.   Configure an ISAKMP policy to determine the ISAKMP parameters that will be used to establish the tunnel.

Step 3.   Define the IPsec transform set. The definition of the transform set defines the parameters that the IPsec tunnel uses, and can include the encryption and integrity algorithms.

Step 4.   Create and apply a crypto map. The crypto map groups the previously configured parameters together and defines the IPsec peer devices. The crypto map is applied to the outgoing interface of the VPN device.

Step 5.   Configure the interface ACL. Usually, there are restrictions on the interface that the VPN traffic uses (for example, block all traffic that is not IPsec or IKE).

Site-to-Site IPsec Configuration: Step 1

The first step in configuring Cisco IOS ISAKMP is to ensure that existing ACLs on perimeter routers, firewalls, or other routers do not block IPsec traffic. Perimeter routers typically implement a restrictive security policy with ACLs, where only specific traffic is permitted and all other traffic is denied. Such a restrictive policy blocks IPsec traffic. Therefore, you must add specific **permit** statements to the ACL to allow IPsec traffic.

Ensure that your ACLs are configured so that ISAKMP, ESP, and AH traffic is not blocked at interfaces used by IPsec. ISAKMP uses User Datagram Protocol (UDP) port 500. ESP is assigned IP protocol number 50, and AH is assigned IP protocol number 51. In some cases, you might need to add a statement to router ACLs to explicitly permit this traffic. You might need to add the ACL statements to the perimeter router by performing the following steps:

Step 1.   Examine the current ACL configuration at the perimeter router and determine whether it will block IPsec traffic:

```
RouterA# show access-lists
```

Step 2.   Add ACL entries to permit IPsec traffic. To do this, copy the existing ACL configuration and paste it into a text editor as follows:

- Copy the existing ACL configuration and paste it into a text editor.

- Add the ACL entries to the top of the list in the text editor.

- Delete the existing ACL with the **no access-list** *access-list number* command.

- Enter configuration mode and copy and paste the new ACL into the router.

- Verify that the ACL is correct with the **show access-lists** command.

If you have a recent version of the IOS, you might also benefit from the named ACL feature, which is also available for numbered ACLs when it comes to editing your ACL so that you do not have to copy and paste it into an external text editor.

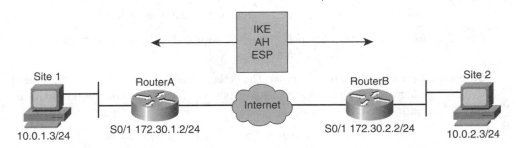

Figure 5-22 *Step 1: Ensure That ACLs Are Compatible with IPsec and Topology*

A concatenated example showing ACL entries permitting IPsec traffic for Router A, shown in Figure 5-22, is as follows:

```
RouterA# show running-config
!
interface Serial0/1
 ip address 172.30.1.2 255.255.255.0
 ip access-group 102 in
!
access-list 102 permit ahp host 172.30.2.2 host 172.30.1.2
access-list 102 permit esp host 172.30.2.2 host 172.30.1.2
access-list 102 permit udp host 172.30.2.2 host 172.30.1.2 eq isakmp
```

Note: Note that the protocol keyword **esp** equals the ESP protocol (number 50), the keyword **ahp** equals the AH protocol (number 51), and the **isakmp** keyword equals UDP port 500.

Site-to-Site IPsec Configuration: Step 2

The second major step in configuring Cisco IOS ISAKMP support is to define a suite of ISAKMP policies. The goal of defining a suite of IKE policies is to establish ISAKMP peering between two IPsec endpoints.

Multiple ISAKMP policies can be configured on each peer participating in IPsec. ISAKMP peers negotiate the acceptable ISAKMP policies before they agree on the SA to use for IPsec.

Use the **crypto isakmp policy** command to define an IKE Phase I policy. IKE policies define a set of parameters that IKE uses during negotiation. Use the **no** form of this command to delete an IKE policy. The command syntax is **crypto isakmp policy** *priority*, where *priority* is a number that uniquely identifies the IKE policy and assigns a priority to the policy. Use an integer from 1 to 10,000, with 1 being the highest priority and 10,000 the lowest.

This command invokes the ISAKMP policy configuration (config-isakmp) command mode.

Note: Assign the most secure policy the lowest priority number so that the most secure policy will find a match before any less-secure policies are configured.

The **crypto isakmp policy** command invokes the ISAKMP policy configuration command mode where you can set ISAKMP parameters. If you do not specify one of these commands for a policy, the default value is used for that parameter. Table 5-4 lists the keywords available to specify the parameters in the policy while you are in the config-isakmp command mode, and displays the default value for the parameters that you do not specifically configure.

Table 5-4 *ISAKMP Parameters*

Parameters	Keyword	Accepted Values	Default Value	Description
encryption	des	56-bit DES-CBC	des	Message-encryption algorithm
	aes	128-bit AES		
	aes 192	192-bit AES		
	aes 256	256-bit AES		
hash	sha	SHA-1 (HMAC variant)	sha	Message-integrity (hash) algorithm
	md5	MD5 (HMAC variant)		
authentication	rsa-sig	RSA signatures	rsa-sig	Peer-authentication method
	rsa-encr	RSA encrypted nonces		
	pre-share	Preshared keys		
group	1	768-bit Diffie-Hellman	1	Key-exchange parameters (DH group identifier)
	2	1024-bit Diffie-Hellman		
	5	1536-bit Diffie-Hellman		
lifetime	*seconds*	Can specify any number of seconds	86400 (second; 1 day)	ISAKMP-established SA lifetime

The current default protection suite offers DES, SHA, DH Group 1, RSA signature, and a lifetime of 86,400 seconds with no volume limit.

Example 5-1 shows an example of configuration of the ISAKMP (IKE) policies that could be negotiated on Figure 5-23. Table 5-4 lists and describes the parameters for the configuration.

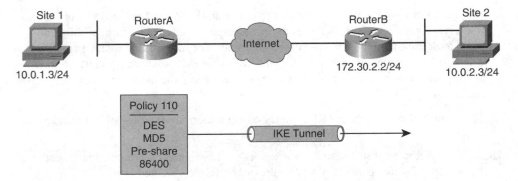

Figure 5-23   *Defining ISAKMP (IKE Phase 1) Policies*

Example 5-1   *Configuring ISAKMP (IKE) Policies*

```
RouterA# configure terminal
RouterA(config)# crypto isakmp policy 110
RouterA(config-isakmp)# authentication pre-share
RouterA(config-isakmp)# encryption des
RouterA(config-isakmp)# group 1
RouterA(config-isakmp)# hash md5
RouterA(config-isakmp)# lifetime 86400
```

IKE Policy Negotiation

ISAKMP peers negotiate the acceptable ISAKMP policies before they agree on the SA to use for IPsec.

When the ISAKMP negotiation begins in IKE Phase 1 main mode, the following occurs:

Step 1.   ISAKMP looks for an ISAKMP policy that is the same on both peers.

Step 2.   The peer that initiates the negotiation sends all of its policies to the remote peer.

Step 3.   The remote peer tries to find a match with its policies. The remote peer looks for a match by comparing its own highest-priority policy against the policies it received from the other peer.

The remote peer checks each of its policies in order of its priority (highest priority first) until a match is found.

A match is made when both policies from the two peers contain the same encryption, hash, authentication, DH parameter values, and when the policy of the remote peer specifies a lifetime less than or equal to the lifetime of the policy that is being compared. If the lifetimes are not identical, the shorter lifetime from the remote peer policy is used. Assign the most secure policy the lowest priority number so that the most secure policy will find a match before any less-secure policies are configured.

Step 4.   If an acceptable match is not found, ISAKMP refuses negotiation, and IPsec is not established. If a match is found, ISAKMP completes the main mode negotiation, and IPsec SAs are created during IKE Phase 2 quick mode.

Figure 5-24 shows the negotiation between Router A and Router B and how the first two policies would be successfully negotiated but the last one could not.

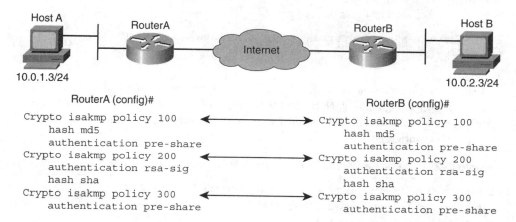

Figure 5-24   *IKE Phase I: Policy Negotiation*

Configuring Pre-Shared Keys

To configure a PSK, use the **crypto isakmp key** global configuration command. You must configure this key whenever you specify PSKs in an ISAKMP policy. Use the **no** form of this command to delete a PSK. The syntax for the command is as follows:

```
crypto isakmp key encryption-type-digit keystring address peer-address
crypto isakmp key encryption-type-digit keystring hostname peer-hostname
```

Table 5-5 lists the command syntax parameter definitions.

Table 5-5   *crypto isakmp Key Command Parameters*

Parameters	Description
encryption-type-digit	Specifies whether the password to be used is encrypted or unencrypted. 0: Specifies that an unencrypted password follows 6: Specifies that an encrypted password follows
keystring	This parameter specifies the PSK. Use any combination of alphanumeric characters up to 128 bytes. This PSK must be identical on both peers.
peer-address	This parameter specifies the IP address of the remote peer.
hostname	This parameter specifies the hostname of the remote peer. This is the peer hostname concatenated with its domain name (for example, myhost.domain.com).

Note: To use the *hostname* parameter, you must configure the ISAKMP identity to use the hostname. Use the **crypto isakmp identity hostname** command in global configuration mode to configure this option. By default, the ISAKMP identity is set to use the IP address.

A given PSK is shared between two peers. At a given peer, you can specify the same key to share with multiple remote peers; however, a more secure approach is to specify different keys to share between different pairs of peers.

Both peers are required to agree on the identity mode, which can be either **address** or **hostname**.

Example 5-2 shows some of ISAKMP and PSK configuration for Router A and Router B in the topology in Figure 5-24. Note that the keystring of *cisco1234* matches. The address identity method is specified. The ISAKMP policies are compatible. Default values do not have to be configured.

Example 5-2   *ISAKMP and PSK Configuration for Router A and Router B*

```
RouterA(config)# crypto isakmp key cisco1234 address 172.30.2.2
RouterA(config)# crypto isakmp policy 110
RouterA(config-isakmp)# hash md5
RouterA(config-isakmp)# authentication pre-share
```

```
RouterB(config)# crypto isakmp key cisco1234 address 172.30.1.2
RouterB(config)# crypto isakmp policy 110
RouterB(config-isakmp)# hash md5
RouterB(config-isakmp)# authentication pre-share
```

Site-to-Site IPsec Configuration: Phase 1

To recapitulate, Example 5-3 shows the comprehensive configuration for Router A and Router B to be successful with the Phase 1 of IPsec.

Example 5-3   *Site-to-Site IPsec Configuration: Phase 1 for Router A and Router B*

```
RouterA(config)# crypto isakmp policy 110
RouterA(config-isakmp)# authentication pre-share
RouterA(config-isakmp)# encryption des
RouterA(config-isakmp)# group 1
RouterA(config-isakmp)# hash md5
RouterA(config-isakmp)# lifetime 86400
RouterA(config-isakmp)# exit
RouterA(config)# crypto isakmp key cisco1234 address 172.30.2.2
```

```
RouterB(config)# crypto isakmp policy 110
RouterB(config-isakmp)# authentication pre-share
RouterB(config-isakmp)# encryption des
RouterB(config-isakmp)# group 1
```

```
RouterB(config-isakmp)# hash md5
RouterB(config-isakmp)# lifetime 86400
RouterB(config-isakmp)# exit
RouterB(config)# crypto isakmp key cisco1234 address 172.30.1.2
```

Note: Policy names and PSK are case sensitive.

Site-to-Site IPsec Configuration: Step 3

A transform set is a combination of individual IPsec transforms that are designed to enact a specific security policy for data traffic. During the ISAKMP IPsec SA negotiation that occurs in IKE Phase 2 quick mode, the peers agree to use a particular transform set for protecting a particular data flow. Transform sets combine the following IPsec factors:

- Mechanism for payload authentication: AH transform

- Mechanism for payload encryption: ESP transform

- IPsec mode (transport mode versus tunnel mode)

Transform sets are limited to one AH transform, one ESP encryption transform, and one ESP authentication transform. To define a transform set, use the **crypto ipsec transform-set** global configuration command. To delete a transform set, use the **no** form of the command. Table 5-6 defines the parameters for the **crypto ipsec transform-set** command, the syntax for which is as follows:

```
crypto ipsec transform-set transform-set-name transform1 [transform2 [transform3]]
```

Table 5-6   crypto ipsec transform-set Parameters

Command	Description
transform-set-name	This parameter specifies the name of the transform set to create (or modify).
transform1, transform2, transform3	This parameter specifies up to three transforms. These transforms define the IPsec security protocols and algorithms.

Example 5-4 shows an example of a transform set configuration on Router A.

Example 5-4   *Transform Set Configuration*

```
RouterA(config)# crypto ipsec transform-set mine esp-des
```

You can configure multiple transform sets and then specify one or more of the transform sets in a crypto map entry. The IPsec SA negotiation uses the transform set that is defined in the crypto map entry to protect the data flows that are specified by the ACL of that crypto map entry. During the negotiation, the peers search for a transform set that has the same criteria at both peers. When such a transform set is found, it is selected and applied to the protected traffic as part of the IPsec SAs of both peers.

When ISAKMP is not used to establish SAs, a single transform set must be used. The transform set is not negotiated.

Transform Set Negotiation

Transform sets are negotiated during quick mode in IKE Phase 2 using the transform sets that you previously configured. You can configure multiple transform sets and then specify one or more of the transform sets in a crypto map entry. Configure the transforms from the most to the least secure, according to your policy. The IPsec SA negotiation uses the transform set defined in the crypto map entry to protect the data flows that are specified by the ACL of that crypto map entry.

During the negotiation, the peers search for a transform set that is the same at both peers, as shown in Figure 5-25. Each of the Router A transform sets are compared against each of the Router B transform sets in succession. Router A transform sets 10, 20, and 30 are compared with Router B transform set 40. The result is no match. All of Router A transform sets are then compared against Router B transform sets. Finally, Router A transform set 30 matches Router B transform set 60. When such a transform set match is found, it is selected and is applied to the protected traffic as part of the IPsec SAs of both peers. IPsec peers agree on one unidirectional transform proposal per SA.

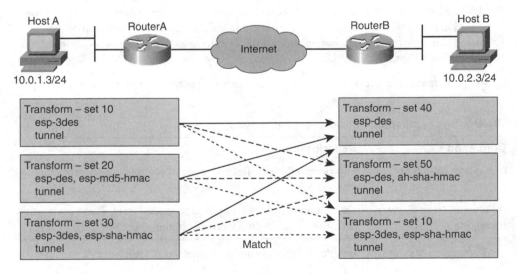

Figure 5-25 *Transform Set Negotiation*

Key Topic

Transform sets are negotiated during IKE Phase 2.

Tunnels by which the encrypted data is transferred are unidirectional, as shown in Figure 5-20, which shows two ESP tunnels (each unidirectional).

Site-to-Site IPsec Configuration: Step 4

Crypto ACLs perform different functions depending on whether the traffic is inbound or outbound to the interface:

- **Outbound:** Selects outbound traffic that IPsec should protect. Traffic that is not selected is sent in plaintext.

- **Inbound:** If desired, you can create inbound ACLs to filter and discard traffic that should have been protected by IPsec.

The crypto ACLs identify the traffic flows that should be protected. Extended IP ACLs select IP traffic to encrypt based on protocol, IP address, network, subnet, and port. Although the ACL syntax is unchanged from extended IP ACLs, the meanings differ slightly for crypto ACLs. That is, **permit** specifies that matching packets must be encrypted, and **deny** specifies that matching packets should not be encrypted. Crypto ACLs behave similarly to an extended IP ACL that is applied to outbound traffic on an interface.

Table 5-7 defines the parameters for the **access-list** command used for extended IP ACLs, the basic syntax for which is as follows:

```
access-list access-list-number { permit ¦ deny } protocol source source-wildcard
destination destination-wildcard
```

Crypto ACL defines which IP traffic the tunnel will protect. The **permit** statement specifies that traffic will be encrypted, and the **deny** statement specifies that the traffic will go out in cleartext.

Key
Topic

Table 5-7   access-list *access-list-number Parameters*

access-list *access-list-number* Command	Description
permit	This option causes all IP traffic that matches the specified conditions to be protected by cryptography, using the policy described by the corresponding crypto map entry.
deny	This option instructs the router to route traffic in plaintext.
protocol	This option specifies which traffic to protect by cryptography based on the protocol, such as TCP, UDP, or ICMP. If the protocol is IP, all traffic IP traffic that matches that permit statement is encrypted.
source and *destination*	If the ACL statement is a **permit** statement, these are the networks, subnets, or hosts between which traffic should be protected. If the ACL statement is a **deny** statement, the traffic between the specified source and destination is sent in plaintext.

Note: Crypto ACLs are the same as normal ACLs, but apply only to the crypto map, and therefore define the interesting traffic to be encrypted. All other traffic passes as plaintext.

Any unprotected inbound traffic that matches a permit entry in the crypto ACL for a crypto map entry that is flagged as IPsec is dropped. This drop occurs because this traffic was expected to be protected by IPsec.

If you want certain traffic to receive one combination of IPsec protection (authentication only) and other traffic to receive a different combination (both authentication and encryption), create two different crypto ACLs to define the two different types of traffic. Different crypto map entries then use these different ACLs to specify different IPsec policies.

Caution: Per recommended practice, you should avoid using the **any** keyword to specify source or destination addresses. The **permit any any** statement is strongly discouraged because this causes all outbound traffic to be protected and all protected traffic to be sent to the peer that is specified in the corresponding crypto map entry. Then, all inbound packets that lack IPsec protection are silently dropped, including packets for routing protocols, NTP, echo, echo response, and so on.

Try to be as restrictive as possible when defining which packets to protect in a crypto ACL. If you must use the **any** keyword in a **permit** statement, you must preface that statement with a series of **deny** statements to filter out any traffic (that would otherwise fall within that **permit** statement) that you do not want to be protected.

Configuring Symmetric Peer Crypto ACLS

You must configure symmetric crypto ACLs for use by IPsec. Both inbound and outbound traffic are evaluated against the same outbound IPsec ACL. The ACL criteria are applied in the forward direction to traffic exiting your router, and the reverse direction to traffic entering your router. When a router receives encrypted packets back from an IPsec peer, it uses the same ACL to determine which inbound packets to decrypt by viewing the source and destination addresses in the ACL in reverse order.

The example shown in Figure 5-26 illustrates why symmetric ACLs are recommended.

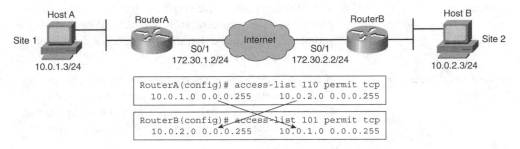

Figure 5-26 *Symmetric Peer Crypto Access Lists*

For site 1, IPsec protection is applied to traffic between hosts on the 10.0.1.0 network as the data exits the Router A S0/1 interface in route to site 2 hosts on the 10.0.2.0 network. For traffic from site 1 hosts on the 10.0.1.0 network to site 2 hosts on the 10.0.2.0 network, the ACL entry on Router A is evaluated as follows:

- Source = Hosts on 10.0.1.0 network

- Destination = Hosts on 10.0.2.0 network

For incoming traffic from site 2 hosts on the 10.0.2.0 network to site 1 hosts on the 10.0.1.0 network, that same ACL entry on Router A is evaluated as follows:

- Source = Hosts on 10.0.2.0 network

- Destination = Hosts on 10.0.1.0 network

The crypto ACLs used by IPsec must mirror-image ACLs because both inbound and outbound traffic is evaluated against the same outbound IPsec ACL.

Key Topic

Site-to-Site IPsec Configuration: Step 5

Crypto map entries that you create for IPsec combine the needed configuration parameters of IPsec SAs, including the following parameters:

- What traffic should be protected by IPsec, using a crypto ACL

- The granularity of the flow to be protected by a set of SAs

- Who the remote IPsec peer is, which determines where the IPsec-protected traffic is sent

- The local address that is to be used for the IPsec traffic (optional)

- What IPsec security should be applied to this traffic, choosing from a list of one or more transform sets

Crypto map entries with the same crypto map name, but different map sequence numbers, are grouped into a crypto map set.

You can apply only one crypto map set to a single interface. Multiple interfaces can share the same crypto map set if you want to apply the same policy to multiple interfaces. If you create more than one crypto map entry for a given interface, use the sequence number (*seq-num*) of each map entry to rank the map entries. The lower the *seq-num*, the higher the priority. At the interface that has the crypto map set, traffic is evaluated against higher-priority map entries first.

You must create multiple crypto map entries for a given interface if any of these conditions exist:

- Different data flows are to be handled by separate IPsec peers.

- You want to apply different IPsec security to different types of traffic (to the same or separate IPsec peers); for example, if you want traffic between one set of subnets to be authenticated, and traffic between another set of subnets to be both authenticated and encrypted. In this case, the different types of traffic should be defined in two separate ACLs, and you must create a separate crypto map entry for each crypto ACL.

■ You are not using IKE to establish a particular set of SAs, and you want to specify multiple ACL entries, you must create separate ACLs (one per permit entry) and specify a separate crypto map entry for each ACL. Although it is possible to establish SAs manually, it is not recommended because the keys never expire. The longer a key is in production, the more vulnerable it becomes.

Use the **crypto map** global configuration command, explained in Table 5-8, to create or modify a crypto map entry and enter the crypto map configuration mode. Set the crypto map entries that reference dynamic maps to the lowest priority in a crypto map set (that is, they should have the highest sequence numbers). Use the **no** form of this command to delete a crypto map entry or set. The command syntax and parameter definitions are as follows:

```
crypto map map-name seq-num cisco

crypto map map-name seq-num ipsec-manual

crypto map map-name seq-num ipsec-isakmp [dynamic dynamic-
map-name]

no crypto map map-name [seq-num]
```

Table 5-8 *crypto map Command Parameters*

Command	Description
cisco	(Default value) This option indicates that Cisco Encryption Technology (CET) will be used rather than IPsec for protecting the traffic specified by this newly specified crypto map entry. Note that CET is end-of-life.
map-name	This parameter defines the name you assign to the crypto map set, or indicates the name of the crypto map you want to edit.
seq-num	This parameter is the number you assign to the crypto map entry.
ipsec-manual	This option indicates that ISAKMP will not be used to establish the IPsec SAs for protecting the traffic specified by this crypto map entry.
ipsec-isakmp	This option indicates that ISAKMP will be used to establish the IPsec SAs for protecting the traffic specified by this crypto map entry.
dynamic	(Optional) This option specifies that this crypto map entry references a pre-existing static crypto map. If you use this keyword, none of the crypto map configuration commands are available.
dynamic-map-name	(Optional) This parameter specifies the name of the dynamic crypto map set that should be used as the policy template.

Table 5-9 *crypto map Configuration Mode Commands*

Command	Description
set	Used with the **peer**, **pfs**, **transform-set**, and **security-association** commands.
peer [*hostname* | *ip-address*]	Specifies the allowed IPsec peer by IP address or hostname.
pfs [group1 | group2]	Specifies DH Group 1 or Group 2.
transform-set [*set_name(s)*]	Specify list of transform sets in priority order. For an **ipsec-manual** crypto map, you can specify only one transform set. For an **ipsec-isakmp** or **dynamic** crypto map entry, you can specify up to six transform sets.
security-association lifetime	Sets SA lifetime parameters in seconds or kilobytes.
match address [access-list-id | name]	Identifies the extended ACL by its name or number. The value should match the *access-list-number* or *name* argument of a previously defined IP-extended ACL being matched.
no	Used to delete commands entered with the **set** command.
exit	Exits crypto map configuration mode.

Use the **crypto map** command in crypto map configuration mode, to define the crypto map entries, with the commands shown in the Table 5-9.

After you define the crypto map entries, you can assign the crypto map set to interfaces using the **crypto map** (interface configuration) command.

Note: ACLs for crypto map entries that are tagged as **ipsec-manual** are restricted to a single permit entry, and subsequent entries are ignored. The SAs that are established by that particular crypto map entry are for a single data flow only. To be able to support multiple manually established SAs for different kinds of traffic, you must define multiple crypto ACLs and then apply each one to a separate **ipsec-manual** crypto map entry. Each ACL should include one **permit** statement that defines the traffic that it must protect.

Figure 5-27 illustrates a topology in which two peers are specified for redundancy, as configured by the crypto map in Example 5-5. If the first peer cannot be contacted, the second peer is used. There is no limit to the number of redundant peers you can configure.

Example 5-5 *crypto map Command Example*

```
RouterA(config)# crypto map mymap 10 ipsec-isakmp
RouterA(config-crypto-map)# match address 110
RouterA(config-crypto-map)# set peer 172.30.2.2
RouterA(config-crypto-map)# set peer 172.30.3.2
RouterA(config-crypto-map)# set pfs group1
```

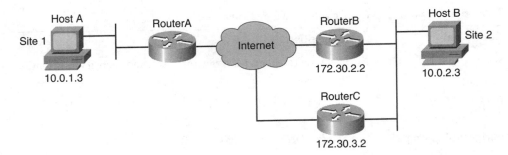

Figure 5-27 *Network Topology for Crypto Map Example*

```
RouterA(config-crypto-map)# set tranform-set mine
RouterA(config-crypto-map)# set security-association lifetime seconds 86400
```

Applying Crypto Maps to Interfaces

In this step, you apply the crypto map to the outgoing interface of the VPN tunnel using the **crypto map** command in interface configuration mode. Use the **no** form of the command to remove the crypto map set from the interface. The command syntax is **crypto map** *map-name*, where *map-name* is the name of the crypto map set to apply to the interface.

Also, make sure that you configure the routing information that is needed to send packets into the tunnel.

All IP traffic passing through the interface where the crypto map is applied is evaluated against the applied crypto map set. If a crypto map entry sees outbound IP traffic that should be protected and the crypto map specifies the use of IKE, an SA is negotiated with the remote peer according to the parameters that are included in the crypto map entry.

Example 5-6 demonstrates how to apply a crypto map.

Example 5-6 *Applying a Crypto Map*

```
RouterA (config)# interface serial0/1
RouterA (config -if)#crypto map mymap
```

Verifying the IPsec Configuration

You can use the Cisco IOS commands explained in Table 5-10 to verify the VPN configuration.

Table 5-10 *IPsec Verification Commands*

Command	Description
show crypto isakmp policy	Displays configured IKE policies
show crypto isakmp sa	Displays current IKE SAs

Table 5-10   *IPsec Verification Commands*

Command	Description
show crypto ipsec transform-set	Displays configured IPsec transform sets
show crypto map	Displays configured crypto maps
show crypto ipsec sa	Displays established IPsec tunnels
debug crypto isakmp	Debugs IKE events
debug crypto ipsec	Debugs IPsec events

show crypto isakmp policy Command

Use the **show crypto isakmp policy** command to display configured IKE policies and the default IKE policy settings. This command, shown in Example 5-7, is useful because it reveals your ISAKMP (IKE) configuration all with one command.

Example 5-7   *show crypto isakmp policy Command Output*

```
RouterA# show crypto isakmp policy
Protection suite of priority 110
        encryption algorithm:   3DES - Data Encryption Standard (168 bit keys).
        hash algorithm:         Secure Hash Standard
        authentication method:  preshared
        Diffie-Hellman group:   #2 (1024 bit)
        lifetime:               86400 seconds, no volume limit
Default protection suite
        encryption algorithm:   DES - Data Encryption Standard (56 bit keys).
        hash algorithm:         Secure Hash Standard
        authentication method:  Rivest-Shamir-Adleman Signature
        Diffie-Hellman group:   #1 (768 bit)
        lifetime:               86400 seconds, no volume limit
```

show crypto ipsec transform-set Command

You can use the **show crypto ipsec transform-set** command, shown in Example 5-8, to show all the configured transform sets. Because transform sets determine the level of protection that your data will have as it is tunneled, it is important to verify the strength of your IPsec protection policy.

Example 5-8   *show crypto ipsec transform-set Example*

```
RouterA# show crypto ipsec transform-set
Transform set AES_SHA: { esp-128-aes esp-sha-hmac }
    will negotiate = { Tunnel, },
```

show crypto map Command

To see all the configured crypto maps, use the **show crypto map** command, shown in Example 5-9. This command verifies configurations and shows the SA lifetime. The **show running-config** command reveals many of these same settings.

Example 5-9   *show crypto map Example*

```
RouterA# show crypto map
Crypto Map "mymap" 10 ipsec-isakmp
        Peer = 172.30.2.2
        Extended IP access list 102
               access-list 110 permit ip host 10.0.1.3 host 10.0.2.3
        Current peer: 172.30.2.2
        Security association lifetime: 4608000 kilobytes/3600 seconds
        PFS (Y/N): N
        Transform sets={ mine, }
```

show crypto ipsec sa Command

One of the more useful commands is **show crypto ipsec sa**, shown in Example 5-10. The output of Example 5-10 relates to the topology of Figure 5-28.

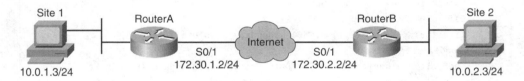

Figure 5-28   *Topology Used for Example 5-10*

When you see that an SA has been established, it indicates that the rest of the configuration is working. Make special note of the *pkts encrypt* and *pkts decrypt* values because they indicate that traffic is flowing through the tunnel.

Example 5-10   *show crypto ipsec sa Command Output*

```
RouterA# show crypto ipsec sa
Interface: Serial0/1
        Crypto map tag: mymap, local addr. 172.30.1.2
        local ident (addr/mask/prot/port): (172.30.1.2/255.255.255.255/0/0)
      remote ident (addr/mask/prot/port): (172.30.2.2/255.255.255.255/0/0)
      current_peer: 172.30.2.2
       PERMIT, flacs={origin_is_acl,}
      #pkts encaps: 21, #pkts encrypt: 21, #pkts digest 0
      #pkts decaps: 21, #pkts decrypt: 21, #pkts verify 0
```

```
    #send errors 0, #recv errors 0
 local crypto endpt.: 172.30.1.2, remote crypto endpt.: 172.30.2.2
 path mtu 1500, media mtu 1500
 current outbound spi: 8AE1C9C
```

The **debug crypto isakmp** and **debug crypto sa** commands are discussed later in the section "Troubleshooting."

Configuring IPsec on a Site-to-Site VPN Using Cisco SDM

The steps to implement an IPsec site-to-site VPN using the Cisco router, as described in the preceding portions of the chapter, can be also performed using the Security Device Manager (SDM), as described in the sections that follow.

Introducing the Cisco SDM VPN Wizard Interface

To select and start a VPN wizard, follow these steps, as illustrated Figure 5-29:

Step 1.   Choose **Configure**.

Step 2.   Choose **VPN** to open the VPN Page.

Step 3.   Choose a wizard from the VPN window. In Figure 5-29, the Site-to-Site VPN Wizard is chosen.

Step 4.   Click the VPN implementation subtype. In Figure 5-29, the Create a Site to Site VPN option is chosen.

Step 5.   Click the **Launch the Selected Task** button to start the wizard.

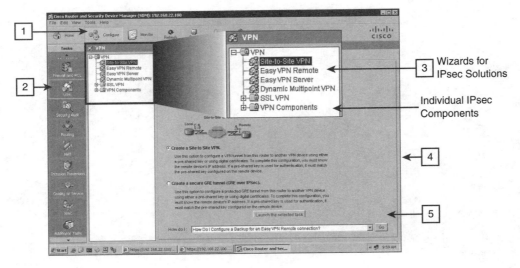

Figure 5-29   *Cisco SDM VPN Wizard Interface*

Site-to-Site VPN Components

The Cisco SDM VPN wizards use two sources to create a VPN connection:

■   User input during a step-by-step wizard process

■   Preconfigured VPN components

The Cisco SDM provides some default VPN components:

- Two IKE policies

- An IPsec transform set for the quick setup wizard

The VPN wizards create other components during the step-by-step configuration process. You must configure some components before you can use the wizards (for example, PKI).

Figure 5-30 illustrates the VPN navigation bar, which contains three major sections:

- VPN wizards
  - Site-to-site VPN
  - Easy VPN Remote
  - Easy VPN Server
  - Dynamic Multipoint VPN

- SSL VPN

- VPN components:
  - IPsec (main component)
  - IKE (main component)
  - Easy VPN Server (optional component): Group Policies and Browser Proxy Settings
  - Public Key Infrastructure (optional component): For IKE authentication using digital certificates

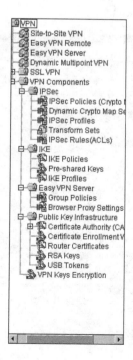

Figure 5-30 *Cisco SDM VPN Navigation Bar*

■   VPN Keys Encryption

This option appears if the Cisco IOS Software image on your router supports type 6 encryption, also referred to as VPN key encryption. You can use this window to specify a master key to use when encrypting VPN keys, such as PSKs, Cisco Easy VPN keys, and Extended Authentication (XAUTH) keys. When the keys are encrypted, they are not readable by someone viewing the router configuration file.

The VPN wizards simplify the configuration of individual VPN components. On the other hand, you can use the individual IPsec components section to modify parameters that may have been misconfigured during the VPN wizard step-by-step configuration.

Using the Cisco SDM Wizards to Configure Site-to-Site VPNs

Use a web browser to start the Cisco SDM on a router. Select the VPN wizard by choosing **Configure > VPN > Site-to-Site VPN**, as shown in Figure 5-31. Follow these steps to create and configure a classic site-to-site VPN:

Step 1.   Click the **Create a Site to Site VPN** radio button on the Create Site to Site VPN tab and click the **Launch the Selected Task** button.

Step 2.   A window displays, which allows you to select the wizard mode, as shown in Figure 5-32:

■   The Quick Setup option uses the Cisco SDM default IKE policies and IPsec transform sets.

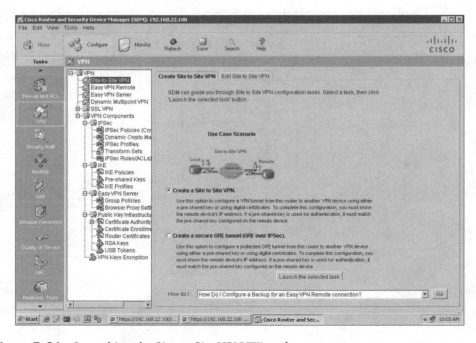

Figure 5-31   *Launching the Site-to-Site VPN Wizard*

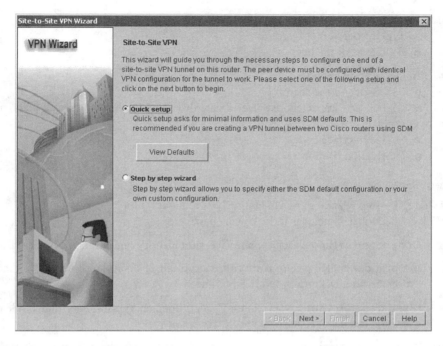

Figure 5-32   *Starting the Site-to-Site VPN Wizard*

- The Step by Step Wizard option allows the administrator to specify all the details.

Step 3.   Click the **Next** button to configure the parameters of the VPN connection.

Quick Setup

The quick setup uses a single window to configure the VPN connection, as shown in Figure 5-33, and includes the following parameters:

- Interface to use for the VPN connection (usually the outside interface)

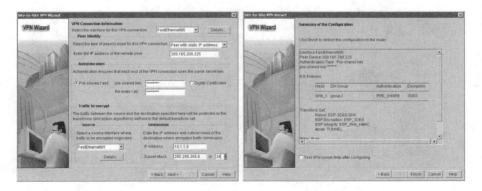

Figure 5-33   *Quick VPN Setup*

- Peer identity information
  - Type of peer
  - IP address of the peer

- Authentication method:
  - PSKs (specify the secret)
  - Digital certificates (choose a certificate that should have been created beforehand)

Traffic to encrypt:
  - Source interface
  - Destination IP subnet

Step-by-Step Setup

The step-by-step wizard, shown in Figure 5-34, requires multiple steps to configure the VPN connection and includes the following parameters:

- **Connection settings:** Outside interface, peer identity, and authentication credentials

- **IKE proposals:** IKE proposal priority, encryption, hashing algorithm, IKE authentication method, DH group, and IKE lifetime

- **IPsec transform sets:** Name, integrity algorithm, encryption algorithm, mode of operation (tunnel or transport), and compression

- **Traffic to protect:** Define single source and destination subnets or define an ACL to use for more complex VPNs

The last task of the step-by-step wizard is to review and complete the configuration.

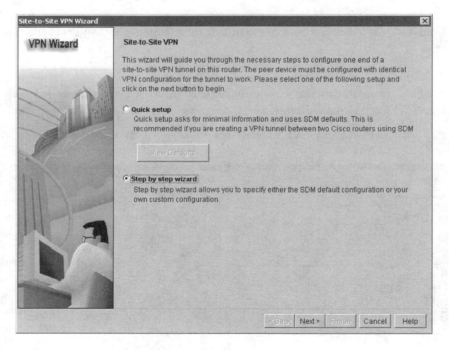

Figure 5-34   *Summary of Quick Setup Configuration*

Connection Settings

The first task in the step-by-step wizard is to configure the connection settings. Follow these steps, shown in Figure 5-35, to configure the connection settings:

Step 1.   Choose the outside interface that is used to connect to the IPsec peer over the untrusted network.

Step 2.   Specify the IP address of the peer.

Step 3.   Choose the authentication method and specify the credentials. Use long and random PSKs to prevent brute-force and dictionary attacks against IKE.

Step 4.   Click the **Next** button to proceed to the next task.

IKE Proposals

The second task in the step-by-step wizard is to configure IKE proposals, as shown in Figure 5-36. Follow these steps to configure the IKE proposals:

Step 1.   To use the IKE proposal that is predefined by Cisco SDM, click the **Next** button (the predefined IKE proposal is chosen by default).

Step 2.   If you want to use a custom IKE proposal, click the **Add** button to define a proposal and specify the following required parameters:

- IKE proposal priority

- Encryption algorithm

- Hashing algorithm

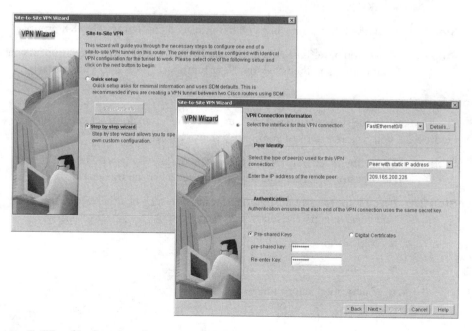

Figure 5-35   *Configuring the Connection Settings*

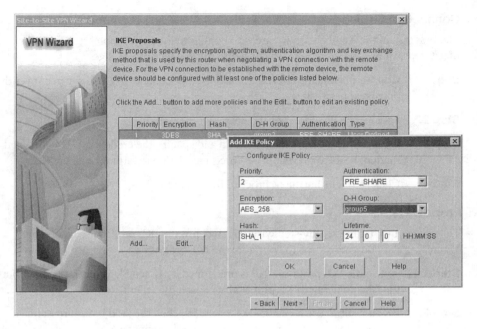

Figure 5-36   *IKE Proposals*

- IKE authentication method

- DH group

- IKE lifetime

Step 3.   Click the **OK** button when you have finished configuring the IKE proposal.

Step 4.   When you have finished with adding IKE policies, choose the proposal you want to use, and then click the **Next** button to proceed to the next task.

Transform Sets

The third task in the step-by-step wizard is to configure a transform set, as shown in Figure 5-37. Follow these steps to configure a transform set:

Step 1.   To use the IPsec transform set that is predefined by Cisco SDM, click the **Next** button (the predefined transform set is chosen by default).

Step 2.   If you want to use a custom IPsec transform set, click the **Add** button to define it and specify the following parameters:

- Transform set name

- Integrity algorithm

- Encryption algorithm

- Mode of operation

- Optional compression

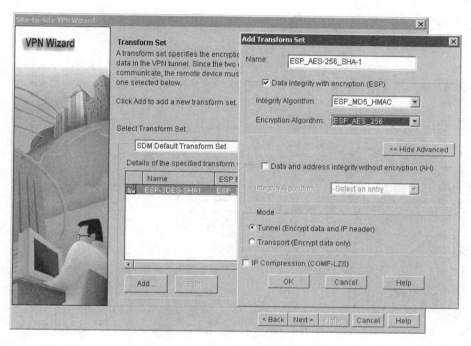

Figure 5-37 *IPsec Transform Sets*

Step 3. Click the **OK** button when you have finished configuring the transform set.

Step 4. When you have finished adding transform sets, choose the transform set you want to use, and then click the **Next** button to precede to the next task.

Defining What Traffic to Protect

The next steps involve using the Cisco SDM to define what traffic the VPN should protect.

Option 1: Single Source and Destination Subnet

To define what traffic needs protection, you can use the simple mode, which allows the protection of traffic between one pair of IP subnets.

To protect the traffic between a particular pair of IP subnets, as shown in Figure 5-38, follow these steps:

Step 1. From the Traffic to Protect window, click the **Protect All Traffic Between the Following Subnets** radio button.

Step 2. Define the IP address and subnet mask of the local network where IPsec traffic originates.

Step 3. Define the IP address and subnet mask of the remote network where IPsec traffic is sent.

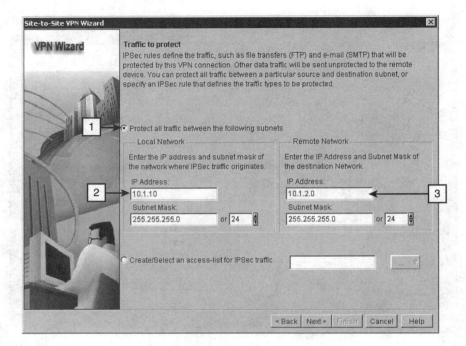

Figure 5-38 *Source and Destination Subnets*

Option 2: Using an ACL

To specify an IPsec rule that defines the traffic types to be protected, as shown in Figure 5-39, follow these steps:

Step 1. From the Traffic to Protect window, click the **Create/Select an Access-List for IPsec Traffic** radio button.

Step 2. Click the ellipsis (**...**) button to choose an existing ACL or to create a new one.

Step 3. If you want to use an existing ACL, choose the **Select an Existing Rule (ACL)** option. If you would like to create a new ACL, choose the **Create a New Rule (ACL) and Select** option.

When you create a new ACL to define traffic that needs protection, you are presented with a window that lists the created access rule entries if any already exist. If none exist, you will be required to create a new rule, as shown in Figure 5-40. To create a new rule, follow these steps:

Step 1. Give the access rule a name and description.

Step 2. Click the **Add** button to start adding rule entries.

Follow these steps to configure a new rule entry, as shown in Figure 5-41:

Step 1. Choose an action from the **Select an Action** list box and enter a description of the rule entry in the Description text box.

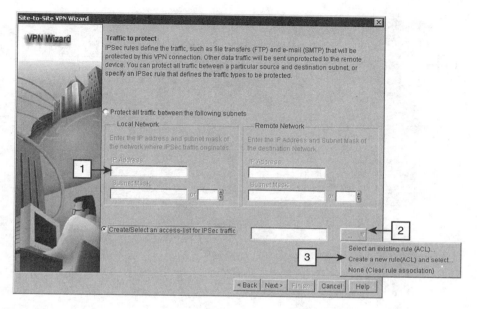

Figure 5-39   *Using an ACL*

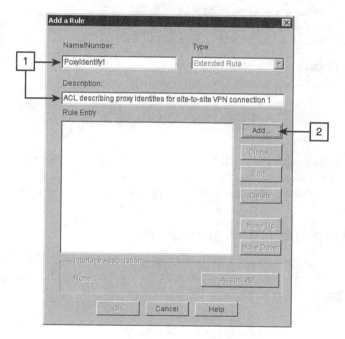

Figure 5-40   *Using an ACL (continued)*

Step 2.   Define the source hosts or networks in the Source Host/Network pane, and the destination hosts or networks in the Destination Host/Network pane. Each rule entry defines one pair of source and destination addresses or networks.

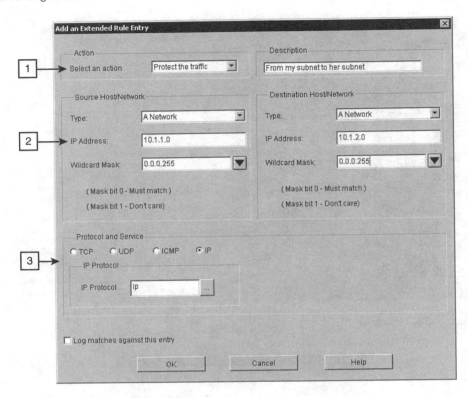

Figure 5-41 *Creating a New Rule*

Note: You must use wildcard bits rather than subnet masks in the Wildcard Mask field.

Step 3. Optionally, you can provide protection for specific OSI protocols by choosing the specific protocol radio box (TCP, UDP, or ICMP) and the desired port numbers. If IP is chosen as the protocol, the rule applies to all IP traffic.

Completing the Configuration

At the end of the configuration, the wizard presents a summary of all the configured parameters, as shown in Figure 5-42. To modify the configuration, click the **Back** button. Click the **Finish** button to complete the configuration.

Testing the Tunnel Configuration and Operation

To run a test to determine the configuration of the tunnel, choose **Configure > VPN > Site-to-Site VPN > Edit Site to Site VPN** and click the **Test Tunnel** button, as shown in Figure 5-43. You can also click the **Generate Mirror** button to generate a mirroring configuration that is required on the other end of the tunnel. This is useful if the other router does not have Cisco SDM and if you have to use the CLI to configure the tunnel.

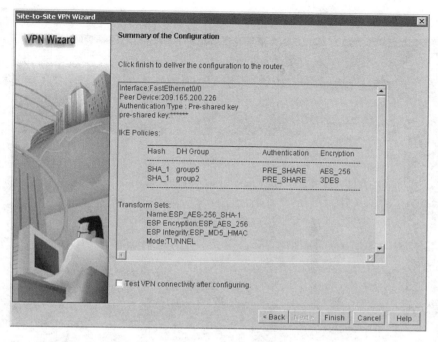

Figure 5-42 *Summary of Step-by-Step Setup Configuration*

Monitoring Tunnel Operation

To see all the IPsec tunnels, their parameters, and status, follow these steps, as shown in Figure 5-44:

Step 1.   Choose **Monitor**.

Step 2.   Choose **VPN Status**.

Step 3.   Choose **IPN Status**.

Advanced Monitoring

The basic Cisco IOS web interface also allows administrators to use the web interface to enter Cisco IOS CLI commands to monitor and troubleshoot the router, as shown in Figure 5-45.

Two of the most useful **show** commands to determine the status of the IPsec VPN connections are as follows:

- **show crypto isakmp sa:** This command displays all the current IKE SAs. QM_IDLE status indicates an active IKE SA.

- **show crypto ipsec sa:** This command displays the settings used by the current SAs. Nonzero encryption and decryption statistics can indicate a working set of IPsec SAs.

Example 5-11 shows some sample output from the **show crypto ipsec sa** command. If this command shows that an SA has been established, it indicates that the rest of the con-

Check VPN status.

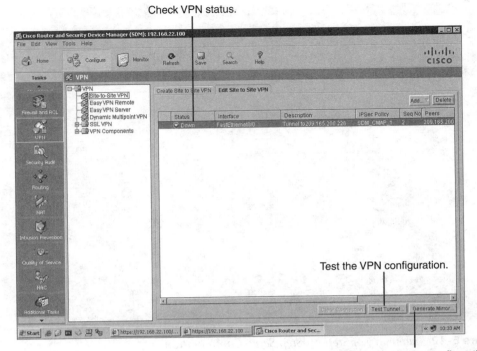

Test the VPN configuration.

Create a mirroring configuration
if no Cisco SDM is available
on the peer.

Figure 5-43　*Testing the Configuration*

figuration is working. Take special note of the *pkts encrypt* and *pkts decrypt* values because these indicate that traffic is flowing through the tunnel.

Example 5-11　*show crypto ipsec sa Output*

```
RouterA# show crypto ipsec sa
interface: Ethernet0/1
    Crypto map tag: mymap, local addr. 172.16.100.100
    local ident (addr/mask/prot/port): (172.16.100.100/255.255.255.255/0/0)
    remote ident (addr/mask/prot/port): (172.16.200.200/255.255.255.255/0/0)
    current_peer: 172.16.200.200
      PERMIT, flags={origin_is_acl,}
    #pkts encaps: 21, #pkts encrypt: 21, #pkts digest 0
    #pkts decaps: 21, #pkts decrypt: 21, #pkts verify 0
    #send errors 0, #recv errors 0
      local crypto endpt.: 172.16.100.100, remote crypto endpt.: 172.16.200.200
      path mtu 1500, media mtu 1500
    current outbound spi: 8AE1C9C
```

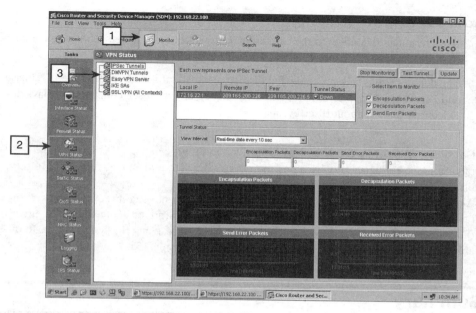

Figure 5-44   *Monitor Tunnel Operation*

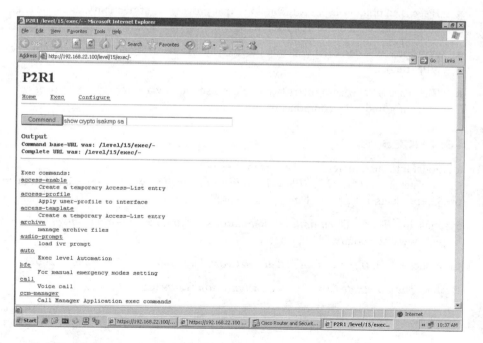

Figure 5-45   *Monitoring Using the Web Interface*

Troubleshooting

Use a terminal to connect to the Cisco IOS router if you want to use debugging commands to troubleshoot VPN connectivity.

The **debug crypto isakmp** command displays detailed information about the IKE Phase 1 and IKE Phase 2 negotiation processes. The **debug crypto ipsec** command displays detailed information about IPsec events.

Caution: Use **debug** commands with caution because the debug processes run the risk of causing performance problems on your devices. Use the **undebug all** command to turn off the debug as soon as possible.

Also to improve throughput, it is recommended that you send loggings to a syslog server rather than the console port. The console port has a bandwidth of 9600 bauds compared to the minimum 10 Mb/s for the Ethernet interface used for reaching the syslog server. To disable logging on the console, use the **no logging console** command.

Summary

The key points covered in this chapters are as follows:

■   IPsec is an ubiquitous VPN technology that provides confidentiality, data-integrity, authentication, and antireplay services.

■   A crypto ACL defines interesting traffic, which is the traffic to be protected by the VPN tunnel.

■   The IPsec VPN wizard offers two choices: user input via a step-by-step process or preconfigured VPN components.

References

For additional information, refer to these resources:

Cisco Systems, Inc. *Cisco IOS IPSEC Introduction*, http://www.cisco.com/en/US/products/ps6635/products_ios_protocol_group_home.html

Systems, Inc. *Export Compliance & Regulatory Affairs: Encryption Control Guidance*, http://www.cisco.com/wwl/export/crypto

Carmouche, J. H. *IPsec Virtual Private Network Fundamentals* (Cisco Press, 2007)

Deal, R. *The Complete Cisco VPN Configuration Guide* (Cisco Press, 2005)

Review Questions

Use the questions here to review what you learned in this chapter. The correct answers are found in the Appendix, "Answers to Chapter Review Questions."

1. Which two modes of SSL VPN are currently available with Cisco IOS?

    a. IPS

    b. Citrix

    c. Clientless

    d. Thin client

2. Which of the following is not a security function provided by IPsec?

    a. Confidentiality

    b. Key management

    c. Antireplay

    d. Authentication

    e. Integrity

3. Which of the following are peer-authentication methods with IPsec?

    a. PSK

    b. RSA signatures

    c. RSA encrypted nonces

    d. HMAC-SHA1

    e. HMAC-MD5

4. Which three modes are used by IKE to secure communications?

    a. Simple mode

    b. Basic mode

    c. Advanced mode

    d. Quick mode

    e. Aggressive mode

    f. Main mode

5. Which command is better suited to show that traffic is flowing through the VPN tunnel?

    a. show crypto map

    b. show crypto ipsec transform-set

    c. show crypto isakmp policy

    d. show crypto ipsec sa

6. Which command would help troubleshoot a Phase I issue?

    a. debug crypto sa

    b. debug crypto phase 1

    c. debug crypto isakmp

    d. show crypto sa

7. Which command would be the most helpful to compare the configuration of peer, ACL, SA lifetime and transform sets?

    a. debug crypto sa

    b. show crypto isakmp sa

    c. show crypto map sa

    d. show crypto map

8. Which of the following is not part of a cryto map configuration?

    a. Peer

    b. Diffie-Hellman group

    c. Transform set

    d. Lifetime

9. Match the Diffie-Hellman group with the size of its prime number.

Groups		Bits	
a.	Group 5	**e.**	768
b.	Group 2	**f.**	163
c.	Group 7	**g.**	1024
d.	Group 1	**h.**	1536

10. Which statement is true regarding how ESP and AH segments are encapsulated in IP packets?

    a. In transport mode, security is provided only for the transport layer and below.

    b. In tunnel mode, security is provided for the complete original IP packet.

    c. In tunnel mode, security is provided only for the transport layer and above.

    d. In transport mode, security is provided for the entire IP packet.

This chapter describes the functions and operations of IDS and IPS systems. This chapter will introduce you to:

■ The underlying IDS and IPS technology that is embedded in the Cisco host- and network-based IDS and IPS solutions

■ Cisco IOS IPS using Cisco SDM

CHAPTER 6

Network Security Using Cisco IOS IPS

Intrusion detection system (IDS) and intrusion prevention system (IPS) solutions form an integral part of a robust network defense solution. Maintaining secure network services is a key requirement of a profitable IP-based business. Using Cisco products and technologies as examples, this chapter defines IDS and IPS and how these systems work.

Introducing IDS and IPS

IDS and IPS work together to provide a network security solution. An IDS captures packets in real time, processes them, and can respond to threats, but works on copies of data traffic to detect suspicious activity by using signatures. This is called *promiscuous mode*. In the process of detecting malicious traffic, an IDS allows some malicious traffic to pass before the IDS can respond to protect the network. An IDS analyzes a copy of the monitored traffic rather than the actual forwarded packet. The advantage of operating on a copy of the traffic is that the IDS does not affect the packet flow of the forwarded traffic. The disadvantage of operating on a copy of the traffic is that the IDS cannot stop malicious traffic from single-packet attacks from reaching the target system before the IDS can apply a response to stop the attack. An IDS often requires assistance from other networking devices, such as routers and firewalls, to respond to an attack.

An IPS works inline in the data stream to provide protection from malicious attacks in real time. This is called *inline mode*. Unlike an IDS, an IPS does not allow packets to enter the trusted side of the network. An IPS monitors traffic at Layer 3 and Layer 4 to ensure that their headers, states, and so on are those specified in the protocol suite. However, the IPS sensor analyzes at Layer 2 to Layer 7 the payload of the packets for more sophisticated embedded attacks that might include malicious data. This deeper analysis lets the IPS identify, stop, and block attacks that would normally pass through a traditional firewall device. When a packet comes in through an interface on an IPS, that packet is not sent to the outbound or trusted interface until the packet has been determined to be clean. An IPS builds upon previous IDS technology; Cisco IPS platforms use a blend of detection technologies, including profile-based intrusion detection, signature-based intrusion detection, and protocol analysis intrusion detection.

The key to differentiating an IDS from an IPS is that an IPS responds immediately and does not allow any malicious traffic to pass, whereas an IDS allows malicious traffic to pass before it can respond.

IDS:

■ Analyzes copies of the traffic stream
■ Does not slow network traffic
■ Allows some malicious traffic into the network

IPS:

■ Works inline in real time to monitor Layer 2 through Layer 7 traffic and content
■ Needs to be able to handle network traffic
■ Prevents malicious traffic from entering the network

IDS and IPS technologies share several characteristics:

■ IDS and IPS technologies are deployed as sensors. An IDS or an IPS sensor can be any of the following devices:
  ■ A router configured with Cisco IOS IPS Software
  ■ An appliance specifically designed to provide dedicated IDS or IPS services
  ■ A network module installed in an adaptive security appliance, switch, or router

■ IDS and IPS technologies typically monitor for malicious activities in two spots:
  ■ Malicious activity is monitored at the network to detect attacks against a network, including attacks against hosts and devices, using network IDS and network IPS.
  ■ Malicious activity is monitored on a host to detect attacks that are launched from or on target machines, using host intrusion prevention system (HIPS). Host-based attacks are detected by reading security event logs, checking for changes to critical system files, and checking system registries for malicious entries.

■ IDS and IPS technologies generally use yes, signatures to detect patterns of misuse in network traffic, although other technologies will be introduced later in this chapter A signature is a set of rules that an IDS or IPS uses to detect typical intrusive activity. Signatures are usually chosen from a broad cross section of intrusion detection signatures, and can detect severe breaches of security, common network attacks, and information gathering.

■ IDS and IPS technologies look for the following general patterns of misuse:
  ■ **Atomic pattern:** In an atomic pattern, an attempt is made to access a specific port on a specific host, and malicious content is contained in a single packet. An IDS is particularly vulnerable to an atomic attack because until it finds the attack, malicious single packets are being allowed into the network. An IPS prevents these packets from entering at all.
  ■ **Composite pattern:** A composite pattern is a sequence of operations distributed across multiple hosts over an arbitrary period of time.

Note: Note that sensors, even inline, might not be completely successful at drop packets of an attack. It is possible that an attack be on its way, if only partially, before even an inline sensor starts dropping packets matching a composite pattern signature. The drop action is much more effective for atomic signatures because the sensor makes a single packet match.

Figure 6-1 shows a sensor deployed in IDS mode and a sensor deployed in IPS mode.

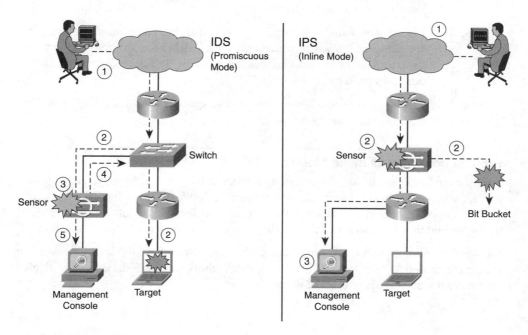

Figure 6-1 *IDS and IPS Operational Differences*

The following are the steps that occur when an attack is launched in an environment monitored by an IDS:

Step 1. An attack is launched on a network that has a sensor deployed in IDS mode.

Step 2. The switch sends copies of all packets to the IDS sensor (configured in promiscuous mode, which is explained later in this section) to analyze the packets. At the same time, the target machine experiences the malicious attack.

Step 3. The IDS sensor, using a signature, matches the malicious traffic to the signature.

Step 4. The IDS sensor sends the switch a command to deny access to the malicious traffic.

Step 5. The IDS sends an alarm to a management console for logging and other management purposes.

The following are the steps that occur when an attack is launched in an environment monitored by an IPS:

Step 1. An attack is launched on a network that has a sensor deployed in IPS mode (configured in inline mode, which is explained later in this section).

Step 2. The IPS sensor analyzes the packets as soon as they come into the IPS sensor interface. The IPS sensor, using signatures, matches the malicious traffic to the signature and the attack is stopped immediately. Traffic in violation of policy can be dropped by an IPS sensor.

Step 3. The IPS sensor can send an alarm to a management console for logging and other management purposes.

Promiscuous Versus Inline Mode

A sensor can be deployed either in promiscuous mode or inline mode. In promiscuous mode, the sensor receives a copy of the data for analysis, while the original traffic still makes its way to its ultimate destination. By contrast, a sensor working inline analyzes the traffic live and therefore can actively block the packets before they reach their destination.

It is worth mentioning that Cisco appliances, such as the Cisco ASA AIP SSM (discussed later in the section, "Cisco ASA AIP SSM"), although advertised as IPS device, can work either in promiscuous mode or in inline mode.

Management Console

The term *management console*, used in this chapter and seen in Figure 6-1, requires some explanation. A management console is a separate workstation equipped with software to configure, monitor, and report on events. The section, "Monitoring IOS IPS," introduces some of Cisco's IPS management solutions.

Table 6-1 lists some of the advantages and limitations of deploying an IDS platform in promiscuous mode.

Table 6-1 *Advantages and Limitations of Deploying an IDS in Promiscuous Mode*

Advantage	Limitation
Deploying the IDS sensor does not have any impact on the network (latency, jitter, and so on).	IDS sensor response actions cannot stop the trigger packet and are not guaranteed to stop a connection. IDS response actions are typically better at stopping an attacker more than a specific attack itself.
The IDS sensor is not inline and, therefore, a sensor failure cannot affect network functionality.	IDS sensor response actions are less helpful in stopping email viruses and automated attackers such as worms.

Table 6-1 *Advantages and Limitations of Deploying an IDS in Promiscuous Mode*

Advantage	Limitation
Overrunning the IDS sensor with data does not affect network traffic; however, it does affect the capability of the IDS to analyze the data.	Users deploying IDS sensor response actions must have a well thought-out security policy combined with a good operational understanding of their IDS deployments. Users must spend time to correctly tune IDS sensors to achieve expected levels of intrusion detection.
	Being out of band (OOB), IDS sensors are more vulnerable to network evasion techniques, which are the process of totally concealing an attack.

Table 6-2 lists some of the advantages and limitations of deploying an IPS platform in inline mode.

Table 6-2 *Advantages and Limitations of Deploying an IPS in Inline Mode*

Advantage	Limitation
You can configure an IPS sensor to perform a packet drop that can stop the trigger packet, the packets in a connection, or packets from a source IP address.	An IPS sensor must be inline and, therefore, IPS sensor errors or failure can have a negative effect on network traffic.
Being inline, an IPS sensor can use stream normalization techniques to reduce or eliminate many of the network evasion capabilities that exist.	Overrunning IPS sensor capabilities with too much traffic does negatively affect the performance of the network.
	Users deploying IPS sensor response actions must have a well thought-out security policy combined with a good operational understanding of their IPS deployments.
	An IPS sensor will affect network timing because of latency, jitter, and so on. An IPS sensor must be appropriately sized and implemented so that time-sensitive applications, such as VoIP, are not negatively affected.

Traffic normalization includes techniques such as fragmentation reassembly to check the validity of the transmission.

Note: Packets that are dropped based on false alarms can result in network disruption if the dropped packets are required for mission-critical applications downstream of the IPS sensor. Therefore, do not be overly aggressive when assigning the drop-action to signature. Also, "drop" discards the packet without sending a reset. Cisco recommends using "drop and reset" in conjunction with alarm.

Table 6-3 summarizes some of the advantages and limitations of an IDS in promiscuous mode and an IPS in inline mode explained earlier.

Table 6-3   *Summary of Advantages and Limitations of IDS and IPS Modes*

	Advantages	Limitations
IDS (Promiscuous Mode)	No impact on network (latency, jitter)	Response action cannot stop trigger packets
	No network impact if there is a sensor failure	Correct tuning required for response actions
	No network impact if there is sensor overload	Must have a well-thought out security policy
		More vulnerable to network evasion techniques
IPS (Inline Mode)	Stops trigger packets	Sensor issues might affect network traffic
	Can use stream normalization techniques	Sensor overloading impacts the network
		Must have a well-thought out security policy
		Some impact on network (latency, jitter)

Types of IDS and IPS Systems

Table 6-4 summarizes the advantages and limitations of the various types of IDS and IPS sensors available.

Table 6-4   *Types of IDS and IPS Sensors*

	Advantages	Limitations
Signature Based	Easy configuration Fewer false positives Good signature design	No detection of unknown signatures Initially a lot of false positives Signatures must be created, updated, and tuned
Policy Based	Simple and reliable Customized policies Can detect unknown attacks	Generic output Policy must be created
Anomaly Based	Easy configuration Can detect unknown attacks	Difficult to profile typical activity in large networks Traffic profile must be constant
Honeypot Based	Window to view attacks Distract and confuse attackers Slow down and avert attacks Collect information about attack	Dedicated honeypot server Honeypot server must not be trusted

- **False negative:** Occurs when the IDS/IPS fails to report an actual intrusive action.
- **False positive:** Occurs when the IDS/IPS classifies an action as anomalous when in fact it is a legitimate action.
  These terms and others are discussed at length in the upcoming section "Signature Alarms."
- **Honeypot:** A system deployed to entice a hacker to attack it and therefore track the hacker's maneuvers and technique.

The sections that follow describe these IDS and IPS sensors in more detail.

Signature-Based IDS/IPS Systems

A signature-based IDS or IPS sensor looks for specific, predefined patterns (signatures) in network traffic. It compares the network traffic to a database of known attacks, and triggers an alarm or prevents communication if a match is found. The signature can be based on a single packet or a sequence of packets. New attacks that do not match a signature do not result in detection. For this reason, the signature database needs to be constantly updated.

> **Note:**   Protocol analysis-based intrusion detection relies on signature-based intrusion detection where the signature performs a check to ensure that the date unit header, flags, payload, and so on respect the protocol.

Signature-based pattern matching is an approach that is rigid but simple to employ. In most cases, the pattern is matched against only if the suspect packet is associated with a particular service or, more precisely, destined to and from a particular port. This matching technique helps to lessen the amount of inspection done on every packet. However, it makes it more difficult for systems to deal with protocols that do not reside on well-defined ports, such as Trojan horses and their associated traffic, which can move at will.

At the initial stage of incorporating signature-based IDS or IPS, before the signatures are tuned, there can be many false positives (traffic generating an alert which is no threat for the network). After the system is tuned and adjusted to the specific network parameters, there will be fewer false positives than with the policy-based approach.

Policy-Based IDS/IPS Systems

In policy-based systems, the IDS or IPS sensor is preconfigured based on the network security policy. You must create the policies used in a policy-based IDS or IPS. Any traffic detected outside the policy will generate an alarm or will be dropped. Creating a security policy requires detailed knowledge of the network traffic and is a time-consuming task.

Policy-based signatures use an algorithm to determine whether an alarm should be fired. Often, policy-based signature algorithms are statistical evaluations of the traffic flow. For example, in a policy-based signature used to detect a port sweep, the algorithm issues an alarm when the threshold number of unique ports is scanned on a particular machine. Policy-based signature algorithms can be designed to analyze only specific types of packets (for example, SYN packets, where the SYN bit is turned on during the handshaking process at the beginning of the session).

The policy itself might require tuning. For example, you might have to adjust the threshold level of certain types of traffic so that the policy conforms to the utilization patterns on the network that it is monitoring. Polices can be used to look for very complex relationships.

Anomaly-Based IDS/IPS Systems

Anomaly-based or profile-based signatures typically look for network traffic that deviates from what is seen "normally." The biggest issue with this methodology is that you first must define what *normal* is. If during the *learning phase* your network is the victim of an attack and you fail to identify it, the anomaly-based IPS systems will interpret that malicious traffic as normal, and no alarm will be triggered next time this same attack takes place. Some systems have hard-coded definitions of normal traffic patterns and, in this case, could be considered heuristic-based systems.

Other systems are built to learn normal traffic behavior; however, the challenge with these systems is eliminating the possibility of improperly classifying abnormal behavior as normal. Also, if the traffic pattern being learned is assumed normal, the system must contend with how to differentiate between allowable deviations, and those deviations that are not allowed or that represent attack-based traffic. Normal network traffic can be difficult to define.

The technique used by anomaly-based IDS/IPS systems is also referred as *network behavior analysis* or *heuristics analysis*.

Honeypot-Based IDS/IPS Systems

Honeypot systems use a dummy server to attract attacks. The purpose of the honeypot approach is to distract attacks away from real network devices. By staging different types of vulnerabilities in the honeypot server, you can analyze incoming types of attacks and malicious traffic patterns. You can use this analysis to tune your sensor signatures to detect new types of malicious network traffic.

Honeypot systems are used in production environments, typically by large organizations that come across as interesting targets for hackers, such as financial enterprises, governmental agencies, and so on. Also, antivirus and other security vendors tend to use them for research.

Tip: Many security experts preach the use of honeypots as an early-warning system to be deployed with your IDS/IPS system, not in lieu of. *Honeyd* is an example of a popular open-source honeypot software. Although honeypots are often found as dedicated servers, it is possible to set up virtual honeypots using VMWare or Virtual PC. Keep in mind that should the honeypot be successfully hacked and used as a launching platform for an attack on a third party, the honeypot's owner could incur downstream liability.

IPS Actions

When an IPS sensor detects malicious activity, it can choose from any or all the following actions:

- **Deny attacker inline:** This action terminates the current packet and future packets from this attacker address for a specified period of time. The sensor maintains a list of the attackers currently being denied by the system. You can remove entries from the list or wait for the timer to expire. The timer is a sliding timer for each entry. Therefore, if attacker A is currently being denied, but issues another attack, the timer for attacker A is reset, and attacker A remains on the denied attacker list until the timer expires. If the denied attacker list is at capacity and cannot add a new entry, the packet is still denied.

- **Deny connection inline:** This action terminates the current packet and future packets on this TCP flow. This is also referred to as deny flow.

- **Deny packet inline:** This action terminates the packet.

- **Log attacker packets:** This action starts IP logging on packets that contain the attacker address and sends an alert. This action causes an alert to be written to the event store, which is local to the IOS router, even if the produce-alert action is not selected. Produce alert is discussed later in a bullet.

■ **Log pair packets:** This action starts IP logging on packets that contain the attacker and victim address pair. This action causes an alert to be written to the event store, even if the produce-alert action is not selected.

■ **Log victim packets:** This action starts IP logging on packets that contain the victim address and sends an alert. This action causes an alert to be written to the event store, even if the produce-alert action is not selected.

■ **Produce alert:** This action writes the event to the event store as an alert.

■ **Produce verbose alert:** This action includes an encoded dump of the offending packet in the alert. This action causes an alert to be written to the event store, even if the produce-alert action is not selected.

■ **Request block connection:** This action sends a request to a blocking device to block this connection.

■ **Request block host:** This action sends a request to a blocking device to block this attacker host.

■ **Request SNMP trap:** This action sends a request to the notification application component of the sensor to perform Simple Network Management Protocol (SNMP) notification. This action causes an alert to be written to the event store, even if produce-alert action is not selected.

■ **Reset TCP connection:** This action sends TCP resets to hijack and terminate the TCP flow.

Note: IP logging and verbose alert traces use a common capture file writing code called libpcap. This is the same format used by the famous packet-capture tool Wireshark (formerly Ethereal); by Snort, a famous freeware IDS; by NMAP, a well-known fingerprinting tool; and by Kismet, a famous wireless sniffing tool.

You can use the reset TCP connection action in conjunction with deny-packet and deny-flow actions. However, deny-packet and deny-connection actions do not automatically cause TCP reset actions to occur.

Event Monitoring and Management

Event monitoring and management can be divided into the following two needs:

■ The need for real-time event monitoring and management

■ The need to perform analysis based on archived information (reporting)

These functions can be handled by a single server, or the functions can be placed on separate servers to scale the deployment. The number of sensors that should forward alarms to a single IPS management console is a function of the aggregate number of alarms per second that are generated by those sensors.

Reporting: Analysis based on archive information

Event monitoring: Real-time monitoring

Experience with customer networks has shown that the number of sensors reporting to a single IPS management console should be limited to 25 or fewer. These customers use a mixture of default signature profiles and tuned signatures. The number of alarms generated by each sensor is determined by how sensitively the sensor is tuned; the more sensitive the tuning, the fewer the alarms that are generated, and the larger the number of sensors that can report to a single IPS management console.

Note: Obviously with the evolution of technology, the limit of 25 sensors reporting to a single IPS management console is constantly being pushed. Check with your vendor for the latest information.

It is essential to tune out false positives to maximize the scalability of the network IPS deployment. Sensors that are expected to generate a large number of alarms, such as those sitting outside the corporate firewall, should log in to a separate IPS management console, because the number of false alarms raised dramatically increases the noise-to-signal ratio and makes it difficult to identify otherwise valid events.

- False positives happen when the IDS/IPS mistakenly takes legitimate traffic for an attack.
- False negatives happens when the IDS/IPS sensor misses an attack.

When implementing multiple IPS management consoles, implement either separate monitoring domains or a hierarchical monitoring structure.

Cisco IPS Management Software

You can use the command-line interface (CLI) to configure an IPS solution, but it is simpler to use a graphical user interface (GUI)-based device manager. The following describes the Cisco device management software available to help you manage an IPS solution.

Cisco Router and Security Device Manager

Cisco Security Device Manager (SDM), shown in Figure 6-2, is a web-based device management tool for Cisco routers that can improve the productivity of network managers, simplify router deployments, and help troubleshoot complex network and virtual private network (VPN) connectivity issues. Cisco SDM supports a wide range of Cisco IOS Software releases and is available free on Cisco router models from the Cisco 850 Series Integrated Services Router to the Cisco 7301 Router.

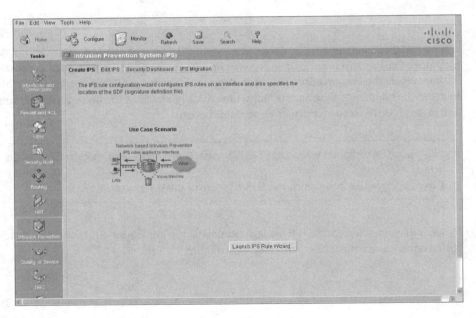

Figure 6-2   *Cisco Router and Security Device Manager*

Cisco Security Monitoring, Analysis, and Response System

Cisco Security Monitoring, Analysis, and Response System (MARS), shown in Figure 6-3, is an appliance-based, all-inclusive solution that enables network and security administrators to monitor, identify, isolate, and counter security threats. This family of high-performance appliances enables organizations to more effectively use their network and security resources.

Figure 6-3   *Cisco Security Monitoring, Analysis, and Response System*

Cisco Security MARS can monitor security events and information from a wide variety of sources, including third-party devices and hosts. With its correlation engine, vector analysis, and hotspot identification, Cisco Security MARS can identify anomalous behavior and security threats, and recommend precision removal of those elements, which leads to rapid threat mitigation. In addition, Cisco Security MARS incorporates a comprehensive reporting engine that provides easy access to information for compliance reporting.

Cisco IDS Event Viewer

Cisco IDS Event Viewer (IEV), referred to also as Cisco IPS Event Viewer, is a Java-based application that enables you to view and manage alarms for up to five sensors. With Cisco IEV, you can connect to and view alarms in real time or in imported log files. You can configure filters and views to help you manage the alarms. You can also import and export event data for further analysis.

Cisco IEV offers a no-cost monitoring solution for small-scale IPS deployments. Monitoring up to five individual IPS devices, Cisco IEV is easy to set up and use, and provides the user with the following:

■   Support for Cisco IPS Sensor Software Version 5.x through Security Device Event Exchange (SDEE) compatibility

■   Customizable reporting

■   Visibility into applied response actions and threat rating

Note: Cisco IEV is being phased out and replaced by Cisco IPS Express manager (http://tinyurl.com/5td7f2).

Cisco Security Manager

Cisco Security Manager is a powerful, but very easy-to-use solution, to centrally provision all aspects of device configurations and security policies for Cisco firewalls, VPNs, and IPS. The solution is effective for managing even small networks that consist of fewer than 10 devices, but also scales to efficiently manage large-scale networks that are composed of thousands of devices. Scalability is achieved through intelligent policy-based management techniques that can simplify administration.

Features of CSM include the following:

■   Auto update for Cisco IOS Release 12.4(11)T2 or later

■   Custom signature templates

■   Signature wizards to create and update signatures

Cisco IPS Device Manager

Cisco IPS Device Manager (IDM) is a web-based configuration tool for network IPS appliances. It is shipped at no additional cost with the Cisco IPS Sensor Software. Cisco IDM implements a web-based GUI.

Note: In May 2008, Cisco announced the release of a new product called Cisco IPS Manager Express. The new Cisco IPS Manager Express (IME), shown in Figure 6-4, is a powerful yet easy-to-use all-in-one IPS management application for up to five IPS sensors. Cisco IME can be used to provision, monitor, troubleshoot, and provide reports for IPS 4200 series sensors, ASA 5500 IPS solution, AIM-IPS on ISRs, and IDSM2 on Catalyst 6500s. To have access to all the capabilities of Cisco IME, it has to be used with sensors running Cisco IPS Software 6.1. With IPS Software Versions 5.1 or 6.0, or IOS IPS, you can use IME to monitor and provide reports only, with limited dashboard support.
Some of the features of Cisco IPS Manager Express are a customizable dashboard, powerful monitoring with real-time and historical viewing, integrated policy provisioning with risk rating, a flexible reporting tool, RSS feed integration, email notification, 75 events per second, and up to five IPS sensors.

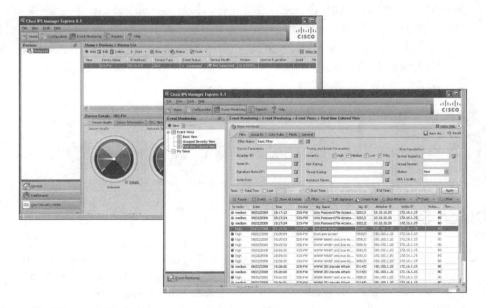

Figure 6-4   *Cisco IPS Manager Express*

Host and Network IPS

IPS technology can be network based and host based. There are advantages and limitations to HIPS compared with network-based IPS. In many cases, the technologies are thought to be complementary.

Host-Based IPS

HIPS audits host log files, host file systems, and resources. A significant advantage of HIPS is that it can monitor operating system processes and protect critical system resources, including files that may exist only on that specific host. HIPS can combine the best features of antivirus, behavioral analysis, signature filters, network firewalls, and application firewalls in one package. Note that the Cisco HIPS solution, Cisco Security Agent (CSA), is signature-free that reduces the maintenance required to be performed on that software.

A simple form of HIPS enables system logging and log analysis on the host. However, this approach can be extremely labor intensive. When implementing HIPS, the CSA software should be installed on each host to monitor all activity performed on, and against, the host. CSA performs the intrusion detection analysis and protects the host.

A Cisco HIPS deployment using CSA provides proactive security by controlling access to system resources. This approach avoids the race to update defenses to keep up with the latest exploit, and protects hosts even on day zero of a new attack. For example, the Nimda and SQL Slammer worms did millions of dollars of damage to enterprises on the first day of their appearance, before updates were even available; however, a network protected with a CSA stopped these attacks without any updates by identifying their behavior as malicious.

Host-based IPS operates by detecting attacks that occur on a host on which it is installed. HIPS works by intercepting operating system and application calls, securing the operating system and application configurations, validating incoming service requests, and analyzing local log files for after-the-fact suspicious activity.

More precisely, HIPS functions according to the following steps, as shown in Figure 6-5:

Step 1.   An application calls for system resources.

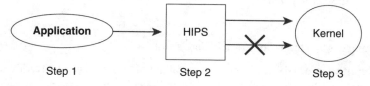

Application → HIPS → Kernel

Step 1   Step 2   Step 3

Figure 6-5   *HIPS Operations Steps*

Step 2. HIPS checks the call against the policy.

Step 3. Requests are allowed or denied.

HIPS uses rules that are based on a combination of known attack characteristics and a detailed knowledge of the operating system and specific applications running on the host. These rules enable HIPS to determine abnormal or out-of-bound activity and, therefore, prevent the host from executing commands that do not fit the correct behavior of the operating system or application.

HIPS improves the security of hosts and servers by using rules that control operating system and network stack behavior. Processor control limits activity such as buffer overflows, Registry updates, writes to the system directory, and the launching of installation programs. Regulation of network traffic can help ensure that the host does not participate in accepting or initiating FTP sessions, can rate-limit when a denial-of-service (DoS) attack is detected, or can keep the network stack from participating in a DoS attack.

The topology in Figure 6-6 shows a typical Cisco HIPS deployment. CSA is installed on publicly accessible servers, corporate mail servers, application servers, and on user desktops. CSA reports events to a central console server that is located inside the corporate firewall. CSA is managed from a central management console.

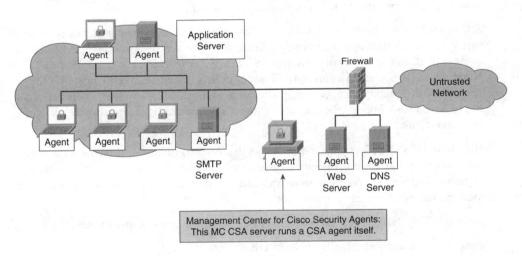

Figure 6-6 *HIPS deployment*

The advantages and limitations of HIPS are as follows:

- **Advantages of HIPS:** The success or failure of an attack can be readily determined. A network IPS sends an alarm upon the presence of intrusive activity but cannot always ascertain the success or failure of such an attack. HIPS does not have to worry about fragmentation attacks or variable Time to Live (TTL) attacks because the host stack takes care of these issues. If the network traffic stream is encrypted, HIPS has access to the traffic in unencrypted form.

- **Limitations of HIPS:** There are two major drawbacks to HIPS:
  - **HIPS does not provide a complete network picture:** Because HIPS examines information only at the local host level, HIPS has difficulty constructing an accurate network picture or coordinating the events happening across the entire network.
  - **HIPS has a requirement to support multiple operating systems:** HIPS needs to run on every system in the network. This requires verifying support for all the different operating systems used in your network.

Network-Based IPS

Network IPS involves the deployment of monitoring devices, or sensors, throughout the network to capture and analyze the traffic. Sensors detect malicious and unauthorized activity in real time and can take action when required. Sensors are deployed at designated network points that enable security managers to monitor network activity while it is occurring, regardless of the location of the attack target.

Network IPS sensors are usually tuned for intrusion prevention analysis. The underlying operating system of the platform on which the IPS software is mounted is stripped of unnecessary network services, and essential services are secured (that is, hardened). The hardware includes the following components:

- **Network interface card (NIC):** Network IPS must be able to connect to any network (Ethernet, Fast Ethernet, Gigabit Ethernet).
- **Processor:** Intrusion prevention requires CPU power to perform intrusion detection analysis and pattern matching.
- **Memory:** Intrusion detection analysis is memory intensive. Memory directly affects the capability of a network IPS to efficiently and accurately detect an attack.

Network IPS gives security managers real-time security insight into their networks regardless of network growth. Additional hosts can be added to protected networks without needing more sensors. When new networks are added, additional sensors are easy to deploy. Additional sensors are required only when their rated traffic capacity is exceeded, when their performance does not meet current needs, or when a revision in security policy or network design requires additional sensors to help enforce security boundaries.

Figure 6-7 shows a typical network IPS deployment. The key difference between this network IPS deployment example and the previous HIPS deployment example is that there is no CSA software on the various platforms. In this topology, the network IPS sensors are deployed at network entry points that protect critical network segments. The network segments have internal and external corporate resources. The sensors report to a central management and monitoring server that is located inside the corporate firewall.

The advantages and limitations of network IPS are as follows:

- **Advantages of network IPS:** A network-based monitoring system has the benefit of easily seeing attacks that are occurring across the entire network. Seeing the attacks against the entire network gives a clear indication of the extent to which the network is being attacked. Furthermore, because the monitoring system is examining

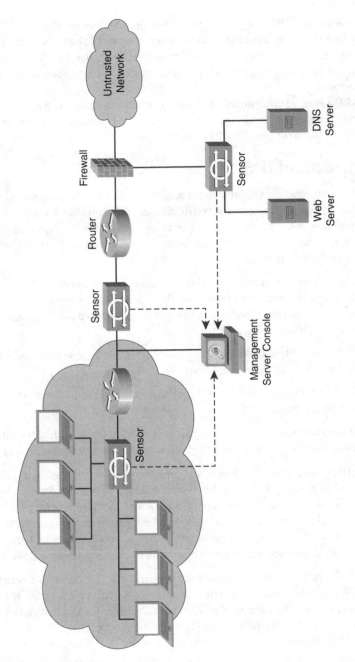

Figure 6-7 *Network-Based IPS Deployment*

only traffic from the network, it does not have to support every type of operating system that is used on the network.

■ **Limitations of network IPS:** Encryption of the network traffic stream can essentially blind network IPS. Reconstructing fragmented traffic can also be a difficult problem to solve. Possibly the biggest drawback to network-based monitoring is that as networks become larger (with respect to bandwidth), it becomes more difficult to place network IPS at a single location in the network and successfully capture all the traffic. Eliminating this problem requires the use of more sensors throughout the network. However, this solution increases costs.

Caution: It is recommended that applications responsible for the management of security, such as syslog servers, IPS alarms, and so on be separated from the main corporate network by a firewall, in essence creating a network management network. Figure 6-8 shows the details of the Enterprise Campus architecture as envisioned by the Cisco SAFE Blueprint. For more information, visit http://www.cisco.com.

Comparing HIPS and Network IPS

Table 6-5 compares the advantages and limitations of HIPS and network IPS.

Table 6-5   *Advantages and Limitations of Host-Based IPS and Network-Based IPS*

	Advantages	Limitations
HIPS	Is host specific	Operating system dependent
	Protects host after decryption	Lower-level network events not seen
	Provides application-level encryption protection	Host is visible to attackers
Network IPS	Cost-effective	Cannot examine encrypted traffic
	Not visible on the network	Does not know whether an attack was successful
	Operating system independent	
	Lower-level network events seen	

A host-based monitoring system examines information at the local host or operating system. Network-based monitoring systems examine packets that are traveling through the network for known signs of intrusive activity. As you move down the feature list toward network IPS, the features describe network-based monitoring features; application-level encryption protection is a HIPS feature, whereas DoS prevention is a network IPS feature.

Note: Network-based monitoring systems do not assess the success or failure of the actual attacks. They only indicate the presence of intrusive activity.
That is where Cisco MARS can be useful. Different sensors might report an intrusion; however, if all those sensors send their individual alarms to a Cisco MARS appliance, it could perform correlation analysis on those different alarms and discover that they are all part, let's say, of a common attack.

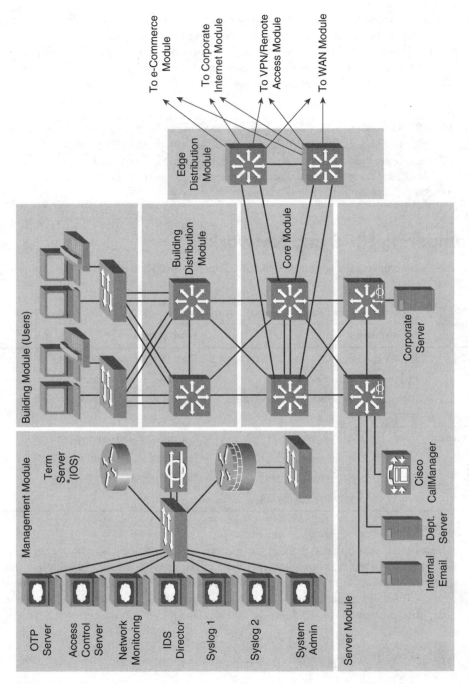

Figure 6-8   *Enterprise Campus Topology with Its Management Module*

Introducing Cisco IPS Appliances

Cisco IPS solutions run on a variety of devices, either as standalone sensors or as a module inserted into another appliance. The following is a brief description of the available Cisco IPS appliances. Each appliance is introduced further later in this section:

■ **Cisco Adaptive Security Appliance Advanced Inspection and Prevention Security Services Module (ASA AIP SSM):** The Cisco ASA AIP SSM uses advanced inspection and prevention technology to provide high-performance security services, such as intrusion prevention services and advanced anti-x services, defined as antivirus and antispyware. The Cisco ASA AIP SSM products include a Cisco ASA AIP SSM-10 module with a 1-GB memory, a Cisco ASA SSM AIP-20 module with a 2-GB memory, and a Cisco ASA SSM AIP-40 module.

■ **Cisco IPS 4200 series sensors:** Cisco IPS 4200 series sensors offer significant protection to your network by helping to detect, classify, and stop threats, including worms, spyware and adware, network viruses, and application abuse. Using Cisco IPS Sensor Software Version 5.1, the Cisco IPS solution combines inline intrusion prevention services with innovative technologies that improve accuracy. As a result, more threats can be stopped without the risk of dropping legitimate network traffic. Cisco IPS Sensor Software includes enhanced detection capabilities and improved scalability, resiliency, and so forth.

■ **Cisco Catalyst 6500 Series Intrusion Detection System Services Module (IDSM-2):** The Catalyst 6500 Series IDSM-2 is part of the Cisco IPS solution. It works in combination with the other components to efficiently protect your data infrastructure. With the increased complexity of security threats, achieving efficient network intrusion security solutions is critical to maintaining a high level of protection. Vigilant protection ensures business continuity and minimizes the effect of costly intrusions.

■ **Cisco IPS Advanced Integration Module (AIM):** Cisco offers a variety of IPS solutions; the Cisco IPS AIM for the Cisco 1841 Integrated Services Router and the Cisco 2800 and 3800 Series Integrated Services Routers is made for small and medium-sized business (SMB) and branch-office environments. Cisco IPS Sensor Software running on the Cisco IPS AIM provides advanced, enterprise-class IPS functions and meets the ever-increasing security needs of branch offices. The Cisco IPS AIM can scale in performance to match branch office WAN bandwidth requirements today and in the future, because IPS functionality is run on its dedicated CPU, thus not hogging the router CPU. At the same time, the integration of IPS onto a Cisco Integrated Services Router keeps the solution cost low and effective for business of all sizes.

Cisco IPS 4200 Series Sensors

The Cisco IPS 4200 series sensors, shown in Figure 6-9, are market-leading dedicated appliances for intrusion detection and prevention, with the highest performance and lowest false alarm rates of the industry. The Cisco IPS 4200 series sensors are focused on protecting network devices, services, and applications. They are capable of detecting sophisticated attacks such as the following:

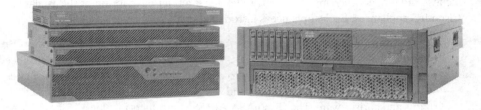

Figure 6-9   *Cisco IPS 4200 Series Sensors*

- Network attacks
- Application attacks
- DoS attacks
- Fragmented attacks
- Whisker (deprecated in favor of Nikto) attacks using IDS-evasive techniques

Cisco ASA AIP SSM

The Cisco ASA AIP SSM, shown in Figure 6-10, provides the intrusion detection and prevention security feature set for the Cisco 5500 series adaptive security appliances. It runs the same Cisco IPS Sensor Software Version 6.0 or later software image as the sensor appliances and, therefore, provides the same security features as the sensor appliance.

Figure 6-10   *Cisco ASA AIP SSM*

The Cisco ASA AIP SSM is available in three models:

- The Cisco ASA AIP SSM-10

- The Cisco ASA AIP SSM-20

- The ASA AIP SSM-40

The Cisco ASA AIP SSM-20 has a faster processor and more memory than the Cisco ASA AIP SSM-10. The Cisco ASA AIP SSM-40 works only in the Cisco ASA 5520 and 5540 and has a maximum throughput of 650 Mb/s.

> **Tip:** Although Cisco markets the AIP SSM as "full-featured intrusion prevention services," it is worth noting that the sensor can operate as an IDS or IPS device. As shown in Figure 6-11, the AIP SSM can be configured in either IDS mode (promiscuous) or in IPS mode (inline).

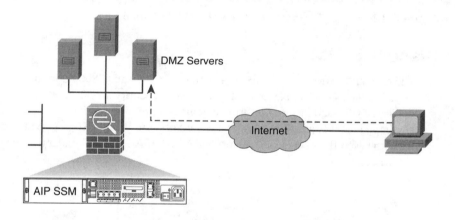

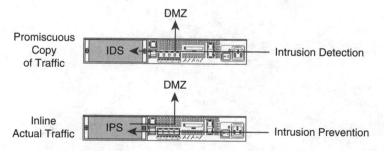

Figure 6-11 *Modes of Operation for Cisco ASA AIP SSM*

Cisco Catalyst 6500 Series IDSM-2

The Cisco Catalyst 6500 Series IDSM-2, shown in Figure 6-12, provides full-featured intrusion protection in the core network fabric device. The Cisco Catalyst 6500 Series IDSM-2 is specifically designed to address switched environments by integrating the IDS functionality directly into the switch. The Cisco Catalyst 6500 Series IDSM-2 runs the same software image as the sensor appliances and can be configured to perform intrusion prevention.

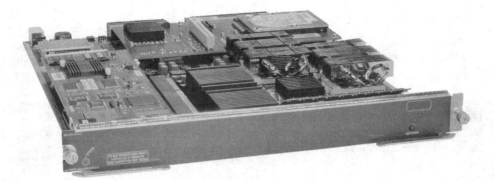

Figure 6-12   *Cisco Catalyst 6500 Series ISDM-2 Module*

Cisco IPS AIM

The Cisco IPS AIM for the Cisco 1841 and Cisco 2800 and 3800 Series Integrated Services Routers, shown in Figure 6-13, is an internal security service module that provides dedicated CPU and memory to offload inline and promiscuous intrusion prevention processing. The AIM runs the Cisco IPS Sensor Software Version 6.0 to provide feature parity with Cisco IPS 4200 series sensors and Cisco ASA 5500 series adaptive security appliances.

Figure 6-13   *Cisco IPS AIM*

By integrating IPS and branch-office routing, Cisco Integrated Services Routers can secure remote branch networks from threats originating from the Internet and reduce the WAN link overload from infected hosts at the branch. The integration of IPS into the branch-office router provides numerous important customer benefits:

- **Physical space savings:** The Cisco IPS AIM occupies the internal AIM slot on the router motherboard and can possibly saves space in the wiring closet.

- **Inline and promiscuous modes:** Both inline and promiscuous IPS inspection modes are supported. Inline mode places the IPS module in the packet path and can be configured to drop violated packets.

- **Common management tool for Cisco IPS solution:** Cisco Security Manager supports Cisco IPS AIM, with the same management tool used on Cisco IPS 4200 series sensors, enabling you to use one centralized management system for both appliance and router sensors.

- **Flexibility in monitoring interfaces:** The Cisco IPS AIM connects directly to the router backplane and can monitor packets coming in and going out of any router interface, including T1, T3, DSL, ATM, Fast Ethernet, and Gigabit Ethernet.

- **In-band management:** An internal Gigabit Ethernet port is used for in-band management of the Cisco IPS AIM CLI and for the web-based management application, Cisco IDM. Access to the IPS AIM can be done through the router console port or through the Secure Shell (SSH) protocol to any Layer 3 interface. No physical management port is required.

- **Simple power and cable management:** Cisco IPS AIM takes advantage of the power options of the router, including DC power and redundant power.

- **Dedicated processor to maximize performance:** Cisco IPS AIM has its own CPU and DRAM for all IPS functions. It offloads the router CPU from processor-intensive tasks, such as deep packet inspection from the host router.

- **Performance:** The Cisco IPS AIM can monitor up to 45 Mb/s of traffic and is suitable for T1, E1, and up to T3 environments.

- **Security in depth:** The Cisco IPS AIM interoperates with security and WAN optimization features such as VPN, firewall, Network Address Translation (NAT), Web Cache Control Protocol (WCCP), and Cisco Wide Area Application Services, and all common Cisco IOS Software functions.

Note: Cisco IOS IPS and the Cisco IPS AIM cannot be used together. Cisco IOS IPS must be disabled when the AIM IPS is installed. Cisco IOS IPS is discussed in the next section of this chapter.

Signatures and Signature Engines

A signature is a set of rules that an IDS and an IPS use to detect typical intrusive activity, such as DoS attacks. You can easily install signatures using IDS and IPS management software such as Cisco IDM. Sensors enable you to modify existing signatures and define new ones.

As sensors scan network packets, they use signatures to detect known attacks and respond with predefined actions. A malicious packet flow has a specific type of activity and signature, and an IDS or IPS sensor examines the data flow using many different signatures. When an IDS or IPS sensor matches a signature with a data flow, the sensor takes action, such as logging the event or sending an alarm to IDS or IPS management software, such as the Cisco SDM.

Signature-based intrusion detection can produce false positives because certain normal network activity can be misinterpreted as malicious activity. For example, some network applications or operating systems may send out numerous Internet Control Message Protocol (ICMP) messages, which a signature-based detection system might interpret as an attempt by an attacker to map out a network segment. You can minimize false positives by tuning your sensors. You can tune built-in signatures (tuned signatures) by adjusting the many signature parameters.

Examining Signature Micro-Engines

A signature micro-engine is a component of an IDS and IPS sensor that supports a group of signatures that are in a common category. Each engine is customized for the protocol and fields that it is designed to inspect and defines a set of legal parameters that have allowable ranges or sets of values. The signature micro-engines look for malicious activity in a specific protocol. Signatures can be defined for any of the supported signature micro-engines using the parameters offered by the supporting micro-engine. Packets are scanned by the micro-engines that understand the protocols contained in the packet.

Cisco signature micro-engines implement parallel scanning. All the signatures in a given signature micro-engine are scanned in parallel fashion, rather than serially. Each signature micro-engine extracts values from the packet and passes portions of the packet to the regular expression engine. The regular expression engine can search for multiple patterns at the same time (in parallel). Parallel scanning increases efficiency and results in higher throughput.

When IDS (promiscuous mode) or IPS (inline mode) is enabled, a signature micro-engine is loaded (or built) on to the router. When a signature micro-engine is built, the router may need to compile the regular expression found in a signature. Compiling a regular expression requires more memory than the final storage of the regular expression. Be sure to determine the final memory requirements of the finished signature before loading and merging signatures.

Note: A regular expression is a systematic way to specify a search for a pattern in a series of bytes.

As an example, a regular expression to be used to prevent data containing .exe or .com or .bat from crossing the firewall could look like this:

".*\.([Ee][Xx][Ee]|[Cc][Oo][Mm]|[Bb][Aa][Tt])".

Note: For the list of currently supported signature micro-engines, refer to the "Lists of Supported Signature Engines" section in the *Cisco IOS Security Guide, Release 12.4* available at http://www.cisco.com/en/US/partner/products/ps6350/ products_configuration_guide_chapter09186a00804453cf.html. This information requires a Cisco.com login.

Table 6-6 summarizes the types of signature engines available in Cisco IOS Release 12.4(6)T. Table 6-7 provides more details on signature engines.

Table 6-6   *Summary of Supported Signature Engines*

Signature Engine	Description
Atomic	Signatures that examine simple packets, such as ICMP and UDP
Service	Signatures that examine the many services that are attacked
String	Signatures that use regular expression-based patterns to detect intrusions
Multi-string	Supports flexible pattern matching and supports Trend Labs signatures
Other	Internal engine to handle miscellaneous signatures

Table 6-7   *Details on Signature Micro-Engines*

Signature Micro-Engine	Description
ATOMIC.IP	Provides simple Layer 3 IP alarms
ATOMIC.ICMP	Provides simple ICMP alarms based on these parameters: type, code, sequence, and ID
ATOMIC.IPOPTIONS	Provides simple alarms based on the decoding of Layer 3 options
ATOMIC.UDP	Provides simple UDP packet alarms based on these parameters: port, direction, and data length
ATOMIC.TCP	Provides simple TCP packet alarms based on these parameters: port, destination, and flags
SERVICE.DNS	Analyzes the Domain Name System (DNS) service

Table 6-7 *Details on Signature Micro-Engines*

Signature Micro-Engine	Description
SERVICE.RPC	Analyzes the remote procedure call (RPC) service
SERVICE.SMTP	Inspects Simple Mail Transfer Protocol (SMTP)
SERVICE.HTTP	Provides HTTP protocol decode-based string engine; includes anti-evasive URL de-obfuscation
SERVICE.FTP	Provides FTP service special decode alarms
STRING.TCP	Offers TCP regular expression-based pattern inspection engine services
STRING.UDP	Offers UDP regular expression-based pattern inspection engine services
STRING.ICMP	Provides ICMP regular expression-based pattern inspection engine services
MULTI-STRING	Supports flexible pattern matching and supports Trend Labs signatures
Other	Provides internal engine to handle miscellaneous signatures

Note: It is recommended that you run Cisco IOS Release 12.4(11)T or later when using Cisco IOS IPS.

Note: Cisco IOS IPS and the Cisco IPS AIM cannot be used together. Cisco IOS IPS must be disabled when the AIM IPS is installed. Cisco IOS IPS is an IPS application that provides inspection capabilities for traffic flowing through the router. Although it is included in the Cisco IOS Advanced Security feature set, it uses the router CPU and shared memory pool to perform the inspection. Cisco IOS IPS also runs a subset of IPS signatures. The Cisco AIM IPS, discussed earlier in this chapter, runs with a dedicated CPU and memory, offloading all processing of IPS signatures from the router CPU. It can load a full signature set and provide enhanced IPS features not available on Cisco IOS IPS.

Signature Alarms

The capability of IDS and IPS sensors to accurately detect an attack or a policy violation and generate an alarm is critical to the functionality of the sensors. Attacks can generate the following types of alarms:

■   **False positive:** A false positive is an alarm triggered by normal traffic or a benign action. Consider this scenario: A signature exists that generates alarms if the enable password of any network devices is entered incorrectly. A network administrator attempts to log in to a Cisco router but enters the wrong password. The IDS cannot distinguish between a rogue user and the network administrator, and it generates an alarm.

■ **False negative:** A false negative occurs when a signature is not fired when offending traffic is detected. Offending traffic ranges from someone sending confidential documents outside of the corporate network to attacks against corporate web servers. False negatives are bugs in the IDS and IPS software and should be reported. A false negative should be considered a software bug only if the IDS and IPS have a signature that has been designed to detect the offending traffic.

■ **True positive:** A true positive occurs when an IDS and IPS signature is correctly fired, and an alarm is generated, when offending traffic is detected. For example, consider a Unicode attack. Cisco IPS sensors have signatures that detect Unicode attacks against Microsoft Internet Information Services (IIS) web servers. If a Unicode attack is launched against Microsoft IIS web servers, the sensors detect the attack and generate an alarm.

■ **True negative:** A true negative occurs when a signature is not fired when nonoffending traffic is captured and analyzed. In other words, the sensor does not fire an alarm when it captures and analyzes "normal" network traffic.

Table 6-8 provides a summary of the alarm types. To understand the terminology, think in terms of "Was the alarm triggered?" A positive means that the alarm was triggered and a negative means that the alarm was not triggered. Thus the expression *false alarm*, which is the same as *false positive* (positive because the alarm was triggered, but false because the intrusion did not happen or the intrusion was not detected by the sensor).

Table 6-8 *Alarm Types*

	Intrusion Occurred/Detected	Intrusion Did Not Occur / Not Detected
Alarm was triggered	True positive	False positive
Alarm was not triggered	False negative	True negative

Alarms fire when specific parameters are met. You must balance the number of incorrect alarms that you can tolerate with the capability of the signature to detect actual intrusions. If you have too few alarms, you might be letting in more suspect packets, but network traffic will flow more quickly. If IPS systems use untuned signatures, they will produce many false positive alarms. You should consider the following factors when implementing alarms that a signature uses:

■ The level assigned to the signature determines the alarm severity level.

■ A Cisco IPS signature is assigned one of four severity levels:

- ■ **Informational:** Activity that triggers the signature is not considered an immediate threat, but the information provided is useful information.
- ■ **Low:** Abnormal network activity is detected that could be perceived as malicious, but an immediate threat is not likely.
- ■ **Medium:** Abnormal network activity is detected that could be perceived as malicious, and an immediate threat is likely.
- ■ **High:** Attacks used to gain access or cause a DoS attack are detected, and an immediate threat is extremely likely.

- ■ You can manually adjust the severity level that an alarm produces.

- ■ To minimize false positives, study your existing network traffic patterns and then tune your signatures to recognize intrusion patterns that are atypical (out of character) for your network traffic patterns. Do not base your signature tuning on traffic patterns that are based only on industry examples. Use an industry example as a starting point, determine what your own network traffic patterns are, and use them in your signature alarm tuning efforts.

Retiring Signatures

Router memory and resource constraints might prevent a router from loading all Cisco IOS IPS signatures. Therefore, it is recommended that you load only a selected set of signatures that are defined by the categories. Because the categories are applied in a "top-down" order, you should first retire all signatures, followed by "unretiring" specific categories. Retiring signatures enables the router to load information for all signatures, but the router will not build the parallel scanning data structure.

Retired signatures are not scanned by Cisco IOS IPS, so they will not fire alarms. If a signature is irrelevant to your network or if you want to save router memory, you should retire signatures, as appropriate. However, be aware that retiring and reinstating signatures are a CPU-intensive process. For more information about this topic, refer to http://www.cisco.com/en/US/docs/ios/12_4t/12_4t11/ips_v5.html.

IPS Best Practices

You should follow some configuration best practices to improve IPS efficiency when deploying IPS in your network.

When setting up a large deployment of sensors, automatically update signature packs rather than manually upgrading every sensor. Then security operations personnel have more time to analyze events. When new signature packs are available, download the new signature packs to a secure server within the management network.

Place the signature packs on a dedicated FTP server within the management network. If a signature update is not available, a custom signature can be created to detect and mitigate a specific attack. You should configure the FTP server to allow read-only access to the files within the directory on which the signature packs are placed only from the account that the sensors will use. The sensors can then be configured to automatically check the FTP server periodically, such as once a week on a certain day, to look for the new signature packs and to update the sensors. You can use an IPS to protect this server from attack by an outside party.

You should stagger the time of day when the sensors check the FTP server for new signature packs, perhaps through a predetermined change window. This prevents multiple sensors from overwhelming the FTP server by asking for the same file at the same time. The need to upgrade sensors with the latest signature packs must be balanced against the momentary downtime—and, therefore, the vulnerability to attack—incurred while upgrading them. Finally, the signature levels supported on the management console must remain synchronized with the signature packs on the sensors themselves.

You should group IPS sensors together under a few larger profiles. Every signature upgrade requires that all new signatures be appropriately tuned on every sensor. Tuning signatures for groups of sensors rather than for each sensor on the network significantly reduces configuration time. This administrative advantage must be balanced against the ability to finely tune sensor configuration by establishing a separate profile for each sensor.

Refer to the release notes of signatures to confirm that the new update will not overwrite the tuning you might have performed on a signature.

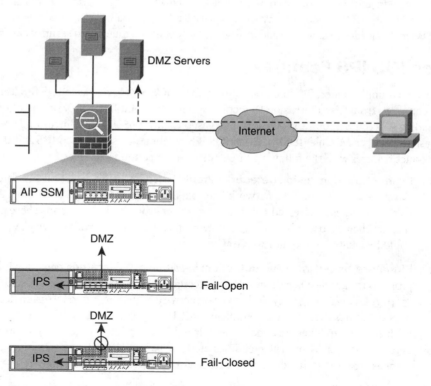

Figure 6-14 *Fail-Open or Fail-Close Approach*

A Great Debate: Fail-Close or Fail-Open?

This is a philosophical debate in which you need to get engaged in for your organization: Should the IPS sensor stop working, do you let the traffic go through or do you stop the traffic? The two opposing philosophies are represented in Figure 6-14, where the network administrator needs to decide whether the traffic will be allowed to flow into the demilitarized zone (DMZ) should the Cisco ASA AIP SSM fail.

It seems that the balance is tilting in favor of the "fail-open" approach with security experts, but each organization has to define and enforce their own policy in this topic.

Note: Readers interested in learning more about generic topics regarding IDS/IPS should consider visiting http://www.searchsecurity.com, more precisely the "Security School," which offers free training modules on different security topics.

Configuring Cisco IOS IPS

Configuring Cisco IOS Intrusion Prevention System (IPS) is a core competency for a network security administrator. In this section, you will learn how to configure Cisco IOS IPS on routers using the Cisco Router and Security Device Manager (SDM). You will also discover that Cisco SDM makes it easy to configure and manage Cisco IOS IPS on routers and security devices.

Cisco IOS IPS Features

Cisco has implemented IPS functions into its Cisco IOS Software. Cisco IOS IPS uses technology from Cisco Intrusion Detection System (IDS) and IPS sensor product lines, including Cisco IPS 4200 series sensors, and Cisco Catalyst 6500 series Intrusion Detection System Services Module (IDSM). Cisco IOS IPS combines existing Cisco IDS and IPS product features with the following three intrusion detection techniques:

- **Profile-based intrusion detection:** Profile-based intrusion detection generates an alarm when activity on the network goes outside a defined profile. With anomaly detection, profiles are created for each user or user group on your system. These profiles are then used as a baseline to define normal user and network activity. A profile could be created to monitor web traffic.

- **Signature-based intrusion detection:** Signature-based intrusion detection is less prone to triggering a false alarm when detecting unauthorized activity. A signature is a set of rules pertaining to typical intrusion activity. Signature-based intrusion detection uses signatures that are based on values in IP, TCP, UDP, and ICMP headers. Network engineers research known attacks and vulnerabilities and then develop signatures to detect these attacks and vulnerabilities on the network. These attack signatures encompass specific traffic or activity that is based on known intrusive activity.

  Cisco IOS IPS implements signatures that can look at every packet going through the network and generate alarms when necessary. A Cisco IOS IPS generates alarms when a specific pattern of traffic is matched or a signature is triggered. You can configure a Cisco IOS IPS to exclude signatures and modify signature parameters to work optimally in your network environment.

A pattern-matching approach searches for a fixed sequence of bytes in a single packet. Pattern matching is a rigid approach but is simple to employ. In most cases, the pattern is matched against a packet only if the suspect packet is associated with a particular service or, more precisely, destined to or from a particular port. For example, a signature might be based on a simple pattern-matching approach such as the following: If <the packet is IPv4 and TCP> and <the destination port is 2222> and <the payload contains the string "foo"> then <fire an alarm>.

■ **Protocol analysis-based intrusion detection:** Protocol analysis-based intrusion detection is similar to signature-based intrusion detection, but it performs a more in-depth analysis of the protocols specified in the packets. A deeper analysis examines the payloads within TCP and UDP packets, which contain other protocols. For example, a protocol such as DNS is contained within TCP or UDP, which itself is contained within IP.

The first step of protocol analysis is to decode the packet IP header information and determine whether the payload contains TCP, UDP, or another protocol. For example, if the payload is TCP, some of the TCP header information within the IP payload is processed before the TCP payload is accessed (for example, DNS data). Similar actions are mapped for other protocols.

Protocol analysis requires that the IPS sensor knows how various protocols work so that it can more closely analyze the traffic of those protocols to look for suspicious or abnormal activity. For each protocol, the analysis is based not only on protocol standards, particularly the RFCs, but also on how things are implemented in the real world. Many implementations violate protocol standards. It is important that signatures reflect common and accepted practice rather than the RFC-specified ideal; otherwise, false results can be reported.

The following attributes describe the primary benefits of the Cisco IOS IPS solution:

■ Cisco IOS IPS uses the underlying routing infrastructure to provide an additional layer of security with investment protection.

■ Because Cisco IOS IPS is inline and is supported on a broad range of routing platforms, attacks can be effectively mitigated to deny malicious traffic from both inside and outside the network.

■ When used in combination with Cisco IDS, Cisco IOS Firewall, virtual private network (VPN), and Network Admission Control (NAC) solutions, Cisco IOS IPS provides superior threat protection at all entry points to the network.

■ Cisco IOS IPS is supported by easy and effective management tools, such as Cisco SDM, Cisco Security MARS, and Cisco Security Manager.

■ Whether threats are targeted at endpoints, servers, or the network infrastructure, Cisco offers pervasive intrusion prevention solutions that are designed to integrate smoothly into the network infrastructure and to proactively protect vital resources.

■ Cisco IOS IPS supports around 2000 attack signatures from the same signature database that is available for Cisco IPS appliances.

Table 6-9 describes the features of Cisco IOS IPS-based signatures.

Table 6-9 *Cisco IOS IPS Signature Features*

Cisco IOS IPS Signature Feature	Description
Regular expression string pattern matching	Enables the creation of string patterns using regular expressions.
Response actions	Enables the sensor to take an action when the signature is triggered.
Alarm summarization	Enables the sensor to aggregate alarms. It does this to limit the number of times an alarm is sent when the signature is triggered.
Threshold configuration	Enables a signature to be tuned to perform optimally in a network.
Anti-evasive techniques	Enables a signature to defeat evasive techniques used by an attacker.

Configuring Cisco IOS IPS Using Cisco SDM

Cisco IOS IPS allows you to manage intrusion prevention on routers that use Cisco IOS Software Release 12.3(8)T4 or later. Cisco IOS IPS monitors and prevents intrusions by comparing traffic against signatures of known threats and blocking the traffic when a threat is detected. Cisco SDM lets you control the application of Cisco IOS IPS on interfaces, import and edit signature files from Cisco.com, and configure the action that Cisco IOS IPS should take if a threat is detected.

The tasks associated with managing routers and security devices are displayed in a task pane on the left side of the Cisco SDM home page, as shown in Figure 6-15. Choose **Configure > Intrusion Prevention** to reveal the intrusion prevention options in Cisco SDM. You can use Cisco SDM to configure Cisco IOS IPS on routers and security devices.

Use the tabs at the top of the Intrusion Prevention System (IPS) window to navigate to the area you want to configure or monitor:

■   **Create IPS:** This tab contains the IPS Rule wizard that you use to create a new Cisco IOS IPS rule.

■   **Edit IPS:** This tab allows you to edit Cisco IOS IPS rules and apply or remove them from interfaces.

■   **Security Dashboard:** This tab allows you to view the Top Threats table and deploy signatures associated with those threats.

■   **IPS Migration:** If the router runs a Cisco IOS Software Release 12.4(11)T or later, you can use this tab to migrate Cisco IOS IPS configurations that were created using earlier releases of the Cisco IOS Software.

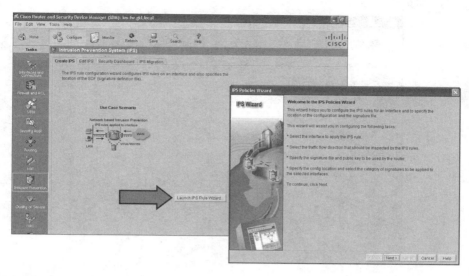

Figure 6-15   *Cisco SDM and IPS Wizard*

Tip: In Cisco SDM, when you see the words *the IPS rule configuration* substitute *the IPS signature configuration*.

Cisco SDM enables you to create a new rule on a Cisco router in two ways: manually through the Edit IPS tab or automatically using the IPS Rule Wizard. The Cisco IOS IPS Deployment Guide recommends using the IPS Rule Wizard. The wizard that is launched does more than just configure a rule; it performs all the Cisco IOS IPS configuration steps.

Follow these steps to configure Cisco IOS IPS on the router or security device using Cisco SDM:

Step 1.   Choose **Configure > Intrusion Prevention > Create IPS**.

Step 2.   Click the **Launch IPS Rule Wizard** button.

Step 3.   Read the Welcome to the IPS Policies Wizard screen, and then click **Next**.

Step 4.   Next, you must choose the interfaces on which you want to apply the Cisco IOS IPS rule by specifying whether the rule is to be applied to inbound traffic or outbound traffic, as shown in Figure 6-16. If you check both the Inbound and the Outbound check boxes, the rule applies to traffic flowing in both directions.

Step 5.   From the Select Interfaces dialog window, choose the router interfaces to which you want to apply the IPS rule by checking either the Inbound check box, Outbound check box, or both, that is next to the desired interface.

Step 6.   Click **Next**.

Step 7.   Cisco IOS IPS examines traffic by comparing it against signatures contained in a signature file. The signature file can be located in router flash memory or on

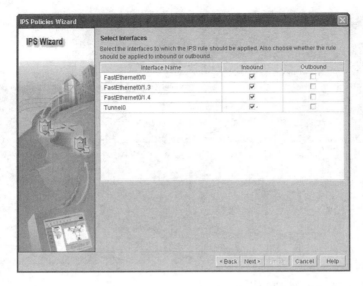

Figure 6-16   *IPS Wizard: Applying Cisco IOS IPS Rule to an Interface*

a remote system that the router can reach. You can specify multiple signature file locations so that if the router is unable to contact the first location, it can attempt to contact other locations until it obtains a signature file.

Step 8.   From the Signature File and Public Key dialog window, in the Signature File pane, click either the **Specify the Signature File You Want to Use with the IOS IPS** or **Get the Latest Signature File from Cisco.com and Save to PC** option and fill in the Signature File or Location text box as appropriate, as shown in Figure 6-17.

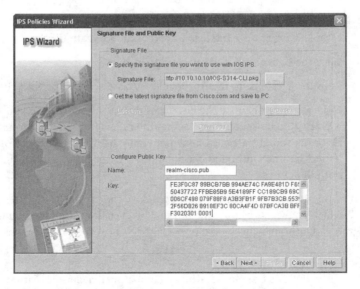

Figure 6-17   *IPS Wizard—Example of Signature File and Public Key*

Note: The appropriate signature file will be in the form of an IOS IPS update package with the naming convention of IOS-S*xxx*-CLI.pkg (where *xxx* is the number of the signature set).

Step 9. If you chose to download the latest signature file from Cisco.com, you will need to click **Download** when you are ready to download the signature file.

The Cisco IOS IPS signature file contains the default signature information present in each update to the file on Cisco.com. Any changes made to this configuration are saved in a delta file. For security, the delta file must be digitally signed. Follow these steps to place the public-key information in the Name and Key fields.

Step 10. Go to the following link to obtain the public key: http://www.cisco.com/pcgi-bin/tablebuild.pl/ios-v5sigup.

Step 11. Download the key to your PC.

Step 12. Open the key in a text editor and copy the text after the phrase *named-key* into the Name field. For example, if the line of text is "named-key realm-cisco.pub signature" copy "realm-cisco.pub signature" to the Name field.

Step 13. Copy the text between the phrase *key-string* and the word *quit* into the Key field. The following output shows what this text might look like:

```
30820122 300D0609 2A864886 F70D0101 01050003 82010F00
3082010A 02820101
00C19E93 A8AF124A D6CC7A24 5097A975 206BE3A2 06FBA13F
6F12CB5B 4E441F16
17E630D5 C02AC252 912BE27F 37FDD9C8 11FC7AF7 DCDD81D9
43CDABC3 6007D128
B199ABCB D34ED0F9 085FADC1 359C189E F30AF10A C0EFB624
7E0764BF 3E53053E
5B2146A9 D7A5EDE3 0298AF03 DED7A5B8 9479039D 20F30663
9AC64B93 C0112A35
FE3F0C87 89BCB7BB 994AE74C FA9E481D F65875D6 85EAF974
6D9CC8E3 F0B08B85
50437722 FFBE85B9 5E4189FF CC189CB9 69C46F9C A84DFBA5
7A0AF99E AD768C36
006CF498 079F88F8 A3B3FB1F 9FB7B3CB 5539E1D1 9693CCBB
551F78D2 892356AE
2F56D826 8918EF3C 80CA4F4D 87BFCA3B BFF668E9 689782A5
CF31CB6E B4B094D3
   F3020301 0001
```

Step 14. Click **Next**.

For Cisco IOS Release 12.4(11) or later, you can specify the following additional options:

■ **Config location:** This information specifies where to store files that contain changes to the Cisco IOS IPS configuration. This information consists of the signature file and the delta file that is created when changes are made to the signature information, as shown in Figure 6-18.

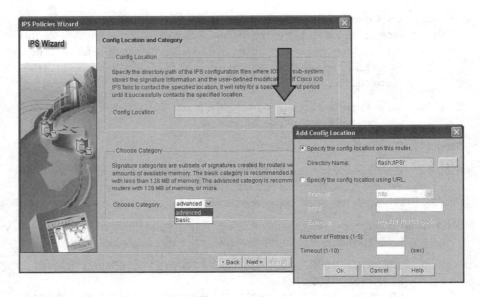

Figure 6-18   *IPS Wizard: Config Location and Category*

■ **Signature category:** The basic signature category is appropriate for routers with less than 128 MB of flash memory, and the advanced signature category is appropriate for routers with more than 128 MB of flash memory.

Follow these steps to specify a location for storing the signature information and what signature category you would like the router to use:

Step 15.   From the Config Location and Category window, in the Config Location section, click the ellipsis (...) button to the right of the Config Location field to display a dialog that allows you to specify a location. After you enter information in this dialog, Cisco SDM displays the path to the location in this field.

Step 16.   Because router memory and resource constraints can prevent the use of all the available signatures, there are two categories of signatures: basic and advanced. In the Choose Category field, choose the category that will allow the Cisco IOS IPS to function efficiently on the router.

Step 17. Click **Finish**. The IPS Policies Wizard confirms configuration as follows:

```
IPS rule will be applied to the incoming traffic on the
following interfaces.
      FastEthernet0/0
      FastEthernet0/1.3
      FastEthernet0/1.4
      Tunnel0
Signature File location:
      tftp://10.10.10.10/IOS-S314-CLI.pkg
Public Key:
    Name:     realm-cisco.pub
    Key:      30820122 300D0609 2A864886 F70D0101
01050003 82010F00 3082010A
 02820101
<output omitted>
Config Location
      flash:/IPS/
Selected category of signatures:
      Basic
```
Figure 6-19 shows actual Wizard Summary windows

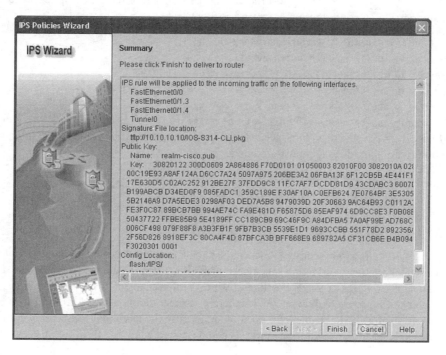

Figure 6-19 *IPS Wizard: IPS Policy Summary*

Configuring Cisco IOS IPS Using CLI

To use the command-line interface (CLI) to specify an IPS rule, use the **ip ips name** *name* command in global configuration mode as follows:

```
router(config)# ip ips name sdm_ips_rule
```

To specify the location of the IPS configuration, use the **ip ips config location** *location* global configuration command, as demonstrated here:

```
router(config)# ip ips config location flash:/ipsdir/retries 1
```

To specify the method of event notification, use the **ip ips notify** global configuration command. The following is an example of event notification sent using Security Device Event Exchange (SDEE), which is a standard developed to communicate an event generated by security devices:

```
router(config)# ip ips notify SDEE
```

> **Note:**   Examples in this section of the chapter dealing with Cisco IOS IPS CLI configuration assume that the signature files are already on the router.

To configure the router to support the default basic signature set use the **ip ips signature-category** global configuration command as follows:

```
Router(config)# ip ips signature-category
Router(config-ips-category)# category all
Router(config-ips-category-action)# retired true
Router(config-ips-category-action)# exit
Router(config-ips-category)# category ios_ips basic
Router(config-ips-category-action)# retired false
```

To apply an IPS rule to an interface, use the **ip ips** *ips_rule_name* command in interface configuration mode as demonstrated here:

```
router(config)# interface Serial0/0/0
router(config-if)# ip ips sdm_ips_rule in
```

Virtual Fragment Reassembly

Virtual Fragment Reassembly (VFR) enables the Cisco IOS Firewall to examine out-of-sequence fragments and reorder the packets into the order. It examines the number of fragments from a same single IP address. When VFR is enabled on a Cisco IOS Firewall, it creates the appropriate dynamic ACLs, thereby protecting the network from various fragmentation attacks. To enable VFR on an interface, use the **ip virtual-reassembly** command in interface configuration mode, as demonstrated here:

```
Router(config)# interface Serial0/0/0
Router(config-if)# ip virtual-reassembly
```

Example 6-1 provides a combined view of the commands shown in the preceding paragraphs.

Example 6-1   *Cisco IOS IPS CLI Configuration*

```
Router(config)# ip ips name sdm_ips_rule
Router(config)# ip ips config location flash:/ipsdir/ retries 1
Router(config)# ip ips notify SDEE
!
Router(config)# ip ips signature-category
Router(config-ips-category)# category all
Router(config-ips-category-action)# retired true
Router(config-ips-category-action)# exit
Router(config-ips-category)# category ios_ips basic
Router(config-ips-category-action)# retired false
!
Router(config)# interface Serial0/0/0
Router(config-if)# ip ips sdm_ips_rule in
Router(config-if)# ip virtual-reassembly
```

Configuring IPS Signatures

Cisco IOS IPS prevents intrusion by comparing traffic against the signatures of known attacks. Cisco IOS images that support Cisco IOS IPS have built-in signatures that the router can use, and you can import signatures for the router to use. Imported signatures are stored in a signature file.

IPS signatures are loaded as part of the procedure to create a Cisco IOS IPS rule using the IPS rule wizard. To view the configured Cisco IOS IPS signatures on the router, choose **Configure > Intrusion Prevention > Edit IPS > Signatures > All Categories**. Because signatures optimize your configuration, confirm that all the correct signatures are loaded on the router or security device. From this window, you can add customized signatures or import signatures that are downloaded from Cisco.com. You can also edit, delete, enable, and disable signatures.

Note: You can import signatures from the router only if the router has a DOS-based file system.

Note: Signature files are available from Cisco at http://www.cisco.com/cgi-bin/table-build.pl/ios-v5sigup-sdm. A Cisco.com login is required for this site.

The signature tree enables you to filter the signature list according to the type of signature that you want to view. To modify a signature, right-click the signature and choose an option from the pop-up menu, as shown in Figure 6-20. To change the severity of the signature, choose **Set Severity To**.

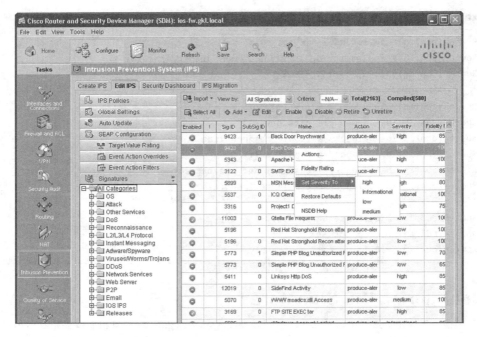

Figure 6-20   *Setting Signature Severity*

Note: Cisco maintains an alert center that provides information about emerging threats. See the Cisco Security Center for more information at http://tools.cisco.com/security/center/home.x.

You can tune a signature configuration using Cisco SDM. To tune a signature, choose **Configure > Intrusion Prevention > Edit IPS > Signatures > All Categories**. A list of available signatures appears.

To modify a signature action, right-click the signature and choose **Actions** from the pop-up menu. The Assign Actions window appears, as shown in Figure 6-21, and displays the actions that can be taken upon a signature match. The available actions depend on the signature, but the following are the most common actions:

■ **Deny Attacker Inline:** Create an ACL that denies all traffic from the IP address that is considered the source of the attack by the Cisco IOS IPS system.

■ **Deny Connection Inline:** Drop the packet and all future packets from this TCP flow.

■ **Deny Packet Inline:** Do not transmit this packet (inline only).

■ **Produce Alert:** Generate an alarm message.

■ **Reset TCP Connection:** Send TCP resets to terminate the TCP flow.

To access and configure signature parameters, choose the signature and then click the **Edit** button in the Cisco SDM Configure Signatures window, as shown in Figure 6-22.

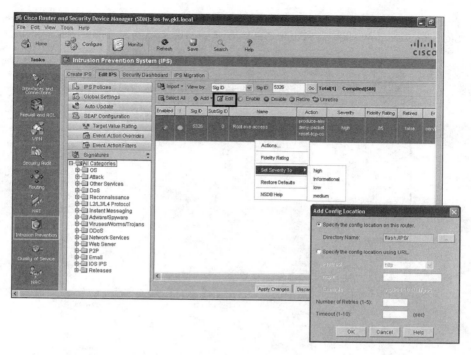

Figure 6-21   *Configuring Signature Actions*

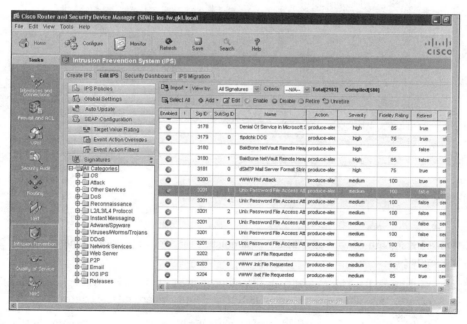

Figure 6-22   *Preparing to Edit the Cisco IOS IDS Signatures*

In the dialog box that results from clicking the **Edit** button in the Cisco SDM Configure Signatures window, shown in Figure 6-23, configure the signature parameters.

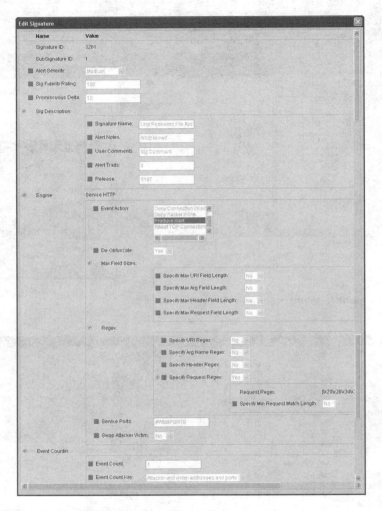

Figure 6-23 *Editing Signatures Using Cisco SDM*

Different signatures will have different parameters that you can modify. The following are common fields.

■ **Signature ID:** This field displays a unique numerical value that is assigned to this signature. This value allows Cisco IOS IPS to identify a particular signature.

■ **SubSignature ID:** This field displays a unique numeric value that is assigned to this subsignature. A subsig ID identifies a more granular version of a broad signature.

■ **Alert Severity:** This field displays the severity of the alert for this signature.

- **Sig Description:** This section includes the signature name, alert notes, user comments, alert traits, and release number.

- **Engine:** This section contains information about what engine the signature uses and characteristics about how the engine operates.

- **Event Counter:** This section displays the event count, the event count key, and whether an alert interval is to be specified. An alert interval allows you to define special handling for timed events.

- **Alert Frequency:** (Not shown in Figure 6-23.) This section has settings to define the frequency of the alert.

- **Status:** (Not shown in Figure 6-23) This section shows whether the signature is enabled and whether the signature is retired.

Monitoring IOS IPS

Figure 6-24 shows how you can use the Security Device Event Exchange (SDEE) protocol and a syslog-based approach to send Cisco IPS alerts. The sensor generates an alarm when an enabled signature is triggered. Alarms are stored on the sensor. A host can pull the alarms from the sensor using SDEE. Pulling alarms from a sensor allows multiple hosts to subscribe to the event "feed" to allow a host or hosts to subscribe on an as-needed basis.

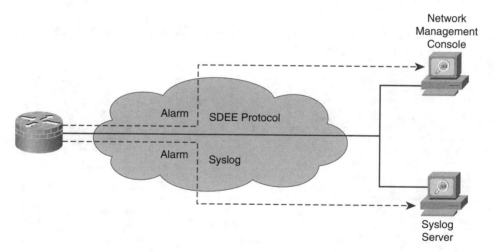

Figure 6-24   *Support for SDEE and Syslog*

The support for SDEE and syslog in the Cisco IOS IPS solution is as follows:

- Cisco IOS Software supports the SDEE protocol. When Cisco SDEE notification is enabled (by using the **ip ips notify sdee** command), by default 200 events can be stored in the event buffer, whose size can be increased to hold a maximum of 1000 events. When you disable Cisco SDEE notification, all stored events are lost. A new buffer is allocated when the notifications are reenabled.

- SDEE uses a pull mechanism. That is, requests come from the network management application, and the IDS and IPS router responds.

- SDEE becomes the standard format for all vendors to communicate events to a network management application.

- You must also enable HTTP or HTTPS on the router, using the **ip http server** command, when you enable SDEE. The use of HTTPS ensures that data is secured as it traverses the network.

- The Cisco IOS IPS router still sends IPS alerts via syslog.

When you use Cisco SDM, you can keep track of alarms that are common in SDEE system messages, including IPS signature alarms. The following is an example of an SDEE system alarm message:

```
%IPS-4-SIGNATURE:Sig:1107 Subsig:0 Sev:2 RFC1918 address
[192.168.121.1:137 ->192.168.121.255:137]
```

The preceding alarm was triggered by the fact that a packet with a private addresses, as listed in RFC 1918, traversed the IPS sensor.

Note: For a complete list of the Cisco IOS IPS system messages, refer to the "Interpreting Cisco IPS System Messages" section in the *Cisco IOS Security Configuration Guide, Release 12.4* available at http://tinyurl.com/3ufo6j.

To view SDEE alarm messages in Cisco SDM, choose **Monitor > Logging > SDEE Message Log**, as shown in Figure 6-25.

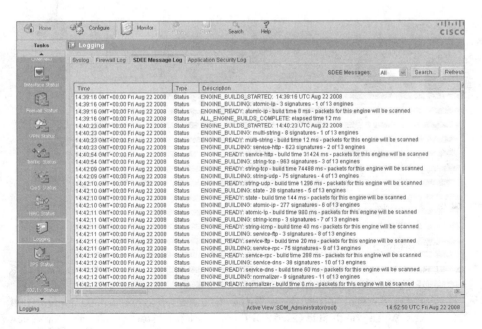

Figure 6-25   *Viewing an SDDE Alarm Message*

To view alarms generated by Cisco IOS IPS, choose **Monitor > Logging > Syslog**, as shown in Figure 6-26.

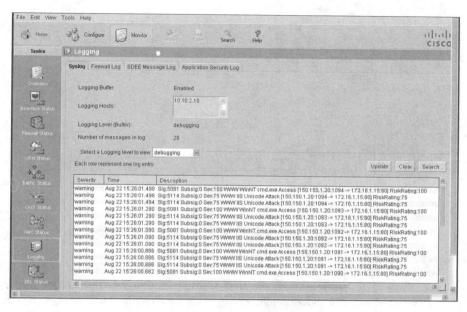

Figure 6-26   *Viewing a Syslog IPS Alarm*

Verifying IPS Operation

To verify the IPS configuration on the router, choose **Configure > Intrusion Prevention > Edit IPS**, as shown in Figure 6-27. The Edit IPS tab shows all the interfaces on the router and whether they are configured for Cisco IOS IPS. If *Enabled* appears in either the Inbound or the Outbound column, Cisco IOS IPS is enabled for that direction of traffic on that interface. If *Disabled* appears in either the Inbound or the Outbound column, Cisco IOS IPS is disabled for that direction on the interface.

Cisco IOS IPS cannot identify the contents of IP fragments when VFR is not enabled, and it cannot gather port information from the fragment to match it with a signature. Therefore, fragments can pass through the network without being examined or without a dynamic ACL being created on the Cisco IOS Firewall. You will remember that VFR enables the Cisco IOS Firewall to examine out-of-sequence fragments. VFR can create the dynamic ACLs necessary to protect against fragment attacks

The VFR status field shows the status of VFR on an interface. If VFR is enabled on the interface, the column displays *On*. If VFR is disabled on the interface, the column displays *Off*.

The Edit IPS tab also contains buttons that enable you to configure and manage Cisco IOS IPS policies, security messages, signatures, and more.

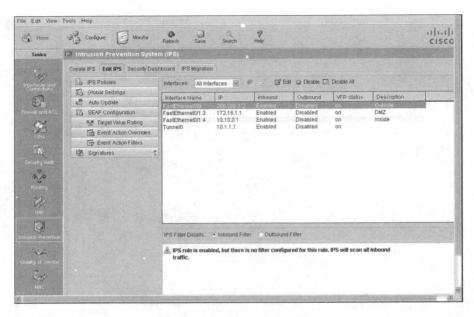

Figure 6-27 *Verifying IPS Policies*

Use the **show ip ips configuration** command to display additional configuration data that is not displayed with the **show running-config** command. Example 6-2 shows some sample output from the **show ip ips configuration** command.

Example 6-2 *show ip ips configuration Command Output*

```
Router# show ip ips configuration
IPS Signature File Configuration Status
    Configured Config Locations: flash:/ipsdir/
    Last signature default load time: 04:39:33 UTC Dec 14 2007
    Last signature delta load time: -none-
    Last event action (SEAP) load time: -none-

    General SEAP Config:
    Global Deny Timeout: 3600 seconds
    Global Overrides Status: Enabled
    Global Filters Status: Enabled

IPS Auto Update is not currently configured

IPS Syslog and SDEE Notification Status
    Event notification through syslog is enabled
    Event notification through SDEE is enabled

IPS Signature Status
    Total Active Signatures: 353
```

```
        Total Inactive Signatures: 1783

IPS Packet Scanning and Interface Status
    IPS Rule Configuration
      IPS name sdm_ips_rule
    IPS fail closed is disabled
    IPS deny-action ips-interface is false
    Fastpath ips is enabled
    Quick run mode is enabled
    Interface Configuration
      Interface FastEthernet0/0
        Inbound IPS rule is sdm_ips_rule
        Outgoing IPS rule is not set
      Interface FastEthernet0/1
        Inbound IPS rule is sdm_ips_rule
        Outgoing IPS rule is not set

IPS Category CLI Configuration:
    Category all:
        Retire: True
    Category ios_ips basic:
        Retire: False
    Category ios_ips:
        Enable: True
    Category ios_ips advanced:
        Enable: True
```

Use the **show ip ips interface** command to display interface configuration data. Example 6-3 displays output from the **show ip ips interface** command, revealing that the inbound IPS audit rule **sdm_ips_rule** is applied to FastEthernet 0/0 and FastEthernet 0/1. There is no rule applied for outgoing traffic on either interface.

Example 6-3   *show ip ips interface Command Output*

```
Router# show ip ips interfaces
Interface Configuration
      Interface FastEthernet0/0
        Inbound IPS rule is sdm_ips_rule
        Outgoing IPS rule is not set
      Interface FastEthernet0/1
        Inbound IPS rule is sdm_ips_rule
        Outgoing IPS rule is not set
```

Use the **show ip ips all** command to display additional configuration data that is not displayed with the **show ip ips configuration** command.

In Example 6-4, the output from the **show ip ips all** command shows that syslog and SDEE notification is enabled, and that there are 693 active signatures and 1443 inactive signatures on the router.

Example 6-4 *show ip ips all Command Output*

```
Router# show ip ips all
IPS Signature File Configuration Status
    Configured Config Locations: flash:ipsstore/
    Last signature default load time: 00:25:35 UTC Dec 6 2007
    Last signature delta load time: -none-
    Last event action (SEAP) load time: -none-

    General SEAP Config:
    Global Deny Timeout: 3600 seconds
    Global Overrides Status: Enabled
    Global Filters Status: Enabled

IPS Auto Update is not currently configured

IPS Syslog and SDEE Notification Status
    Event notification through syslog is enabled
    Event notification through SDEE is enabled

IPS Signature Status
    Total Active Signatures: 693
    Total Inactive Signatures: 1443

IPS Packet Scanning and Interface Status
    IPS Rule Configuration
      IPS name myips
    IPS fail closed is disabled
    IPS deny-action ips-interface is false
    Fastpath ips is enabled
    Quick run mode is enabled
    Interface Configuration
      Interface FastEthernet0/1
        Inbound IPS rule is not set
        Outgoing IPS rule is myips

IPS Category CLI is not configured

IPS Category CLI is not configured
```

Summary

This chapter described how intrusion detection system (IDS) and intrusion prevention system (IPS) technology embedded in Cisco host- and network-based IDS and IPS solutions fight Internet worms and viruses in real time. More precisely, you have learned how

- A signature is a set of rules that an IDS and an IPS use to detect typical intrusive activity.

- To use Cisco SDM to configure Cisco IOS IPS on the router or security device, choose **Configure > Intrusion Prevention > Create IPS** in Cisco SDM and click the **Launch IPS Rule Wizard** button.

- Cisco IOS IPS combines existing Cisco IDS and IPS product features.

- To configure Cisco IOS IPS on the router or security device, click the **Launch IPS Rule Wizard** button in Cisco SDM.

- Cisco IOS IPS prevents intrusion by comparing traffic against the signatures of known attacks.

- Cisco IOS IPS alarms are communicated using SDEE and syslog.

- The command **show ip ips all** displays all the available IPS information.

References

For additional information, refer to these resources:

Cisco Systems, Inc. *Cisco Intrusion Prevention System: Introduction*, http://www.cisco.com/go/ips

Cisco Systems, Inc. *Cisco Security Monitoring, Analysis and Response System: Introduction*, http://www.cisco.com/go/mars

Cisco Systems, Inc. *Cisco Security Agent: Introduction*, http://www.cisco.com/go/csa

Cisco Systems, Inc. Cisco Intrusion Detection System Event Viewer 3DES Cryptographic Software Download, http://www.cisco.com/cgi-bin/tablebuild.pl/ids-ev

Cisco Systems, Inc. *Cisco IOS Intrusion Prevention System (IPS): Cisco IOS IPS Supported Signature List in 4.x Signature Format*, http://www.cisco.com/en/US/partner/products/ps6634/products_white_paper0900aecd8039e2e4.shtml

Cisco Systems, Inc. Software Download: Cisco IOS IPS, http://www.cisco.com/cgi-bin/tablebuild.pl/ios-sigup

Cisco Systems, Inc. Software Download: Cisco IDS Management Center - Version *4.x* Signature Updates, http://www.cisco.com/cgi-bin/tablebuild.pl/idsmc-ids4-sigup

Cisco Systems, Inc. *Cisco IOS Security Configuration Guide, Release 12.4: Configuring Cisco IOS Intrusion Prevention System* (IPS), http://tinyurl.com/3ufo6j

Cisco System, Inc. Tools & Resources: Software Download, Cisco IOS IPS Signature Package for SDM 2.4, http://www.cisco.com/cgi-bin/tablebuild.pl/ios-v5sigup-sdm

Cisco System, Inc. Cisco Security Center, http://tools.cisco.com/security/center/home.x

Cisco Systems, Inc. *Cisco IOS Security Configuration Guide, Release 12.4: Configuring Cisco IOS Intrusion Prevention System (IPS)*, http://www.cisco.com/en/US/products/ps6350/products_configuration_guide_chapter09186a00804453cf.html

SearchSecurity.com. http://searchsecurity.techtarget.com/

Review Questions

Use the questions here to review what you learned in this chapter. The correct answers are found in the Appendix, "Answers to Chapter Review Questions."

1. Which two modes of IPS operations are currently available with Cisco IDS and IPS solutions? Select all that apply.

    a. Out-of-band

    b. Promiscuous

    c. Multicasting

    d. Inline

2. Which device cannot be an IDS or IPS sensor?

    a. A Cisco router configured with IPS software

    b. A Cisco VPN concentrator configured with IPS software

    c. An appliance specifically designed to provide dedicated IDS or IPS services

    d. A IDS/IPS network module installed in a Cisco ASA or in a switch or in a router

3. Which general patterns of misuse do IDS and IPS technologies look for? (Choose all that apply.)

    a. Atomic pattern

    b. Molecular pattern

    c. Intrusive nonces

    d. Composite pattern

    e. Composition pattern

4. Which of the following is not a type of IDS or IPS sensor?

    a. Signature based

    b. Policy based

    c. Transgression based

    d. Anomaly based

    e. Honeypot based

5. What are signature engines?

    a. A set of rules that an IDS and an IPS use to detect typical intrusive activity

    b. A full-feature intrusion prevention located in the core network fabric device

    c. An internal security service module that provides dedicated CPU and memory to offload intrusion prevention processing.

    d. A component of an IDS and IPS sensor that supports a group of signatures that are in a common category

6. Reorder the steps taken by a host-based IPS.

    a. HIPS checks the call against the policy.

    b. An application calls for system resources.

    c. Requests are allowed or denied.

7. Which of the following are advantages of a network-based IPS?

    a. Cost-effective

    b. Provides application-level encryption protection

    c. Is host specific

    d. Analyzes lower-level network events

    e. Not visible on the network

8. Which IPS card could integrate into a Cisco 1841?

    a. Cisco IDSM-2

    b. Cisco ASA AIP SSM

    c. Cisco IPS AIM

    d. Cisco IPS 4200 series sensor

9. What is an IPS signature?

    a. A message digest encrypted with the sender's private key

    b. A set of rules used to detect typical intrusive activity

    c. A binary pattern specific to a virus

    d. An appliance that provides anti-x services

10. Compiling a regular expression found in a signature requires more memory than the final storage of the regular expression. True or False?

    a. True

    b. False

This chapter focuses on several additional aspects of network security: LAN, storage-area network (SAN), voice, and endpoints. This chapter emphasizes Layer 2 and host security to provide a much more comprehensive coverage of the important issues involved in securing an enterprise. Topics covered in this chapter include the following:

- Current endpoint protection methods, such as HIPS, integrity checkers, operating system protection, and the Cisco NAC Appliance

- Risks and countermeasures for SAN security

- Risks and countermeasures to IP telephony

- Layer 2 attacks against network topologies and protocols

CHAPTER 7

LAN, SAN, Voice, and Endpoint Security Overview

The term *endpoint* is used in a variety of ways in different contexts. For this chapter, an endpoint is considered an individual computer system or device that acts as a network client. Common endpoints are laptops, desktops, and personal computing devices, such as personal digital assistants (PDA). In addition, servers can be considered endpoints.

Hidden Endpoints

When we think of endpoints, we tend to think about those visible devices, such as workstations, laptops, servers. However, as network security professionals, we should also think about those hidden endpoints such as printers, and the security concerns they pose.

Who thinks about the consequences of changing the IP address of a networked printer to that of the default gateway would have on the network?

Read the article titled *Hidden Endpoints: Mitigating the Threat of Non-Traditional Network Devices* at http://www.searchsecurity.com if you want to learn more about the security of hidden endpoints.

Examining Endpoint Security

The Cisco strategy for addressing host security, and therefore network and enterprise security, is based on three broad elements:

- **Endpoint protection:** New behavior-based technology is available with Cisco Security Agent that protects endpoints against threats that are posed by viruses, Trojan horses, and worms.

- **Cisco Network Admission Control (NAC):** The Cisco NAC solution ensures that every endpoint complies with network security policies before being granted access to the network. Cisco NAC provides access to compliant devices, and ensures that noncompliant devices are denied access, placed in quarantine, or given restricted access to resources.

■ **Network infection containment:** To address the newest attack methods that can compromise your network, containment focuses on automating key elements of the infection response process. The Cisco Self-Defending Network (SDN) elements of the Cisco NAC, Cisco Security Agent, and intrusion prevention system (IPS) provide this service.

An endpoint security strategy is necessary because software has historically had weaknesses. Secure (trustworthy) software is designed to protect data and withstand attack attempts. Historically, "secure" software has been used only with the military and in critical commercial systems. Generally, this type of software is custom software.

You can make software more trusted by hardening it. Hardening is often done, but requires documentation of the internal software components, which is not commonly provided by vendors.

> **What Is *Hardening*?**
> System hardening refers to the steps a network administrator takes to minimize security vulnerabilities that might be inherent to a system. System hardening includes installing patches, closing unneeded ports, and removing nonessential software. Hardening might also involve tweaking particular software, such as on a FTP server, allowing only "blind FTP," where a user can upload to a folder but cannot download. Only the administrator can read the content of the upload folder. This protects against users just "parking" their files on an FTP server to later come and retrieve them.

There are two main areas of focus for secure software:

■ Security of operating systems

■ Security of applications that run inside an operating system

Operating System Vulnerabilities

Operating systems provide basic security services to applications:

■ Trusted code and trusted path ensure that the integrity of the operating system code base is not violated, and provide the user with a way of using the system that bypasses any possible Trojan horse's fake trusted path.
  Trusted code refers to the assurance that the operating system code is not compromised. An operating system might provide integrity checking of all running code by using Hashed Message Authentication Code (HMAC) or digital signatures. Also, integrity verification of add-on software might be necessary at installation. Digital signatures could be used here, too.
  Trusted path refers to a facility that assures that the user is using a genuine system and not a Trojan horse. The trusted path mechanism guarantees that data entered by a user is protected from unauthorized programs. A prime example of a trusted path is the Ctrl-Alt-Del key sequence for logging in to Windows NT, Windows 2000, and Windows XP, which is called *secure attention sequence*. This sequence is guaranteed to take you to the genuine password prompt and thus bypasses *fake* logging prompt.

■ Privileged context of execution provides some identity authentication and certain privileges based on the identity of the user, such as the rights being set differently if you log as *guest* or as *administrator* on a Windows workstation.

- Process memory protection and isolation provides separation from other users and their data.

- Access control to resources ensures confidentiality and integrity of data.

An attacker can subvert all of these services. If either trusted code or a trusted path is not present or is compromised, the operating system and all applications can be easily subverted by hostile code. In addition, an operating system might be made more vulnerable if there is a need to provide support for legacy protocols.

Modern operating systems provide each process with an identity and privileges. Privilege switching is possible during program operation or during a single logon session. For instance, UNIX has the **suid** (**set-UID**) facility, and Windows has the **runas** utility.

Using *runas*

Catching malware could be the result of doing a simple task on a system where one has elevated privileges, such as web browsing while being logged in as administrator on a server. Using the **runas** option in Windows XP can be used to protect against the problem described in the preceding paragraph. By right-clicking the application and selecting **runas**, you could select an alternative account with less privilege to run an application.

The following techniques help protect an endpoint from operating system vulnerabilities:

- **Least privilege concept:** Ideally, to better protect the endpoint, the least privilege concept should be followed; a process should never be given more privilege than is necessary to perform a job. In real life, this concept is usually not honored, which is a source of many vulnerabilities.

- **Isolation between processes:** An operating system should provide isolation between processes. This isolation can be virtual or physical. For instance, memory protection can be done in hardware. Some trusted operating systems provide isolation via "logical execution compartments." This *logical execution compartment* is best experienced nowadays when a program hangs and you can terminate only that one application. In the past, with older operating systems that were not enforcing process isolation, if one application was hanging, the operating system was also hanging.

- **Reference monitor:** A reference monitor is an access control concept that refers to a mechanism or process that mediates all access to objects. The reference monitor provides a central point for all policy decisions. A reference monitor typically implements auditing functions to keep track of access. In addition to the reference monitor that typically exits in an operating system, Cisco Security Agent functions essentially as a reference monitor.

- **Small verifiable pieces of code:** For all security functionality, the idea is to have small, easily verifiable pieces of software that are managed and monitored by a reference monitor.

Note: The Cisco NAC solution and Cisco Security Agent combine to provide protection against operating system vulnerabilities.

Application Vulnerabilities

Most attacks target applications, or the data they are protecting, or both. Attacks can be one of the following two types:

- **Direct:** In a direct attack, the attacker fools the application into performing a task with the privileges of the application.

- **Indirect:** In an indirect attack, the attacker first compromises another subsystem and attacks the application through the compromised subsystem (privilege escalation).

The more privileges the application has, the more damage it can do to its sensitive data and the whole host system.

Note: Cisco Security Agent prevents both types of attacks, direct and indirect.

The ultimate target of an attacker is often an application running on a host that processes sensitive data the attacker wants to obtain. When an attacker has the option of communicating directly with the application hosting sensitive data, the application must be suitably protected against this potential threat. Attackers seek to obtain permissions to read or write to sensitive data, thereby compromising confidentiality and integrity; they might want to cause a denial-of-service (DoS) attack in a specific application.

An attacker may attack an application directly by finding a flaw in the application and by-passing its access controls to obtain read or write access to sensitive data. The complexity of current applications makes such flaws common. In addition, secure development is too costly or not feasible for many businesses.

In another scenario, an attacker gains access to sensitive data through a chain of compromises of other system components. For example, an attacker first obtains basic user-level access to the system on which the sensitive data resides. Then, by exploiting a flaw in any local application, the attacker attains system administration privileges (known as privilege escalation). Using these privileges, the attacker might be able to read or write to most objects on the system, including sensitive data of the target application.

Buffer Overflows

An application must carefully verify user application input. The input might contain improperly formatted data, control sequences, or too much data.

Buffer Overflow Definition
"Buffer overflow vulnerabilities are based on an attacker sending more data to a vulnerable program than the original software developer planned for when writing the code for the program" is the definition given by Ed Skoudis in a great security book titled *Counter Hack Reloaded*, Second Edition (Prentice Hall, 2006).
Another excellent source of reference is *Penetration Testing and Network Defense*, by Newman and Whitaker (Cisco Press, 2005).

Buffer overflows are a common exploitation method that try to overwrite memory on an application stack by supplying too much data into an input buffer. Initially, it is not easy to discover how to initiate a buffer flow and use it to exploit a system, but once found, attackers can prepackage exploit code for widespread use by script kiddies who use easy-to-find and easy-to-use hacking tools.

A buffer overflow is an anomalous condition in which a program writes data beyond the allocated end of a buffer in memory. Buffer overflows usually arise from a bug and the improper use of languages such as C or C++ that are not memory safe. One consequence of the overflow is the overwriting of valid data.

Buffer overflows are a commonly exploited computer security risk. Because program control data often sits in the memory areas adjacent to data buffers, executing a buffer overflow condition can make the computer execute arbitrary (and potentially malicious) code that is fed back to the program as data.

A variant of a buffer overflow is a heap overflow. The heap is a stack that is dynamically allocated by the application at runtime and typically contains program data.

Figure 7-1 shows a basic and generic representation of memory address space.

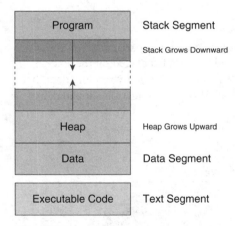

Figure 7-1 *Memory Address Space*

Note: Cisco Security Agent prevents buffer overflows by intercepting application programming interface (API) calls to the operating system kernel and rejecting any such call that could interfere with the proper functioning of the operating system.

Buffer overflows are perhaps the most common method of application subversion on the Internet today.

Basics of a Typical Buffer-Overflow Exploit

An attacker tries to subvert a program function that reads input and calls a subroutine. The exploitable program function does not perform input length checks and allocates a fixed amount of memory for data, as shown in Figure 7-2.

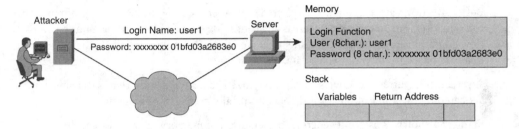

Figure 7-2 *Buffer Overflow: Preparation*

When an application makes a subroutine call, it places all input parameters on the stack. To return from the subroutine, the return address is also placed on the stack by the calling function. An attacker can overwrite the return address by sending data that is longer than the fixed memory space on the stack that the application allocated, as shown in Figure 7-3.

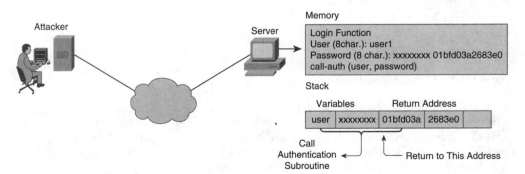

Figure 7-3 *Buffer Overflow: Attack*

Because of this overwrite, the application returns to an attacker-supplied address, pointing to the malicious code of the attacker, as shown in Figure 7-4. This code is also supplied as part of the overly long input. Arbitrary code can therefore be executed with the privileges of the application.

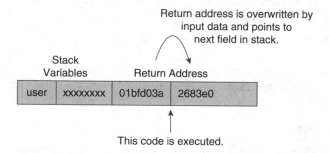

Figure 7-4 *Buffer Overflow: Outcome*

Types of Buffer Overflows

Buffer overflows are mostly used to *root* a system by executing arbitrary codes or to cause a DoS attack. Rooting a system is most easily accomplished with either remote root or local root buffer overflows. Remote root buffer overflows are the more dangerous of the two because if your system is vulnerable, an attacker can "own" it in a matter of seconds. The most dangerous worm attacks have exploited remote root buffer overflows.

Note: "Rooting a system" involves hacking a system so that the attacker has root, or superuser, privileges.

Note: The most common tool used for rooting a system are rootkits, which come in two categories:

- **Application-mode rootkits:** Separate applications on a system, which are therefore more easily detectable

- **User-mode rootkits:** An altered part of the existing kernel and therefore don't run as a separate application that could be detected by host-based security software

Local root buffer overflows usually require some assistance in distributing the exploit in the form of a virus that is transported by email or possibly a Trojan horse–infected executable.

Note: A majority of the software vulnerabilities that are discovered are buffer overflows. Reports suggest that two out of every three software vulnerabilities that are identified by Computer Emergency Response Team (CERT) are buffer overflows.

Buffer overflows are usually the primary conduit through which viruses, worms, and Trojan horses do their damage. For example, the most serious worms, such as SQL Slammer and Code Red, exploit remote root buffer overflows. On the other hand, viruses tend to take advantage of local root buffer overflows. Increasingly, Trojan horses tend to resemble viruses by exploiting local root buffer overflows.

Worms

Worms are a particularly dangerous type of hostile code. They replicate themselves over networks by independently exploiting vulnerabilities. Worms usually do not require user participation and can spread extremely fast.

Major components of a worm attack are

- **Vulnerability:** A worm installs itself using an exploit vector (email attachment, Trojan horse, or remote root buffer overflow) on a vulnerable system.

- **Payload:** Once the device is infected with a worm, the attacker has access to the host, and it is usually a privileged access. Attackers can also use a local exploit to escalate their privilege level.

- **Propagation mechanism:** After gaining access to a device, the worm replicates itself and chooses new targets.

Usually, worms are self-contained programs that attack a system attempting to exploit vulnerability. Upon successful exploitation, the worm copies itself from the attacking host to the newly exploited system and the cycle begins again.

Viruses

Viruses are pieces of malicious code that piggyback on legitimate programs or content. They usually replicate by attaching themselves to other software. Viruses usually require end-user activation and can lay dormant for an extended period and then activate at a specific time or date. They can be destructive or harmless (benign). They can be programmed to mutate to avoid detection (polymorphism).

The virus code is attached to some executable by the creator (for example, a freeware game). Somehow, that executable circulates to other computers (for example, by USB flash drive or email attachment) or to a file downloaded from an FTP site. When a victim runs the infected executable, the virus is loaded into memory and can now infect other executables on that computer.

A simple virus might install itself at the first line of code of the executable, such that starting the executable jumps right to the code for the virus. The virus might first check the disk for executables it has not yet infected and then infect them. Then, it might do any number of things ranging from harmless (displaying a picture to the screen) to subtly modifying files on the disk.

Trojan Horses

A Trojan horse is a program that appears to be normal and useful, but which contains hidden, malicious code that exploits the privileges of the user that runs it. Games are often trojanized in this manner. When running the game, the game works, but in the background, the Trojan horse has been installed on the victim system and continues running after the game has been closed.

The Trojan horse concept is flexible:

■ A Trojan horse might cause immediate damage.

■ A Trojan horse might provide remote access to the system (a back door).

■ A Trojan horse might perform actions as instructed remotely, such as "send me the password file once per week."

Custom-written Trojan horses (for example, Trojan horses with a specific target) are hard to automatically detect.

Tip: Cisco Security Agent is very effective at defeating viruses, worms, and Trojan horses.

Phases of a Generic Attacks

The following is an explanation of the generic phases found in most attacks:

1. **Probe phase:** This phase identifies vulnerable targets. The goal of this phase is to find computers that can be subverted. Internet Control Message Protocol (ICMP) ping scans map networks, and scans and identifies operating systems and vulnerable software. Hackers can obtain passwords using social engineering, dictionary attack, brute-force attack, or network sniffing.

2. **Penetrate phase:** Exploit code is transferred to the vulnerable target in this phase. The goal of this phase is to get the target to execute the exploit code through an attack vector, such as a buffer overflow, ActiveX, or Common Gateway Interface (CGI) vulnerability, or an email virus.

3. **Persist phase:** After the attack is successfully launched in memory, its code tries to persist on the target system. The goal of this phase is to ensure that the attacker code is running and available to the attacker even if the system reboots. This ability is achieved by modifying system files, making Registry changes, and installing new code.

4. **Propagate phase:** Next, the attacker attempts to extend the attack to other targets. This phase looks for vulnerable neighboring machines. Propagation vectors include emailing copies of the attack to other systems and uploading files to other systems using file shares or FTP services, active web connections, and file transfers through Internet Relay Chat (IRC).

5. **Paralyze phase:** During this phase, actual damage is done to the system. Files can be erased, systems can crash, information can be stolen, and distributed DoS (DDoS) attacks can be launched.

Notable Worm and Virus Attacks

Table 7-1 lists a cross-reference of worm and virus attacks over the past 20 years, with some of the differences in how they accomplished the various phases of attack used by hackers. Note how often similar methods are used.

Table 7-1   *Worms and Viruses: The Past 20 Years*

	Morris	Love Bug	Code Red	Slammer	MyDoom	Zotob	MS RPC DNS 0Day	Koobface
Year	1988	2000	2001	2003	2004	2005	2007	2008
Probe Phase	Scan for Finger daemon (fingerd)	N/A	Scan for MS IIS server	N/A	N/A	Scan for MS directory services	Scan or endpoint Mapper query	N/A
Penetrate Phase	Buffer overflow in fingerd	Arrive as email attachment	Buffer overflow in IIS	Buffer overflow in SQL and MSDE	Arrive as email attachment	Buffer overflow in UpNp service	Buffer overflow in RPC service	Caught on a social networking site
Persist Phase	Execute script to download code	Create executables and edit Registry	Execute script to download code	N/A	Create executables and edit Registry	Create executables and edit Registry, download code	Execute payload to download code	Copy and execute self and edit Registry
Propagate Phase	Look for addresses and spread to new victim	Open address book and email copies	Pick new addresses and spread to new victim	Pick new addresses and spread to new victim	Open address book and email copies	Start FTP and TFTP services, look for addresses, and spread to new victim	Look for addresses and spread to new victim	Add links pointing to malicious sites to social networking sites
Paralyze Phase	Lots of processes slow system	Worm spreads	Lots of threads slow system	Lots of packets slow network	Worm spreads	Delete Registry keys and files, terminate processes	Worm spreads	Worm spreads

IronPort

Cisco IronPort security appliances, shown in Figure 7-5, protect enterprises against Internet threats, with a focus on email and web security products, which are two of the main sources of endpoint threats.

Figure 7-5   *IronPort: Email and Web Security Appliances*

The following are the three major security appliance products that IronPort offers:

■ **IronPort C-series:** Email security appliances

■ **IronPort S-series:** Web security appliance

■ **IronPort M-series:** Security management appliance

IronPort SenderBase

At the heart of IronPort's success is IronPort SenderBase (http://www.senderbase.org). SenderBase is the first and largest email traffic monitoring service. SenderBase collects data from more than 100,000 Internet service providers (ISP), universities, and corporations around the world. SenderBase measures more than 120 different parameters for any email server on the Internet. This massive database receives more than five billion queries per day, with real-time data streaming in from every continent, from both small and large network providers. SenderBase has the most accurate view of the sending patterns of any given mail sender because of the size of the database, and conversely the database has remained the largest in the world because of the accuracy of the data. IronPort licenses SenderBase data to the open-source community and other institutions that are participating in the fight against spam.

IronPort C-Series: Email Security Appliances

The IronPort C-series email security appliances are in production at 8 of the 10 largest ISPs and more than 20 percent of the largest enterprises in the world. These systems have a demonstrated record of unparalleled security and reliability. The same code base that powers the largest customers of IronPort is available in all the IronPort email security appliances, to protect the email systems of enterprises of all sizes. By reducing the downtime associated with spam, viruses, and a wide variety of other threats, these products enable the administration of corporate mail systems and reduce the burden on technical staff. IronPort email security appliances support and protect your email systems—not only from the threats of today, but also from those certain to evolve in the future.

The C-series is an all-inclusive Mail Transfer Agent (MTA) that provides the following services:

- Antispam
- Antivirus
- Policy enforcement
- Mail routing

Figure 7-6 shows a before and after network topology using IronPort C-series.

Note: The C-series has interesting features such as its Multidimension Pattern Recognition (MPR), which lets it detects image-based spam, by looking diligently for "polka dots." Image-based spam typically has impurity in the form of dots in the image. MPR breaks down images in subparts and hunts for those polka-dot patterns to identify previously documented image-based spam messages. Techniques such as MPR make IronPort email security appliances the most sophisticated systems available today.

IronPort S-Series: Web Security Appliances

The IronPort S-series is the fastest web security appliance in the industry. Spyware has quickly evolved to become one of the most significant corporate security issues. More than 80 percent of corporate PCs are infected with spyware, yet less than 10 percent of corporations have deployed perimeter spyware defenses. The speed, variety, and maliciousness of spyware and web-based malware attacks have highlighted the importance of a robust, secure platform to protect the enterprise network perimeter from such threats. The IronPort S-series appliances combine a high-performance security platform with the exclusive Web Reputation technology of IronPort and the breakthrough Dynamic Vectoring and Streaming (DVS) engine of IronPort, a new scanning technology that enables signature-based spyware filtering. Robust management and reporting tools deliver ease of administration and complete visibility into threat-related activity.

Figure 7-7 shows a before and after network topology using IronPort S-series.

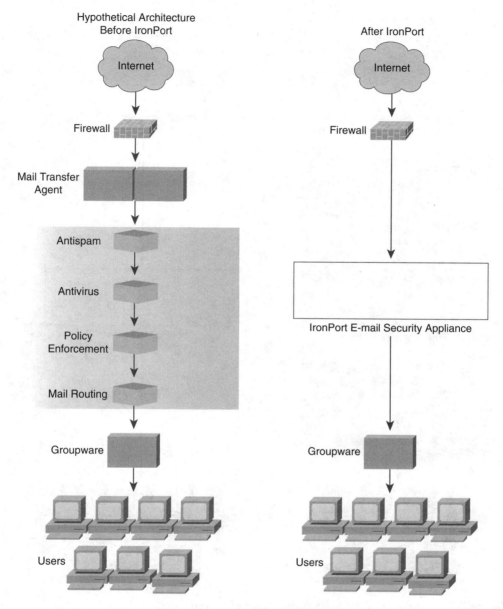

Figure 7-6   *IronPort Email Security Appliance: Before and After*

Note: IronPort multilayer security uses the following three stages to permit or deny Internet traffic:

1. It checks websites against a Web Reputation checklist and blocks infected sites.

2. It filters malicious content using the IronPort antimalware system.

3. It detects and blocks communication with outside host servers by using a Layer 4 traffic monitor.

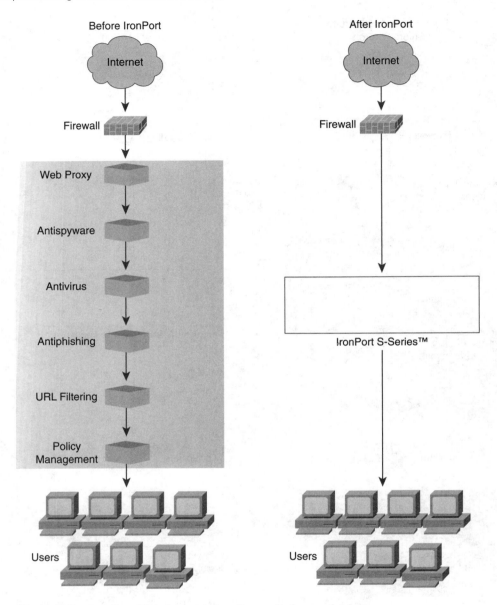

Figure 7-7   *IronPort Web Security Appliance: Before and After*

IronPort M-Series: Management for C and S Series

The IronPort M-series appliance acts as a centralized location for spam quarantine and centralized statistics, reporting and tracking for the C- and S-series of appliances.

Cisco NAC Products

The purpose of Cisco Network Access Control (NAC) is to allow only authorized and compliant systems (whether managed or unmanaged) to access the network and to enforce network security policy. In this way, Cisco NAC helps maintain network stability. NAC provides four key features:

- Authentication and authorization

- Posture assessment (evaluating an incoming device against the policies of the network)

- Quarantining of noncompliant systems

- Remediation of noncompliant systems

Cisco NAC products come in these general categories:

- **NAC framework:** The NAC framework uses the existing Cisco network infrastructure and third-party software to enforce security policy compliance on all endpoints. The NAC framework is a system that is suited for high-performance network environments with diverse endpoints. These environments require a consistent LAN, WAN, wireless, extranet, and remote-access solution that integrates into the existing security and patch software, tools, and processes. Different devices in the network, not necessarily one device, can provide the four key features of NAC.

- **Cisco NAC Appliance:** The Cisco NAC Appliance solution condenses the four key NAC functions into an appliance form and provides a turnkey solution to control network access. This solution is a natural fit for medium-scale networks that require a self-contained, turnkey solution. Cisco NAC Appliance is especially ideal for organizations that need simplified and integrated tracking of operating system and antivirus patches and vulnerability updates. Cisco NAC Appliance does not require a Cisco network.

Table 7-2 summarizes the differences between NAC framework and Cisco NAC Appliance.

Table 7-2   *NAC Framework Versus Cisco NAC Appliance*

NAC Framework	Cisco NAC Appliance
Software module embedded within NAC-enabled products, such as switches, routers, and so on	In-band or out-of-band Cisco NAC Appliance solution that can be used on any switch or router platform
Integrated framework leveraging multiple Cisco and NAC-aware vendor products	Self-contained turnkey solution

NAC Framework

Figure 7-8 displays components of a NAC framework that is used to provide compliance-based access control. NAC functions, including authentication, authorization, and accounting (AAA), scanning, and remediation, are performed by other Cisco products, such as a Cisco Secure Access Control Server (ACS), or partner products such as TrendMicro.

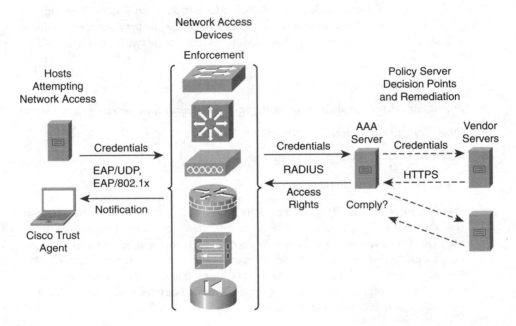

Figure 7-8 *NAC Framework*

QualysGuard, released by Qualys, a Cisco partner, can automatically audit hosts to determine their security position.

The goal of both the NAC framework and the Cisco NAC Appliance is to admit on to the network only those hosts that are authenticated and have had their security posture examined and approved. The net result of such a thorough examination before allowing connectivity is a tremendous reduction in total cost of ownership (TCO) because only known, secure machines are allowed to connect. Therefore, laptops that have been on the road for weeks and have possibly been infected or were unable to receive current security updates cannot connect into the network and unleash a DoS attack.

In Figure 7-8, the network devices function as the enforcement layer. They force the clients to authenticate and then query a RADIUS server for authentication and authorization. The RADIUS server can query other devices, such as a TrendMicro antivirus server, and reply to the network enforcers. If everything is up to standard, the host is identified and admitted to the network.

Cisco NAC Appliance: Components

The Cisco NAC Appliance consolidates all the functions of the NAC framework into a single network appliance fulfilling all the same roles. The following are the major components of the Cisco NAC Appliance and the tasks they accomplish:

- **Cisco NAC Appliance Server (NAS):** Cisco NAS is a device that is used to perform network access control. This security enforcement device is implemented at the network level. It can be implemented in-band or out-of-band, in Layers 2 or Layer 3, as a virtual gateway or as a real IP gateway, and it can be deployed centrally or around the globe. The Cisco NAS performs device compliance checks as users attempt to access the network.

- **Cisco NAC Appliance Manager (NAM):** Cisco NAM is a centralized administrative interface that is used by technical support personnel. The Cisco NAM provides a web-based interface for creating security policies and managing online users. It can also act as an authentication proxy to authentication servers on the back end. Administrators can use it to establish user roles, compliance checks, and remediation requirements. The Cisco NAM communicates with, and manages, the Cisco NAS, which is the enforcement component of the Cisco NAC Appliance.

- **Cisco NAC Appliance Agent (NAA):** Cisco NAA is client software that facilitates network admission. This lightweight, read-only agent runs on an endpoint machine. It performs a deep inspection of the security profile of a local machine by analyzing Registry settings, services, and files. Through this inspection, it can determine whether a device has a required hotfix; and can then run the correct antivirus software version and other security software, such as Cisco Security Agents. For unmanaged assets, the Cisco NAA can be downloaded as needed.

- **Ruleset updates:** Automatic updates are used to keep the security level high by always providing the latest virus updates, software patches, and so on, for quarantined hosts.

The Cisco NAC Appliance extends NAC to all network access methods, including access through LANs, remote-access gateways, and wireless access points. The Cisco NAC Appliance also supports posture assessment for guest users.

Cisco NAC Appliance provides the following benefits:

- It recognizes users, their devices, and their roles in the network. This occurs at the point of authentication, before malicious code can cause damage.

- It evaluates whether machines are compliant with security policies. Security policies can include specific antivirus or antispyware software, operating system updates, or patches. The Cisco NAC Appliance supports policies that vary by user type, device type, or operating system.

- It enforces security policies by blocking and isolating noncompliant machines. A network administrator will be advised of the noncompliance and will proceed to repair the host.

Noncompliant machines are redirected into a quarantine area, where remediation occurs at the discretion of the administrator.

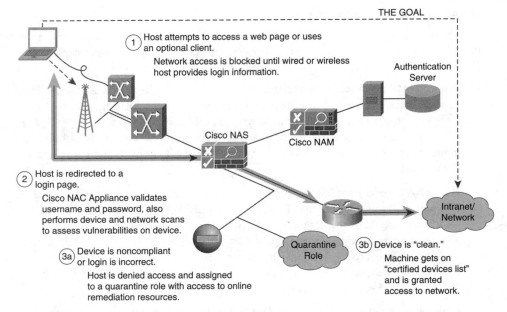

Figure 7-9   *Cisco NAC Appliance Process Flow*

Figure 7-9 illustrates the Cisco NAC Appliance process:

1. The user attempts to access a network resource.

2. The user is redirected to a login page.

3. The host is authenticated and optionally scanned for posture compliance.
   a.   If not compliant, the host is quarantined to a VLAN where the host can be patched and become compliant.
   b.   If compliant, the host is granted access to the network.

The Cisco NAA is the software interface that users sees when they interact with the Cisco NAC Appliance. Figure 7-10 shows the three windows that a user sees.

1. The first window the user sees is the initial logon window, where the user enters the username and password, and the system is scanned for compliance.

2. If the scan fails, the user is granted temporary access and will see the You Have Temporary Access window.

3. If remediation is available, the Please Download and Install the Required Software window is presented, inviting the user to install the necessary software to become compliant.

Cisco Security Agent

Cisco Security Agent, a host intrusion prevention system (HIPS) product, is software that provides endpoint security by providing threat protection capabilities for server, desktop, and point-of-service computing systems. Because a single management console can support up to 100,000 agents, it is a highly scalable solution.

Login Screen

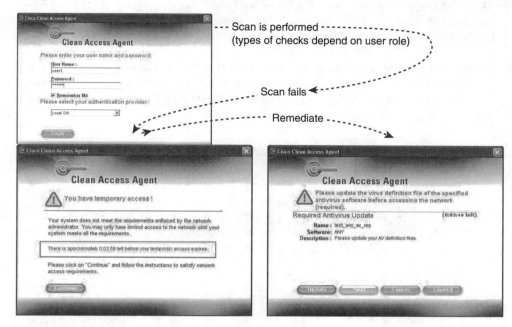

Figure 7-10   *Cisco NAC Appliance: Process Flow*

Figure 7-11   *Cisco Security Agent Architecture*

The Cisco Security Agent architecture model consists of two components, as shown in Figure 7-11:

- **Management Center for Cisco Security Agents:** Management Center for Cisco Security Agent enables you to divide network hosts into groups by function and security requirements, and then configure security policies for those groups. Management Center for Cisco Security Agent can maintain a log of security violations and send alerts by email or pager.

- **Cisco Security Agent:** The Cisco Security Agent component is installed on the host system and continuously monitors local system activity and analyzes the operations of that system. Cisco Security Agent takes proactive action to block attempted malicious activity and polls the Management Center for Cisco Security Agent at configurable intervals for policy updates. Obviously, the Management Center should also run CSA.

Tip: You can configure an administration workstation to securely connect to the Management Center for Cisco Security Agent by using a Secure Sockets Layer (SSL)–enabled web interface.

When an application needs access to system resources, it makes an operating system call to the kernel. Cisco Security Agent intercepts these operating system calls and compares them with the cached security policy, as shown in Figure 7-12. If the request does not violate the policy, it is passed to the kernel for execution.

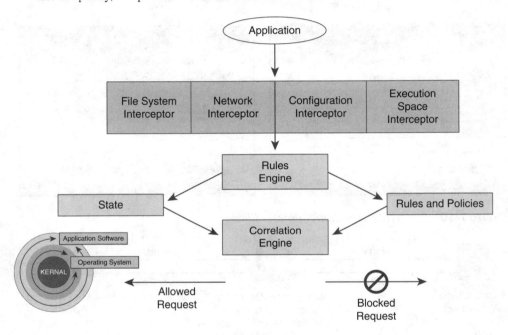

Figure 7-12   *Application, Kernel, and Interceptors*

If the request violates the security policy, Cisco Security Agent blocks the request and takes the following actions:

■   An appropriate error message is passed back to the application.

■   An alert is generated and sent to the Management Center for Cisco Security Agent.

Cisco Security Agent correlates this particular operating system call with the other calls made by that application or process, and correlates these events to detect malicious activity.

Cisco Security Agent provides protection through the deployment of four interceptors:

■   **File system interceptor:** All file read or write requests are intercepted and allowed, or denied, based on the security policy.

■   **Network interceptor:** Network driver interface specification (NDIS) changes are controlled and network connections are cleared through the security policy. The number of network connections that are allowed within a specified time can also be limited to prevent DoS attacks.

- **Configuration interceptor:** Read/write requests to the Registry in Windows or to *rc* configuration files on UNIX are intercepted. This interception occurs because modification of the operating system configuration can have serious consequences. Therefore, Cisco Security Agent tightly controls read/write requests to the Registry.

- **Execution space interceptor:** This interceptor maintains the integrity of the dynamic runtime environment of each application by detecting and blocking write requests to memory that is not owned by the requesting application. Attempts by one application to inject code, such as a shared library or dynamic link library (DLL) into another are also detected and blocked. The interceptor also detects buffer-overflow attacks. This results in maintaining the integrity of dynamic resources, such as the file system and configuration of web services. In addition, the integrity of highly dynamic resources, such as memory and network I/O, is preserved.

Cisco Security Agent Interceptors

By intercepting communication between applications and the underlying system, Cisco Security Agent combines the functionality of the following traditional security approaches:

- **Distributed firewall:** The network interceptor performs the functions of a host firewall.

- **HIPS:** The network interceptor teams with the execution space interceptor to provide the alerting capability of a HIPS, with the proactive enforcement of a security policy.

- **Application sandbox:** An application sandbox is an execution space in which you can run suspect programs with less-than-normal access to system resources. This security service is provided by a combination of file system, configuration, and execution space interceptors.

- **Network worm prevention:** The network and execution space interceptors provide worm prevention without a need for updates.

- **File-integrity monitor:** The file system and the configuration interceptors act as a file-integrity monitor.

Table 7-3 summarizes the Cisco Security Agent interceptors.

Table 7-3   *Cisco Security Agent Interceptors*

Security Application	Network Interceptor	File System Interceptor	Configuration Interceptor	Execution Space Interceptor
Distributed firewall	✓			
Host intrusion detection	✓			✓
Application sandbox	✓			✓
File-integrity monitor		✓	✓	

The default policies on Cisco Security Agent implement all of these security features. Customers can easily create or change policies; however, the default policies instantly provide all of these protections.

Cisco Security Agent Attack Response

Malicious attacks come in thousands of varieties, and new attacks are constantly being devised to exploit newly discovered vulnerabilities.

An analysis of the logical progression of an attack helps illustrate how almost every attack intends to gain control of core mechanisms in the target system. Table 7-4 provides an overview of the different phases of attacks. Significant differences exist between the attack mechanisms used in the probe and penetrate phases compared to the attack mechanisms used in the persist phase.

Table 7-4   *Malicious Behavior Identified and Stopped by CSA Classified by Attack Phases*

Attack Phase	Attack Actions
Probe	Ping scans
	Port scans
Penetrate	Transfer exploit code to target
Persist	Install new code
	Modify configuration
Propagate	Attack other targets
Paralyze	Erase files
	Crash system
	Steal data

The first two stages change continuously, with new vulnerabilities being discovered and custom exploits being created almost every day. Combating attacks at the probe and penetrate phases requires constant updating of malicious IPS signatures and firewall defenses as these attacks evolve. Attacks at these early phases also lend themselves to evasion techniques, such as Unicode encoding of web strings or overlapping packet fragments. The mutability of attacks at the penetrate stage requires a significant amount of interpretation, because false alarms that require time-consuming review by a security administrator can be generated.

In contrast, attack mechanisms in the persist phase and the later phases are comparatively stable. The malicious activities of an attacker are limited, and an attack involves making a system call to the kernel to access the system resources. The malicious code can attempt to modify the operating system, modify files, create or alter network connections, or violate the memory space of active processes. The list of potential attacks on system resources has remained stable. These attacks use different vectors to access the target systems.

Because consistently identifying attacks in their early phases is nearly impossible, Cisco Security Agent focuses on providing proactive security by controlling access to system resources. This approach avoids the need for updating defenses to keep up with the latest attack and protects hosts from a new attack. For example, the Nimda and Slammer worms caused millions of dollars of damage to enterprises on the first day of their appearance, before updates were available; but Cisco Security Agent stopped these attacks by identifying their malicious behavior without any updates.

Endpoint Security Best Practices

Trusted operating systems exist, but are expensive and can be cumbersome to support. Their appropriate use would be for critical servers or workstations. Although there has been some progress in the past 10 years, the default configuration of a typical modern operating system is still quite untrustworthy. Operating system hardening should be considered mandatory for use in sensitive environments. A hardened system resists an attacker when alternate paths to sensitive data are attempted.

Network access controls (firewalls) should be used to limit the exposure of hosts. You should allow only necessary traffic to reach sensitive machines.

Security add-ons, such as integrity checkers, IPSs, and host firewalls, are recommended for systems that perform important services.

Design applications with security in mind from the start:

- Apply the least privilege principle.

- Use modularization and multiple tiers of application functionality, spread over multiple servers.

To manage host and application risks, use multiple protection methods together to form a multilayered security system. A multilayered security system does not rely on a single security mechanism to perform a function, because that mechanism might be compromised. Instead, different security mechanisms provide a similar protection function and back each other up. This applies universally to any security system and is considered good practice in a security design.

The following are application protection methods:

- Application access controls (enforcing least privilege) coupled with secure programming is the most significant cornerstones of application security. Secure development is typically expensive and slow. With the creation of safer high-level languages and the awareness of developers to security issues in programming, many current systems can provide high levels of application security. Most stock software still in use today by many businesses is vulnerable to simple attacks to defeat its security.

- Cryptography, if used properly, can provide confidentiality, integrity, and authenticity guarantees for data. Cryptographic methods often protect data when it is outside the control of the application, such as when the data on the disk drives is encrypted and can only be read by the application. More commonly, all data between the client and the server is encrypted, providing confidentiality over an unsafe network.

- Do not trust data from outside sources, and always perform strict input validation.

- Assume that users of the application may be malicious (which is not always the case).

Examining SAN Security

Storage-area networks (SAN) offer a solution to the increasing costs of network and server downtime. Because the main purpose of everything in network security is to secure data, now that data is residing on a SAN, it is essential that you secure the SAN.

Defining SANs

A SAN is a specialized network, as shown in Figure 7-13, that enables fast, reliable access among servers and external storage resources. In a SAN, a storage device is not the exclusive property of any one server. Rather, storage devices are shared among all networked servers as peer resources. Just as you can use a LAN to connect clients to servers, you can use a SAN to connect servers to storage resources, servers to each other, and storage resources to storage resources.

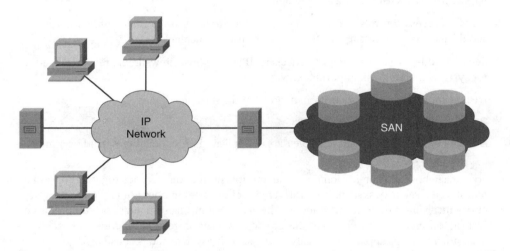

Figure 7-13   *A Enterprise Network with a SAN*

A SAN does not need to be a physically separate network; it can be a dedicated subnet that carries only business-critical I/O traffic between servers and storage devices. A SAN, for example, would not carry general-purpose traffic such as email or other end-user applications. It would be limited to I/O traffic, such as reading a file from a disk or writing a file to a disk.

By taking this type of network approach, you avoid the unacceptable compromise and performance reduction inherent in a single network for all applications.

Network and server downtime cost companies large sums of money in business and productivity losses. At the same time, the amount of information to be managed and stored is increasing dramatically every year.

eDiscovery: The Need for SAN

Electronic discovery has taken on new importance following the amendments to the Federal Rules of Civil Procedure that became effective December 1, 2006. The rules now stipulate that organizations must safe-keep electronic information, such as email, instant message dialogues, and so on, in case of civil litigation. Organizations must also keep the metadata related to the electronic information. Metadata includes the date the file was created, the author, date modified, and so on.

Keeping copies of electronic information for a certain number of year requires large storage infrastructures, contributing to the popularity of SANs.

SANs offer an answer to the increasing volume of data that must be stored in an enterprise network environment. They offer high-performance access without the burden of having to manage local attached storage. Implementation of a SAN enables users to offload storage traffic from the daily network operations and establish a direct connection between storage media and servers.

SAN Fundamentals

SANs are evolving rapidly in the enterprise infrastructure to meet three primary business requirements:

- Reduce capital and operating expenses

- Increase agility to support changing business priorities, application requirements, and revenue growth

- Improve long-distance replication, backup, and recovery to meet regulatory requirements and industry best practices

Cisco can help IT managers meet these requirements with an enterprisewide approach to deploying scalable, highly available, and more easily administered SANs.

Cisco solutions for intelligent SANs are an integral part of an enterprise data center architecture and provide a better way to access, manage, and protect growing information resources across a consolidated Fibre Channel, Fibre Channel over IP (FCIP), Internet Small Computer Systems Interface (iSCSI), Gigabit Ethernet, or optical network.

Most of the major SAN transport technologies are based on the Small Computer Systems Interface (SCSI) communications model. In many ways, a SAN can be described as the merging of SCSI and networking. The SCSI command protocol is the de facto standard that is used extensively in high-performance storage applications. The command part of SCSI can be transported over a Fibre Channel SAN or encapsulated in an IP packet and carried across IP networks.

There are three major SAN transport technologies:

- **Fibre Channel:** This technology is the primary SAN transport for host-to-SAN connectivity. Traditionally, SANs have required a separate dedicated infrastructure to interconnect hosts and storage systems. The primary transport protocol for this interconnection has been Fibre Channel. Fibre Channel networks primarily provide a serial transport for the SCSI protocol.

- **iSCSI:** This technology maps SCSI over TCP/IP and is another host-to-SAN connectivity model that is typically used in the LAN. The basic idea of iSCSI is to leverage an investment in existing IP networks to build and extend the SANs. This is accomplished by using the TCP/IP protocol to transport SCSI commands, data, and status between hosts or initiators and storage devices or targets, such as storage subsystems and tape devices.

- **FCIP:** FCIP is a popular SAN-to-SAN connectivity model that is often used over the WAN or metropolitan-area network (MAN). SAN designers can use the open-standard FCIP protocol to break the distance barrier of current Fibre Channel solutions and enable interconnection of SAN islands over extended distances.

In computer storage, a logical unit number (LUN) is an address for an individual disk drive and, by extension, the disk device itself. The term is used in the SCSI protocol as a way to differentiate individual disk drives within a common SCSI target device, such as a disk array.

Key Topic

Hosts need a LUN to access a disk.

LUN masking is an authorization process that makes a LUN available to some hosts and unavailable to others. LUN masking is implemented primarily at the host bus adapter (HBA) level. LUN masking that is implemented at this level is vulnerable to any attack that compromises the HBA, such as tampering with the HBA driver command in an attempt to eventually access the SAN.

The security benefits of LUN masking are limited because with many HBAs it is possible to forge source addresses. LUN masking is mainly a way to protect against misbehaving servers corrupting disks that belong to other servers.

For example, Windows servers that are attached to a SAN will sometimes corrupt non-Windows volumes by attempting to write Windows volume labels to them. By hiding the LUNs of the non-Windows volumes from the Windows server, this can be prevented, because the Windows server does not even realize the non-Windows volumes exist.

Note: Today, LUNs are typically not individual disk drives, but are virtual partitions (or volumes) of a redundant array of independent disks (RAID) set.

A world wide name (WWN) is a 64-bit address that Fibre Channel networks use to uniquely identify each element in a Fibre Channel network.

Zoning can use WWNs to assign security permissions. Zoning can also use name servers in the switches to either allow or block access to particular WWNs in the fabric.

The use of WWNs for security purposes is inherently unsecure because the WWN of a device is a user-configurable parameter. Zoning that uses WWNs is susceptible to unauthorized access, because the zone can be bypassed if an attacker is able to spoof the WWN of an authorized HBA. An HBA is an I/O adapter that sits between the bus of the host computer and the Fibre Channel loop, and manages the transfer of information between the two channels.

In storage networking, Fibre Channel zoning is the partitioning of a Fibre Channel fabric into smaller subsets. If a SAN contains several storage devices, one device should not necessarily be allowed to interact with all the other devices in the SAN.

Zoning is sometimes confused with LUN masking, because they seek the same objectives. However, zoning is implemented on fabric switches, whereas LUN masking is performed on endpoint devices. Zoning is also potentially more secure. Zone members "see" only other members of the zone. Devices can be members of more than one zone.

In Figure 7-14, three zones have anywhere from two to four members per zone. All the members of ZoneC also belong to other zones. ZoneA has four members: Host1, Disk1, Disk2, and Disk3. ZoneB has two members: Host2 and Disk4. ZoneC has three members: Host2, Disk1, and Disk3. All the members of ZoneC belong to two zones.

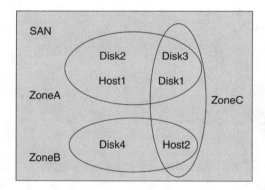

Figure 7-14   *Fibre Channel Fabric Zoning*

Note: Zoning applies only to the switched fabric topology; it does not exist in simpler Fibre Channel topologies.

A virtual storage-area network (VSAN) is a collection of ports from a set of connected Fibre Channel switches that form a virtual fabric. You can partition ports within a single switch into multiple VSANs. In addition, multiple switches can join any number of ports to form a single VSAN. In this manner, VSANs strongly resemble VLANs. Like VLANs, traffic is tagged with the VSAN ID as it crosses Inter-Switch Links.

Note: A SAN island refers to an isolated group of switches used to connect hosts to storage devices.
VSAN is a section of a SAN that has been broken up into logical sections, also called partitions.

VSAN is an approach used by Cisco Systems. Routing between VSAN is done through Inter-VSAN Routing (IVR).

As shown in Figure 7-15, physical SAN islands are virtualized onto common SAN infra-structure.

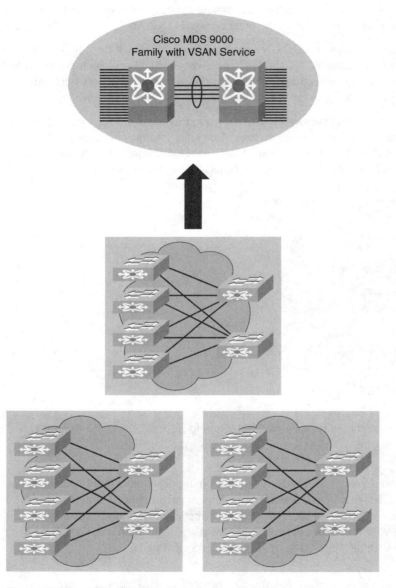

Figure 7-15 *Virtual SANs*

VSANs were originally invented by Cisco, but they have now been adopted as an ANSI standard.

SAN Security Scope

Three areas that you should protect to secure SANs are the SAN fabric, the hosts, and the actual disks. To provide this security, it is important to focus on six areas:

- **SAN management access:** Secure the management services used to administer the SAN.

- **Fabric access:** Secure access to the fabric from devices.

- **Target access:** Secure access to targets and LUNs.

- **SAN protocol:** Secure the protocols used in switch-to-switch communications.

- **IP storage access:** Secure FCIP and iSCSI.

- **Data integrity and secrecy:** Encrypt data as it crosses networks and encrypt data that is stored on disks.

SAN Management Access Security

Security for SAN management focuses on protecting against the following:

- **Disruption of switch processing:** The disruption of switch processing can be accomplished with a DoS attack, which causes excessive load on the CPU and thus causes it to be unable to react to fabric events.

- **Compromise of fabric:** Compromised fabric stability is caused by changed configurations, lost configurations, or both that could result in changes to the configured services or ports.

- **Compromise of data integrity and confidentiality:** Data compromise is the breaching of the actual data, either compromising integrity or confidentiality.

Many of the fabric and target access security features, explained next, are just as relevant to SAN protocol security as they are to fabric and target access security. In addition to these, switches should include additional SAN protocol security functions such as a capability to reject disruptive fabric-reconfiguration requests from rogue misconfigured or new unconfigured switches being attached to an existing fabric.

SAN Fabric and Target Access Security

Security for fabric access and target access should focus on three main things:

- **Application data integrity:** If unauthorized access is gained to application data, integrity and confidentiality have both been breached. It is conceivable that there will also be availability concerns if the data is corrupted or deleted.

- **LUN integrity:** If the LUN is compromised, either accidentally or intentionally, data can be lost and availability can be threatened.

- **Application performance:** Application performance security should focus on unnecessary I/O or fabric events that affect availability.

VSANs and zones are complementary technologies that work well together as a security control in a SAN. The first step in configuring these complimentary protocols is to associate the physical ports with a VSAN, much like associating switch ports with VLANs, and then you logically divide the VSANs into zones.

There are two main methods of zoning:

■ **Soft zoning:** Restricts only the fabric name services, showing a device only an allowed subset of devices. Therefore, when a server looks at the content of the fabric, it will see only the devices it is allowed to see. However, any server can still attempt to contact other devices on the network based on their address.

■ **Hard zoning:** In contrast to soft zoning, this method actually restricts communication across a fabric. This zoning is more commonly used because it is more secure.

In Figure 7-16, there are two VSANs, each with multiple zones. Disks and hosts are dedicated to VSANs, although both hosts and disks can belong to multiple zones within a single VSAN. However, disks and hosts cannot span VSANs.

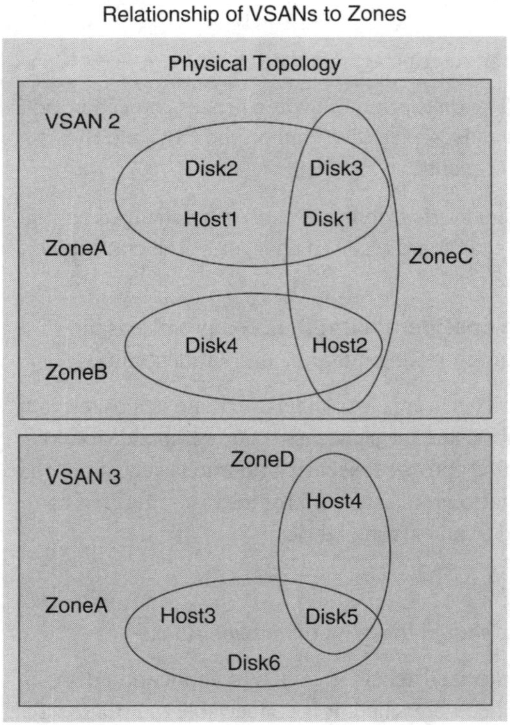

Figure 7-16 *Virtual SANs*

IP Storage and Transmission Security

To secure data transmission and data storage, a number of techniques are used. iSCSI leverages many strategies common to IP networking. For example, IP access control lists (ACL) are analogous to Fibre Channel zones, VLANs are similar to VSANs, and IEEE 802.1X port security resembles Fibre Channel port security.

For data transmission security, a number of encryption and authentication protocols are supported, such as Diffie-Hellman Challenge Handshake Authentication Protocol (DH-CHAP), Fibre Channel Authentication Protocol (FCAP), Fibre Channel Password Authentication Protocol (FCPAP), Encapsulating Security Payload (ESP), and Fibre Channel Security Protocol (FC-SP).

FCIP security leverages many IP Security (IPsec) features in Cisco IOS-based routers:

- IPsec for security over public carriers

- High-speed encryption services in specialized hardware

- Firewall filtering

Examining Voice Security

This section examines the business drivers for VoIP, the required components, and the service issues. This section also examines the security implications of VoIP on IP networks.

VoIP Fundamentals

VoIP is the transmission of voice traffic over IP-based networks. IP was originally designed for data networking, but its success in data networking has led to its adaptation to voice traffic.

VoIP has become popular largely because of the cost savings it provides compared with traditional telephone networks. On traditional telephone networks, most people pay a flat monthly fee for local telephone calls and a per-minute charge for long-distance calls. VoIP calls are placed using the Internet, with most Internet connections being charged a flat monthly fee. Using the Internet connection for both data traffic and voice calls can allow consumers to get rid of one monthly bill. For international calls, the monetary savings can be enormous.

Note: The generic term *VoIP* describes the transmission of voice traffic over an IP-based network. The term *IP telephony*, however, is a superset of VoIP. IP telephony includes all the add-on activities to VoIP such as call procedures, dialing, signaling, and quality of service, to name a few.

The business advantages that drive implementations of VoIP networks have changed over time. Starting with simple media convergence, these advantages have evolved to include the convergence of call-switching intelligence and the total user experience.

Originally, return on investment (ROI) calculations centered on toll-bypass and converged-network savings. Although these savings are still relevant today, advances in voice technologies allow organizations and service providers to differentiate their product offerings by providing advanced features.

The following are some of the VoIP business drivers:

- **Cost savings:** Traditional time-division multiplexing (TDM), which is used in the public switched telephone network (PSTN) environment, dedicates 64 kb/s of bandwidth per voice channel. This approach results in bandwidth being wasted when there is no voice to transmit. VoIP shares bandwidth with multiple logical connections, which allows a more efficient utilization of bandwidth, thereby reducing bandwidth requirements. A substantial amount of equipment is needed to combine 64-kb/s channels into high-speed links for transport across the network. Packet telephony statistically multiplexes voice traffic alongside data traffic. This consolidation results in substantial savings on capital equipment and operations costs.

- **Flexibility:** The sophisticated functionality of IP networks allows organizations to be flexible in the types of applications and services that they provide to their customers and users. Service providers can easily segment customers. This segmentation helps service providers provide different applications, custom services, and rates depending on the traffic volume needs of the customer and other factors.

- **Advanced features:** The following are some examples of the advanced features that current VoIP applications provide.
    - **Advanced call routing:** When multiple paths exist to connect a call to its destination, certain paths may be preferred based on cost, distance, quality, partner handoffs, traffic load, or other considerations. Least-cost routing and time-of-day routing are two examples of advanced call routing that can be implemented to determine the best possible route for each call.
    - **Unified messaging:** Unified messaging improves communications and boosts productivity. It delivers this advantage by providing a single-user interface to messages that have been delivered over a variety of mediums. For example, users can read their email, hear their voice mail, and view fax messages by accessing a single inbox.
    - **Integrated information systems:** Organizations are using VoIP to affect business process transformation. Centralized call control, geographically dispersed virtual contact centers, and access to resources and self-help tools are examples of VoIP technology that have enabled organizations to draw from a broad range of resources to service customers.
    - **Long-distance toll bypass:** Long-distance toll bypass is an attractive solution for organizations that place a significant number of calls between sites that are charged long-distance fees. In this case, it might be more cost-effective to use VoIP to place those calls across the IP network. If the IP WAN becomes congested, the calls can overflow into the PSTN, ensuring that there is no degradation in voice quality.
    - **Encryption:** Security mechanisms in the IP network enable the administrator to ensure that IP conversations are secure. Encryption of sensitive signaling header fields and message bodies protects the packet in case of unauthorized packet interception.
    - **Customer relationship:** The capability to provide customer support through multiple mediums, such as telephone, chat, and email, builds solid customer satisfaction and loyalty. A pervasive IP network allows organizations to provide contact

center agents with consolidated and up-to-date customer records along with the related customer communication. Access to this information allows quick problem solving, which in turn, builds strong customer relationships.

Figure 7-17 shows the basic components of a packet voice network:

- **IP phones:** IP phones provide IP voice to the desktop.

- **Gatekeeper:** (Not shown in Figure 7-17.) The gatekeeper, also known as a Cisco Multimedia Conference Manager (MCM), provides Call Admission Control (CAC), bandwidth control and management, and address translation.

- **Gateway:** The gateway provides translation between VoIP and non-VoIP networks, such as the PSTN. Gateways also provide physical access for local analog and digital voice devices, such as telephones, fax machines, key sets, and PBXs.

- **Multipoint control unit (MCU):** The multipoint control unit provides real-time connectivity for participants in multiple locations to attend the same videoconference or meeting.

- **Call agent:** The call agent provides call control for IP phones, CAC, bandwidth control and management, and address translation. Cisco Unified Communications Managers and Cisco Unified Communications Manager Business Edition both function as the call agents.

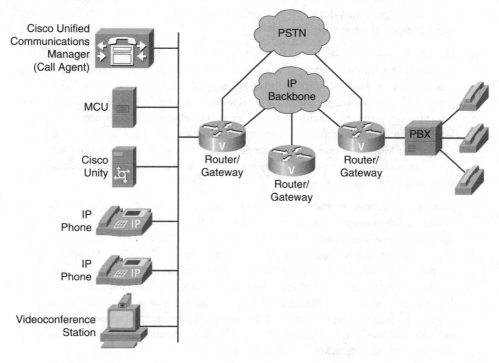

Figure 7-17   *Components of a VoIP Network*

- **Application servers:** Application servers provide services such as voice mail and unified messaging (which is provided by Cisco Unity).

- **Videoconference station:** The videoconference station provides access for end-user participation in videoconferencing. The videoconference station contains a video-capture device for video input and a microphone for audio input. The user can view video streams and hear the audio that originates at a remote user station.

Other components, such as software voice applications, interactive voice response (IVR) systems, and softphones, provide additional services to meet the needs of enterprise sites.

The following are some of the major VoIP protocols:

- **H.323:** This is an ITU standard protocol for interactive conferencing. H.323 was originally designed for multimedia in a connectionless environment, such as a LAN. H.323, is an umbrella of standards that define all aspects of synchronized voice, video, and data transmission. H.323 defines end-to-end call signaling.

- **Media Gateway Control Protocol (MGCP):** This is a method for PSTN gateway control or thin device control. Specified in RFC 2705, MGCP defines a protocol to control VoIP gateways that are connected to external call control devices, referred to as call agents. MGCP provides the signaling capability for less-expensive edge devices, such as gateways, that may not have implemented a full voice-signaling protocol such as H.323. For example, any time an event such as off hook occurs at the voice port of a gateway, the voice port reports that event to the call agent. The call agent then signals that device to provide a service, such as dial-tone signaling. The call agent controls the gateway.

- **H.248:** This is a joint IETF and ITU standard that is based on the original MGCP standard. The H.248 protocol, also known as Megaco, defines a single gateway control approach that works with multiple gateway applications, including PSTN gateways, ATM interfaces, analog-like and telephone interfaces, IVR servers, and others. The Megaco protocol provides full call control intelligence and implements call-level features such as transfer, conference, call forward, and hold. The basic operation of the Megaco protocol is similar in nature to MGCP; however, the Megaco protocol provides more flexibility by interfacing with a wider variety of applications and gateways.

- **Session Initiation Protocol (SIP):** SIP is a detailed protocol that specifies the commands and responses to set up and tear down calls. SIP also details features such as security, proxy, and transport (TCP or User Datagram Protocol [UDP]) services. SIP and its partner protocols, Session Announcement Protocol (SAP) and Session Description Protocol (SDP), provide announcements and information about multicast sessions to users on a network. SIP defines end-to-end call signaling between devices. SIP is a text-based protocol that borrows many elements of HTTP, using the same transaction request and response model, and similar header and response codes. It also adopts a modified form of the URL addressing scheme that is used within email that is based on Simple Mail Transfer Protocol (SMTP).

- **Real-Time Transport Protocol (RTP):** RTP is an IETF standard media-streaming protocol. RTP carries the voice payload across the network. RTP provides sequence numbers and time stamps for the orderly processing of voice packets.

- **RTP Control Protocol (RTCP):** RTCP provides out-of-band control information for an RTP flow. Every RTP flow has a corresponding RTCP flow that reports statistics on the call. RTCP is used for quality of service (QoS) reporting.

- **Secure Real-Time Protocol (SRTP):** SRTP provides encryption, message authentication and integrity, and replay protection to the RTP data in both unicast and multicast applications that a VoIP device transmits. This eliminates the need to use IPsec to encrypt VoIP streams.

- **Skinny Client Control Protocol (SCCP):** SCCP is a Cisco proprietary protocol used between Cisco Unified Communications Manager and Cisco IP phones. Some other vendors are beginning to support SCCP. With the SCCP architecture, the vast majority of the H.323 processing power resides in an H.323 proxy known as the Cisco Unified Communications Manager. The end stations (IP phones) run what is called the skinny client, which consumes less processing overhead. The skinny client communicates with the Cisco Unified Communications Manager using connection-oriented (TCP/IP-based) communication to establish a call with another H.323-compliant end station. Once the Cisco Unified Communications Manager has established the call, the two H.323 end stations use connectionless (UDP/IP-based) communication for audio transmissions.

Table 7-5 provides a summary of the major VoIP protocols.

Table 7-5   *Major VoIP Protocols*

VoIP Protocol	Description
H.323	ITU standard protocol for interactive conferencing; evolved from H.320 ISDN standard; flexible, complex
MGCP	Emerging IETF standard for PSTN gateway control; thin device control
Megaco/H.248	Joint IETF and ITU standard for gateway control with support for multiple gateway types; evolved from the MGCP standard
SIP	IETF protocol for interactive and noninteractive conferencing; simpler but less mature than H.323
RTP	IETF standard media-streaming protocol
RTCP	IETF protocol that provides out-of-band control information for an RTP flow
SRTP	IETF protocol that encrypts RTP traffic as it leaves the voice device
SCCP	Cisco proprietary protocol used between Cisco Unified Communications Manager and Cisco IP phones

Note: G.711 and G.729, not mentioned in this section, are responsible for the digitalization and compression of voice.

H.323 devices can call each other without the help of any other devices. SIP can also do peer-to-peer without additional infrastructure; this is not scalable. Scalability dictates the use of a SIP registrar.

MGCP devices cannot call each other directly; they need a call agent, such as Cisco Call Manager. The call agent controls the gateway. The VoIP gateway converts voice calls, in real time, between the PSTN and the IP network.

Voice Security Threats

The following are some of the common threats to VoIP networks:

- **Unauthorized access to voice resources:** Hackers can tamper with voice systems, user identities, and telephone configurations, and intercept voice-mail messages. They could also do toll fraud. If hackers gain access to the voice-mail system, they can change the voice-mail greeting, which will have a negative impact on the image and reputation of the company. A hacker who gains access to the PBX or voice gateway can shut down voice ports or change voice-routing parameters, affecting voice access into and through the network.

- **Compromise of network resources:** The goal of a secure network is to ensure that applications, processes, and users can reliably and securely interoperate using the shared network resources. Because the shared network infrastructure carries voice and data, securing access to the network infrastructure is critical to securing voice functions. Because IP voice systems are installed on a data network, they are potential targets for hackers who previously targeted only PCs, servers, and data applications. Hackers are aided in their search for vulnerabilities in IP voice systems by the open and well-known standards and protocols that are used by IP networks.

- **DoS attacks:** DoS attacks are defined as the malicious attacking or overloading of call-processing equipment to deny access to services by legitimate users. Most DoS attacks fall into one of three categories:
  - **Network resource overload:** This type of attack involves overloading a network resource that is required for proper functioning of a service. The network resource is most often bandwidth. The DoS attack uses up all available bandwidth, causing authorized users to be unable to access the required services.
  - **Host resource starvation:** This type of attack involves using up critical host resources. When use of these resources is maximized by the DoS attack, the server can no longer respond to legitimate service requests.
  - **Out-of-bounds attack:** This type of attack involves using illegal packet structure and unexpected data, which can cause the operating system of the remote system to crash. One example of this type of attack may be to use illegal combinations of TCP flags. Most TCP/IP stacks are developed to respond to appropriate

use: They are not developed for anomalies. When the stack receives illegal data, it may not know how to handle the packet and may cause a system crash.

- **Eavesdropping:** Eavesdropping involves the unauthorized interception of voice packets or RTP media streams. Eavesdropping exposes confidential or proprietary information that is obtained by intercepting and reassembling packets in a voice stream. Numerous tools are used by hackers to eavesdrop.

Spam over IP Telephony

Spam over IP Telephony (SPIT) also referred to VoIP spam, is unsolicited and unwanted bulk messages broadcast over VoIP to the end users of an enterprise network. In addition to being annoying and having the potential to significantly affect the availability and productivity of the endpoints, high-volume bulk calls that are routed over IP can be difficult to trace and have the capacity for fraud, unauthorized use, and privacy violations.

Up to now, there have not been a great many instances of VoIP spam, but there is great potential for it to become a major problem. SPIT could be generated in a similar way to email spam with botnets, targeting millions of VoIP users from compromised machines.

Spam has been a problem for years, and unsolicited commercial and malicious email spam now makes up the majority of email worldwide. In Europe in 2006, according to analysts Radicati, 16 billion spam messages were sent each day, representing 62 percent of all European email messages, and this figure is expected to increase to 37 billion spam emails a day by 2010. There is a concern in some circles that VoIP will suffer the same fate as email, and IP telephony would then become unusable.

Another concern about SPIT is that email antispam methods will not work. The real-time nature of voice calls will make dealing with SPIT much more challenging than email spam. New methods are going to have to be invented to address SPIT problems.

Note: Authenticated Transport Layer Security (TLS) stops most SPIT attacks because endpoints accept packets only from trusted devices.

An example of SPIT would be marketing or malicious phone calls made on a regular basis. The calls are infrequent enough, so they bypass any thresholds, but are frequent enough to affect employee productivity.

Fraud

Two common types of fraud in VoIP networks are vishing and fraud.

Vishing (voice phishing) uses telephony to glean information, such as account details, directly from users. One of the first reported cases of vishing affected PayPal. Victims first received an email pretending to come from PayPal asking them to verify their credit card details over the phone. Those who called the number were then asked to enter their credit card number using the keypad. Once the credit card number had been entered, the perpetrators of this fraud were free to steal money from the account of their victims.

Scams such as this are not just a danger for VoIP users, but the lower cost of making voice calls will make them much more popular than with standard phone systems. Users still trust the telephone more than the web, and by using spamming techniques, attackers can call thousands of people for very little cost every day.

Toll fraud is the theft of long-distance telephone service by unauthorized access to a PSTN trunk (an "outside line") on a PBX or voice-mail system. Toll fraud is a multibillion-dollar illegal industry, and all organizations are vulnerable. Theft can also be defined as the use of the telephony system, by both authorized and unauthorized users, to use voice network resources to access unauthorized numbers, such as premium-rate numbers.

This fraud is not new and PBXs have always been vulnerable. The difference is that few people could hack into PBXs, compared to the numbers of people actively breaking into IP systems.

To protect against such fraud, it is important to use features that exist in Cisco Unified Communications Manager, such as dial-plan filters, partitions, or forced authorization codes (FAC), to control phone calls.

SIP Vulnerabilities

The increasing adoption of SIP for VoIP is expected to open up a completely new front in the security war. SIP is a protocol that offers little inherent security. Some of its character-istics also leave it vulnerable to hackers, such as using text for encoding and SIP exten-sions that can create security holes.

Examples of hacks for SIP include registration hijacking, which allows a hacker to inter-cept incoming calls and reroute them; message tampering, which allows a hacker to mod-ify data packets traveling between SIP addresses; and session teardown, which allows a hacker to terminate calls or carry out a VoIP-targeted DoS attack by flooding the system with shutdown requests.

Defending Against VoIP Hacking

Many IP security solutions can be implemented only on Layer 3 (IP) devices. Because of protocol architecture, the MAC layer (Layer 2) offers little or no inherent security. Understanding and establishing broadcast domains is one of the fundamental precepts in designing secure IP networks. Many simple, yet dangerous attacks can be launched if the attacking device resides within the same broadcast domain as the target system. For this reason, IP phones, VoIP gateways, and network management workstations should always be on their own subnet, separate from the rest of the data network and from each other.

Protect IP Telephony with Voice VLAN

To ensure communications privacy and integrity, voice media streams must be protected from eavesdropping and tampering. Data-networking technologies, such as VLANs, can segment voice traffic from data traffic, enabling you to prevent access to the voice VLAN from the data VLAN. Using separate VLANs for voice and data, as shown in Figure 7-18, prevents any attacker or attacking application from snooping or capturing other VLAN

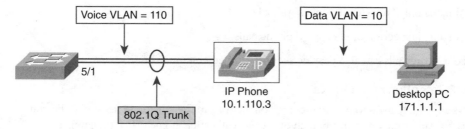

Figure 7-18 *Separate Voice VLAN*

traffic as it traverses the physical wire. Also, by making sure that each device connects to the network using a switched infrastructure, you can render packet-sniffing tools less effective for capturing user traffic.

Using voice VLANs to logically segment voice and data traffic is an industrywide accepted best practice. As much as possible, devices that are identified as voice devices should be restricted to dedicated voice VLANs. This approach ensures that they can communicate only with other voice resources. More important, voice traffic is kept away from the general data network, where it could be more easily intercepted or tampered with. In addition, having a voice specific VLAN makes it easier to apply VLAN access control lists (VACL) to protect voice traffic.

By understanding the protocols used between devices in the VoIP network, you can implement affective ACLs on the voice VLANs. IP phones send only RTP traffic to each other; they never have a reason to send TCP or Internet Control Message Protocol (ICMP) traffic to each other. IP phones do send a few TCP and UDP protocols to communicate with servers. You can stop many of the IP phone attacks by using ACLs on the voice VLANs to watch for deviations from these principles.

Firewalls inspect packets and match them against configured rules. It is difficult to specify ahead of time which ports will be used in a voice call because the ports are dynamically negotiated during call setup.

Protect IP Telephony with Firewalls

Cisco ASA Appliances inspect voice protocols to ensure that SIP, SCCP, H.323, and MGCP requests conform to voice standards. Cisco ASA Appliances can also provide the following capabilities to help protect voice traffic:

- Inspect protocols to ensure SIP, SCCP, H.232 and MGCP requests conform to standards

- Prevent inappropriate SIP methods from being sent to Cisco Unified Communications Manager

- Rate limit SIP requests

- Enforce the policy of calls according to whitelists, blacklists, caller/called party and SIP uniform resource identifier

- Dynamically open ports for Cisco applications

- Enable only "registered phones" to make calls

- Enable inspection of encrypted phone calls

Cisco IOS firewalls can also provide security unified communication.

Protect IP Telephony with VPNs

VPNs are widely used to provide secure connections to the corporate network. The connections can originate from a branch office, a small office, home office (SOHO), a telecommuter, or a roaming user. Then IPsec can be used for authentication and confidentiality services. To facilitate performance, it is recommended that VPN tunnels terminate inside of a firewall, as shown in Figure 7-19. You can then use the firewall to inspect and protect the plaintext protocols.

Frequently asked questions about voice over VPN generally deal with overhead and delay, which have an impact on the QoS for the call.

Note: One important consideration to remember is the absence of QoS when deploying VPNs across the Internet or a public network. Where possible, QoS should be addressed with the provider through a service level agreement (SLA). An SLA is a document that details the expected QoS parameters for packets transiting the provider network.

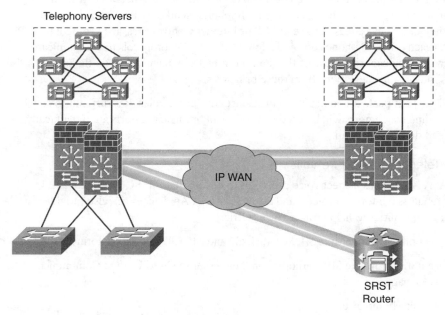

Figure 7-19   *IP Telephony with VPNs*

Voice communications do not work when even a modest amount of latency is present. Because secure VPNs encrypt data, they can create a throughput bottleneck when they process packets through their encryption algorithm. The problem usually gets worse as security increases.

VoIP and either Advanced Encryption Standard (AES), Data Encryption Standard (DES), or Triple DES (3DES) encryptions are fully compatible with each other as long as the VPN delivers the necessary throughput. Internationally, corporations can run into other factors. The U.S. Department of Commerce places restrictions on the export of certain encryption technology. Usually, DES is exportable, whereas 3DES and AES are not, but regulations take numerous forms, from total export exclusions that are applied to certain countries, to allowing 3DES export to specific industries and users. Corporations with VPNs that extend outside the United States should find out whether their VPN provider has exportable products and how export regulations affect networks built with those products.

Note: Cisco Unified Survivable Remote Site Telephony (SRST) provides Cisco Unified Communications Manager with fallback support for Cisco IP phones that are attached to a Cisco router on your local network. Cisco Unified SRST enables routers to provide call-handling support for Cisco IP phones when they lose connection to remote primary, secondary, or tertiary Cisco Unified Communications Manager installations or when the WAN connection is down.

Protect IP Telephony Endpoints and Servers

Signed firmware and configuration files are among the defenses that are built in to Cisco IP telephony products. You can also harden the IP phones by disabling specific features and functions that could be used to compromise the phone. Things you should think about disabling on the Cisco IP phone, especially those located in public areas such as office lobbies, airport gates, and so on, include the PC port, settings button, speakerphone, and web access.

When securing your voice traffic, do not forget to secure the voice application servers. The current version of Cisco Unified Communications Manager is a hardened appliance that disables unnecessary services, disables default usernames, allows only signed images to be installed, has Cisco Security Agent installed, and supports secure management protocols.

By combining the transport security provided by secure LANs, firewalls, and VPNs with the application and host security features available with the Cisco Unified Communications Manager and Cisco IP phones, it is possible to have a highly secure IP telephony environment.

Mitigating Layer 2 Attacks

Like routers, both Layer 2 and Layer 3 switches have their own set of network security requirements. Access to switches is a convenient entry point for attackers who are intent on illegally gaining access to a corporate network. With access to a switch, an attacker can set up rogue access points and protocol analyzers, and launch all types of attacks from within the network. Attackers can even spoof the MAC and IP addresses of critical servers to do a great deal of damage.

Basic Switch Operation

Unlike hubs, switches can regulate the flow of data between their ports by creating "instant" networks that contain only the two end devices communicating with each other at that moment in time. When end systems send data frames, their source and destination addresses are not changed throughout the switched domain. Switches maintain content-addressable memory (CAM) lookup tables to track the source MAC addresses located on the switch ports. These lookup tables are populated by an address-learning process on the switch. If the destination MAC address of a frame is not known, or if the frame received by the switch is destined for a broadcast or multicast MAC address, the switch forwards the frame to all ports. Because of their capability to isolate traffic and create instant networks, you can use switches to divide a physical network into multiple logical segments, or VLANs, using Layer 2 traffic segmenting.

Layer 2 is the data link layer in the OSI model and is one of seven layers designed to work together but with autonomy. Layer 2 operates above the physical layer, but below the network and transport layers, as shown in Figure 7-20.

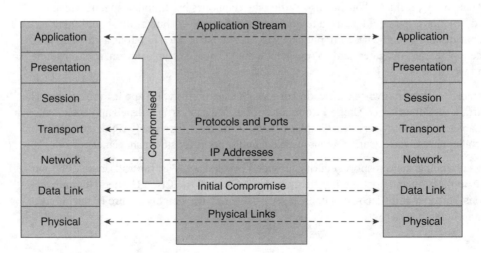

Figure 7-20 *Domino Effect If Layer 2 Is Compromised*

Layer 2 independence enables interoperability and interconnectivity. However, from a security perspective, Layer 2 independence creates a challenge because a compromise at one layer is not always known by the other layers. If the initial attack comes in at Layer 2, the rest of the network can be compromised in an instant. Network security is only as strong as the weakest link—and that link might be the data link layer.

Mitigating VLAN Attacks

A VLAN is a logical broadcast domain that can span multiple physical LAN segments, as shown in Figure 7-21. Within the switched internetwork, VLANs provide segmentation and organizational flexibility. You can design a VLAN structure that lets you group together stations that are segmented logically by functions, project teams, and applications without regard to the physical location of the users. You can assign each switch port to only one VLAN, thereby adding a layer of security. Ports in a VLAN share broadcasts; ports in different VLANs do not share broadcasts. Containing broadcasts within a VLAN improves the overall performance of the network.

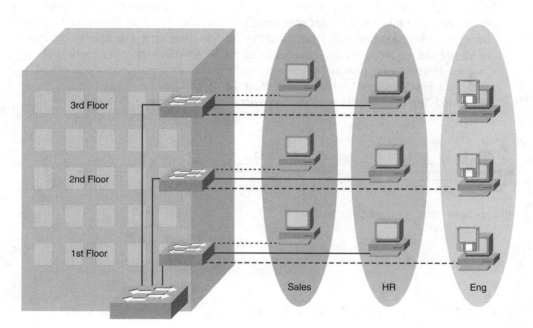

Figure 7-21   *VLAN Overview*

Within the switched internetwork, VLANs provide segmentation and organizational flexibility. Using VLAN technology, you can group switch ports and their connected users into logically defined communities, such as coworkers in the same department, a cross-functional product team, or diverse user groups sharing the same network application.

A VLAN can exist on a single switch or span multiple switches. VLANs can include stations in a single building or multiple-building infrastructures. VLANs can also connect across WANs.

VLAN Hopping

The VLAN architecture simplifies network maintenance and improves performance. However, VLAN operation opens the door to abuse. VLAN hopping allows traffic from one VLAN to be seen by another VLAN without first crossing a router. Under certain circumstances, attackers can sniff data and extract passwords and other sensitive information at will. The attack works by taking advantage of an incorrectly configured trunk port. By default, trunk ports have access to all VLANs and pass traffic for multiple VLANs across the same physical link, generally between switches. The data moving across these links may be encapsulated with IEEE 802.1Q or ISL.

VLAN Hopping by Rogue Trunk

In a basic VLAN hopping attack, the attacker takes advantage of the default automatic trunking configuration on most switches. The network attacker configures a system to spoof itself as a switch. This spoofing requires that the network attacker be capable of emulating either ISL or 802.1Q signaling along with Dynamic Trunking Protocol (DTP) signaling, as shown in Figure 7-22. By tricking a switch into thinking it is another switch that needs to trunk, an attacker can gain access to all the VLANs allowed on the trunk port. To succeed, this attack requires a configuration on the port that supports trunking, such as **auto**. As a result, the attacker is a member of all the VLANS that are trunked on the switch and can "hop" (that is, send and receive traffic) on all of those VLANs.

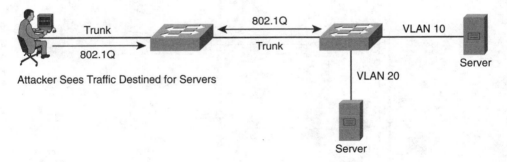

Figure 7-22 *VLAN Hopping by Rogue Trunk*

A VLAN hopping attack can be launched in one of two ways:

■ **Spoofing DTP messages from the attacking host to cause the switch to enter trunking mode:** From here, the attacker can send traffic tagged with the target VLAN, and the switch then delivers the packets to the destination.

■ **Introducing a rogue switch and turning trunking on:** The attacker can then access all the VLANs on the victim switch from the rogue switch.

The best way to prevent a basic VLAN hopping attack is to turn off trunking on all ports except the ones that specifically require trunking. On the required trunking ports, disable DTP (auto trunking) negotiations and manually enable trunking.

VLAN Hopping by Double Tagging

The double-tagging (or double-encapsulated) VLAN hopping attack takes advantage of the way that hardware on most switches operates. Most switches perform only one level of 802.1Q decapsulation and allow an attacker, in specific situations, to embed a hidden 802.1Q tag inside the frame. This tag allows the frame to go to a VLAN that the outer 802.1Q tag did not specify. An important characteristic of the double-encapsulated VLAN hopping attack is that it works even if trunk ports are set to **off**.

A double-tagging VLAN hopping attack follows four steps, as shown in Figure 7-23:

Step 1.   The attacker sends a double-tagged 802.1Q frame to the switch. The outer header has the VLAN tag of the attacker, which is the same as the native VLAN of the trunk port. For the purposes of this example, assume that this is VLAN 10. The inner tag is the victim VLAN, VLAN 20.

Step 2.   The frame arrives on the switch, which looks at the first 4-byte 802.1Q tag. The switch sees that the frame is destined for VLAN 10 and sends it out all VLAN 10 ports (including the trunk), because there is no CAM table entry. The switch does not add a VLAN 10 tag to the frames because VLAN 10 is the native VLAN, and as specified by the 802.1Q specification, native VLAN traffic is not tagged. At this point, the second VLAN tag is still intact and has not been inspected by the first switch.

Step 3.   The frame arrives at the second switch but has no knowledge that it was supposed to be for VLAN 10.

Step 4.   The second switch looks only at the 802.1Q tag (the former inner tag that the attacker sent) and sees that the frame is destined for VLAN 20 (the victim VLAN). The second switch sends the packet on to the victim port, or floods it, depending on whether there is an existing CAM table entry for the victim host.

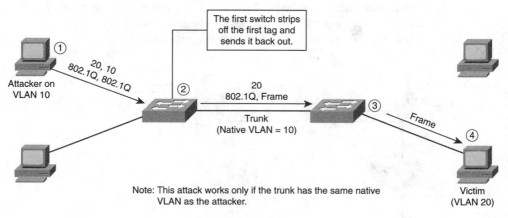

Figure 7-23   *VLAN Hopping by Double Tagging*

It is important to note that this attack, as shown in Figure 7-23, is unidirectional and works only when the attacker and trunk port have the same native VLAN. Thwarting this type of attack is not as easy as stopping basic VLAN hopping attacks. The best approach is to ensure that the native VLAN of the trunk ports is different from the native VLAN of the user ports.

To prevent a VLAN hopping attack that uses double 802.1Q encapsulation, the switch must look further into the packet to determine whether more than one VLAN tag is attached to a given frame. Unfortunately, the ASICs that most switches use are only hardware optimized to look for one tag and then switch the frame. The issue of performance versus security requires administrators to balance their requirements carefully.

Mitigating VLAN hopping attacks that use double 802.1Q encapsulation requires several modifications to the VLAN configuration. One of the more important elements is to use a dedicated native VLAN for all trunk ports. This attack is easy to stop if you follow the best practice that native VLANs for trunk ports should never be used anywhere else on the switch. Also, disable all unused switch ports and place them in an unused VLAN.

You have the following options to control trunking for ports:

- For links that you do not intend to trunk across, use the **switchport mode access** interface configuration command to disable trunking.

- For links that you do intend to trunk across, take the following actions:
  Use the **switchport mode trunk** interface configuration command to cause the interface to become a trunk link and use the **switchport nonegotiate** interface configuration command to prevent the generation of DTP frames.
  Use the **switchport trunk native vlan** *vlan_number* interface configuration command to set the native VLAN on the trunk to an unused VLAN. The default native VLAN is VLAN 1.

Preventing Spanning Tree Protocol Manipulation

Even though redundant designs, shown in Figure 7-24, can eliminate the possibility of a single point of failure causing a loss of function for the entire switched or bridged network, you must consider problems that redundant designs can cause.

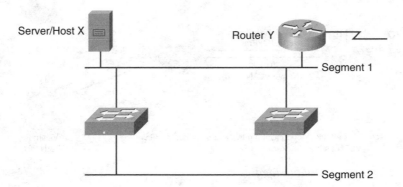

Figure 7-24   *Redundant Topology*

Some of the problems that can occur with redundant links and devices in switched or bridged networks are as follows:

- **Broadcast storms:** Without some loop-avoidance process in operation, each switch or bridge floods broadcasts endlessly. This situation is commonly called a broadcast storm.

- **Multiple frame transmission:** Multiple copies of unicast frames may be delivered to destination stations. Many protocols expect to receive only a single copy of each transmission. Multiple copies of the same frame can cause unrecoverable errors.

- **MAC database instability:** Instability in the content of the MAC address table results from copies of the same frame being received on different ports of the switch. Data forwarding can be impaired when the switch consumes the resources that are coping with instability in the MAC address table.

Layer 2 LAN protocols, such as Ethernet, lack a mechanism to recognize and eliminate endlessly looping frames. Some Layer 3 protocols implement a Time to Live (TTL) mechanism that limits the number of times a Layer 3 networking device can retransmit a packet. Lacking such a mechanism, Layer 2 devices continue to retransmit looping traffic indefinitely.

A loop-avoidance mechanism is required to solve each of these problems.

Spanning Tree Protocol (STP) provides loop resolution by managing the physical paths to given network segments. STP allows physical path redundancy while preventing the undesirable effects of active loops in the network. STP is an IEEE committee standard defined as 802.1D.

STP behaves as follows:

- STP forces certain ports into a standby state so that they do not listen to, forward, or flood data frames, as seen in Figure 7-25, where one switch has a port in blocking mode. The overall effect is that only one active path exists to the other network segment at any time.

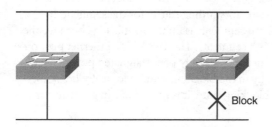

Figure 7-25   *Loop Resolution with STP*

- If there is a problem with connectivity to any of the segments within the network, STP reestablishes connectivity by automatically activating a previously inactive path, if one exists.

STP performs three steps to provide a loop-free logical network topology:

Step 1. Elects one root bridge:

STP has a process to elect a root bridge. Only one bridge can act as the root bridge in a given network. On the root bridge, all ports are designated ports. Designated ports are normally in the forwarding state. When in the forwarding state, a port can send and receive traffic. In Figure 7-26, switch X is the root bridge.

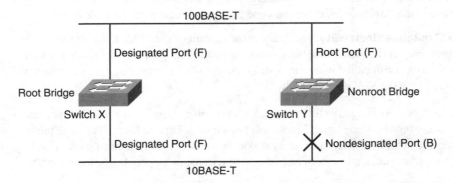

Figure 7-26   *STP Operation and Resulting Topology*

Step 2. Selects the root port on the nonroot bridge:

STP establishes one root port on each nonroot bridge. The root port is the lowest-cost path from the nonroot bridge to the root bridge. Root ports are normally in the forwarding state. Spanning-tree path cost is an accumulated cost that is calculated on the bandwidth. In Figure 7-26, the lowest-cost path to the root bridge from switch Y is through the 100BASE-T Fast Ethernet link.

Step 3. Selects the designated port on each segment:

On each segment, STP establishes one designated port. The designated port is selected on the bridge that has the lowest-cost path to the root bridge. Designated ports are normally in the forwarding state, forwarding traffic for the segment. In Figure 7-26, the designated port for both segments is on the root bridge because the root bridge is directly connected to both segments. The 10BASE-T Ethernet port on switch Y is a nondesignated port because there is only one designated port per segment. Nondesignated ports are normally in the blocking state to logically break the loop topology. When a port is in the blocking state, it is not forwarding traffic but can still receive traffic.

Figure 7-26 shows STP operations and the resulting topology.

Switches and bridges running the spanning-tree algorithm exchange configuration messages with other switches and bridges at regular intervals (every two seconds by default). Switches and bridges exchange these messages using a multicast frame called the bridge protocol data unit (BPDU). One of the pieces of information included in the BPDU is the *bridge ID* (BID).

STP calls for each switch or bridge to be assigned a unique BID. Typically, the BID is composed of a priority value (2 bytes) and the bridge MAC address (6 bytes). The default priority, in accordance with IEEE 802.1D, is 32,768 (1000 0000 0000 0000 in binary, or 0x8000 in hex format), which is the midrange value. The root bridge is the bridge with the lowest BID.

Note: A Cisco Catalyst switch uses one of its MAC addresses from a pool of MAC addresses that are assigned either to the backplane or to the supervisor module, depending on the switch model.

In Figure 7-27, both switches are using the same default priority. The switch with the lowest MAC address is the root bridge. In Figure 7-26, switch X is the root bridge with the default priority of 0x8000 (hex,) or 32,768 in decimal, and a MAC address of 0c00.1111.1111.

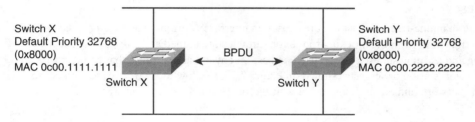

Figure 7-27   *STP: Root Bridge Selection*

Figure 7-28 shows how a network attacker can use STP to change the topology of a network so that it appears that the network attacker host is a root bridge with a higher priority. The attacker sends out BPDUs with a better bridge ID, and as a result, becomes the root bridge. Now all the traffic for this switch domain passes through the new root bridge, which is actually the attacker system.

By manipulating the STP root bridge parameters, network attackers hope to spoof their system, or a rogue switch that they add to the network, as the root bridge in the topology. To do this, the network attacker broadcasts out STP configuration and topology change BPDUs in an attempt to force spanning-tree recalculations. The BPDUs sent out by the system or switch of the network attacker announce that the attacking system has a lower bridge priority. If successful, the network attacker becomes the root bridge and sees a variety of frames that otherwise would not be seen.

Note: This attack can be used against all three security objectives of confidentiality, integrity, and availability.

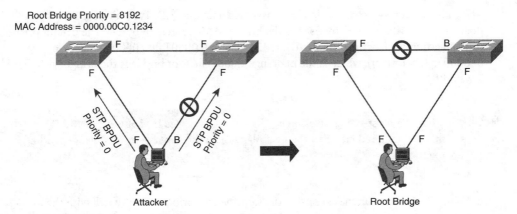

Figure 7-28   *STP Manipulation*

PortFast

The spanning-tree PortFast feature causes an interface configured as a Layer 2 access port to transition from the blocking to the forwarding state immediately, bypassing the listening and learning states. You can use PortFast on Layer 2 access ports that connect to a single workstation or server, as shown on Figure 7-29, to allow those devices to connect to the network immediately, instead of waiting for spanning tree to converge.

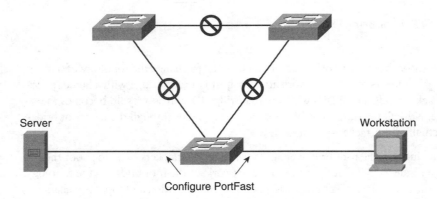

Figure 7-29   *Using PortFast*

If a port that is configured with PortFast receives a BPDU, spanning tree can put the port into the blocking state by using a feature called BPDU guard.

Caution: Because the purpose of PortFast is to minimize the time that access ports must wait for spanning tree to converge, it should be used only on access ports. If you enable PortFast on a port connecting to another switch, you risk creating a spanning-tree loop.

Table 7-6 lists the commands that you use to implement and verify PortFast on an interface.

Table 7-6   *PortFast Commands*

Command	Description
Switch(config-if)# **spanning-tree portfast**	Enables PortFast on a Layer 2 access port and forces it to enter the forwarding state immediately.
Switch(config-if)# **no spanning-tree portfast**	Disables PortFast on a Layer 2 access port. PortFast is disabled by default.
Switch(config)# **spanning-tree portfast default**	Globally enables the PortFast feature on all nontrunking ports.
Switch# **show running-config interface** *type slot/port*	Indicates whether PortFast has been configured on a port.

Mitigating STP Vulnerabilities

To mitigate STP manipulation, use the BPDU guard and root guard enhancement commands available on Cisco switches to enforce the placement of the root bridge in the network and enforce the STP domain borders.

BPDU Guard

The STP BPDU guard feature is designed to enable network designers to keep the active network topology predictable. BPDU guard is used to protect the switched network from the problems that may be caused by the receipt of BPDUs on ports that should not be receiving them. The receipt of unexpected BPDUs might be accidental or might be part of an unauthorized attempt to add a switch to the network.

BPDU guard is best deployed toward user-facing ports to prevent rogue switch network extensions by an attacker.

The global command to activate BPDU guard on all ports with PortFast enabled is as follows:

```
Switch(config)# spanning-tree portfast bpduguard default
```

In Figure 7-30, the attacker starts sending out spoofed BPDUs in an effort to become the root bridge. Upon receipt of a BPDU, the BPDU guard feature disables the port.

Note: Another command used to prevent BPDU filtering, which prevents a port from sending and receiving BPDUs is following the interface command:

```
Switch(config-if)# spanning-tree bpdufilter enable
```

Be careful when you enter the **spanning-tree bpdufilter enable** command; it overrides the PortFast configuration, explained previously.

This command has three states:

■   ```Switch(config-if)# spanning-tree bpdufilter enable```
This command state unconditionally enables BPDU filtering on the interface.

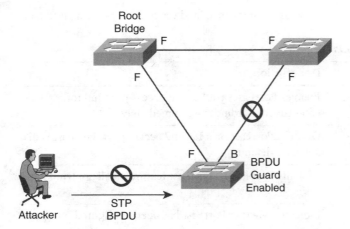

Figure 7-30   *BPDU Guard*

- ■   `Switch(config-if)# `**`spanning-tree bpdufilter disable`**
  This command state unconditionally disables BPDU filtering on the interface.

- ■   `Switch(config-if)# `**`no spanning-tree bpdufilter`**
  This command state enables BPDU filtering on the interface if the interface is in operational PortFast state and if you configure the **spanning-tree portfast bpdufilter default** command.

Root Guard

The root guard feature of Cisco switches is designed to provide a way to enforce the placement of root bridges in the network. Root guard limits the switch ports out of which the root bridge can be negotiated. If a root guard–enabled port receives BPDUs that are superior to those that the current root bridge is sending, that port is moved to a root-inconsistent state, which is effectively equal to an STP listening state, and no data traffic is forwarded across that port.

Because an administrator can manually set the bridge priority of a switch to zero, root guard might seem unnecessary. However, setting the priority of a switch to zero does not guarantee that switch will be elected as the root bridge, because another switch could have a priority of zero and a lower MAC address, and therefore a lower BID.

Root guard is best deployed toward ports that connect to switches that should not be the root bridge.

The command to enable root guard on a per-interface basis is as follows:

`Switch(config-if)# `**`spanning-tree guard root`**

In Figure 7-31, the attacker starts sending out spoofed BPDUs in an effort to become the root bridge. Upon receipt of a BPDU, the switch with the root guard feature configured on that port ignores the BPDU and puts the port in a root-inconsistent state. The port will recover as soon as the offending BPDUs cease.

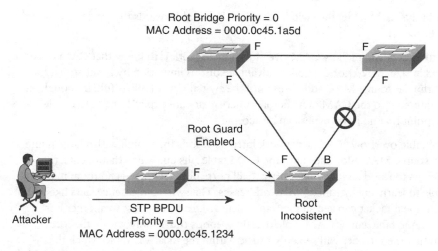

Figure 7-31 *Root Guard*

Confirming Spanning-Tree State

To display information about the state of spanning tree, use the **show spanning-tree summary** command.

Example 7-1 shows that BPDU guard is enabled.

Example 7-1   show spanning-tree summary *Command Output*

```
Switch# show spanning-tree summary
Root bridge for: Bridge group 1, VLAN0001, VLAN0004-VLAN1005
 VLAN1013-VLAN1499, VLAN2001-VLAN4094
EtherChannel misconfiguration guard is enabled
Extended system ID is enabled
Portfast is enabled by default
PortFast BPDU Guard is enabled
Portfast BPDU Filter is disabled by default
Loopguard is disabled by default
UplinkFast is disabled
BackboneFast is disabled
Pathcost method used is long
<output omitted>
Switch#
```

CAM Table Overflow Attacks

The CAM table in a switch contains the MAC addresses that can be reached off a given physical port of a switch and the associated VLAN parameters for each. When a Layer 2 switch receives a frame, the switch looks in the CAM table for the destination MAC address. If an entry exists for the MAC address in the CAM table, the switch forwards the frame to the MAC address port designated in the CAM table. If the MAC address does not exist in the CAM table, the switch acts like a hub and forwards the frame out every port on the switch.

The key to understanding how CAM-overflow attacks work is to know that CAM tables are limited in size. MAC flooding takes advantage of this limitation by bombarding the switch with fake source MAC addresses until the switch CAM table is full. If enough entries are entered into the CAM table before other entries are expired, the CAM table fills up to the point that no new entries can be accepted.

In a CAM table overflow attack, a network intruder floods the switch with a large number of invalid source MAC addresses until the CAM table fills up. When that occurs, the switch begins to flood all incoming traffic to all ports because there is no room in the CAM table to learn any legitimate MAC addresses. The switch, in essence, acts like a hub. As a result, the attacker can see all the frames sent from a victim host to another host without a CAM table entry. CAM table overflow floods traffic only within the local VLAN so that the intruder will see only traffic within the local VLAN to which the intruder is connected. If the intruder does not maintain the flood of invalid source MAC addresses, the switch eventually ages out older MAC address entries from the CAM table and begins to act like a switch again.

In Figure 7-32, the macof program is running on Host C. This tool floods a switch with packets that contain randomly generated source and destination MAC and IP addresses. Over a short period, the CAM table in the switch fills up until it cannot accept new entries. When the CAM table fills up, the switch begins to flood all frames that it receives.

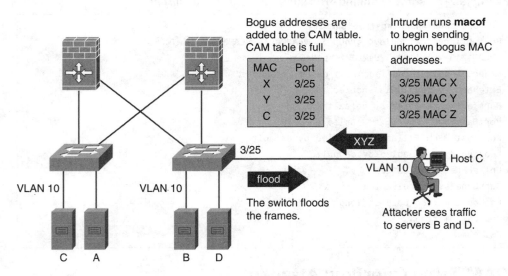

Figure 7-32   *CAM Table Overflow Attack*

As long as macof is left running, the CAM table on the switch remains full. When this happens, the switch begins to flood all received frames out every port so that frames sent from any host are also flooded out of port 3/25 on the switch.

The CAM table overflow attack can be mitigated by configuring port security on the switch. With port security, you can either statically specify the MAC addresses on a particular switch port or you can allow the switch to dynamically learn a fixed number of MAC addresses for a switch port. To statically specify the MAC addresses on switch ports is far too unmanageable a solution for a production environment; however, allowing the switch to dynamically learn a fixed number of MAC addresses for a port is a more administratively scalable solution.

MAC Address Spoofing Attacks

MAC spoofing attacks involve the use of a known MAC address of another host to attempt to make the target switch forward frames destined for the remote host to the network attacker. By sending a single frame with the source Ethernet address of the other host, the network attacker overwrites the CAM table entry so that the switch forwards packets destined for the host to the network attacker instead. Until the host sends traffic, it does not receive any traffic. When the host sends out traffic, the CAM table entry is rewritten once more so that it moves back to the original port.

Figure 7-33 shows how MAC spoofing works. In the beginning, the switch has learned that Host A is on port 1, Host B is on port 2, and Host C is on port 3. Host B (attacker) sends out a packet identifying itself with the source MAC address of Host A. This traffic causes the switch to move the location of Host A in its CAM table from port 1 to port 2. Traffic from Host C destined to Host A is now visible to Host B and not to Host A.

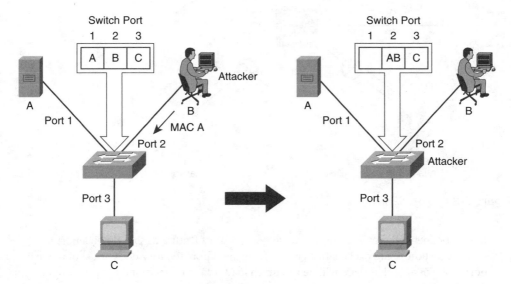

Figure 7-33   *MAC Address Spoofing Attack*

This attack can also be mitigated using port security.

Using Port Security

You can use the port security feature to restrict input to an interface by limiting and identifying the MAC addresses of the stations that are allowed to access the port. When you assign secure MAC addresses to a secure port, the port does not forward packets with source addresses outside the group of defined addresses.

Port security allows you to statically specify MAC addresses for a port or permit the switch to dynamically learn a limited number of MAC addresses. By limiting the number of permitted MAC addresses on a port to one, you can use port security to control unauthorized expansion of the network.

When a secure port receives a packet, the source MAC address of the packet is compared to the list of secure source addresses that were manually configured or autoconfigured (learned) on the port. If a MAC address of a device attached to the port differs from the list of secure addresses, either the port shuts down until it is administratively enabled (default mode) or the port drops incoming packets from the unsecure host. The behavior of the port depends on how you configure it to respond to a security violation. In Figure 7-34, traffic from Attacker 1 and Attacker 2 will be dropped at the switch because the source MAC addresses of these frames do not match MAC addresses in the list of secured (allowed) addresses.

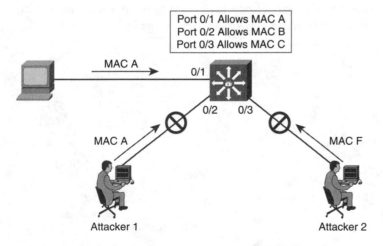

Figure 7-34   *Port Security*

It is recommended that you configure the port security feature to shut down a port instead of just dropping packets from insecure hosts. If port security does not shut down a port, it is possible that there will be too much load from an attack, and the port will be disabled anyway.

Note: For specific guidelines and limitations on port security configuration, refer to the *Cisco Catalyst Switch Configuration Guide.*

Tip: Port security protects against too many MAC address per ports and can dictate which MAC address is allowed to connect against which port. However, if the hacker spoofs the MAC address permitted on that port, he will gain access to the network. If you are concerned by spoofed MAC addresses, then consider implementing an 802.1X authentication solution.

To configure port security on an access port, follow these steps (see Table 7-7 for command details):

Table 7-7   switchport port-security *Command Parameters*

Parameter	Description
mac-address *mac-address*	(Optional) Specify a secure MAC address for the port by entering a 48-bit MAC address. You can add additional secure MAC addresses up to the maximum value configured.
vlan *vlan-id*	(Optional) On a trunk port only, specify the VLAN ID and the MAC address. If no VLAN ID is specified, the native VLAN is used.
vlan access	(Optional) On an access port only, specify the VLAN as an access VLAN.
vlan voice	(Optional) On an access port only, specify the VLAN as a voice VLAN. Note: The **voice** keyword is available only if voice VLAN is configured on a port and if that port is not the access VLAN.
mac-address sticky [*mac-address*]	(Optional) Enable the interface for sticky learning by entering only the **mac-address sticky** keywords. When sticky learning is enabled, the interface adds all secure MAC addresses that are dynamically learned to the running configuration and converts these addresses to sticky secure MAC addresses. Specify a sticky secure MAC address by entering the **mac-address sticky** *mac-address* keywords. Note: Although you can specify a sticky secure MAC address by entering the **mac-address sticky** *mac-address* keywords, it is recommended that you use the **mac-address** *mac-address* interface configuration command to enter static secure MAC addresses.

Table 7-7 **switchport port-security** *Command Parameters*

Parameter	Description
maximum *value*	(Optional) Set the maximum number of secure MAC addresses for the interface. The maximum number of secure MAC addresses that you can configure on a switch is set by the maximum number of available MAC addresses allowed in the system. The active Switch Database Management (SDM) template determines this number. This number represents the total available MAC addresses, including those used for other Layer 2 functions and any other secure MAC addresses configured on interfaces. The default setting is 1.
vlan [*vlan-list*]	(Optional) For trunk ports, you can set the maximum number of secure MAC addresses on a specific VLAN. If the **vlan** keyword is not entered, the default value is used. **vlan:** set a per-VLAN maximum value. **vlan** *vlan-list*: set a per-VLAN maximum value on a range of VLANs separated by a hyphen or a series of VLANs separated by commas. For nonspecified VLANs, the per-VLAN maximum value is used.

Step 1.   Enter interface configuration mode:

```
Switch(config)# interface FastEthernet 0/8
```

Step 2.   Configure the interface as an access interface:

```
Switch(config-if)# switchport mode access
```

Note: With an interface in the default mode (dynamic desirable), it cannot be configured as a secure port.

Step 3.   Enable port security on the interface:

```
Switch(config-if)# switchport port-security [mac-address mac-address
[vlan {vlan-id | {access | voice}}] ] | [mac-address sticky [mac-
address| vlan {vlan-id | {access | voice}}]] [maximum value [vlan
{vlan-list | {access | voice}}]]
```

Step 4.   (Optional) Set the maximum number of secure MAC addresses for the interface:

```
Switch(config-if)# switchport port-security maximum value
```

Note: The range is 1 to 132; the default is 1.

Step 5.   (Optional) Set the violation mode. This is the action to be taken when a security violation is detected:

```
Switch(config-if)# switchport port-security violation {protect |
restrict | shutdown | shutdown vlan}
```

Table 7-8 provides the details of the **switchport port-security violation** command parameters.

Table 7-8 **switchport port-security violation** *Parameters*

Parameter	Description
protect	(Optional) Set the security violation protect mode. When the number of secure MAC addresses reaches the limit allowed on the port, packets with unknown source addresses are dropped until you remove a sufficient number of secure MAC addresses or increase the number of maximum allowable addresses. You are not notified that a security violation has occurred.
restrict	(Optional) Set the security violation restrict mode. When the number of secure MAC addresses reaches the limit allowed on the port, packets with unknown source addresses are dropped until you remove a sufficient number of secure MAC addresses or increase the number of maximum allowable addresses. In this mode, you are notified that a security violation has occurred. Specifically, a Simple Network Management Protocol (SNMP) trap is sent, a syslog message is logged, and the violation counter increments.
shutdown	(Optional) Set the security violation shutdown mode. In this mode, a port security violation causes the interface to immediately become error disabled and turns off the port LED. It also sends an SNMP trap, logs a syslog message, and increments the violation counter. When a secure port is in the error-disabled state, you can bring it out of this state by entering the **errdisable recovery cause psecure-violation** global configuration command, or you can manually reenable it by entering the **shutdown** and **no shut down** interface configuration commands.
shutdown vlan	Set the security violation mode to per-VLAN shutdown. In this mode, only the VLAN on which the violation occurred is error-disabled.

Tip: When a secure port is in the error-disabled state, you can bring it out of this state by entering the **errdisable recovery cause** *psecure-violation* global configuration command, or you can manually reenable it by entering the **shutdown** and **no shutdown** interface configuration commands.

Step 6.   (Optional) Enter a static secure MAC address for the interface with this command:

```
Switch(config-if)# switchport port-security mac-address mac-address
```

Note: Repeat this command as many times as necessary for each secure MAC address.

Step 7.   (Optional) Enable sticky learning on the interface with this command:

```
Switch(config-if)# switchport port-security mac-address sticky
```

Use the **no switchport port-security** interface configuration command to return the interface to the default condition of not being a secure port. The sticky secure addresses remain part of the running configuration. To remove the sticky secure addresses from the running configuration, use the **no mac-address** *mac-address* command.

Use the **no switchport port-security maximum** *value* interface configuration command to return the interface to the default number of secure MAC addresses.

Use the **no switchport port-security violation {protect | restrict}** interface configuration command to return the violation mode to the default condition (shutdown mode).

You can use port security aging to set the aging time for static and dynamic secure addresses on a port. Each port supports two types of aging:

■   **Absolute:** The secure addresses on the port are deleted after the specified aging time.

■   **Inactivity:** The secure addresses on the port are deleted only if the secure addresses are inactive for the specified aging time.

You can use this feature to remove and add secure MAC addresses on a secure port without manually deleting the existing secure MAC addresses and still limit the number of secure addresses on a port. Also, you can enable or disable the aging of statically configured secure addresses on a per-port basis.

Use the **switchport port-security aging {static | time** *time* **| type {absolute | inactivity}}** command to enable or disable static aging for the secure port, or set the aging time or type. Table 7-9 provides the details of the **switchport port-security again** parameters.

Table 7-9   switchport port-security aging *Parameters*

Parameter	Description
static	This command option enables aging for statically configured secure addresses on this port.
time *time*	This command option specifies the aging time for this port. The range is 0 to 1440 minutes. If the time is 0, aging is disabled for this port.
type absolute	This command option sets the aging type to absolute. All the secure addresses on this port age out exactly after the time (minutes) specified and are removed from the secure address list.
type inactivity	This command option sets the aging type to inactivity. The secure addresses on this port age out only if there is no data traffic from the secure source address for the specified time period.

Example 7-2 shows a typical port security configuration for a voice port. Two MAC addresses are allowed, and they are to be learned dynamically. One MAC address is for the

IP phone, and the other IP address is for the PC connected to the IP phone. Violations of this policy result in the port being shut down, and the aging timeout for the learned MAC addresses is set to two hours.

Example 7-2 *Port Security Configuration*

```
Switch(config-if)# switchport mode access
Switch(config-if)# switchport port-security
Switch(config-if)# switchport port-security maximum 2
Switch(config-if)# switchport port-security violation shutdown
Switch(config-if)# switchport port-security mac-address sticky
Switch(config-if)# switchport port-security aging time 120
```

Use the **show port-security** command to view port security settings for the switch, including violation count, configured interfaces, and security violation actions.

Use the **show port-security** [**interface** *interface-id*] command to view port security settings for the specified interface, including the maximum allowed number of secure MAC addresses for each interface, the number of secure MAC addresses on the interface, the number of security violations that have occurred, and the violation mode.

Example 7-3 shows that port security is enabled on port fa0/12 with a maximum MAC address count of 2. Currently, there are no MAC addresses learned on that port, and the violation action has been set to shut down the port.

Example 7-3 **show port-security** *Command Output*

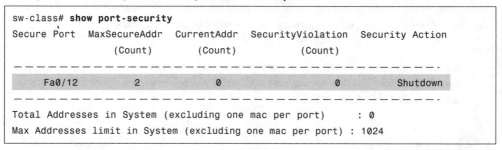

```
sw-class# show port-security
Secure Port  MaxSecureAddr  CurrentAddr  SecurityViolation  Security Action
             (Count)        (Count)      (Count)
 ------------------------------------------------------------------------
    Fa0/12        2             0              0              Shutdown
 ------------------------------------------------------------------------
Total Addresses in System (excluding one mac per port)    : 0
Max Addresses limit in System (excluding one mac per port) : 1024
```

Example 7-4 demonstrates output from the **show port-security interface fa0/12** command, revealing that a violation has occurred, which means that more than one MAC address has been seen on the port. The port has been shutdown because of this policy violation, as confirmed by the *secure-down* port status.

Example 7-4 **show port-security interface fa0/12** *Command Output*

```
sw-class# show port-security interface fa0/12
Port Security              : Enabled
Port status                : Secure-down
Violation mode             : Shutdown
Maximum MAC Addresses      : 1
Total MAC Addresses        : 2
```

```
Configured MAC Addresses    : 0
Aging time                  : 120 mins
Aging type                  : Absolute
SecureStatic address aging  : Disabled
Security Violation Count     : 1
```

Use the **show port-security** [**interface** *interface-id*] **address** command to view all the secure MAC addresses that are configured on all switch interfaces, or on a specified interface, with aging information for each address.

Example 7-5 shows that port fa0/12 is in VLAN 1 and has a secured MAC address of 0000.ffff.aaaa, which means that the host with the 0000.ffff.aaaa MAC address can connect to port fa0/12.

Example 7-5 show port-security address *Command Output*

```
sw-class# show port-security address
Secure Mac Address Table

———————————————————————————————————————————————————————-.
Vlan    Mac Address       Type             Ports    Remaining Age    •
                                                      (mins)

——    ——————.            ——               ——.      ——————.
  1     0000.ffff.aaaa    SecureConfigured   Fa0/12      -
———————————————————————————————————————————————————————-.
Total Addresses in System (excluding one mac per port)     : 0
Max Addresses limit in System (excluding one mac per port) : 1024
```

Network managers need a way to monitor who is using the network and where they are. In Figure 7-35, if port Fa2/1 is secure, an SNMP trap will be generated when MAC D disappears from the CAM table of the switch.

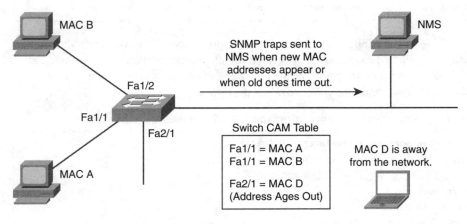

Figure 7-35 *Notification of Intrusions*

The MAC address notification feature sends SNMP traps to the network management station (NMS) whenever a new MAC address is added to, or an old address is deleted from, the forwarding tables. MAC notifications are generated only for dynamic and secure MAC addresses.

MAC address notification allows the network administrator to monitor MAC addresses that are learned and MAC addresses that age out and are removed from the switch.

Use the **mac address-table notification change** global configuration command to enable the MAC address notification feature on the switch.

Additional Switch Security Features

The sections that follow describe the additional security features that are available with Cisco switches.

Switched Port Analyzer

You can analyze the network traffic that passes through ports or VLANs by using Switched Port Analyzer (SPAN) or Remote Switched Port Analyzer (RSPAN) to send a copy of the traffic to another port on the switch, or to a port on another switch, that has been connected to a network analyzer or other monitoring or security device. SPAN copies (or mirrors) traffic received or sent (or both) on source ports or source VLANs to a destination port for analysis. SPAN does *not* affect the switching of network traffic on the source ports or VLANs. You must dedicate the destination port for SPAN use. Except for traffic that is required for the SPAN or RSPAN session, destination ports do not receive or forward traffic.

An intrusion detection system (IDS) has the capability to detect misuse, abuse, and unauthorized access to networked resources. You can use SPAN to mirror traffic to another port where a probe or an IDS sensor is connected, as shown in Figure 7-36. When an IDS sensor detects an intruder, the sensor can send out a TCP reset that tears down the intruder connection within the network, immediately removing the intruder from the network.

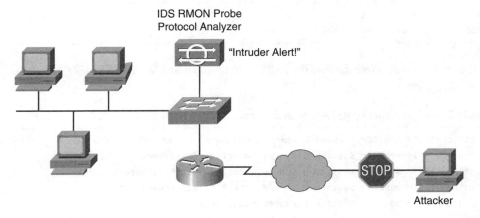

Figure 7-36   *Switched Port Analyzer*

Example 7-6 shows how to set up SPAN session 1 for monitoring source port traffic to a destination port. First, any existing SPAN configuration for session 1 is deleted, and then bidirectional traffic is mirrored from source port Gigabit Ethernet 0/1 to destination port Gigabit Ethernet 0/2, retaining the encapsulation method.

Example 7-6   *Setting Up SPAN*

```
Switch(config)# no monitor session 1
Switch(config)# monitor session 1 source interface gigabitethernet0/1
Switch(config)# monitor session 1 destination interface gigabitethernet0/2
encapsulation replicate
Switch(config)# end
```

Note: Should you need ingress traffic to be passed on that SPAN port, use the following command:
Switch(config)# **monitor session 1 destination interface gigabitethernet0/2 encapsulation replicate ingress untagged vlan 5**

An IPS sensor configured with an EventAction of TCP reset is an example of a typology where the SPAN port needs to accommodate ingress traffic.

Remote SPAN

Figure 7-37 shows that an RSPAN VLAN has been created for the forwarding of traffic from switch to switch to reach the IDS, which analyzes the traffic for malicious behavior. Source ports for the spanned traffic are found on all three switches resulting in the IDS examining traffic that is forwarded by all of these devices. As the attacker traffic leaves the router, a copy of it will be forwarded to the IDS for examination.

To configure RSPAN, you start by configuring the RSPAN VLAN. Example 7-7 shows the command to create VLAN 901 and configure it as an RSPAN VLAN.

Example 7-7   *Setting Up Remote SPAN*

```
Switch(config)# vlan 901
Switch(config-vlan)# remote-span
```

Next, it is necessary to configure the RSPAN source ports and VLANs. Example 7-8 shows a variety of sources.

Example 7-8   *Configuring RSPAN Source Ports*

```
Switch2(config)# monitor session 2 source interface fastethernet1/1 - 3 rx
Switch3(config)# monitor session 2 source interface fastethernet 5/15 , 7/3 rx
Switch4(config)# monitor session 2 source interface gigabitethernet 1/2 tx
Switch5(config)# monitor session 2 source interface port-channel 102
Switch6(config)# monitor session 2 source filter vlan 2 - 3
Switch7(config)# monitor session 2 destination remote vlan 901
```

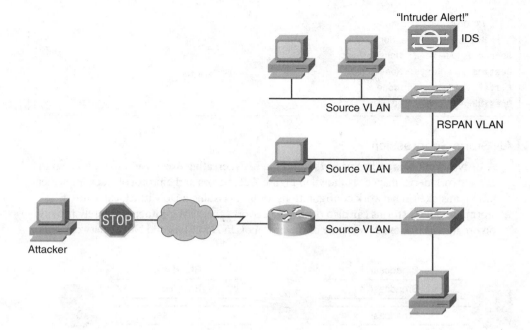

Figure 7-37   *Remote SPAN*

Finally, you configure the RSPAN traffic to be forwarded out an interface toward where the IDS resides. Example 7-9 configures traffic that is destined for VLAN 901 to be forwarded out interface FastEthernet 1/2.

Example 7-9   *Configuring Remote SPAN Traffic Toward a Specific Interface*

```
Switch(config)# monitor session 2 source remote vlan 901
Switch(config)# monitor session 2 destination interface fastethernet 1/2
```

To display an RSPAN configuration, use the **show monitor session** command. Example 7-10 shows that the FastEthernet interfaces 1/1, 1/2, and 1/3 are configured as source ports to only receive traffic, and VLAN 901 is configured as the RSPAN VLAN.

Example 7-10   show monitor session *Command Output*

```
Switch2# show monitor session 2 detail
Session 2
— — — — — —
Type : Remote Source Session
Source Ports:
    RX Only:        Fa1/1-3
    TX Only:        None
    Both:           None
Source VLANs:
    RX Only:        None
```

```
    TX Only:        None
    Both:           None
Source RSPAN VLAN: None
Destination Ports: None
Filter VLANs:       None
Dest RSPAN VLAN:    901
```

LAN Storm Suppression

A LAN storm occurs when packets flood the LAN, creating excessive traffic and degrading network performance, as shown in Figure 7-38. Errors in the protocol-stack implementation, mistakes in network configurations, or users issuing a DoS attack can cause a storm. Broadcast storms can also occur on networks that have protocols that rely heavily on broadcasts (for example, some of the protocols in AppleTalk and Novell networking).

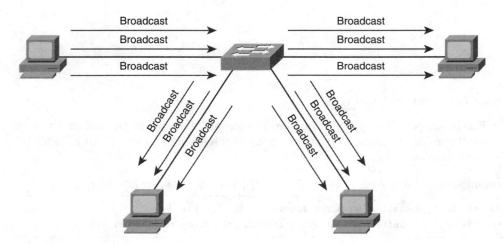

Figure 7-38 *LAN Storm*

By limiting the number of incoming broadcast, multicast, and unicast frames on each port, the processing and forwarding of frames is limited. Storm control (or traffic suppression) limits the number of incoming frames by monitoring packets that pass from an interface to the switching bus and determines whether the packet is unicast, multicast, or broadcast. The switch counts the number of packets of a specified type received within the one-second time interval and compares the measurement with a predefined suppression-level threshold. Storm control blocks traffic on a port when the rising threshold is reached.

For example, on a Catalyst 3550 switch when a multicast storm occurs, the networking device blocks all traffic (broadcast, multicast, and unicast traffic) except for control traffic, such as BPDU frames. By default, when a broadcast or unicast storm occurs, the networking device blocks only the broadcast or unicast traffic. This blocking includes traffic that might be necessary in the network, such as routing protocol traffic. Therefore, you must assess the required thresholds on each port against their potential for attack and assess the required traffic for normal network operation. Also, the network should be designed and configured to remove or limit the normal broadcast and multicast traffic.

Use the **storm-control** interface configuration command to enable storm control on an interface and set the threshold value for each type of traffic. You can enter the storm-control suppression level as a percentage of total bandwidth of the port, as a rate in packets per second at which traffic is received, or as a rate in bits per second at which traffic is received.

When you specify the traffic suppression level as a percentage (up to two decimal places) of the total bandwidth, the level can be from 0.00 to 100.00. A threshold value of 100 percent means that no limit is placed on that type of traffic. A value of 0.0 means that all traffic of that type on that port is blocked.

Threshold percentages are approximations because of hardware limitations and the way in which packets of different sizes are counted. Depending on the packet sizes that make up the incoming traffic, the actual enforced threshold might differ from the configured level by several percentage points.

Note: Storm control is supported on physical interfaces. Since Cisco IOS Software Release 12.2(25), you can also configure storm control on EtherChannel port channels. When you configure storm control on an EtherChannel, the storm control settings propagate to the EtherChannel physical interfaces.

The full command syntax for the **storm-control** command is as follows:

```
storm-control {{broadcast ¦ multicast ¦ unicast} level {level [level-low] ¦ bps
bps [bps-low] ¦ pps pps [pps-low]}} ¦ {action {shutdown ¦ trap}}
```

Table 7-10 shows the details of the **storm-control** command.

Table 7-10   storm-control *Command Parameters*

Parameter	Description
broadcast	This parameter enables broadcast storm control on the interface.
multicast	This parameter enables multicast storm control on the interface.
unicast	This parameter enables unicast storm control on the interface.

Table 7-10   storm-control *Command Parameters*

Parameter	Description
level *level* [*level-low*]	Specify the rising and falling suppression levels as a percentage of total bandwidth of the port: *level*: Rising suppression level, up to two decimal places. The range is 0.00 to 100.00. Block the flooding of storm packets when the value specified for level is reached. *level-low*: (Optional) Falling suppression level, up to two decimal places. The range is 0.00 to 100.00. This value must be less than or equal to the rising suppression value. If you do not configure a falling suppression level, it is set to the rising suppression level.
level bps *bps* [*bps-low*]	Specify the rising and falling suppression levels as a rate in bits per second at which traffic is received on the port: *bps*: Rising suppression level, up to 1 decimal place. The range is 0.0 to 10000000000.0. Block the flooding of storm packets when the value specified for bps is reached. *bps-low*: (Optional) Falling suppression level, up to 1 decimal place. The range is 0.0 to 10000000000.0. This value must be equal to or less than the rising suppression value. You can use metric suffixes such as **k**, **m**, and **g** for large-number thresholds.
level pps *pps* [*pps-low*]	Specify the rising and falling suppression levels as a rate in packets per second at which traffic is received on the port: *pps*: Rising suppression level, up to 1 decimal place. The range is 0.0 to 10000000000.0. Block the flooding of storm packets when the value specified for *pps* is reached. *pps-low*: (Optional) Falling suppression level, up to one decimal place. The range is 0.0 to 10000000000.0. This value must be equal to or less than the rising suppression value. You can use metric suffixes such as **k**, **m**, and **g** for large-number thresholds.
action {**shutdown** | **trap**}	The action taken when a storm occurs on a port. The default action is to filter traffic and to not send an SNMP trap. The keywords have these meanings: **shutdown**: Disables the port during a storm **trap:** Sends an SNMP trap when a storm occurs The **trap** and **shutdown** options are independent of each other.

If you configure the action to be taken as **shutdown,** the port is error disabled during a storm, and you must use the **no shutdown** interface configuration command to bring the interface out of this state.

When a storm occurs and the action is to filter traffic, if the falling suppression level is not specified, the switch blocks all traffic until the traffic rate drops below the rising suppression level. If the falling suppression level is specified, the switch blocks traffic until the traffic rate drops below this level.

Use the following command to verify the storm control settings:

```
show storm-control [interface][{broadcast ¦ multicast ¦ unicast ¦ history}]
```

Layer 2 Best Practices

The following list suggests Layer 2 security best practices. All of these suggestions are dependent on your security policy:

- Manage switches in as secure a manner as possible (SSH, OOB, permit lists, and so on).

- Always use a dedicated VLAN ID for trunk ports.

- Do not use VLAN 1 for anything.

- Set all user ports to nontrunking (unless you are using Cisco VoIP).

- Use port security where possible for access ports.

- Selectively use SNMP and treat community strings like root passwords.

- Enable STP attack mitigation (BPDU guard, root guard).

- Use Cisco Discovery Protocol only where necessary (with phones it is useful).

- Disable all unused ports and put them in an unused VLAN.

It is important to manage switches like routers, using secure protocols or out-of-band methods if policy permits it. Because VLAN 1 is a known management VLAN, it is recommended that you avoid using it. Turn off services that are not necessary and ports that are not being used. Implement the various security services that have been covered in this chapter as necessary and as supported by your hardware. Turn Cisco Discovery Protocol (CDP) off on ports that do not connect to network devices, with the exception of ports that connect to Cisco IP phones.

Summary

Layer 2 security is often an overlooked aspect of network security. It is important for security practitioners to remember that all software is vulnerable to poor programming. Buffer overflows can be the worst of these problems. The goals of endpoint security include protection from viruses, worms, and Trojan horses. SAN and voice security are also increasingly important because these technologies are growing in popularity in the modern enterprise.

The major points covered in this chapter are as follows:

■ An endpoint is an individual computer system or device that acts as a network client.

■ Cisco offers different security appliances such as IronPort Systems, Cisco NAC Appliance, Cisco ASA, and Cisco MARS.

■ A SAN is a specialized network that enables fast, reliable access among servers and external storage resources.

■ VoIP is the transmission of voice traffic over IP-based networks. Hackers can tamper with voice systems, user identities, and telephone configurations and intercept voice-mail messages.

■ Assigning voice traffic to specific VLANs to logically segment voice and data traffic is an industrywide accepted best practice.

■ Always use a dedicated VLAN ID for trunk ports and do not use VLAN 1 for anything. Also, set all user ports to nontrunking (unless you are using Cisco VoIP).

■ Use port security where possible for access ports and enable STP attack mitigation (BPDU guard, root guard).

■ VLAN hopping and MAC spoofing attacks are possible on switched networks and measures should be put in place to protect against those attacks.

References

For additional information, refer to these resources:

Cisco Systems, Inc. *Cisco Catalyst 6500 Series Switches: Private VLAN Catalyst Switch Support Matrix*, http://tinyurl.com/2w22d6

Cisco Systems, Inc. *Securing Networks with Private VLANs and VLAN Access Control Lists*, http://www.cisco.com/warp/public/473/90.shtml

Cisco Systems, Inc. *LAN Security: Introduction*, http://tinyurl.com/594lpb

Cisco Systems, Inc. *Identity Based Networking Services Solution*, http://www.cisco.com/en/US/netsol/ns340/ns394/ns171/ns75/networking_solutions_sub_sub_solution_home.html

Cisco Systems, Inc. *Catalyst 6500 Release 12.2SXH Software Configuration Guide: Configuring Private VLANs (PVLANs)*, http://www.cisco.com/en/US/docs/switches/lan/catalyst6500/ios/12.2SX/configuration/guide/pvlans.html

Cisco Systems, Inc. *Catalyst 4500 Series Switch Cisco IOS Software Configuration Guide, 12.1(13)EW: Configuring Private VLANs*, http://tinyurl.com/5mhtdl.

IronPort Systems. http://www.ironport.com

Cisco Systems, Inc. *Cisco Security Agent Introduction*, http://www.cisco.com/go/csa

Cisco Systems, Inc. *Network Admission Control Introduction*, http://www.cisco.com/go/nac

Cisco Systems, Inc. *Storage Networking Introduction*, http://www.cisco.com/go/storagenetworking

Cisco Systems, Inc. *Data Center Networking*, http://www.cisco.com/go/datacenter

Storage Network Industry Association. http://www.snia.org

ANSI T11 FC Projects. http://www.t11.org/index.htm

Vacca, J. R. *The Essential Guide to Storage Area Networks* (Prentice Hall, 2001)

Wallace, K. *Cisco Voice over IP (CVOICE) Self-Study* (Cisco Press, 2007)

Review Questions

Use the questions here to review what you learned in this chapter. The correct answers are found in the Appendix, "Answers to Chapter Review Questions."

1. A buffer overflow exploit tries to do which of the following?

    a. Extract data from vulnerable host

    b. Overwrite memory on the stack of an application

    c. Disguise itself as a worm

    d. React as a Trojan horse

2. IronPort products provide protection against what? (Choose the three best answers.)

    a. Buffer overflows

    b. Spam

    c. Malware

    d. Sniffing

    e. Privilege escalation

    f. Spyware

3. Which of the following are Cisco NAC Appliance characteristics? (Choose two.)

    a. Software module embedded with NAC-enabled products

    b. Self-contained solution

    c. In-band solution that can be used on any Cisco switch or router

    d. Integrated framework leveraging multiple vendor products

4. Define logical unit number (LUN).

    a. A worldwide name 64-bit address that Fibre Channel networks use to uniquely identify each element in a Fibre Channel network

    b. A collection of ports from a set of connected Fibre channel switches

    c. An address for an individual disk drive and, by extension, the disk device itself

    d. An I/O adapter that sits between the bus of the host computer and the Fibre Channel loop

5. Factors motivating the installation of a VoIP infrastructure include which of the following? (Choose three.)

    a. Cost savings

    b. Simplicity

    c. Flexibility

d. Advanced features

e. Carefree maintenance

6. Which of the following is *not* a valid statement regarding assigning voice traffic to specific VLANs?

a. To logically segment voice and data traffic to increase.

b. To ensure communication privacy and integrity.

c. It is seldom used in the industry.

d. It makes it easier to apply VLAN access list.

7. Which of the following commands should not be used on a trunk port when attempting to protect against VLAN hopping?

a. switchport mode access

b. switchport mode trunk

c. switchport nonegotiate

d. switchport trunk native vlan

8. Which two commands best protects a switched network from a hacker who is trying to preempt an election of the Spanning Tree Protocol?

a. spanning-tree portfast bpduguard

b. spanning-tree portfast default

c. spanning-tree guard root

d. swithport port-security violation

9. Which command limits the number of MAC addresses communicating through the same switch port?

a. switchport mode access

b. switchport port-security maximum

c. switch port-security mac-address sticky

d. switch port-security violation

10. Which feature could be used to facilitate the use of an IDS sensor on a switched network?

a. IronPort

b. Cisco Network Admission Control

c. Switched Port Analyzer

d. Storm control

11. Which best describe the concept of least privilege?

   a. Having small, easily verifiable pieces of software

   b. An access control concept that refers to a mechanism that mediates all access to object

   c. An operating system that provides isolation between processes

   d. A process that is never given more privilege than is necessary to perform a job

12. Which two Cisco solutions when combined provide protection of operating system vulnerabilities?

   a. Cisco CSA

   b. Cisco NAC

   c. Cisco ASA

   d. Cisco MARS

13. Why should you worry about Layer 2 security?

   a. Switches cannot regulate the flow of data between their ports.

   b. You don't have to worry about Layer 2 security because it is lower than the IP layer and that most attacks happen at the network layer.

   c. Domino effect.

   d. VLANs are a Layer 3 function in a switch, and therefore, as with any other Layer 3 processes, it can be easily hacked.

14. Put the following steps of a VLAN hopping attack in the proper order.

   a. The frame arrives at the second switch but has no knowledge that it was supposed to be for VLAN 10.

   b. The second switch looks only at the 802.1Q tag (the former inner tag that the attacker sent) and sees that the frame is destined for VLAN 20 (the victim VLAN). The second switch sends the packet on to the victim port, or floods it, depending on whether there is an existing CAM table entry for the victim host.

   c. The attacker sends a double-tagged 802.1Q frame to the switch. The outer header has the VLAN tag of the attacker, which is the same as the native VLAN of the trunk port. For the purposes of this example, assume that this is VLAN 10. The inner tag is the victim VLAN, VLAN 20.

   d. The frame arrives on the switch, which looks at the first 4-byte 802.1Q tag. The switch sees that the frame is destined for VLAN 10 and sends it out all VLAN 10 ports (including the trunk), because there is no CAM table entry. The switch does not add a VLAN 10 tag to the frames because VLAN 10 is the native VLAN, and as specified by the 802.1Q specification, native VLAN traffic is not tagged. At this point, the second VLAN tag is still intact and has not been inspected by the first switch.

15. For which reason should IP phones, VoIP gateways, and network management work-stations be on their own subnet?

    a. Many simple, yet dangerous attacks can be launched if the attacking device resides within the same broadcast domain as the target system.

    b. Devices are easier to manage if they are located on their own subnet.

    c. It is easier to set SSH access rules in the Cisco security appliances for a distinctive subnet.

    d. With separate subnets, VLANs can be used to control the access to the physical network.

Answers to Chapter Review Questions

Chapter 1

1. a, b, e.
2. a, d, e.
3. a = f, b = e, c = d.
4. a = p, b = k, c = m, d = i, e = o, f = l, g = j, h = n.
5. Step 1 = c, Step 2 = e, Step 3 = g, Step 4 = a, Step 5 = f, Step 6 = d, Step 7 = b.
6. d.
7. b.
8. a.
9. a, c, e, f.
10. a.
11. f.
12. b.
13. c.
14. c, d, b, a.
15. d.
16. a, f; b, e; c, d.
17. a.
18. c.
19. a = c, b = d.
20. a = h, b = f, c = g, d = e.
21. b, d, e, a, c.
22. b.
23. b.
24. a.
25. d.

Chapter 2

1. a, c, d.
2. c.
3. a, d.
4. b.
5. d.
6. a.
7. c.
8. c.
9. False.
10. b.
11. d.
12. a.
13. b.
14. c.
15. b.
16. d.
17. c.
18. c.
19. a.
20. d.

Chapter 3

1. b.
2. d.
3. a = 1, b = 4, c = 2, d = 3.
4. a.
5. a, d.
6. b, c.
7. d.
8. b.
9. b, a, d, c.
10. b.
11. d.
12. a.
13. d.
14. a.

Chapter 4

1. b.
2. a, c, d.
3. a, b, c.
4. d.
5. a, c.
6. d.
7. a.
8. a.
9. c.
10. a.
11. c.
12. c.
13. d.

Chapter 5

1. c, d.
2. b.
3. a, b, c.
4. d, e, f.
5. d.
6. c.
7. d.
8. b.
9. a = h, b = g, c = f, d = e.
10. b.

Chapter 6

1. b, d.
2. b.
3. a, d.
4. c.
5. d.
6. b, a, c.
7. a, d, e.
8. c.
9. b.
10. True.

Chapter 7

1. b.
2. b, c, f.
3. b, c.
4. b.
5. a, c, d.
6. c.
7. a.
8. a, c.
9. b.
10. c.
11. d.
12. a, b.
13. c.
14. c, d, a, b.
15. a.

Index

B

C

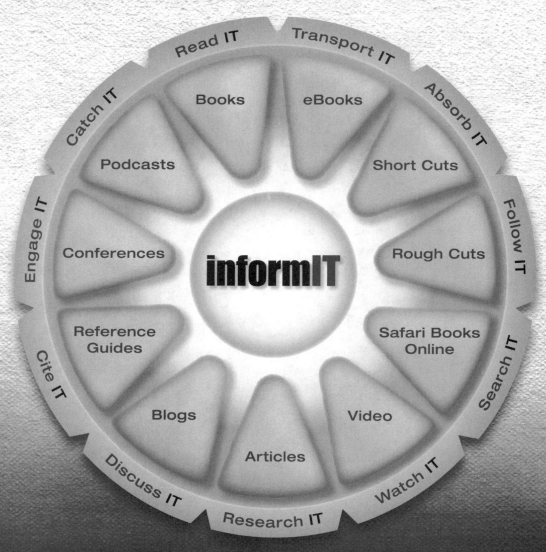

FREE Online Edition

Your purchase of **Authorized Self-Study Guide Implementing Cisco IOS Network Security (IINS)** includes access to a free online edition for 45 days through the Safari Books Online subscription service. Nearly every Cisco Press book is available online through Safari Books Online, along with more than 5,000 other technical books and videos from publishers such as Addison-Wesley Professional, Exam Cram, IBM Press, O'Reilly, Prentice Hall, Que, and Sams.

SAFARI BOOKS ONLINE allows you to search for a specific answer, cut and paste code, download chapters, and stay current with emerging technologies.

Activate your FREE Online Edition at www.informit.com/safarifree

> **STEP 1:** Enter the coupon code: QHTUIVH.

> **STEP 2:** New Safari users, complete the brief registration form.
> Safari subscribers, just log in.

If you have difficulty registering on Safari or accessing the online edition, please e-mail customer-service@safaribooksonline.com